Ontario since Confederation: A Reader

Ontario since Confederation contains some of the most recent scholarship in the field of post-Confederation Ontario history. This comprehensive collection, the first of its kind to be published in almost a decade, is intended primarily to introduce students to new areas of debate and new methodologies in Ontario history.

The articles range widely over the political, economic, and social history of the province, encompassing both traditional and newly emerging topics. They focus on the theme of 'state and society,' describing and articulating the interactions between social values and ideals, political action, and government bureaucracies from diverse perspectives. The collection raises fundamental questions about the role, nature, and development of the modern bureaucratic state. How pervasive was the influence of the state? Does the state determine or reflect social values? To what degree, and in what manner, could the powers of the state successfully be resisted?

Focusing specifically on Ontario history, contributors address the paradoxical relationship between provincial and national history. Some essays explore the influence of the federal government on the province in areas such as pollution management, native rights, and welfare. Other chapters discuss issues of interracial relationships, the family, and unwed motherhood.

The variety of topics and approaches represented in this collection attests to the diversity of Ontario and the rich social fabric of its history.

EDGAR-ANDRÉ MONTIGNY is teaching at the Department of History, Wilfrid Laurier University and Ryerson Polytechnical University.

LORI CHAMBERS is an associate professor in the Department of Women's Studies at Lakehead University.

Ontario since Confederation

A Reader

Edited by Edgar-André Montigny
and Lori Chambers

UNIVERSITY OF TORONTO PRESS
Toronto Buffalo London

© University of Toronto Press 2000
Toronto Buffalo London
Printed in Canada

ISBN 0-8020-8234-3 (paper)
ISBN 0-8020-4444-1 (cloth)

Printed on acid-free paper

Canadian Cataloguing in Publication Data

Main entry under title:

Ontario since Confederation : a reader

ISBN 0-8020-4444-1 (bound)   ISBN 0-8020-8234-3 (pbk.)

1. Ontario – History – 1867– . I. Montigny, Edgar-André.
II. Chambers, Anne Lorene, 1965– .

FC3061.O577 2000   971.3'03   C00-930539-4
F1058.063 2000

'"Cultivation" and the Middle-Class Self: Manners and Morals in Victorian
Ontario' by Andrew Holman appears in revised form in his book, *A Sense of
Their Duty: Middle-Class Formation in Victorian Ontario Towns* (Montreal and
Kingston: McGill-Queen's University Press, 2000). Parts of 'Families, Institu-
tions, and the State in Late-Nineteenth-Century Ontario' by Edgar-André
Montigny appeared in chapters 4 and 5 of his book, *Foisted upon the Govern-
ment? State Responsibilities, Family Obligations, and Care of the Dependent Aged in
Late-Nineteenth-Century Ontario* (Montreal and Kingston: McGill-Queen's
University Press, 1997). A version of 'Citizen Participation in the Welfare State:
The Recreation Movement in Brantford, 1945–1957' by Shirley Tillotson
appeared in the *Canadian Historical Review* 75, 4 (1994): 511–42.

University of Toronto Press acknowledges the financial assistance to its
publishing program of the Canada Council for the Arts and the Ontario Arts
Council.

University of Toronto Press acknowledges the financial support of the
Government of Canada for its book publishing activities through the Book
Publishing Industry Development Program (BPIDP).

Contents

Preface

Ontario since Confederation: A Reader is a collection of essays dealing with the history of Ontario. Although that may seem a straightforward statement of fact, it is by no means obvious what the subject matter of such a collection should be. There is considerable debate over what constitutes 'Ontario' history.

For some, Ontario history simply refers to the history of the province of Ontario. According to this definition, Ontario is but one region of the many that make up Canada. Many historians have found this 'limited' definition of Ontario history problematic. As Michael Piva puts it, while no one denies that Ontario is a region of sorts, it is a region that seems to defy description or analysis.[1] Firm portrayals of Ontario's distinctive regional character are rare. It becomes difficult to determine which topics would be included in a history of 'Ontario as a region' when few people are certain what defines Ontario as a region.

One of the main reasons why Ontario has not been clearly defined as a region is that, until recently, many Ontarians failed to regard Ontario as a region at all. Instead, any sense of regional pride was so closely associated with national pride that Ontario and Canada were almost blended into one entity, with many Ontarians assuming that what was best for Ontario was best for the nation.[2] Accordingly, most historians of Ontario did not see themselves as Ontario historians. As Peter Oliver argues, for most of the twentieth century 'there seems to have been a tacit, almost unthinking assumption that a regional approach to Ontario history was neither necessary nor appropriate.'[3] The one clear aspect of Ontario's historical identity that historians could agree on was a confident acceptance of the province's dominant role in Canadian Confederation. The fact that so many Ontario politicians played a leading role in defining and defending Canadian na-

tional ideals only helped to blur the distinction between the national identities and a sense of a specific Ontario identity.[4] For this reason, few of
Ontario's historians felt that Ontario was merely a region. Instead, they
treated their subject as a kind of provincial equivalent to Canada as whole.[5]

According to this definition, the subject matter of Ontario history was not
the region of Ontario alone but of all Canada. This approach has made it
extremely difficult for historians to decide where Ontario history ends and
Canadian history begins. Therefore, any collection that purports to deal
with Ontario history is bound to be criticized by some for being too local in
scope, and by others for including too much 'national' history that does not
focus on local Ontario issues. Recognizing this dilemma, *Ontario since Confederation* sidesteps the thorny question of whether Ontario is merely
one region among the many that make up Canada, or whether it is more
than a region, one tied closely to national activities and ideals. Rather, the
purpose of this collection is simply to bring together a series of new essays
and recently published articles that focus on Ontario. It showcases work
from established scholars, promising young members of the profession,
and graduate students, bringing together innovative writing on traditional
topics and path-breaking work in new areas of inquiry.

For the purposes of this volume, any activity or event that occurred
within Ontario, or had an impact on the development or character of the
province, was recognized as being part of Ontario's history. In some cases
the material is local in nature, dealing solely with provincial or even
municipal activities; in others the actions of the federal government loom
large. In this way, we hoped that the paradox of Ontario history could be
addressed. Ontario is a region with its own local and even parochial history. At the same time, it is more than a region. The interaction between
Ontario history and national history is clearly something that cannot be
ignored. Only by blending the two approaches can a collection capture the
dual nature of Ontario.

Despite the duality or diversity of this collection, the unifying theme of
'state and society' ensured that the articles shared a common concern with
the interaction between social values and ideals on the one hand and
political action and government bureaucracies on the other. From a wide
range of perspectives, and exploring several superficially unrelated topics,
the essays included in this collection all ask fundamental questions about
the role, nature, and development of the modern bureaucratic state. How
pervasive has the influence of the state been? Has the state determined or
reflected social values? To what degree, and in what manner, has the power
of the state been successfully resisted?

These essays are but a small example of the exciting new scholarship on the history of Ontario. Even if Ontario's status as a region is uncertain and its identifying characteristics remain undefined, interest in every aspect of Ontario's economic, social, and political history is high. Numerous scholars are now willing to call themselves Ontario historians.

This volume was a collaborative effort. The contributors donated their time, energy, and talent. The demands of work and family often intervened, and in some cases it would have been reasonable for authors to abandon this project in favour of more pressing priorities. Yet they carried on, sometimes under circumstances that were far from ideal, and we appreciate their commitment. As editors of the collection, the most exciting aspect of the project was being exposed to the wealth and breath of new research on the history of Ontario. Even more rewarding was the opportunity this project offered us to get to know the various scholars personally. The diversity of styles, personalities, and interests the authors represent attests to the diversity of Ontario and the rich fabric of its history.

We also wish to thank the many people who do not appear as contributors, but who were crucial in preparing the collection. They guided us to the historians who finally prepared the essays, advised us on topics to select, and counselled us on how best to avoid the many pitfalls that can befall a project of this scope. Special thanks are due to Emily Andrew, Jill McConkey, Frances Mundy, and senior editor Gerry Hallowell for offering us the opportunity to prepare this collection and for helping us to see it through to completion. Despite the many obstacles and frustrations involved in editing a collection of this size, it was a most worthwhile and enriching experience. We certainly learned much about Ontario in the process. We hope the collection proves as useful to others.

We dedicate this collection to 'our little ones,' Catherine and Geoffrey Chambers-Bedard and Maude Montigny-Gibbs.

NOTES

1 Michael Piva, ed., *A History of Ontario* (Toronto: Copp Clark Pitman, 1988), 1.
2 Peter Oliver, *Public and Private Persons: The Ontario Political Culture, 1914–34* (Toronto: Clark Irwin, 1975), 8.
3 Ibid., 8.
4 Allan Smith, 'Old Ontario and the Emergence of a National Frame of Mind,' in F.H. Armstrong, H.A. Stevenson, and D.J. Wilson, eds., *Aspects of Nineteenth-Century Ontario* (Toronto: University of Toronto Press, 1974), 194.
5 Sid Wise, 'Ontario's Political Culture,' in Donald C. MacDonald, ed., *Government and Politics of Ontario*, 3rd ed. (Scarborough, Ont.: Nelson, 1985), 160–1.

Ontario since Confederation: A Reader

Patterns of Gendered Labour and the Development of Ontario Agriculture

MARGARET DERRY

Agriculture, the occupation of the majority of people in Ontario before 1920, reflected gendered patterns of labour.[1] But these characteristics shifted as farming developed between 1780 and 1920 within the province. When a major upheaval in gendered work patterns occurred in the late nineteenth and early twentieth centuries, for example, it seems significant that the transition occurred at the same time that fundamental shifts in Ontario farming practices were taking place. The evolution of farming, then, may help to explain how gender functioned in agricultural production. I will illustrate in this article how the development of market focus and of crop and livestock farming, together with the adoption of innovations between 1780 and 1920, can be related to a transformation in the way men and women worked on farms in Ontario.

Before 1860 all agricultural labour was either 'male' or 'female' oriented. Work could clearly be identified by these terms when men and women performed different agricultural tasks. Male farm labour normally revolved around the cultivation of field crops and the breeding, raising, and feeding of hogs, beef cattle, and horses. Female farm labour was concerned primarily with dairy cattle and poultry: women fed chicks and calves, bred poultry, collected eggs and regulated sitting hens, slaughtered poultry, selected suitable dairy cows, did the milking, and made both butter and cheese. The masculinization of arable agriculture and this sexual division of livestock agriculture had evolved over centuries in Europe, and the patterns had been carried forward from there to the New World. There were times, however, when men and women worked together in these gendered tasks, suggesting that a sexual division in farm work did not always exist. When the labour was communal, the masculine and feminine nature of the tasks became more concealed. Men helped women with female farm work, and women helped men with male farm work. When men milked cows or made butter, they were helping women with female work. When women worked in the fields, they did so under the supervision of men. The superficial fact that there was often no rigid or ubiquitous pattern to the way actual tasks were done tended to hide the underlying gendered patterns that existed even in shared labour.

From the 1780s to 1860 a shift in farming practices, from equal emphasis on livestock and wheat production to greater emphasis on wheat cultivation, evolved on colonial farms. As might be expected, farming and the gendering of work interacted with each other during this period. Before the American Revolution, northern New York and Vermont farm families (who later became the Loyalists and who, before 1800, made up the majority of the Ontario farm families) had raised fodder crops, kept livestock, and planted wheat. It seems that women had played an important role in that animal and farm economy and had been recognized as producing units within the family. The migration of these families to the part of the colony of Quebec that would later become Ontario resulted in the general loss of their livestock. There were not enough animals to support an extensive livestock industry, nor was there an adequate market, either domestic or foreign, for animal products.[2] Wheat was in demand in Europe by 1800 and, by the mid-nineteenth century, in the United States as well. Canada West (later Ontario) farms began to focus on the production of wheat. Wheat farming became highly valued when it guaranteed significant amounts of cash income: by 1850 it appeared that three-quarters of the cash income of farms was generated by wheat.[3] Because men were responsible for the cultivation of field crops, wheat farming was traditionally a male occupation. Women could and did work on the land, but it was always in a 'help' capacity.[4] The relative decline of livestock farming as a cash generator, along with the emphasis on wheat cultivation, changed the position of women within the farm family unit and polarized the relative value of men's and women's work. It was male agriculture that was valued.

Because wheat produced the greatest share of the recorded cash income in the colonial period, most surviving source material focuses on wheat farming. Based on this documentation, historians have made a number of different conclusions about the role of wheat in the economy, the nature of farming practices, and the commercialization of farming generally. Wheat, for example, has been seen as a staple. As an internationally marketable product, wheat was believed not only to drive the economic engine of the province but to be the major sector of the agricultural economy.[5] More recent scholarly work on colonial farming in Canada West has shown that wheat was not as dominant in agricultural production as earlier research had indicated.[6] During the wheat era, livestock farming survived and was significant in an unobtrusive way in the farm economy.[7] The livestock market, unlike that of wheat, tended to be predominantly local or domestic in nature. A considerable portion of that livestock sector was female generated because it was in butter, cheese, eggs, and poultry – the agricultural production of women.

Women, then, continued to play a role in the farm economy, even after the emphasis on wheat overshadowed their contribution. Livestock farming did not receive much contemporary attention and generated little documentation. It is therefore difficult to establish what role income from women's industries played in the overall welfare of the farm family before 1860, though it seems it was important. Evidence about women's farm income that emerges later in the century suggests that in this earlier period women had made a reasonable amount of money from their work and that this had been an important complement to the cash brought in by wheat. The same evidence also implies that women controlled the money generated by these female industries and maintained hegemony over them, devalued as they were.[8] The rise of wheat and the decline of livestock farming did not end the existence of male and female activities, but the skewed nature of the historical record might partially explain the subsequent academic exaggeration of the importance of wheat and of male agriculture in early Ontario farming.

Patterns of gender and labour, which interacted with the rise of wheat, reveal that certain characteristics were connected to the export and domestic arms of the economy. The fact that men dominated the international market for wheat, while women concurrently played an important role in certain aspects of the local market, is significant because this sexual division between the two markets partially explains the evolution of the devaluation of female farm work. Foreign and some local markets were linked to male work, while local markets alone were linked to female work. The male–foreign market linkage was also associated with commercialism, and the female–local market with self-sufficiency. Men were commercial farmers because they raised saleable products, which also tended to be directed at the international market. Women were not commercial farmers, or so contemporary men believed, because women produced food for the farm family and sold only the surplus and only to the local market. Any income generated by women was therefore discounted, and as a result tended to remain hidden and be devalued.

During these same years, significant changes were taking place in the better-known, masculine wheat sector of agriculture, specifically in the mechanization of field work. Wheat cultivation drove the development of the early Ontario implement industry in the 1850s.[9] Reapers, mowers, and threshers were all built in what would be southern Ontario in increasing numbers. Yet these developments mechanized the work of men only. Mechanization, as a form of adopting technological innovations, became linked to males. This linkage would become significant with the new emphasis on livestock farming in the late nineteenth century.

By 1870 more livestock were raised in Ontario in response to better, particularly foreign, markets.[10] Wheat cultivation now went hand in hand with the production of fodder crops (animal feed) and stock keeping. Emphasis on livestock was as great as, or even greater than, the emphasis on wheat. Agricultural experts were delighted with this new orientation because intensive wheat cultivation, via a rotation system of wheat-fallow-wheat, had so drained the province's fields of fertility that crop yields declined rapidly during the mid-century. By 1851 about 90 per cent of fall wheat averaged 16 bushels an acre in Canada West, while yields earlier in the century were normally around 30 to 40 bushels an acre.[11] Stock farming guaranteed the production of fertilizer through animal manure. Shifts in land use reflected the rise in livestock farming, as more and more acres between 1870 and 1920 were planted in fodder crops. Better crop rotation systems – some with cycles as long as seven years – accompanied the cultivation of these plants. Table 1 reflects the rise of livestock husbandry, showing the increase in the production of fodder crops such as oats, fodder corn, and hay for animal feed, and the reduction in human food grains such as wheat and barley.

Successful livestock production depended on more than meeting the requirements of fodder crop husbandry. Men and women had many decisions to make about which livestock to raise, in what combination, and for what purpose. Animal husbandry relied on separate farming systems for each species. Hog farming, for example, was completely different from dairy or beef cattle farming. Hogs could be raised in conjunction with either, but required different breeding and housing facilities from those for any type of cattle. Good stock from different species did not result from the same breeding or rearing principles, either. Distinct breeds of hogs supplied different levels of fat in their meat, and that quality influenced the success their carcasses would yield in the bacon trade. Beef cattle were produced by a complex system in which some farms bred the stock and others fed them until they were ready to be killed. Dairy cows could be selected for their ability to produce milk and/or to fatten.[12] Poultry showed varying abilities to generate eggs or meat, and the characteristics for one purpose tended to be antagonistic to the other. Specific knowledge was required for the perpetuation of any one species, and the skills for successful livestock production were not easily transferable.

TABLE 1
Ontario Crops (acres planted in 000s)

Year	Wheat	Barley	Oats	Fodder Corn	Hay and Clover
1871	1,366				1,691
1881	1,930	849	1,375	207	2,529
1890	1,322	701	1,882	224	2,462
1900	1,446	578	2,399	511	2,527
1914	804	579	2,777	710	3,415
1921	692	413	2,761	563	3,456

SOURCE: *The Agricultural Gazette*, 1916, 804; Ian Drummond, *Progress without Planning: The Economic History of Ontario from Confederation to the Second World War* (Toronto: University of Toronto Press, 1987), table 3.1; and *Report* of the Bureau of Industries, Ontario, *Sessional Paper* 26 (1901): 25, 26, 29, 32.

The rise of livestock farming after 1870 would ultimately have a profound effect on the role of women in agriculture. Female hegemony began to decline after men argued successfully that dairying and, later, poultry raising should become part of the male sphere, so these industries could be more commercially viable and more oriented to foreign markets. Because shifts in poultry production would follow a similar pattern after dairying had become male, a review of the defeminization of dairying will serve to explain the process.

The revolution of the cheese industry after 1870, through factory rather than farm manufacture and male rather than female control of the process, began the masculinization of dairying.[13] The association of masculinity with dairying accompanied male hegemony in the cheese industry generally. Reports of the Dairymen's Associations in Ontario adamantly stated that good dairymen were 'manly,' 'nationalistic' Canadians. Masculinization led to the phenomenal success of cheese in the Canadian foreign economy. Cheese exports surpassed all others until 1900.[14] In spite of these changes in the cheese industry, though, dairying was still not entirely a male industry. Women continued to dominate the manufacturing side of the other major arm of dairying – butter. In 1890 only about 3 per cent of Canadian butter was made by men in factories, called creameries, and by 1920 almost half the butter was still made by women on farms.[15] Butter production remained focused on the domestic market. In 1910, for example, only 3.7 million pounds of butter, out of Canada's total production of 202 million pounds, were exported.[16]

Butter manufacture could be said to be commercially motivated in spite of its female, local market orientation because of its role in the economy. The butter output of Canada was consistently greater in volume than the output of cheese, and Ontario produced more butter than any other province.[17] Butter income seems to have been significant for a farm family. Patterns in Ontario, seen in the farming practices described in reports to the Agricultural and Arts Association for the prize farm competitions of the 1880s and 1890s, imply that women's monetary contribution to the farm family unit through butter was significant.[18] Unfortunately, very few diaries from Ontario farms discuss the issue. Some evidence of just how significant it could have been in Ontario is suggested in an Ohio document. The diary of a woman living on a beef farm in Ohio in the late 1880s reveals that she made between 21 and 30 per cent of the farm income through butter from her separately run dairy herd of Jersey cows and eggs from poultry of her breeding.[19]

Contemporaries continued to see female production as non-commercial 'pin money' and of little significance. A study of gender in Ontario's butter industry between 1880 and 1920 indicates that women's work in dairying was associated with inferior production, antiquated techniques, and a hindrance to the forward 'manly' nature of more modern, scientific approaches.[20] The association of female work with poor farming made contemporaries believe that female labour explained the slow advancement of dairying technology. It was thought that men would mechanize male, but not female, work. As early as 1891 the dairy professor of the Ontario Agricultural College argued that farmers 'had to have the horses and the reaping and mowing machines and the driving sheds and everything else they wanted while their wives had to get along' without improved equipment.[21] 'It has only been said a few million times that the farmer will buy machinery for himself, but not his wife,' noted the *Farmer's Advocate* in 1920.[22] The problem of dairy mechanization and gender is a complex one, as is any discussion of technology and its relation to women.[23] Dairying mechanization remained slow compared with that in crop farming, and it has been suggested by recent scholars as well as by contemporary agriculturalists that there was a connection to the predominantly female labour in dairying.[24]

One important technological invention for the dairy industry – the home centrifugal cream separator – revealed something of the complexity of women's relationship to mechanization. Cream separation technology remained primitive throughout most of the nineteenth century. The centrifugal cream separator was invented in Denmark in 1879, and in the 1880s a small version of the machine was available for use on farms. It became commercially viable for Ontario farms after 1890, and its ramifications extended far beyond butter making to providing sweet skim milk as a nourishing food for chickens, calves, and hogs. Since women used these machines, we cannot say that superior technology automatically removed them from traditional work. Still, a study of advertisements in farm journals confirms that women did not control the process by which technology spread: men clearly made decisions about the purchase of the machines.[25]

Female involvement was not the main reason dairy technology lagged. For one thing, mechanization of the dairy industry had to wait for advancements in areas outside dairying. A few examples of improvement necessary for the modernization of dairying were changes in transportation and refrigeration, and better understanding of bacteriology and both human and animal health. Men at the time seemed blinded to the reality of this situation and pleaded for the removal of women from the manufacture of butter and the transition to the production of creamery butter under male control. They also supported the development of more commercial markets abroad.

By the late nineteenth century, severe labour shortages made the adoption of mechanical innovations critical for better agricultural production. Implements originally developed for wheat production now expanded to fodder crops in general. The farm implement industry developed rapidly in the last half of the nineteenth century in Ontario, and new technology between 1870 and 1920 reduced the work involved with livestock as well. In the 1880s windmills made the watering of stock easier. By 1914 manure spreaders, which were horse drawn and had beaters to throw manure, reduced the labour of spreading manure. In search for even more innovation, farm families began to take a greater interest in the biological improvement of livestock. But wherever vestiges of female control of livestock remained, certain patterns persisted. The level of improvement in cattle breeding, for example, tended to reflect the male or female involvement with that species. Dairy cattle were slow to improve as long as women were involved in their care or in the manufacture of butter. Beef cattle, in contrast, were seen earlier as candidates for biological improvement via superior breeding methods.[26] Women's labour and a lack of innovation could be linked.

The participation of women in agricultural education provides an excellent example of their removal, after 1870, from their traditionally hegemonic position in certain aspects of farm work. By 1905 reports made by the Women's Institutes and by Macdonald College, the female arm of the Ontario Agricultural College, indicate that all education labelled as agricultural for women was focused on topics within the home. All true agricultural training, in contrast, was directed at men. Even short courses in farming work that was historically practised by women – fruit growing, butter dairying, and poultry raising – were designed to attract men and boys rather than women and girls. Advertisements in farm journals make this trend abundantly clear. A young woman, Laura Rose, did teach dairying at the Ontario Agricultural College. What is strange, however, is that little association is made in the agricultural press between her work and women's dairying. This same dichotomy between descriptions of the training of women and the work everyone knew they did on farms has been documented for the agricultural college at Cornell University in the United States.[27]

The fact that farm women engaged in agricultural work, yet received no education for that pursuit, struck some women as ridiculous. One farm woman wrote to *The Canadian Live-Stock and Farm Journal* in 1890 stating that 'we read and hear much about the necessity of education for farmers' sons, so as to incline them to love and honour the noble vocation of their fathers, but as yet we have heard little, if anything, about giving farmers' daughters an education that would better fit them for the important position of farmers' wives. I do not know why,' she continued, 'agricultural colleges should not [be] open to women and men on the same terms.'[28] It was not until 1918 that a woman was allowed into the full program at the Ontario Agricultural College. George Creelman, president of the college, wrote to the first female student in the program, Susannah Chase of Nova Scotia: 'I have taken a long time to consider your application for admission to our Third Year in Agriculture for the reason that we have never had a woman take any of our long course work up to this time. Professor Cummings gives you a strong recommendation and urges me to try the experiment, and I see no reason why you should not be admitted to the course.'[29]

The National Council of Women did little to support female farm work, despite the establishment in 1899 of a Standing Committee on Agriculture.[30] When J.W. Robertson, a dairying expert who served as the dairy professor at the Ontario Agricultural College and then as the dairy commissioner for Canada, was asked to speak to the members of this committee, he had nothing to say about the direct contribution of women to the butter industry. Instead, he concentrated on the role of the farm wife in the domestic sphere.[31]

Although women continued to make butter, they were less likely after 1900 to retain the remuneration generated by that product. We do not have the statistical data necessary to prove that statement, but numerous comments in the contemporary press support its truth. An American survey also implied that the trend existed. A survey done in the United States in 1920 revealed that while 60 per cent of farm women churned butter in 1920, only 11 per cent received payment for it.[32] Canadians believed that this same statistic applied to Ontario.

In the first two decades of the century there was a great deal of discussion in the farm press about the position of women on farms. Inheritance practices, educational issues, remuneration problems, and the lack of respect in the farm press for agricultural work done by women all commanded attention. After the 1880s, women, especially young women, also left farms in increasing numbers. The female side of this rural depopulation may at least partially have been triggered by the transition of traditional female agricultural spheres to male control. 'We hear a great deal about keeping the boys on the farm and giving the boys a chance. This is all right but how often do we hear about keeping the girls on the farm and giving the girls a chance? Yet year by year the girls are leaving the farm, mainly because they desire a chance for some sort of economic independence,' noted one farm woman.[33] In 1911 one township about 25 miles from Toronto was described as being full of bachelor farmers because the women these men should have married were all in American and Canadian cities, working as dressmakers, stenographers, and nurses.[34] 'The schools that formerly had 50 pupils, today do not average 12' in this area, a farm journal noted that same year.[35]

After 1920, views about women's unequal position suddenly vanished in the press. It is arguable that the exhausting war years partially explain this silence, or it may reflect the general lack of interest in feminism during the next decade. But there may be a more fundamental issue at work. The persistent emphasis in the literature had been on farm work itself, not on the broader social issues concerning women. By 1920 the transition to male control was complete, and with it disappeared any expression of female resentment in the farm press. The attempt to reverse the trend to male control that had fired female discontent had failed.

Farming became male gendered when livestock agriculture became a completely male enterprise through the gendering of all accountability as male. Separate hegemonic farming spheres ended, and the internal dynamics of the family with respect to gender and hierarchy changed. Under these conditions, agricultural production was focused on the export market. While a large and sophisticated domestic market after 1910 would ultimately reduce the old linkage of commercial agriculture to the export market exclusively, these new perceptions did not change gendered attitudes to commercialization. Commercial agriculture was still seen as male.

Under these conditions, women were not removed from farm labour: it was merely their role that changed. Their control of the work disappeared and they became helpers in the industries for which they had once been responsible. A study on milking patterns by gender in Ontario in this period, for example, indicates that the defeminization of dairying was accompanied by the removal of women from milking, but not from milking operations. The American survey of 1920 suggests that while one-third of farm women might milk, three-quarters of them might do the cleaning up. This pattern demonstrates women's new capacity in agriculture generally: to help. A recent survey of women's farm work in Ontario has confirmed that men still dominate the functioning of all production, and women still serve as helpers. Moreover, women's work still tends to be with livestock rather than in crop husbandry.[36] The hegemonic position of women that existed before 1870, when they controlled a significant local market for butter, cheese, eggs, and poultry, has apparently ended for good. The process of change in gendered farm labour reveals that the decline of women's position in agriculture was not caused by their removal from farm work, but by the loss of their accountability in certain livestock industries.

Between 1780 and 1920, the changes in farming activities were entangled with the way men and women worked on farms. The earliest farm families to arrive in Ontario had practised both male and female agriculture, but conditions in the new country caused a decline in livestock farming and an increase in wheat cultivation. The result of this shift in farm practices was a devaluation of the female spheres of agriculture. Women, however, continued to control their devalued industries. A more basic transition in the position of women in farming occurred in the late nineteenth and early twentieth centuries, along with the shift to a more equal emphasis on livestock and wheat farming. The move to an export-driven agriculture and the perceptions about the commercialization of farming that had originated in the wheat era were part of the changes in practices and outlook that began about 1870.

Men took control of women's traditional agricultural spheres in certain aspects of the livestock industry. But the introduction of innovations could also be gendered. The mechanization process and agricultural education both showed gendered patterns. The slowness of certain aspects of animal farming to keep pace with other arms of livestock husbandry – for example, the improvement of dairy cows compared with the improvement of beef cattle – can also be partially explained by gendered responsibility. The real shift in the way men and women worked on farms during the last two hundred years actually occurred in what was known as the early mixed-farming period: 1870 to 1920. Fundamental to that evolution was the masculinization of accountability of all agricultural industries. Once the transition was in place, it became more difficult to understand that the role of women in agriculture, while it might have been hidden by certain preconceived gendered ideas about the nature of commercial agriculture, had once been significant.

NOTES

1 See R. Sandwell, 'Rural Reconstruction: Towards a New Synthesis in Canadian
   History,' *Histoire sociale/Social History* 27 (1994): 1–32, for an excellent review of
   the literature on agricultural history in North America. Certain characteristics
   of the historiography of Ontario agriculture should be pointed out in a little
   more detail. First, studies of rural Ontario have tended to focus only on the
   pre-Confederation period, a fact that makes our knowledge of farming in the
   post-Confederation era very limited. Second, most work done on agriculture in
   the province within any time frame has tended to concentrate on the economic
   performance of farming. Third, in conjunction with the point above, there is
   very little material on actual agricultural techniques in any era. A few examples of pre-Confederation work on agriculture are J. McCallum, *Unequal
   Beginnings: Agriculture and Economic Development in Quebec and Ontario until
   1870* (Toronto: University of Toronto Press, 1980), and D. McCalla, *Planting the
   Province: The Economic History of Ontario, 1784–1870* (Toronto: University of
   Toronto Press, 1993). One example of the studies that focus on the economy
   and the pre-Confederation era is: D. McCalla, 'The Internal Economy of Upper
   Canada: New Evidence on Agricultural Marketing before 1850,' *Agricultural
   History (AH)* 59 (1985): 397–416. The most notable material on the post-
   Confederation era is M. McInnis, 'Perspectives on Ontario Agriculture, 1867–
   1930,' *Canadian Papers in Rural History (CPRH)* 8 (1992): 17–128. The standard
   work on agricultural practice in Ontario is R. Jones, *History of Agriculture in
   Ontario, 1613–1880* (Toronto: University of Toronto, 1946). See also M. Derry,
   'The Development of a Modern Agricultural Enterprise: Beef Cattle Farming in
   Ontario, 1870–1924' (PhD thesis, University of Toronto, 1997). Good examples
   of social studies are D. Gagan, *Hopeful Travellers: Families, Land, and Social
   Change in Mid-Victorian Peel County, Canada West* (Toronto: University of
   Toronto Press, 1981), M.G. Cohen, *Women's Work, Markets, and Economic Development in Nineteenth-Century Ontario* (Toronto: University of Toronto Press,
   1988); and T. Crowley, 'Rural Labour,' in P. Craven, ed., *Labouring Lives: Work
   and Workers in Nineteenth-Century Ontario* (Toronto: University of Toronto
   Press, 1993), 13–102.
2 From M. Leung, 'The Meaning of Loyalism' (PhD thesis in progress, University
   of Toronto, 1998), and M. Leung, 'The Loyalist as Immigrant Farmer,' Paper
   presented at the Canadian Historical Association Conference, 1998.
3 McCallum, *Unequal Beginnings*, 4.
4 See, for example, *The Farming World*, 1 September 1904, 27, and *Farming World
   and Canadian Farm and Home*, 1 September 1904, 645.
5 McCallum, in *Unequal Beginnings*, is probably the best known and most recent
   strong advocate of this approach. The staples approach as an explanation of all
   aspects of the Canadian economy has persisted in scholarly work on the development of Canada. The approach originated with Harold Innis in the 1930s.

6 McCalla, *Planting the Province* and 'The Internal Economy of Upper Canada,' and McInnis, 'Perspectives on Ontario Agriculture, 1867–1930.'

7 McCalla, in *Planting the Province*, describes the strength of the local farm trade.

8 See, for example, *Farming World and Canadian Farm and Home*, 15 September 1904, 707; 9 December 1908, 14; 16 December 1908, 14; *Farm and Dairy and Rural Home*, 14 January 1909, 17.

9 See McCallum, *Unequal Beginnings*, and G. Winder, 'Following America into Corporate Capitalism: Technology and Organization of the Ontario Agricultural Implement Industry to 1930' (PhD thesis, University of Toronto, 1991).

10 See M. Derry, *Ontario's Cattle Kingdom: Purebred Breeders and Their World, 1870–1920* (Toronto: University of Toronto Press, forthcoming), for the role of the foreign market on the development of livestock enterprises.

11 McCallum, *Unequal Beginnings*, 4, 20; and K. Kelly, 'Wheat Farming in Simcoe County in the Mid-Nineteenth Century,' *Canadian Geographer* 15 (1971): 97.

12 See Derry, 'Development of a Modern Agricultural Enterprise,' for a discussion about the production of beef stock and the relationship of dairying to that production. See also M. Derry, 'The Role of Purebred Breeder/Ordinary Farmer Conflict in the Rate of Herd Improvement – A Study of Cattle Farming in Ontario, 1870–1920,' Association of Living Farms and Agricultural Museums, *Proceedings*, 1998.

13 See H. Menzies, 'Technology in the Craft of Ontario Cheesemaking: Women in Oxford County circa 1860,' *Ontario History (OH)* 86 (1995): 293–304.

14 C.P. Stacey, *Canada and the Age of Conflict*, volume 1 (Toronto: University of Toronto Press, 1984), 360–2.

15 Cohen, *Women's Work*, 106; *Proceedings* of the Select Committee of the House of Commons to Inquire into Agricultural Conditions, 1924, Part 11, 1583.

16 Census of Canada, 1911, volume IV, xci, lxxxix; and K. Norrie and D. Owram, *A History of the Canadian Economy* (Toronto: Harcourt Brace, 1991), 319.

17 Narrie and Owram, *A History of the Canadian Economy*, 319.

18 This pattern can be seen in detailed reports of the agricultural practices on farms submitted for prizes given by the Agriculture and Arts Association over this period.

19 V. McCormick, *Farm Wife: A Self-Portrait, 1886–1896* (Ames: Iowa State University Press, 1990), 94. See also V. McCormick, 'Butter and Egg Business: Implications from the Records of a Nineteenth-Century Farm Wife,' *Ohio History* 100 (1991): 57–67.

20 M. Derry, 'Gender Conflicts in Dairying: Ontario's Butter Industry, 1880–1920,' *OH* 90 (1998): 31–47.

21 Ontario, *Sessional Papers*, 1891, no. 36, 165.

22 *Farmer's Advocate*, 26 August 1920, 1482.

23 See, for example, J.A. McGaw, 'Women and the History of American Technology,' *Signs* 7 (1982): 799–828.

24 F. Bateman, 'Labor Inputs and Productivity in American Dairy Agriculture,

1850–1910, A Quantitative Analysis,' *Journal of Economic History* 28 (1968): 209–11.

25 See Derry, 'Gender Conflicts.'

26 For more on the way dairy and beef cattle improved, see Derry, 'Development of a Modern Agricultural Enterprise.'

27 K.R. Babbitt, 'The Productive Farm Woman and the Extension Home Economist in New York State, 1920–1940,' *AH* 67 (1993): 83–101.

28 *The Canadian Dairyman and Farming World*, 16 December 1908, 14.

29 University of Guelph Archives, George C. Creelman Papers, letter dated 6 June 1918.

30 National Council of Women of Canada, *President's Memorandum*, 1899, 19.

31 National Council of Women, *Yearbook*, 1899, provides speeches given to the ladies by Professor Robertson and Dr Mills, president of the Ontario Agricultural College.

32 *Advocate*, 26 August 1920, 1482.

33 *Farm and Dairy*, 26 January 1911, 16

34 Ibid., 13 April 1911, 19.

35 Ibid., 26 January 1911, 16

36 L.I. Carbert, *Agrarian Feminism: The Politics of Ontario Farm Women* (Toronto: University of Toronto Press, 1995), 53–7.

Putting Flesh on the Bones: Writing the History of Julia Turner

AFUA COOPER

Practitioners of the new women's history are producing accounts that articulate their subjects' oppression and victimization along with their agency and power as these women attempt to create meaningful lives for themselves. Such an approach enables historians to construct a more holistic view of women's historical experiences.[1] The case of Julia Turner, a Black woman who taught in Essex County, Ontario, during the middle and late nineteenth century, is instructive. Her life and work provide an opportunity to study the dialectical interplay of women's oppression, subordination, and agency as these aspects are informed by gender, class, race, family, and marital status and the world of paid employment.

Methodological Approaches in Constructing Black Women's History

The metaphor of the skeleton is apt not only in finding a methodology to construct a history of Julia Turner but in allowing us to consider approaches for the study of Black women's history in Canada. Most of the sources for this essay are archival: data came from school superintendents' reports, the manuscript censuses of 1851, 1861, 1871, 1881, and 1891, a probate document from the surrogate court in Sandwich, and the Sandwich assessor's rolls from 1870 to 1899, which detail Turner's tax contributions. Newspaper articles, specifically from the *Voice of the Fugitive*, were used. The minute book of the trustees of the Amherstburg Black school (King Street school) was also invaluable in constructing Turner's history. A personal testimony, in the form of a letter to the American Missionary Association, came from Turner herself. In the probate document, Jordinia Turner, Julia's sister, gave a brief family history that also stands as a form of personal testimony.

Oral evidence was useful in helping me to write this history. I conversed with Sylvia Jackson, Jordinia's granddaughter, about Turner's life and family background. Though I had no formal interview with Mrs Jackson, the evidence she provided was useful in helping me anchor Turner in a poor, working-class family in the Black community of nineteenth-century Essex County. Secondary sources also helped. History texts about African Canadian women and men and about white women provided the historical, racial, and gender contexts in which to place Turner and helped to elucidate her life.

Black Women in Canadian History

Most historians no longer bemoan the exclusion of 'women' from history because, over the past twenty-five years, valiant 'restoration' work has been done in white women's history. The same cannot be said, however, for Black women's history in Canada.[2] Until recent years, the focus in Canadian women's historical studies has been on white, middle-class women. And because this 'whiteness' has not been broken down by race, an analysis of race is missing from the narratives. As a result, the history of Black woman and other minorities has been marignalized, if not made outright invisible, in Canadian historical writing. Sherry Edmunds Flett puts it well in her study of Black women in British Columbia: 'The lives of African Canadian women have been reduced to being mere illustrations or "add-ons" within feminist history.'[3] For a truly inclusive women's history, we need a redefinition of the term *woman*. This new definition would have to consider the various factors that make up woman: gender, race, class, socioeconomic stature, and sexuality in all their differences.[4]

Because Canadian women's history developed as a field of inquiry that focused on white women, there are few studies that centre on the experiences of Black women.[5] American historian Darlene Clark Hine states in her discussion of the development of African American women's history that Black women, belonging as they do to two subordinate groups in society, tend to 'fall between the cracks' of Black history, with its male focus, and women's history, with its white women focus.[6] This situation was not rectified until Black female historians started to place Black women at the centre of historical inquiry. The same cannot be said of African Canadian women's history, for although there is a well-developed field of white women's history in Canada, African Canadian history as a branch of legitimate historical inquiry is virtually non-existent. Given this state of affairs, the conclusion that can be drawn for Black women's history is that it has dropped into a huge crater.[7]

Black feminist historians cannot wait for a field of Black Canadian women's history to come into being on its own; we must develop one. Numerous sources for Black women's history abound and, with the recent explosion of white women's history in Canada and the development of African women's history, the historian of Black women's history in Canada has at her or his disposal a variety of methodologies, theories, and interpretive frameworks drawn from women's history, gender history, and social history. In addition, because the field of African Canadian women's history is relatively uncharted, we are in the process of developing our own theoretical approaches and methodologies.

This essay on Julia Turner, then, is an exploration in methodology, interpretive frameworks, and theoretical issues. It attempts to provide an integrated analysis of how race, gender, class, family, and marital status made their impact on the life, employment, and work choices of one woman. It is located, then, at the intersection of African Canadian history, women's history, and the history of teaching in Canada. As Gisela Bock notes in *Gender and History*: 'Women's history holds the possibility of doing much more than recovering a history of women's past lives. It can shed light on gender relations and provide new understandings of general history.'[8]

Family Origins

Julia Turner was the second child born to Henry and Rosina Turner in Ontario. Rosina and Henry fled from slavery in West Virginia and Kentucky, respectively, with two young daughters and arrived in Ontario in 1828. Their first child born in Ontario was a girl named Mary Jane Crawford.[9] Julia was born in 1831 and was followed by nine more children, two of whom died in infancy. The history of African Americans, both slave and free, leaving the United States to settle in Ontario and Canada has been documented elsewhere, so it is not necessary to relate it here.[10] Suffice it to say that Rosina and Henry Turner were part of that group of Black Americans who created an American diaspora in Ontario, one that eventually became Canadianized.

The Turner family is listed in the 1861 census report for Amherstburg. It lists only four children: Julia, aged 30, Jordinia, 17 (spelt 'Georgina' by the enumerator), Louisa, 13, and Henry, 22. The senior and junior Henry are listed as labourers, but no occupation was given for Rosina or any of her daughters. This lack of information on occupation for the women in the family was a common feature of the census records. Enumerators, in keeping with the prevailing gender ideology of man as breadwinner, tended not to note the occupation of women in a household considered to be male headed. Women and their work were thereby made invisible. In fact, Julia Turner had at this point been teaching school for a number of years.

The Turners were of 'humble' background. According to the census, they lived in a half-storey frame house and had six pigs, two cows, and two horses. The real and personal value of Henry Turner's estate was $160. Because of the prevailing gender ideology, Julia's salary as a teacher would not have been included in the counting of the family's wealth by the census taker. The father of the family, Henry Turner, was listed as a labourer, which meant that his wages were low. Having several young children to support most probably meant that the family was struggling 'to make ends meet.' However, Sylvia Jackson related that when Henry and Rosina came to Ontario in 1828 they opened a grocery store and a rooming house in Amherstburg, and that they also made and sold carpets. She did not know for how long the couple operated these enterprises, but if they were still engaged in such activities in 1861, the enumerator did not report it.[11]

The census taker also reported that every one of the enumerated family members was born in the United States, though research has indicated this was not the case. Since many, if not most, of the Black families in Ontario were of American origin, it was felt by the census takers that 'anyone who was Black' must have been born in the United States. This perception has served to deny African Canadians a Canadian identity, since members of the dominant group constantly saw them as newcomers. And because African Canadians were imagined as newcomers, their role in the making and shaping of Canadian history has been effectively denied.[12] Like many other Black Ontarians, the Turners were identified as Baptists.

The census is not the only source for uncovering the presence of the Turners in Amherstburg. The list for Captain Caldwell's Company of Coloured Volunteers at Amherstburg reveals that Henry Turner served as a sergeant in active duty during the Upper Canadian Rebellion from 27 December 1837 to 25 January 1838.[13] This information supports the oral evidence given by family members of the early arrival of Henry and Rosina into the province.

Having several young children to care for, Rosina and Henry Turner had to come up with various survival strategies. In nineteenth-century Ontario one such strategy was for older children to engage in some kind of paid employment, whether this meant working as an apprentice or labourer for boys, and, for girls, going into domestic service or, as the century matured, into teaching. Julia, being one of the senior children in her family, went out to work at an early age. By the time she was fourteen she was teaching at a Black separate school in Essex County.[14]

Gender, Race, and Work: Teaching in Nineteenth-Century Ontario

Julia Turner's presence in the teaching force at this early age is recorded in a letter she wrote to George Whipple, field secretary of the American Missionary Association, asking for financial help for a Black school in the town of Amherstburg.

Amherstburg
Jan. 25th, 1853

Dear Sir,

I have forwarded this letter to you by recommendation to solicit aid in behalf of a school in Amherstburg. their [sic] is a school in this place kept in Mr Rice's[15] mission house by a young man by the name of James Underwood. As to the teacher they are satisfied with his teaching but are dissatisfied with the course he has taken by going to the mission house.[16] As he was paid twenty dollars per month by the trustees of the incorporation, they feel dissatisfied under those circumstances and having known their disapproval of that course to the trustees, they [the trustees] refuse to hear them, being rather in favour of his course and partial to Mr Rice.

They [the parents] have requested me to apply for assistance in carrying on their school in the coloured Wesleyan Church which I shall teach and the number of scholars are from thirty-five to forty, which I shall take up if I can be supported. They will pay what they can, but having to their taxes to pay to the other school whither they send or not, but by not sending will be exempted from paying the rate bill which they will pay to their own teacher if they can get assistance from you.[17]

They say you would assist them if they would come under the AMA society. As for myself, I have been teaching in Canada for eight years and for some of them I have received twenty four dollars per year for two years and I had the promise [of] more but the people were too poor, I could not bear to distress them. I have taught five years ... in one settlement by the name of Mount Pleasant to which if I do not get support in town will teach.

It is a large settlement of coloured people and a large quantity has moved there within the two years time, to give you sir, an idea of the number that have [sic] gone in that settlement since the fugitive bill has passed.[18] I have received from them last year, for the first time $72 for the year so I can say thank God, times are getting better ... As to my assertions and character as a schoolteacher, you can inquire of Mr Peden, minister of the Presbyterian church, Mr A. Binga, pastor of the Baptist church ...

I am your humble servant,

Julia Turner

p.s. I will teach either place that you will support me in, Amherstburg or Mount Pleasant.[19]

Turner's letter makes for wonderful reading in aspects of African Canadian social history in Essex County in particular and Ontario in general. It highlights the tensions and the partisanship that plagued certain Black communities with special regard to education: the fight between parents and trustees, which for many Ontario communities became a constant theme, with the teacher caught in the middle; and the recurring tensions between missionaries and their congregations. It sheds light on the state of education for Black children in Essex, and it also reveals the poverty of many of the Black settlers, especially those newly arrived from the United States. Much of this poverty was engendered by the dislocation and disruption that the Fugitive Slave Law caused for Black families. In the letter, Turner presents herself as a devoted and dedicated teacher who emphathizes deeply with the parents. More important for our purpose is what Turner reveals about her long teaching experience in Canada. The letter was written at the beginning of 1853 and, if she had been teaching for eight years, she began in 1845, when she was fourteen years of age.

Schoolteaching is one of the richest areas of women's history in Canada and one of the most developed fields of women's history. By the last quarter of the nineteenth century in several provinces, teaching had become essentially a women's occupation. The entry of so many young women into teaching had to do with the limited job opportunities available to women at this time. Teaching was one of the few professions that courted and encouraged women, and, gradually, women became a majority among elementary school teachers. Canadian historians have documented and analysed this phenomenon well, even though the focus has been on white women teachers.[20]

Julia Turner was part of that initiative of women becoming teachers as the educational state expanded. Although teaching probably functioned as a survival strategy for her and her family, other forces were at work to propel her into the world of teaching. The growth of the Black population through natural increase and emigration from the United States meant that there was a rapid increase in the number of Black children for whom educational facilities had to be provided.[21] Turner points in her letter to the inadequacy of such facilities. Moreover, the real fact and persistence of separate schooling for Black children in much of the province exacerbated the educational difficulties that they and their parents already faced.

Separate Schooling in Nineteenth-Century Ontario

As early as 1828 Black parents in Ontario protested against the lack of schooling for their children, and by 1838 Black children in Brantford, Amherstburg, and other places were attending separate schools.[22] This de facto segregation in education became a fact of life for many Black children, though their access to schooling varied. In Toronto and other towns and hamlets in the east, Black children, attended school with white children, but not so in the western and southern portion of the province. In these regions, of which Essex County was a part, racial segregation in education was the norm.

Propelled by the vision of Egerton Ryerson, Canada West's energetic superintendent of education, public education expanded in the 1840s. During this period a series of laws recognized separate schooling for religious groups and, in 1850, the crowning piece of legislation enshrined in law separate schooling for Blacks.[23] Although Blacks were given permission to set up their own schools if they desired, whites often insisted that Blacks leave the common schools and set up their own separate schools. School segregation based on race was already a reality before 1850, but white school supporters used the separate school act as the most effective weapon in their fight to expel all Black children from the common schools. When Blacks declined, many whites began to prevent Black students from physically entering the public schools. White school trustees also began to gerrymander districts to prevent Black children from attending schools deemed to be white.[24] The combined action of these groups resulted in numerous Black children not receiving any kind of formal education.[25]

Black parents, teachers, and other supporters responded to this situation in a number of ways, primarily by setting up schools for their children.[26] In both Canada and the United States, the Black community made a valiant effort in educating and attempting to educate the children. This effort produced both pride and bitterness.[27] As a young female teacher, Julia Turner in Mount Pleasant and elsewhere was responding to the educational needs and demands of a her community. A major part of this response was premised on the imperative of race uplift.

Race Uplift in Ontario

Race uplift, an ideology articulated by the Black middle class in the nineteenth century and one that most Blacks eventually subscribed to, entailed 'acting for the good of the race' and thereby 'elevating' it.'[28] Blacks who had the means were called upon to help their less-fortunate fellows. Uplift was best expressed and manifested in the realm of education. Linda Perkins underscores the centrality of this ideology in Black educational efforts in her discussion of Black women and uplift: 'Since the intellectual inferiority of the race was the primary justification for slavery ... blacks sought as a central goal in their mission of uplift to improve their education to help dispel the widespread myth of the dull black intellect.'[29]

Most Blacks, slave and free, felt that if the race were educated, the oppression it experienced from white society would lessen. Henry Bibb used classic uplift language when he wrote in the *Voice of the Fugitive* that, with the acquisition of education, Black people would be 'strengthened and elevated.'[30] Uplift doctrine reigned full force in the Black teaching community, as most teachers expressed the view that one of their main desires was to elevate their oppressed brethren.[31] They still went into teaching with pragmatic aims and expected to be paid for their labours so they could support themselves and their family members. But many times teachers were not paid, simply because the parents did not have the money or the aid that some of the schools received from the province was not adequate or not forthcoming.[32] Yet these teachers pressed on. What kept most of them in the school in spite of insufficient remuneration was the uplift ideology.

Since uplift was an ideology that most in the Black community subscribed to, it was not necessary to be a teacher to want to help fellow brothers and sisters. The Turners were farmers, or worked in agriculture, and most of the Black settlers pursued similar paths.[33] Other people, such as newspaper publishers, medical doctors, and Black intellectuals, all vigorously espoused the uplift doctrine.[34]

Thus, in the early stages of the establishment of the Black communities in the province, it did not seem to matter if the teachers were as young as fourteen. What mattered was that they knew more than their charges and had the necessary literacy and numeracy skills. For Julia Turner and her family, however, her entry into the workforce was perhaps first dictated by economic considerations rather than the impulse of race elevation. Would a young teenage girl have internalized the concept of uplift sufficiently to be inspired by it and incorporate it in her praxis? For much of the nineteenth century, children went out to work at an early age; Turner was part of this momentum. Yet, given the fact of the racial oppression that Black people encountered in Canada, including the lack of educational opportunities,

Turner was forced at an early age to consider uplift in both theory and practice.

Julia Turner, Teacher

There is no evidence that Turner received the aid she requested from the American Missionary Association. One year later, however, she assumed the position of teacher at the Amherstburg Black school for a salary of £50 per annum.[35] From this meagre salary she was responsible for providing the classroom space and the fuel. The teacher before Turner, James Underwood, taught the Black school in Isaac Rice's mission house, but, given the controversy with the parents, Turner did not continue the school there. Turner found an alternative space, but it was an uncomfortable structure, as Benjamin Drew, the Boston abolitionist who was touring 'Black Ontario,' discovered when he stopped in Amherstburg in 1855. Drew's description of the Amherstburg Black school says volumes about Turner's working conditions and the state of education for Black children in Canada West:

> A separate school has been established here, at their own request:[36] their request was given them, but leanness went with it ... There was an attendance of twenty-four – number on the list, thirty. The school-house is a small, low building and contains neither blackboard nor chair. Long benches extend on the sides of the room, with desks of corresponding length in front of them. The whole interior is comfortless, and repulsive. The teacher, a colored lady,[37] is much troubled by the frequent absences of the pupils, and the miserably tattered and worn-out conditions of the books ... The teacher appeared to bear up as well as she could under her many discouragements: but the whole school adds one more dreary chapter to the 'pursuit of knowledge under difficulties.'[38]

Turner's working conditions were not poor and dreary simply because she was a Black woman working in a Black school. Conditions were wretched in many of the province's fledgling schools, but there was hope of improvement as the educational enterprise expanded and as the state began to take education more seriously and allot more money for the education of its young. However, race was a crucial factor in the process. White schools improved; most Black schools did not. Over time, primarily because of poor government funding, conditions worsened in many of the Black separate schools.[39]

Drew tells us that Turner was troubled by the difficulties she and her students encountered. Black children were taught in a facility that was dilapidated and lacked the necessary learning apparatus. The superintendent's reports of 1855 and 1856 confirmed some of Drew's observations. The 1856 report noted that the school lacked blackboards and maps. The school is described as 'old' and 'rented.' In comparison, the white school had eight maps and a blackboard.[40] This report confirmed the low priority that the provincial government accorded the Black schools. By and large, the needs of the whites were given first priority.

The absence of relevant teaching apparatus in the Black school raises some important pedagogical questions. Since maps and blackboards were missing, how did Turner teach subjects that required the use of these things? On a personal level, did she continue living with her parents while she taught at the Amherstburg school? It is likely that she was still living at home, since she was teaching in her home town, receiving a pitiful salary, and remained unmarried. She had a number of young siblings, and it is feasible to assume that her earnings went a long way in helping her family out.[41]

At the time of her tenure at the Amherstburg school, Turner held a third-class county certificate. She did not attend the Normal School, so must have obtained her certificate from a county institute. These institutes held summer courses at various places in the county. Examinations were held at the courthouse in Sandwich, the seat of Essex County. Although in 1855 she held the lowest county certificate, which implied that her level of educational training was not extensive, she had been teaching for over ten years.

Turner continued at the Amherstburg school until the end of 1856, when she was forced out of the school by the parents, trustees, and other school supporters. According to the minutes of the school trustees, on 12 January 1856 'a petition was received from the coloured people on the subject of employing a male teacher instead of a female. It was agreed to call a meeting of the coloured people on Monday evening next to consider the matter. A balance of $167.00 being due to Miss Turner and it was agreed the same should be paid.'[42] The trustees give no indication as to why parents and others wanted a male teacher instead of Julia Turner. Did they believe that a man would be a better teacher? Did they feel that Turner and other female teachers were incompetent? Did it have to do with a developing belief in the province that men were better managers of children? Some historians have noted that 'rural authorities worried about the ability of women teachers, particularly if they were young, to manage schools attended by young men and about the ability of women to "govern" children in general.'[43] Those who favoured the 'men as better managers' position felt that men could give more advanced training and discipline, especially to older boys. Since the minutes do not give the reason for the male preference, we can only assume and speculate. What is certain is that sexism was at the base of Turner's dismissal.

How does one explain this kind of sexism in the Black Amherstburg community? Was it reflective of the larger southwestern Ontario Black community? Mary Ann Shadd, while teaching school in Chatham, wrote to George Whipple of the American Missionary Association and expressed the view that Chatham Blacks had a preference for male teachers. She said that the Chathamites had a 'prejudice' against female teachers.[44] This is a strange charge considering the crucial role Black women played in setting up schools in Ontario and the number of Black women teachers. How can this paradox be explained?[45] James Horton notes that many free Blacks, despite economic limitations and racial constraints, sought to model the gender conventions articulated by white society. Even though lack of employment opportunities for Black men dictated that most Black women would work for a wage, the preference, in subscription to the ideal espoused by separate sphere ideology, was for women to remain at home and be 'model housewives.' Male editors at Black newspapers were at the forefront of pushing the separate ideology ideal. However, Horton notes that these same men also exhorted Black women to undertake reform and uplift work.[46]

Turner continued on in the midst of the controversy until 18 December 1856. At the beginning of the new year a man, John B. Williams, replaced her at the Amherstburg school. It was not until 1869, thirteen years after the firing of Turner, that the Amherstburg separate school trustees hired another woman as a teacher, though they hired women as assistants.[47]

From the end of 1856 to 1861, Turner's name seems not to be listed in any of the superintendents' reports for separate schools in Essex County. What did she do in these years? Did she continue teaching? Did she leave the province? Did she change occupation? Seeking different employment was not an uncommon route for teachers. Some became seamstresses, some went to work full time on the farm, and some became domestics.[48] It is possible that Turner continued teaching. The schools' reports are not the most reliable sources for tracking down a teacher or following the activity of a separate school. Not all Black schools received government aid. Some were run solely by Black parents, or with the help of missionary associations. These schools would not make it into the government's report.

In 1862 Turner emerges as a teacher with a second-class certificate at the Black separate school in Anderdon. She may well, then, have continued in teaching during the years her name was absent from the superintendents' reports. She had upgraded her school certificate, and would most likely not have done so if she had not been in the education business.[49] Turner remained at Anderdon for only one year. In 1863 she started teaching at the Sandwich separate school, where she was to spend the rest of her teaching life.

The separate school at Sandwich had a troubled history. Mary Bibb, on arriving in Sandwich in 1850, started a school in her home for the Black children of the area because they were being driven from the common school by whites and had no access to schooling. Bibb's school later became 'public' when she applied for and received a small subsidy from the province. However, the school floundered owing to a lack of financial resources. Sometime in 1853 the government reactivated the school, but it was closed again a year later.[50] The Black children of Sandwich went without a common school until 1859, when, after years of agitation by their parents, the trustees for the town opened a school for them. Turner was the third teacher to be appointed to the Sandwich school since its opening. She was paid $200 for her services that year. The Sandwich trustees, like those in several other places, did not spend much money on the separate school. Turner instructed her charges in the 'coloured church.' The province, then, did not fully support the school, and the community had to 'pitch in' to make the school viable.

Turner again worked to upgrade her credentials and in 1866 she was awarded a first-class certificate. In 1869, the last year that the superintendents' reports were filed, Julia Turner was still at Sandwich and the school was still being kept in the Black Methodist Church.[51]

Turner continued on at Sandwich until her retirement. In the 1871 and 1881 censuses, her name appeared in the town of Sandwich as 'schoolteacher.' In the latter year she was fifty years old and had taught Black children for more than thirty-five years. She is listed in the 1891 census, but no profession is given, so presumably she had retired. It is quite possible that Turner taught well after 1881, when she was last listed as a schoolteacher. If so, she could have taught for forty years or more – a phenomenal record, given that, in the mid and late nineteenth century, most teachers did not spend more than four years in the occupation.[52] Turner devoted most of her life to teaching and became a 'career woman' before the term was invented. Another point is instructive: she taught for her whole career in rural schools. Turner's story alerts us to the fact that the history of teaching in Ontario and Canada must be rewritten to include Black women, many of whom devoted decades to the occupation and helped to give it a professional 'image' at a time when teaching was often seen as an interlude before marriage.

The bulk of Turner's teaching career occurred during the post-Confederation period, after 1867. Within the new nation state, the position of Black people was to be even more tenuous than it was under the old order. Blacks became even more marginalized. With the end of the American Civil War and the abolition of slavery, many white Canadians felt that the 'Black' problem was over. Abolition was interpreted by many whites to mean that Blacks would no longer be seeking refuge on Canadian soil. It never seemed to occur to Canadian whites that American Blacks would want to come to Canada as immigrants, in the same way that Europeans and white Americans were coming. Even though several hundred African Canadians of American stock went to the United States during the Reconstruction to find lost relatives, pursue better opportunites, and help in the building of a new society, the bulk of Black Ontarians, even those who were American born, remained in Ontario. Their children and grandchildren were Canadians and saw Canada as home. This post-Confederation Black community became more and more invisible as a vibrant nationalism emerged which did not see Black people as part of the Canadian nation-building ethos. Blacks now faced extreme discrimination in employment, education, and other areas of life. One of the paradoxes of post-Confederation Canada is that, as European immigrants flooded to country to take up opportunities provided by an expanding agricultural and industrial sector, Black Canadians were denied these opportunities and many families sunk into poverty.[53]

As a result, hundreds of Black Canadians from both the Maritimes and Ontario went south to the United States to find work and other economic opportunities. In the United States, racial segregation was enshrined in law, and African Americans continued to feel the sting of racial oppression. Yet because of the size of the population and the Jim Crow laws, American Blacks were able to establish their own institutions and to provide employment for themselves along with educational, social, and other opportunities. In Canada there was no official colour bar, yet African Canadians were consistently denied the opportunity by white society to improve their lives. Many of the hundreds who migrated to the United States in the post-Confederation era were able to find a 'larger world' there.[54]

The post-Confederation era did not augur well for either Black women or Black men, in spite of the new economic opportunities that resulted from the industrialization of the country. Historian Jane Errington, in assessing the impact of this new mode of production on women, notes: 'Between 1870 and 1920, as the Canadian economy became industrialized and urbanized, women were ... drawn to the growing towns and cities of the new nation, where factories, shops, and mills promised adventure, greater personal and economic independence.'[55] But the 'generic woman' Errington is talking about is white. Black and other racial minority women were not allowed in these factories, shops, or mills. Oral accounts from Black women about their life and work experiences, and those of their mothers in the first half of this century, attest to this discrimination. Their stories detail their exclusion from the new industrial opportunities right up to the outbreak of the Second World War. It was not until this period that Black women were allowed in the factories. As Marjorie Lewsey, with stinging irony, testifies: 'We weren't allowed to go into factory work until Hitler started the war.'[56] It was the labour shortage occasioned by the war, not a civil rights impulse, which dictated the 'integration' of the workforce in terms of race and sex.

In the post-Confederation era in which Julia Turner taught, Black women who worked outside the home were concentrated in the fields of teaching and domestic work. For Black men who were not farmers, or who did not pursue other independent work activities, a 'racially split' labour market developed. Black men were primarily employed as railway porters. They found it almost impossible to find any other kind of public employment.[57]

Given the lack of job opportunities that existed for Blacks as a whole, and Black women in particular, the fact that Julia Turner was a consistent wage earner for over thirty-five years was a stunning achievement. She fought sexual and racial oppression to live as best she could in the world. She must have been aware of how her race and sex were perceived by white society: that the most suitable employment for Black women was as a domestic worker. She must also have been equally aware of her status as a consistent wage earner and of the difficulties Blacks faced in gaining viable paid employment.

Turner did not conform to the stereotypes that were put on her gender and her race in nineteenth-century North America. She created her own reality and, though she did not leave many written records behind, it is clear that her sense of self was quite developed. Her longevity in teaching must have created in Turner a tremendous amount of self-confidence, self-esteem, and pride.

The fact that Turner worked solely in separate schools points to the nature of racial oppression and race relations in Canada. In some places, Black teachers could be found teaching in white schools, but only in areas where there were few Black families and teachers were sorely needed.[58] Whites sometimes instructed in Black schools, but, by and large, Black teachers worked in Black schools and perhaps preferred it that way. Evidence shows that Black teachers clung tenaciously to their jobs in Black schools, for the Black school was one of the few areas in which they could find permanent jobs.[59]

In addition, in most instances Black parents preferred that Black teachers instruct their children.[60] The flip side was the unlikeliness that white trustees and white-dominated school boards would hire a Black teacher to teach in a largely white school. The fact that it was only in 1913 that the Windsor School Board hired its first Black teacher, Ada Kelly, points to the racialized nature of teaching in Ontario, a situation that did not ease in the later period.[61] As late as the post-1945 era, Fern Shadd Shreve reported that when she graduated from Normal School, she taught in a school that for all intents and purpose was a Black school. Yet, after returning to work following the birth of her son, and with the dismantling of the Black school, she could not find a job in a white school. 'Black teachers were not allowed to teach in white schools,' she said.[62]

Turner gave most of her life to one of the very few professions opened to women at that time. It was true that women in teaching were underpaid and overworked, but, as historians have pointed out, it was one of the few areas that 'welcomed' women. Many women knew they were exploited by the school officials, but they nonetheless used teaching as a vehicle to acquire independence, and as a real and positive alternative to marriage. Teaching provides an excellent example of the way women used an exploitative situation to acquire independence and power. For Turner it was a site where race, class, economic stature, and gender were inextricably linked.

Family and Marital Status

Turner did not marry. She started her work life as a 'daughter in the house,' and at some point moved out to establish her own hearth. According to the Sandwich assessor's roll for 1870, she was living by herself and paying the school tax for a property she had purchased on East Bedford Street. It would therefore be safe to conclude that Turner began living on her own when she took up the teaching position at the Sandwich school.

Once Turner began to live on her own, she had to continue working. Teaching for her was not a stopgap before marriage and motherhood. It would appear that the consistent manner in which she strove to upgrade her teaching credentials meant that she saw teaching as a lifelong occupation. Her rejection of marriage also indicates that she became conscious of herself as a breadwinner, and as one capable of supporting herself. Clearly she saw teaching as a way to 'make her way in the world,' a way to support herself and live independently.

African diasporic scholar Filomina Chioma Steady, in her work on the historical experiences of African-descended women, identifies two dominant measures – self-reliance and a survival strategy imperative – that Black women used to combat racial, gender, and class tyranny. These values, according to Steady, have become institutionalized in many African and

African-descended communities. Given the multiple forms of oppression that Turner faced as a Black woman in the mid and late nineteenth century, it becomes apparent that she articulated these two values in her quest to overcome social inequities and to live as fully human as possible.[63]

The fact that Turner did not marry does not mean that she missed out on love or sexual relationships. She may well have chosen to remain single. Historians of women teachers have chronicled the loss of independence and income that women teachers experienced when they married. The potential loss of income loomed large as a reason why many female teachers chose not to marry. Also, for women used to looking after themselves, even on a small salary, the thought of having to succumb to male authority within a marriage, and accepting the inherent inequalities in most heterosexual marriages, was something many found unappealing.

As was to be expected, Turner remained close to her family. The 1891 census revealed that her sister Jordinia (spelt 'Georgina' in the census) was living with her. Jordinia was married at this time and had children, but her husband is not listed as being part of the household. According to the census, Jordinia was also working as a servant. Perhaps a dislocation in her immediate family situation necessitated her living with her sister and working to support herself and her children.[64]

For much of the 1870s, 1880s, and 1890s, children lived with Turner. They may have been family members, children of her siblings. It is also probable that they were Jordinia's children and that Turner helped to support them both financially and emotionally.[65] Turner must also have had a circle of friends, part of which may have come from her church community. Various records show that she was a Baptist. Given the religiosity of the period, especially among Black people, one can easily surmise that Turner was a practising Christian and a faithful Baptist, and that she helped to organize social activities for her church and participated in church affairs. Her uplift work would have extended beyond the classroom.

Julia Turner, A Wealthy Woman

On 10 November 1900 Julia Turner died at Amherstburg from heart failure and an enlarged thyroid.[66] She had died 'intestate,' which meant that she did not leave a will. Five weeks later an application was filed in the surrogate court at Sandwich by attorney Arthur St George Ellis to administer Turner's estate. The persons named on the document as her heirs were two brothers, James and William, two sisters, Rosina Monroe and Jordinia Matthews, a niece, Estella Thomas, and a nephew, Walter Viney. Her real estate was valued at $4200; her personal estate and effects at less than $1800.[67] According to this document she owned property in Amherstburg, Sandwich, Malden, and Colchester.

The probate document, read along with the tax records, clearly reveals that Turner invested and speculated in real estate. The assessment rolls for Sandwich show that, beginning in 1870, she began to acquire property in that town and, by 1899, owned at least five lots of varying size and value.[68] At the time of her death she owned only two properties in Sandwich, but several in at least three other townships, placing her among those who paid the highest taxes in Essex County. Family lore has it that, along with liquor magnate Hiram Walker, Turner was one of the county's leading taxpayers.

Clearly, Turner not only saved the money she earned as a teacher but invested in property. The probate document speaks volumes about the kind of woman Turner was. She persisted in teaching for over thirty-five years and used her exploitation and subordination to 'raise herself in the world.' Through teaching and the force of her own personality she was able to transcend in varying degrees racial, sexual, and class oppression. Here was a person who was born poor, but died relatively well off. Perhaps that in itself is not so unusual, but when racial oppression and the sexist nature of the society are considered, Turner's accomplishment truly must be described as phenomenal.

NOTES

1 See Linda Gordon's discussion, 'U.S. Women's History,' in *The New American History*, a pamphlet published by the American Historical Association in 1997.
2 The outpouring of works on white women's history, both French and English, in the past two decades is staggering, and two examples will suffice: Veronica Strong-Boag, *The New Day Recalled: Lives of Girls and Women in English Canada, 1919–1939* (Toronto: Penguin, 1988); the Clio Collective, *Quebec Women: A History* (Toronto: Women's Press, 1987). Recently, attention has shifted to include women of non-English and non-French backgrounds. See Jean Burnet, *Looking into My Sister's Eyes* (Toronto: Multicultural History Society of Ontario, 1986); Barbara Latham and Roberta Pazdro, eds., *Not Just Pin Money: Selected Essays on the History of Women's Work in British Columbia* (Victoria: Camosun College, 1984); Franca Iacovetta and Mariana Valverde, eds., *Gender Conflicts: New Essays in Women's History* (Toronto: University of Toronto Press, 1992). Though attention is paid in these studies to 'immigrant women' and some women of colour, the main focus is still on white women. The authors have failed to develop adequately in their texts an analysis in which race is part of

the consideration of gender. Gender is usually perceived as 'something belonging' to white women.

3 Sherry Edmunds Flett, '"Abundant Faith": 19th Century African Canadian Women on Vancouver Island' (unpublished paper), 3.

4 Gail Cuthbert Brandt deals with some of these issues and the state of Canadian women's historiography in 'Postmodern Patchwork: Some Recent Trends in the Writing of Women's History in Canada,' *Canadian Historical Review* 62, 4 (1991): 441–70.

5 I am not suggesting that there be separate areas for each category of women or that white women's history be 'decentred' to make the experiences of Black women and women of colour visible. The centre can be 'constantly and appropriately' pivoted. See Elsa Barkley Brown, 'African-American Women's Quilting: A Framework for Conceptualizing and Teaching African-American Women's History,' *Signs* 14, 4 (1989): 921–2. Brown acknowledges Bettina Aptheker, *Tapestries of Life: Women's Work, Women's Consciousness and the Meaning of Daily Life* (Amherst: University of Massachusetts Press, 1989), for this concept of looking at history from 'numerous centers and thus to maintain the reality that all these centers exist simultaneously.'

6 Darlene Clark Hine, *Hine Sight, Black Women and the Reconstruction of American History* (Bloomington: Indiana University Press, 1994), xxvi.

7 The following works, centring Black women's experiences, have been critical in making Canadian women's historical writing more inclusive. Sylvia Hamilton, 'Our Mothers Grand and Great: Black Women of Nova Scotia,' *Canadian Woman Studies* 4, 2 (1982): 32–7; Adrienne Shadd, '300 Years of Black Women in Canadian History: Circa 1700–1980,' *Tiger Lily* 1, 2 (1987): 4–13; Myriam Merlet, 'Black Women Immigrants,' in Kathleen Storrie, ed., *Women: Isolation and Bonding, The Ecology of Gender* (Toronto: Methuen, 1987), 159–75; Esmeralda Thornhill, 'Focus on Black Women,' *Socialist Studies* 5 (1989): 26–36; Agnes Calliste, 'Canada's Immigration Policy and Domestics from the Caribbean: The Second Domestic Scheme,' *Socialist Studies* 5 (1989): 133–65; Makeda Silvera, *Silenced: Talks with Working Class Caribbean Women about Their Lives and Struggles as Domestic Workers in Canada*, 2nd ed. (Toronto: Sister Vision Press, 1989); Dionne Brand, *No Burden to Carry: Narratives of Black Women Working in Ontario, 1920s to 1950s* (Toronto: Women's Press, 1991); Afua Cooper, 'The Search for Mary Bibb, Black Woman Teacher in Nineteenth-Century Canada West,' *Ontario History* 83, 1 (1991): 39–54, reprinted in Darlene Clark Hine, Wilma King, and Linda Reed, eds., *'We Specialize in the Wholly Impossible': A Reader in Black Women's History* (Brooklyn: Carlson Publishing, 1995), 171–85; Peggy Bristow, Dionne Brand, Linda Carty, Afua Cooper, Sylvia Hamilton, and Adrienne Shadd, *'We're Rooted Here and They Can't Pull Us Up': Essays in African Canadian Women's History* (Toronto: University of Toronto Press, 1994/ 1999); Suzanne Morton, 'Separate Spheres in a Separate World: African Nova

Scotia Women in Late-19th-Century Halifax County,' in Janet Guilford, ed., *Separate Spheres: Women's World in the 19th-Century Maritimes* (Fredericton: Acadiensis Press, 1994), 185–210; Shirley J. Yee, 'Gender Ideology and Black Women as Community-Builders in Ontario, 1850–1870,' *Canadian Historical Review* 75, 1 (1994): 53–73; Judith Fingard, 'From Sea to Rail: Black Transportation Workers and Their Families in Halifax, c. 1870–1916,' *Acadiensis* 24, 2 (1995): 49–64; Kenneth Donovan, 'Slaves and Their Owners in Ile Royale, 1713–1760,' *Acadiensis* 25, 1 (1995): 3–32; Carol B. Duncan, '"Dey Give Me a House to Gather in Di Chil'ren": Mothers and Daughters in the Spiritual Baptist Church' *Canadian Woman Studies* 18, 2 and 3 (1998): 126–31.

8 Gisela Bock, 'Women's History, Gender History,' *Gender and History* (1989): 7.

9 See documents filed in the surrogate courts of Essex County regarding Julia Turner's property. Jordinia Turner relates a brief family history in these documents. Archives of Ontario (AO), probate documents, Julia Turner, GS1–741.

10 See Robin Winks, *The Blacks in Canada: A History* (1971; reprint, Montreal and Kingston: McGill-Queen's University Press, 1997).

11 Personal conversation with Mrs Jackson, March 1991.

12 Colin Thomson, *Blacks in Deep Snow: Black Pioneers in Canada* (Don Mills, Ont.: J.M. Dent, 1979).

13 Metropolitan Toronto Reference Library, Black Canadian Militia file.

14 For a discussion on the extreme youthfulness of Ontario's early female teachers, see Marta Danylewycz, Beth Light, and Alison Prentice, 'The Evolution of the Sexual Division of Labour in Teaching: A Nineteenth-Century Ontario and Quebec Case Study,' *Histoire sociale/Social History* 26, 31 (1983): 81–109, particularly 93, 96, and 97.

15 Isaac Rice was a white missionary maintained by the American Missionary Association in Amherstburg. He started one of the first schools for Black children in that town. However, Rice soon came in conflict with some of the parents and members of his congregation. See Jason H. Silverman and Donna J. Gillie, '"The Pursuit of Knowledge under Difficulties": Education and the Fugitive Slave in Canada,' *Ontario History* 74 (1982): 97.

16 Trustees developed a notorious reputation because of their parsimonious attitudes with regard to spending money on schools and school programs. By having the Black school in Rice's mission house, they would not have to build or rent a suitable building in which to conduct the school. The trustees must also have felt that the mission house was 'ideal' since Rice had earlier started a school there for Black youths.

17 Schooling at this time was supported by the taxpayers. The rate bill was one kind of tax designed by school officials to help with the salaries of the teacher. Turner hints at the current dilemma that many Black parents faced in getting an education for their children: though they paid the school tax, their children were often chased from the common schools by whites who did not want their

children to mix with Black children. Black parents could not withhold their taxes, but could withhold the rate bill. Parents often sued the trustees or the government for the lack of educational opportunities for their children. See H.W. Arthur, 'Civil Liberties – Public Schools – Segregation of Negro Students,' *Canadian Bar Review* 41 (September 1963): 453–7; Claudette Knight, 'Black Parents Speak: Education in Mid-Nineteenth-Century Canada West,' *Ontario History* 89, 4 (1997): 269–84.

18 The Fugitive Slave Bill became law in the American Congress in September 1850. It granted slave owners the power to hunt and capture slaves who they claimed had run away from them. This right caused great panic and fear among Blacks in the northern states, many of whom were escaped slaves who had been living in freedom for a long time. Numerous families fled to Ontario because of this law. Alarmed at the proscriptive laws against them, many free families also left. Fred Landon, 'The Negro Migration to Canada after the Passing of the Fugitive Slave Act,' *Journal of Negro History* 5 (1920): 22–36.

19 Original copy of the letter is at the American Missionary Association's Archives, Amistad Research Center, Tulane University, Louisiana.

20 Bruce Curtis, *Building the Educational State in Canada West, 1836–1871* (London, Ont.: Althouse Press, 1988); Alison Prentice, 'The Feminization of Teaching in British North America and Canada, 1845–1875,' *Histoire sociale/Social History* 8, 15 (1975): 5–20; and Janet Guilford, 'Separate Spheres: The Feminization of Public School Teaching in Nova Scotia, 1838–1880,' in her *Separate Spheres*, 119–44.

21 Historian Michael Wayne notes that by 1861 at least 40 per cent of the Black children in Ontario was born in the province: 'The Black Population of Canada West on the Eve of the American Civil War: A Reassessment Based on the Manuscript Census of 1861,' in Franca Iacovetta, Paula Draper, and Robert Ventresca, eds., *A Nation of Immigrants: Women, Workers, and Communities in Canadian History, 1840–1960s* (Toronto: University of Toronto Press, 1998), 64, 65.

22 See William Riddell, 'Petition of People of Colour of Ancaster,' *Journal of Negro History* 15 (1930): 115–16. Alison Prentice and Susan Houston, *Schooling and Scholars in Nineteenth-Century Ontario* (Toronto: University of Toronto Press, 1988), 300; Silverman and Gillie, 'Pursuit of Knowledge under Difficulties,' 95–112.

23 For details of the Common School Act, which legislated separate schooling for Blacks, see J. George Hodgins, *Documentary History of Education in Upper Canada*, 9: 1850–1851 (Toronto: L.K. Cameron, 1902), 24–5, 38–9.

24 'Petition of Black Residents of Euphemia against Boundary Changes to Exclude Them from the White School,' AO, RG 2 C6c, Incoming General Correspondence to the Department of Education, 9 August 1853.

25 See Silverman and Gillie, 'Pursuit of Knowledge under Difficulties' and Knight, 'Black Parents Speak.'

26 Afua Cooper, 'Black Teachers in Canada West, 1850–1870: A History' (MA thesis, University of Toronto, 1991).

27 Carter G. Woodson, *Education of the Negro prior to 1860* (New York: Arno Press, 1968); Silverman and Gillie, 'Pursuit of Knowledge under Difficulties'; Cooper, 'Black Teachers in Canada West'; and Yee, 'Gender Ideology and Black Women.'

28 Those who exhorted Blacks to uplift the race appealed to both women and men. Because of racial oppression, both sexes were convinced of the need for elevating the race. Most of the exhorters seem to have been men, but, owing to racial and sexual oppression, they had more access to the means of public expression and left more written records behind than women. The women who did leave records showed that they, too, supported and engaged in uplift activities. See Linda Perkins, 'Black Women and Racial "Uplift" prior to Emancipation,' in F.C. Steady, ed., *The Black Woman Cross-Culturally* (Cambridge, Mass.: Schenkman Books, 1981) 317–34; James Oliver Horton, 'Freedom's Yoke: Gender Conventions among Antebellum Free Blacks,' *Feminist Studies* 12, 1 (1986): 51–76.

29 Perkins, 'Black Women and Racial "Uplift,"' 323.

30 *Voice of the Fugitive*, 15 January 1851.

31 Cooper, 'Black Teachers in Canada West,' 95–6. Ronald Butchart also examines uplift in the work of some African American teachers he studied; see his '"We Can Best Instruct Our Own People": New York African Americans in the Freedmen's Schools, 1861–1875,' *Afro Americans in New York Life and History* (January 1988): 33.

32 For a discussion of several teachers who kept on teaching despite inadequate remuneration, see Cooper, 'Black Teachers in Canada West,' 81–98.

33 A large majority of the young female teachers in Ontario, Black and white, were farmers' daughters. Prentice and Houston, *Schooling and Scholars*, 170.

34 One could argue that uplift was a middle-class ideology, given the push that came from the Black intelligentsia. This class privilege gave it access to print. Still, I maintain that, even though the Black middle class presented its opinions as *the* Black opinion, poor and working-class people, given the racist nature of the society, willingly supported and promoted uplift. For a Black intellectual position, see Martin Delany, *The Condition, Elevation, Emigration, and Destiny of the Colored People of the United States* (1852; reprint, New Hampshire: Ayers Co., 1988). Delany wrote this book before he came to live in Ontario, but residence in the province did not change his view, as his actions on behalf of Kent's Black community testified.

35 See AO, McCurdy Collection, King Street School, Amherstburg, Minutes of Public School Trustees, 1851–82.

36 In fact, Amherstburg's Blacks fought segregated schooling and refused to set up a separate school when Ryerson advised them to do so in 1846. They firmly

believed in integrated education and desired to send their children to the local schools. But the whites would not agree. Finally, unable to 'beat down white prejudice,' Amherstburg's Blacks capitulated and set up a separate school by 1851. AO, RG 2 cbc, Robert Peden to Egerton Ryerson, 23 February 1846; RG 2 C1, Egerton Ryerson to Isaac Rice, 5 March 1846; see also Silverman and Gillie, 'Pursuit of Knowledge under Difficulties.'

37 The minutes of the Amherstburg Trustees reveal that it was Julia Turner who was the 'colored lady teacher' at the time of Drew's visit to the Amherstburg school. See AO, McCurdy Collection, Minutes of Public School Trustees.

38 Benjamin Drew, *Narratives of Fugitives Slaves in Canada* (Boston: Jewett & Co., 1856), 348

39 For the poor condition of the province's schools as the educational state got into full gear, see Prentice and Houston, *Schooling and Scholars*, 210–12.

40 See AO, RG 2 17, superintendent's reports, 1855, 1856, Amherstburg, Essex County.

41 One study shows that, by 1881, well over half the female teachers in at least seven Ontario counties were daughters living at home. Danylewycz, Light, and Prentice, 'Sexual Division of Labour,' 100.

42 See AO, McCurdy Collection, Minutes of Trustees.

43 Danylewycz, Light, and Prentice, 'Sexual Division of Labour,' 85.

44 American Missionary Association, Shadd to Whipple, 6 August 1861.

45 The prejudice against women teachers in Western society can probably be traced back to Saul of Tarsus's injunction against the practice: 'Let not a woman teach, nor to usurp authority over the man, but to be in silence,' says the man who later became St Paul. In his view, patriarchal civilization would crumble if women stepped into the public realm and 'uttered.' Their silence ensured their subordination to male authority.

46 Horton, 'Freedom's Yoke,' 51–76.

47 The hiring of Black women as assistants after Turner's firing lends credence to my suspicion that Turner was fired because trustees and parents became 'anxious' about a woman in charge of their children. This fear probably derived from the belief that a woman could not instill the 'proper discipline' in their children.

48 Mary Bibb, for example, became a dressmaker after her first school foundered in Sandwich. She advertized her business in the *Voice of the Fugitive* from July to December 1852.

49 Another possibility is that Turner worked at home while at the same time studying to raise the level of her education. When she obtained a second-class certificate, she reapplied for work in the system.

50 For a history of Mary Bibb and the Sandwich school, see Afua Cooper, 'Black Women and Work in 19th-Century Canada West: Black Woman Teacher Mary Bibb,' in Bristow et al., *'We're Rooted Here and They Can't Pull Us Up,'* 143–70.

51 See AO, RG 2 17, Superintendent's Reports for Essex, 1863–9.

52 Danylewycz, Light, and Prentice, 'Sexual Division of Labour in Teaching,' 97.

53 Robin Winks calls this period, from 1865 to 1930, the 'nadir' in the Black historical experiences in Canada. See his *Blacks in Canada*, 288–336.

54 See James Walker, *A History of Blacks in Canada* (Quebec: Government of Canada Publication, 1980), 67–8.

55 Jane Errington, 'Pioneers and Suffragists,' in Sandra Burt, Lorraine Code, and Lindsay Dorney, eds., *Changing Patterns: Women in Canada* (Toronto: McClelland & Stewart, 1993), 70.

56 Dionne Brand, 'We weren't allowed to go into the factory until Hitler started the war': The 1920s to the 1940s,' in Bristow et al., *'We're Rooted Here and They Can't Pull Us Up,'* 179.

57 Agnes Calliste, 'Sleeping Car Porters in Canada: An Ethnically Submerged Split Labour Market,' in Laurel MacDowell and Ian Radforth, eds., *Canadian Working-Class History* (Toronto: Canadian Scholars' Press, 1992), 673–92.

58 For example, Emmaline Shadd taught in a Scottish Gaelic community in Peel County. The fact that Shadd was extremely light-skinned and did not have 'Negroid' features perhaps helped her to gain acceptance by this community. Her photograph suggests that she could, if she wanted to, pass for white. Shadd stayed in Peel for a year, after which she left, married, and retired from teaching. The case of Walter Rolling bears on this point. Rolling, descended from Black pioneers who homesteaded in the Aurora area in the 1830s, became the principal of a white school in 1895. Aurora had few Black families and perhaps whites there did not see someone like Rolling as a threat. A teacher/ principal was also needed for the school. On Shadd, see Cooper, 'Black Teachers in Canada West,' 113; on Rolling, see Carl Finkle, 'Walter Rolling: Black School Principal,' *Akili: Journal of African Canadian Studies* (March 1995): 14–15.

59 Alfred Whipper and Aaron Highgate, two Black teachers, fought hard for their jobs in the Chatham separate school when the white trustees tried to oust them from it. See note 60.

60 Black parents protested in 1859 when the Chatham school trustees fired the two Black teachers of the separate school, Aaron Highgate and Alfred Whipper, and hired a white teacher, Peter Nichol. The trustees justified their action by claiming that Nichol was the most qualified because he had a first-class teaching certificate. The Black parents objected angrily, arguing that their children needed Black teachers as they served as better role models. For them, a first-class certificate was not as important as having a Black person in charge. See Cooper, 'Black Teachers in Canada West,' 59–60.

61 See 'Ada Kelly Whitney's Story' in the kit *Black Women in Canada: Past and Present*, compiled by Marguerite Alfred and Pat Staton (Toronto: Green Dragon Press, 1997).

62 Brand, *No Burden to Carry*, 272.

63 See Steady, *Black Woman Cross-Culturally*, 22–4. Rosalyn Terborg-Penn elaborates on Steady's research and theory in her article, 'Through an African Feminist Lens: Viewing Caribbean Women's History Cross-Culturally,' in Verene Shepherd, Bridget Brereton, and Barbara Bailey, eds., *Engendering History: Caribbean Women in Historical Perspective* (Kingston, Jamaica: Ian Randle, 1995), 3–19.

64 Jordinia at some point in her life also taught school. It could be that after she married she left teaching, but had to continue in paid employment to help her family.

65 See AO, GS 976, Assessors' rolls for Sandwich from 1875 to 1899.

66 AO, MS 935, reel 96, Vital Statistics Records, Death Registration. The fact that Turner died in Amherstburg indicates that she may have been ill for some time and moved to her home town to be cared for by family members.

67 AO, GS 1, 741, application filed in the surrogate court of Essex County, 15 December 1900.

68 AO, GS 976, Assessors' rolls, Town of Sandwich, Essex County, 1870–99.

The Wikwemikong First Nation and the Department of Indian Affairs' Mismanagement of Petroleum Development

RHONDA TELFORD

In the 1860s, Charles T. Dupont, Indian agent at Manitowaning, authorized outsiders to develop the unrelinquished oil and gas resources of the Wikwemikong First Nation on Manitoulin Island. A high-ranking official in the Crown Land Department – William Spragge, the deputy superintendent of Indian Affairs – collaborated with Dupont to bring his illegal and fraudulent leases into operation. Against this blatant colonial appropriation of Aboriginal property stood the Wikwemikong First Nation, which opposed the efforts of the Indian Department to control and regulate its petroleum resources through consistent declarations of sovereignty and by issuing its own unilateral leases. Nevertheless, Indian Department mismanagement and appropriation continued to affect the Wikwemikong First Nation negatively into the twentieth century.

The Wikwemikong reserve occupies the easternmost section of land on Manitoulin Island. The Wikwemikong First Nation, which includes Ottawa, Potawatami, and Ojibwa peoples, did not sign the Manitoulin Treaty in 1862; it therefore retained its Aboriginal title and rights to the entire island and all the out-islands. The island is unceded Aboriginal territory.[1]

The year 1857 marked the first oil boom in Canada at Oil Springs, Ontario. By October 1862 and the conclusion of the Manitoulin Treaty, the boom at Oil Springs had been eclipsed by another close by at Petrolia. The non-Natives and their settler government were obsessed with the sticky black substance and its development. Aboriginal people, however, had always known where the petroleum was located and had shared this information with non-Natives. Native people were the original discoverers of this oil and the first to have sacred and commercial uses for the substance.

Early Aboriginal Knowledge and Use of Petroleum

The Native people of Manitoulin Island collected oil from seepages on the surface of the earth and skimmed it from the water. The Ottawa, Ojibwa, and Potawatami, who valued oil for its healing properties, shared their knowledge with missionaries, prospectors, and settlers. These Native groups told the Jesuits of two oil springs on Wikwemikong in the vicinity of Smith's Point during the 1600s.

Minerals, including oil and gas, were intimately connected to the spirit world, especially Michipichieu and his serpent companions, and were thereby associated with dreaming, medicine, and health. Michipichieu appears as the Great Lynx on land, but can also swim underwater and live in the caverns beneath the surface of the land. As the keeper of the minerals, he links water, submerged land, islands, and the places under the earth's surface to the Aboriginal people. He is the manifestation of the subsurface and submarine in Aboriginal thought. According to F.W. Major, a later commentator, the Ottawa believed the sticky black petroleum came 'from the entrails of the Great Manitou in which "rock oil" was found that cured all human diseases.' The Aboriginal disclosure of the location of the petroleum led to the first oil boom on Manitoulin in the mid-1860s, only two years after the treaty. William Baby, who received the first government licence near Smith's Point, acknowledged previous Aboriginal knowledge and use of the oil.[2]

Native groups consumed and distributed the petroleum locally and commercially in the form of oil medicine. The Seneca, for example, had been selling oil medicine to non-Natives at exorbitant prices since at least 1627. During the 1830s the Chippewa and Moravian peoples living in the vicinity of the Thames River and the Bear Creeks also sold oil medicine to local settlers.[3] By the 1850s and 1860s, however, oil was desired not so much as a medicine by non-Natives but as a lubricant and illuminating fluid. First Nation citizens on Manitoulin Island were more than willing to make deals and to prosper from the development of their ancient oil pools so long as they controlled the terms of leasing and the amount of compensation.

The Development of Petroleum on Manitoulin Island, 1864–1949

William Baby claimed to have permission from the Wikwemikong First Nation to explore for and develop oil over an area of 375,000 acres.[4] It is not known what the First Nation demanded in return for this privilege, but the Indian Department refused to recognize leases unilaterally negotiated by

Native groups. Baby and an associate also applied for a government lease in the fall of 1864, covering a smaller area 10 miles wide across the waterfront and 7 miles deep.

A bitter struggle ensued between First Nation citizens and the Indian Department over who would control and profit from the exploitation of the oil. Charles Dupont, the Indian agent for Manitoulin Island and the north shores, possessed several applications in addition to Baby's. He was supposed to hold a council of the Wikwemikong First Nation to obtain a blanket surrender of its oil and gas rights. Although Dupont fixed the date of this council for early 1865, he realized after he held preliminary discussions with individual Native people on the issue that they would not agree to conduct business through either himself or the department. Father Stanipeaux, one of the local priests, confirmed his suspicions. Dupont therefore reported to his superiors that the Wikwemikong viewed itself as a sovereign, 'separate and distinct Nation ... very jealous of relinquishing any of their rights, by appearing to consent to the Right of [the Crown] ... to exercise any control over the Reserves.' He saw the Wikwemikong people as troublesome and independent simply because he could not control them.[5] When they insisted on conducting business for themselves, Dupont treated them with the greatest 'hatred' and disdain. Finally, in 1868 he was removed from office because of his behaviour towards the Wikwemikong First Nation, his bloody assault on a priest, and his irregular land dealings.[6]

Dupont's first attempt to secure the oil and gas rights of the Wikwemikong people in council was unsuccessful because the chiefs and principal men refused to show up. Dupont later informed the Indian Department that the Wikwemikong people would not lease oil through the government. In assessing Aboriginal behaviour, he stated that 'their impression is that as owners of the soil they have a right to lease these locations directly from themselves and that if they attend any council or grant any permission to the Government to lease them for them they part with an imaginary title they have to distinct and independent nationality.'[7] Given Dupont's dislike of Aboriginal people, the opposition and obvious sovereignty of the Wikwemikong First Nation must have annoyed him. His comments, here as elsewhere, indicate that Native people viewed control over their minerals as an aspect of their inherent sovereignty. This issue of sovereignty, more than any other reason, is why the Indian Department tried, but failed, to prohibit Native control.

Dupont arranged for a second vote and council to be held in May when Baby and his associate could be on the reserve, but because the position of the First Nation had not changed, he was not optimistic that it would succeed. He foresaw correctly that if the Wikwemikong Nation asserted its sovereignty through the negotiation of independent leases that did not lead to extinguishment of title, other First Nations under his superintendence on the north shores would also seek this right and subvert the purpose of the Indian Department.[8]

The second vote was a complete failure for Dupont, who had postponed it for three days because Baby and his associate could not be present. This action was not ethical: none of the self-interested developers should have been present at the vote. Only forty-five Wikwemikong citizens from a total population of between six and seven hundred were in attendance at the council, and Dupont was shouted down by Father Chone, who was representing and speaking for the Indians. Dupont was unable to read the terms of the government's oil lease and was presented instead with a lease containing terms acceptable to the Wikwemikong people: Baby and his associate would have exclusive rights to develop the entire reserve, but all revenues generated were to be paid to the First Nation through Chone. Dupont, who was always concerned about the *appearance* of government power over the First Nations, did not accept either of these terms. He pointed out that Baby had already proposed to 'amalgamate' with other applicants. In effect, this meant that Baby would sublet the oil and thereby usurp control of leasing from the Indian Department. Likewise, if Chone and the Native peoples unilaterally controlled all the moneys generated, they, and not the Indian Department, would control the profits. The bureaucratic insistence on both the superficial and the real control of unceded natural resources was part of the way the government appropriated control of natural resources, including minerals, fish, game, water, shorelines, and timber. This posturing clearly indicated that the government understood the importance of, and sought to impose the appearance of, Crown control over First Nations so it could argue, then, or later, that First Nations were subordinate and not equal players. The response and actions of the Wikwemikong people indicate that they also understood this play.[9]

Although Dupont failed to obtain Aboriginal consent at this vote, the Indian Department licensed Baby and his associate in June 1865 to 'begin operations' on 70 square miles of the Wikwemikong reserve.[10] This licence was not valid: it breached government rules with regard to non-Native resource development on reserve land. The Indian Department was aware of this fact and continued to instruct Dupont to obtain the consent of the First Nation. Even though some Wikwemikong citizens had negotiated an independent lease with Baby, the department could not legally issue a licence because it had not obtained Aboriginal consent to do so. There could hardly be a stronger demonstration of Wikwemikong sovereignty than this authority to refuse to give consent. The First Nation never did give consent, either at the time or later, for the department's licence to Baby.

Dupont believed that he would obtain a blanket surrender of oil rights in a third vote, though he noted it would have been easier if Baby and his associate had not already started operations. There is no doubt that the Indian Department was trying to cover its back by continuing attempts to legitimize Baby's illegitimate lease after the fact.[11] Dupont, claiming he would collect fees of $20 for each licence from developers, and $50 for each location, advised the department not to invest the fees, but to pay out all the moneys, not only the interest, to First Nation members. He asserted that this course of action might aid the department in obtaining a surrender of the oil rights. Evidently, Dupont intended to use money from this development to bribe the First Nation into agreement.[12]

Dupont was told to expedite the surrender. He therefore held a council with Wah Ka Kizhok, the most influential chief, to arrange a vote date. When the chief replied that the people were fishing and would not return for some time, the date was set for early in 1866.[13]

By the fall of 1865, Dupont noted that $3 had accrued to the First Nation from dues on twelve barrels of oil. Under the terms set by the Indian Department, Aboriginal benefit amounted to only 25 cents per barrel. Dupont said he would take this money to council and pay the First Nation, as a way of gaining its consent. Yet this return was negligible, amounting to well under 1 cent for each First Nation member. In the same period, one barrel of oil was worth $12 at the Bothwell oilfields to the southwest. If Manitoulin oil was worth about the same, the Indian Department secured dues worth one-forty-eighth the value of a Bothwell barrel. Even if a barrel of Manitoulin oil was worth half the Bothwell price, the percentage authorized by the department as compensation was too low. This ridiculous sum is an example of the poor management skills of the Indian Department and, more important, a breach of fiduciary obligation.

In spite of Dupont's earlier statements about fees for licences and locations, this small rent of 25 cents per barrel appeared to be the only monetary provision made by the department for the benefit of the First Nation. Baby described the rent to be paid to the Wikwemikong First Nation as 'trifling' and noted that the company would retain all the oil produced. There was no provision for a portion of the oil to be returned to the First Nation for lighting or other purposes. Indeed, so pleased was Baby with the extraordinarily good deal the department had allowed him that he touted the lack of benefits to the First Nation as one of the great 'advantages' of the company.[14]

These comments are taken from Baby's first annual report, which Dupont sent to the Indian Department. They indicate that Baby was reporting his oil exploits to a government that had not yet obtained Aboriginal consent for its licence. Only a few days later, Baby and his associates petitioned to obtain two additional oil locations. Dupont advised the department to support this expansion,[15] even though no Aboriginal consent was sought in advance and no consent had yet been obtained for the first area.

In the period between November 1865 and early January 1866, when the next vote was scheduled, Dupont continually discussed lease terms and their advantages with individual First Nation citizens and employed Fred Lamorandiere to help him. Lamorandiere had applied on more than one occasion for oil rights and had earlier been identified as an associate of Baby. Dupont cancelled the third vote because neither Lamorandiere nor Ironside could attend, leaving him without an interpreter. Dupont noted that the chiefs wanted the meeting to take place anyway and would provide their own interpreter. Dupont refused to go, however, and proposed a new meeting three days later. Several Wikwemikong citizens found this position unacceptable and held their own council after trying unsuccessfully to force Dupont to attend.[16]

The chiefs and people agreed to meet Dupont on the 19th for a vote on the oil issue. About two hundred people were present. Dupont attempted to convince them of the advantages of agreeing to a blanket lease for oil and gas purposes and to warn them that they did not have the right to stop the development of oil, which was a public resource.[17] He purposely misconstrued the situation, for he well knew that the First Nation was anxious to develop its oil and gas as long as it was in control of the negotiations and setting the terms. Had Dupont been authorized by the Indian Department to threaten the First Nation as he did? Oil and gas were not, like gold or silver, royal minerals, and the basis on which the government tried to appropriate them for public benefit is not clear. Moreover, these subsurface resources were unrelinquished Aboriginal property.

At the meeting, Dupont failed to gain the consent of any of the people, who, in any case, did not constitute a majority of eligible voters. In spite of this constraint, he told the First Nation that leases would be authorized anyway. He also reported to Spragge that the First Nation would eventually come around:

> Finding them obstinate in refusing to consent, after four hours discussion I broke up the Council, informing them that the general issue of licenses was determined upon by the Department + I had no doubt they would soon see that their interests were promoted by this step.
>
> I am happy to say that I do not believe any resistance whatever would be

made on their part to this step ... [and suggested that some Chiefs were in favour].[18]

The contradictory nature of this statement is evident. There is no prior evidence to suggest that any chief favoured leasing through the Indian Department.

Only three days after the third unsuccessful council, Spragge instructed Joseph Wilson, the land agent at Sault Ste Marie, to meet Dupont at Wikwemikong for the purpose of procuring a blanket surrender of oil rights over the entire island or, at least, a smaller area.[19] This surrender would require a fourth vote. It is not known whether such a council was held: Dupont does not mention one involving Wilson.

In April 1866 the Indian Department authorized Dupont to secure a surrender of rights and to negotiate the terms of lease for the Lake Huron Oil Company. There is no record of this case, but Dupont reported in May that he had obtained Aboriginal consent for William Pristow to explore for and develop oil over an area of 2000 acres.[20] He provided no further details. Unlike all his other reports on his attempts to gain First Nation consent, Dupont gave no particulars about arranging the alleged council, the date when it was held, or what transpired there. He did not state whether the First Nation was involved in setting the terms of the lease. It is therefore questionable whether he obtained consent at all.

In June 1866 seventy-two heads of Wikwemikong families petitioned the governor general for Dupont's removal, complaining of his high-handed, rude, and insolent manner. They criticized his practice of inciting the Indians to riot, when using this pretext to jail their chiefs. Obviously, Dupont had his own agenda on the reserve and did not hesitate to manipulate circumstances to gain his ends. The petition also indicated that the First Nation viewed the Treaty of 1862 as fraudulent and called for its abrogation. The Indian Department did not respond to these complaints.[21]

In spite of the strenuous efforts of Dupont and the Indian Department to bar Wikwemikong members from negotiating independent oil leases, it is clear that such agreements were being made. In July, Dupont warned a developer, Mr Moylan, to cease all private communications with Wikwemikong First Nation citizens, no matter who initiated them. Moylan complied with these instructions once the chiefs were informed of a council arranged for the beginning of August, by Dupont, to secure Aboriginal consent to Moylan's proposals. On 4 August Dupont reportedly obtained this consent, not only for Moylan and his associate but for others as well, including Baby and his associates. It is not known if the alleged consent to Baby and his associates was for their first location or for different ones.

Baby had several locations and more than one company operating on Manitoulin. Dupont failed to mention the number of voters, whether they were all eligible voters, and whether they constituted a majority of the eligible voting members. He did not specify the terms of the leases or whether there had been Aboriginal input in their negotiation.[22] Shortly thereafter, the Indian Department authorized several additional licences. No separate surrenders appear to have been obtained, and Dupont reported no councils or votes.[23]

By the end of the oil season in 1866, Baby's Company, Great Manitoulin Oil, had produced sixty-two barrels, at an unknown value. Under the less-than-beneficial arrangement made by the department, the Wikwemikong First Nation received only 25 cents on each barrel. Thus, six or seven hundred people received a mere $15.50, less than $2\frac{1}{2}$ cents each – for the development of their oil under what likely remained an unauthorized departmental lease.[24] This sum in no way represented fair market-value compensation.

After 1866 Baby abandoned his oil developments for about two and a half years, thereby breaching the terms of his lease. Regardless, he applied for its reactivation, and Spragge supported him. It is not known whether the lease was in fact resumed, but Spragge made no mention of obtaining Aboriginal consent.[25] Such a resumption should have required a new council and vote, not only because Baby's actions had abrogated the lease but because the Indian Department never appears to have obtained consent for the first one.

As we have seen, the department took no action on the petition of the Wikwemikong First Nation which charged Dupont with mismanagement of its affairs. In August 1867, however, Dupont assaulted Father Sims so violently that he 'bled profusely.' An investigator ordered by the governor general to examine Dupont's activities accused the agent of being 'tyranical, overbearing and unjust towards the Indians and with having systematically treated the Indians with contempt and derision.' He reported that 'Dupont has been in the habit of treating the Indians with great harshness and from his whole demeanour during the Investigation I am convinced that so far from having the least sympathy with the unfortunate race over whom he had been placed in authority he entertains for them the greatest contempt.' In addition, Dupont had been speculating in the lands on Manitoulin Island which he was supposed to be managing for the benefit of the First Nations there. He was removed from office some time in the spring of 1868.[26]

Before the oil developments of the 1860s, Aboriginal people had been moved to Manitoulin Island as part of an agricultural experiment under the 'civilization' policy. The experiment had failed[27] long before the 1862 treaty, when the Native groups on the western portion of the island allegedly agreed to relinquish their land. Still, the Indian Department and Dupont vigorously attempted to relocate many of the island's people to this location or others. At least one reason was Dupont's knowledge of mineral deposits at or near the traditional locations of some Aboriginal communities. This was the case at Mi-teh-skewe-di-gang, where, in May 1865, Dupont reported that D.C. Thompson had applied to mine lead on 400 acres. Noting that some Native peoples wanted to locate their reserve at Mi-teh-skewe-di-gang, Dupont informed Thompson that he would ensure that the reserve was situated so as to exclude the designated acres. A Mr A. Howland also sought an oil site there.[28]

Similarly, Dupont strongly encouraged Native people living at Sheguiandah to move to Manitowaning, even though they did not want to, so the area could be sold as mineral or oil lands. In July 1865 he received an application from Isaac Laidlaw for permission to explore for oil or salt wells at several locations, including Sheguiandah. In August an application for coal oil was received from Howland. When Rev. Sims, the same man Dupont would assault in 1866, applied for land for a mission at Sheguiandah, he was told that the area, if granted, would exclude mineral and petroleum rights.[29]

Interest in Wikwemikong oil was not renewed until the late 1890s, when the island was 'subjected to [a] deliberate government search for any new resources that might bear commercial development.' Because of this push, the Wikwemikong First Nation allegedly released its oil and gas rights to the department in 1898. The explorations of an American company, which had obtained very favourable leases from the Indian Department, caused a short-lived rush on the western side of the island.[30]

Around 1904 the Indian Department granted a 10,000-acre lease to Philomen Poirier and a 50,000-acre lease to the Great Northern Oil and Gas Company.[31] There is no evidence that the department held a council to vote on this surrender of oil and gas rights. Either it took no surrender at all or it relied on the 1898 surrender, now nearly seven years old. On 20 April 1909 very unusual and broad patents were issued, conveying all oil and gas presently known to exist on the reserve as well as all future deposits that might be discovered. In all, 60,000 acres of land with oil and gas rights were confirmed 'in fee simple' to the patentees. The patents were subject to an 8 per cent royalty at the well's mouth and contained three conditions: no surface rights were granted except as expressed; Aboriginal labour was to be used; and timber was not to be wasted.[32] The meaning of the first condition is not clear, since land and oil were granted, under both patents, in fee simple. That Canada allowed such wording to pass is but one example of the gross incompetence of the Indian Department

The status of Wikwemikong as land protected under the Royal Proclamation of 1763 was now in jeopardy because of actions by the Department of Indian Affairs itself. The patents purported to transfer land, oil, and gas to non-Natives in fee simple. Yet the First Nation had not agreed to a land surrender, nor did it sanction the permanent alienation of its oil and gas in 1898. The terms of these patents represented a breach of federal fiduciary obligation.

Poirier sunk a 500-foot well at Smith's Point near Manitowaning and reportedly struck oil. He suspended operations and capped the well during the winter. After his cap blew, however, spectacular reports of oil were circulated widely in the press and resulted in a large influx of American oil speculators to the island. In December 1917 Poirier 'transferred' all his rights under the patent to the Great Northern.[33] By 1938 Canada wanted both patents abrogated because no real development had occurred at Wikwemikong. It was not known if the Great Northern still existed. The Indian Affairs Branch erroneously believed that the other patent was held by the widow of Senator Poirier, who, at any rate, refused to relinquish it. The superintendent of reserves and trusts called the situation 'a fiasco' and asserted, 'the oil and gas rights affected by these two patents are gone beyond recall save some extra-judicial procedure.'[34]

Between 1938 and 1942 Canada talked about abrogating the Great Northern patent through legislation, but did not act. In the fall of 1942 the company's solicitor informed Ontario that it would resume oil development on Manitoulin. Ontario supported the company in its plan, and Canada did nothing.[35] It is not known why the branch allowed the company to regain standing on the reserve or why the original patent was to be resurrected. Why was a *new* patent not negotiated? In addition to the objectionable fee simple clause, the original patent sanctioned an inadequate royalty of 8 per cent of the oil produced, and there were no cash rentals. The terms were highly prejudicial to the interests of Wikwemikong, especially since much better terms could be had just to the southeast of Manitoulin Island.[36]

Initial work was started and terminated by the Ivy Drilling Company operating on behalf of the Great Northern. The First Nation could see, however, that there had been no real mineral development. Indian agent C.R. Johnston wanted to prevent the Great Northern from regaining its powers, since its activities on the reserve were viewed as 'unfair.'[37] Company inactivity continued throughout 1944. When Ottawa urged cancellation of the charter, the provincial deputy minister of justice concurred. Under the previous arrangement, oil and gas rights reverted to Canada, but this time oil rights would fall to the province.[38] The matter remained unresolved until November 1948, when Ontario finally cancelled the patent by order in council.

The 60,000 acres now lay in provincial hands. Ontario agreed to relinquish its rights over the land, but demanded that someone pay the full amount of back taxes owed by the Great Northern.[39] Indian Affairs wanted the whole matter with Ontario cleared up as quickly as possible, claiming it was impossible to make the local Native council understand the 'legal position' of the lands in question. What this likely meant was that the council refused to accept the 'legal position' by which the branch had caused its lands and oil to fall into federal mismanagement.

The final solution to this problem, arranged by the Indian Affairs Branch, merely added insult to injury. J.S. McLaughlin, representing an unidentified company, successfully applied to the branch for a permit to explore for oil and gas over 68,824 acres of the Wikwemikong Reserve, paying $6882.40 to the First Nation in rental fees. But, to obtain the right to issue such a permit, Indian Affairs had to secure a conveyance of the oil and gas from Ontario. This transaction activated Ontario's value-for-value policy, and the province demanded that Ottawa pay the Great Northern's back taxes amounting to $3000. The branch told McLaughlin it would pay the back taxes from the permit money it received from his company. These terms were acceptable to McLaughlin, whose client eventually filed for rights to explore for oil and gas on the terms noted above.[40]

It is not clear from the records whether the First Nation agreed to lose half its permit money to Ontario for the back taxes of the Great Northern Company. Neither is it clear that the First Nation agreed to the continued development of its oil or the terms offered by McLaughlin. If the Indian Affairs Branch really had the best interests of the Wikwemikong at heart, it should have paid the back taxes with its own money, or sued the Great Northern. It should also have asked the First Nation if it wanted to surrender its oil and gas rights again under a new arrangement with McLaughlin.

Conclusion

Petroleum development on Wikwemikong was badly mismanaged by the Indian Department, first as part of the colonial government and then, after 1867, as part of the nation state. While Indian agent Dupont and Deputy Superintendent Spragge cooperated in failed attempts to legitimize highly questionable oil leases, the Wikwemikong First Nation issued its own leases. At the centre of this disagreement was the sovereignty of both the Wikwemikong Nation and the Crown/nation state, and the struggle between them for the control of and profit from the development of subsurface minerals. This particular struggle is one example of many between First Nations and government over the ownership, control, and beneficial interest in natural resources.

The Indian Department and its representatives needed to maintain an appearance of state power over the First Nations and over their land and resources. Neither the developers nor the Aboriginal people and their allies could be seen to be independently leading the exploitation of resources or controlling the profits. Rather, there was to be state appropriation of natural resources, including minerals, timber, fish, game, water, and shorelines.

During the second wave of petroleum development on Wikwemikong, the actions of the Indian Affairs Branch are equally reprehensible. Indeed, the branch sacrificed the best interests of the Wikwemikong First Nation to its own interests and those of Ontario. Instead of benefiting fully from the McLaughlin permit, the First Nation, after years of suffering under the federal patents to Poirier and the Great Northern, would receive only half the rental. To recover oil and gas rights over the 60,000 acres it had foolishly granted in fee simple to the Great Northern, Canada paid the company's back taxes. First Nation moneys should not have been used for this purpose. The branch did not pay for its mistake with its own money, nor did it make either company pay. Instead, it used the McLaughlin rental money to pay for its error, and $3882.40, rather than $6882.40, was put into the general funds of the Wikwemikong First Nation. Indian Affairs proved itself unfit to manage the affairs of Wikwemikong citizens.

NOTES

1 For the Indian Department version of these treaties, see Canada, *Indian Treaties and Surrenders* (1891; reprint, Calgary: Fifth House Publishers, 1992), surrender nos. 45 and 94, 1:112 and 235.

2 Metropolitan Toronto Reference Library, Baldwin Room, 'Prospectus of the Great Manitoulin Oil Company, Manitoulin Island, Lake Huron,' 1865, 17. See also F.W. Major, *Manitoulin: The Isle of the Ottawas* (1934; reprint, Gore Bay: Recorder Press, 1974), 64. Francis Assikinack, 'Legends and Traditions of the Odahwah Indians. By F. Assikinack, A Warrior of the Odahwahs. Read before the Canadian Institute, December, 1857,' in *The Canadian Journal of Industry, and Art: Conducted by the Editing Committee of the Canadian Institute*. New Series, number 13. January, 1858 (Toronto: Canadian Institute, 1858).

3 'Petroleum Down the Centuries,' *Imperial Oil Review*, March/April 1934, 17. Elma Gray and Leslie Robb Gray, *Wilderness Christians* (Toronto: Macmillan,

1956), 136. Ian Drummond, *Progress without Planning* (Toronto: University of Toronto Press, 1987), 93. Earle Gray, *The Great Canadian Oil Patch* (Toronto: McLean Hunter, 1970), 34.

4 'Prospectus of the Great Manitoulin Oil Company,' 17.

5 See, for example, National Archives of Canada (NA), RG 10, vol. 574, 281–2, Dupont to Spragge, 19 January 1866, where the American, Osow wah me meke, refuses to agree to surrender oil rights unless the Department of Indian Affairs agrees to sanction the removal of M. Baptiste, a Wikwemikong resident who was forced from his home two or three years earlier for his part in agreeing to the 1862 treaty. Further references to the Baptiste issue can be found in Dupont's letters and Spragge's replies. See also Douglas Leighton, 'The Manitoulin Incident of 1863: An Indian-White Confrontation in the Province of Ontario,' *Ontario History* 69, 2 (1977): 113–24. Numerous other references occur which attest to Dupont's aversion towards American Natives: see NA, RG 10, vol. 574, 301, Dupont to Hon. A. Campbell, superintendent general, 27 March 1866. Here Dupont stereotypes all Americans at Wikwemikong as 'a source of trouble + ringleaders in every disturbance + by their evil influence have induced a seditious spirit among a portion of our own Indians.' The 18 June 1866 petition from the Wikwemikong Indians also indicates that Dupont insulted the Canadian chiefs by calling them 'Americans.' NA, RG 10, vol. 574, 71.

6 NA, RG 10, vol. 574, 71–3, petition from Wikwemikong, 18 June 1866.

7 Ibid., 153, letter, Dupont to Spragge, 8 February 1865.

8 Ibid., 159, Dupont to J.R. Berthelot, 13 February 1865; 191–2, Dupont to Spragge, 25 April 1865.

9 Ibid., 199–202, Dupont to Spragge, 6 May 1865.

10 Ibid., vol. 723, 81–2, memo from Spragge: 'An application from the Great Manitoulin Oil Company to resume their operations for oil &c. A Report by the Deputy Superintendent of Indian Affairs sanctioned by order in council 11 May 1869,' 11 May 1869. Also, vol. 574, 263, reference to fact of licence: Dupont to Spragge, 22 November 1865; vol. 574, 202, reference to area involved: Dupont to Spragge, 6 May 1865.

11 NA, RG 10, vol. 574, 248, Dupont to Spragge, 20 October 1865.

12 Ibid., 248–9, Dupont to Spragge, 20 October 1865.

13 Ibid., 261, Dupont to Spragge, 15 November 1865.

14 'Prospectus of the Great Manitoulin Oil Company,' 18–19. Other applicants sought to be granted similar terms. See NA, RG 10, vol. 364, Donald McDonald to Spragge, 31 July and 11 September 1865.

15 NA, RG 10, vol. 574, 263, Dupont to Spragge, 22 November 1865.

16 Ibid., 278, Dupont to Spragge, 19 January 1866. Dupont enclosed the minutes of this council in his report to Spragge, but no copy remains on file. Neither is there a copy in Spragge's correspondence.

17 Ibid., 280, Dupont to Spragge, 19 January 1866.

18 Ibid., 282, Dupont to Spragge, 19 January 1866.

19 Ibid., vol. 616, 3–4, Spragge to Dupont, 22 January 1866, and 8–10, Spragge to Joseph Wilson, 22 January 1866.

20 Ibid., vol. 574, 311, Dupont to Spragge, 25 May 1866.

21 Ibid., vol. 616, 70–3, Wiki petition, 18 June 1866. The petition states that Commissioner William McDougall asked them for their lands, but they refused. A few days later, on 6 October, other men came and spoke to some Native people, who were finally intimidated into surrendering the land. The petitioners maintained that the majority of people were against the surrender and that only a few chiefs signed. The Wikwemikong First Nation were not signatories to the 1862 treaty, which allegedly shared the west half of the island with the Crown. See NA, RG 10, vol. 616, 132–3, Spragge to Dupont, 8 August 1866.

22 Ibid., vol. 574, 339, Dupont to Moylan, 29 July 1866; 341, Dupont to Tomah, head chief, and other chiefs and Indians at Wikwemikong, 31 July 1866; 350, Dupont to Spragge, in Campp Oil Springs, Manitoulin Island, 4 August 1866.

23 Ibid., vol. 616, 162, Spragge to Dupont, 14 August 1866.

24 Ibid., 314–16, Spragge to Dupont, 6 Feb. 1867.

25 Ibid., vol. 723, 81–2, memo from Spragge, 11 May 1869: 'An application from the Great Manitoulin Oil Company to resume their operations for oil &c. A Report by Deputy Superintendent ... sanctioned by order in council 11 May 1869.'

26 Ibid., vol. 722, 'Report of Secretary of State on Mr C.T. Dupont's conduct towards the Rev. Mr Sims & Indians generally,' nd. The assault occurred around August 1867. Dupont was removed from office during the first half of 1868. See ibid., 477, memo from Spragge, 16 September 1868: 'Memo by the Deputy Sup. of IA, On application in behalf of the Indians of Point Grondine I.R.'; 360–2, memo by Spragge: 'Memo by the Deputy Superintendent of Indian Affairs relative to complaints against Mr C.T. Dupont,' 7 October 1867; 391–3, 'Report of Secretary of State on Mr C.T. Dupont's conduct towards the Rev'd Mr Sims & Indians generally,' 2 March 1868.

27 Leighton, 'The Manitoulin Incident of 1863,' 113–16.

28 NA, RG 10, vol. 574, 205, Dupont to Spragge, 15 May 1865; 229, Dupont to A. Howland, Esq., Quebec, 19 August 1865; and 232–3, Isaac Howland to Dupont, 3 August 1865.

29 Ibid., 337, Dupont to Spragge, 7 July 1866; 228, Isaac Laidlaw to Dupont, 24 July 1865; 229, Dupont to A. Howlan, 19 August 1865; 229, and 232–3, Isaac Howland to Dupont, 3 August 1865. See also Dupont to Alfred Bouttler, New Market, 1 April 1867. The latter applied for oil lands in Shiguiandah as well: ibid., 289–90, Dupont to Rev'd. J.N. Sims, Church of England Missionary, 8 January 1866.

30 W.R. Wightman, *Forever on the Fringe: Six Studies in the Development of the Manitoulin Island* (Toronto: University of Toronto Press, 1982), 144–5.

31 NA, RG 10, vol. 7643, F. 20019–4, pt 1, 1935–47, memo of D.J. Allan, superintendent, Reserves and Trusts, to C.W. Jackson, chief executive assistant, 21 October 1938.

32 Ibid.

33 Ibid., pt 2 (Wikwemikong), 1947–9, Deputy Minister (presumably Department of Mines and Resources) to Deputy Minister, Department of Justice, 1 February 1948.

34 Ibid., pt 1, 1935–47, memo of Allan to Jackson, 21 October 1938.

35 Ibid., memo of Allan to Jackson, 13 November 1942.

36 Ibid., vol. 6994, F. 471/20–6–7–46, pt 1, memo of Kehoe, IAB, Mines and Resources, to Allan, 6 July 1945; and Allan to Imperial Oil, 10 January 1947.

37 Ibid., vol. 7643, F. 20019-4, pt 1, C.R. Johnston, Indian agent, to D.J. Allan, 11 June 1943.

38 Ibid., Kehoe to Allan, 13 September 1944.

39 Ibid., pt 2, J.S. McLaughlin (counsel for unidentified company) to IAB, 5 October 1949.

40 Ibid., Acting Director, Indian Affairs Branch, to J.S. McLaughlin, November 1949; Ernest Lilley (McLaughlin's client) to D.J. Allan, 25 November 1949.

The Other Side: *The Rhetoric of Labour Reform in Toronto during the 1870s*

CHRISTINA BURR

During the early 1870s, in a period of economic growth and industrialization in Ontario, trade union membership increased, new unions were organized, the important struggle for shorter hours occurred, and the institutional framework for the labour movement was put into place. Toronto Local 3 of the Cooper's International Union provided the impetus for the organization of the Toronto Trades Assembly in April 1871. The following spring the journeymen members of the TTA were embroiled in the provincewide struggle for shorter working hours, a campaign that became known as the nine-hours movement.[1]

On 12 April 1871 delegates from the various trade organizations in the city met in the Iron Moulders' Hall and formally organized the Toronto Trades Assembly. Twenty-eight-year-old John Hewitt, an Irish Protestant immigrant who had already amassed considerable knowledge about labour reform while working in New York for three years in the late 1860s, and who would emerge as a leading spokesmman and idealogue during the nine-hours campaign, was elected president.[2] John Dance of the Iron Moulders' Union was chosen vice president, and James S. Williams of the Typographical Union became recording secretary. Both Dance and Williams had been born in London, England. The identification of Toronto labour reformers with the United States and Britain, and their knowledge of the labour reform movement in those countries, helped to shape the rhetoric of the nascent Toronto labour movement.[3]

In the midst of the nine-hours movement, which was launched by Hamilton workers on 27 January 1872, Hewitt provided the impetus for the founding of a labour newspaper in Toronto. Established as a cooperative newspaper, the first issue of the *Ontario Workman* appeared on 18 April 1872, with James S. Williams as editor. The *Workman* was published weekly until 9 April 1874, but was organized as a cooperative venture for only six months. In September 1872 John A. Macdonald, in an effort to attract working-class voters, secretly loaned Williams and his partners, Joseph C. McMillan and David Sleeth, the money to purchase the paper. All of the men were known Conservative Party supporters.[4]

In response to the rhetoric of employers which negatively defined working men as a class to be feared (most notably from George Brown, editor of the *Globe* and Grit politician), labour reformers were confronted with the task of building a positive working-class identity. The class dimension of the nine-hours campaign has already been documented in Canadian labour history.[5] In this essay, the language of labour reformers and the coded sets of representations by which they defended the morality of the working class and articulated their own gender ideals of working-class manhood are explored. In opposition to the rhetoric of employers, labour reformers articulated a counter-discourse that emphasized worker independence and commitment to the collective goals of trade unionism. These goals were accomplished, at least in part, through the institutional framework of the TTA and through workers' fiction and poetry published in the *Ontario Workman*.

The language of labour reformers during the early 1870s created a positive image of working-class manhood for purposes of mobilizing working-class support and combatting the opponents of the nascent labour movement. Labour reformers presented a distinctive masculine subject organized around the honest, skilled, Anglo-Saxon working man who struggles against the evils of capitalist exploitation. The masculinity of the working man was not completely autonomous, however, and its content was influenced by the dominant middle-class culture.

The role of the nineteenth-century labour reformer was to educate working-class men and to transform them into concerned citizens, workers, trade unionists, husbands, and fathers. A handful of intellectuals and reform-oriented journalists attempted to create an alternative 'serious' working-class fiction and labour press, unlike the 'penny dreadfuls' or dime novels favoured by workers during their leisure hours. The representations of male workers in working-class fiction were counter to the images of working men presented in the writings of middle-class reformers.[6] In response to the subjection of workers in the factory and the workshop, working-class narratives reversed discourses that disparaged workers and trade unionism. These narratives opened up a space for counter-identification, which empowered rather than victimized male workers.

Melodrama was used to educate workmen in the cause of labour reform. *The Other Side*, a novel by American labour reformer Martin Foran, for example, was published in the *Ontario Workman* in weekly instalments between 27 June 1872 and 27 February 1873. The subject of the working man was partially dealt with in the discourses of the state, the trade union, the workplace, and the family, but it was also less formally, yet effectively, constructed through literature.

Rethinking Labour Reform in Toronto during the Early 1870s

During the spring of 1872 George Brown played a prominent role in mobilizing employer resistance to the nine-hours movement through his editorials in the *Globe*. He spearheaded the organization of an employers' association, which was named the Master Printers' Association. Brown also had the striking printers in his employ prosecuted for conspiracy to combine.[7] A follower of Manchester liberalism, Brown reduced the issue to one of the simple operation of the economic law of supply and demand. 'It is a question of profit and loss as between the employer and the employed,' he argued; 'it is one that may well be discussed on social and moral grounds; but there is no law in morals or philosophy that makes eight or nine hours' labour right, and ten hours' wrong.' In his editorials, Brown suggested that workers had a right to bargain with employers for shorter hours and higher wages, but he indicated that if employers decided to make a bargain for a ten-hour work day, there was no injustice in their position.[8]

Brown denounced the arguments in favour of a reduction in working hours made by labour reformers at nine-hour rallies throughout southwestern Ontario in the spring of 1872. He classified the speakers who addressed the crowds gathered at these rallys as 'foreign agitators' or 'the agents of English trades' unions who make money out of labour agitation.' Another even more dangerous class, Brown suggested, were those men 'of dreamy, imaginative character, who form exaggerated notions of the evils of manual labour and vague aspirations after a different and what they consider a much higher life.' He used Charles Kingsley's fictional character Alton Locke, which was loosely based on the life of Thomas Cooper, the Chartist poet and editor of *The Chartist Rushlight*, as a symbol of the danger he believed this group of workmen posed to society.[9]

In his editorials, Brown challenged the credibility of the nine-hour activists. 'What is the ambition of every working man but himself to become one of those capitalists on whose hoards so many look with no little jealousy?' he asked.[10] He relied on the dominant middle-class discourse of self-help, and emphasized that a large proportion of the capitalists in this country began their careers as artisans or workers for wages and by 'hard saving and self-reliance' became employers.[11] In opposition to the hard-saving and self-reliant 'capitalist,' Brown described the 'handicraftsman' as a worker who relied almost exclusively on brute strength and knew little of mental effort. In his view, any man who refused to work ten hours a day was a 'loafer' who did not properly carry out his 'manly' obligations in the public realm or provide adequately for his family. He did not agree that a reduction in working hours would necessarily be used for purposes of self-help, education, or a healthier home life. Rather, he asserted that an increase in leisure time would only heighten the moral degeneration among the working class by giving them more time to frequent the tavern and the billiard hall.[12] Thus, Brown transformed the issue of a reduction in working hours into a problem of lack of moral fibre among working-class men.

During the early 1870s Toronto labour reformers confronted the task of constructing a positive working-class masculine identity. In doing so, they emphasized that their efforts were not isolated, but were, as John Hewitt stated at the 15 February rally, 'on the heels of the noble working men of Great Britain and those in the United States.'[13] Later, at another demonstration held in the city's East Market Square, on the evening of 24 April, Hewitt referred to the 'cosmopolitan feeling' among working men and suggested that 'they were losing that local and sectional feeling which used to characterize them.'[14]

Canada's colonial relationship with Britain was incorporated into labour-reform discourse and used to define a community that included Canadian working men. Rather than the 'foreign agitators' depicted by Brown, Toronto labour reformers indicated that the nine-hours movement derived from the 'mother country,' and that, as members of the 'great Anglo-Saxon race,' working men should endeavour to put themselves on an 'equality' with their 'brethren at home.' The labour reformers promoted identification with the nine-hours movement as a 'duty' owed by workers to the mother country.[15]

Poetry was used by articulate workers to construct a working-class variant of patriotism. The first issue of the *Ontario Workman* included a poem entitled 'Canada.' It was written especially for the *Workman* and was signed 'Canadian.' In the opening stanza the anonymous bard expressed the patriotic and political ideals of Anglo-Canadian labour reformers:

> Canadian hearts, let us be loyal,
>   And remain 'neath England's wing
> Till she can no longer guard us
>   Then to Canada e'er cling.
> Patriot's love and heal inspire us
>   To maintain our country's rights;

Yield – no, never, to our formen,
Though we come to bloody fights.

May that time be ages distant –
Ever here at peace remain!
Never may Canadian freemen
Fell the haughty tyrant's chain.
Heaven smile upon our country –
Guard it with thy righteous wand!
Make it great as nations have been –
Might as its Mother Land![16]

Patriotism, which embraced the notions of duty, obligation, and sacrifice for Canada and the 'mother country,' was expected of male workers, but, as this verse suggests, working men also had rights as citizens and as 'freemen.' Contrary to the rhetoric of employers, notably George Brown, which excluded or 'otherized' working-class men, Toronto labour reformers constructed their own variant of national identity, using a disourse that emphasized working men's obligations to the British Empire and their role as 'the mainstay of the country.'

This construction of the working man as vital to the project of nation building applied to 'white' workers only. In 1874, when the Mackenzie Liberal government announced that Chinese labourers were being considered to complete the Canadian Pacific Railway, this particular group of workers was targeted for exclusion by the TTA. The editor of the *Ontario Workman* stated outright that the government should not use 'cheap Chinese labor,' and that a 'great injustice would be done to the white population of the country.' Racist rhetoric was used to define Chinese labourers as undesirable immigrant workers.[17]

During the early 1870s labour reformers united white Anglo-Saxon working men around the demand for universal manhood suffrage, so they might eventually win their full rights as citizens. They drew on both the tradition of British constitutionalism and Painite egalitarianism, and spoke of 'the universal rights of man.' Williams indicated that, in politics, the motto of labour reformers was 'first, Man, and then Property.'[18] The existing franchise based on property qualification was targeted as a relic of the feudal age, and independence became a powerful masculine ideal. Labour reformers rejected the rhetoric of liberal political economy which compared working men to 'serfs.' In rejecting the qualification for the vote based on property, labour reformers spoke of themselves as 'free men' with a 'natural right' to the vote.

Power was reinvested in the individual in labour reformers' constructions of manliness. Qualification for the franchise, Hewitt suggested, should 'no longer be measured by that old dreg of feudalism,' but 'rather on the basis of intelligence, morality and worth, which alone constitute true manhood.' In another letter to the editor of the *Ontario Workman*, Hewitt used satire to criticize the existing system of suffrage based on property. 'Whether the man so admitted is a wise man or a fool it matters not,' he wrote; 'don't you see he is a man of property?' He continued: 'Whether he be a person of high moral character, or a profligate person, never mind; Don't you see the property; upon this the law has made him free, how dare you further question the man's respectability.'[19]

Toronto's male trade unionists applauded a bill introduced in the provincial legislature in January 1873 to extend the vote to every man who received an annual income from any calling of not less than $300 in any city or town, and of $200 in any village or township.[20] This measure, Williams wrote, 'will give votes to a large class of young men, clerks, students, professional men, mechanics and others, who have hitherto been excluded from voting because they are not on the assessment roll.'[21] Women, many of whom also worked for a wage, were omitted from the proposed suffrage amendments and from labour reformers' comments on the proposed legislation.

Toronto labour reformers also confronted the employer-worker relationship. Their critique of the new industrial order was based on the labour theory of value.[22] 'Labor is both superior and prior to capital, and alone originally produces capital,' editor Williams stated in the *Ontario Workman*.[23] Elements of the older pre-industrial ideology of the mutuality of interests between worker and employer, and the skilled working man's property of skill and control over his labour, were retained, however. 'The interests of both classes are bound together,' Williams concluded. 'If either one is harmed, the other must ultimately suffer.' Toronto trade unionists stated at nine-hours rallies and in the *Ontario Workman* that they believed in 'a fair day's work for a fair day's pay.'[24]

Toronto labour reformers referred to the 'nobility of labour' and the 'dignity of labour,' in contradistinction to employers' efforts to 'master' the labour force. In pre-industrial social relations, the term *master* meant a 'master of the craft,' who had also perhaps acquired his own shop. With industrial capitalism, the term was redefined to mean a 'master of men.' In a letter to the editor of the *Ontario Workman*, journalist John McCormick ridiculed 'money-grubbers' who believed, 'We the employers of labor, are your masters, you are our servants, and we have the right to dictate to you the terms upon which you shall labor and live or exist.' For McCormick the very term *master* was an abomination, for man was systematically robbed and held cheap by current social relations of production, and by laws that placed property first and man second.[25] Another correspondent, who used the *nom de plume* 'Wood Worker,' wrote that he was highly amused to read in the *Globe* that carriage makers Messrs Hasson and Guy called themselves 'master' carriage makers. Neither of the manufacturers possessed the skills of a craftsman, yet, according to 'Wood Worker,' they cried out the loudest against benefitting skilled workmen. The correspondent concluded his letter with a evocation of workers' power as craftsmen: 'Let the mechanics of Ontario be true to each other, and we will teach those brainless, self-styled Masters, that the workmen of Ontario know their power, and are determined to use it.'[26]

During the early 1870s the 'body politic' emerged as a site of political intervention for Toronto labour reformers.[27] In addition to investing power in the body through their articulation of labour as the source of all capital, labour reformers constructed a whole series of codes of disciplinary individuality over the mind. Among nineteenth-century labour reformers few words enjoyed more popularity than the word *manly*, with its connotations of dignity in labour, respectablility, and defiant egalitarianism. 'Self-help' and 'self-elevation' were consistently cited as crucial to the objectives of the labour movement. This goal was reinforced in workers' poetry.[28] A stanza of 'A True Mechanic,' written for the *Ontario Workman*, suggests:

The man who polishes heart and mind,
While he frames the window and shapes the blind,
And utters his thoughts with an honest tongue,
That is set as true as his hinges are hung,
He is the nobleman among
   The noble band of mechanics.[29]

The allegory mixes the images of the skill and precision required in the builder's craft with the building of the 'frame' of the 'noble' workman which required honesty and a pure heart.

Although the notion of 'self-help' articulated by labour reformers in the editorials, letters, poetry, and improving literature published in the *Ontario Workman* embraced many aspects of dominant middle-class constructions, including a Christian belief in the building of a moral character, humility, honour, and a commitment to honest hard work, there were still important discrepancies between the classes. Labour reformers criticized the measurement of success as represented by the boy who rises from poverty to become a millionaire, such as the American Jacob Astor. The fallacy of the middle-class ideal was in the manner of acquiring success. The labour reformers argued that under the prevailing social system, wealth could not be acquired without chicanery in bargaining and disregard for workers. 'The standard of success is a false one,' Williams wrote. 'It is impossible for one man to get rich without causing others to suffer. It is proverbial that just and generous men do not get rich.'[30]

'Self-elevation,' incorporating both moral and intellectual improvement, was promoted as the way to a better life for working men. The rhetoric of progress and self-culture, not unlike that of the late Victorian middle class, was used by Toronto labour reformers to sustain a radical critique of employers during the nine-hours campaign. At a nine-hours rally held in the Music Hall on 14 February 1872, Andrew Scott, a member of the Machinists' and Blacksmiths' Union, suggested that progress could only be made if workmen had the time to cultivate their intelligence. This goal of self-elevation, Scott observed, required a reduction in working hours to provide workers with the necessary leisure time.[31]

Labour reformers were confronted with the problem of the need to reconcile self-elevation with the collective objectives of labour organization. They suggested that the growth of intelligence among workmen was needed to promote understanding of the importance of cooperation to the workers' cause. Cooperation among working-class men could only be furthered through the progress of intelligence. The short-lived Canadian Labor Protection and Mutual Improvement Association, organized by the leaders of the Nine-Hours League in April 1872, provided the institutional framework for the discourse of self-elevation. The intent of the organization was to elevate the intelligence of workmen and to promote workers' common interests across local and trade boundaries.[32] Intelligent, sober, industrious, and independent, mechanics would ultimately combine and save the country from monopolies and corrupt politicans.

The cooperative goals of Toronto labour reformers did not easily incorporate unskilled labourers, however. An 'Ex-Labourer' wrote that 'while the artisans and tradesmen of all classes are asserting the rights of labor and manhood, the laborers *par excellence* – the men of the pick and shovel, of the crowbar and hod – are, I regret to say, lying in a state of lethargy and supineness.' He attributed the situation to a lack of organization.[33] A Labourers' Union was organized in Toronto in May 1873, but it apparently had a marginal presence in the TTA because its leadership was drawn from the ranks of skilled trade unionists.[34]

Among labour reformers, individual elevation and self-education included a commitment to domesticity and sobriety. Opponents of a reduction in working hours argued that if workers were given more leisure time, they would only spend it drinking and gambling. They targeted those male workers who spent their time away from home and in the pub. 'If the laborer thus released applies his leisure hour to his own domestic business, to his garden or his shop, to his needed rest or the education of his children ... to almost anything except dissipation, idleness and debauchery – it will prove a blessing,' Williams remarked.[35] In a subsequent editorial, Williams attributed the propensity to drink among workmen to the monotony and drudgery of incessant labour, and, for this reason, he concluded that moral suasion could never succeed and a strict prohibitary law was necessary.[36] The rhetoric of domesticity was used to defend the morality of male workers in the larger political context, and was integral to the positive masculine identity for working men constructed by labour reformers.[37]

Williams suggested that reading the *Ontario Workman* by the home fire after a day of toil was a suitable way for working-class men to promote self-elevation and the cultivation of domesticity – although this remark was probably intended, at least in part, to increase subscriptions. 'We want to help one another, as far lies in our power,' he wrote, 'to share more fully in the rich fund of edification, refinement and elevating enjoyment to be found in the literature of our age.'[38]

The Other Side: Melodrama and Labour Reform

On 23 May 1872 Williams announced that the president of the Coopers' International Union (CIU), Martin Foran, had consented to the publication of his novel, *The Other Side*, in serial instalments in the *Ontario Workman*. Williams pronounced enthusiastically: 'Something of this kind is what we have long wanted, as the whole field of story writing has been occupied and controlled in class interests, and every workingman should hail with joy the advent of one of themselves into the literary world, who is not only well able to use his pen in the field of fiction, but willing to take up the cause of labor, and battle for its rights with literary ability against the acknowledged champions in this great and powerful range of thought.'[39] Foran was a familiar figure among the organized workers of Toronto. He corresponded on several occasions with the TTA, and he was acquainted with John Hewitt through their respective involvement in the CIU. Earlier, in May 1871, the TTA had arranged for Foran to deliver a public lecture on education and labour reform.[40]

In the introduction to *The Other Side*, Foran provided two reasons for writing the novel. First, he shared with other labour reformers the belief that, 'if the laboring class could be made a *reading* class, their social and political advancement and amelioration would be rapid and certain.' He pointed to the 'popular taste among the masses' for fiction, especially those whose education was limited and did not include 'a classical training.' Rather than disparage the love of fiction and dime novels among the working class, Foran used the novel to encourage workmen to develop their intellectual side. For nineteenth-century labour reformers, intellectual development was essential to the attainment of complete manhood.[41] Foran's second objective was to counter the anti–trade union rhetoric used by the popular British novelist Charles Reade in a melodrama entitled *Put Yourself in His Place*, which was published serially in *Cornhill Magazine* in seventeen instalments beginning in March 1869.[42]

Trade unionism was given a dramatically different representation in Foran's novel. In his introductory remarks, Foran admitted that many of the measures and means employed by workmen to redress grievances were 'neither born of justice nor wisdom.' Before these men were condemned, however, he urged that their side of the story be told. Foran criticized Reade for 'not delineating both sides of the subject, in not putting himself in the places of all the characters in his story.' *The Other Side*, therefore, was both instructional and defensive in its intent.[43]

Foran followed the conventions of melodrama closely in the novel. Melodrama was the dominant modality in the nineteenth century. As Martha Vicinus has argued, 'it was important as a psychological touchstone for the powerless, for those who perceived themselves as "the helpless and unfriended."' 'Social and economic conditions were unstable during much of the nineteenth century,' she writes; 'melodrama acknowledged this and seemed to demonstrate how difficult circumstances could be endured and even turned to victory.'[44] Melodrama was immensely popular among later nineteenth-century working-class audiences who were seeking to comprehend the social transformations wrought by industrial capitalism.

In their fiction, labour reformers departed somewhat from the stereotypical characterization and plotting of melodrama and emphasized the political implications of the situation. When working-class audiences identified with the tragedies suffered by the honest-hearted mechanic hero, this empathy reinforced perceptions of working-class oppression. These writings, which focused on the manly and virtuous mechanic hero and his many misfortunes, were intended to mobilize workers to support the collective goals of the labour movement.[45]

Each literary genre employs certain textual strategies that cue readers to expect a particular kind of discursive experience. Melodrama denotes the indulgence of excessive emotionalism, inflated rhetoric, overt villainy, merciless persecution of the good, and the final reward of virtue – all exaggerated expressions of right and wrong, remarkable and improbable coincidences, dark plottings, suspense, and numerous plot twists. [46] Nineteenth-century melodrama was organized around a binary world of good and bad, rich and poor, male and female, and was bounded by faith in a universe ruled by morality. Evil drives the plot by unleashing a betrayal of the moral order. The hand of Providence insures the triumph of good, but only after the virtuous hero or heroine was sorely tried. Romance and sexual desire were integral to this drama of persecuted innocence and virtue triumphant. Villains were always destroyed, providing the reader with catharsis and, finally, solace. A potent dogma of democracy assured equality among all men, but only if they retained a pure heart.

Foran created a facsimile of himself in his manly worker hero, Richard Arbyght, a young farm-bred cooper.[47] Like all melodramas, a series of tragedies befall the young hero. Richard's father is robbed and murdered on a roadside as he journeyed homeward. Completely devastated by the death of her husband, Irene Arbyght soon dies of a broken heart. Orphaned at the age of nine, young Richard is taken in and raised by Squire Stanly. The squire is Foran's ideal of the sturdy, honest, intelligent farmer that existed previous to widespread urban and industrial development. Foran indicates that the squire is of the 'old school of political economists' who believe 'that our laws should be so framed and administered that they would tend to better advancement of the toiling masses, and the greater glory of the nation.' The squire and the pure country life are associated with good, in contrast to the evils and dangers of the city for workmen and their families.

Deprived of the inheritance that would have allowed him to continue his education, Richard must learn a trade. He is apprenticed to a local cooper. Artisanal pride in craftsmanship is reinforced in the narrative. Richard 'was especially fond of excelling in skilled and superior workmanship.' At the age of twenty, the hero is fully six feet tall, sinewy and strong, with 'a quick, elastic movement, and fiery, dark eye.' His countenance is 'open and expressive, his demeanor dignified and grave, his mind inquisitive, his heart brave and sympathetic.' His every look and movement 'gave assurance of the greatness and goodness of that noblest attribute of man – SOUL.' While Foran's worker hero was inflicted with some of the same signifiers as the hero of bourgeois fiction – specifically, courage and a sympathetic heart – the 'mechanic accents' are different.[48] Manliness for the worker hero in Foran's melodrama incorporated craft skill and trade-union membership. The upper-case type of the word *SOUL* in the copy published in the *Ontario Workman* reinforces the idea that for labour reformers, manliness was not based on wealth.

The hero, Richard, subsequently relocates to Chicago. The villain, a tyrannous employer named Alvan Relvason, who was described by Foran as 'the typical employer,' is introduced when Richard secures a position in Relvason's shop. A few days later, employer and worker confront each other in the shop. Annoyed by what he interprets as Richard's impudence, Relvason reminds him, 'you are the employed and I the employer.' Richard in turn responds, 'I would have you remember that I, too, am a MAN as well as you.' Richard tells Relvason that they are 'equals' who meet as buyer and seller: 'I have a commodity which you desire to purchase and which I am willing to sell for a consideration which you are disposed to give in exchange for it.' In opposition to the dominant political economy, Foran suggests a labour theory of value.

With the aid of two trusted workmen, Richard secretly organizes the journeymen coopers into a union. The villain, Relvason, discovers that a union has been organized and he schemes to destroy it. He threatens to dismiss any worker who refuses to sign an ironclad agreement. In the binary world of melodrama, and consistent with the politics of labour reform, Relvason is the antithesis of virtue. He is an example of 'abnormal humanity,' and is described metaphorically as 'ghoulish,' a 'leviathan,' 'knavishly cunning,' and a 'monster.'

The workers, of course, refuse to abandon their union. In contrast to the representation of trade unionists presented by Reade, the mechanics who support the union in Foran's novel are classified as 'manly.' They also have a distinctive physical appearance from years of hardship and toil, 'a young old look,' Foran writes, 'a dull, oppressive, heavy expression, seen only on those who toil ten hours or more per day.' Commitment to family and nation are integral to Foran's construction of the manly and honest working man: 'the honest man who married and brought up a large family did more service than he who continued single and only talked of population.' Trade unionists were depicted by Foran as men who love their children, and for this reason they willingly, even cheerfully, endure lives of never-ending toil.

Relvason issues an ultimatum that Richard must either abandon the union or be fired. Concerned with the plight of his union brothers, and consistent with the heroic ideal of self-sacrifice typical of melodrama, Richard decides to leave the trade. 'He did not regard it good unionism for one man to throw a hundred men out of employment, and stop their children's supply of bread.' The hero's hardships mount. He is blacklisted by the employers and unable to secure another position.

Race and national identity are interwoven into the novel's overarching theme of the importance of union solidarity to the cause of labour reform. In searching for employment, Richard is told by one anti-union employer that if his men 'dare' to organize, he will discharge them all and fill their places with cheaper Chinese workers. The employer remarks that the men in his shop are of his own 'nationality' and that he feels obligated to keep them on. Richard responds that these national ties would quickly deteriorate as soon as the men questioned his right to dictate to them what their labour is worth. Foran, however, excludes Chinese workers from his ideal of the unity of male workers under trades unionism.

Frustrated by the unwillingness of any employer to hire him, Richard returns to his boardinghouse, where he finds Alexander Fargood waiting for him. Fargood agrees to give Richard a job. Foran presents his concept of the ideal employer in the character of Fargood: 'The bearing of the employer was never that of a *master*. In a word the relations existing between these two men were pre-eminently those that should ever exist between all employers and employees: MUTUAL OR RECIPROCAL INDEPENDENCE AND DEPENDENCE.'[49] Like other nineteenth-century writers of working-class fiction, Foran recreated a world of artisanal independence rather than developing a critique of proletarianization under industrial-capitalist social relations.[50]

While the political objectives of labour reform were at the forefront of Foran's narrative, the plot of *The Other Side* centres around the unresolved tragedy of the Arbyght family and the romance between Richard and Vida Geldamo – the daughter of a banker. In Vida, Foran presents what he suggests is the 'true woman.' Vida is described as having all of woman's spiritualized nature: 'She was all goodness, all loveliness – an angel.' This ideal of femininity is analogous to middle-class constructions of womanhood which value feminine purity above wealth. Vida in all her goodness of heart could never believe 'that the possession of money made the heart warmer ... or the soul purer.' In the conflict between marriage based on property and romantic love, Mr Geldamo favours property. He orders Vida to marry Mr Allsound, who, although not as morally worthy as Richard, is a man of property. In the spirit of heroic self-sacrifice characteristic of melodrama, Richard resolves not to see Vida again in view of the barrier erected between them 'by caste and wealth.' Vida becomes despondent, and then seriously ill from a broken heart. Her father relents and agrees to let her marry Richard, but the young hero must first prove himself capable of building a home.

Like all melodramas, moral virtue triumphs in *The Other Side*. The villain, Relvason, is destroyed. The hero, Richard, discovers that it was Relvason who murdered his father. He also wins the hand of Vida Geldamo. While it appears that romantic love has triumphed over the traditional idea of marriage based on property, their union is sanctioned only after her father loses all of his money in a business downturn. While sexuality based on heterosexual desire triumphs over property, Foran was unable to overcome the class tensions emerging from the fictional marriage of a working-class man to a woman from a wealthy family.[51] Arbyght and Geldamo establish their own business and employ several men who are treated as 'social equals.' The novel concludes with trade unionism flourishing in the city. 'Through its agency,' Foran writes, 'workingmen are fast becoming more thoughtful, more industrious, more temperate, and are making fearful strides in mental and moral worth and social elevation.'

The Other Side becomes caught up in the central paradox of melodrama. Although the domestic ideal is defended against the evils of industrial-capitalist society under the belief that a universal moral order would prevail, the moral order championed in the melodrama is in fact a reflection of dominant middle-class gender and class values. Foran never proposed that the existing social order be overthrown, and, for him, the home remains the symbol of moral permanence and feminine purity. Also, the relationship between this literature and working-class and middle-class cultures remains ambiguous. In trying to create a work that measured up to the criteria of the bourgeois literary community, Foran also neglects the ethnic variables in working-class culture.

Conclusion

By August 1872 the nine-hours movement had been defeated and, by the end of the decade, labour reform's initial upsurge in Toronto had been crushed by a combination of economic recession, stifled militancy, trade union isolation, and Tory domination.[52] During the early 1870s, however, Toronto labour reformers defined the social subjectivity of the honest working-class mechanic, a description that encompassed their own distinct class-based representation of manliness. The masculine rhetoric of labour reformers, with its emphasis on progress, citizenship, and self-culture, was not entirely unlike that of the late Victorian middle class, but it was inscribed with a distinctively working-class politic. It sustained a radical critique of employer-worker relations under the prevailing social relations of production. To define their status as citizens, and to make the case for universal male suffrage, Toronto labour reformers maintained that they held property in their labour. In this way, Toronto labour reformers, like their British counterparts, articulated a notion of class that excluded women and children.[53] Toronto labour reformers also drew on their colonial relationship with Britain to shape their notion of class. Patriotism, which embraced a sense of 'Britishness' stemming from Canada's colonial status, was incorporated into their discourse of working-class manhood.

Alongside the institutions of labour reform, working-class fiction, poetry, and improving literature guided workers in the collective goals of the labour movement and provided instructions on how to be a 'good' trade unionist, worker, citizen, husband, and father. This rhetoric was an important part of the cultural world of Toronto workers, and part of the strategy used to challenge employers' incursions on the long-established rights of skilled mechanics.

An emphasis on sobriety and domesticity was elaborated in the early 1870s. Domesticity functioned to defend the morality of working men against attacks from employers. The working-class man as father and husband was an integral part of the positive masculine identity constituted by Toronto labour reformers during this period. Yet labour reformers never successfully resolved the tension between the private, and powerless, domestic sphere and the public world of work. The ideal of domesticity, as found at the conclusion of working-class melodramas, never translated into a resolution of the problems created for working-class families by the growth of industrial capitalism. For most working-class families, domesticity was an illusion, as few families were able to survive on the wage of a single male breadwinner. During the 1870s, furthermore, the plight of women workers was rarely mentioned. It was only in the 1880s, with the rise of the Knights of Labor in Toronto, that women workers were put onto the political agenda of the labour movement.

Although labour reformers constructed a national identity that outlined an imagined community which incorporated all workers, unskilled and Chinese labourers were effectively excluded. The labour reform movement of the early 1870s functioned to promote the social and political interests of one segment of the working class – namely, skilled Anglo-Saxon working men – and ultimately fragmented as much as it consolidated the working class.

NOTES

1 National Archives of Canada, MG 28 I 44, 'The Toronto Trades Assembly, How It Originated,' Toronto Trades Assembly (TTA), Minutes, vol. 6, February 1871.
2 Gregory S. Kealey, *Toronto Workers Respond to Industrial Capitalism, 1867–1892* (Toronto: University of Toronto Press, 1980), 325; John Battye, 'The Nine Hour Pioneers: The Genesis of the Canadian Labour Movement,' *Labour/Le Travailleur* 4 (1979): 32. Hewitt was also active in the Orange Order, and he was a Conservative Party supporter.
3 Kealey, *Toronto Workers*, 130.

4 *Ontario Workman*, 5 September 1872; Kealey, *Toronto Workers*, 138; Ron Veruh, *Radical Rag: The Pioneer Labour Press in Canada* (Ottawa: Steel Rail, 1988), 19–23.

5 Kealey, *Toronto Workers*, 124–45; Bryan D. Palmer, *A Culture in Conflict: Skilled Workers and Industrial Capitalism in Hamilton, Ontario, 1860–1914* (Montreal: McGill-Queen's University Press, 1979), 125–52; Battye, 'The Nine Hour Pioneers,' 25–56.

6 Michael Denning, *Mechanic Accents: Dime Novels and Working-Class Culture in America* (London: Verso, 1987); Mary Grimes, *The Knights in Fiction: Two Labor Novels of the 1880s*, afterword by David Montgomery (Urbana and Chicago: University of Illinois Press, 1986), 1–23; Martha Vicinus, *The Industrial Muse: A Study of Nineteenth Century British Working-Class Literature* (New York: Barnes and Noble, 1974); Anna Clark, 'The Rhetoric of Chartist Domesticity: Gender, Language, and Class in the 1830s and 1840s,' *Journal of British Studies* 31 (January 1992): 62–88; Frank William Watt, 'Radicalism in English-Canadian Literature since Confederation' (PhD dissertation, University of Toronto, 1957).

7 J.M.S. Careless, *Brown of the Globe: Statesman of Confederation 1860–1880*, vol. 2 (Toronto and Oxford: Dundurn, 1989), 288–300.

8 *Globe*, 16 and 27 February, 23 March, and 20 May 1872.

9 Ibid., 20 May 1872; Louis James, *Fiction for the Working Man, 1830–50* (London: Oxford University Press, 1963), 48–9; Catherine Gallagher, *The Industrial Reformation of English Fiction: Social Discourse and Narrative form 1832–1867* (Chicago: University of Chicago Press, 1985), 88–110.

10 *Globe*, 16 February 1872.

11 See Leonore Davidoff and Catherine Hall, *Family Fortunes: Men and Women of the English Middle Class, 1780–1850* (Chicago: University of Chicago Press, 1987), 229–71.

12 *Globe*, 16 February and 23 March 1872.

13 Ibid., 15 February 1872.

14 *Ontario Workman*, 25 April 1872.

15 Ibid.

16 Ibid., 18 April 1872.

17 Ibid., 22 January 1874.

18 Ibid., 18 April 1872.

19 Ibid., 6 March 1873, 31 October 1872. This demand for universal manhood suffrage was reiterated in editorials and in several letters to the editor of the *Ontario Workman*. However, the Macdonald government's long-awaited franchise bill, read for the first time in 1869 and announced in the Speech from the Throne in the spring of 1873, and again in the fall, was dropped in the crisis surrounding the Pacific Scandal.

20 The Election Act of 1868 gave the vote to male British subjects, twenty-one years of age and older, who owned, rented, or occupied real estate assessed at a minimum of $400 in cities, $300 in towns, and $200 in villages and townships. The bill passed by the Mowat government in 1874 added males with an annual

income of at least $400, without regard to real estate, to the list of eligible
voters, together with a new category of 'enfranchised Indians.' Attempts to
extend the municipal franchise to women in 1875 and 1877 were defeated,
although married and single women with property gained the right to vote for
school trustees in 1850. Catherine Cleverdon, *The Woman Suffrage Movement in
Canada*, 2nd ed. (Toronto: University of Toronto Press, 1974), 22; Randall
White, *Ontario, 1610–1985: A Political and Economic History* (Toronto and London: Dundurn, 1985), 143.

21 *Ontario Workman*, 30 January 1872.
22 Palmer, *A Culture in Conflict*, 99–100; Kealey, *Toronto Workers*, 130.
23 *Ontario Workman*, 22 August 1872.
24 *Globe*, 15 February 1872; *Ontario Workman*, 15 August 1872, 10 April and
     4 September 1873.
25 *Ontario Workman*, 23 May 1872. During the early 1870s McCormick, an Irish
     Catholic, was a correspondent for Patrick Boyle's *Irish Canadian*. In 1880 he
     published a pamphlet entitled *Conditions of Labour and Modern Civilization*,
     much of it reprints of his columns. The articles contain an extensive critique of
     Malthusianism and liberal political economy.
26 *Ontario Workman*, 18 April 1872.
27 Michel Foucault has argued that during the late nineteenth century the body
     became directly involved as a political field. See Michel Foucault, *Discipline and
     Punish: The Birth of the Prison*, translated by Alan Sheridan (1975; reprint, New
     York: Vintage Books, 1979), 25–6.
28 See also Vicinus, *The Industrial Muse*, 95.
29 *Ontario Workman*, 4 July 1872.
30 Ibid., 29 January 1874.
31 *Globe*, 15 February 1872.
32 *Ontario Workman*, 9 May and 26 September 1872.
33 Ibid, 23 May 1872.
34 TTA, Minutes, 2 May 1873; *Ontario Workman*, 26 June 1873.
35 *Ontario Workman*, 23 January 1873. Peter Bailey has argued that working-class
     culture was more additive than substitutive, and that workers engaged in the
     concurrent pursuit of 'thinking and drinking.' Although I agree with Bailey's
     argument, my intent here is to illustrate how labour reformers used the rheto-
     ric of working-class respectability and sobriety for political purposes. See Peter
     Bailey, '"Will the Real Bill Banks Please Stand Up?" Towards a Role Analysis
     of Mid-Victorian Working-Class Respectability,' *Journal of Social History* 12, 3
     (1979): 336–53.
36 *Ontario Workman*, 8 January 1874.
37 For a similar argument concerning Chartist domesticity, see Clark, 'The Rheto-
     ric of Chartist Domesticity,' 62–88.
38 *Ontario Workman*, 18 April 1872.
39 Ibid., 23 May 1872.

40 TTA, Minutes, 19 May 1871; *Coopers' Journal* 2, 7 (1871). The lecture was attended by approximately one thousand mechanics and toilers representing various branches of industry.

41 *Ontario Workman*, 27 June 1872.

42 Charles Reade, *Put Yourself in His Place* (1896; reprint, London: Chatto and Windus, 1902). Reade's novel portrayed the decay of the aristocracy and the rise of the manufacturing middle class in the fictional city of Hillsborough. The hero, Henry Little, a cutler and inventor of tools and machinery, is driven out of town for neglecting to 'square' himself with the trade and join the Edge-Tool Forgers' Union. Reade characterizes trade unionists as blackguards and ruffians – 'skilled workmen at violence.' In the aftermath of a series of threats, beatings, warning letters, and explosions all secretly arranged by union leaders, Little sets up a small forge in an ancient, unused country church. Unemployed cutlers hired by union officials to drive Little away, or else kill him, are frustrated by the timely arrival of Squire Raby. The title of the novel is explained by another character, Dr Amboyne, a philanthropically inclined physician, who in treating Little's injuries urges him to 'put himself in his place.' Amboyne advises Little to consider all the angles of an issue, and to situate 'Life' before the relations of 'Labor and Capital.' Malcom Elwin, *Charles Reade* (1931; reprint, New York: Russell & Russell, 1969), 201–2; Elton E. Smith, *Charles Reade* (Boston: Twayne Publishers, 1976), 20.

43 *Ontario Workman*, 27 June 1872.

44 Martha Vicinus, '"Helpless and Unfriended": Nineteenth-Century Domestic Melodrama,' *New Literary History* (autumn 1981), 131.

45 Vicinus, *The Industrial Muse*, 114; Denning, *Mechanic Accents*, 173–5.

46 Peter Brooks, *The Melodramatic Imagination: Balzac, Henry James, Melodrama, and the Mode of Excess* (New Haven and London: Yale University Press, 1976), 11–14; Vicinus, 'Nineteenth-Century Domestic Melodrama,' 127–43; David Grimsted, 'Melodrama as Echo of the Historically Voiceless,' in Tamara K. Hareven, ed., *Anonymous Americans: Explorations in Nineteenth-Century Social History* (Englewood Cliffs, NJ: Prentice-Hall, 1971), 80–98.

47 Born in 1840, Martin Foran grew up in rural Pennsylvania, where his father owned a farm and a cooper shop. After a brief stint in the cavalry, Foran taught school briefly and worked as an oil-field hand. In 1868 he moved to Cleveland, where he found work as a journeyman cooper. He helped to organize the International Coopers' Union and the Industrial Congress while simultaneously attending law school. In 1882 Foran, a Democrat, was elected to Congress. He was re-elected twice before retiring to private law practice in 1899. David Montgomery, *Beyond Equality: Labor and the Radical Republicans* (New York: Knopf, 1967), 214–15.

48 Denning, *Mechanic Accents*, 82–3. Denning borrows the term *accents* from Voloshinov, a Soviet language theorist associated with the circle of Mikhail

Bakhtin. These theorists argue that the ambiguity of ideological signs comes not only from their rhetorical character but from the different class accents with which they are inflected.

49 *Ontario Workman*, 22 August 1872. Emphasis in the labour press reprint.

50 Vicinus, 'Nineteenth-Century Dometic Melodrama,' 139.

51 Foucault described this power relationship as the 'deployment of sexuality.' See Michel Foucault, *The History of Sexuality*, vol. 1: *An Introduction*, translated by Robert Hurley (New York: Vintage Books, 1978), 106–8.

52 Bryan D. Palmer, *Working-Class Experience: Re-thinking the History of Canadian Labour, 1800–1991*, 2nd ed. (Toronto: McClelland & Stewart, 1992), 112–16; Battye, 'The Nine Hour Pioneers,' 51–6.

53 For a discussion of the British context, see Anna Clark, 'Manhood, Woman-hood, and the Politics of Class in Britain, 1790–1845,' in Laura L. Frader and Sonya O. Rose, eds., *Gender and Class in Modern Europe* (Ithaca and London: Cornell University Press, 1996), 263–79.

Families, Institutions, and the State in Late-Nineteenth-Century Ontario

EDGAR-ANDRÉ MONTIGNY

Just as the state has enacted major changes in the social welfare system during the last fifty years, so the second half of the nineteenth century also witnessed a significant transformation in poor-relief policies. During this period the Ontario government came to accept a great deal of responsibility for the care of the ill, the insane, the destitute, and the dependent aged. For the most part, the government focused on providing institutional forms of care, often purposely eliminating all alternatives. By the end of the nineteenth century, however, these policies had backfired, as the absence of alternatives created an ever increasing demand for institutional care which forced the government to re-evaluate its commitment to the various groups of dependent people who sought relief.

Rather than attempting to re-establish alternative forms of care, the government decided simply to force families to care for their dependent members. The result was a campaign to reduce the financial burden represented by social welfare responsibilities, such as institutional care, by blaming increasing costs on irresponsible families who refused to carry out their care-giving obligations. Although these policies applied to a wide variety of dependent populations, the dependent aged and their families were the most affected by changes in the way assistance was offered. By the end of the century the aged were the focus of most policy discussions. For this reason, policies affecting the dependent aged will be used as a case study to illustrate the impact of late nineteenth-century developments in Ontario's provincial welfare environment on the dependent populations who required assistance and their families.

Until the last decades of the nineteenth century, most Ontarians who required public assistance received local outdoor relief. This assistance consisted of donations of cash or of food, fuel, or clothing, provided in their own home through a combination of the informal charity of neighbours and more formal contributions from the local municipal or township council. Since most of the communities providing this relief possessed only limited resources, these outdoor relief systems were far from ideal. The assistance was rarely sufficient to do more than keep a person alive, but the system was flexible. Both the community and the local government generally understood that although families should have the primary responsibility for caring for their dependent members, particularly the aged, there was a definite limit to how much the community could expect a family to do. In most instances the community was willing to assist families with their care-giving obligations, mainly to ensure that they were able to continue in their task.

By the end of the nineteenth century these communal relief systems had, for the most part, ceased to function. While population growth and migration may have weakened community bonds, it appears that the demise of local communal relief systems was due mainly to provincial policy changes that favoured, promoted, and even enforced a shift towards institutional modes of care. Although the full impact of this shift would not be felt until after Confederation, the legislative framework that allowed for it began to develop in 1837.

Before 1837 there were no institutional modes of relief to turn to. By mid-century, even, only Toronto and Kingston were served by institutions that accepted aged people and were capable of housing more than a handful of people.[1] Twenty years later, there were still fewer than twenty private charitable homes and sixty-one public institutions in the province; of the latter, fifty-three were prisons. It was not until the 1880s that institutional care became the standard form of public assistance available for the aged. Nevertheless, the opening of the Toronto House of Industry in 1837 and the Toronto Lunatic Asylum in 1838 marked the first steps in a process that eventually eliminated outdoor relief, emphasized the notion that the aged were properly a familial as opposed to a community responsibility, and forced the aged poor who could not be supported by kin to segregate themselves from their communities in order to receive public assistance.[2]

One of the prime motives behind the initial construction of institutions for the care of the poor and disabled was cost. Starting in the 1830s, massive immigration, combined with economic upheavals and transformations, contributed to a substantial rise in the incidence of unemployment and poverty in the province. The cost of providing relief to the masses of needy people escalated beyond the means of the private charity organizations that had previously managed to care for these people.[3] District magistrates also found that they lacked the funds to distribute outdoor relief, such as pensions or grants, to all the aged and needy persons who petitioned them for aid.[4] It was in this environment of fiscal desperation that the provincial government found itself compelled to assume responsibility for the destitute.[5]

The government could have provided financial assistance to private charities and local district and municipal councils, allowing them to continue providing outdoor relief to the poor and to people who were caring for the ill and the aged. Instead, the provincial authorities decided to focus poor-relief efforts on establishing and encouraging the use of institutions. This shift, Richard Splane elaborates, was largely due to the strength of the movement towards institutional care, and away from outdoor relief, which was gaining ascendancy on both sides of the Atlantic.[6] Moreover, as the incidence of destitution increased, so, too, did popular distrust of the poor.[7] As has frequently been explained, nineteenth-century attitudes towards the poor came to blame poverty and misfortune on personal faults. Hence, charity organizations felt not only that generous assistance would harm the poor but that the poor would take advantage of any assistance that was too easily available.

After 1837, private charities increasingly came to rely on government funding, and municipal and district councils found themselves unable to cope with the demands for assistance they received. Under these circumstances the provincial government established a spiralling degree of control over public assistance for the poor.[8] As more control over poor-relief policy was placed in the hands of the government, institutions dominated larger segments of the poor-relief landscape.

Legislation, such as the 1838 House of Industry Act, placed the authority over institutions in the hands of the province, thus reducing the influence of local authorities over poor-relief decisions.[9] After 1834, various municipal incorporation acts defined the responsibilities of town councils towards the poor solely in terms of, and in some cases specifically limited the provision of poor relief to, institutional care.[10] In addition, the 1849 Municipal Incorporation Act, while it granted some authority relating to poor relief to county councils, restricted municipal powers by putting in question the right of municipalities to tax themselves for the support of the poor.[11] Together, these actions effectively removed control of poor-relief efforts from local authorities. Henceforth, the poor were increasingly subjected to the dictates of provincial policy decisions.[12]

The province, meanwhile, refused to acknowledge any responsibility for outdoor relief, even after 1871, when the government had ample revenues to fund such activities.[13] Instead, it chose to limit spending to the construction of provincial institutions, such as asylums, and to assist private charity groups who emphasized institutional care.[14] In fact, the inspector of prisons and public charities, J.W. Langmuir, declared that communal relief systems promoted ineffectual 'unsystematic charity.' He advocated the elimination of outdoor relief as a means of encouraging the construction of county houses of industry, which he felt should assume the burdens of municipal poor relief.[15]

The government formalized its dedication to institutional care in 1874 with the passing of the Charity Aid Act, which focused provincial funding for private charity organizations on those who provided institutional relief. In a move that put municipal outdoor relief efforts at a distinct disadvantage, provincial assistance was, in most cases, allotted solely on the basis of the number of people resident in any given charitable institution. Institutions were not eligible to receive funding for any people they decided to assist outside the establishment.[16] As one report noted, 'outdoor-relief seems to go for nothing, and the government assistance is given exclusively on the number of permanent paupers assisted. The more permanent these are so much greater the public help!'[17] This trend was of particular significance to the aged. One 1879 report declared that of the applicants for outdoor relief in Toronto, a majority of the women were beyond middle age and nearly all the men were old and infirm.[18] It was clear that any reduction in outdoor relief payments would affect the aged more severely than any other group and force them, more than any other group, into institutions.

Although provincial policies were increasingly obliging aged people in need of public assistance to enter institutions, few institutions were constructed specifically for the elderly. At the same time, specialized facilities were established for other groups, such as children and women.[19] As the size of the aged population in Ontario grew rapidly, and at a much faster rate than the number of beds in public institutions, most non-specialized institutions, such as Houses of Industry, 'swiftly found themselves depositaries for the decaying and the decrepit.'[20]

Local authorities, meanwhile, could do little to combat the trend towards institutionalization. Mary Stokes has outlined how municipal authorities found that, after the passing of the Municipal Corporations Act, or 'Baldwin Act,' in 1849, their autonomy in many areas was reduced. Increasingly municipalities came under the power of the central authorities, especially in regard to their spending. Using the powers granted to them by the 'Baldwin Act,' provincial authorities regularly imposed new responsibilities – and expenses – on municipal authorities without offering any compensation.[21] These duties put additional pressure on municipal finances and left even less money available for discretionary spending such as outdoor relief.

With little influence and limited finances, the counties and municipalities of the province found themselves less able to distribute funds within local communities either to help people care for those who could not care for themselves or to provide pensions that would enable people, many of them aged, to remain independent. As non-institutional relief received no support from provincial authorities, county and municipal councils were forced to seek cost-saving methods of assisting the poor. In this regard, Langmuir and other provincial officials promoted institutional relief as being more effective and less costly than outdoor relief. Hence, the goal of reducing municipal poor-relief spending became a strong catalyst for constructing institutions.

Although some council members supported the construction of houses of industry because they genuinely believed the poor would be better cared for in an institution, most focused their arguments on the possibility that 'establishing a Poor House would be a great saving to the county.'[22] Almost all the surviving municipal material on houses of industry is concerned with the costs of running the institutions, not the quality of care being given to the residents. In the counties of Kent, Leeds and Grenville, and Lanark, for instance, most house of industry correspondence was concerned with calculating how much each municipality owed the county council for housing indigents, and with expelling paupers from municipalities that did not contribute to the institution's expenses.[23] Caring for the poor became a second priority to ensuring that all 'unjust impositions on this charity' were avoided.[24]

It is evident that municipalities envisaged institutional relief as a replacement for, rather than as a compliment to, outdoor relief. Municipalities frequently reduced their spending on outdoor relief drastically once institutional forms of relief were made available. In Brantford, for example, both the county council and the municipal council distributed funds for outdoor poor relief. Once municipal funds were diverted towards maintaining a house of industry, however, local assistance to groups providing outdoor poor relief was reduced or halted. As the *Brantford Courier* reported, the construction of the house of industry will 'remove the Ladies Aid Society from any further responsibility in the matter of charitable donations, at least as far as the city grant is concerned.'[25] Once the Ladies Aid Society municipal grant was eliminated, the society was no longer able to assist the local poor by distributing outdoor relief. As a result, people previously being supported in their own homes were forced to enter the newly constructed house of industry.

Two investigations of municipal poor relief were carried out in 1874 and 1888. These reports indicated that the number of people assisted by municipal relief declined between the two dates, despite the massive population growth experienced in most of the province.[26] In addition, reports of the sums local county councils gave to each pauper during the same period reveal a general trend towards smaller disbursements. While the provincial average for outdoor relief payments was $10 per head in 1874,[27] once a house of industry was opened in 1883, Welland County officials usually granted no more than $6 in aid to any one person.[28] Other reports suggest that, by the 1880s, most municipalities distributed between $3 and $8 to each person on their charity list.

It also appears that certain councils were less willing to provide aid to people who were caring for others. In Lanark County in 1862, for instance, five people received between $20 and $76 each as compensation for caring for indigent or insane individuals.[29] By the 1880s there is little record of similar payments being made. These changes were certainly related to the establishment of county houses of industry, most of which were constructed after 1874. Although the information available from newspaper reports and municipal records is far from conclusive, the existing evidence suggests that the amounts given as outdoor relief to the poor were most likely to decrease in localities that had recently constructed some type of institution to care for the poor.

Lincoln County, for instance, paid between $5 and $10 a month in outdoor relief to each person on its destitute and insane charity list. In this manner the county council distributed an average of $1078.65 a year on outdoor relief between 1882 and 1886. In 1887, however, the council spent only $381 on poor relief, and, after 1888, spending fell to less than $100 a year.[30] The main reason for this drastic drop in outdoor relief payments was the opening of the Lincoln County House of Industry in January 1887. Between 1884 and 1887, council was assisting between fourteen and twenty people a year. Between 1888 and 1891 it assisted only one (see table 1). With the opening of a local institution, Lincoln County's recipients of poor relief were cut off from local relief payments and no new names were added to the list.

In effect, the county ceased to distribute outdoor relief once the house of industry was constructed. And, because the house of industry was the only source of public assistance available to them after 1887, people requiring support had no choice but to enter the institution. Although the existing records list most persons entering the institution only as 'an indigent,' Mrs Bowman, Elizabeth Howell, and Mrs Spears, who were receiving outdoor relief before 1887, were listed as having been sent to the house of industry between January and June 1887.[31] It is likely that several of the other 'indigents' were also people formerly on the outdoor relief list.

TABLE 1
Outdoor Relief Payments in Lincoln County between 1882 and 1891

Recipient	1882 Jan.	1882 June	1884 Jan.	1884 June	1885 Jan.	1885 June	1887 Jan.	1887 June	1891 Jan.	1891 June
Terryberry					████████*					
Caugh								████████		
Shelley						██████████████				
Isaubacker		████████████████████████████████								
Burghart		████████								
Gregory						█████████████████████				
Howell						██████████████████████████				
Simmerman	██									
Bowmann				████████████████████████████████						
Spears								▪ ▪ ▪		
Cook	██									
Wilcox	██									
Finn	██									
Wilkinson	██									
Dolan	██									
Mellow									███	
Slough	██									
Turl	████████████████████████████████████									
Schwabb					████████████████████*					
Osbourne	██									

SOURCE: AO, RG 21, Municipal Records, Lincoln County Clerk, Treasurer's Letterbook: see expenses for Insane and Destitute, 1884–91.
NOTES: ████ length of time person was receiving outdoor relief.
   * died.

The house of industry was expensive to build, but the institution's daily maintenance did not cost the county much more than it had previously been spending on outdoor relief. It also allowed the county to support a few more people. According to the 1891 census, the institution housed twenty-one people. More significant, however, while the province limited the amount the county could spend on outdoor relief by refusing to offer provincial grants for such activities, the county received a $4,000 legislative grant in 1891 to assist it with the expenses of maintaining the poor in an institution.[32] Financially, institutionalizing the poor made a great deal of sense for Lincoln County. Little mention is made, however, of the quality of care people received in an institution that was constructed specifically to save money.

As municipalities provided less assistance for the non-institutionalized poor, and as people caring for the elderly found it more difficult to receive assistance from their local municipalities, it became increasingly difficult for aged persons to remain in their own homes and for other people to provide care for them. Although municipalities never completely halted outdoor relief payments, evidence indicates that the portion of the population assisted by such funds declined drastically during the last quarter of the century. As a result, outdoor relief became a less viable means of support for the aged.[33]

This process was exacerbated by the fact that the immediate impact of the government's refusal to recognize outdoor relief as a legitimate subject of provincial support was to encourage the construction of new institutions at the expense of local communal relief systems. There were only four publicly assisted charity establishments in 1866, but thirty-three in 1893. By the end of the century this number had risen to nearly one hundred.[34] Since municipalities reduced or even eliminated their outdoor relief efforts once an institution was established nearby, each additional institution led to a further reduction in the amount of outdoor assistance available to the aged poor and their families. Basically, the provincial government's insistence on putting all public funds into institutional care effectively eliminated outdoor relief as an option for anyone needing more than temporary aid.[35] The disappearance of outdoor aid forced many persons who required long-term assistance, which was often the case with the elderly, to enter institutions.

Although anti-outdoor-relief policies in Ontario were not as brutally enforced as those in other jurisdictions, such as England or some American states, the refusal of the provincial government to assist people outside institutions still forced numerous aged people to enter houses of industry, houses of refuge, and old age homes. The insistence that institutions were the only way to provide public assistance to the needy increased the number of people requiring institutional care by eliminating other viable options.[36] It also created undue hardships for many poor people and their families because, although the provincial policies eliminated most alternative forms of relief, the government failed to provide sufficient institutional facilities to accommodate all the people who needed care.

While government policies directed all those in need of assistance towards institutions, the province did little more than encourage counties to provide adequate facilities to accommodate all those in need. Often outdoor relief was eliminated before anyone could ensure that the people who had formerly been assisted in this manner could be accommodated in an institution. In some municipalities, for instance, outdoor relief had been limited to people requiring temporary or emergency assistance before a house of industry had been erected to care for those individuals who needed more long-term support.[37]

Once again this problem developed largely because of provincial funding policies. Although the province agreed to assist establishments that provided institutional care for the poor, it did not, until 1890, provide funds to assist counties with the cost of constructing institutions. Houses of industry saved counties money in the long run, but they were usually expensive to construct. Lincoln County, for example, spent almost $28,000 over a four-year period to construct and prepare its house of industry to receive residents.[38] This cost deterred many counties from establishing a house of industry, while others reduced outdoor relief expenditures in order to accumulate funds with which to commence constructing an institution. The overall effect of these trends was to limit the amount of support available to the aged and their families outside institutions, without ensuring that institutional care expanded to keep up with the demand for care. Hence, in public institutions, there were never anywhere near the number of beds required to accommodate all the aged people who needed care.[39] As a result, the institutions that did exist were forced to adopt rigid entrance requirements and to refuse entry to anyone who did not meet the specifications.[40]

Despite restrictive admission policies, the aged came to constitute an ever increasing segment of the province's institutionalized population. Provincial policies left elderly people with nowhere else to go. Forcing the aged into institutions, however, had far more serious consequences than merely removing them from their homes and segregating them from their communities. The institutionalization of the aged population affected not only how the aged lived but also how they were perceived by institution administrators, government officials, and the public in general. Institutions focused attention on the desperate and needy elderly, thereby making the most decrepit and dependent segment of the aged population the most visible.[41] As a result, an image of the elderly as incapacitated, unproductive, and helpless was created and confirmed.[42] Thereafter, officials and administrators often implemented policies for the aged which were based on this impression.

These policies, which tended to have a significant impact on the future of many aged people and their families, rarely bore any relation to the experience and situation of the vast majority of the aged population that resided outside institutions. However, government officials, who tended to formulate policies based on what was visible to them, rarely saw the vast number of non-institutionalized aged people. They knew only the elderly who filled the rooms and corridors of the province's houses of industry and houses of refuge.

When only the institutionalized aged were considered, it appeared that a large portion of the elderly population was destitute and without families

able or at least willing to care for them. Despite attempts to limit the
number of aged people admitted into institutions, both the number of
elderly within their walls and the portion of the institutionalized population they represented grew steadily during the final decades of the nineteenth century. It appeared to officials that there was no end to the number
of aged people who needed public care. The main explanation officials
could find for this increase in the number of aged people needing care was
that families and communities were using institutions as a means of evad-
ing their obligations towards the aged. The fact was, however, that regardless of how many elderly people crowded into the province's institutions,
they were never more than a small minority of the total aged population.

Nevertheless, it was possible for government officials to argue that families were institutionalizing the aged at an ever increasing rate during the
1890s. At the beginning of the decade, the elderly formed a minority of the
population within institutions. By the end, this was no longer the case. The
number of old people in institutions grew and came to form a large portion
of the province's institutionalized population. The fact that the institutionalized elderly population was increasing during a period when the government was building more institutions, many specifically designed to shelter
aged people, added further weight to the government's argument.

Census reports indicate that in 1891 there were 152,488 persons in
Ontario who were over the age of sixty. In September of the same year,
the inspector of prisons and public charities reported that there were 1260
beds in government-funded charitable institutions likely to shelter aged
people.[43] In addition, there were 3318 beds in the various provincial asylums for the insane. Altogether, there was potential accommodation for
4478 aged persons. Even if every one of these beds had been occupied by
someone over the aged of sixty, this number would have represented only
3.5 per cent of the province's total aged population.

In fact, the number of elderly people in these institutions was much
smaller. At no time, for instance, did the aged constitute more than 20 per
cent of the insane asylum population. Between 1888 and 1896 the elderly
represented only 15 per cent of the total number of people admitted to all
provincial asylums.[44] Also, as table 2 demonstrates, an 1889 investigation
indicated that aged people accounted for fewer than half of the residents of
the province's county houses of industry.[45] The number of old people in
Ontario's institutions in 1891, then, represented no more than 2 per cent of
the total aged population of the province.

Over the course of the 1890s, however, the aged population within public
institutions grew to the point that, by the turn of the century, the elderly
constituted approximately 80 per cent of the population of Ontario's houses

TABLE 2
Number of Aged People Reported as Resident in Houses of
Industry in Ontario, 1889

County	Total Inmates	Aged Inmates	Per Cent Aged
Brant	60	unknown*	unknown*
Elgin	109	46	42.2
Lincoln	52	19	36.6
Norfolk	75	19	25.3
Middlesex	127	60	47.2
Waterloo	118	72	61.1
Welland	59	35	59.3
Wellington	77	54	70.1
York	157	78	49.7
Total	774*	383	49.4

NOTE: *Brant was not included in the total calculations.
SOURCE: *Ontario Sessional Paper*, no. 61, 1889.

TABLE 3
Number of Beds Available in Ontario's
Houses of Refuge, 1889–99

Year	Total Number of Beds
1889	1,260
1891	1,349
1893	1,706
1895	1,917
1897	2,120
1899	2,268

SOURCE: AO, Annual Report, 1889–9,
'Report of the Inspector of Prisons and
Public Charities upon Houses of
Refuge.'

of refuge and 70 per cent of the province's county houses of industry.[46] This increase occurred even though the decade was a period of institution building. The number of houses of refuge, county houses of industry, and other publicly funded charitable institutions in the province rose from sixty-two at the beginning of the decade to nearly one hundred in 1901. In houses of refuge alone the number of beds almost doubled, increasing from 1260 to 2268 (see table 3). In total, provincial institutions could accommodate as many as 4485 persons by the end of the century.[47] At the same time, almost 2000 new beds were added to provincial asylums for the insane. In all, this figure represented an 80 per cent increase in the number of aged people who could potentially be housed in a public institution. When the aged population of these institutions grew despite their enlarged capacity, it is not surprising that government officials concluded, at least initially, that the aged were being sent to institutions at an ever increasing rate and that the burden on the public treasury would soon become unbearable. In truth, this was not the case.

The problem was that the new accommodations in provincial institutions came nowhere near keeping pace with the even more dramatic increase in the total number of aged people in the province. Between 1891 and 1901 the number of people over the age of sixty grew by over 30,000, to a total of 182,735 persons. Even though the number of beds increased during the 1890s, provincial institutions could still shelter no more than 3 per cent of Ontario's aged population.

Thus, while officials blamed the ever increasing numbers of old people located in public institutions on the willingness of families to abandon the aged, the portion of the total aged population being sent to institutions changed little between 1891 and 1901. Despite government reports, even if the aged had filled every bed in every institution, the vast majority of them would never have seen the inside of one of these places. Rather than any deterioration of the sense of familial responsibility towards the aged, a rough estimate indicates that for every aged individual in an institution, there were at least thirty-three others being cared for by kin or living on their own.

Nevertheless, in a manner that would be echoed a century later, Ontario officials acted on the assumption that aged people were being institutionalized needlessly. They argued that 'the number of aged and infirm people who can work very little or not at all is not a large one. The number of those of this class who have no friends to support them,' and hence may become candidates for institutionalization, 'is still smaller.'[48] While this may have been true, the government assumed that anyone who had 'friends,' a term that referred to relatives as well as non-related people, was not a candidate for institutionalization. Thus, even the minority of the aged population that sought the shelter of institutions because they truly needed assistance often found that restrictive admission policies denied them access to care. If one could not enter an institution, there were, by the 1890s, few alternative forms of care available. One observer commented that it was often so difficult to obtain admission to a house of industry that it 'was easier for an aged infirm pauper to get into jail than into [an] institution.'[49]

It was common, for instance, for institutions to adopt policies that denied access to institutions to any person from outside the region served by the establishment. People who lived in counties that had no house of industry were left with no place to go. Institutions also demanded that residents be easy to care for and that they behave appropriately. These requirements affected the aged more severely than others because the elderly frequently suffered from illnesses or senility, which made them difficult to care for or troublesome. As one house of industry inspector pointed out, the aged residents were 'in many cases most trying patients.'[50]

It was the aged with kin, however, who suffered the most from the fact that, in attempting to limit the cost of maintaining people in public institutions, government officials tried to reduce the number of elderly persons eligible for institutional care. As a result, institutional administrators expressed the view that the aged were not proper candidates for institutions. Instead, it was argued, they should be cared for by their families.[51] In a manner that reflected the new emphasis on the self-supporting family and the increased responsibility that late nineteenth-century society placed on individual families with regard to the care of dependent individuals, officials began to argue that if public shelters were made accessible, they would 'take away ... the filial obligation for the support of aged parents which is the main bond of family solidarity.'[52]

In the name of supporting familial responsibilities, institution officials often tried to locate relatives in order to force them to take responsibility for their aged kin. Often when relatives were discovered, inmates were discharged into their care as they were no longer seen to be fit candidates for public charity. This was the case with one destitute old woman in Ottawa who had found refuge in the Protestant Orphans' Home. As Lorna McLean explains, the woman had lived in the home for one year when it was discovered that she had two sons to support her. She was dismissed and sent to her children.[53] Unlike communal support networks which recognized that families were not always able to care for an aged relative without assistance, institutional care givers demanded that families look after their aged regardless of their financial ability. These tactics ignored the fact that a person whose relatives were able or willing to provide care would probably not have arrived at the institution.

One could argue that the government officials could not possibly have been unaware of the inaccuracy of their statements. Surely they should have realized that the very economic crisis that was causing bureaucrats to advocate cost-cutting measures was also having a major impact on the working class. As David and Rosemary Gagan explain, during the 1890s, working-class incomes and standards of living fell, causing individual and familial distress.[54] The government itself reported in 1895 that, 'owing to the general depression in business and consequent hard times during the past years, the number of paupers has greatly increased.'[55] The same downturn certainly had an impact on families' ability to care for dependent relatives.

The government appears to have ignored these facts. Legislators and bureaucrats rarely understood that many families, especially among the working class, lacked the physical or financial resources required to care for an aged relative. Government officials, for the most part, belonged to elite families, and they tended to base their ideas of family care on the situation found in their own homes. As with many of the traditional views of family life in the past, the ideal image of family care for the aged was the reality only for wealthy families. This image included a large family that was able to 'easily manage' the care of an infirm, ill, or senile older person because several kin were available to help with those relatives who required assistance. Also, unlike the majority of the population, the wealthy could provide care for ill kin without worrying about the financial strain such actions might place on the family.

It could also be argued that, despite their personal biases, government officials could not ignore the needs of working-class voters. It appears, however, that the working class could be effectively ignored by bureaucrats and legislators alike. Universal manhood suffrage was a recent innovation in Ontario, Oliver Mowat having made the reform only in 1888. Despite this increased voting power, as well as the activities of working-class political movements, it appears that the interests of working men were systematically neglected by Liberals and Conservatives alike. The Knights of Labor tried to elect working-class men to the legislature to ensure that it would 'take some interest in the welfare of the class,'[56] but this working-class political movement was organized in only a few locations and was never very successful. By 1894 the Knights were described as 'devastated.'[57] Although the activities of the some working-class political groups forced Conservatives and Liberals to pass certain pieces of labour legislation, they achieved little with regard to improvements in social policy or social spending.

Ignoring both the circumstances and the needs of the dependent elderly and their working-class families, the government instead pursued policies that were more in line with views of middle-class reformers. They emphasized the theory of the ideal family and were also concerned with moral, urban, and social reform. In almost all their activities, these reformers displayed a distinct lack of understanding or sympathy for the poor. When working-class families failed to live up to middle-class notions of acceptable behaviour or to carry out what the reformers felt were their proper responsibilities and obligations, many reformers, instead of reconsidering their assumptions, advocated the use of state intervention to force the lower classes to conform to the reformers' ideals.[58]

In the realm of care giving for the dependent aged, government policy

makers appear to have accepted the basic premise of the reformers' arguments, perhaps because it was a convenient justification for cost-cutting
measures. Social spending, which represented 32.4 per cent of provincial
expenditures in 1893, made up only 14.7 per cent of spending by 1911.[59]
Since over 70 per cent of the social welfare budget consisted of expenditures
on institutions, especially mental hospitals and government-funded charitable institutions such as county houses of industry and houses of refuge,
these cuts, could not help but affect the availability and quality of institutional care for the aged. To justify these cuts the government argued it
would be better for everyone if families carried a larger share of the burden.
In making this demand on families, however, the state was enforcing a
notion of the ideal family that was completely beyond the capacities of most
of the families that would be affected by government social policies or
institutional regulations. It was also based on a distorted image of the past.

Institutional adminstrators ignored the fact that families that may previously have been able to provide care for the aged, largely because they were
assisted by their community, were no longer able to do so because their
communities could not assist them. Provincial policies had worked to eliminate municipal outdoor relief for the poor and aged, and in the process
served to reduce the effectiveness of the communal support networks that
had accompanied these formal relief systems. Institutional care was established to replace community relief, but various fiscal restraints, combined
with ideologies of familial responsibilities, prevented many needy aged
people from gaining access to these institutions. Large numbers of elderly
people were left dependent on relatives who were totally unable to care for
them. Hence, the combination of the province's preference for institutional
care and the emergence of an ideology that emphasized the self-supporting
family left many aged people with no form of support. These casualties of
'the great social transformation' usually found themselves destitute and
homeless. As one late nineteenth-century Canadian social commentator
noted, 'we build large buildings to accommodate unfortunates, but we
initiate no system whereby the aged and the needy will be able to live
without begging.'[60] When begging failed, many homeless old people found
themselves imprisoned in local jails.

Nineteenth-century laws in Ontario permitted county magistrates to con-
fine homeless old people in the local jail as vagrants. While in earlier
decades the aged formed only a small portion of jail inmates, by the later
decades of the century it was clear that, in many jails, elderly vagrants
comprised a large portion of the inmates. The increase in the number of old
people in jails was almost certainly a direct consequence of two trends:
provincial policies that limited public relief for the aged to institutional

care, and an increasing emphasis on familial responsibility for the aged that limited the access of the elderly to institutions.

In the 1890s, determining the boundary between state responsibilities and family obligations towards the aged became a key element in provincial policies concerning the institutionalization and support of Ontario's elderly people. Basically, the government faced a situation that was very similar to the problem facing the province's legislators today: the question of dealing with a rapid increase in the demand for institutional accommodation for the province's aged population during a period of fiscal restraint. The nineteenth-century solution to this problem was to blame the situation on the irresponsibility of families. The government insisted that the increasing number of aged people in institutions was obvious evidence that families were shirking their duties and attempting to force on the state responsibilities that properly belonged to the family. In response, the government simply restricted the admission of old people to institutions and declared that the care of the aged was a family obligation. In defining the boundaries between family obligations and state responsibilities in this manner, the Ontario government argued that, before the creation of provincially funded institutions, the aged were the sole responsibility of their families. It was not unreasonable, therefore, in a time of fiscal crisis, for the state to request that families once again assume the responsibilities they had formerly carried out.

In fact, the provincial government was doing more than merely returning to the family those responsibilities that it had previously carried out. Traditionally, rather than being solely a family responsibility, the aged had been viewed as a legitimate concern of the entire community. Friends, neighbours, and members of the community in general assisted families in the performance of their caring functions. When the Ontario government argued that the care of the aged was the obligation of the family, it was, in fact, attempting to redefine the boundary between state responsibilities and family obligations in a manner that placed a far greater share of responsibility on the family than had previously been the case.

Defining the care of the elderly in this manner, however, allowed the government to justify its refusal to increase public expenditures on institutional accommodation for the dependent aged. By promoting an image of families shirking their duties and foisting their aged on the state, the government generated sympathy for policies that were really intended to reduce the state's responsibility for the poor and reduce social welfare spending. Similarly, the high levels of poverty, destitution, and dependency reported among Ontario's elderly population at the end of the last century were often the result of changes in government policy and the large-scale transfer of the state's responsibility for the aged to the family. Turning government responsibilities into family obligations may have reduced social welfare expenditures, but these policies often ignored the fact that families were rarely able to bear the degree of responsibility now placed on them. The result was widespread suffering among both the dependent aged population and their families.

NOTES

1 Lorna McLean, 'Single Again: Widow's Work in the Urban Family Economy, Ottawa, 1871,' *Ontario History* 83, 2 (1991): 127.

2 Allan Irving, 'The Master Principle of Administering Relief: Jeremy Bentham, Sir Francis Bond Head, and the Establishment of the Principle of Less Eligibility in Upper Canada,' *Canadian Review of Social Policy* 23 (1989): 16–17; also Rainer Baehre, 'Paupers and Poor Relief in Upper Canada,' *Historical Papers* (1981): 79.

3 Baehre, 'Paupers and Poor Relief,' 59.

4 See David Murray, 'The Cold Hand of Charity: The Court of Quarter Sessions and Poor Relief in the Niagara District, 1828–1841,' *Canadian Law in History Conference* (Carleton University, June 1987): 201–38; and Ruth Bleasdale, 'Class Conflict on the Canals of Upper Canada in the 1840s,' *Labour/Le Travailleur* 7 (1981): 14.

5 For evidence of a similar financial crisis in local poor relief in the United States, see Raymond Mohl, 'Three Centuries of American Public Welfare, 1600–1932,' *Current History* 65 (1973): 8.

6 Richard Splane, *Social Welfare in Ontario, 1793–1893* (Toronto: University of Toronto Press, 1965), 70.

7 See Joan Underhill Hannon, 'Poor Relief in Antebellum New York State: The Rise and Decline of the Poorhouse,' *Explorations in Economic History* 22 (1985): 234.

8 For reference to this process in England and Europe, see J.S. Zainaldin and P.L. Tyor, 'Asylums and Society: An Approach to Industrial Change,' *Journal of Social History* 13 (1979–80): 40.

9 Baeher, 'Paupers and Poor Relief,' 75.

10 Splane, *Social Welfare in Ontario*, 72.

11 Ibid., 74.

12 Elizabeth Wallace, 'The Origin of the Social Welfare State in Canada, 1867–1900,' *Canadian Journal of Economics and Political Science* 16 (1950): 384; see also Philip Lee and A.C. Benjamin, 'Intergovernmental Relations: Historical and Contemporary Perspectives,' in *Fiscal Austerity and Aging: Shifting Governmen-*

tal Responsibility for the Elderly, edited by Carroll Estes and R. Newcomer (London: Sage Publications, 1983): 60.

13 Splane, *Social Welfare in Ontario*, 12.

14 Kenneth Bryden, *Old Age Pensions and Policy Making in Canada* (Montreal: McGill-Queen's University Press, 1974), 22.

15 Splane, *Social Welfare in Ontario*, 109.

16 Ibid., 104; see also Carole Haber, *Beyond Sixty-Five: The Dilemma of Old Age in America's Past* (Cambridge: Cambridge University Press, 1983), 85.

17 City of Toronto Archives (CTA), SC 35, Series H, 'Report on Asylums and Hospitals,' *Globe*, 6 February 1877.

18 Ibid., 'The Charity System,' *Globe*, 24 December 1879.

19 Stormi Stewart, 'The Elderly Poor in Rural Ontario: Inmates of the Wellington County House of Industry, 1877–1907,' *Journal of the Canadian Historical Association* (Charlottetown, 1992), 224.

20 Andrew Scull, *Museums of Madness: The Social Organization of Insanity in Nineteenth-Century England* (London: A. Lane, 1979), 40.

21 See Mary Stokes, 'Local Government in the Shadow of the Law: The Municipal Corporation as Legal Actor in Canada West/Ontario, 1850–1870' (unpublished paper, University of Western Ontario, 1987), especially 28–32 and note 70; also Mary Stokes, 'Petitions to the Legislative Assembly of Ontario from Local Governments, 1867–77: A Case Study in Legislative Participation,' *Law and History Review* 11, 1 (1993): 169, 176.

22 Archives of Ontario (AO), RG 21, Municipal Records, Ontario County Clippings Album, June 1878.

23 Ibid.; RG 21, Municipal Records, series F-1886, Raleigh Township, House of Industry Reports; RG 21, Municipal Records, Lanark County, House of Industry Management Board Minutes; RG 21, Municipal Records, series F-1740, Leeds and Grenville, January 1893; and RG 21, Municipal Records, series F-1740, box 16, file 4, Leeds and Grenville, 1857.

24 Ibid., series F-1740, 1883, file 111B, Leeds and Grenville.

25 'Ladies Aid Society,' *Brantford Courier*, 19 January 1887.

26 Splane, *Social Welfare in Ontario*, 109.

27 Ibid.

28 See *The Newmarket Era*, March and April 1883; *Brantford Daily Courier*, 20 December 1888; in the fall of 1887, the Burford Town Council gave out $123, an average of $5 per person.

29 *Perth Courier*, 7 January 1862.

30 AO, RG 21, Municipal Records, Lincoln County, Clerk Treasurer's Letterbook:' see payments for Destitute and Insane

31 Ibid.: see expenses for the Industrial Home, 166, 466, and 468.

32 Ibid., 1882–93; House of Industry, Expense Book.

33 This trend was discovered in Philadelphia by Haber, *Beyond Sixty-Five*, 85; for England, see Zainaldin and Tyor, 'Asylums and Society,' 40.

34 Splane, *Social Welfare in Ontario*, 84.

35 CTA, SC 35, series H, *Globe*, 12 October 1877.

36 Andrew Scull, 'A Convenient Place to Get Rid of Inconvenient People: The Victorian Lunatic Asylum,' in A.D. King, ed., *Buildings and Society* (London: Routledge & Kegan Paul, 1980), 39; see also J.B. Williamson, 'Old Age Relief Policies prior to 1900: The Trend Towards Restrictiveness,' *American Journal of Economics and Sociology* 43, 3 (1984): 369–84; and Benjamin Klenbaner, 'Poverty and Relief in American Thought,' *Social Services Review* 38 (1964): 399.

37 AO, RG 21, Municipal Records, Ontario County, Newsclippings Album, June 1877.

38 Ibid., Lincoln County, Clerk Treasurer's Letterbook.

39 Bryden, *Old Age Pensions and Policy Making in Canada*, 35.

40 Stewart, 'The Elderly Poor in Rural Ontario,' 35.

41 Stephen Katz, 'Alarmist Demographics: Power, Knowledge and the Elderly Population,' *Journal of Aging Studies* 6, 3 (1992): 213.

42 Carole Haber, 'The Old Folks at Home: The Development of Institutional Care for the Aged in Nineteenth-Century Philadelphia,' *The Pennsylvania Magazine of History and Biography* 110, 2 (1977): 249; see also Haber, *Beyond Sixty-Five*, 126.

43 See AO, Annual Report of the Inspector of Prisons and Charities for the Province of Ontario (Annual Report) 1891. Beds in institutions such as orphanages, lying-in hospitals, Magdalene asylums, schools for the deaf and blind, and reformatories were excluded from this total, given that they were unlikely to house older individuals.

44 Annual Report, 1897.

45 See *Ontario Sessional Papers*, no. 61, 1889.

46 See Annual Report, 'On Houses of Refuge for the Province of Ontario,' 1896; and D.C. Park and J.D. Wood, 'Poor Relief and the County House of Refuge System in Ontario, 1880–1911,' *Journal of Historical Geography* 18, 4 (1992): 446.

47 Annual Report, 1901.

48 CTA, SC 35, series H, 'Provision for the Poor,' *Globe*, 20 October 1877.

49 Ibid., 'Remodel It,' *Evening Star*, 20 September 1897.

50 AO, RG 21, Municipal Records, series F-1551, Brant County, Correspondence, 2 January 1905.

51 See Ann Shola Orloff, *The Politics of Pensions* (Madison: University of Wisconsin Press, 1993), 163–6, for an example of how this sentiment became embedded in relief practices. See also Diane Matters, 'Public Welfare Vancouver Style, 1910–20,' *Journal of Canadian Studies* 14, 1 (1979): 11.

52 Judith Husbeck, *Old and Obsolete: Age Discrimination and the American Worker, 1860–1920* (New York: Garland Press, 1989), 170.

53 McLean, 'Single Again,' 144.

54 David Gagan and Rosemary Gagan, 'Working Class Standards of Living in Late-Victorian Urban Ontario: A Review of the Miscellaneous Evidence on the

Quality of Material Life,' *Journal of the Canadian Historical Association* (1990), 180.

55 *Ontario Sessional Papers*, no. 11, '27th Annual Report on the Common Gaol, Prisons and Reformatories,' 1895, xii.

56 Gregory Kealey and Brian Palmer, *Dreaming of What Might Be: The Knights of Labor in Ontario, 1880–1900* (Toronto: New Hogtown Press, 1987), 206.

57 Ibid., 247.

58 See Marianna Valverde, *The Age of Light, Soap and Water: Moral Reform in English Canada, 1885–1925* (Toronto: McClelland & Stewart, 1991), introduction.

59 Allan Moscovitch and Glenn Drover, 'Social Expenditures and the Welfare State: The Canadian Experience in Historical Perspective,' in *The Benevolent State: The Growth of Welfare in Canada*, edited by Allan Moscovitch and Jim Albert (Toronto: Garamond Press, 1987), 18–19.

60 Norman Patterson, 'Canadian People, A Criticism,' *Canadian Magazine* 12 (1899): 135.

Oliver Mowat, Patronage, and Party Building

S.J.R. NOEL

Oliver Mowat was exceptional among the politicians of his time in many respects, not the least of which was his frank and sophisticated defence of the idea of party politics. In the nineteenth century, in Ontario as elsewhere, political parties were generally held in low regard. Many believed they had no legitimate place in politics, and their allegedly sinister and corrupting influence was commonly deplored by the press, by the informed public, and even by the most partisan of politicians. In particular, their presence in Ontario politics was a source of vociferous opposition by those who favoured 'non-partisan' government. Denunciations of parties as unnecessary, 'puerile,' and 'noxious' intrusions into provincial politics were commonplace at election time, as were appeals to voters to elect the 'best' candidates irrespective of party. It took considerable political and intellectual courage to argue, as Mowat did, in favour of a politics based on disciplined political parties.

Mowat's thinking on this question was undoubtedly influenced by his experience as a member of the Parliament of the United Canadas, where a lack of party cohesion and an unmanageable contingent of nominally 'independent' members (whose votes in practice were for sale to the highest bidder) had led to chronic instability and, in Mowat's view, a travesty of responsible government. As early as 1858 he had concluded, as he confided to his friend Alexander Mackenzie, that 'the only principle on which free government appears to be capable of being worked [is] the distinction of parties.'[1] By the time he assumed power as premier of Ontario in 1872, his views were fully developed and he made no secret of them. 'I confess that I do attach a great deal of importance to party,' he stated in his first throne speech debate, 'but I do not place party before country ... I am for party because I believe – because I know – that the interests of the country are best advanced by means of a well-organized party, founded on well-recognized principles ... Our whole system of government involves party as a necessity.'[2]

It is against this background that Mowat's role as the great and innovative party builder of nineteenth-century politics must be understood. It was grounded in long-held conviction and a clear grasp of the theory of responsible parliamentary government. One of his main priorities after becoming premier was to construct a new type of political party – one that would be an efficient and reliable instrument of political power, whose disciplined structure would make responsible government truly workable. The question was, by what means could such a party be built?

At first glance, the material that Mowat found immediately to hand was not very promising. Behind him in the House sat the same motley collection of reformers, radical Grits, ministerialists, and 'independents' of uncertain allegiance who had doomed every Liberal attempt to govern for a quarter of a century. Subjected to pressure or inducements, parliamentary formations of this kind in the past had always fallen apart, and there was no reason to think that this one would not do so as well. Mowat's answer to this problem, which had plagued every government since 1841, was to construct an extraparliamentary organization that would give the Liberal Party a solid, permanent, and influential presence in every riding in the province. It would be a formal means of choosing Liberal candidates and an election machine responsible for getting these candidates elected – and it would also enable Mowat, as party leader, to impose a previously unknown degree of party discipline. Those elected would succeed through the efforts of the Liberal machine and would thus be bound into a tightly knit, hierarchical organization.

By the 1870s Ontario was ripe for such a development because of the increasing size of the electorate. There was both general population growth and a progressive widening of the franchise, which the Mowat government actively promoted. An enlarged electorate, however, does not necessarily dictate any single response in the political system. The pace and type of change that take place may vary widely, depending on the constitutional framework, past experience of party rule, and, in general, the operative norms and expectations of the political culture.[3] Ontario, in the early years of Confederation, was a particularly fascinating seed-bed of party structures. Two distinct variants of machine-type party organization arose there, more or less simultaneously: the federal Conservative machine of John A. Macdonald and the provincial Liberal machine of Oliver Mowat. The result was two broadly different patterns of party organization and two broadly different styles of party leadership. Both leaders relied heavily on political patronage as the glue that held together their respective parties, but the way in which they used it varied strikingly.

There can be no doubt, however, that of the two parties and leaders, it was the Conservatives and Macdonald who controlled incomparably the greater share of patronage resources, since at Confederation seemingly all of the richest spoils of office had fallen into the federal maw. Macdonald was thus amply supplied with the means he needed to strengthen and expand the Conservative Party organization – in effect, to complete the task to which he had devoted so much time and effort during the Union era. He had been the most assiduous, and on the whole the most effective, party organizer of that era. Better than any of his contemporaries, he had learned to use patronage as a means of knitting together the always potent (but endemically anarchic) conservatism of the districts with the precarious coalition of Tories and moderates who constituted the Conservative Party in Parliament. His efforts, while extraordinary for their time and in many respects the key to his political success, were also almost entirely idiosyncratic and personal: insofar as there was a Conservative 'organization,' he was it.[4]

Not surprisingly, Macdonald's approach to party building in the post-Confederation era followed essentially the same pattern. In other words, the Ontario Conservative Party machine was built by formalizing – and enriching with new federal patronage – the bonds that already existed between the party leadership and the local elites, whether Tory or 'progressive' conservative, whom Macdonald had always cultivated. Yet while the local elites were unquestionably the party's vital core, they were rarely the party's creatures. Their power and prestige, in fact, typically predated their involvement in the party, and often their positions in commerce and local government enabled them to sustain substantial networks of their own. They were quasi-independent local notables in their own right, and they expected party leaders to bargain with them for their support. Dealing with them could be a trial: it required brokerage skills of a high order, a personal touch – and usually a great deal of Macdonald's famous 'soft sawder' – to keep them in line; yet no Conservative leader could contemplate fighting an electoral battle without them.

Mowat had few pre-existing resources to draw upon. The Liberal or 'Reform' Party outside the legislature was not so much a party as a semi-organized 'tendency,' in that it was composed of a large but amorphous body of 'reform opinion,' a number of supporting newspapers, and a miscellany of constituency electoral committees or associations that varied widely in their levels of activity and effectiveness. Its local leadership tended to be difficult to coordinate for electoral purposes, and often drawn towards temperance, anti-Catholic, or other single-issue diversions. There was the unresolved question of whether Ontario's seemingly narrow range of powers under the British North America Act gave it either sufficient reason or sufficient resources to sustain the existence of political parties of any kind, let alone to sustain an ambitious attempt to build a new kind of party from the ground up. Yet in spite of these apparent disadvantages, over the course of Mowat's first four years in the premiership a working prototype of a new Liberal Party machine was put in place in Ontario which was in many respects organizationally superior to its Conservative counterpart.

Although not averse to incorporating traditional local elites into its structure, Mowat's Liberal machine was for the most part forced to create its own cadre of riding-level officers. They were recruited for the most part from among the ranks of the respectable, progressive, upwardly mobile members of the community, who generally had solid roots in their ridings. Unlike their Conservative rivals, they owed their political influence less to any independent social eminence or commercial importance than to their Liberal Party connections. The result was a party apparatus that was more amenable to direction from the top, and a party in the legislature that was dependent upon it for electoral support and thus more easily whipped into line. Over the following decade this party organization would be developed into an instrument that was without peer as an efficient electoral machine.

Initially, the significance of the rise of Mowat's new Liberal machine was obscured by the coincidence, after 1873, of having a Liberal government in Ottawa. After the return to power of Macdonald and the Conservatives in 1878, it soon became evident that the Mowat machine was by no means dependent on federal Liberal support for its continued existence. On the contrary, as it showed in the 1879 Ontario general election, it was perfectly capable of operating effectively without it. Mowat had always taken care, even during the interval of complete federal-provincial Liberal hegemony, to base his machine's operation primarily on the downward flow of provincial patronage, which, under his aegis, was systematically increased in volume and variety. The process through which this patronage flow was managed, however, should be viewed in the context of the times.

Mowat was the foremost exponent of 'provincial rights' among his contemporaries. His victories over the federal government, in a series of constitutional cases, were instrumental in decentralizing the structure of the Canadian federation. Yet to concentrate too narrowly on this aspect of his premiership is to miss the other essential thrust of his approach to governing: the greater centralization of power within Ontario. There is, moreover, an essential connection between the two. Ultimately, it was only the Liberal Party's hold on the Ontario electorate that enabled Mowat to challenge the federal government from a position of strength; and the vital machinery of that party had been created primarily through the consolidation of power and patronage within the Ontario government's own undisputed constitutional sphere, particularly vis-à-vis the municipalities. On the face of it, the latter was a politically dangerous course to pursue, for it seemed to run directly counter to the spirit of localism that had for so long been a pronounced feature of the Ontario political culture.

In Mowat's view, however, efficient administration and centralization went hand in hand. Although the idea of local autonomy was still too entrenched to be attacked directly, in practice it could be overridden by appealing to another long-established value of the political culture – the idea, dating back to the original Loyalist founders of the province in the eighteenth century, of government as a benefactor of local communities. This was Mowat's approach. From the time he took office, there poured forth from his ministry a stream of centralizing acts and regulations in such diverse areas as health, education, liquor licensing, and agriculture. These reforms not only produced local benefits but also amounted cumulatively to a new definition of the role of the province – a definition which, even after the passage of more than a century, remains recognizable in the basic contours of Ontario government.

For Mowat, centralization was always justified on the grounds of greater administrative efficiency. But it also meant projecting the presence of the Ontario government directly and formally into the local constituencies on a scale previously unknown. Provincially appointed commissioners, inspectors, agents, and trustees multiplied in number, many replacing municipal officials in fields taken over by the province. Since all these officers owed their positions directly to patronage, they naturally tended to be partisan supporters of the Liberal Party, giving it a more solid and extensive extraparliamentary structure than any of the old Upper Canadian political groupings, Reform or Conservative, that had preceded it. That structure, moreover, remained for a long time unshaken by even a temporary interruption of its hold on office. As a result, Sir John Willison observes: 'For over a generation no Conservative was appointed to the public service in Ontario. Although fitness in appointments was seldom disregarded, the Civil Service was an essential portion of the organized political machinery of the Mowat Administration.'[5]

In fact, the first statement is not strictly true. It is a mark of the new sophistication that Mowat brought to the administration of patronage that – much like a modern-day premier, for example, and in sharp contrast to the approach of his predecessors – he always sought to give at least a modicum of credibility to Liberal claims of non-partisanship by appointing a certain number from the other party. Of some 230 liquor commissioners appointed to 1883, for example, at least 23 were known Conservatives.[6] But there can be no doubt that Willison's conclusion is essentially correct. Indeed, nowhere is the process of centralization more clearly demonstrated, and nowhere is the connection between centralization and the growth of the Liberal Party's 'political machinery' more immediately obvious, than in the area of liquor licensing.

In 1876 legislation was enacted which effectively stripped the municipalities of their longstanding power to license and regulate the sale of alcoholic beverages and, instead, transferred jurisdiction to the province.[7] Mowat's basic technique of administration, in this as in other areas of policy, was to apply a set formula. Under the new act (known as the 'Crooks Act' – not in judgment of its ethics, but after the provincial treasurer, Adam Crooks), the government was to appoint three liquor commissioners for every city, town, and electoral division in Ontario. These officials would assume responsibility for the distribution of local tavern, bar, hotel, and other similar licences. Further, the number of such licences that could be granted in each locality would be restricted by means of a formula based on population: one licence for each 250 of the first 1000 of population and one additional licence for each 400 of population above 1000.

While the act went some way towards mollifying the temperance movement, its effect on the Liberal Party was more important by far. At a stroke, a cadre of loyal Liberal office holders was created and distributed across the province in careful parallel structure to the electoral system. These men would fill the crucial intermediate positions as the party machine expanded to its full pyramidal shape. At the same time, liquor licences were turned into valuable assets that the machine controlled. The holders of these assets were necessarily placed in a patron-client relationship with the Liberal district bosses who filled the commissionerships, with predictable consequences: 'The liquor regulations were tempered to the behaviour of licence-holders. An adequate display of zeal for the Government was a fair guarantee of security when licences were renewed. Inactivity was tolerated. Open rebellion was often punished.'[8] Licence holders' ties to the machine were further reinforced and placed on a continuous face-to-face basis by a corps of provincially appointed liquor inspectors who replaced the local officials who had previously enforced the liquor regulations. These inspectors were all lower-level Liberal Party operatives.

The Conservatives had not been slow to perceive the political implications of the Crooks Act and had tried desperately to rally popular support

against it. In what would become a constant Conservative refrain over the
next twenty years, they denounced the trend towards greater centralization
as 'fraught with danger for the liberty of the people' and staunchly defended the maintenance of local autonomy. In their view, the act's partisan
purpose was clear:

> In plain words, it proposes to put the trade under the surveillance of the
> politicians; for, as politics go now, the commissioners and inspectors ap-
> pointed to regulate the traffic will, without doubt, be political partisans of
> local might and celebrity, and skilled in the low arts of electioneering and
> ward chicanery ... No sensible man, whatever his opinions may be as to the
> use and abuse of intoxicating liquor, will approve of this sweeping and
> despotic proposition. We know too well what desperate things petty govern-
> ment officers will do to please their patrons at election times.[9]

Their efforts, however, met with scant success. Many local governments
were not in fact unhappy to be relieved of a jurisdiction they found increasingly difficult to administer and full of political pitfalls, especially in communities where the temperance movement exerted strong pressure.
Moreover, the pill of centralization was sugar-coated by guarantees to the
municipalities of generous financial compensation for their loss of power,
to be paid out of surplus licence revenues.

The basic blueprint of the Mowat machine is plain: it was designed
specifically to facilitate central control. And the ultimate controller was
Mowat himself, whose position as premier was immeasurably strengthened. Unlike earlier premiers, he had no need to bargain in the lobbies of
the legislature with capricious independents and local patrons who would
never lend more than their conditional or nominal support to any leader.
Instead, for the first time, 'the most influential Liberals in the Province and
the humblest were subject alike to the will of the Premier.' The suppression
of factionalism was also dramatic, for his pre-eminence in Cabinet as in
party was beyond challenge: 'He said that the Cabinet was a band of
brothers; so it was, but he was the Elder Brother, the undisputed head of the
household. The scholarly Crooks, the ebullient Fraser, the stormy Hardy,
the clever Ross, all sat in the family carriage, but Mowat drove.'[10]

Yet for all the importance of patronage in securing his place in the
driver's seat, it would be wrong to conclude that Mowat's use of it was
either excessive or corrupt. In spite of the frequently asserted claim of the
Conservative press that 'Sir Oliver ... is more responsible than any other
man in Canada for the introduction of the methods of Tammany and the
spoils system,' Mowat was no Boss Tweed, nor was his Liberal machine

modelled after Tammany Hall.[11] In Ontario an ethical line was drawn between patronage and corruption that was generally understood and accepted, even if its precise location was unmarked and often hotly disputed in particular cases. Conservatives and Liberals alike considered it a perfectly normal part of politics for the victorious party to reward its own supporters with public appointments. Where the controversy arose was usually over whether this or that individual who had been given a post was an honest and deserving recipient or a mere 'boodler.' On such questions, needless to say, opinion tended to divide along party lines.

But if there was room for disagreement on cases, it was at least agreed in principle that rewards ought not to be given to corrupt or incompetent party hacks solely on the basis of services rendered – or still less, services claimed or sevices promised. Mowat was adamant on this point, and there were no exceptions. The typical grassroots operation of the machine may be seen in Elgin County: 'James Coyne, after his defeat by Andy Ingram (a Tory) in 1886 became the manager of patronage in the riding until he pulled out a plum for himself: county registrar. Coyne followed very definite criteria in sifting applicants: capability, proven party service, proven support from party colleagues. As well he was careful to make a fair distribution across all areas of the riding.'[12] These were not just the Elgin criteria: they applied everywhere across the province. And Coyne's own plum was likewise not his for the picking: it had to be vetted by those above him in the hierarchy.

At the higher levels of the system, however, additional considerations came into play. Liberal backbenchers (or local patronage agents such as Coyne in ridings held by the opposition) were allowed a fair degree of personal discretion in dealing with the minutiae of patronage, such as the employment of labourers on public works, for such discretion was important to their standing in the community. But in the case of even minor public service appointments they could only transmit their recommendations upward to a more senior level of the party hierarchy, usually to a member of the Cabinet. There the competing claims of the various ridings (and sometimes, within ridings, of the various townships) would be balanced and, if no more was involved than the filling of an existing post, a decision might be made at that level: Cabinet ministers too had their prestige to maintain.

It was understood by all, however, that the overriding authority belonged to the premier. He dealt directly with all appointments of a highly lucrative, honorific, or politically sensitive nature, as well as with a great many others that were less important but which, out of caution on the part of underlings, or on his own initiative, were deemed to require his attention. Finally, he alone regulated the amount of patronage in the system: hence, any requests or recommendations that went beyond the filling of existing posts to the creation of new ones were automatically referred to him. A request for the appointment of additional magistrates in Southwold Township, for example, received this characteristically Mowatian reply: 'Your letter of the 25th June to Mr. Hardy [Provincial Secretary] about new Magistrates has been transferred to me. I find there are already 49 Magistrates in the commission for Southwold, or one for every 106 of the population, while the ordinary rule is that of Magistrates acting and not acting one for every 250 is sufficient.'[13] Once again there was the familiar invocation of a formula and the implicit judgment that provincewide standards ought to prevail over local particularisms. Such formulas were not absolutely rigid, but neither were they easily bent, since the integrity of the system depended on their general application. Certainly, personal appeals for variance were not encouraged. Mowat's letter continued: 'When I had the pleasure of seeing you here recently, we had some conversation about additional Magistrates. I took no note of what passed, and the effect of it has escaped my memory.'[14]

Obviously, not every liberal appointee was blessed with outstanding competence and sterling character, nor was every Liberal patronage agent impeccably honest and judicious in his dealings. Yet there were standards that had to be observed. From the top down there was an undeviating insistence that public duties be faithfully and honestly performed, that contractors give value for money, that the party not be embarrassed. This is not to say that there were no infractions – but when they came to light, punishment was swift and severe, and the same standard applied at every level. Even so senior a Liberal as Archibald McKeller, a quintessential machine politician who had risen through the ranks to become Mowat's commissioner of agriculture and public works, was summarily banished to a minor post when his habit of buying votes and other flagrant peccadillos exposed the administration to charges of 'McKellarism' – a clever opposition coining that threatened to stick in the public mind.

Then, as now, the use of patronage – like the use of alcohol – was constrained not only by the law but also by the values of the community. A party machine that offended those values through abuse or excess was liable to do itself serious and perhaps irreparable damage. One of Mowat's greatest political assets was his sensitivity to those values and his willingness to work within the limits set by them; he seemed to know instinctively where the boundaries of patronage lay. No party boss has ever been more effective in ensuring that patronage was used efficiently and productively. In nearly a quarter of a century in the premiership, 'the little Christian

Statesman' – as his more shameless acolytes were fond of referring to him – was never seriously tainted by the whiff of corruption.

Patronage was an inescapable part of nineteenth-century Ontario politics. The question was not whether it would be used by those in political power but whether it would be used responsibly and to what end. Under Mowat, the Liberal Party was built into a formidable political machine through the use of patronage, but at the same time, it was designed in such a way that it also served as the means by which patronage could be used with restraint and in accordance with the values of Ontario society. The Liberal machine was structured hierarchically, rested on a broad base of local appointees, and was well integrated into the social and economic fabric of local communities. At all levels, those who worked for it were subject to the scrutiny and discipline of those immediately above them in the hierarchy, and ultimately of the premier himself. Abuses were not tolerated, and strict performance criteria had to be met by Liberal office holders. On the whole, the Liberal machine was not the dispenser of the richest plums of patronage – most of these, such as Senate seats, were controlled by the federal parties – but it did possess a sufficient supply of modest plums to support a lean and efficient operation. While not a perfect microcosm of Ontario society, it was fairly representative. The rewards it offered were within the reach of ordinary citizens who wished to become active in the political process, and it was possible to start at the bottom and rise through the ranks.

Oliver Mowat's modern reputation rests, justifiably, on his unsurpassed record of achievement during his twenty-four years as premier – in many respects the formative years of the province of Ontario. Though his role as party leader is less well known, it was no less important, for it was his success as the builder and leader of the Liberal Party machine which enabled him to stay in power for so long and to govern so effectively. His type of party organization, moreover, ultimately prevailed over its rivals. It became, and long remained, the dominant Canadian model of party organization, not only in Ontario but also in other provinces and in federal politics.

NOTES

1 C.R.W. Biggar, *Sir Oliver Mowat: A Biographical Sketch* (Toronto: Warwick & Ritter, 1905), 1: 76–7.
2 Ibid., 176–7.
3 There is a considerable body of theory in political science relating to political

parties and party machines. For a more theoretical treatment of this subject, see S.J.R. Noel, *Patrons, Clients, Brokers: Ontario Society and Politics, 1791–1896* (Toronto: University of Toronto Press, 1990), 275–9.

4 See Gordon T. Stewart, *The Origins of Canadian Politics* (Vancouver: UBC Press, 1986), 67–90.

5 John Willison, *Reminiscences Personal and Political* (Toronto: McClelland & Stewart, 1919), 95–6.

6 This figure was accepted by the Conservatives themselves in their 1883 election pamphlet, 'Facts for the People.' See University of Western Ontario, D.B. Weldon Library, *Ontario Political Pamphlets, 1878–1900*, vol. 4.

7 *Journals of the Legislative Assembly of Ontario* 9: 1875–6, 209–10.

8 Willison, *Reminiscences*, 93.

9 Toronto *Mail*, 26 January 1876.

10 J.E. Middleton and F. Landon, *The Province of Ontario: A History 1615–1927* (Toronto: Dominion Publishing, 1927), 1: 447.

11 Tammany Hall is the name of the notoriously corrupt political machine that controlled the government of New York City from the mid-nineteenth century until well into the twentieth century. Boss Tweed was its leader from 1857 to 1871. See Seymour J. Mandelbaum, *Boss Tweed's New York* (New York: J. Wiley, 1965).

12 Barbara A. McKenna, 'Farmers and Railwaymen, Patronage and Corruption: A Volatile Political Mix in Turn of the Century Elgin County,' *Ontario History* 74 (1982): 225.

13 D.B. Weldon Library, Coyne Papers, Mowat to J.H. Coyne, 29 September 1888.

14 Ibid.

'Cultivation' and the Middle-Class Self: Manners and Morals in Victorian Ontario

ANDREW C. HOLMAN

It is not in the quiet and calmness of the study chamber, or when sitting by the fireside ... that the true features of character betray themselves; but it is in the hurry, the bustle, the turmoil of a busy, active existence, that we see the man. Then we can discern whether his be an upright, virtuous, and noble character that may command our admiration and respect, or whether his be a nature as repels us, and fills us with contempt and aversion.

John Scrimger, 'Ambition,' an essay read to the
Galt Mechanics' Institute, February 1869[1]

Social identity has recently become a topic of considerable debate and discussion among social historians seeking to reconstruct the ways in which ordinary people defined themselves in the past.[2] The question of reconstructing social identity has been a particularly slippery one for students of the middle class in nineteenth-century North America. The paradox of the middle class is that, although its members – professionals, merchants, manufacturers, clerks, and master artisans – acted in many ways like a distinctive 'class unto themselves,' they seldom openly acknowledged a sense of class consciousness. Indeed, the central tenets of middle-class discourse were individualism, self-help, and even 'the denial of the significance of class.' Scholars have convincingly inferred the existence of middle-class awareness from common behavioural patterns, such as residential segregation, associational life, and family strategy, but they have found little class language that *admitted* as much.[3]

Who, or what, did members of the Victorian middle class think they were? What were their sources of social identity and distinctiveness? Did they ever express them? One clue to these questions exists in the concept of and discourse about 'cultivation,' a standard of behavioural propriety and an important ingredient of 'self' among middle-class contemporaries. This essay examines the concept of cultivation and the construction of a sense of self among male members of the middle class in Galt and Goderich, Ontario, from the 1850s to the 1890s. In this discussion, three points are significant. First, the discourse about cultivated behaviour provides historians with exceptional evidence of middle-class consciousness, a somewhat elusive commodity. Second, cultivation was a gendered ideal and, as such, provided separate standards of public conduct for middle-class men and women. For middle-class men, cultivated behaviour was a measure of masculinity. Third, it is clear that, while informed by regional, national, and international currents, cultivated behaviour was constructed and negotiated locally among fellow townsmen. Victorian norms of personal conduct were forged by class and gender dictates and by place. For men, the principal space for this form of class expression was the public arena. From 1850 to 1890, middle-class men constructed an unofficial code of locally acceptable and masculine public conduct.

In Victorian Galt and Goderich, the middle class was a phenomenon as new as the towns themselves. First settled at the confluence of Mill Creek and the Grand River in the mid-1820s, Galt grew quickly, from 2248 residents in 1851, to 3827 in 1871, and 7535 by 1891. The development of local industry was responsible principally for this growth: mid-century artisanal endeavours in grist- and sawmilling, weaving, and blacksmithing grew into large, concentrated, industrial manufactories of axes, iron castings, machinery, woollens, flour, and textiles. A Waterloo County atlas boasted in 1881 that Galt was 'the most important manufacturing town in Western Ontario,' and, in the words of an 1890 commentator, 'the Manchester of Canada.'[4] Goderich enjoyed a less mercurial rise and a more mixed pattern of growth. It was founded in 1827 as the headquarters for the Canada Company's operations in the Huron Tract, but it was forced to find its own *raison d'être* in 1852, when the company's offices were moved, unceremoniously, to Toronto. In the 1850s and 1860s, Goderich ran on the business from its Lake Huron port, on a handful of mills and foundries, and most important, on the professional business from its position as the Huron County seat: court proceedings, land surveying, and the local jail. In the late 1860s salt mining and flour milling grew in importance, but by the mid-1870s American tariffs and a general recession produced an economic decline from which the town could not recover. Consequently, a population of 1329 in 1851 had reached 4564 by 1881, but slipped to 3829 in 1891. By the 1880s Goderich had earned the oft-repeated descriptions of 'sleepy' and 'decidedly conservative.'[5]

These towns in the late nineteenth century nurtured environments for opportunity and change. Economically, they were open arenas for enterprise or, in the words of C. Wright Mills, a 'testing field for heroes.'[6] They held great potential for an emerging middle class – 'new' men in new places – to succeed or to fail. They were also crucibles in which social identities were created and diffused. In these years, Galt's and Goderich's manufacturers, merchants, professionals, and clerks forged an identity rooted in workplace authority. Moreover, they translated and broadcast this authority into the social sphere through their control of the local state, education, philanthropy, temperance, and other voluntary associations.[7] They constructed, too, a language of proper behaviour – the language of cultivation.

This discourse was public and, almost by definition, male. Middle-class journalists, editorialists, clergy, and letter writers, almost all men, chimed in on what it meant and should mean to think and act in respectable and masculine ways. For these middle-class Victorian Ontarians, cultivation meant, quite simply, a cluster of prescribed values and behavioural standards. Cultivation was a way of trumpeting one's personal respectability and worthiness of status in these local societies. Cultivated performance in society constituted a significant standard of class expression and gendered behaviour.

The middle-class ideal of cultivation in Victorian Canada was hardly a unique social construction. Rather, the character of the Canadian middle class in this era should be seen as part of a larger discussion in the North Atlantic world over proper middle-class behaviour, in which the principal participants were British and American commentators.[8] Throughout the Victorian era, a handful of American and British journalists sparred over the reputed quality of their respective middle classes, part of which involved the ideal of cultivation. British writers held that democracy had vulgarized and degraded the manners and morals – the 'character' – that Americans had inherited.

Americans begged to differ. 'Manners are the mirror of a people's mind,' Boston Unitarian minister Orville Dewey wrote in the *Christian Examiner* in 1844. 'And we believe that each class in this country as compared with its respective class abroad, will be found from its relative position, to have manners more manly and sincere and more just, as between man and man; the higher less assumption, the lower less sycophancy; the middling classes decidedly more cultivation.'[9] When British littérateur Matthew Arnold branded the American and British middle classes alike as philistine in 1883, the editor of *The Nation* was quick to respond. 'What Mr. Arnold has not yet seen is a middle class which feels itself as good as any class ... A middle-class without an aristocracy above it must of necessity ... differ from a middle-class with such an aristocracy, must be superior to it, must have ... more independence ... more sweetness and light, and a great deal less of that narrow, conventional habit of mind usually denounced as Philistinism.'[10] Over the course of this debate, commentators constructed two polar caricatures: the established, stolid British middle class and its more fluid, more animated American counterpart.

Throughout the Victorian era, commentators placed the character of the Canadian middling ranks within the terms of this discussion. In the first place, Canadian society, like American, was democratic and lacked a formal aristocratic upper class in the European sense. Unlike America, however, the tone of Canadian democracy was less vulgar and hurried, and more predictable, facts that produced a kind of hybrid middle-class culture. 'The Canadian,' John White observed in his Sketches from America in 1870, 'is a sort of middle term between the Englishman and the American. He is not so absorbed and so eager in his industrialism as the American. If his aspirations are limited to getting up some straight and narrow ladder of life, at least he climbs it more quietly, more patiently, and with less intense agony of struggling.'[11]

But the ideal of cultivation was more than an abstract subject of purely academic debate. In Victorian Ontario towns, that ideal served as a tool of class distinction; in places like Galt and Goderich, merchants, manufacturers, professionals, and white-collar workers gave expression to their status through the ways in which they presented themselves. To be cultivated in urbanizing Victorian Ontario signified a decision to conduct oneself personally in circumscribed ways, distinctive in many respects from the excessive personal behaviours of the vulgar rich and the barren poor. Cultivation was a hallmark of membership in the middling ranks, or, at least, an indication of one's social ambitions.

But cultivation had a second role, beyond its function as a source of middle-class cohesion. Cultivation, broadly speaking, was a middle-class prescription for local society. 'Manners and deportment are not a matter of mere personal taste and choice, but belong to the sphere of duty,' William Clark asserted in his 1893 essay 'Conduct and Manner' in The Canadian Magazine. 'A good man has no right to make goodness repulsive.'[12] Good manners, like industry, fraternalism, self-improvement, and sobriety, was a message that the local middle class spread to others in society. Mannerliness, ostensibly, was achievable by people from all social ranks and a potential source of social order. Most important, the message of cultivation lacked the kinds of media that industry, fraternalism, self-improvement, and sobriety enjoyed. The middle class prescribed cultivated behaviour not mainly through vehicles like benevolent societies, fraternal orders, self-improvement clubs, or temperance organizations, but more subtly in myriad ways.

Members of the middle classes in Victorian Ontario developed their own ideal of cultivation from many sources, inherited and otherwise. Members of the Canadian middle class, like their American counterparts, were voracious readers and much of their idea about cultivation would have been gleaned from journals, novels, and etiquette books from Britain and America.[13] Proper etiquette in society paralleled professional codes of conduct (written and conventional) that existed among physicians, lawyers, and clergymen.[14] But cultivation as a middle-class value was also negotiated locally, face to face, in nineteenth-century towns, where town size, social structure, and the conduct of wealthy locals could be influential factors in determining the local meaning of the term.[15] In Galt and Goderich in the years 1850–90, cultivation had particular local expression and resonance; here, ideas of cultivation were made manifest in newspaper editorials and letters, public oratory in Mechanics' Institutes and Literary Societies, private correspondence, and by personal example.

Cultivation was, perhaps, the most often employed term among many that popular journals in the Anglo-American world used to describe middle-class society; respectable, civil, genteel, and refined were other such expressions. Cultivation was an omnibus term that described to Victorians a web of ideas about proper conduct, dress, speech, and deportment in society – that is, how to be respectable *externally*.[16] It defined the middle-class way of being, a new, refined self-image that declared members' place in a modernizing world. Central to middle-class identity in these years was, in Victorian writer Richard Grant White's words, 'an elegance of outward seeming.'[17] The elements of nineteenth-century cultivation were numerous and wide-ranging. To the middle class, 'good manners' encompassed personal appearance, body management (or carriage), speech, emotional control, table etiquette, and disciplined spectatorship. In much of the contemporary literature, it was these aspects that commentators pointed to as evidence of true gentility, rather than those of inherited wealth and paraded foppery.[18]

Middle-class standards of deportment were gendered, as men and women aspired to different forms of cultivated performance. Masculinity among middle-class men was measured by the possession of a number of different characteristics in Victorian Canada. 'Manly' men performed a series of important roles that established authoritatively their relationships to family members and to civil society as a whole: breadwinner, billpayer, companion, patriarch, worker, and, often, clubman. True manliness, contemporary writers noted, was to be found in men who straddled the public/private divide judiciously – neither overly domesticated nor too often absent from home. In each realm, standards of manly behaviour were constructed, expected, and dutifully performed.[19] Cultivated behaviour belonged peculiarly to the public realm. Among middle-class men in Galt and Goderich in the years 1850–90, three behavioural elements were in particular most often discussed: appearance, carriage, and demeanour. To these might be added a fourth measure of propriety: presentation of home and garden – a physical extension of the refined male self.[20]

'It is one of the blessings of this new country,' Catherine Parr Traill reported assuredly to Britons in *The Canadian Settlers Guide* in 1854, 'that a young person's respectability does by no means depend upon ... points of style in dress.'[21] Her comment was intended undoubtedly to indicate the openness of Canadian democracy to potential British emigrants, and the relative absence of class fetters. Otherwise laudible, it stretched the truth. In Ontario towns from the 1850s, personal appearance (styles of dress, coiffure, and adornment) were indeed important measures of one's place in society, a reflection of one's true self. As much as in Britain or America, personal appearance in urbanizing Victorian Ontario was a central element of male middle-class presentation.

Dress was the most conspicuous aspect of cultivated personal appearance. Clothes were expected to be simple, sincere, and bright reflections of the character of their wearers. The most respectable clothes demonstrated taste, reserve, dignity, and humility. For men, respectable apparel in the mid-Victorian period was usually represented in drab colours: grey, black, or dark blue waistcoats, with white shirts, ties, and trousers.[22] Clothes were designed to produce a sense of genteel anonymity, rather than to attract special interest. 'The golden rule in dress is to avoid extremes,' the author of 'Deportment in Social Intercourse' argued in Galt's *Nut=Shell* in 1890. 'Do not choose garments that would render you conspicuous.' Cultivation in dress, rather, was measured in style, fit, and an overall tone 'quiet and modest.' Above all, readers were reminded, all garments must be unsoiled and jewellery should be worn only on the most celebrated occasions.[23]

Local tailors and milliners in Galt and Goderich were careful to meet these standards and regularly advertised their stock as the latest in respectable fashion from London and New York. If these styles did not satisfy, most of them offered to custom make fashions to suit local needs.[24] Even so, extravagant dress constituted an occasional cause for concern among the respectable ranks. Some felt that slavish adherence to fashion was unbecoming to people whose first concerns in dress should be simplicity. 'Why Follow All the Fashions in Dress?' the *Dumfries Reformer* wondered in September 1873, while one Goderich contemporary was even more blunt. 'I think [they] should give up changing the fashions all together.' Furthermore, clerks and other young male social climbers were sometimes criticized publicly for dressing above their station. For the most marginal members of the middle class, cultivated dress was one of a few tenuous claims to status and thus prone to overstatement.[25]

Proper appearance meant also that middle-class bodies were to be regularly washed – every day in the summer and 'quite often' in the winter. Teeth, likewise, were to be carefully brushed every night and morning, and fingernails kept scrupulously clean: 'People of culture give special attention to the appearance of their fingernails,' one essayist noted, '[and t]o neglect this indicates vulgarity.'[26] Nor was hair to be neglected. Clean and well brushed, it was also to be neatly cut and kept regularly trimmed. If a man chose to grow a beard, 'nature's ornament to a man's face,' it must be similarly cared for. In Galt and Goderich, middle-class men entrusted their hair to a number of local barbers and hairdressers of various reputations. If they did not suit, Galt and Goderich residents might rely on other services, such as the itinerant hair-goods manufacturer, Professor Dorenwend, and his 'immense stock of hair goods ... frontispieces ... switches &c., Gents, wigs and toupees, – all shades – all sizes – all prices.'[27]

The issue of where a man might properly part his hair occasioned some public discussion in the *Signal* in March 1884. Close cropping and parting on the side were almost universal practices, one contributor, 'Addenda,' noted, but they should not be seen as the only acceptable way for the cultivated to wear their hair. 'When I, one of the old school, am told that because I will persist in parting my hair in the centre, I am guilty of dandyism, of dudism, and every other "ism" that a respectable member of society should not be guilty of, I want to raise my goosequill aloft and place my protest on record. Gentle reader, I think I have said enough to conclusively prove that, although every man has the right to draw the line in hair parting where it suits ... the proper place to do so is back from the centre of the forehead.' In doing this, 'Addenda' concluded, neither he nor fellow centrists – Huron MPP Alexander McLagan Ross, Alexander McDougall Allan, Town Clerk Peter Adamson, or even Bismarck – could be mistaken.[28]

Apart from personal appearance, middle-class etiquette prescribed proper personal carriage, by which contemporaries meant countenance, gait, and composure. The principal goal of proper carriage was to make evident one's inner dignity. Upright posture reflected upright morality. Middle-class men were admonished to 'command themselves' – to create the feelings they wished to exude through personal control. To contemporaries, a respectable countenance was much more than a proper appearance; middle-class men were expected not only to look genteel but to seem it as well, so as to be comfortable and confident with the personal trappings of middle-class status. In this aspiration, at least some Goderich residents could take pride. 'I have been on the streets of Toronto, London, Hamilton, New York and other places, and I never enjoyed such a walk as I had on Goderich Square,' Dr D.C. Murray of Appin, Middlesex County, reported in January 1890. 'Every face I saw had an air of comfort and respectability about it.'[29]

When it came to gait, strict rules applied as well. Cultivated men were advised to walk with poise and dignity and to avoid both haughty and dandylike strides. Of proper walks, Clark noted in 1893, 'there are two false kinds ... the one which is put on – the pompous look and strut, adopted for the most part with a view to impressing others; the other, the spontaneous outcome of a man's egregious self-importance.' A respectable walk showed both ease of movement and purpose. A proper gait was both even and smooth. Men were to take large steps, which provided evidence of bodily control, while women were advised to be elegant, light, meandering walkers. Their fluidity symbolized their sensitivity. For both, there should be no sign of hurry.[30]

Personal demeanour, or the ways in which one presented one's personality, was the third measure of middle-class respectability in Victorian Galt and Goderich. Proper demeanour involved social intercourse, speech, and gesture: in short, what was to be said, and how, whether between strangers or friends. Cultivated speech was to be at all times sincere, natural, unaffected, tactful, and unselfish. Middle-class men were admonished to display a 'gentle, humble, kindly spirit which is productive of a true, not a servile, deference and thoughtfulness towards the opinions, the feelings and the interests of others.'[31] Proper demeanour exhibited the ability to express inner feelings outwardly in a modest, respectable way. The golden rule, in manners as in much of middle-class culture, was self-control.

Though cultivated conversation was meant to express true sentiments, extreme feelings, such as jealousy, hilarity, and anger, were to be suppressed in favour of maintaining a veneer of propriety. Tasteful wit and jest were welcome, buffoonery and clownishness decried. 'There is a difference between the jocularity of a gentleman and that of a vulgarian,' Clark noted.[32] Similarly, heated arguments were to be avoided; commentators advised that polished gentlemen could back away in dignity and honour, however unsatisfying that might prove in the immediate instance. Resort to fisticuffs, of course, constituted the worst example of losing emotional control and the ultimate breach of public conduct.[33]

Aside from the proper tone of speech, content was important too. In public, middle-class men and women were admonished to converse on elevated topics. 'There are two very respectable persons of whose culture we despair,' the *Canadian Presbyter* announced in 1851: 'mere men of business, whose talk even in society is of stocks and goods and discounts; and mere housekeepers, whose talk is of servants, and new rec[i]p[e]s for puddings, and the prices of bread and butter!'[34] Gossip was to be scrupulously avoided, as were religion and politics. Indeed, any topic that had the potential to cause offence was dangerous territory. Advice literature stopped short, however, of providing a list of acceptable topics. Other than reminders to 'talk wisely, not foolishly,' middle-class men and women were on their own.[35]

To converse cultivatedly, of course, one required a polished education. Education, to the middle class, had more than instrumental value; it was the cornerstone of polite conversation and a mark of gentility. 'Education, we say, prepares us for society,' a correspondent to the *Signal* said in January 1865. 'We soon perceive the difference between the educated and the uneducated; the former with how much ease and how fluently he converses on any subject, while the latter seems timid, as though he was not quite sure of what he was saying ... Glad we ought to feel that we are not shut up in utter ignorance, – that we are in a refined and intelligent part of the world, where education is prospering on either side of us.'[36] Cultivated learning was available through many facets in Victorian Galt and Goderich, but most conspicuously through three: the school systems proper, unstructured learning at home, and the matrix of literary and debating societies, Christian associations, and Mechanics' Institutes that offered 'rational recreation' to local town dwellers interested in respectable intellectual fare.

From the 1840s on, many Upper Canadians were hopeful that the system of grammar schools and public schools being established in the province could be relied upon for teaching not just the basics of reading, writing, and arithmetic, but also the elements of polished expression. The goals of central school promoters, such as Rev. Egerton Ryerson, to use the province's school system to improve the manners and conversation of the young and to 'create a respectable class,' were echoed by local school supporters and by principals and teachers in the central and ward schools in Galt and Goderich as well. 'Education,' the *Signal* editor could note as early as 1863, 'is indispensible in the gradual but certain elevation of the middle and lower classes,' and Goderich was second to no place in this respect. 'Our beautiful Central school [is] amply furnished with everything calculated to impress indelibly upon the youthful mind the rudiments of knowledge, together with those subtle associations which are not driven out of the mind even by the anxiety of maturer years.'[37]

In Galt, William Tassie's Grammar School (later the Galt Collegiate) was a locus of gentlemanly training and an institution that contemporary

Galtonians spoke of with some pride, despite the fact that the majority of the students (all boys) came from outside the town. Tassie had a definite view of what constituted proper public deportment and sought to instill it in his charges by pedagogy and other means if necessary. 'It was his object to make us gentlemen,' James Kerr recalled in 1915. 'Manliness, sincerity, truthfulness, perseverance, diligence, thoroughness, were qualities that he himself possessed, and these he succeeded in imprinting on the hearts and minds of scores of hundreds of boys.'[38] By the 1890s the Galt Business College made a similar claim. 'The influences thrown about students of the College are such that cannot fail to make a decided impression for good upon their minds. There is but one rule for young men: to conduct themselves as gentlemen.'[39]

In addition to formal schooling, home instruction was expected to provide middle-class members with finish. Etiquette manuals and popular commentary reiterated the need for middle-class homes to be, in effect, little charm schools, with all the equipment necessary for proper instruction. 'It was once said by an eminent writer, "if I would ascertain a man's character, I would simply ask to look at his books,"' the *Signal* editor noted in November 1852.[40] The middle-class parlour was the setting for the enterprise of self-instruction, and parents were to take the utmost care in the selection of books for home consumption. Home reading was a serious pursuit; books were important tools of moral and intellectual growth, not mere articles of consumption. History and biography were considered most instructive and enlightening by middle-class contemporaries, but travel books, geography, and natural science were appropriate as well. Most problematical were novels. The message to those seeking to become cultivated through home study was plain, as Louise Stevenson notes: 'Avoid thoroughly vicious books and read as much as you can.'[41]

In places like Galt and Goderich, the popular equation of knowledge with enlightened masculine behaviour was recognized and promoted. Thomas Cowan's essay 'Working and Thinking,' written in 1869 and read before the Galt Literary and Debating Society, is evidence of this sentiment locally. 'The possession of intelligence will enable you to estimate external polish at its true value ... True politeness ... [exists] in the complete education of the whole man, PHYSICALLY, MORALLY AND INTELLECTUALLY.' Among Cowan's recommendations to club members were admonitions to set apart a portion of every day for home study in mental and moral culture, and to choose books written by the ablest thinkers of modern and ancient times. 'Young men,' the *Signal* echoed in July 1863, 'spend the greater part of your pocket money in books, study to be intelligent, industrious and persevering in your calling ... and ... you will be useful and respected members of society.'[42] The middle-class quest for respectable reading material was widely recognized. Newspaper editors advertised the contents of recent periodicals, perhaps in part to assure parents and other potential subscribers of their respectable nature. This drive was apparent to booksellers (local and non-local) as well. The Signal bookstore advertised its full stock of literature in 1862: 'Doctors, Lawyers, Clergymen, Mechanics ... may obtain almost any desired book at a bargain.' In Goderich, non-local booksellers found a market as well. Dissatisfied, perhaps, with local offerings, Goderich cultivators formed a branch of the Home Knowledge Association, a wholesale book club, in February 1888.[43]

A cultivated mind was something that middle-class Victorian males also pursued in formal associations organized for reading, debating, lecturing, and being lectured to. In the 1850s, Galt was host to three such bodies, a number that grew to six by 1891; Goderich had two self-improvement associations in the 1850s, and four by 1891. Among these, Mechanics' Institutes and Young Men's Christian Associations were, perhaps, the most effective ones, and the series of literary and debating societies was conspicuous too. These institutions provided spaces in which ordinary townspeople could experience literary, scientific, and philosophical study at the most basic level. As such, they were instruments employed by middle-class aspirants to provide the stuff and style of intellectual culture.[44]

Lectures given under the auspices of local self-improvement societies were carefully invited from respectable public speakers and prominent local members. Topics were moral and practical. Galt Mechanics' Institute lectures on 'Electricity' and 'Insects of North America,' like those given in the Goderich institute on 'Chemistry' and 'Railroads, Gravel Roads and Local Improvements,' alternated with more philosophical fare, such as lectures in the Galt institute and YMCA on 'Modern Infidelity' and 'John Howard,' and in Goderich on 'Social Progress.' Public debates were championed by contemporaries as excellent forums of instruction and articulation: training grounds for the cultivation of the middle-class man. 'To young men more especially we would say that during the long winter evenings attendance at those meetings will prove of great assistance in acquiring instruction combined with a readiness of utterance necessary to every one aspiring to take a position in the community in which he lives,' the *Reformer* editor suggested. In these years, Galt and Goderich debating associations entertained a wide variety of topics, moral and political, such as the benefits of poor laws, the relationship of party to good government, the relative strengths of the sword and the pen, and the effects of inventions on the condition of the working class. In Goderich, the debate format was changed on occasion to that of a mock Parliament, complete with Cabinet ministers, leaders, caucuses, and a question period.[45]

Mental culture was promoted at these places also by providing books and space for unstructured reading. In Galt the Mechanics' Institute library and reading room received an increase in visitors and loans in almost every year, according to annual reports, and in Goderich the library and reading room flourished. Their directors assured the public repeatedly that only the most respectable literature lined the libraries' stacks, and special scrutiny was used in selecting fiction, widely recognized as the most dangerous literary form. 'Your committee,' the Galt Mechanics' Institute Report for 1865 stated, has 'the satisfaction of knowing that the greatest care has been exercised in the selection of these fictitious writings, and that all works of an immoral or doubtful tendency have been rigorously excluded.'[46]

In both Galt and Goderich, membership figures grew steadily in the mid-Victorian period. Membership was, moreover, decidedly male and middle class. 'It does not seem to be generally known,' Galt Mechanics' Institute secretary M.T.W. Wright reported on behalf of the committee in 1871, 'that ladies are as welcome to the Library and Reading Room as gentlemen. It is true we have one or two lady subscribers, but the number is much smaller than your committee think would avail themselves of the privilege if the fact above mentioned was more widely known.' Observations like Wright's were telling. Though no overt regulations excluded women from pursuing self-improvement in these associations, they were nevertheless *de facto* male, public institutions and a reflection of the currency of separate-spheres thinking in Victorian Ontario towns. Moreover, these self-improvement societies began as and remained, largely, institutions for the middle class, or those already on their way to reaching that status. The *Signal* remarked: 'Although the library and reading room go under the name, "Mechanics' Institute," ... the mechanics of the town patronize it to a very limited extent.' Of 153 names on the Goderich Institute's librarian's books in 1883, only 24 were those of mechanics or unskilled workers. The presumed effects of free reading, lectures, and debates in these Mechanics' Institutes and debating societies reinforced popular prescriptions for respectable, masculine behaviour.[47]

For all this action and discussion, cultivation might have seemed abstract to middle-class residents of Galt and Goderich. The figures in popular journals, novels, clothing advertisements, and etiquette manuals were, after all, two-dimensional, fictitious models. But the Victorian notion of cultivation was modelled as much on local figures as it was on a cultural ideal. Both towns were home to residents who provided real, living examples of cultivated performance that might be emulated. Certain individuals in Galt and Goderich were living examples of middle-class prescriptions for culti-vated, manly behaviour. The celebrated Galt Presbyterian minister, Rev. John Bayne, his many obituaries held, was a model of propriety. 'In his dress ... he was particular,' Rev. A. Cunningham Geikie recalled. 'He hated foppery ... but he was a gentleman, and liked to look like one. In society his manners were easy ... they had a tinge of ... dignity.'[48] The legacy of George Langdale Marwood, a Goderich lake vessel captain, was not so much his considerable contributions to Goderich society as town councillor, philanthropist, clubman, or capitalist, the *Signal* eulogized in 1853, though he performed these roles well. 'More than all he had gained the esteem and confidence of all classes by his unassuming amiable traits and character.'[49]

To what extent these examples – institutional and personal – had real influence in pushing local respectables to become cultivated is difficult to gauge, particularly given the paucity of memoirs, detailed correspondence, and diaries of young men from these two towns. One illuminating exception was provided by Andrew McIlwraith, a Galt bookkeeper and diarist in the late 1850s and early 1860s. For McIlwraith, trained as a draughtsman and patternmaker, these years were fraught with insecurity, both economic and psychological. Lack of permanent employment forced him to travel for work to Hamilton, Sarnia, and New York City, and kept him from achieving economic independence and, accordingly, real manhood. This liminality, in turn, prohibited him (in the short term at least) from marrying the woman he loved. '[I am] Feeling kind of crippity crappity on the subject of Mary,' McIlwraith wrote (and subsequently overscored) in his diary in early 1858. '[I] blame myself for not being more of a man.'

Interestingly, McIlwraith's diary provides evidence of the centrality of cultivation, especially self-improvement, both inside and out. Cultivation, clearly, was to him an important ingredient for achieving independence and becoming a real man. Throughout the diary, McIlwraith notes spending non-work time attending church, lectures, and singing lessons, hunting, walking, and debating. In his short stay in Dundas, McIlwraith was appointed secretary of the Mechanics' Institute, and in Galt he became a regular borrower of the local institute's books. 'Called in at the library in the evening and got "Self-Help" by Samuel Smiles,' he noted in February 1861. '[I] was at the reading room in the evening,' he noted a year later, 'and got an interesting volume entitled "Brief Biographies" by Mr Smiles.' Alternatively, volumes on ornithology, draughting, and business, among others, captured his attention. 'Had a walk about ... and purchased a book of etiquette, etc. from a young Scotchman,' he noted while in New York City in December 1857.[50] For McIlwraith and his contemporaries, cultivation represented both an end and a means to an end: a goal worthy of pursuit and a method for attaining a respectable stature in local society.

Respectable appearance and affable conduct represented to many middle-class men a symbol of social station. Proper deportment was, to many, a window of sincerity; a polished exterior, as etiquette manuals asserted, reflected a noble and honest interior. In a period when urban growth, transiency, immigration, and emigration were fluid, and towns and cities became increasingly anonymous, an identifiable middle-class appearance was a measure of familiar territory – a man who could be *trusted*.

Despite these elaborate codes of conduct, middle-class etiquette was hardly foolproof. There emerged in this period a number of pretenders in middle-class guise who preyed upon the trust and sincerity of local respectables. Historians John F. Kasson and Karen Halttunen have documented this phenomenon in large American cities, such as New York, in the nineteenth century. The existence of confidence men and other social hypocrites and class traitors underlined the fragility of genteel performance as a true measure of social worth.[51] Ontario towns were not immune to middle-class pretenders. If the confidence games played in places like Galt and Goderich were less frequent than those in Gotham, their effect upon and general threat to the middle class were as deeply felt. Galt lenders bilked by the imposter 'Lieutenant Carter' in 1858 were no doubt vindicated when his apprehension in Port Hope for similar misdeeds was reported in the local press weeks later.[52] In Goderich the antics of a deserter from the Union Army, William Webber, who established himself locally in 1863 as a provisioner, had similar effect. He possessed all the social graces expected among the genteel, cultivated classes in Goderich. 'Webber was soon spoken of as a good sort of fellow in his way, and his pretty better-half was remarkable as a leader of the middle class ... [He] contrived to win the confidence of the whole community, especially as he appeared to be strictly upright in all his dealings.' But having borrowed money to the amount of $1000 from local citizens to 'enter into a little butter speculation,' Webber ended the charade and skedaddled. 'We must say,' the *Signal* admitted shortly after the incident, 'that we did not expect so much rascality could lurk within such a sleek exterior.'[53]

If their credence in the semiotics of middle-class etiquette was shaken by these episodes, it seems it was not shaken to pieces. Members of the middling ranks continued to rely on etiquette as a yardstick of respectability and seem to have had little interest in alternative external measures of internal character. Galt and Goderich played host to a number of phrenologists (itinerant and local), for example, during their heyday in the 1850s and 1860s, but the inexactness of their 'science,' the prevalence and news of frauds in their midst, and the opposition of the regular medical profession ensured their demise locally. 'The lower strata of society is continually throwing to the surface men [of] depraved appetites,' the *Reformer* editor noted of phrenologist Professor Hagarty's visit to Galt in 1858.[54] In short, dress, speech, and deportment seemed to provide a much fuller account of a man than did a reading of his cranial bumps by someone whose own character was in question.

Middle-class cultivation extended beyond a man's person to his abode. The ways in which a man fashioned his own home environment was a subject of notice among those well versed in acceptable public conduct. The size and appearance of his home was to reflect his social station, a physical statement that paralleled the language of cultivated behaviour. Notable here, of course, is the fact that men's responsibility for a cultivated home in this discourse encompassed normally its exterior only; houses' interiors ventured into middle-class women's prescribed domain.[55]

To the middle-class mind, propriety and orderliness were important measures, reflections of homeowners' pragmatic values. To be rejected were an overly ostentatious appearance or an opulent presentation. Middle-class homes were not to be unadorned, but decorated in measured, natural refinement. A moderate number of bushes of varying size and neatly mown grass were considered appropriate; a well-pruned tree, even better. Well-kept yards and gardens were credits to the homeowner and the neighbourhood. 'The citizen whose dwelling, however humble, is kept neat and trim, and beautified by even a few tastefully placed trees, shrubs, vines and flowers, is regarded somewhat as a public benefactor,' Galt homeowner James Young wrote in his 1894 essay 'Canadian Homes and Their Surroundings,' 'for his place is not only a source of pleasure to himself and his family, but adds to the attractiveness of his town or neighborhood.'[56]

In Galt, local topography and the prevalence of handsome stone dwellings among the local middle class occasioned many remarks from both visitors and civic boosters. In the 'valley city,' 'adjacent ridges are dotted with many fine private residences conspicuous among which are those of ... [lawyer] A.T.H. Ball, [industrialist] Hugh McCulloch, James Young, MP, Dr Kerr, [lawyer] F.G. Allenby, and [industrialist] John Goldie.'[57] Similarly, in Goderich by the 1870s, middle-class homes were a mark of civic pride. The comments made by visitors about Goderich homes and gardens were most often complimentary, a fact that local boosters seized upon in their own promotions. 'The town is a pretty sight ... with many fine houses and summer residences, with gardens and ornamental grounds,' an 1889 Board of Trade publication boasted. Alongside carefully written accounts of local enterprises were pen-and-ink sketches of the residences of William McLean, merchant Charles A. Humber, bank manager R.S. Williams, barrister Philip Holt, physician Thomas F. McLean, merchant J.M. Shepherd, grocer D.C. Strachan, dentist Malcolm Nicholson, cattle dealer Robert McLean, and a rendering of barrister-politician Malcolm Colin Cameron's 'The Maples,' with its conservatory, hot and cold grapery, artistic grounds and fountains – 'one of the most complete and charming homes in the West.'[58] Travellers' accounts confirmed this impression, qualified only with the occasional complaint that the practice of constructing high board fences around some private residences obstructed the view of their 'tasty' gardens.[59]

The *Signal* promoted domestic beautification in Goderich, both by observing regularly the construction of new, attractive homes by prominent local businessmen and professionals and by pushing locals to clear their weeds, 'an eye-sore to the people of this town.' The journal also published British and American copy on home adornment, such as 'Orchard and Garden,' a column 'devoted to the improvement of suburban and country homes.' The Town Council chipped in as well in May 1888, donating free trees to all citizens who would plant them.[60]

From the 1850s to the 1890s, the ideal of cultivation enjoyed considerable currency among middle-class men in Galt and Goderich. Proper appearance, carriage, and deameanour, and tastefully presented homes and gardens served as indicators of a sense of shared values about masculine behaviour and the importance of class cohesion. They served as symbols of class distinction, exterior markers of where individuals stood socially in the world. They also operated as standards of masculine propriety and badges of civic respectability. Cultivated performance helped congeal an identity locally among the first generation of middle-class men in Galt and Goderich. 'Good manners,' for men especially, developed in these years as a code of respectability. It was a discourse, written, spoken, and acted out in such local contexts as Victorian Galt and Goderich, which helped middle-class men define themselves culturally. Cultivation remains an important key to unlocking the elusive sense of social identity that the Victorian Ontario middle class both ascribed to and prescribed to others.

NOTES

An earlier version of this essay was presented at the Canadian Historical Association conference at Brock University, St Catharines, Ontario, in June 1996. The argument is developed further in *A Sense of Their Duty: Middle-Class Formation in Victorian Ontario Towns* (Montreal and Kingston: McGill-Queen's University Press, 2000).

1 'Ambition,' [Galt] *Dumfries Reformer*, 24 February 1869.
2 On this debate, see Geoff Eley, 'Is All the World a Text? From Social History to the History of Society Two Decades Later,' in Terrence J. McDonald, ed., *The*

Historical Turn in the Human Sciences (Ann Arbor: University of Michigan Press, 1996); Neville Kirk, 'History, Language, Ideas and Post-Modernism: A Materialist View,' *Social History* 19, 2 (1994): 221–40; Patrick Joyce, *Democratic Subjects: The Self and the Social in Nineteenth-Century England* (Cambridge: Cambridge University Press, 1994) and 'The End of Social History?' *Social History* 20, 1 (1995): 73–91; Geoff Eley and Keith Nield, 'Starting Over: The Present, the Post-Modern and the Moment of Social History,' *Social History* 20, 3 (1995): 355–64.

3 Stuart Blumin, 'The Hypothesis of Middle-Class Formation in Nineteenth-Century America: A Critique and Some Proposals,' *American Historical Review* 90, 2 (1985): 299–338, and *The Emergence of the Middle Class: Social Experience in the American City, 1760–1900* (New York: Cambridge University Press, 1989). See also Peter Stearns, 'The Middle Class: Toward a Precise Definition,' *Comparative Studies in Society and History* 21 (1979): 377–96; Mary Ryan, *Cradle of the Middle Class: The Family in Oneida County, New York, 1790–1865* (New York: Cambridge University Press, 1984); Richard Sennett, *Families against the City: Middle Class Homes of Industrial Chicago, 1872–1890* (Cambridge, Mass.: Harvard University Press, 1970).

4 McMaster University, Mills Memorial Library, Manuscript Census of the Canadas, 1851 [microfilm]; Manuscript Census of Canada, 1871, 1891 [microfilm]; *Historical Atlas of Waterloo and Wellington Counties* (Toronto: Belden, 1881), 8, and 'The Town of Galt,' *Industries of Canada, Historical and Commercial Sketches* (Toronto: M.G. Bixby, 1890), 105.

5 *Historical Atlas of Huron County* (Toronto: Belden, 1879), vi.

6 C. Wright Mills, *White Collar: The American Middle Classes* (New York: Oxford University Press, 1951), chapter 3.

7 For a fuller discussion of this process, see Andrew C. Holman, 'Aspects of Middle-Class Formation in Victorian Ontario Towns: Galt and Goderich, 1850–1891' (PhD dissertation, York University, 1995).

8 See Andrew Holman, '"Cultivation" and the Middle-Class Self in Nineteenth-Century America,' *Canadian Review of American Studies* 23, 2 (1993): 183–93; Christopher Mulvey, *Transatlantic Manners: Social Patterns in Nineteenth-Century Anglo-American Travel Literature* (Cambridge: Cambridge University Press, 1990).

9 Orville Dewey, 'On American Morals and Manners,' [Boston] *Christian Examiner* 36 (March 1844): 276–7.

10 *The Nation* 957 (1 November 1883): 367. The quotation is a paraphrasing of *The Nation*'s argument and response to [London] *The Spectator* 56 (17 November 1883): 1474.

11 John White, *Sketches from America* (London: S. Low, Son, and Marston, 1870), 120. See also 'A Lesson on Young Americans,' [London, Ontario] *The Family Circle* 6, 2 (1882): 30; Samuel Phillips Day, *English America: or Pictures of Canadian Places and People* (London: T. Newby, 1864), 251.

12 William Clark, 'Conduct and Manner,' [Toronto] *The Canadian Magazine of Politics, Science, Art & Literature* 1, 1 (1893): 24.

13 It is difficult to determine the currency of etiquette manuals in Galt and Goderich in these years; however, there is some evidence of their presence. See 'Hand Book for Home Improvement,' *Reformer*, 11 May 1864.

14 See Waterloo County Medical Association, *Constitution of the Waterloo County Medical Association, adopted 10 December 1872* (Waterloo: The Association [1872]); Richard A. Willie, '"A Proper Ideal during Action": Fraternity, Leadership and Lifestyle in Winnipeg Lawyers' Professional Culture, 1878–1900,' *Journal of Canadian Studies* 27, 1 (1992): 58–72.

15 See *Signal*, 23 October 1891; Charles Stewart's poem 'Tell It Not You Are Poor,' *Reformer*, 9 March 1881; 'The "Poor Rich Man,"' *Reformer*, 13 October 1881; Holman, 'Aspects.'

16 In *Worcester's Dictionary of the English Language* (Philadelphia: J.B. Lippincott, 1881), for example, the terms *cultivation, refinement,* and *mannerliness* are each used to define one another, along with the terms *civility, elegance,* and *polish.*

17 Richard Grant White, 'Class Distinctions in the United States,' [Boston] *North American Review* 137 (1883): 234.

18 See, for example, 'The True Gentleman,' [Montreal] *The Saturday Reader* 1, 2 (16 September 1865): 24; 'Who Is a Gentleman?' *The Family Circle* 5, 9 (March 1882): 134; 'Aristocratic Notions,' *The Family Circle* 7, 9 (3 November 1883): 126. Locally, Galt and Goderich had their own self-styled gentry, whose elegance exceeded the respectable limits of cultivation. See A Lady in Galt, 'Society As It Is,' *Galt Reporter*, 27 March 1857; 'Society News,' *Reformer*, 23 November 1870; Robina Lizars and Kathleen Macfarlane Lizars, *In the Days of the Canada Company: The Story of the Settlement of the Huron Tract and a View of the Social Life of the Period, 1825–1850* (Toronto: W. Briggs, 1896), 318–22.

19 Scholars have asserted that masculinity was undergoing a crisis in Victorian Britain and the United States as gender roles came to be altered by new work roles and the push for women's rights. See Mark C. Carnes and Clyde Griffen, eds., *Meanings for Manhood: Constructions of Masculinity in Victorian America* (Chicago: University of Chicago Press, 1990); J.A. Mangan and James Walvin, eds., *Manliness and Morality: Middle-Class Masculinity in Britain and America, 1800–1940* (Manchester: Manchester University Press, 1987); Michael Roper and John Tosh, eds., *Manful Assertions: Masculinities in Britian since 1800* (London: Routledge, 1991); E. Anthony Rotundo, *American Manhood: Transformations in Masculinity fron the Revolution to the Modern Era* (New York: Basic Books, 1993). Masculinity in places like Galt and Goderich must have been affected by larger patterns and attitudes in the Anglo-American world, even as men formed their own locally negotiated versions of acceptable, masculine conduct. See 'Manliness,' *Reformer*, 23 July 1885.

20 Cultivated feminine behaviour was negotiated locally too, but with less fan-

fare, reflecting, it seems, the idea that, given women's principally private roles, less tutelage in public matters was required. The discourse for women that did exist was, however, produced by men. See 'True Womanhood,' *Reformer*, 29 April 1857; 'Women's Rights,' ibid., 7 March 1855; 'Adhesiveness in Women,' ibid., 12 December 1855; 'YMCA Lecture ... "Woman, Her Sphere in the Dominion,"' ibid., 8 January 1868; 'True Womanhood,' *Signal*, 12 September 1890.

21 Catherine Parr Traill, *The Canadian Settler's Guide* (1855; Toronto: McClelland & Stewart, 1969), 9.

22 John F. Kasson, *Rudeness & Civility: Manners in Nineteenth-Century Urban America* (New York: Hill and Wang, 1990); Karen Halttunen, *Confidence Men and Painted Women: A Study of Middle-Class Culture in America, 1830–1870* (New Haven: Yale University Press, 1982).

23 'Deportment in Social Intercourse,' [Galt] *The Nut=Shell* 1, 2 (February 1890): 1.

24 See, for example, 'Habbick's Show Room,' *Reformer*, 11 May 1864; 'J.A. Reid & Bro.,' *Goderich Illustrated Signal-Star* (Board of Trade Edition), 25 May 1889.

25 'Why Follow All the Fashions in Dress?' *Reformer*, 10 September 1873; Goderich, Huron County Historical Museum, Papers of Eloise A. Skimmings, 1859–1912, 'Cousin Lizzie,' Goderich, to Richard Skimmings, Bermuda, 6 February 1869; 'Adolphus Tiffics, Esq. By a Poor Young Man,' *Signal*, 28 April 1865.

26 'Deportment in Social Intercourse,' 2–3.

27 'Prof. Dorenwend to be Here,' *Signal*, 25 April 1890.

28 'Addenda's Articles,' *Signal*, 23 March 1884.

29 'What He Thinks of Goderich' *Signal*, 31 January 1890.

30 Clark, 'Conduct and Manner' 27. See also 'Self-Confidence' *Reformer*, 26 November 1885.

31 Clark, 'Conduct and Manner,' 27.

32 Ibid., 28.

33 Unless, of course, it was in defence of respectable women or family members. See 'A Word Not Unneeded,' *Reformer*, 14 July 1855; 'Chivalric,' ibid., 30 July 1879.

34 'Society,' *Canadian Presbyter* 1 (1851): 338–9.

35 Clark, 'Conduct and Manner,' 29.

36 'On Education,' *Semi-Weekly Signal*, 24 January 1865. 'Desireable as it may be for young men to shun the extravagance of the aesthete, and to despise the shams of society,' another Victorian commentator noted, 'they cannot afford to neglect the courtesies of life; and they do well who, while devoting their energies to mathematics and the classics, pay a little attention to the cultivation of manners. It is while young that manners are made; the most strenuous efforts will not remedy or eradicate in after life the gaucheries formed in youth.' J.M. Loes, 'Education and Good Manners,' [Toronto] *The Week*, 27 September 1888.

37 'The Educational Advantages of Goderich,' *Semi-Weekly Signal*, 13 March 1863; Alison Prentice, *The School Promoters: Education and Social Class in Mid-Nineteenth-Century Upper Canada* (Toronto: McClelland & Stewart, 1977), chapter 3.

38 James E. Kerr, 'Recollections of My Schooldays at Tassie's,' *Waterloo Historical Society* 3 (1915): 22–3.

39 *The Galt Business College, Galt, Ont.* (Hamilton: Spectator Printing Co., 189?), 18.

40 'Popular Institutions,' *Signal*, 18 November 1852.

41 Louise L. Stevenson, *The Victorian Homefront: American Thought and Culture, 1860–1880* (New York: Twayne Publishers, 1991), 46. See also John Laing, 'The Morality of Our Country,' *Canadian Presbyter* 2 (1851): 364.

42 'Working and Thinking,' *Reformer*, 10 November 1869; 'Twenty-Five Cents,' *Semi-Weekly Signal*, 3 July 1863.

43 *Semi-Weekly Signal*, 18 November 1862; 'The Home Knowledge Association,' ibid., 3 February 1888. See also 'The Editor's Table,' ibid., 9 August 1889; 'Literary Notices,' ibid., 29 May 1885; 'Godey for November,' *Reformer*, 29 October 1856; 'Godey's Lady's Book, for February,' ibid., 15 January 1862.

44 See Holman, 'Aspects,' 329–45; Oisin P. Rafferty, 'Apprenticeship's Legacy: The Social and Educational Goals of Technical Education in Ontario, 1860–1911' (PhD dissertation, McMaster University, 1995), chapter 3.

45 'The Literary Society,' *Reformer*, 24 October 1866; Holman, 'Aspects,' 340–1.

46 'Galt Mechanics' Institute,' *Reformer*, 17 January 1866. In both Galt and Goderich, the Mechanics' Institute secretaries published annual reports (usually in January) in the local newspapers detailing membership, library holdings, and other sundry business.

47 Ibid., 18 January 1871; 'Mechanics' Institute,' *Signal*, 1 June 1883. This pattern emerges clearly in even a cursory scan of members' characteristics. See Ontario Archives, Galt Mechanics' Institute Membership Book, 1879–89.

48 A. Cunningham Geikie, 'A Colonial Sketch of Dr John Bayne of Galt,' *The British and Foreign Evangelical Review* 93 (July 1875).

49 'Died,' *Signal*, 4 August 1853.

50 Kitchener Public Library, Grace Schmidt Room, Diary of Andrew McIlwraith, 1857–1862 [typescript].

51 Kasson, *Rudeness & Civility*; Halttunen, *Confidence Men and Painted Women*.

52 'Pranks of an Imposter,' *Reformer*, 9 June 1858; 'Lieu. Carter Jugged,' ibid., 23 June 1858. See also 'A Swindler in Galt and Guelph,' ibid., 29 January 1862; 'A Confidence Operator,' ibid., 8 September 1875; 'Skipped Out,' ibid., 24 November 1881; 'The Hersman Case,' ibid., 1 December 1881.

53 'Confidence Game Extraordinary,' *Semi-Weekly Signal*, 16 October 1863. See also 'Gone Where the Eagle Screameth,' ibid., 10 October 1871; 'No They Don't,' ibid., 17 October 1871; 'Insurance Frauds,' *Signal*, 9 August 1876; 'A Well-Known Swindler,' ibid., 30 August 1889.

54 'Infidel Principles,' *Reformer*, 19 May 1858.

55 Annmarie Adams, *Architecture in the Family Way: Doctors, Houses, and Women, 1870–1900* (Montreal and Kingston: McGill-Queen's University Press, 1996). There is some evidence, however, that this aspect was not so clearly gendered as the others. 'Character,' Galt minister James A.R. Dickson observed in 1885, derives from 'all the appointments of the house,' interior and exterior. 'It is breathed by the pictures on the walls, by the literature on the tables, by the furnishing of the rooms, by the flowers of the garden, by the demeanour and deeds of the parents; in a word, by all the ordering of home life.' *Working for the Children, in the Home and in the Sunday School* (Toronto: J. Young, 1885), 53. See also Margaret Marsh, 'Suburban Men and Masculine Domesticity, 1870–1915,' in Carnes and Griffen, eds., *Meanings for Manhood*, 111–27.

56 James Young, 'Canadian Homes and Their Surroundings,' The *Canadian Magazine of Politics, Science, Art & Literature* 3, 6 (1894): 514.

57 *Reformer*, 11 April 1877.

58 *Goderich Illustrated Signal-Star* (Board of Trade Edition), 25 March 1889. Similarly, the *Historical Atlas of Huron County* published, alongside a history and map of the town, pen-and-ink sketches of Goderich's leading men and their residences.

59 'A Walk about Town,' *Semi-Weekly Signal*, 29 May 1863.

60 See 'Orchard and Garden,' *Signal*, 23 January 1891. In Galt, the *Reformer* offered 'Farm and Garden.' See *Reformer*, 8 January 1891.

The State, Public Education, and Morality: Evaluating the Results of School Promotion, 1893–1896

DAVID G. BURLEY

In December 1896 George W. Ross, minister of education for Ontario, asked the province's public school inspectors to report on the 'moral tone of the Public Schools.' In the previous twenty years, since the creation of the Department of Education, he wondered, had the schools been able to fill the expectations placed upon them to create a moral, respectable, and responsible citizenry? 'In the education of the youth of the country,' the minister asserted, 'it is of the first importance that the School System maintained by the State should aim at the development of the highest citizenship ... The forces which lie at the foundation of the best and strongest character are moral and religious.'[1] This was Ross's third inquiry into the condition of public education, following one in 1893 on 'the progress ... in school-room work,' and another in 1895 on health and sanitation.[2] Totalling more than four hundred pages in the annual reports, the responses to the three surveys constituted a discourse on discipline. In it, inspectors attempted to systematize their observations and bring them into line with their assumption that the state possessed sufficient power to form a public culture within the educational space of the public school.

Ross wished to reflect on his accomplishments as minister of education. Between his appointment as minister in 1883 and his becoming premier in 1899, he sought effective state administrative control over all levels and functions of education in Ontario – from kindergarten to university, from textbooks to teacher certification. His predecessors, Egerton Ryerson and Adam Crooks, had begun the process, but Ross achieved completion. For him, the structural integration of schooling was essential for implementing a curriculum aimed at forming moral character and for training the teachers to deliver it.[3]

In his three surveys, Ross set the parameters for evaluating a generation of public education. Their topics may have seemed distinct, and Ross may not have consciously anticipated their totality. Still, the ability of the schools to form moral character in the students depended on the moral character and professional attainments of the teachers and the wholesome and aesthetically uplifting quality of the school environment. Ross began in 1893 with a straightforward inquiry into the effectiveness of teaching. As an afterthought, he questioned the quality of school premises and the interest of trustees, and asked, 'Are teachers improving in culture, in professional skills, in personal neatness? ... Are they becoming better "character builders?"'[4]

Piqued by the responses he received, Ross initiated subsequent surveys. Were teachers and students healthy? Were school grounds and premises, especially the toilet facilities, conducive to learning and character formation? In the third survey, Ross wanted to know whether truancy was increasing; whether students were less quarrelsome and boisterous, more courteous, truthful, and straightforward, kinder to animals, and tidier and cleaner in their habits; and whether they were more easily disciplined without corporal punishment and more trustworthy when out of their teachers' presence. The importance that Ross placed on teachers was evident in the detailed questions he asked about them. 'Has the moral tone of the teaching profession improved since you became Inspector?' 'How many teachers have been suspended, use alcohol, attend Church, teach Sunday School?' Further, he wanted to know how teachers controlled their charges and how they sought to effect moral improvement among them. As well, inspectors were asked whether clergymen offered religious instruction and whether teachers could contribute more instruction of this sort.[5] The questions asked whether students had internalized discipline, and assumed one could judge pupils' moral responsibility from their public behaviour.

The objective of public education was to internalize authority in the young in the form of self-motivated morality. Thereby, the state could more easily exercise discipline over its citizens, and good behaviour would no longer depend on deference to immediate authority. Because Ross believed that teachers should demonstrate moral responsibility, he wanted to know about their after-school activities, their habits, and their participation in religious life, all areas where they were beyond the scrutiny and censure of the inspectorate. Not only did their actions outside the classroom extend their ability to uplift the public, but their example impressed the public with the quality of instruction within the classroom. Beneath the particulars of Ross's questionnaire, it is not difficult to discern, as did several of his respondents, a more general and profound inquiry concerning the cultural achievements of power. If the moral level of pupils and teachers had indeed improved, then the state had supplanted both parental and church authority in character formation and succeeded where earlier agencies of education were thought to have failed. If public schooling had achieved moral improvements, then the state had created an educated citizenry in accordance with what it believed to be its own interests: the state could form the people whose civic responsibility it was to elect the officers of the state. As well, the inspectors knew implicitly that questions about teachers, teaching, and teacher training evaluated the significance of gender and the growing female presence in the classroom, a presence that had increased to more than two-thirds of the profession.[6] Finally, the surveys asked inspectors to present state actions as a historical narrative of moral progress.

Historians have found the administration of education after 1871 a less compelling problem than the arguments used to justify compulsory state education amid local resistance to bureaucratic control. Logically, it helps to know the objectives before evaluating their outcome. Alison Prentice's classic study, The School Promoters, argued that those advocating state schooling hoped to create 'almost perfect human beings, a generation better than the one which had gone before.' Educationalists understood this goal as character formation, one of leading students to acquire proper manners of behaviour and expression, to express Christian conviction, to strive for and respect property.[7] Bruce Curtis further emphasized that public schooling constituted an essential element in state building. Not only did state schools define a 'public' but the state also superimposed an administrative grid on civil society aimed at regulation, transformation, and inculcation of a bourgeois cultural hegemony.[8] Subsequently, Curtis examined the careers of the agents of bourgeois cultural hegemony, the first generation of school inspectors in the 1840s. By their position, these men, 'typically respectable, Anglo-Saxon men of property,' were well situated 'to promote and, at times, to enforce their cultural conceptions, their moral standards, their sense of justice, and their aesthetic sense as models for the rest of society.'[9]

Prentice's and especially Curtis's studies presumed an effective state, one able to develop, articulate, and administer an increasingly complex institution of social control. Robert Gidney and Winnifred Millar in their study of secondary education during the period disputed the capacity of the state to determine educational change so effectively. Instead, they argued that the interests and demands of its middle-class clientele formed the character of the high school, often in ways that subverted the intentions of centralized bureaucratic authority.[10] Robert Lanning, in one of the few articles on the era after school promotion, examined the 1896 moral survey. His concern, different from this essay's purpose, was to describe the understanding of moral education held by late nineteenth-century educators. He concluded, in terms consistent with the earlier work of Prentice and others, that a later generation of educationalists, like the school promoters, sought indirect methods to form a morality among students that would be expressed in citizenship consistent with the class interests of the dominant class.[11]

This essay is concerned more generally with the morality presumed to be imparted by state education and its evaluation among teachers as well as students. The intent is to demonstrate that once the apparatus of the educational state had been erected, school administrators were themselves concerned with charting its boundaries of effective surveillance and discipline.

The inspectors' responses to Ross's survey varied: some answered the questions directly and sequentially with little elaboration or reflection, while others were more discursive. The latter, often more critical than the former about actual achievement, reflected on many of the assumptions and expectations implicit in the survey. Thus, the apparently dissenting and qualified reports revealed a greater understanding of the exercise and, ironically, shared the ambitions for state power that motivated it. Reading against the grain, finding dissenting themes in the discourse, reveals the reservations of those who hoped for more.

A number of the inspectors, especially those with some years of experience, took their report as an opportunity to reflect on the nature of state-directed moral education. D.A. Maxwell, an inspector for nineteen years, began by speculating about the state's authority to compel school attendance and to enforce morality. He posited that 'the wealth and power of a nation does not consist in its material possessions but in the worth of the individuals composing it,' and that 'the preservation of society demands that every on-coming citizen shall be a contributor to the national worth.' It followed, then, that 'civilized people' have sought the best means to prepare their children for citizenship and have taxed themselves to achieve that end. The unwillingness of some families to exercise parental responsibilities, along with the inadequacy of the church, meant that the state had to assume the pre-eminent role in education.

Maxwell distinguished moral instruction, in contrast to both religious and ethical instruction, as the best education for citizenship. Theological disagreement made any definition of the content of religious education difficult. Similarly, the substance of ethical education was open to dispute, depending on its definition in social or in individualistic terms. Despite these disagreements, all citizens could accept a number of propositions on which to base moral education: the capacity of sane persons to distinguish right from wrong; the founding of right in some supernatural order; the superiority of Christianity; and the possibility of educating individuals to distinguish right and wrong more effectively. This last point represented the main task of moral education.[12]

Few of the inspectors theorized like Maxwell, although they all shared his understanding that moral education should contribute to an appreciation of right and wrong. They understood that Ross's concern focused on the observable behaviour of children and teachers. Overwhelmingly, they reported that the morality of both teachers and students had improved over the previous twenty years. Typical of the uncritical approbation was Rev. Thomas McKee's belief that, in Simcoe South, 'the students are improving every year not only intellectually and physically, but esthetically and morally ... In a word the pupils are more manly and womanly than ever before.' W.J. Carson responded with incredulity: 'Any man who thinks that children are not better behaved now than they formerly were would do well to have himself carefully examined by a physician who is a specialist in nervous and mental disease.'[13]

Such judgments implicitly created a history in which childhood in previous times appeared crude and even cruel. William Carlyle recollected, for example: 'I have to go back several years to find a school not amenable to discipline. Rudeness of behavior ... is rapidly disappearing. The boorishness, the slovenly style of dress, the negligence as to personal cleanliness and appearance, offensively present once, are now noticeably absent.'[14] Reports that fighting was infrequent implied that previously it had been more common. 'Fifteen or twenty years ago,' J.A. Craig recalled, 'every school had its bully. This character was not only the pet of the school, but often the pet of the section. To-day the youth who takes pride in his pugilistic ability is looked upon with contempt.' No one shared M.J. Kelly's opinion that the old way was not 'without its good moral effect when the sneak, the humbug or the bully got his deserts.'[15]

Although all the respondents accepted the idea that boys had a need to struggle and test themselves against others, they noted that these contests had been transferred to the athletic field – a development that the 1895 Sanitary Report had commended. Inspectors approved of the health benefits and discipline acquired in athletics, and encouraged teachers to promote sports and participate in them themselves.[16] They disagreed, however, over the merits of organized athletic clubs. A minority thought them too exclusive: rather than cultivating a spirit of helpfulness, the clubs sustained the 'manly vice' of excluding those weak in competitive ability. The majority viewed them not merely as 'a means of developing muscular power, but ... as a means of developing true manliness ... [B]oys will learn to manage business affairs of after life in a business way in the organization and management of a good sporting club.'[17] Sports and games, then, provided an outlet for youthful energies that previously had provoked fighting.

Comments about the treatment of animals also implied a more violent childhood in previous decades. Inspector David Fotheringham believed that changes in the curriculum, especially literature such as *Black Beauty*, published by humane societies, had improved the sensibilities of children. According to historian Harriet Ritvo, kindness to dumb creatures became, for Victorians, an expression of more general social obligations.[18] Inspectors, too, saw a broader significance in the humane treatment of animals when they coupled their observations with statements about courtesy shown to the elderly and the infirm. John Dearness, for example, thought that children were 'more considerate and humane in their treatment of dumb animals and of aged, weak and imbecile persons.' That fowl, dogs, and pigs rummaged in the school yard for the scraps of students' lunches suggested to Thomas Gordon of Grey West that these creatures had no reason to avoid children.[19]

The humane treatment of animals manifested what one inspector termed the students' 'kinder feelings and more refined tastes.' More pleasing surroundings, school grounds, and classrooms contributed to 'the cultivation of the esthetic faculty.' Another respondent recommended decorating the blackboards 'with wreaths and borders of beautiful designs in variegated colors.' Inserted among these decorations were mottoes expressing the virtues of 'self denial, self sacrifice, self development, self application, nobility of purpose and aim ... [W]ith refining influences around, children instructively become more attentive to personal appearance and habits.' For J.A. Craig, improvements in the classroom, and by effect among students, could be attributed to the teacher; 'a neat, smart, tidy female teacher,' he claimed, 'works wonders by example.' But George Ross regretted that such refinements were much too scarce and, in many instances, 'the school walls are entirely devoid of the ordinary attractions of a private room.'[20]

The inspectors disagreed, however, in deciding whether the more refined, orderly, peaceable, and humane behaviour of children marked real moral improvement. M.J. Kelly wondered whether the positive changes were more than 'skin-deep.' Likewise, J.C. Morgan questioned whether a valid criterion for improvement was 'the external and visible one of action.' He explained: 'We find among the pupils a general external appearance of respect, with a painful absence of real reverence for anything human or divine. We meet with less immorality which can be seen and punished, but this is not accompanied by any real increase of purity.' For Kelly and Morgan, the inner state could not be equated so easily with the outer.[21]

Teachers had to contend with children's nature, which especially in the case of boys could express its force brutishly. 'Human nature and child nature,' C.W. Chadwick believed, 'are very much the same now as they were twenty years ago.' Improvement depended entirely on the teacher, and weakness could allow inherent bad behaviour to reappear. 'A trespassing animal, whether bird or beast,' David Robb disclosed, 'is still subject to pretty rough usage, and often pays the penalty with its life. It is almost impossible to induce boys to believe that reptiles and some noxious animals should not be tortured to death.' Another opined that 'the propensity to kill is still strong.'[22] That some schoolboys retained a blood lust does not necessarily contradict the inspectors' overall judgment on the humane treatment of animals. Rather, it acknowledged the temptations to which students might succumb without their teachers' vigilance.

Beyond adult surveillance, the children's character showed more truly. Rev. W.H.G. Colles lamented their copying at examinations and their indulgence in that 'secret filthiness as too often evidenced by the condition of outbuildings.' In 1895 he had complained to Ross that 'objectionable cuttings and pencillings [sic]' defaced the walls of outhouses. 'We may do much by teaching the children ... to abhor evil and to love the good and the pure, but so long as the average, not to say the worst, school closets of our Province remain as they are, a strong counter influence exists, paralyzing to some extent the good seed sown, and silently suggesting evil which may escape the vigilance of teachers.' The condition of outhouses presented a quandary to school officials, since a respect for modesty and privacy in meeting those basic bodily functions limited the equally important need for supervision. Boys, especially, could not all be trusted when they absented themselves from the classroom. Away from the teacher's gaze they could not only disregard the principles of personal and public hygiene but could deface the walls and scar them with foul obscenities. Where only a partition separated facilities for the two sexes, boys could torment girls on the other side or even invade their privacy by peeping through chinks in the wall. F.L. Michell complained that 'double closets are too common, and hence modesty – the crown of womanhood – is not encouraged.'[23]

Responsibility for the moral contamination that flowed from defiled outhouses rested with the teacher, and female teachers had proved particularly inadequate. J.C. Morgan explained that 'it requires a teacher of some power and influence, whose vigilance is as sleepless as his abhorrence for obscenity or profanity is profound, to cope successfully with the evil.' As Morgan's use of the masculine pronoun implies, he judged young women lacking in the experience and perhaps too modest to inspect, let alone investigate and discuss, the outhouse activities of their male students. 'I find it impossible,' complained James B. Grey, 'to get young female teachers to inspect the closets regularly, or talk to the boys about the necessity and propriety of keeping these places clean.'[24] The inspectors did keep the outhouse problem in perspective: it was troubling not because of its magnitude, but because it proved the dependence of morality on surveillance.

A more common moral failure was cheating on school assignments and examinations. According to Albert Odell, students did not seem to recognize the appropriation of another's work as an offence. Yet, to him, dishonesty in assignments and examinations portended more serious transgressions in later life. In a perverse way, cheating exposed just how deeply important educational attainment had become in the public mind. W.S. Clendenning criticized the stress on examinations: 'so much attention has to be paid to ... preparation for examinations – the teachers being goaded on by public opinion often contrary to their better judgments – that direct moral instruction is generally set aside.'[25] With a sensitivity to the fears that preyed on young minds, W.E. Tilley wondered whether cheating might well arise as a side-effect of the other qualities of character that public schooling stimulated. Both parents and teachers prodded children to diligence in their studies by emphasizing the need to pass examinations to advance in school and in later life. Understandably, then, 'the pupils perhaps, being a little beyond their depths, and it may be, somewhat hampered by over many studies, from a fear of disgrace, a desire to make a step forward though not quite ready for it, or a natural love of approbation, especially that of teacher and parent, make use of means to pass the examinations that do violence to their conscience and tend to undermine their integrity.'[26]

Because departmental examinations were so important in Ontario's school system, Ross considered cheating a troublesome sin. Elsewhere in his 1896 report, he justified examinations as a necessary guarantee of the 'commercial value' of the certificates issued for various achievements. More than that, they connoted progress towards realizing ambitions in life and demonstrated the potential of the credential holder, regardless of family background, to enter the professions.[27] Pervasive cheating on schoolwork and examinations debased the state's credentials and, as significantly, raised concerns about the state's ability to compel moral behaviour.

Fortunately, the inspectors' replies gave the minister no reason to conclude that cheating was out of control, but he may have felt concern in reading the remarks of William Tytler. To the Guelph inspector, more serious was the unwillingness of students to report malefactors or to supply teachers with information when queried about incidents. 'By the schoolboy's standard of morality,' the false profession of no knowledge constituted but a 'venial' sin.[28] Yet the reluctance to incriminate one's peers marked the limit of the identification with and submission to authority that teachers were urged to cultivate through moral instruction.

Ross had recognized that moral behaviour might depend too heavily on present authority, and he wondered to what extent students could be trusted in the absence of teachers and to what extent teachers' authority depended on corporal punishment. Nearly all inspectors agreed that corporal punishment had become less necessary, but that the ability to trust students in the absence of a teacher varied considerably, not with the class but with the teacher. Even the best-ordered group of students might revert to the disorderly conduct of a former era if the quality and ability of the teacher deteriorated.[29]

Inspectors considered that indirect or incidental moral instruction contributed most effectively to the maintenance of order and to character formation. D.A. Maxwell identified three ways to deliver such instruction. First, the ability of the child to apply energy to a single task cultivated the self-control needed to resist temptation, do one's duty, and distinguish right from wrong. Second, teachers influenced their students at an unconscious level, as 'the heart speaks to the heart by its own signs, conveying thought not always defined by the intellect.' And, third, the orderly social relations of the school and the messages conveyed in school texts revealed the merits of the rule of law.[30] History lessons could be very useful in this instruction.[31] From the past, children learned 'that the loyal citizen looks first to the general good and determines that what is harmful to others is not good for himself ... that freedom or liberty is possible only to him who makes his conduct conform to the well-being of others as well as of himself.' In other words, individualism and self-interest were to be subordinated to the social will as embodied in the legislative acts of the state.[32]

Unfortunately, the 1893 survey on pedagogy had found that history was probably the subject taught least satisfactorily and that students remained uninspired. Put bluntly, 'nearly every teacher seems to hate history.' Teachers were themselves to blame: 'Water cannot rise above its own level, neither can the teacher. His ability to inspire a love for the good, the true and the beautiful depends entirely on his own appreciation of them.' Few knew or read history and, though improving, 'culture' was generally lacking. Most inspectors admitted that, given the youth of teachers, the almost complete turnover in the province's teaching complement every four or five years, and, implicitly, the gender of teachers, little cultural sophistication or personal certainty about cultural values could be expected. As Donald McCaig put it, 'the teaching profession ... is more effeminate with less strong manliness and womanliness' than before.[33]

As a result, the general management of the schools had to compensate for the immaturity of teachers. James McBrien, for example, encouraged incidental moral lessons in the schools of Ontario County. 'The spirit of our discipline is constantly to throw the pupil on his own responsibility and to lead him to do right because it is right. We have no faith in police or constable duty in school management. Therefore, as the self-government of the pupil increases, the government of the teacher decreases until it is zero.' Children were bound to commit transgressions until they had achieved self-government, and so, of necessity, 'the school-room is a court of justice held daily,' in which the teacher exercised judicious care in settling disputes and exacting punishment. McBrien counselled his teachers to lead offenders to judge themselves by giving them a day or so to reflect on their unacceptable behaviour. Once they had acknowledged their guilt and recanted, they were pardoned. 'Mercy is the fairest attribute of power ... Severity of punishment creates fear, and fear promotes secretiveness, a prolific source of deception or practical lying.' Not all, however, confessed their errors. Then the teacher should not hesitate 'to throw the united opinion of the whole school against the misconduct of a certain one and, thus, crush it out of existence. Here we have united action in the best interests of the commonwealth, just as society [is] united to destroy any vice or sin that threatens its welfare.'[34]

J.B. Grey had misgivings about levelling public opinion against offenders. Teachers in his district were advised to discipline children privately, and if some misbehaviour proved especially common, teachers were to direct an appropriate moral lesson to the entire school or class. Thereby, individual offenders were reprimanded without being humiliated publicly, while all students were given notice that they were suspected of being potential offenders and would be punished for their sins. By implication, the failure of the one could easily be the failure of the many, and the effect was to make everyone more wary of transgression.[35]

Because moral instruction relied so heavily on indirect methods and because student behaviour seemed to vary directly with the quality of the teacher, Ross wanted to know whether the moral qualities of teachers had also improved over the last two decades. Inspectors generally reported even more favourably about the moral standing of teachers than they had about children. The need for improvement had not been great, but they did remind Ross that, in the past, some teachers (presumably from the context, male teachers) had been less than temperate. William Carlyle remembered, 'When I first assumed the duties of inspection there were a number of teachers, some prominent in the profession, regarding whom informal complaints reached me of dissolute habits. The number has grown less and less until there is but one.' Similarly, another respondent was pleased that 'the day of the tippling teacher is gone.'[36]

Archibald Smirle attributed moral improvement among teachers to two factors: high expectations and careful policing. 'There is no other class in the community, save the clergy, from whom so high a standard of morality is exacted as from teachers,' he wrote. 'Offences that are readily overlooked in other callings, will drive a teacher from the ranks ... cancel his certificate.'[37] That few inspectors reported the need to cancel certification no doubt confirmed their view of the effectiveness of community pressure.

But M.J. Kelly disputed that the morally corrupt had become less so: 'The leopard has not changed his spots, nor will he.' And J.C. Morgan questioned whether community pressure produced real moral conviction among teachers. Increasingly, he believed, people displayed 'a careful regard to outward observances, to the decencies of nineteenth-century civilization,' without any real 'active religious life, and correspondingly little of the power which comes from deep thinking and ripe experience ... Our teachers (however correct their observance of the externals may be), are neither cold nor hot, but lukewarm.' Holding few beliefs strongly and fervently themselves, teachers were unable to instill any sincerity of inner conviction in their students.[38]

Other inspectors shared Morgan's concern. W. Mackintosh blamed the limited success in forming moral character among students on the immaturity of teachers. 'Character can only be formed by character,' he observed. 'So long as the great majority of schools continue to be controlled by teachers with little experience and less maturity of thought and habit, no matter how amiable, respectable and bright they are, so long will these schools fail to do well the work which alone justifies their support by taxation – preparation for citizenship and for the duties and responsibilities of life.'[39] And, of course, though he did not say so explicitly, these young, inexperienced, immature teachers were mostly women.

M.J. Kelly was perhaps the most sceptical respondent – least sanguine about the innovations in teacher education and generally critical of the increasing number of young women in the schools. To him, the formation of boys' character was the most important goal of education and required the teacher's good example as a role model. Like John Locke, whom he cited, Kelly believed that 'the first requisite of a teacher is that he should be a gentleman, and gentlemen, like poets, are born not made.' The teacher should join 'his' pupils in sports and games in order to influence them: thereby the teacher 'is for the nonce a boy himself and is known to be genuine in all things.' Women by their sex were excluded from gentlemanly status and from such influence over their male charges. The surfeit of women teachers seeking employment would diminish the moral tone of the profession just as oversupply had degraded the 'ancient and honorable professions of medicine and law.'[40]

Ross acknowledged that the turnover and the consequent limited experience and culture of third-class teachers was a problem, but he argued that raising the non-professional (or academic) standards for certification and lengthening the professional program of the county model schools would improve teachers.[41] He had a vested interest in defending basic teacher training. In 1876 he had himself, as provincial inspector and chair of the Central Committee's Sub-Committee on Model Schools, assumed specific responsibility for the county model schools and had prepared the model school curriculum.[42] Again in 1884, not long after becoming minister of education, he had revised the model schools' course of study and had spelled out in departmental regulations week-by-week lesson plans to be delivered to aspiring teachers.[43]

Ross was also convinced that the model schools, especially because they were coeducational, provided in effect a term of moral probation. As J.J. Tilley, provincial model school inspector, reported to his minister, coeducation 'refines the man, strengthens the woman, restrains both, and prepares woman equally with man for the broadest and highest sphere of usefulness.' In seventeen years, Ross pointed out, 20,984 young men and women had gone through the program 'with no other restraint than their own sense of propriety and ... not a single one had to be subjected to discipline for immorality of any kind.'[44]

Many of the school inspectors shared Ross's evaluation of the model and normal schools and their utility in promoting professional development. W.E. Tilley defended the training they gave teachers in channelling the potentially negative characteristics of child nature into positive directions. 'The teacher who has been trained in the proper management of the children, knowing that the fear of punishment, the desire for gain, and love of approbation, are the great causes of falsehood, deceit and dishonesty, will use the greatest care and watchfulness to detect what may be the child's times of special temptation to err, and will use his best endeavors to lead the timid, the ambitious or the sensitive child in ways unobserved by him or his classmates, around difficulties which without such leading would in all probability land him in some disastrous pitfall.'[45]

Others were not so favourably disposed to the county model schools. Much of their quality depended on the particular principal's direction. Both inspectors in Hastings County, for example, criticized the school there for not doing good work and the principal for not being 'a thoroughly live man.'[46] As well, the survey of progress in teaching, by noting several subjects inadequately taught, cast doubts on the effectiveness of the third-class professional training. Reading, the most basic primary skill, came in for particular attention. Many inspectors doubted whether teachers sufficiently understood their training in the phonic method to apply it in their classrooms. Consequently, many teachers still relied on the 'look and say' method (the nineteenth-century's whole-language approach) and encouraged pupils to relate written words to pictorial representations of objects.[47] Other inspectors thought that teacher training presented methods suited to ideal situations, and did not encourage the development of the teacher's judgment and ability to tailor instruction to the peculiarities of the class. As a result, one observed, 'teachers of the third-class are generally slaves to methods used in the Model Schools which they attended.'[48]

Perhaps this slavishness convinced school inspectors that teachers should not be given additional responsibilities to provide religious instruction. From Ryerson's time, various denominations had objected to the secularism of state education. Indeed, the evaluation of morality sought by Ross presupposed a system of character formation that displaced the church from any substantial role. If any in the survey was a 'trick question,' it was the one asking about the frequency of school visitation and religious instruction by local clergymen. The school regulations permitted any clergyman to offer religious instruction after school to children of his denomination, providing parents agreed.[49] The opportunity for such instruction and the informal inspection that occurred from visits during the regular day demonstrated the state's willingness to reach accommodation with the church in what had previously been its exclusive domain. Thus, evidence of regular visits legitimated the state's engagement in moral education. The absence of visitation, as was more frequently reported, could be taken as clerical approval for state initiative, at the same time as it also revealed the inadequacies of the church in providing moral education. The inspectors' responses ranged from a regret that visits occurred so infrequently to derision of the church's real commitment to religious instruction.

Typical of clerical indifference was York North, where clergymen had never visited the schools unless invited to do so. Nor had they ever expressed a desire to engage in more of this work. Several inspectors thought that trustees and teachers would welcome such visits, but none had ever been requested. J.J. Craig regretted somewhat sarcastically that 'the Protestant clergy are apparently so busied with other important matters that they can spare no time to enter our school rooms. The Roman Catholic clergymen visit frequently.' Because of their reluctance to visit, J.C. Morgan had little patience for them and thought them grossly misinformed. 'With few exceptions,' he argued, 'the ministers are clamoring loudly for more opportunities for giving religious instruction, whilst they are ignorant of and blind to, or else they persistently ignore and contemptuously neglect those which have been offered to them.'[50]

Ross's question about the reaction to teachers offering more religious instruction may have anticipated this report on the dereliction of the clergy. In soliciting his inspectors' advice, he tried to tread more warily than in 1884, when he had made some religious instruction obligatory. Regulations that year called for the school day to begin with prayer and to end with a reading from the Holy Scriptures and another prayer. To this end, he had authorized a collection of Scripture readings for classroom use. The controversy that arose over the 'Ross Bible,' as these readings were derogated by critics, is generally well known,[51] although its pedagogical significance has not always been appreciated. The Bible, in Ross's judgment, was not 'suited to the capacity of children,' hence religious education based on it did not provide the best moral instruction for character formation. Instead, texts were needed that were appropriate to a child's level of understanding, were organized historically so the narrative presented continuity, and varied in style and material so as to hold the children's interest.[52]

One advantage of having religious instruction in the schools was that those who were expert in teaching, 'at least, in an ideal sense,' would deliver it. Personally, Ross was a religious man who accepted that 'Christianity is the basis of our school system, and therefore its principles should pervade it throughout.' But he preferred to appropriate the benefits of a moral, Christian education for the state, not for the institutional churches. In his 1888 report, he had quoted Egerton Ryerson: 'All theories which make the State the servant of the Church, are, as all history demonstrates, degrading to the former and corrupting to the latter.' Ross went on himself to explain that 'the position of the State in religious matters is more passive than positive,' protecting each denomination's right to propagate its distinctive understanding of the Christian faith, while favouring none with financial support and binding none to attendance.[53] However, he did accept that 'the whole social fabric rests upon well-established principles of moral or religious belief. Our relations to our fellow-men, the laws which regulate our conduct as citizens, in fact every outward act as well as inner motive, comes within its purview. To frame a system of education ... without providing for some form of religious instruction would be to disregard one of the most important elements of education requisite for citizenship, viz., power of religion over life and conduct.'[54] Religious instruction, then, was of interest to the state because of its utility in promoting socially responsible behaviour.

Ross's questions concerning church attendance and Sunday school instruction by public school teachers were intended to judge their fitness for a greater role in religious education. The general opinion of the inspectors was that a large majority of their teachers were regular church members and that many already taught Sunday school.[55] Nonetheless, few of the reports encouraged more formal religious instruction in the public schools.

Overwhelmingly, the inspectors urged the minister not to introduce any changes because they feared an outburst of sectarianism, similar to 'the criminally senseless crusade against the Scripture readings a few years ago.' Most considered teachers unqualified by their youth, inexperience, and lack of training to undertake Bible teaching. J.C. Morgan sarcastically predicted that teachers at present would likely give 'expositions ... more originally bizarre than orthodox.' Better training, more careful Bible study, and improved texts, he thought, would only lead teachers to commit themselves more strongly to sectarian doctrinal peculiarities. More seriously, inspectors thought that few teachers were able to meet the reactions of denominational watch guards. 'There is so much dogma, denominationalism, and doctrine taught from the pulpits,' J.A. Craig observed, 'that no teacher, even if he were an angel, could give expositions of the Scripture and steer clear of the rocks.' If division within the church made religious instruction difficult in the state's schools, the failure of the church to reach 'the multitudes of children who never or seldom attend its services' rendered it inadequate in cultivating moral development.[56] Just as clergymen had failed to take advantage of their privilege of visitation, so, too, the denominations had rendered the church not just ineffective but destructive in religious and moral instruction.

A few of the school inspectors questioned the usefulness of religious instruction. Opening and closing exercises might produce a calm and quiet tone in the classroom conducive to industrious study, but, as D.A. Maxwell put it, 'Goody-goody talk can never develop manly behavior.' W.E. Tilley doubted that it was effective as a means of social control. Ignorance of right and wrong was not the problem. 'The dishonest and vicious ... have [not] formed those habits of thought and action which would enable them to live up to their knowledge ... Rather would we place our confidence in the quiet suggestion, the gentle reproof, or the kindly word of the loving sympathetic teacher.'[57] Habit rather than rationality, indirect rather than direct action, promised better results.

Like their school promoting counterparts of a generation earlier, Ross's inspectors remained critical of the family in forming those habits of good behaviour. Thomas Hilliard, for example, regretted that there remained 'a fraction of our pupils whose hereditary tendencies and home training have alike been defective.' The failure of such families manifested itself in the continuing problem of irregular attendance and truancy. Frederick Burrows blamed 'the almost criminal apathy of parents,' while J.H. Smith was not alone in denouncing 'indulgent parents [for] allowing their children to absent themselves from school for the most trivial reasons.'[58]

At the same time, the inspectors were perhaps less optimistic than their predecessors about the ability of the schools to overcome negative parental influence. One lamented, 'As to truthfulness ... more depends on home training than on teachers.' Another opined that 'there will always be truants as long as there are imperfect homes.' W.E. Tilley remonstrated that those who placed too much faith in the public school's capacity for moral instruction ignored the stages of child development. 'We must guard against the too common error of placing the whole responsibility of [moral] training on the teacher ... The moral faculties manifest themselves much earlier than do the higher faculties of the intellect, and hence the child may be considered as either *won or lost* before he enters the school room, and even after the school life of the child begins, the time he spends under the teacher's eye is short compared with that which is spent in the environments of home.'[59]

For school inspectors, especially in urban centres, the limitations of public schooling when confronted with negative parental influences justified greater use of the state's coercive power. They supported the legislation of 1891 that had provided for the appointment of truant officers to enforce compulsory attendance.[60] If anything, they wanted even stronger enforcement and recommended larger salaries for truant officers and penalties for non-performance of duty. W.F. Chapman judged truancy to be on the increase in Toronto because of his inability to get persistent offenders sent to industrial schools. Similarly, J.H. Knight thought that the requirement that municipalities bear the cost of maintaining youths in industrial schools made authorities unwilling to enforce the legislation to its full measure. 'Had the cost been borne by the Province ... it might have prevented at least one murder and a great many other crimes.'[61]

The recommendation of public school inspectors that more punitive measures might ultimately be necessary to enforce moral behaviour came as an admission of the limitations of public schooling. An earlier generation of educationalists, committed to building the educational state, had promised much from the promotion of public schools. No longer addressing their discourse to parents and taxpayers, Ross's officials could confide in their minister and acknowledge the weaknesses that had become evident in administering the educational state.

Were children and teachers in 1896, as the inspectors reported to George W. Ross, really more moral than they had been twenty years earlier? Even if it were possible to make such a judgment, the responses to the minister's questionnaire would not provide the most objective evidence. In the end, the truth would remain elusive, but that hardly matters. Of more interest is the 'discursive fact' that Ross sought to resolve a discourse initiated in Ontario at least a generation earlier. Could the state, through the institution of the public school, so reconstruct individual character that the moral precepts of good citizenship might be implanted in the very selves of children who passed through the system? By the last decade of the nineteenth century, a second generation of students, a generation whose parents had themselves been compelled in their youth to attend state schools, had settled into their seats to learn. Surely the effects of moral education ought to have been visible in their character and behaviour?

Ross's inspectors would not close this discourse of power; perhaps as its products themselves, they could not. Nearly all of them acknowledged the achievements of the state in improving the moral character of students and teachers, yet many tempered the optimism with a variety of warnings. For some, there were practical reservations about the effectiveness of teacher training, ever more young women in the profession, and the disruptive consequences of a surplus of teachers. Others baulked as they recognized the practical magnitude of the challenge, especially in overcoming the negative effects of what they considered parental irresponsibility and neglect. Recourse to truancy legislation was itself an admission of deficiency. But the most substantive concerns came from those who found moral education itself limited by its focus on behaviour as the test of results. The state might well discipline the physical person and cultivate, and, if need be, coerce, respectable demeanour and orderly behaviour. But did actions accurately reveal the inner self? Were actions enough? Or did moral conduct rest solely on the individual's awareness of surveillance?

Ross had tentatively linked moral education to religious instruction, providing divine guidance for the individual in making his or her choices. Like his predecessor, Egerton Ryerson, he had sought a common Christianity that might be codified as a juridical standard.[62] Sectarianism and serious doubts about the ability of teachers resulted in the marginalization of religious instruction to symbolic opening and closing exercises. Consequently, religious observance had been reduced for those most in need of it to 'a silent Saturnalia of quiet and irreverent license.'[63] Regrettably, with moral education severed from religious instruction, the behaviour of students was left to rely solely on what Michel Foucault termed *subjectivation* – that process by which the individual, through the exercise of personal will, limits that part of his or her freedom of action that constitutes the object of moral practice. Thereby, the individual defines a personal relationship to a specific moral precept, decides on action, and personally monitors compliance.[64] Having displaced the church in proclaiming its responsibility for character formation, the state, then, could not easily depend on the tools of religion to aid it in achieving its goal.

The state, secure in its ability to gather knowledge about moral behaviour, could not be certain about its interpretation. It could not be certain whether the behaviour it observed was the product of moral conviction or an effective concealment of inner reality by those aware that they might be under surveillance.

NOTES

1 Province of Ontario, Sessional Papers (OSP), 1897, no. 1, 'Report of the Minister of Education (Ontario) for the Year 1896,' xv.

2 OSP, 1896, no. 2, 'Report of the Minister of Education (Ontario) for the Year 1895,' xiii; OSP, 1894, no. 3, 'Report of the Minister of Education (Ontario) for the Year 1893,' 1.

3 Ross offered a summary of his first decade as minister in his report for 1893: OSP, 1894, no. 3, xl–l. For historians' overviews of Ross's administration as minister of education, see David G. Burley, 'George William Ross,' *Dictionary of Canadian Biography*, 14: *1911 to 1920* (Toronto: University of Toronto Press, 1998), 888–95; Douglas Dart, 'George William Ross: Minister of Education for Ontario, 1883–1899' (MA thesis, University of Guelph, 1971); Robert M. Stamp, *The Schools of Ontario, 1876–1976* (Toronto: University of Toronto Press, 1982), 26–50. On one of the many issues concerning textbook authorization, see Oisin P. Rafferty, 'Balancing the Books: Brockerage Politics and the *"Ontario Readers"* Question, *Historical Studies in Education/Revue d'histoire de l'education* 4 (spring 1992): 79–96. On the controversies over language of instruction, see Chad Gaffield, *Language, Schooling, and Cultural Conflict: The Origins of the French-Language Controversy in Ontario* (Kingston and Montreal: McGill-Queen's Unversity Press, 1987).

4 OSP, 1894, no. 3, 2.

5 OSP, 1897, no. 1, xv.

6 OSP, 1886, no. 5, 'Report of the Minister of Education (Ontario) for the Year 1885,' xvii; OSP, 1900, no. 12, 'Report of the Minister of Education (Ontario) for the Year 1899,' vi.

7 Alison Prentice, *The School Promoters: Education and Social Class in Mid-Nineteenth Century Upper Canada* (Toronto: McClelland & Stewart, 1977), 4, 84.

8 Bruce Curtis, *Building the Educational State: Canada West, 1836–1871* (London, Ont.: Althouse Press, 1988), 366–80.

9 Bruce Curtis, *True Government by Choice Men? Inspection, Education, and State Formation in Canada West* (Toronto: University of Toronto Press, 1992), 7. For an evaluation of Curtis's earlier work, see Donald Soucy, 'Interpreting Schooling in Nineteenth-Century Ontario,' *Historical Studies in Education/Revue d'histoire de l'education* 3 (fall 1991): 275–84.

10 R.D. Gidney, *Inventing Secondary Education: The Rise of the High School in*

Nineteenth-Century Ontario (Kingston and Montreal: McGill-Queen's University Press, 1990), 315–18. See also R.D. Gidney and W.P.J. Millar, 'Rural Schools and the Decline of Community Control in Late Nineteenth-Century Ontario,' *Proceedings of the 4th Annual Agricultural History of Ontario Seminar*, 1979, 70–91. Earlier articles by Gidney and Douglas A. Lawr argued similarly for an appreciation of local influence on the evolving school system: 'Bureaucracy vs. Community? The Origins of Bureaucratic Procedure in the Upper Canadian School System,' *Journal of Social History* 13 (1981): 438–57, and 'Who Ran the Schools? Local Influence on Educational Policy in Nineteenth-Century Ontario,' *Ontario History* 72 (1980): 131–43.

11 Robert Lanning, 'Assessing Morality: The Ontario Provincial Survey of 1896,' *Journal of Educational Thought* 26 (April 1992): 5–21, and 'Mapping the Moral Self: Biography, State Formation and Education in Ontario, 1820–1920' (PhD thesis, University of Toronto, 1990).

12 OSP, 1897, no. 1, 138–9.

13 Ibid., 153, 196, 220.

14 Ibid., 183–4.

15 Ibid., 125, 168, 172, 175, 211, 215, 219.

16 Ibid., 163, 191; OSP, 1896, no. 2, 218.

17 OSP, 1896, no. 2, 179, 201, 223.

18 Harriet Ritvo, *The Animal Estate: The English and Other Creatures in the Victorian Age* (Cambridge, Mass.: Harvard University Press, 1987), 126–7, 135.

19 OSP, 1897, no. 1, 147, 177, 197, 208.

20 Ibid., 135, 172, 188, 208–9. Ross had hoped for such aesthetic improvement when, in 1885, he set aside the first Friday in May as Arbor Day, a day on which the energies of the students were directed to the clean up and improvement of the school grounds. As well, beginning in 1898, he had his inspectors issue diplomas for school premises that met departmental standards, including those for 'cleanliness and adornment.' OSP, 1899, no. 2, 'Report of the Minister of Education (Ontario) for the Year 1898,' xxix–xxxii.

21 OSP, 1897, no. 1, 125, 193.

22 Ibid., 158, 166, 206, 223.

23 OSP, 1896, no. 2, 199, 205, 224; OSP, 1897, no. 1, 161.

24 Ibid., 189, 209, 220.

25 OSP, 1897, no. 1, 125, 127, 128, 178, 181, 191, 206, 221, 223.

26 Ibid., 135.

27 Ibid., xxxi–xxxiv.

28 Ibid., 214.

29 Ibid., 212.

30 Ibid., 141.

31 Robert N. Berard, 'Moral Education in Nova Scotia, 1880–1920,' *Acadiensis* 14 (autumn 1984): 61. See also William Brickman, 'The Teaching of Secular Moral

Values in the Nineteenth Century: U.S.A., England, France,' *Paedagogica Historica* 12 (1972): 381.

32 OSP, 1894, no. 3, 23, 68, 136; OSP, 1895, no. 4, 'Report of the Minister of Education (Ontario) for the Year 1894,' xxxii.
33 Ibid., 16, 19, 29, 43, 46, 53, 56, 75, 114, 135, 210.
34 OSP, 1897, no. 1, 127, 161, 181–2.
35 Ibid., 176.
36 Ibid., 160, 183–4.
37 Ibid., 130, 144, 175.
38 Ibid., 125, 193.
39 OSP, 1894, no. 3, 31–2; OSP, 1897, no. 1, 154.
40 OSP, 1897, no. 1, 125–6, 133, 166, 169.
41 OSP, 1895, no. 4, xxvi.
42 On Ross's appointment to the Central Committee, see 'The Central Committee,' *Toronto Mail*, 22 August 1877; 'Mistatements Regarding the Central Committee,' Toronto *Globe*, 5 September 1877; Stamp, *The Schools of Ontario*, 6–7. On his involvement with the model schools, see R.D. Gidney, 'George Paxton Young,' *Dictionary of Canadian Biography*, 9: *1881 to 1890* (Toronto: University of Toronto Press, 1982), 943; OSP, 1878, no. 5, 'Annual Report of the Normal, Model, High and Public Schools of Ontario for the Year 1876, with Appendices by the Minister of Education,' 168–9, 179; OSP, 1879, no. 5, 'Annual Report of the Public and High, also of Normal and Model Schools of the Province of Ontario, for the Year 1877, with Appendices by the Minister of Education,' part 2: 62, 70–2; OSP, 1880, no. 5, 'Annual Report of the Minister of Education on the Public, Separate, and High Schools, also on the Normal and Model Schools, of the Province of Ontario, for the Year 1878,' 104–15; OSP, 1881, no. 5, 'Annual Report of the Minister of Education of the Province of Ontario on the Public (Including Separate), and High Schools, also on the Normal and Model Schools for the Training of Teachers, for the Year 1879,' 124–8.
43 OSP, 1885, no. 5, 'Report of the Minister of Education (Ontario) for the Year 1884,' 92–113.
44 OSP, 1895, no. 4, xxxi; OSP, 1897, no. 1, 135, 144, 146, 157, 240–2.
45 OSP, 1897, no. 1, 135.
46 OSP, 1894, no. 3, 34, 37.
47 Ibid., 8, 11, 15, 18.
48 Ibid., 18, 21.
49 OSP, 1897, no. 1, xxviii.
50 Ibid., 163, 195, 197, 199–200, 204, 208, 215, 222, 224.
51 See Dart, 'George William Ross,' 1–36; A. Margaret Evans, *Sir Oliver Mowat* (Toronto: University of Toronto Press, 1992), 234–8.
52 OSP, 1886, no. 5, xxxiv.

53 OSP, 1888, no. 7, 'Report of the Minister of Education (Ontario) for the Year 1887,' xlv.

54 *Speech of the Hon. George W. Ross, Minister of Education, at His Nomination, October 11, 1886* (Toronto: np, 1886), 14.

55 OSP, 1897, no. 1, 143.

56 Ibid., 129, 137, 138, 173, 184, 188, 194, 195.

57 Ibid., 136, 140, 165.

58 Ibid., 128, 174, 204, 224, 218.

59 Ibid., 134, 190, 223.

60 Ibid., 145. On the truancy legislation and rules for truant officers, see OSP, 1892, no. 11, 'Report of the Minister of Education (Ontario) for the Year 1891,' 62–4. In his study of Victoria Industrial School, Paul W. Bennett has remarked upon a similar change in tone and practice. 'What began in 1887 as a child rescue venture dedicated to moral rehabilitation evolved gradually into a punitive school of educational rehabilitation.' Bennett has attributed this evolution to a change in the population of the school after the closing of the Penetang Reformatory in 1904 and the introduction of a juvenile justice system that 'criminalized' many children. He does not consider these changes as consequences of a critique of the original regime at the school. 'Taming "Bad Boys" of the "Dangerous Class": Child Rescue and Restraint at the Victoria Industrial School, 1887–1935,' *Histoire Sociale/Social History* 21 (May 1988): 74, and 'Turning "Bad Boys" into "Good Citizens": The Reforming Impulse of Toronto's Industrial School Movement, 1883 to the 1920s,' *Ontario History* 78 (September 1986): 209–15.

61 OSP, 1897, no. 1, 198, 212.

62 Curtis, *Building the Educational State*, 109–12.

63 OSP, 1897, no. 1, 194.

64 Michel Foucault, *The History of Sexuality*, 2: *The Use of Pleasure* (New York: Vintage, 1986), 25–32.

The Case of the 'One Good Chinaman': Rex v. Charles Lee Hing, *Stratford, Ontario, 1909*

MONA-MARGARET PON

On 2 October 1909 the Stratford *Daily Herald* printed this eye-catching headline: '15-YEAR OLD STRATFORD GIRL ESCAPES FROM CHINESE JOINT.' The story that followed was as gripping as its title promised:

> It appears that Charlie Lee Hing kept a laundry in Stratford [in 1907] where he employed a 13 year old orphan girl at large wages to help in the laundry. The girl ... alleges that a few days after she entered his employ the Chinaman assaulted her. Lately he has kept the 'Gold Dollar' restaurant in Woodstock and by a letter to this child offering big wages and saying there were other girls in his employ she was induced to work for him again last Monday. On Wednesday last she claims that he again brutally assaulted her. The child returned to Stratford yesterday in a stupor. Two local doctors examined her and found she had been drugged.[1]

Although some readers in 1909 might have been shocked and appalled, most would not have found this story incredible or fantastic. Indeed, this scenario might have serviced many social reform projects popular at the time – confirming yellow perilist fears, fuelling anti-Chinese immigration campaigns, and vindicating concerns of the dangers confronted by working single women, especially those employed by Chinese men. At first glance this 'little girl' and her horrific encounter with Hing seemed a perfect fit with the pattern of fiendish Chinese behaviour so often complained of in British Columbia and, more recently, in Toronto.

This story, as reported, ought to have played out according to a predictable script. A predatory Chinaman had lured, drugged, and raped an innocent, white girl. Justice would be served. But what if the victim was not a 'maidenly girl'[2] and the accused was not a 'fiendish Chinaman'? The result, in this case, was an extraordinary criminal trial in which the main characters defied easy categorization and no one did what might have been expected. For the historian, the outcome is a complex case study highlighting the unresolved tensions among race, class, and gender, complicated further by sex and sexuality. What becomes apparent in *Rex v. Charles Lee Hing* is that a discussion on race, sex, and interracial sex cannot be carried on without class analysis. As the array of social hierarchies come into play, everything is misaligned and turned around: the Chinaman goes free.

The criminal indictment case file for *Rex v. Charles Lee Hing* can be found among the court records housed at the Archives of Ontario. Researchers who have used these records will be familiar with the unpredictable nature of each individual file's contents. In this case, historians will be simultaneously elated and disappointed by their findings. An exhilarating discovery will be the twenty-one letters written between 1907 and 1909 by the complainant to the prisoner which were entered as evidence in Hing's defence. Unfortunately, the case file does not contain the preliminary testimonies sworn before the Stratford police magistrate or the trial transcripts. Nonetheless, the case file, other court records such as the judge's benchbook and the court minute books, together with newspaper reports, contain important pieces to reconstruct this rape trial. The case provides a unique opportunity to explore the dynamics of early twentieth-century practices and attitudes surrounding racial hierarchies, class biases, and patriarchal privileges.

On 1 October 1909 a working-class, white woman named Daisy Reid laid information against a Chinese man, Charles Lee Hing. Reid swore out that Hing first raped her in 1907 while she was ironing in his Stratford laundry. She alleged that he again assaulted her a few days before in Woodstock while she was working in his restaurant. Hing was arrested the next day in Woodstock and escorted to Stratford. On the 4th, evidence was taken in camera before a police magistrate, Reid's letters to Hing were entered as defence evidence, and Hing was committed to stand trial at the upcoming assize courts. Hing's first application for bail was denied. The judge reportedly said that 'in view of the difference between the Chinese and Canadian standards of morals, Chinamen should not be allowed to employ girls of the tender age of the complainant.'[3] On 26 October Hing was granted bail of $300 in cash and $3000 in cash bonds. According to the Toronto *Globe*: 'The Judge remarked that the fact of the girl being in the Chinaman's employ made the offence more serious' and hence the steep bail.[4] At the trial, Hing was indicted on the charge of raping Daisy Reid in the year 1907. Based on the testimonies and evidence, the presiding judge instructed the jury that 'the charge could not be substantiated under any statute and it would be absolutely unsafe to ... make a conviction.'[5] Without leaving their seats, the jury acquiesced. At 9 pm on 17 November 1909, following a five-hour trial, the 'Chinaman [was] a Free Man.'[6]

This is the basic chronology derived from news accounts. An examination of how this case was reported in newspapers and a closer look at Reid's letters will add greater complexity and density to this narrative. At the time the crown attorney, stymied by the 'peculiar' nature of the case, foresaw 'a good deal of difficulty'[7] to come in the trial; a newspaper proclaimed it 'most curious';[8] and the trial judge described it as the most puzzling he had ever come across.[9] This case, which, on the surface, ought to have ignited great moral indignation on behalf of the victim, instead aroused widespread bewilderment. The source of puzzlement stemmed from an ill fit between the 'predatory Chinaman' archetype and the evidence at hand; between what ought to have happened and the finer details. From beginning to end, Hing's behaviour and character would not be reconciled with the supposed perils wrought by his kind.

In news reports, Hing was described as a thirty-two-year-old, Presbyterian widower.[10] In 1909 he had been in Canada for almost sixteen years and, according to the Woodstock *Daily Sentinel*, was 'looked upon by many of the Chinamen in the district as a friend [and an] advisor.'[11] According to the Toronto *Daily Star*, Hing 'was regarded as a very respectable Chinaman. His education appeared to be above the average of his class.'[12] Educated or not, Charles Lee Hing would have made a striking physical presence in Stratford or Woodstock. At the time of the trial, both cities were racially and ethnically homogenous, composed mostly of immigrants from the British Isles.[13]

In the early twentieth century the large majority of Chinese in Canada were still on the west coast.[14] In 1911 there were only 2766 Chinese in all of Ontario, and they were scattered throughout the northern and southern regions.[15] According to the 1911 census data, Toronto's Chinese population of 1036 was the largest in Ontario. The community of 162 in Ottawa and 160 in Hamilton were the next largest enclaves of Ontario Chinese.[16] The 1901 census enumerated only five Chinese in Stratford and eight in Woodstock.[17] In 1911 this number increased just slightly to thirteen and sixteen, respectively.[18]

Despite the small numbers of Chinese in Stratford and Woodstock, neither city would have been immune to the various forms of anti-Chinese racism virulent in British Columbia and often echoed in Toronto.[19] News reports taken 'off the wire,' intense lobbying in Ottawa to restrict Chinese immigration, and the vocal efforts of social and moral reform groups to curtail Chinese civil rights in Canada all served to diffuse the 'yellow peril' myth. Relying heavily on rhetoric and *a priori* reasoning, anti-Chinese arguments held that *all* Chinamen were inherently prone towards immoral and criminal behaviour. The individual Chinese person was subsumed within a larger collectivity, which, in turn, was invested with values and habits deemed inferior and repulsive.

By the time of Hing's trial, alleged consequences of Chinese immigration into Canada had coalesced into a fatalistic paradigm, a predicted pattern of social, moral, and economic decline. This model interwove such themes as the fall of Canadian democratic institutions, the ruin of white labour, the Chinese inability to assimilate, and the debauchery and degradation of decent white women. It was on this latter theme that the Stratford press initially based its story-telling, case-reporting strategy.[20] However, this storyline was thwarted by a non-conformist cast of characters.

From a legal standpoint, the situation seemed equally unclear. In the 1906 Canadian Criminal Code, under the heading 'crimes against the person or reputation,' three indictable unlawful carnal knowledge offences were listed.[21] The first was the charge of rape – that is, having carnal knowledge of a woman not being the accused's wife and without her consent. The second was attempted rape, and the third was committing rape on a woman, who was not a spouse, under the age of fourteen.[22] The point of contention between the prosecution and the defence was Reid's age in 1907, the year of the alleged assault.

According to Reid, she turned fifteen on 18 September 1909.[23] If this claim were true or, more important, if it could be proven by the crown attorney, the charge against Hing would have been statutory rape, since the age of sexual consent was fourteen. This charge not only carried a different punishment from rape but also omitted the need to address the issue of female consent.[24] Thus, if Reid was underage in 1907, and if Hing had sexual relations with her, he was liable for criminal indictment whether or not she gave her consent. Determining Reid's age, however, proved a difficult task for the Crown. She was adopted and, at the time of the trial, her foster mother was dead. Reid herself could not produce a birth certificate and could give only her word that she was under age. But this assertion was deemed insufficient by the prosecution. L.H. Bradford, king's counsel in this case, 'thought it advisable to procure the evidence of some one other than Daisy Reid as to her age.'[25] Inquiries into this matter turned up that Reid was seventeen years old in 1909, and thus of legal consenting age in 1907.[26]

Concern over verifying Reid's age and the Crown's reluctance to base its case on her word arose after preliminary testimonies had been sworn and the letters to Hing had been produced as defence evidence. Reid had initially tried to deny authorship of these letters,[27] but this lie proved to be a futile attempt at self-protection. Reid was wise beyond her years: she understood that the letters could, and would, be used against her in public and in a court of law. Scholars of Canadian legal, social, and women's history have shown that a woman's character is placed on trial even, or especially, when she is the complainant in a sexual assault case.[28] This convention has held true in different historical time periods and geographic settings. The rape trial held in Stratford was not an exception. Daisy Reid, her moral character, and her reputation did not stand up well under social and legal scrutiny. On many counts, social conventions were in a state of disarray.

The problem was that Hing would not conform to the behavioural expectations of the 'predatory Chinaman,' while Reid seemed repeatedly and unabashedly to breech the moral codes accorded to her race and sex. Race, class, gender, and sexual lines were crossed and criss-crossed. But these boundaries were fault lines and, as this case pointed out, the spaces on either side were not as self-contained, stable, and well defined as had been assumed. News writers and editors employed their own strategies when dealing with these zigzagging lines and demarcated their own moral boundaries.

Soon after Hing's arrest an interesting competitive dynamic emerged between the Stratford and Woodstock newspapers. Stratford, home of the victim, quickly positioned Reid in the role of the underaged, exploited, orphan child lured, drugged, and raped by a Chinese man.[29] Woodstock, current home of the accused, responded with articles recounting his side of the story.[30] The Woodstock *Sentinel* did not deny that an assault may have occurred in 1907 in Stratford, but was quick to point out that no evidence existed of 'any misconduct upon the part of the Chinaman while she was working in Woodstock last week.'[31] While Stratford may have housed a 'terrible Chinese joint,' Woodstock, at least, was free of such vice and crime.

The two newspapers engaged in repartee. The *Sentinel* claimed that the Stratford *Herald* was 'considerably excited by the case' to the point that its journalistic judgment was clouded and its 'version' of the story near ridiculous.[32] 'Et tu,' responded the *Herald*, claiming that the paper 'there' could barely 'disguise its sympathy with the accused.'[33] Beneath this 'professional' jostling is an example of what historian Karen Dubinsky has termed 'moral boosterism,' wherein sex-related crimes were used as a gauge to measure an area's general moral condition and the efficacy of the local police and citizenry as keepers of law and moral order.[34] The issue of debate was not *if* an assault had occurred but *where* – in which city, which county – had this transgression taken place. From the onset, Reid's allegations and the relationship between this white woman and her Chinese employer were invested with broader social and moral implications. Aspects of anti-Chinese rhetoric were propounded by the *Herald* and conditionally endorsed by the *Sentinel*. In the early days of October, however, the basic structural integrity of the yellow peril myth would begin to buckle under the internal contradictions of this particular case. Three days after Hing's arrest, Reid's letters had become public knowledge and property.

On 5 October the *Sentinel* printed a long front-page story describing the 'conflicting lot of evidence ... heard in the Stratford police court yesterday.' 'The evidence,' continued the report, 'showed that Hing had been most generous in his treatment of the girl.' The *Sentinel* recounted how Reid repeatedly wrote to the prisoner claiming she was 'hard up' and asking for dresses, shoes, money, and employment at Hing's restaurant in Woodstock.[35] On 13 October the *Sentinel* quoted directly from the letters:

> In one letter she thanked 'Charlie' for a birthday present. Hing said he had sent her $1. In the same she proposed to come to him at Woodstock and said 'Don't tell anyone, but me and you will have a good time.'
>
> 'When I come to Woodstock I can get a coat, hat, and shoes and we will have a swell time, Charlie if you don't tell,' is a quotation from another alleged letter.[36]

The Stratford paper printed, verbatim, the 5 October story run by the *Sentinel*. However, the *Herald* tucked the report onto page 4 and cast editorial doubt on its accuracy with the preface: 'His Side of It Spread Large by One of Woodstock's Papers.'[37] Although the Stratford daily was more reticent in broadcasting the contents of Reid's letters, their existence could not be ignored. One week later, the Stratford paper reported: 'The girl in her affidavits both admits and denies having written some letters put in as evidence.'[38]

Reid's letters can be read from different angles and perspectives. In 1909 they were used by Hing's lawyer to exculpate his client and to blemish Reid's credibility as a Crown witness. For historians these letters are remarkable sources for many different reasons. They provide a partial glimpse into the life of one young, working-class woman in early twentieth-century, small-town Ontario. Finding documentary evidence created by women, and especially those living on the economic fringes of society, is often a daunting task for historians. In this light, Reid, quite unintentionally, bequeathed to us a rare historical treasure. She often chatted about her days, recounting her leisure and wage-earning activities. She included tidbits on special events happening in Stratford and told anecdotes about her and

Hing's common acquaintances. There was the time, for example, when Lee John was run over by a horse and rig, and another when the Avondale cemetery was decorated and the whole town turned out for a marching band parade.[39] We know that Reid attended Sunday school, enjoyed moving pictures, liked snowfalls and 'good sleighing,' and became tired when the weather turned 'awful hot.'[40] We know also that she continued working for Chinese men after Hing had moved away from Stratford in 1907. As an unskilled, female worker, there were limited wage-earning options available to her. She worked long days – 'from 7 or 7.30 till night' – and she worked sporadically.[41]

In the first letter, dated 4 June 1907, she told Hing that 'Lee John and Bang have been kind to me so far.'[42] Six months later, however, she wrote the following: 'I came very near quitting work for Lee John but I could not get a good job last week. But I think the beginning of the New Year I may get a really good steady job and not far away from home and next Spring I am going to try get mother to come down ... and I will work for you[.] How would you like that?'[43] The new year came to pass and Reid was still in Stratford. Only two of the letters on file were written in 1908, and it is unclear where, and by whom, Reid was employed. Then in February 1909 she wrote: 'I am not working for Hong any more but I think I will try and go and learn the millinery business in a few days.'[44] It does not appear that she acquired this new skill. Throughout 1909 Reid's life was undergoing some difficult changes, and her increasing anxiety was reflected in her correspondence to Hing.

Written over three years, Reid's letters help us trace her relationship with a Chinese man. What becomes increasingly clear as one reads through these twenty-one pieces of correspondence is that Hing was considered to be a friend of the Reid family. He was constantly urged to visit their home in Stratford and made to feel welcome over holidays such as Christmas or New Year's. Many of the notes opened with the salutation: 'We received your ever welcome letter and was glad to hear from you,' implying that his correspondence was shared with her foster mother and brother, Charles Reid. Once, in 1907, when the post office mislaid one of Hing's letters, Daisy Reid wrote: 'I am very sorry I did not get it before. Mother thought it was strange you didnot [*sic*] write before this.'[45] Thus, at least in the earlier years, their letter-writing relationship was not carried on in any covert or devious fashion. The clandestine tone of her writing began to emerge in the letters written from June 1909 through to the end of September, just before Hing's arrest.

Daisy Reid's foster mother, who had been ill for some time, died on 9 June 1909.[46] Daisy and her foster brother were then moved to Greenville,

Michigan, to live with other siblings. Throughout this period, as Reid's life became less predictable and increasingly out of her control, she turned to Hing for assistance. Letters written to him in these months grew increasingly demanding, conspiratorial, and even desperate. The press focused on these letters and, indeed, they posed the most damage to the Crown's case and to Reid's moral character. Part of Reid's difficulty was that she had to stop working for wages in order to care for her mother and the house. Without her own income, she started asking Hing to send her things. Such requests were not uncommon, but while she was working she had usually asked for trivial items such as fancy chocolate boxes or picture postcards to add to her collection.[47] When her mother became unable to eat, Reid asked Hing to send a roast chicken. She explained to him: 'The doctor told us to get a nice chicken & I tried but couldnot [sic] get one ... it is bad to bother you Charlie but I couldnot get one anywhere.'[48] Given the long-term relationship between Hing and the Reid family, he may have seemed a natural supporter to whom Daisy Reid could turn.

On 5 June 1909 Reid wrote to Hing from Stratford: 'Mother has been very sick and she can not live but a few hours more. My sister and two brothers are home. I will try and come down and see you because [we] will go to Greenville about next Saturday. Charlie would you be kind enough to send me a little money as I want a new dress. I have not been able to work much. When you answer this letter you must register it and do not sign your name.'[49]

One day before her foster mother's death, Reid responded to a letter from him: 'Charlie I would love to come and work for you but I half [sic] to go to Greenville with my brother and sister but when I get a new dress I will come and see you a day before we go away. Well will you try and give me a little money at once and I will try my best to work for you. Answer at once and don't sign your name.'[50] Then from Greenville, Reid wrote: 'Mother died last Wednesday ... at 7 o'clock and we all came with the body to Greenville Michigan. They are going to bury her this afternoon at 3 o'clock. We received the chicken very safely. I came here to live with my sister and I think I will try and go back to Stratford as soon as I can.'[51] On 10 September 1909 Reid began to plan her escape. She wrote to Hing:

> I will have to go to school in January and all the time after then and this is my only chance to come & work for you and see you for a while. I am feeling better now ... My sister does not want me to go but I told her I knew a girl down in Woodstock ... But if I come I will half [sic] to be very careful of myself as I will have an operation in my stomach at Stratford Hospital in December ... Don't tell anyone I am coming because then there will be terrible trouble if my

brother finds out & do not sign your name to the letter. (Be sure) ... Answer so I get it Wednes. morning as I am afraid she might get it.[52]

On the 16th she wrote again: 'Received your letter. Thanks for birthday present. I will leave here a week from next Tuesday for Woodstock to work ["to work" is crossed out] don't tell anyone but me & you will have a good time. Am feeling better now ... Do not write any more now.'[53]

The last letter in Hing's case file is undated, but appears to accompany an envelope postdated 22 September 1909. In it Reid wrote:

Got in with my sister today noon. If you send me the $6.00 for fare for my sister she goes home on Monday and send me a ticket and I will come & work for a while answer at once for sure. Answer at once

> Address
> Daisy R
> Stratford Ont.[54]

She told friends she was going to Port Dover and, instead, took the train to Woodstock. She was with Hing for two days before, suddenly, she returned to Stratford. There she was examined by doctors, told she had been drugged, and became a ward of the Children's Aid Society. Under the guidance of a Reverend W.A. Gunton, she swore to the rape. Until this time she had never told anyone of Hing's 'mistreatment.' Thus, concluded the Woodstock *Sentinel*, the alleged assault was a 'case of his word against hers.'[55] Unfortunately for Reid, the defence and the press had three years' worth of her written words. In court, each of her twenty-one letters was read aloud and Reid was subjected to a two-hour cross-examination.[56] Shortly thereafter, Hing was acquitted.[57] But had he, at some time, coerced Daisy Reid into sexual relations?

In this case of he said/she said, not only did Daisy Reid inadvertently say a lot but she often said the wrong things. Under oath, she tried to deny writing the letters to Hing, and in the process she perjured herself. These letters were damning pieces of evidence. They were read as being overly familiar, intimately confidential, and even 'couched in affection.' Once these letters became public property, the Stratford press retreated from her defence. Had the letters not existed or had they not been produced as evidence, the original storyline crafted by the Stratford *Herald* – the young girl rescued from Chinese joint scenario – might have held water. But in her writings Reid revealed what was considered to be a terrible moral flaw: she yearned for pretty things, things she could not afford to buy for herself. Then she asked a Chinese man to provide her with these fineries. It was all too easy, really, to see Daisy Reid not as the victim of a horrific sexual crime, but as a 'good times girl.' She had either consented to perform sexual acts with a Chinese man, in exchange for presents and promises, or she had willingly placed herself at peril.

If Reid had told someone about the 1907 rape, the Crown's case would not have rested solely on her word. The grand jury, remarking on the case and the final verdict, highlighted the uncorroborated nature of the prosecutorial evidence.[58] In its final report on the case the Stratford *Herald* hypothesized that if Reid had made complaints to a friend or to her foster mother, the outcome might have been different.[59] Thus, according to this paper, even the testimony of a woman from her grave might have undermined the credibility of Charles Lee Hing. But Reid had never told on Hing, and there was no one to speak on her behalf, to lend credence to her claims.

Hing, on the other side, was able to gather impressive resources to his defence, drawing from both the Chinese and the English-speaking communities in southern Ontario. Stratford and Woodstock papers referred to Hing's wide assortment of supporters, ready to finance a vigorous defence.[60] And the *Herald* cautioned Reid supporters to be on the alert. Hing's $3000 bond was paid by a Jim Lee living in Toronto.[61] Hing's brother and nephew, harking from Brantford and Hamilton, respectively, were in constant attendance to lend support.[62] On the day of Hing's trial the courtroom was packed with curious spectators and crowded with Hing's advocates. According to the *Sentinel*, many prominent professional and business men were on hand to testify for the prisoner, but most were never even summoned to the stand.[63] Hing's lawyer called only three witnesses. Hing testified on his own behalf, and the other two, Woodstock's police chief and Presbyterian church minister, were character witnesses.[64] Law and moral order fell on the side of the defendant – the Chinese man.

If Hing were white, he would have been on level standing with any of Stratford's and Woodstock's white middle class. He was, after all, a self-made Christian man. But he was Chinese. He had worked past the economic constraints oppressive to most Chinese immigrants. He had crossed into the economic class of men who had power and authority, as the employer, over a white woman. Charles Lee Hing accomplished something that Chinese immigrants were mythically incapable of – he assimilated. Hing became the beneficiary of what Barrington Walker has termed the 'residual benefits of white patriarchy.'[65] By virtue of his sex, but compromised by his race, Hing was given partial access to the privileges of white male prerogatives. The patriarchal circle had closed, leaving Daisy Reid, a white woman, on the outside.

Against the odds, Charles Lee Hing had become a respectable Chinese in

Canada. This one man's seemingly exemplary life history flew in the face of a predicted pattern of Chinese behaviour. How could he be explained within the yellow peril paradigm? Hing was a frontal assault on a belief system based on knowing and legislating Chinese immigrants as a single predictable entity. How could it be maintained that Hing and other Chinamen like him were few and far between, and that stringent immigration policies were necessary? To maintain effectiveness, anti-Chinese rhetoric needed to reconcile Hing and the 'predatory Chinaman' stereotype. Towards this end, the One Good Chinaman theory operated as a conceptual loophole out of the structural rigidity of the yellow peril paradigm. This loophole made it possible, within a race-conscious and racially organized culture, to deal with those like Hing: the anomalies, the blips inside the pattern. And the cunning of the theory was that it left the paradigm intact. Herein, Daisy Reid played a strategic role. She was the escape out of the loophole and back into the paradigm. She embodied the dangers and the consequences of interracial liaisons. Reid was a fallen woman, and a Chinese man, albeit an exceptional one, was the cause of her ruination. Physically, with her body and her outrageous sex, Reid formed a bridge between the theory and the paradigm, connecting Hing to the rest of the yellow race. In her ruined state, she protected and proved the paradigm's validity. In juxtaposition to the exceptional Hing there was Daisy Reid – 'Yet Another Bad Girl.'[66] Operating in tandem, the existence of one archetype made the other viable.

The idea of the One Good Chinaman made it possible for the *Sentinel* to alternate between stories defending Hing's (and hence Woodstock's) good reputation and stories describing loathsome Chinamen in Montreal who held innocent white girls as captive sex slaves.[67] There was no contradiction, and the truth of the latter story need not be questioned because Hing was a rare exception to the Chinese rule. Even the Stratford *Herald* contributed to the construction of the exceptional Charlie Lee Hing, describing the accused as 'rather a fine looking Oriental, well-dressed in American style, and indeed [he] is a splendid specimen of the well-to-do Americanized Chinese.'[68] The Toronto *Daily Star* condescendingly, and ironically, given the charges against him, described Hing as a 'superior Celestial' and a 'good Christian boy.'[69]

Then there was Daisy Reid – a white woman who worked for a Chinaman. Sympathies Reid may have garnered because of her struggling working-class background were offset by her having worked in a Chinese business. This choice of occupation, and her tenacious pursuit of it, placed her among the lowest of working-class women. By becoming affectionate with her Chinese employer, by transgressing racial boundaries, she also forsook her white racial privileges. For all these reasons, she was excluded from the 'maidenly girl' category. Thus, in the multifariousness of social hierarchies brought to bear on the case, Reid retained no leverage, no claim to credibility or respectability. She left the space wide open for Hing to stake his claims in class and gender superiority. But what of his race? What happened was a reverse ricochet effect whereby Hing's Chineseness rebounded onto Reid and damaged her case and her reputation. In the end it was Reid, in her proximity to Hing, who suffered the consequences of anti-Chinese racism. She was the casualty, the object lesson, in this conceptual deployment of the One Good Chinaman theory.

But this is not the end of the story. In the Charles Lee Hing criminal case file there is one small clue pointing towards a tragic aftermath. On file is a letter dated 11 October 1910, almost one year after Hing's acquittal, in which G.G. McPherson, the Stratford crown attorney, had the following request made to the registrar at Osgoode Hall in Toronto:

> Rex vs. Charles Lee Hing
>
>   This case was I understand tried last November at Stratford and certain exhibits were put in. There is now an enquiry to be held at Stratford in connection with an inquest and Mr. McPherson the Crown Attorney wishes to have the exhibits forwarded to him. Will you please have them sent accordingly to Mr. McPherson.[70]

A handwritten notation tells us that this request was fulfilled. Another letter dated 19 October indicates that all exhibits were being returned from Stratford to Toronto. Newspaper reports help to fill in some of the gaps concerning an inquest held in 1910 which somehow involved Daisy Reid, Charles Lee Hing, and the letters she had begun writing to him years before.

On 22 September 1910 the Stratford *Daily Herald* printed the following story:

>   Body of Infant Found in Attic of Ontario St[reet] House ... The remains are those of a new-born or a few days' old baby ... From a cursory examination coroner J.P. Rankin, who was called in could not tell whether the babe had been still-born or how it had come to its death. He estimated that it had been there about a year or a considerable number of months.[71]

The finder of the body, a young man named Harry Dockerill, had been in the attic searching for some lost pigeons and accidentally placed his hand on the infant's skull. The Dockerills, who lived directly beneath the attic, had been bothered by a 'faintly apparent but inexplicable odor' for some time. This mystery was solved. It now remained to determine the cause of death and those who were responsible for the infant's birth and death.

In its first report the *Herald* constructed a general scenario of this 'gruesome discovery.' There was no floor in the attic and the body was found lying, unclothed and uncovered, in between two joists. The Dockerill family had been in the house for only the past three months. Before their occupancy, the house had been vacant. A year previously, however, 'at the time when the body is supposed to have been put there, an old lady, who has since died, was living in the lower apartments, Mrs. Reid by name. Since, however, the body was found in the attic, it could have been put there without her being any the wiser, as there is a stair-case up the outside, to the second storey.'[72] Beyond this information, the *Herald* could speculate no further. A coroner's hearing into the matter could not be called until the crown attorney, who was away on business, returned to Stratford.

The initial inquest was held on 4 October and a dozen witnesses were called forth, including previous and current tenants, the owner, an architect, a coroner, a health inspector, and a police officer. The following information came to light. The remains were of a fully formed infant so decomposed that it was impossible to determine its sex. It was estimated that the body had been there from at least one year up to a year and a half. Next to the remains were an old valise, which was closed but unclasped, and also an edition of the Stratford *Daily Herald* dated 10 September 1909. The architect described the building's layout, explaining that the attic could only be accessed by the apartment in the west end of the house. The owner and previous tenants helped to reconstruct the history of occupancy and to account for the children born to tenants over the past two years. It came out that an elderly Mrs Reid had lived in the west end of the house and that she had an adopted daughter. One witness had known Daisy Reid and stated: 'Daisy had worked in a Chinese laundry.' The inquest was then adjourned until 18 October, at which time important documentary evidence would be produced and out-of-town people contacted.[73]

The out-of-towners were Reid and Hing. The important documents were Reid's letters, which once again became pivotal evidence in a criminal investigation. Details on the inquest hearings are sketchy. The Stratford paper ran only three stories, while the Woodstock *Sentinel* never reported on the inquest. The paper and the city no longer had a vested interest in Hing, for he had moved on. The attorney general's efforts to track him down as a witness led to uncertain ends. Hing's lawyer from 1909 thought he was in Toronto, while other sources claimed he might be in Brantford.[74] Daisy Reid was still a ward of the Children's Aid Society and living with a family in Niagara Falls. CAS officials recommended that an officer be sent to bring her to Stratford. Although a CAS representative was present at the second inquest, it is unclear whether Hing or Reid was in attendance. Reid's letters did, however, make it to the hearing. But once again the letters failed to secure a criminal conviction, this time in Daisy Reid's favour. The inquest was held in camera, but insufficient evidence existed to place responsibility for the infant's death. The coroner's jury returned an 'open verdict' to the effect that 'an unknown child came to its death by means unknown.'[75] A few days later Reid's letters were returned to Toronto and replaced in the *Rex v. Charles Lee Hing* criminal case file.

Although it is not unreasonable or impossible to believe that Daisy Reid gave birth, it is difficult to determine the date of the infant's birth and the identity of the biological father. Was the child born in the spring of 1909, before her foster mother died and Daisy moved from Stratford to Michigan? Was Daisy referring to her pregnancy when she wrote about a stomach operation scheduled for December 1909?[76] If this was so, and if she was accurate in calculating the date of conception, she would have been seven or eight months pregnant in November, at the time of Hing's rape trial. Perhaps, however, this operation was unrelated to a pregnancy.

Another possibility is that Daisy Reid gave birth in September 1909. Given that a newspaper dated 10 September 1909 was found next to the body, it is likely that the infant was placed in the attic sometime after its publication. On the 10th, Reid had written to Hing from Greenville, Michigan, planning and plotting her departure. In this letter she mentioned the operation, but told Hing, 'I am feeling better now.'[77] In the next letter, she reiterated the exact same message.[78] If the infant was born in September, Reid would have conceived in the beginning of 1909. In a letter written in February, Reid had said: 'I am not working for Hong anymore.'[79] Then, two months later, she wrote to Hing: 'Charlie Hong is going to move in a couple of weeks.' This letter, which contained little else of obvious significance, was entered as Exhibit 1 for the defence case.[80] Had she told Charles Lee Hing she was pregnant? In June 1909, when her letters became secretive and desperate, she would have been five or six months pregnant. Was her changing body becoming more difficult to hide as she was asking Hing for a new dress, for a place to which she could escape? It is unclear whether the trial lawyers and presiding judge were aware that she had been pregnant. There is no mention of a child in the judge's notes or in the newspapers. She might, however, have confessed to the birth while she swore out her preliminary testimony, which was taken in closed court. Had Daisy Reid been coerced into sexual intercourse and impregnated by this other Chinese man, Charlie Hong? Where did Charles Lee Hing fit into these affairs?

Despite all the research historians can do, there are some fundamental questions we may never answer. Did Reid and Hing have sexual contact? Let us say they did and that it was consensual sex. Why did Reid accuse him of rape? Did the rape charge stem from Reid's resentment, guilt, shame, or anger at having to go through the motions of sexual intercourse in order to acquire things – the dress, shoes, hat, the money, and the employment – things she needed and desired? Consent, as a legal category and construct, absolved the judge and jurors from considering reasons why Reid may have sexually complied against her deeper wishes. Or was the accusation of rape the most expedient and socially accepted explanation for making love with a Chinese man? Was Reid 'found out' and her rape charge an instinctive response to being caught in a socially despised relationship?

What if Hing was guilty of the crime, and Reid had felt too frightened, too helpless, to report his assault? Would the 'not guilty' verdict have been passed if Hing had not been an 'Americanized Chinaman,' a prominent, respected, and Christian businessman with the economic resources to launch a strong defence case? What if Reid had come from a solid middle-class family, rather than being of 'unknown parentage'[81] and residing in tenement housing? Recall that Reid was identified by a witness at the 1910 coroner's inquest by the words, 'Daisy worked in a Chinese laundry.' Through elliptical thinking, this phrase not only encapsulated her employment record but alluded to her sexual history and questioned her moral character. What if Reid had kept and produced the letters she had received from Hing? To what words, hints, subtle pleas, or threats did Reid respond when she promised never to forget him?[82]

Who would have thought that things would turn out as they did? How could a Chinese man accused of raping a teenaged, white woman go free? Perhaps, however, the outcome should not be such a surprise. Daisy Reid was no match for Charles Lee Hing, the One Good Chinaman.

NOTES

I would like to thank several grant agencies that funded my work: the Social Sciences and Humanities Research Council, Toronto Chinese Businessmen's Association, Federation of Chinese-Canadian Professionals (Ontario), Canadian Federation of University Women, and Robert F. Harney Memorial Trust Fund. I am grateful to Phillip Bird for taking the time and having the enthusiasm to talk and work through historical 'conundrums.'

1 Stratford *Daily Herald*, 2 October 1909, 1.

2 For a discussion on this concept of the 'maidenly girl' and its diametric opposite, the 'designing woman,' see Karen Dubinsky, *Improper Advances: Rape and Heterosexual Conflict in Ontario, 1880–1929* (Chicago: University of Chicago Press, 1993).

3 Woodstock *Daily Sentinel*, 13 October 1909, 1; also in Toronto *Globe*, 13 October 1909, 5.

4 Toronto *Globe*, 27 October 1909, 7.

5 Stratford *Daily Herald*, 18 November 1909, 1.

6 Woodstock *Daily Sentinel*, 17 November 1909, 1.

7 Archives of Ontario (AO), RG 22 unprocessed files, County of Perth, miscellaneous correspondence, 1903–11, box 4, L.H. Bradford to G.G. McPherson, 11 November 1909.

8 Woodstock *Daily Sentinel*, 2 October 1909, 1.

9 Ibid., 17 November 1909, 1.

10 Ibid., 13 October 1909, 1; Toronto *Daily Star*, 4 October 1909, 1; Toronto *Globe*, 13 October 1909, 5; Stratford *Daily Herald*, 12 October 1909, 1.

11 Woodstock *Daily Sentinel*, 5 October 1909, 1.

12 Toronto *Daily Star*, 4 October 1909, 1.

13 In 1901 there were 113 'Negroes' in Woodstock, and this number dropped to 60 in 1911. Although the African-descent population in Stratford was much smaller, this city tended to have a slightly larger Eastern European population than did Woodstock. *Census of Canada*, 1901, vol. 1, table 11: Origins of the People, 338–9.

14 For general histories of Chinese immigration and settlement in Canada, see Anthony Chan, *Gold Mountain* (Vancouver: New Star Books, 1983); David Chuenyan Lai, *Chinatowns: Towns within Cities in Canada* (Vancouver: UBC Press, 1988); Peter S. Li, *The Chinese in Canada* (Toronto: Oxford University Press, 1988); Edgar Wickberg et al., *From China to Canada: A History of Chinese in Canada* (Toronto: McClelland & Stewart, 1982).

15 *Census of Canada*, 1911, vol. 2, table 7: Origins of the People by Sub-districts, 204–5. In Northern Ontario, for example, there were 165 Chinese in the District of Thunder Bay and Rainy River, and 149 in the Nipissing District. Ibid., table 8: Origins of the People by District, 336–7.

16 Ibid., table 7: Origins of the People by Sub-districts, 248–9; 234–5; 218–19.

17 *Census of Canada*, 1901, vol. 1, table 11: Origins of the People, 338–9. In the 1901 census, Chinese and Japanese were enumerated under one single category. It is safe, however, to assume that these numbers for Stratford and Woodstock refer to Chinese immigrants. In 1911, when the two groups were categorically distinguished, there was one Japanese person in Woodstock and none in Stratford. *Census of Canada*, 1911, vol. 2, table 7: Origins of the People by Subdistrict, 234–5, 238–9.

18 In 1911 the total population in Stratford was 12,946, and in Woodstock, 9320. *Census of Canada*, vol. 2, table 7: Origins of the People by Sub-districts, 238–9, 234–5.

19 For discussions on attitudes towards Chinese in Canada, see Kay J. Anderson, *Vancouver's Chinatown: Racial Discourse in Canada* (Montreal: McGill-Queen's University Press, 1990); Gillian Creese, 'Exclusion or Solidarity? Vancouver Workers Confront the "Oriental Problem,"' *BC Studies* 80 (1988–9): 24–51; M. Pon, 'Like a Chinese Puzzle: The Construction of Chinese Masculinity in *Jack Canuck*,' in Joy Parr and Mark Rosenfeld, eds., *Gender and History in Canada* (Toronto: Copp Clark, 1996), 88–100; Patricia Roy, *A White Man's Province: British Columbia Politicians and Chinese and Japanese Immigrants, 1858–1914* (Vancouver: UBC Press, 1989); Peter Ward, *White Canada Forever: Popular Attitudes and Public Policy toward Orientals in British Columbia* (Montreal: McGill-Queen's University Press, 1978).

20 For studies on the moral panic surrounding relations between white women and Chinese, and the various ways in which this panic was manipulated to instigate anti-Chinese policies and laws, see Constance Backhouse, 'White Women's Labour Laws: Anti-Chinese Racism in Early 20th Century Canada,' *Law and History Review* 14 (1996): 315–68; Carolyn Strange, *Toronto's Girl Problem: The Perils and Pleasures of the City, 1880–1930* (Toronto: University of Toronto Press, 1995); Mariana Valverde, *The Age of Light, Soap, and Water: Moral Reform in English Canada, 1885–1925* (Toronto: McClelland & Stewart, 1991); James W.St.G. Walker, *'Race,' Rights and the Law in the Supreme Court of Canada: Historical Case Studies* (Toronto: Osgoode Society for Canadian Legal History and Wilfrid Laurier Press, 1996).

21 For a concise description and analysis of the history of Canadian sexual assault laws, see Constance Backhouse, 'Nineteenth-Century Canadian Rape Law, 1800–92,' in David H. Flaherty, ed., *Essays in the History of Canadian Law*, vol. 2 (Toronto: University of Toronto Press, 1983), 200–47.

22 *Selected Chapters of the Revised Statutes of Canada, 1906, and Amendments, 1907–1909, Relating to the Criminal Law* (Ottawa 1909), 72–3.

23 AO, Judges' Benchbooks, RG 22-491-1-13, Justice Teetzel, 22 June 1909–March 1910, box 2, 171. In a letter to Hing dated 10 September 1909 Reid wrote, 'my birthday is Saturday week,' but made no reference to her age. AO, Criminal Assize Indictment Case Files, RG 22-392-0-5107, box 122 (hereafter Case Files).

24 In 1909 the punishment for committing rape on a woman was death or life imprisonment, and for statutory rape it was life imprisonment with the lash. Canadian Criminal Code, section 301, chapter 146.

25 AO, RG 22 unprocessed files, County of Perth, miscellaneous correspondence, 1903–11, box 4, L.H. Bradford to G.G. McPherson, 11 November 1909.

26 Ibid., Chief of Police, Greenville, Michigan, to Bradford, 1 November 1910.

27 Woodstock *Daily Sentinel*, 13 October 1909, 1; Toronto *Globe*, 13 October 1909, 5.

28 See, for example, Backhouse, 'Nineteenth-Century Canadian Rape Law'; Dubinsky, *Improper Advances*; Strange, *Toronto's Girl Problem*.

29 Stratford *Daily Herald*, 2 October 1909, 1.

30 Woodstock *Daily Sentinel*, 5 October 1909, 1.
31 Ibid.
32 Ibid., 4 October 1909, 1.
33 Stratford *Daily Herald*, 6 October 1909, 4.
34 Dubinsky, *Improper Advances*, 67–8.
35 Woodstock *Daily Sentinel*, 5 October 1909, 1.
36 Ibid., 13 October 1909, 1.
37 Stratford *Daily Herald*, 6 October 1909, 4.
38 Ibid., 12 October 1909, 1.
39 Case Files, letters dated 4 June, 19 July, 4 August 1907.
40 See, for example, ibid., letters dated 11 July, 18 September, 18 November, 19 June, 11 August 1907.
41 Ibid., letter dated 27 October 1908.
42 Ibid., letter dated 4 June 1907.
43 Ibid., letter dated 18 November 1907.
44 Ibid., letter dated 10 February 1909.
45 Ibid., letter dated 7 November 1907.
46 In her letters, Reid had referred to her mother's bouts of ill-health since 1907.
47 Case Files, letters dated 11 August and 7 November 1907, 27 November 1908.
48 Ibid., letter dated 27 May 1909.
49 Ibid., letter dated 5 June 1909.
50 Ibid., 8 June 1909.
51 Ibid., letter dated 15 June 1909.
52 Ibid., letter dated 10 September 1909.
53 Ibid., letter dated 16 September 1909.
54 Ibid., letter dated 22 September 1909.
55 Woodstock *Daily Sentinel*, 5 October 1909, 1.
56 Ibid., 17 November 1909, 1.
57 Ibid.;´ Stratford *Daily Herald*, 18 November 1909, 1; AO, Judges' Benchbooks, RG 22-491-1-13, box 2, Justice Teetzel, 22 June 1909–March 1910, 171–3.
58 AO, Supreme Court of Ontario Criminal Assize Clerk Reports, County of Perth, RG 22-391, 15 November–18 November 1909.
59 Stratford *Daily Herald*, 18 November 1909, 1.
60 Woodstock *Daily Sentinel*, 7 October 1909, 1; Stratford *Daily Herald*, 8 October 1909, 1.
61 AO, RG 22 unprocessed files, County of Perth, miscellaneous correspondence, 1903–11, box 4, 24 November 1909.
62 Stratford *Daily Herald*, 5 October 1909, 4.
63 Woodstock *Daily Herald*, 17 November 1909, 1.
64 AO, Judges' Benchbooks, RG 22-491-1-13, Justice Teetzel, 22 June 1909–March 1910, box 2, 173.
65 Barrington Walker, 'Sexual Conflict, Black Patriarchy, and the Law: Reading the Story of George and Eliza Ross in Ontario's Criminal Case Files, Essex

County, Ontario, 1882,' paper presented at Canadian Historical Association, Ottawa, June 1998.

66 I am indebted to Carolyn Strange for pointing out the co-dependence of these two social constructs.

67 Woodstock *Daily Sentinel*, 15 November 1909, 1.

68 Stratford *Daily Herald*, 4 October 1909, 1.

69 Toronto *Daily Star*, 4 October 1909, 1.

70 Case Files, G.G. McPherson to A.F. McLean, 11 October 1910.

71 Stratford *Daily Herald*, 22 September 1910, 1.

72 Ibid.

73 Ibid., 5 October 1910, 1.

74 AO, RG 22 unprocessed files, County of Perth, miscellaneous correspondence, 1903–11, box 4.

75 Stratford *Daily Herald*, 19 October 1910, 1.

76 Case Files, letter dated 10 September 1909.

77 Ibid.

78 Ibid., letter dated 16 September 1909.

79 Ibid., letter dated 10 February 1909.

80 Reid's letter, entered as Exhibit 1, reads as follows:

Stratford Ont
April 21st [1909]

Dear Friend Charlie

We recieved your ever welcome letter and was glad to hear from you. We are all well hoping to find you the same. I should of [*sic*] answered your letter sooner but have been busy and did not get time. How is you business now. did you get many presents for Easter I got quite a few Charlie Hong is going to move in a couple of weeks.

Well I guess I must close for now as I am making some blouse waists answer soon

Yours Truly
D.

For a list of exhibits, see Case Files, 'List of Exhibits filed on the trial of this action 16th day of November 1909.'

81 Woodstock *Daily Sentinel*, 13 October 1909, 1.

82 Case Files, letter dated 19 July 1907.

'By Every Means in Our Power': Maternal and Child Welfare in Ontario, 1900–1945

CYNTHIA R. COMACCHIO

The development of a modern public health system in Ontario owes much to the province's children. In the opening years of the twentieth century, growing public sensitivity to infant and maternal health, as harbingers of the province's (and the nation's) future status, motivated a reform campaign that eventually manifested itself in social policy and the state structures necessary to support it. Ontario, as the most populous, urbanized, and industrialized of the provinces, containing both national and provincial capitals within its boundaries, was also the leader in national health and welfare concerns. It was the first to establish a specialized child welfare division in its Department of Health. During the interwar years, Ontario's newly reconfigured Department of Health was widely lauded as the Canadian exemplar in modern health systems, particularly in its child and maternal welfare programs.

Much of Ontario's leadership role can be credited to the efforts of, and within, its capital city. By 1920 Toronto had the best-organized municipal public health apparatus in Canada, a large part of which was devoted to the cause. Toronto's Hospital for Sick Children was also the first pediatric hospital in Canada, and one of the earliest established in North America. The pre-eminent Canadian pediatrician of the day, and the campaign's unofficial 'grandmaster,' was the hospital's Dr Alan Brown, who acted as an official consultant to the federal government and to various provincial governments. Much of the pediatric research, and most of the childrearing advice literature integral to the campaign's goals, emanated from Toronto and Ottawa.

Finally, the central role played by Dr Helen MacMurchy, at both the provincial and the federal levels, ensured that much of the campaign's story is Ontario based. MacMurchy's declaration of its purpose – 'To glorify, dignify, and purify motherhood, by every means in our power' – helped to rally national attempts to save mothers and infants from preventable illness and death. Physician, health activist, author of the Ontario Board of Health's critical series of infant mortality reports in the years 1910– 13, and first chief of the Child Welfare Division of the federal government's new health department in 1919, MacMurchy was ideally positioned to issue this call to arms.

Organizing the Crusade: The Problem and Its Solutions

Unfolding within an international movement, the campaign to save Ontario's mothers and babies was closely modelled on earlier initiatives in the United States, Great Britain, and France. Operating largely under the aegis of Social Gospel reform, the campaign aimed to lower the horrific infant and maternal mortality rates. Each year, one in five Canadian infants died from common respiratory and intestinal ailments in the first twelve months. MacMurchy's *Report on Maternal Mortality* (1928) also estimated that 1500 mothers across the nation died annually because of complications in childbirth.[1] Though scant and frequently impressionistic, contemporary statistics confirmed that this loss was a class mortality, afflicting primarily the ill-fed, ill-housed, often recently arrived families of workers. The sense of urgency about these deaths was heightened by influential pseudoscientific theories of the time. Eugenicists sounded dire warnings about the imminent degeneration – even devolution – of Canadian society, owing to ill-advised marriages and unconsidered reproduction, ill-informed child care and childrearing practices, and the reckless intermingling of the 'races.' Illness and deviance appeared endemic. Recognizing the enormity of the problem and its threat to social order, middle-class reformers looked to the state to intervene in the process of social reproduction.[2]

Social critics of the time understood that reproduction encompassed more than the biological function and included the socialization, physical maintenance, and emotional nurture of all family members. The family, therefore, played a crucial social role.[3] Discounting the environmental and subjective components of health, factors that all too often hinged on family economics, early twentieth-century doctors explained the crisis epitomized by high infant and maternal mortality as a 'failure of motherhood.' Too many mothers, especially those distinguished by 'race' and social class, were ignorant about their all-important reproductive duties. Since it is impossible to make dependent infants and children responsible for their own health and upbringing, mothers had to be made responsible. Medical supervision and regulation, doctors argued, offered the best hope for improved 'racial' prospects. Doctors therefore became the foremost proponents of a 'modern, scientific motherhood' as the answer to a perceived crisis in the family that translated into a crisis in the social order. Given the stakes depicted by those intent on such regulation, society and the state were obliged to support it.[4]

The regulation of reproduction, doctors argued, required nothing less than a state-funded, professionally directed, actively interventionist and 'scientific' program. Such a program would ensure the health of prospective 'mothers of the land' and produce healthy infants, its first objective. But it would also, as all nature of maternalist reformers believed, encourage the 'proper' nurture, maintenance, and socialization of those infants in the interests of continued national progress and economic productivity. Science and technology were restructuring the world. Childhood, too, had to be reconfigured to reflect evolving social needs and aspirations, and to eradicate the difficulties that doctors attributed to improper, inferior, and outmoded childrearing practices.[5]

As the movement's ideologues, strategists, and administrators, the emergent caste of family experts represented by medical doctors was not merely performing its defined role in guarding the nation's health. In striving to modernize motherhood, and consequently childhood, doctors were leading a collection of professional and lay supporters to intervene in the process of social change. They were intent on using science and state intervention as cloaks of modernity, but their 'modern' rhetoric only thinly disguised continuities with past concepts of the ideal society. The ideal projected by the child welfare campaigners, with doctors in the lead, was a modern motherhood and childhood that preserved traditional power relations.

The concerns of public health reformers about communicable diseases, especially as they affected infants and young children, are borne out by the statistics of those years. Although they probably underestimate the true incidence of illness and its outcome, the statistics at least allow an impression of the impact of communicable diseases on the population. In Ontario, between 1902 and 1911, with an average of 2000 reportable deaths per year, it is clear that these diseases claimed at least one in six children under fourteen years, and one in ten under five years. The highest death rate was in the first year of life, where the toll was nearly double that for the second year and for the entire five-to-nine age group. In 1922 respiratory and contagious diseases accounted for nearly 23 per cent of all deaths under one year, with diarrhea and enteritis comprising another 18 per cent.[6] Many Ontario families understood firsthand the suffering wrought by ill health and early death.

International bacteriological research had pinpointed the three leading causes of infant mortality: prematurity and congenital debility, intestinal disorders, and respiratory diseases.[7] The all-too-common intestinal problems appeared to provide the most promising approach and practical strategy, since medicine remained far more effective in its preventive than in its curative aspects until the advent of antibiotic therapy during the Second World War. Doctors contended that most of these illnesses, often called 'summer complaint' because their incidence peaked during that season, were directly attributable to the spreading practice of bottle-feeding. More and more women, they charged, were shirking their maternal – and 'patriotic' – breastfeeding duties. If they did not yet know precisely why artificially fed infants were dying from intestinal infections or how to isolate the specific organism and name it, doctors were firmly convinced of the link between infant feeding and infant death, especially in working-class households. Few such children enjoyed regular medical supervision, and their mothers were thought to be particularly ignorant of simple hygienic principles. True improvement in child health and welfare called for the kind of education and supervision that only medical professionals could effectively supply. The 'problem' thus defined was best approached through public education, attempts to regulate the milk supply, and continued voluntary efforts.[8]

What really turned public attention towards saving Ontario's mothers and babies was Dr Helen MacMurchy's series of infant mortality reports, commissioned by the Ontario government between 1910 and 1913. Shocking their readers across the land, the reports revealed that death had claimed 6932 children under one year in the wealthiest province in 1909, or more than 10 per cent of the 52,629 children born that year. Toronto alone suffered 230 deaths per 1000 live births. Although associated primarily with intestinal diseases, as MacMurchy argued, this mortality actually stemmed from a wide range of societal causes. Ignorance, poverty, and inadequate medical assistance were foremost among them. She concluded that only 'national action, government action, collective action, not individual action, can save the baby.'[9] As the first systematic, large-scale surveys of the extent and nature of the problem, MacMurchy's reports effectively set the tone and pace for the campaign that ensued.

Growing public concern about infant mortality sparked organized movements to clean up the milk supply, or at least to provide pure milk for the most vulnerable. Milk depots, or 'babies' dispensaries,' were modelled on their late nineteenth-century counterparts in Britain, France, and the United States. Organized women, including such groups as the local and provincial councils of the National Council of Women, the rural Women's Institutes, and the Imperial Order Daughters of the Empire (IODE), also inaugurated related programs involving home visitors (usually municipal nurses, but sometimes volunteers), supervisory baby clinics, public lectures on child care, and 'Little Mothers' classes in schools. Some groups arranged medical assistance for poor mothers in childbirth, as well as layettes for newborn babies and housekeeping and nursing help during the traditional ten-day 'laying-in' period after birth. In Toronto, well-baby clinics were established in 1912 at the Evangelia and University Settlement Houses in the heart of the city's immigrant district. In accordance with medical ideas and objectives, these clinics did not offer treatment, but focused on instructing mothers in modern child care. By 1915 Toronto had organized a separate Division of Child Hygiene in its municipal Public Health Department, under the direction of Dr Alan Brown and the Hospital for Sick Children.[10]

The First World War constituted a turning point for this developing campaign. War naturally drew attention to the population as a biological resource, enhancing existing anxieties about social reproduction. The casualties of war, affecting some 60,000 'future fathers of the race,' magnified concerns about 'race suicide' and the depletion of 'the better stock,' as white Anglo-Celtic middle-class Canadians classified themselves. The Great War also renewed social commitment to 'regeneration' through reform, especially where the besieged family was concerned. Canadians who witnessed the federal government's management of the war economy, including such 'philanthropic' programs as the maintenance of soldiers' dependants, were impressed by the peacetime possibilities that state intervention appeared to hold out.[11]

The voluntarist efforts on behalf of infants and mothers initiated by women's organizations were helpful, but insufficient to meet the great need. In the wake of war and the social turmoil that followed, the 'crisis in the family' demanded a state-funded, professionally directed, and 'scientific' plan to ensure the health of prospective mothers, who would then produce an abundance of healthy infants. Avowedly regulatory in design and scope, this program would also foster the 'proper' nurture, maintenance, and socialization of infants, thus assuring the nation's future glory in this brave new postwar world. Since the problem of child welfare was defined in terms of 'health' in its broadest sense – physical, mental, moral, social, and economic – then who better to lead these noble efforts than the newly organized, newly scientific (as they proclaimed themselves) medical profession?[12]

By 1915, in most urban areas, the original babies' dispensaries had evolved into general clinics for the supervision and maintenance of the health of infants and preschool children. The clinics and visiting nurse programs evolving in Ontario cities in the early war years were the foundation for a broader network of child and maternal welfare services during the interwar period. But the expansion of these services under municipal auspices, and their supervision by the new provincial Division of Maternal and Child Hygiene, did not bring about a significant change in their strategy, structure, or function. By the war's end in 1918, child welfare had become a joint enterprise of medicine and newly created agencies at the municipal, provincial, and federal levels of government. Women continued to help in their voluntary capacity, largely by supporting and promoting government-run campaigns based on three hallmark services: publication and dissemination of free educational literature, visiting public health nurses, and well-baby clinics. The campaign's leadership, however, was firmly in the hands of medical professionals and municipal agencies overseen by the newly activist provincial Department of Health.

The Family and the State: Defining a Modern Relationship

The Great War transformed a loose coalition of reformers into a focused campaign under professional direction, and, increasingly, state control. The key issue was maternal ignorance; the solution, education by health professionals; and the principal instrument, the state. The British North America of Act 1867 had made little specific provision for public health matters, assigning exclusive jurisdiction for health and welfare to provincial and municipal governments. From the time of its own inception in that Confederation year, the Canadian Medical Association passed regular resolutions calling for the creation of a dominion health department to provide leadership and coordination. Pressure from organized medicine and various reformist organizations went unheeded until 1919. The department then created was intended to cooperate with the provincial, territorial, and other health authorities 'with a view to the coordination of the efforts proposed or made for preserving and improving the public health, the conservation of child life, and the promotion of child welfare.'[13]

The federal department's declared commitment to child welfare was reinforced in 1920, when a separate child welfare division was created under the direction of Dr Helen MacMurchy. The federal government also inaugurated the Council on Child Welfare (later the Canadian Welfare Council), with Charlotte Whitton as its executive secretary. All nationally organized agencies engaged in any aspect of child welfare work were entitled to representation on the council, a voluntary body that received some federal funding for its educational services. By the Second World War, it had become the nation's central social service tribunal.[14]

The decade between 1912 and 1922 saw the expansion and professionalization of public health activity in Ontario, now the pre-eminent
province in the area of modern public health organization. The Public
Health Act of August 1912 strengthened provincial supervision over municipal health boards; seven district officers were appointed as full-time
supervisors of public health across the province. More important, growing
emphasis on child welfare in reform and medical circles led to the creation
in 1916 of the Child Welfare Bureau. The first of its kind in Canada, it was
hailed as a demonstration of what a modern provincial government could
do on behalf of public health and welfare. Rhetoric aside, and obliged to
operate within wartime budgetary restraints, the bureau's work was actually limited to sending one nurse across the province with its 'Child Welfare Special,' a specially outfitted exhibit clinic on wheels. In these early
years, demonstration work was performed largely in hopes of convincing
resident medical practitioners to become personally involved in establishing local clinics.[15]

As part of the government's postwar reconstruction plans, the Ontario
Board of Health was restructured in 1920. The Division of Public Health
Nursing was incorporated with that of Maternal and Child Hygiene in
1921, on the premise that the campaign's goals were best attained through
an intensive and coordinated system of public health nursing focused on
'teaching health in homes, clinics and schools.' Public health nurses specially trained in maternal and child welfare were sent in pairs to carry the
campaign to the furthest reaches of the province. Although there was no
fixed plan, the aim was to have the nurses provide three months' demonstration in each locality. These temporary excursions into smaller communities and isolated areas were intended to awaken a sense of need that
might be addressed by the hiring of a municipal public health nurse.[16] In
addition, the new Division of Health Education was devoted entirely to
promoting preventive measures through literature, exhibits, films, radio
talks, and special lectures. By 1925, school health services had been removed from the Department of Education and incorporated into the Division of Maternal and Child Hygiene. Within five years of its creation, this
division had taken charge of the needs of Ontario mothers and children
from conception through puberty, in explicit acknowledgment of the
campagn ideal that 'the first point in any scheme for public health is
emphasis on intelligent maternity ... children can grow up only once.'[17]

Widely considered the prototype for municipal child welfare work, Toronto's efforts were unrivalled anywhere in Canada. The city's Hospital for
Sick Children played a far-reaching role in both the provincial and the
national campaigns, thanks largely to its physician-in-chief, the indomita-

ble Alan Brown. Brown became director of Toronto's Division of Child Hygiene in 1914. When he became chief of the hospital in 1919, it was a simple matter to link clinic work throughout the city with the hospital. All doctors and nurses staffing the twenty-eight clinics established between the wars were trained and supervised through the children's hospital. By the early 1920s, Brown was child health consultant to the School of Hygiene at the University of Toronto and to the federal and provincial health departments, 'thus enabling practically all phases of children's work and problems to be guided from the children's hospital.' Toronto also provided the best prenatal supervision in the province. The city's general hospitals were operating prenatal clinics in the early 1920s, while the municipal board sent twenty special nurses on home visits to expectant and new mothers.[18]

The diagnostic services offered by province and municipality consisted of well-baby clinics, occasional preschool clinics, a few prenatal clinics in larger centres, and home visits by nurses. Both clinics and home visits were, by strict definition, instructional and supervisory. This stress on prevention and education necessitated precise guidelines in order to avoid conflict with private practitioners. Only well babies were allowed to attend clinics, so their mothers could benefit 'from such health instruction as the public health nurse may properly give.' Any child who showed evidence of a physical defect was referred to its own family physician, though many of those in attendance were unlikely to have such care except in extreme cases.[19]

Once pledged to the preservation of infant life, doctors natually committed themselves to greater involvement in the physiological and emotional aspects of maternity. MacMurchy's influence again made itself felt. Her 1928 report for the federal government, *Maternal Mortality in Canada*, confirmed that Canada had the fourth-highest rate of the nineteen nations that could provide similar statistics. Ontario's maternal mortality, at 5.6 per 1000, slightly exceeded the national rate. Doctors surmised that women's diffidence about prenatal care was the major impediment to be overcome by public education. One possibility for providing affordable and accessible medical care for pregnant women was the trained and licensed midwife. This option garnered much support from women's organizations, particularly those such as the Women's Institutes and the United Farm Women that knew first hand the difficulties confronting mothers in rural and frontier communities. Midwives were also an important component of parallel campaigns in Great Britain and the United States. Even though the majority of births in Canada before the Second World War took place at home, and despite estimates that as many as 40 per cent were unattended by trained medical professionals, the Canadian Medical Association and its provincial bodies firmly opposed the licensing of midwives, who had been outlawed in Ontario since the 1860s. They were successful in preventing enabling legislation.[20]

Contemporary class and gender ideals, rather than any purely scientific assessment of the health problems of parturient women, necessitated that child and maternal welfare be defined as inseparable. In order to produce healthy children who would adapt readily to the modern order and realize its splendid potential, motherhood had to be modernized. Ultimately, the doctors' ambivalence about the extent of their own responsibility for maternal mortality, their resolute abhorrence of trained midwives, and their inclination to the all-encompassing maternal ignorance explanation meant that the prenatal aspects of the child welfare campaign were the least organized and developed. Some attempts were made to improve obstetrical training and practice and to provide a modicum of prenatal supervision, but maternal education remained the panacea.[21]

Despite the federal initiatives in the years immediately after the First World War, the primary responsibility for public health remained in provincial hands. As such, the federal government managed to sidestep accountability for creating, maintaining, or directing health care programs beyond its commitment to restricted lump-sum funding. Meanwhile, the expanding health and welfare needs of an increasingly industrial and urban society gave rise to an imbalance between the provincial and local governments' responsiiblities in this area and their ability to fund needed services. By the time of the Second World War, the publicity campaign waged by succeeding Ontario governments had persuaded a number of municipalities to take up child welfare and public health nursing work on a permanent basis. On the whole, however, the results were disappointing. In 1921, the first year of organized provincial demonstration work, twenty-four municipalities had public health nurses and child welfare clinics; by 1938, the number had increased only to thirty-six, not including the twenty-eight clinics boasted by the city of Toronto. Although many municipalities proclaimed support for child welfare projects, most of them eventually declined to participate because of budgetary considerations.[22]

The role of the state was given much rhetorical significance in child welfare circles, but it was always cautiously defined. If governments at all levels gradually expanded their participation in the campaign during the interwar years, their involvement was restricted to the administration and direction of educational measures. Child welfare advocates never interpreted their favourite emblem of the child as 'national asset' to mean direct state responsibility for the health of mothers and children. It meant, instead, a new obligation on the part of mothers with regard to their duty to the nation.

Maternal education was not 'the easy way' so much as an approach that fitted the limitations of its proponents' position and outlook. It allowed doctors greater scope for their professional authority. Just as important, it upheld traditional concepts of feminine roles at a time when political enfranchisement and new opportunities in education and employment were challenging those constructs. Motherhood was a science and 'a profession of the highest order,' not merely a biological or instinctual function. As physicians argued, 'Intelligent motherhood alone can give to the infant that which neither wealth nor state nor yet science can offer with equal benefit to mother or child.' The goal of scientific motherhood dictated both the campaign's direction and its measures throughout its course. In a wider sense, it also shaped new relationships between doctors and mothers, mothers and children, and, ultimately, women, the family, and the state.

Scientific Motherhood: Training Ontario Mothers in Childhood Management

The response to the crisis in the family signified by infant and maternal mortality was a maternalism depicted as regenerative while operating in a fundamentally regulatory manner. Medicine and the state would see that mothers were 'educated': modernized, upgraded, re-formed, in effect, so that families could meet the needs of modern industrial society while preserving their traditional form and relationships.[23] If mothers accepted their 'national duty,' they could minimize 'inefficiency and waste' at their source by improving the health of their children through expert-designed scientific child care methods. Once physical welfare was assured in infancy, they could manage and train their children along the path to healthy, productive, and efficient adulthood.[24] By promoting and facilitating 'scientific motherhood,' the state could best do its work 'to see that the rights of the children are not ignored and that the mothers have the opportunity given them of learning how best to rear their children.' The result would be a modern Canada defined by the favourable implications of modernity, rather than its adverse ones: progress, efficiency, productivity, and the triumph of reason signified by advances in science and technology. The enthusiastic maternalist platforms of various reform organizations, women's groups, and voluntary agencies, and the establishment of a federal health department and a provincial division with stated commitments to child welfare by the early 1920s, facilitated popular acceptance of attempts to 'modernize' motherhood.[25]

The clinics, home nursing visits, and advice literature that became the campaign's signature services were meant to complement but never to replace regular attendance by the family physician. Despite the fact that most of the client families could not avail themselves of such medical care, the clinics' foremost advice to all classes of mothers was that they should see their doctors regularly and take no counsel from non-professional, traditional sources, such as their own network of family, friends, and neighbours. The clinics were purely diagnostic and advisory. No treatment was permitted. Mothers were often required to have the written permission of their regular physicians before attending. Nurse visits to homes were also advisory, and limited to 'demonstration' of child care techniques in order to impress on mothers the value of raising children and keeping house in the sanctioned 'scientific' way, the only 'proper' way. Child welfare nurses were kept under close surveillance by the public health departments for any suspected overstepping of bounds, usually respecting artificial feeding, which was supposed to be exclusively limited to doctors' prescription. And disclaimers were published on every piece in the extensive, government-produced body of parenting literature to the effect that, while 'expert' in origin, this information was meant to serve as a 'guideline' only. Mothers were repeatedly warned that each individual case demanded the personal attention and specific consultation of the physician.

Through the medium of advice literature, predominantly medical in authorship or at least in inspiration, directives for 'perfect parenting' were issued. During the interwar years, this literature was produced apace by medical professionals, new health and welfare agencies at all levels of government, and in conjunction with private insurance companies and voluntary health and social service organizations. It was further popularized in the advice columns and 'women's pages' of mass-circulation magazines and newspapers, through government-produced radio shows and short films, and by public health nurses who held 'demonstrations' at baby clinics and in homes. The advice strove to establish doctors as maternal mentors, to associate maternalism with national interest, and to reformulate motherhood – and, consequently, childhood.[26] Science and state lent the weight of their combined authority to social constructions depicting the ideal mother, the ideal child, and ideal family relationships.

Although disparaging modern women, this doctor-designed educational crusade called for the creation of a new, improved, scientific mother, a thoroughly modern mother befitting the new industrial order. 'Management,' an almost solely masculine role, was the core concept. Just as 'efficiency' and 'productivity' became keywords of modern industry, scientific management ideas were transferred to the home. Modern motherhood was infused with the spirit of industry, with its unrelenting demands for regularity, repetition, scheduling, systematization, discipline, and productivity, effectively transforming children – it was hoped – into 'little machines.' The tremendous public admiration for science and technology made this outcome desirable: the machine represented the most evolved human type, the most 'modern' of all.

Even while recognizing the limits of education, child welfare workers believed that their efforts were making a definite impact on their target audience. Growing numbers of mothers were being reached. By the close of the Depression decade, it appeared to nurses that 'we are dependent upon a public which is becoming increasingly more interested and better informed.'[27] There was also a real sense in the popular press that parenthood and childhood were in transition. For some, the changes were not altogether positive: 'most children nowadays ... never are children at all.' They passed their childhood in rigorous training for greater things than simple play would allow. Just as motherhood was being 'professionalized' according to the experts' regulations, so childhood was becoming an intensely specialized and 'managed' event.[28]

Working-class commentators, meanwhile, argued that, under 'a properly organized social system,' children 'with bodies ruined by lack of food and attention' would not exist. Workers were urged to 'look at the deaths which are preventable and yet go on, and ask yourself is it worth wearing out the only life you have in bolstering a thoroughly rotten system, which exists for the benefit of the few?' Only by realizing their own power and standing together could workers 'forever abolish the spectre of dread which now haunts every working-class mother.'[29] Women's labour groups were particularly active in lobbying for improvements in health care. In 1932 the Women's Canadian Labour Council passed a resolution supporting 'the principle and practice of state medicine.' The United Women's Educational Federation of Ontario and the United Farm Women passed similar resolutions and sent delegations to petition municipal and provincial governments to 'get measures through in the interests of women and children.'[30]

Many of the surviving letters to the Council on Child and Family Welfare indicate that mothers were attempting to apply these precepts of modern childrearing. Especially grateful for such advice were mothers in isolated rural and outpost communities. As one wrote, 'it means a whole lot to rural mothers to have such a splendid advice and assistance offered to us free and from a reliable source.' Another expressed similar thanks: 'There was so much in them that is especially helpful to me as we are on a farm and it is not just as convenient to get advice as in the city.'[31] Some mothers, however, complained forcefully that, notwithstanding the benefits of free advice literature, not nearly enough was being done. As efforts to subsume the Division of Child and Maternal Welfare within the federal health department commenced in the late 1930s – another Depression-induced rationalization measure – even the information services were threatened. A northern Ontario woman regarded this cutback as evidence of the government's hypocrisy, amounting to callous disregard about the plight of the nation's mothers and children. While agreeing that information was helpful, she stressed that mothers needed affordable and accessible medical service above all else:

> The government is a poor blind and horribly ignorant affair that is too busy with the petty details of its today to think of the nation of tomorrow ... if you were a bunch of real statesmen and nationbuilders rather than a scraggly bunch of cheap politicians you would be thinking of building the nation some backbone for its future ... do the doctors boss you or do you boss the doctors? Isn't it possible for you to pass a law saying that every doctor must examine every maternity patient before they are paid by them. You are in a position to allow clever young people to have healthy clever babies and a foundation for a grand new nation. What are you going to do about it?[32]

Canada's most famous children of all time were born to a large rural family of francophone Catholics living in Corbeil, near North Bay, Ontario, in May 1934. It is doubtful that any children have ever been raised as meticulously 'by the book' as were the Dionne quintuplets. Shortly after their birth, the Ontario government declared itself the true parent of the newborn Dionnes and separated them legally and physically from their family. All rhetoric to the contrary, the Dionnes were not dealt with as children in need of state protection; they were scenic wonders requiring public management for the public good more than for their own benefit. In the depths of Depression gloom, the marvel of the five sweet little sisters epitomized the potential of an idealized childhood. And the quints' early childhood was very much of the idealized 'little machine' variety. The Ontario government kept the infants sequestered across the road from the family farm in a custom-built hospital, with the latest medical technology, round-the-clock nursing care, and the unremitting surveillance of the renowned medical and psychological specialists of the day. With its observation rooms and souvenir shops, 'Quintland' soon drew as many tourists as Niagara Falls – some 400,000 in 1938 alone. None of the experts, including Dr Alan Brown and University of Toronto child psychologist William Blatz, expressed any qualms about the negative long-term effects of such a 'public' upbringing, with its performative aspects, its enforced separation from family, and the children's effective institutionalization. When they were ultimately returned to their parents, the latter were unable and, more important, unwilling to modify their childrearing values and objectives, rooted in rural French-Canadian and Catholic tradition. The results were the quints' tragic alienation from their parents, the emotional difficulties they encountered as adults, and the sorrow and public humilition of all family members. The fate of the Dionne sisters suggests how 'scientific childrearing,' in this case taken to extremes beyond the possibilities of most parents, ended in the objectification of the children themselves.[33] Although the Dionnes became the ideal representation of 1930s childhood, they were deprived of anything remotely like an ideal childhood themselves.

If there was no revolution in the true sense of the word, new trends in childrearing were definitely making themselves felt in Ontario during the interwar years. The modernization of the parent-child relationship was mediated by the retention of those cultural patterns that parents found personally significant. If mothers of all origins shared common concerns for their children's health and common interest in learning better methods to ensure it, those most vulnerable – according to the doctors' own classifications of what constituted maternal vulnerability, deemed 'ignorance' – were also the least satisfied with the means undertaken to improve their families' welfare.

Good Intentions Notwithstanding: The Campaign's Limitations

Early twentieth-century assessments of the Canadian infant mortality problem reflected the social and medical considerations of the British and American studies inspiring them. They repeated a complicated and confused logic that recognized the link between poverty and ill health, but refused to see poverty itself as the primary cause.[34] They also refused to give much thought to the true costs of fee-for-service health care, which effectively removed regular medical supervision – exactly what they were so vehemently promoting – from the reach of many families. A 1918 survey by the Dominion Bureau of Statistics found that 46 per cent of the labour force of seven major industries earned less than $20 per week; a doctor's attention cost at least $5, not including drugs or dental care. Costs for medical attendance at childbirth ranged from $15 to $25, constituting a full week's wages for many breadwinners, already hard-pressed to support their families without some wage supplementation by other family members.

The Canadian Medical Association consistently maintained that, by comparison with other professional incomes, the average medical income was 'not excessive.' Yet the 1920s were years of unprecedented medical affluence. An association study of two districts in Ontario served by five hundred physicians reported that the physicians' average gross annual income from 1925 to 1930 was $6262.78, comparing favourably with the $1024 average annual earnings of industrial workers.[35] Organized medicine was profoundly opposed to anything resembling 'state medicine,' which was seen as a direct threat to professional autonomy and an omen of 'Bolshevism.'

The economic collapse of the 1930s naturally made matters worse for families already living on the margins. Identifying herself only as 'A Worried Expectant Mother,' a woman from Wabewawa in Northern Ontario wrote a heart-wrenching letter to the federal health department in 1932. She assured officials undoubtedly used to such pleas that she was not writing to beg food or clothing, 'though I am in need of both.' As she told it, the imminent delivery of her sixth child was the 'thing that worries me the most.' At the age of twenty-five, she had already borne five children in as many years, all without medical help, at great cost to her health and with much risk to the infants. No doctor would come to her isolated homestead for less than $25, a sum far beyond her family's means. 'It is a tragic thing,' she concluded, 'that the mothers of the land must suffer.'[36] Similar plaintive personal stories from other parts of Canada provide stark testimony of the close relationship between material circumstances and individual and familial health. Poverty not only prevented the seeking of medical help but also kept parents from obtaining the necessary corrections for their children's health defects even when these were diagnosed. A survey of twelve Ontario cities by the provincial health department in 1930 revealed a delay of a year or more in securing the necessary medical attention in 45.5 per cent of cases. The reason was inability to pay for treatment.[37]

Only when the market failed doctors as much as other working Canadians during the Great Depression did the medical profession invoke state responsibility for health care, and then only as an emergency relief measure. It was estimated that nearly 3 million Canadians were 'medically indigent' by 1935. Managed by the Ontario Medical Association, the system implemented in the province that year was the largest organization of medical relief services in Canada, serving an estimated 50,000 people per month. Ironically, it was only due to the combination of economic collapse and professional pressure that many Ontario families were able to obtain the medical care beyond their reach in better times.[38]

As the campaign expanded and flourished nationally, doctors continued to discount and dismiss the role of environmental factors in infant and maternal mortality. They were also inclined to downplay or ignore the simple fact that many Canadian women either did not have access to, or could not afford, medical care during pregnancy, childbirth, and the critical first years of the infant's life. The official stand of doctors and state health officials did not waver throughout these years, even when they could not deny the need or the outcome of not meeting it. The explanation for high infant and maternal mortality, they insisted, lay with the mothers themselves. The poor were providing the victim's sanction by refusing to take responsibility for their own health and welfare and that of their children. They had to be made responsible by means of 'a better and broader education in all that relates to the child and child life.' Paradoxically, while mothers were the source of the problem, they were also its principal solution.

Given the need to balance conflicting options and to work around the divergent interests represented by women, medicine, labour, and government, it is not surprising that the child welfare campaign was restrained within such boundaries. For all the language of efficiency and productivity, its measures were often inefficient and less than productive. With the exception of the medical relief program necessitated by the Depression emergency, few public initiatives on behalf of mothers and children materialized before the Second World War. Neither organized women, nor farm and labour groups, had the political representation and influence necessary to persuade governments to take action that smacked of 'state medicine' in a time of ambivalence about the state's role in welfare, and of medicine's opposition.

One of the most serious complications arising from expanding medical involvement in child welfare involved the relationship of doctors (almost exclusively male) and nurses (exclusively female). The point of contention was the nurses' role in delivering the child welfare message while respecting bounds delimited according to the doctors' professional expertise and private practice. Doctors agreed that nurses were the essential liaison between mothers and medicine. Far from the relationship being one of peers, however, the doctors were adamant that both nurses and mothers were to be subordinate and obedient to the doctors in charge. Above all, nurses were to carry out doctors' orders and see that they were obeyed by mothers.[39]

There was some reason for doctors to suspect that nurses occasionally overstepped these bounds. Mothers were increasingly taking up bottle-feeding, which was supposed to be by doctor's prescription only. Many of them, however, enjoyed no more regular medical supervision than that provided through nurse-run clinics and nurse visits. Some nurses felt compelled to provide the necessary instructions for making formula, and otherwise took steps in the direction of 'treatment' rather than simply weighing and 'checking' babies and advising mothers. Physician anxiety about these possibilities periodically threatened the campaign, to the point where the Division of Maternal and Child Hygiene grasped every opportunity to reassure doctors that the scope and function of public health nurses were carefully delimited and monitored by the department itself. Nursing director Mary Power recognized that, 'in spite of the fact that both workers, public health nurses and practising physicians, are seeking the same goal by parallel roads, there exists in some places a lack of sympathy between the two groups which I am convinced is based on misunderstanding.'[40] The fact that the provincial health department was sponsoring the touring nurses and actively promoting their efforts may have persuaded some physicians to participate in clinic demonstrations, if only to avoid unfavourable publicity. In the face of widespread indifference, and even hostility on the part of doctors, it seemed to nurses that their child welfare victories were won in spite of physicians and not with their assistance. Nurses felt themselves to be 'angels without wings' who were subjected to undue criticism, 'often captious,' for all their hard labour and dedication.[41] More than just a problem of appropriate doctor/nurse relationships, the conflict was also rooted in the clash between the medical autonomy signified by private practice and the perceived state encroachment through public health services.

The government-sponsored programs on behalf of child and maternal welfare were strongly weighted on the side of making mothers accept their responsibilities, while downplaying the state's reciprocal obligation. Nowhere was this inequality more apparent than in the province's rural and outpost districts. The problems of transportation and communication in a difficult climate were aggravated by the primitive outpost conditions of northern frontier communities, the so-called New Ontario. Even the rural areas of the more populous south only benefited from medical programs to the degree of their proximity to an urban centre. The province established a skeleton framework of public health services for its sparsely populated regions, but only ten municipalities in all Ontario in 1936 had a full-time medical officer of health. Out of a population of 3.6 million, only one-third lived in areas where public health services had adequate direction.[42]

In addition to distance and cost, there was little municipal organization in much of New Ontario. Existing municipal governments were unable to finance child welfare efforts, and federal and provincial governments were at an impasse on this jurisdictional issue. For many families outside the province's cities and larger towns, health care proved to be the scarcest resource of all. The Canadian Medical Association was so concerned about the lack of doctors in rural districts that it repeatedly urged the provincial government to place and maintain recent medical graduates in these outlying areas. The association's pleas went unheeded. Beyond conferring with Ontario health officials, encouraging discussion in the Dominion Council of Health, and publishing a special supplement to MacMurchy's *The Canadian Mother's Book,* no federal action was taken either.[43]

By 1926 the Ontario health department had decided that the advantages of 'such service as is available' should first be extended to the districts of Northern Ontario that were unable to supply it for themselves. Diagnostic clinics for infants and preschoolers were held at the request of local medical practitioners or in conjunction with the nurses' regular field work. These nursing services could not begin to cover the population's needs, obviously, and were often restricted to school inspection alone. Throughout the interwar years, at least half the province did not enjoy the health protection offered by a public health nursing program. For all its efforts, the provincial health department could not compel the municipalities to accept their responsibility for the health of their people. The administrators explained municipal reluctance in terms of popular ignorance and false economy, but the reports of local medical officers of health repeatedly pointed to financial constraints as the true source of non-compliance.[44]

Voluntary organizations attempted to fill the void where official agencies were unwilling or unable to provide medical services. The Red Cross Hospital-on-Wheels operated in Northern Ontario's most isolated districts. The first of these outpost centres was opened at Wilberforce in 1921. By 1940 twenty-nine centres were in operation. Red Cross nurses also provided prenatal supervision and attended confinements in areas where no doctor was available.[45] It was frequently difficult to reach the neediest mothers; the problem of geographic isolation was compounded by their poverty and the burden of daily work they bore. In her summary of conditions in the Thunder Bay district in 1922, a provincial nurse reported that the area's young women were typically in poor physical condition, with equally sorry results for their children's health. Referring specifically to the 'entire lack of obstetrical care' in the area, she pointed out that 'there have been many who have had six or seven children without proper care and are beginning to realize that many of their ailments and suffering have been caused by their lack.' This situation was encountered repeatedly. The district health officer for North Bay reported that home visiting, limited as it was, was 'unsatisfactory' because of the poverty that prevented mothers from making the necessary expenditures to put the nurses' recommendations into practice.[46]

Despite, and even because of, the conditions peculiar to less settled areas, nurses were even more 'messengers of mercy' for the residents of rural settlements, villages, and resource communities. Conditions in some areas were so pitiable that there was little hope of improving maternal and infant health by means of the vaunted educational methods. In North Hastings County in 1925, a nurse noted that 'stagnation of industry, lack of education, bad housing, overcrowding, immorality, intermarrying and the many evils which follow in its train are some of the most outstanding problems of the district and are the direct result of isolation and poverty.' Coupled with this was 'the daily struggle for a mere existence on land so rocky that in some localities, farming is practically impossible.' The nurses' moral sensibilities may have been offended by what they saw in some impoverished homes, but they were sensitive to the desperation of these people and the magnitude of their daily struggle. They understood that destitution did not provide fertile ground for health education. Diagnosis of health problems and recommendations for treatment were futile for those who lacked the ways and means to obtain remedies. Under these circumstances, the nurses felt, there simply was 'not much use in going back.' Lessons in healthful living were best concentrated 'on the small number who might be taught and helped.'[47] More than any of the campaign's other participants, the nurses who took its precepts directly to the families of Ontario were forced to confront its limitations.

In 1928 the United Farm Women of Ontario tried to politicize the issue of medical care for women and children in rural and outpost areas through petitions to the federal and provincial governments. Contrary to prevailing medical views, the women stressed that 'the chief cause of our appalling death rate of mothers at childbirth is economic, the remedy of which is slow.' To address 'this calamity,' they indicated their support for public education and improved medical training and obstetrics, but also called for maternity insurance and state placement and subsidization of doctors.[48] But the only request on behalf of rural mothers and children that was answered by the state was a wholehearted commitment to the dissemination of health information. An attempt to make advice literature more relevant to rural and outpost mothers actually confirmed both the extent of their need and the state's unwillingness to meet it. The supplement to *The Canadian Mother's Book*, also written by MacMurchy, proposed to advise rural women on 'what to do if baby arrives before the doctor does.' MacMurchy never referred directly to midwives, and insisted that neither her supplement nor neighbours should substitute for the doctor, since they were intended to help only 'until the doctor comes.' It must have been small consolation to anxious expectant mothers for whom this impending arrival was little more than fantasy. Nurses found that newly delivered mothers maintained supervision over household and family 'although in bed,' and that many took up their normal labours, including field work, much too soon after confinement. There was also the difficulty of paying for medical care even when it was otherwise available. The few physicians settled in these districts were at times leery of attending to poor families, especially during the Depression, when their own incomes were declining.[49]

The campaign's directors were well aware of the gaps between their aspirations and the practical efforts conceived to attain them. In 1932 the Ontario government's public health field staff conducted a survey of 'the effectiveness of child health services' in the province. They found that parents were very interested in the well-being of their children in every location visited, and that publications, clinics, and nurse visits were reaching an increasing number of Ontario families. In qualitative terms, however, such services remained seriously deficient. In many Ontario towns, nothing was carried out on any systematic basis.[50]

With its own findings underlining the ineffectiveness of existing measures, the provincial government was persuaded to take steps to set up a permanent public health service, with emphasis on child and maternal welfare work, for an impoverished area of eastern Ontario. The first rural health unit was established for the eastern counties of Stormont, Glengarry, Prescott, and Russell. Two-thirds of the funds for the Eastern Ontario Health Unit were contributed by the municipalities involved, and one-third by the province. If the new, permanent health unit represented significant progress by comparison with the temporary, periodic demonstration work that had preceded it, its actual services remained centred on education. The unit centralized child and maternal welfare work for its counties, without expanding the scope or nature of that work. The problems recognized by the provincial nurses in the early 1920s persisted. The unit's directors were quickly forced to concede, as had the nurses before them, that many of the client families' health problems were so aggravated by social and economic difficulties that any effort was destined to be fruitless.[51]

For some poor families, the assistance delivered was simply too little, too late. However grateful she may have been for the nurse's help, one expectant mother lost two daughters to bronchitis in one week. As a visiting nurse recounted, 'She had not had the doctor as she cannot afford it ... it seemed very hard losing the two children so near together. It was a pathetic sight to see the little body wrapped in a sheet lying on a wooden bench in the corner with a lamp burning at the head and a piece of new-patched quilt on the wall to improve the place and the mother's thanks for the help that we had been to her was very touching.'[52]

As such stories demonstrate, educating mothers in scientific childrearing was in itself far from easy. But, as an essential component of modern science, education inspired both medical support and popular faith in an age of scientific advance and seeming progress. Education also corresponded to middle-class aspirations for reforming Canadian families. It enhanced specific professional status concerns while protecting the system. The focus on education fit well with the social welfare philosophy prevailing in government circles and the determination of the federal government to make the municipalities and provinces accept their responsibilities in this area. The comparatively low cost of educational efforts speaks for itself as a motivating factor. Certainly the cost-effectiveness of social welfare programs grew in importance during the Depression. In the end, despite all good intentions, issues of authority, control, and responsibility limited the effectiveness of the campaign's hallmark services and suggested to some of its participants that education was an inappropriate and ineffective solution to the problem. Whatever the campaigners could muster in the form of instruction in modern methods could not compensate for the real health needs of many Ontario families.

Conclusion: Effects and Prospects

By the end of the Depression decade, the child welfare campaign was diminishing in intensity. The massive reorganization necessitated by the outbreak of the Second World War meant that governments at every level directed all resources to the war effort. This war, too, would prove an important breakthrough. Lessons learned from the Depression experience, full-scale state intervention for the war effort, and public pressure about postwar reconstruction pushed and pulled the nation towards the welfare state. It seemed that Canadians who had suffered through the 1930s with minimal state assistance were not going to sacrifice themselves and their children in another war unless money could also be found to better their lives during peacetime.

Mackenzie King's Liberal government was at last prepared to consider the need for effective, coherent, social security legislation. McGill University social scientist Leonard Marsh was asked to prepare a report for the House of Commons Committee on Reconstruction and Rehabilitation. His *Report on Social Security for Canada*, presented to the committee in 1943, attempted to establish a justifiable social minimum for all Canadians. The report proclaimed that children 'should have an unequivocal place in social security policy.' After much criticism and consternation, the Family Allowances Act was passed in 1944. Produced the same year as the Marsh Report, Dr J.J. Heagerty's health insurance recommendations for the Committee on Reconstruction, with their comprehensive measures for health insurance and public health grants, were largely jettisoned because of the perpetual inability of the provincial and federal governments to agree on fiscal terms. Just as important, if their own Depression experience encouraged some doctors to look favourably on state medicine, the majority continued to insist that complete state control of health care services would undermine the quality of medical care and consequently the health status of the people. Further measures would have to await the economic affluence and 'baby boom' of the 1950s.

Doubtless, many Ontario mothers and their children gained from the programs initiated by provincial and municipal health departments during the interwar years, despite their recognized limitations. Ontario's health department coordinated and supervised child welfare measures unmatched anywhere in Canada. But beyond distributing free vaccine and literature and sending nurses on demonstration tours, its major goal was to encourage municipalities to hire their own nurses and establish their own clinics and visiting services. Nonetheless, the campaign's attempts to awaken public, official, and professional interest inspired greater efforts towards pure milk legislation, antiseptic conditions at delivery, improved hospital techniques, and prenatal and well-baby supervision.

By the end of the Second World War, most Ontario towns were served by some form of public health nursing. More county health units were created to minister to the needs of unorganized rural and outpost districts. The clinic and visiting nurse services continued, expanding into municipalities just acquiring public health organization. Their function was educational, as always, but a 1946 amendment to the Public Health Act allowed each expectant mother to obtain one free complete prenatal medical examination from the physician of her choice. By 1950 the proportion of free prenatal examinations in relation to live births was 60 per cent. Maternal deaths in Ontario reached an all-time low in 1946 of 1.64 per cent, with the infant death rate also falling to a historic low of 18.8 per 1000 live births.[53] While there was still a long way to go in all these areas, Ontario families at mid-century enjoyed far more health care options than they had had even twenty years earlier. The statistical improvement for mothers and children was obviously a related outcome.

It is also clear that, in striving towards the twin goals of saving babies and modernizing mothers, doctors gave scientific authorization to traditional gender roles and the traditional family, supported by the power of the state.[54] The maternalist ideals at the basis of the child welfare campaign affected the way that Canadians regarded motherhood, and the way that governments shaped social policy. But neither ideals nor attempts at state regulation of maternity necessarily made women the passive and submissive 'patients' that doctors wanted them to be. Far from simply taking in the entire 'modern motherhood package' presented by the new experts and state agencies, women recognized the limits of these ideas and practices. Ultimately, the way that most women raised their children had more to do with the material circumstances of their lives, and how these factors constrained their choices, than with any amount of advice or medical supervision provided through baby clinics, nurse visits, and, especially, through heaps of free literature.[55] In many ways, however, the campaign's understandings of gender, motherhood, family, and the role of the state in related concerns have persisted. They continue despite their obvious inadequacies in the face of the sociocultural changes that have taken place since Dr Helen MacMurchy first issued her pleas for collective action on behalf of Ontario's mothers and children.

NOTES

Many thanks are due to the Social Sciences and Humanities Federation of Canada for the Post-doctoral Research Fellowship, 1992, which helped immensely in the research for my book, *Nations Are Built of Babies: Saving Ontario's Mothers and Children, 1900–45* (Montreal and Kingston: McGill-Queen's University Press, 1993), from which this essay is drawn.

1   Recent examples of the historiography on maternalism include the pathbreaking work by T. Skocpol, *Protecting Soldiers and Mothers: The Political Origins of Social Policy in the United States* (Cambridge, Mass.: Belknap Press, 1992); G. Bock and P. Thane, eds., *Maternity and Gender Policies: Women and the Rise of European Welfare States* (London: Routledge, 1991); S. Koven, and M. Michel, eds., *Mothers of the New World: Maternalist Politics and the Origins of Welfare States* (New York: Routledge, 1993); H. Marsland, L. Marks, and V. Fildes, eds., *Women and Children First: Maternal and Infant Welfare in International Perspective* (London: Routledge, 1992); and S. Pedersen, *Family, Dependency, and the Origins of the Welfare State* (Cambridge: Cambridge University Press, 1993). For Canada, see Comacchio, *Nations Are Built of Babies*; and K. Arnup, *Education for Motherhood: Advice to Mothers in Twentieth-Century Canada* (Toronto: University of Toronto Press, 1994). For Quebec, see D. Baillargeon, 'Fréquenter les "Gouttes de Lait": L'expérience des mères montréalaises, 1910–1965,' *Revue d'histoire de l'Amérique française* 50, 1 (1996) 29–68; A. Lévèsque, *Making and Breaking the Rules: Women in Quebec, 1919–39*, translated by Y.M. Klein (Toronto: McClelland & Stewart, 1994), especially chapter 1. On Helen MacMurchy, see D. Dodd, 'Advice to Parents: The Blue Books, Helen

MacMurchy, M.D., and the Federal Department of Health,' *Canadian Bulletin of Medical History* 8, 2 (1991): 203–30. On social reform in Canada, see R. Allen, *The Social Passion* (Toronto: University of Toronto, 1971); N. Sutherland, *Children in English-Canadian Society: Framing the Twentieth-Centry Concensus* (Toronto: University of Toronto Press, 1976); M. Valverde, *The Age of Light, Soap and Water: Moral Reform in English Canada, 1885–1925* (Toronto: McClelland & Stewart, 1991); and the essays in L. Kealey, ed., *A Not Unreasonable Claim: Women and Reform in Canada, 1880s–1920s* (Toronto: Women's Press, 1979).

2 Dr P.H. Bryce, 'The Scope of a Federal Department of Health,' *Canadian Medical Association Journal (CMAJ)* 10, 1 (1920): 3; Dr A. Meyer, 'The Right to Marry: What Can a Democratic Civilization Do about Heredity and Child Welfare?' *Canadian Journal of Mental Hygiene* 1, 2 (1919): 145; Dr H. MacMurchy, 'The Parent's Plea,' ibid., 1, 3 (1919): 211. See also MacMurchy's reports for the Ontario government, 'The Feeble-Minded in Ontario,' in Ontario, *Sessional Papers*, 1907–15, annually; and MacMurchy, *Sterilization? Birth Control?* (Toronto: King's Printer, 1934). All these texts use blatant class and race arguments to explain perceived social degeneration.

3 Charges of maternal ignorance and negligence run rampant through the medical and social service journals of the early twentieth century. Some examples include the editorial, 'Save the Children,' *Canada Lancet* 40, 10 (1907): 934; editorial, 'The Health of the Child,' *CMAJ* 2, 7, (1912): 704; Dr B.F. Royer, 'Child Welfare,' *Canadian Public Health Journal (CPHJ)* 12, 8 (1921): 293; and Dr H. MacMurchy, 'A Safety League for Mothers,' *Social Welfare* 13, 9 (1931): 184. These themes are further developed in Comacchio, *Nations Are Built of Babies*. See also Baillargeon, 'Frequenter les gouttes de lait.' The long-standing debates about the theoretical significance of domestic labour and its nature and relationship to production are complicated, unrelenting, and largely unresolved. For an overview of these debates, which commenced in the mid-1960s, see P. Armstrong, and H. Armstrong, *Theorizing Women's Work* (Toronto: Garamond, 1990), 67–97.

4 Dr C. Hodgetts, 'Infantile Mortality in Canada,' *CMAJ* 1, 8 (1911): 720; Dr H. MacMurchy, *Infant Mortality: Third Special Report* (Toronto: King's Printer, 1912), 30.

5 S.M. Carr Harris, 'Reasons for Parental Education,' *The Canadian Nurse* 22, 6 (1926): 312–14; A. Mackay, 'Caring for the Children,' *Maclean's*, 15 August 1928, 25; Dr E.K. Clarke, 'Community Responsibility for Habit Training in Children,' *Social Welfare* 13, 11 (1931): 228; and K.W. Gorrie, 'Parent Education and Social Work,' *Canadian Child and Family Welfare*, 11, 5 (1936): 33–4.

6 Reportable diseases were smallpox, scarlet fever, diphtheria, measles, whooping cough, typhoid, tuberculosis, infantile paralysis, and cerebrospinal meningitis: Ontario Board of Health, *Annual Report*, 1912, 12–13. See also Ontario, Department of Health, *Annual Report*, 1940. In 1921, children under fifteen

years constituted 30.8 per cent of the population of Ontario. In 1932, communicable diseases were still responsible for 600 deaths annually in Ontario, concentrated in the under-ten age group; see M.A. Ross, 'The Mortality in Ontario of Four Communicable Diseases of Childhood,' *CPHJ* 23, 7 (1932): 340.

7 Dr J.H. Mason Knox, 'Infant Care,' *CMAJ* 23, 8 (1933): 151.

8 Charges of maternal ignorance and negligence run rampant through the medical and social service journals of the early twentieth century. Some examples include the editorial, 'Save the Children,' *Canada Lancet* 40, 10 (1907): 934; editorial, 'The Health of the Child,' *CMAJ* 2, 7, (1912): 704; Dr B.F. Royer, 'Child Welfare,' *CPHJ* 12, 8 (1921): 293; and Dr H. MacMurchy, 'A Safety League for Mothers,' *Social Welfare* 13, 9 (1931): 184.

9 Dr H. MacMurchy, *Infant Mortality: First Special Report* (Toronto: King's Printer, 1910); *Second Special Report* (1911); *Third Special Report* (1912).

10 Editorial, 'Baby Clinics,' *CPHJ* 4, 2 (1913): 94; Dr G. Smith, 'The Result of Three Years' Work in the Department of Child Hygiene, Toronto,' *CPHJ* 9, 7 (1918): 310–13.

11 Dr A. Brown, 'Infant and Child Welfare Work,' *CPHJ* 9, 4 (1918): 149; see also A.W. Coone, 'The Child as an Asset,' *Social Welfare* 1, 2 (1918): 38; and Dr P.H. Bryce, 'Infant Mortality and Disease,' *Social Welfare* 1, 6 (1919): 133.

12 On the role of doctors in social and moral reform campaigns, see A. McLaren, *Our Own Master Race: Eugenics in Canada, 1885–1945* (Toronto: McClelland & Stewart, 1990), 8, 28–9; and Valverde, *The Age of Light, Soap and Water*, 47.

13 See, for example, editorial, 'Railways and Typhoid,' *CMAJ* 1, 3 (1911): 261; editorial, 'A Dominion Minister of Health,' *Canada Lancet* 37, 1 (1903): 243; and editorial, 'The Lives of the People,' *CPHJ* 4, 7 (1913): 422–3.

14 Dominion Department of Health, *Report of the Deputy Minister*, 1922, 22; editorial, 'Child Welfare Activities in Canada,' *CMAJ* 11, 5 (1921): 396. The council received $10,000 annually from the federal government. It changed names several times: originally the Canadian Council on Child Welfare, it became the Council on Child and Family Welfare in 1931, and the Canadian Welfare Council in 1935.

15 Ontario, Board of Health, *Annual Report*, 1919, 37–42.

16 Archives of Ontario (AO), RG 10, 30–A-L, box 11, file 11.3, typescript, undated, unsigned, 'Maternal and Child Hygiene.' Each of the eight public health nurses was paired with a Red Cross nurse and sent to a district for a three-to-six-month tour. See also Board of Health, *Annual Report*, 1921, 171; and 1922, *Report of Associate Director Beryl Knox*, 177–9.

17 'Canada's Health,' *Canadian Congress Journal* 19, 9 (1940): 41. The board became the Department of Health in 1924.

18 Smith, 'The Result of Three Years' Work,' 313; E.M. Forsythe, 'Child Welfare Clinics,' *CPHJ* 9, 4 (1918): 170. By the end of the period the city health board employed ninety-six nurses.

19 AO, RG 10, 30-A-1, box 6, file 6-4, Public Health Nursing, Historical Literature, undated typescript, probably early 1920s, outlining official goals in establishing child welfare clinics in Ontario; see also box 1, file 1.7, typescript, unsigned, 'Living Conditions in Belleville,' 22 March 1922.

20 Drs H.E. Young and J.T. Phair, 'Maternal Mortality in Canada,' *CPHJ* 19, 3 (1928): 135; Dr G. Fleming, 'The Future of Maternal Welfare in Canada,' Dominion Council of Health, *Report of the 26th Meeting*, June 1933, 3–4. In Ontario, midwifery was outlawed as early as 1875.

21 Dr J.T. Phair, 'Radio Talk,' *CPHJ* 18, 3 (1927): 133; 'Preliminary Trends,' *Canadian Welfare Summary* 15, 5 (1940): 55.

22 Board of Health, *Annual Report*, 1922, 177–9; see also AO, RG 62, 1-f-1-b, box 473, Correspondence, 'List of Municipalities Employing Public Health Nurses.'

23 On the social influence of doctors in Canadian history, see W. Mitchinson, *The Nature of Their Bodies: Women and Their Doctors in Victorian Canada* (Toronto: University of Toronto Press, 1991); McLaren, *Our Own Master Race*, 9, 28–9; Valverde, *The Age of Light, Soap and Water*, 47; Lévesque, *Making and Breaking the Rules*, 14.

24 C. Lasch, *Haven in a Heartless World: The Family Besieged* (New York: Basic Books, 1977), and J. Donzelot *The Policing of Families* (New York: Pantheon, 1979). For Canada, see the seminal work of Sutherland, *Children in English Canadian Society*. V. Strong-Boag describes the tutoring in medicine to allay maternal 'amateurism' in *The New Day Recalled: Lives of Girls and Women in English Canada, 1920–1939*, 149. On infant and maternal mortality, see S. Buckley, 'Efforts to Reduce Infant and Maternal Mortality between the Wars,' *Atlantis* 4 (1979); S. Buckley, 'Ladies or Midwives?' in Kealey, ed., *A Not Unreasonable Claim*; S. Buckley, 'The Search for the Decline of Maternal Mortality,' in W. Mitchinson and J.D. McGinnis, eds., *Essays in the History of Canadian Medicine* (Toronto: McClelland & Stewart, 1988); N. Lewis, 'Creating the Little Machine,' *BC Studies* 56 (1982–3); and N. Lewis, 'Reducing Maternal Mortality in British Columbia,' in B.K. Latham and R.J. Pazdro, eds., *Not Just Pin Money: Selected Essays on the History of Women's Work in British Columbia* (Victoria: Camosun College, 1984).

25 Dr H. MacMurchy, 'The Baby's Father,' *Canadian Public Health Journal* 9, 7 (1918): 315. MacMurchy is actually citing Dr John Burns, who presided over Britain's First National Council on Infantile Mortality in 1906; see Deborah Dwork, *War Is Good for Babies and Other Young Children: A History of the Infant and Child Welfare Movement in England* (London: Tavistock, 1987), 114.

26 To name just a few examples of the advice literature: the federal government's Division of Child and Maternal Welfare produced *The Canadian Mother and Child*; the Ontario government produced *The Baby*; and the Canadian Welfare Council published a series of newsletters entitled *Prenatal Letters, Postnatal Letters*, and *Preschool Letters*. The 'Letters' series circulated, with various up-

dates, throughout the 1920s and 1930s; *The Canadian Mother and Child* remains in publication today. Advice manuals included Dr A. Brown, *The Normal Child, Its Care and Feeding* (Toronto: Macmillan, 1923); and Dr F.F. Tisdall, *The Home Care of the Infant and Child* (New York: Harper, 1931). Brown and Tisdall, Canada's foremost paediatricians during this period, worked out of Toronto's Hospital for Sick Children; with Dr T.H. Drake, they were the creators of Pablum. See also J. Mechling, 'Advice to Historians on Advice to Mothers,' *Journal of Social History* 9, 1 (1973): 65; and V. Strong-Boag, 'Intruders in the Nursery,' in J. Parr, ed., *Childhood and Family in Canadian History* (Toronto: McClelland & Stewart, 1982), 169–73.

27 Toronto City Hall Archives, RG 11, box 1, file 1, Historical Material on Maternal and Child Health, A. Thomson, 'Changing Practices in Public Health Nursing,' undated manuscript, 1930s, 1.

28 For example, R. Howe, 'A Woman's Place,' *Industrial Banner* 20 February 1920; and 'Leave Jack and Jill Alone,' *Canadian Congress Journal* 10, 1 (1931): 41.

29 J. Farrant, 'What of My Children?' *Canadian Trade Unionist*, 30 August 1932.

30 'Women Urge State Medicine,' ibid., 29 February 1932; 'Women Are Needed in the Labour Movement,' *The People's Cause*, 27 April 1926. On labour women's efforts, see J. Naylor, *The New Democracy* (Toronto: University of Toronto Press, 1991).

31 National Archives of Canada (NA), MG 28, I 10, vol. 35, file 168, Letters to the Canadian Welfare Council, from Norwich, Ontario, 25 August 1933; London, 21 August 1933; Rainy River, 1 April 1929, expressing a father's gratitude; Toronto, September 1933; and Kapuskasing, 16 December 1935. Although various government reports remark on the great number of letters sent to the council by mothers across the land, few seem to have survived.

32 Ibid., RG 29, vol. 991, file 499-3-2, pt 3, Canadian Welfare Council, from Sudbury, 8 January 1937. No reply was found.

33 For a discussion of the quintuplet's daily schedule and observations on their behaviour, see Dr W. Blatz, D. Millichamp, et al., *Collected Studies on the Dionne Quintuplets* (Toronto: University of Toronto Press, 1937), and Dr W. Blatz, *The Five Sisters: A Study of Child Psychology* (Toronto: McClelland & Stewart, 1938). See also L. Dempsey, 'What Will Become of Them?' *Chatelaine*, June 1937. Strong-Boag, 'Intruders in the Nursery'; P. Berton, *The Dionne Years* (Toronto: Penguin, 1977); and the special issue of *Journal of Canadian Studies* 29, 4 (1994–5), especially M. Valverde, 'Families, Private Property and the State: The Dionnes and the Toronto Stork Derby,' 15–35.

34 See, for example, Drs A. Brown and G. Campbell, 'Infant Mortality,' *CMAJ* 4, 8 (1914): 693. Brown received his postgraduate training in pediatrics under the renowned American pediatrician Dr L. Emmett Holt at the Babies' Hospital of New York; he was consultant to the Toronto Board of Health, and the federal and provincial Divisions of Maternal and Child Hygiene of the respective

health departments; he was physician in chief at Toronto's Hospital for Sick Children, 1920–50; chair of the Department of Paediatrics, School of Medicine, University of Toronto; and one of the founders of the Canadian Society for the Study of Diseases of Children (1920), later the Canadian Paediatric Society. Campbell did his postgraduate training at the Hospital for Sick Children, and was first director of the Division of Child Hygiene, Toronto Board of Health, 1913–14.

35 'Changes in the Cost of Living in Canada from 1913–1937,' *Labour Gazette*, June 1937, 819–21; Canadian Medical Association, *Annual Report*, 1934, 62; see also D. Naylor, *Private Practice, Public Payment: Canadian Medicine and the Politics of Health Insurance, 1911–1966* (Montreal and Kingston: McGill-Queen's University Press, 1986), 47.

36 NA, RG 29, vol. 991, file 499-3-2, pt 2, Canadian Welfare Council, letter to Minister of Health, signed 'A Worried Expectant Mother,' Wawbewawa, Ontario, 10 July 1935.

37 Dr J.T. Phair, 'Effectiveness of Child Health Programs in Ontario by Survey Methods,' *American Journal of Public Health* 30, 1 (1933): 127.

38 Canada, House of Commons, *Debates*, 25 January 1935, 204; League for Social Reconstruction Research Committee, *Social Planning for Canada* (Toronto: T. Nelson, 1935), 390.

39 AO, Pamphlet Collection, Dr J.T. Phair, 'Report of a Survey of the Services Extended by the Health Department of the City of Toronto,' December 1943, 2; AO, 16383, 3–14, Ontario Welfare Council, *Annual Report*, January 1930, Report of the Child Welfare Committee; also Dr A.M. Jeffery, 'The Private Physician Looks at Public Health Nursing,' *CPHJ* 23, 10 (1932): 459–60.

40 M. Power, 'The Scope of the Public Health Nurse,' Division of Maternal and Child Hygiene and Public Health Nursing, *Bulletin*, September–October 1924, 20.

41 B.E. Harris, 'The Public Health Nurse Looks at Herself,' *CPHJ* 23, 10 (1932): 467. On nursing, see K. McPherson, *Bedside Matters* (Toronto: Oxford University Press, 1997).

42 National Committee for Mental Hygiene, *A Study of the Distribution of Medical Care and Public Health in Canada* (Toronto: Department of National Health 1939), 82. Also Dr D.R. McClenahan, 'Observations on Rural Public Health Work in Ontario,' *CPHJ* 23, 4 (1932): 170–1.

43 See, for example, CMA, *Annual Report*, 1931, 324; ibid., 1933, 415; also editorial, 'Go Rural Young Man,' *The Canadian Doctor* 5, 5 (1939): 21–6; Department of Pensions and National Health, *Report of the Deputy Minister*, 1923, 39; House of Commons, *Debates*, 3 March 1930, 223; D. Mickleborough, 'Health Services Outside the City,' *Social Welfare* 14, 6 (1933): 197.

44 Ontario, Department of Health, *Annual Report*, 1927, 24; National Committee, *Study of the Distribution of Medical Care*, 84.

45 CMA, *Annual Report*, 1934, 34; AO, RG 10, 30–A-3, box 16, Public Health
   Nursing Field Reports, Apsley file, June 1935; also W.F. Marshall, 'The Red
   Cross Outposts,' *The Canadian Nurse* 26, 3 (1930): 128–30; An Ontario Outpost
   Nurse, 'Experiences in a Red Cross Outpost,' ibid., 22, 2 (1926): 76–7.

46 AO, RG 62, F-2, vol. 488, Field Reports, G. Bastedo, 'Public Health Work in the
   Thunder Bay District,' 19 September 1922; Department of Health, *Annual
   Report*, 1927, 70; M.E. Wilkinson, 'The Rural Community and the Nursing
   Outpost,' *The Canadian Nurse* 22, 6 (1926): 306–8.

47 AO, RG 10, 30-A-1, box 1, Field Reports, E. Corbman, Hastings County file,
   17 March 1925, 1–5; RG 62, F-2, vol. 488, Field Reports, G. Bastedo, 'Thunder
   Bay District,' 3.

48 Department of Pensions and National Health, *Annual Report*, 1928–9, 126.

49 Dr. H. MacMurchy, *Supplement to the Canadian Mothers' Book* (Ottawa: King's
   Printer, 1923), 139; Dr W. Woolner, (Ayr, Ontario), 'Medical Economics in
   Rural Districts of Ontario,' *CMAJ* 24, 3 (1934): 307; Dr W.E. Park, 'Rural Medi-
   cal Relief,' *CMAJ* 24, 4 (1934): 438.

50 AO, RG 10, 30–A-1, box 7, file 7, Division of Maternal and Child Hygiene and
   Public Health Nursing, *Annual Report*, 1933, Dr J.T. Phair, director, and Edna
   Moore, chief public health nurse, 'A Survey of the Effectiveness of Child
   Welfare Measures,' 3.

51 AO, RG 10, 30-A-3, box 3, Eastern Health Unit file, 'Varied Activities of Health
   Unit in 1937,' newspaper clipping, unknown source; also, 'Report on Child
   Welfare Work in the Eastern Ontario Health Unit,' 1937, 1.

52 AO, RG 62, f-2, box 488, Field Reports, I.J. Grenville, Report of Visit to
   Thessalon, December 1920–March 1921.

53 Ontario, Department of Health, *Annual Report*, 1950, 6, 79–81; also *Annual
   Report*, 1982, 'The Fifth Decade,' discusses advances in public health during the
   1940s and 1950s.

54 See M. Ladd-Taylor, *Mother-Work: Women, Child Welfare and the State* (Urbana:
   University of Indiana Press, 1993), 6, 189, for American developments parallel-
   ling these in Canada.

55 For examples, see the letters from dissatisfied mothers to the federal govern-
   ment's Division of Child and Maternal Welfare and the Canadian Welfare
   Council, expressing both gratitude for information and public health nurse
   visits and the need for provision of real medical care: Comacchio, *Nations Are
   Built of Babies*, 209–11. Similar letters from American mothers can be found in
   M. Ladd-Taylor, ed., *Raising a Baby the Government Way* (New Brunswick, NJ:
   Rutgers University Press, 1993).

Indian Reserves v. Indian Lands: Reserves, Crown Lands, and Natural Resource Use in Northeastern Ontario

JEAN L. MANORE

Today, non-Native Canadians generally believe that 'Indian lands' are synonymous with Indian reserves. This, however, is not the Native view of Indian lands. For many First Nations, the lands they claim are the lands that were used by their ancestors. Even those First Nations that have signed treaties in which land surrenders supposedly took place still claim rights of access and use, if not ownership, to their traditional territories. This view of the treaties stands in stark contrast to those of the federal and provincial governments. They argue that the Indian signatories surrendered all their title and rights to the land covered by the treaty, except for their reserved areas.

In addition to this profound dissonance between Native and non-Native perceptions of what constitutes Indian lands and of the proper interpretation of treaties is a disagreement over where Native and non-Native activities are to be allowed. Historically, Native economic activities were strictly defined by non-Native governments as hunting, fishing, and trapping. They were to take place only in areas where there were no non-Native activities – especially industrial ones. In effect, Native activities were to be segregated from non-Native activities, and were to take place ideally only on Indian reserves. Any Native activities off reserve would be limited and subject to the same legislative authority and regulation as non-Native activities. Many First Nations, however, wanted to include employment opportunities that were offered within the industrial economy into their traditional way of life. Reserves were places they could completely call their own, while the rest of the land was to be shared.

Historians and others have commented on these dissonant views, mostly in an effort to explain non-Native government policies towards Indian lands and peoples. In general, many have concluded that the non-Native view of restricting Indian lands and activities to Indian reserves has been unjust and, by implication, wrong. They have grounded their conclusions of injustice on ethnocentric interpretations by the federal and provincial governments of treaties, Aboriginal rights and title, and the Indian peoples themselves. This difference of opinion, however, goes beyond simple political narrow-mindedness.

First Nations experience the land in a different way than the non-Native governments. The former largely experiences the land through use – for example, through harvesting the living resources; the latter experiences it through control – through claiming ownership of the land and administering it. Thus, more than ethnocentrism or a 'cultural' dissonance is at work here; there is also a 'cognitive' dissonance, as each group knows or experiences the land differently.[1] Despite attempts by the non-Native governments to eliminate the Indian idea of land and Native use of it, it is clear from an examination of the historical record of treaties and their applications in Canada that each of these cognitive conceptualizations of the land continues largely intact to the present day.

When the Ontario and federal governments negotiated Treaty 9 with the Northern Cree and Anishnabe[2] in 1905–6 and 1929–30, for example, they agreed to set aside certain parcels of land for each of the signatory First Nations. According to the federal and provincial understanding of the treaty, each First Nation was to choose its own reserve and 'settle' within its boundaries. Yet, despite the establishment of the reserves, the northern First Nations continued to use or harvest the resources of the land and waters over a much broader area; they continued to live, work, and camp 'off reserve' on a regular basis. Even today, this level of activity remains largely intact, despite the sporadic attempts of the federal and provincial governments to restrict Indian movements and activities off-reserve in the northeast and elsewhere. Consequently, the Treaty 9 First Nations can and do argue that the treaty did not limit their use of the land to the reserve areas. They are not alone. Other First Nations, treaty and non-treaty, make the same argument. Hence, First Nations' understanding of Indian lands is, on a practical level at the very least, much broader than that delimited by reserves. As a result, one could argue that reserves are in essence non-Native constructions superimposed over a landscape of more ancient custom and usage.

Thus, First Nations' continued use of the resources of a vast stretch of territory points to a weakness in the limited conceptualization of Indian lands as strictly Indian reserves – a weakness that the federal and provincial governments are slowly recognizing in their current negotiations with First Nations for land and resource management agreements. Yet because the

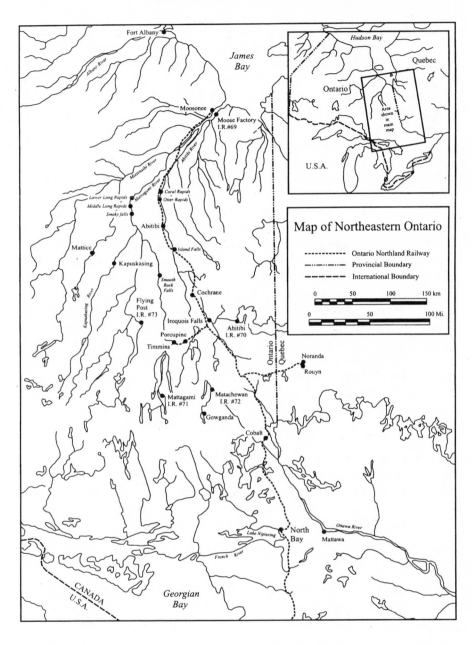

Map of Northeastern Ontario

- - - - - - - - - Ontario Northland Railway
- · - · - · - · - Provincial Boundary
- - - - - - - - - International Boundary

| 0 | 50 | 100 | 150 km |
| 0 | 50 | 100 Mi. |

non-Native orthodox view of Indian lands as reserves persists, there is significant resistance within government, and by large sectors of the non-Native public, to these initiatives. An examination of the causes and history of these conflicting views of Indian land, using Treaty 9 and northeastern Ontario as a representative example, will provide a timely context for these negotiations and perhaps lead to a greater understanding of the historic relationship between Native and non-Native peoples and the land.

The Aboriginal peoples who inhabit northeastern Ontario are Cree and Anishnabe. In early contact times, these First Nations relied on hunting, fishing, and gathering for their food supplies. The seasonal availability of these living resources contributed to the mobile existence of the bands, as they travelled to their traditional lakes and rivers to fish in the warmer months of the year, and inland to their traditional lands to hunt for game in winter.[3] By the late eighteenth century, fur traders from both the North West Company and the Hudson's Bay Company were trading regularly with Native people in the Moose-Mattagami drainage basin. It has been argued that the intense competition between the two fur-trading companies created pressures on the Native peoples to increase their trapping activities.[4] Certainly, during this time, many Native individuals and families did develop some dependency on European traders and their goods and also began to settle near or adjacent to trading posts, as occurred around Fort Matawagamingue (Mattagami).[5] They did not, however, abandon their traditional pursuits and continued to depend on the land and resources for their survival. This way of life is amply illustrated by a quotation from an Ontario survey report written in 1901:

> There was good soil around Fort Mattagami and northwards and over to the east along the Grassy River there were many cabins belonging to Indians who made their summer homes there and were attempting to grow their own supplies. They were not too successful at this because they had to delay planting until the finish of their hunting season in June. But they did well with fish. Whitefish spawned in the river just before the Indians went out again to their hunting grounds for the winter and they caught great quantities in nets.[6]

When non-Native industrial activities such as mining, lumbering, and generating hydroelectricity spread into northern Ontario, they conflicted with and disrupted the traditional lifestyles of the northern First Nations to a far greater degree than had the post-contact fur trade. The Cree and Anishnabe consequently complained to government officials, pointing out that the resource developers were trespassing on their lands. As a result, the federal and Ontario governments realized the need to negotiate an agreement with the First Nations for land-use rights. The mechanism adopted by all the parties to reach agreement was the treaty.

Treaty 9, initially signed during the summers of 1905 and 1906, contained three key clauses that set the framework for future confusion over Native and non-Native rights to lands and resources within the treaty area. Within these clauses, the ambiguous wording allowed for both the Native and the non-Native view of Indian lands.

The first of these clauses stipulated that reserves should be laid aside for each of the signatory bands,

> the same not to exceed in all one square mile for each family of five or in like proportion for larger or smaller families, and the location of the said reserves was arranged between His Majesty's Commissioner and the chiefs and head men, as was described in the schedule of reserves, the boundaries to be hereafter surveyed and defined.

Furthermore,

> such portions of the reserves as may at any time be required for public works, buildings, railways or roads of whatsoever nature may be appropriated for that purpose by His Majesty's Government of the Dominion of Canada, due compensation being made to the Indians for any improvements thereon.

In addition to the reserve lands, the First Nations were to have

> the right to pursue their usual vocations of hunting, trapping and fishing throughout the tract surrendered ... subject to such regulations as may from time to time be made by the governments of the country, acting under the authority of His Majesty, and saving and excepting such tracts as may be required or taken up from time to time for settlement, mining, lumbering, trading or other purposes.[7]

These three clauses are the linchpin on which the cognitive dissonance of the Native and non-Native societies rest. According to the federal government, the lands occupied by the First Nations were to be surrendered for the purposes of opening up the territory for settlement and resource development when required. Those lands that remained in Indian hands – the reserves – were to be the only remaining Indian lands: the only ones to which they had a continuing claim.

Behind this simple division of land between Native and non-Native constituencies lay numerous cultural assumptions on the part of the non-

Native governments about Indians and Indian land. After the treaty was signed, the federal and provincial governments viewed Indian lands solely as Indian reserves, and any lands that were to be used for industrial development or state-building purposes became non-Indian lands. Further proof of this distinction comes from another clause in Treaty 9 which stipulated that no reserves were to contain water power sites capable of generating energy over 500 horsepower. What is of paramount importance in interpreting the treaty, however, is not that the Treaty 9 territory could be divided neatly into Native and non-Native areas, but that much of the Treaty 9 area remained in an undeveloped state – as crown land – and therefore remained outside this seemingly straightforward dichotomy. As long as the land remained undeveloped, then, according to the third clause of the treaty noted above, the First Nations could continue to pursue their traditional activities: that is, they could continue to exercise their Aboriginal hunting and fishing rights off the reserves. In doing so, their way of knowing the land continued intact, including knowing the land beyond a reserve's boundaries.

Even today this perception is valid because large areas of Treaty 9 continue to be free of industrial development. To illustrate how this cognitive dissonance manifested itself in the Treaty 9 territory, we can look at two issues that continue to be of great importance to Native and non-Native people: reserves and hunting and fishing activities.

Before Treaty 9 Indian reserves could be 'officially' recognized, they had to be surveyed and confirmed by the federal and Ontario governments. In most cases, the surveys were readily confirmed, but there were several instances in which the provincial government disputed the surveyor's suggested boundaries. In each case, the objections arose because projected reserves contained within them areas compatible for development activities.

Abitibi Indian Reserve 70, for example, was confirmed by order in council in 1907, with an addition confirmed in December 1910. Confirmation, however, was not automatic. Abitibi was a reserve in which mining claims had been allotted before the survey of the reserve. In May 1908 J.D. McLean of the Department of Indian Affairs wrote to Aubrey White of the Ontario Department of Lands and Forests informing him that the surveyor of Indian Reserve 70 noted that he 'found a number of mining claims staked out and in one case preparations were being made apparently for active work.'[8] McLean, uncertain how to deal with these claims, asked White for direction.[9] As a result, discussion took place between officials in Indian Affairs and their counterparts in Lands and Forests. By July 1909 it was agreed that the Indians of Abitibi would receive another tract of land at the northwest corner of their reserve in exchange for the mining locations situated within their original reserve boundaries.[10] Thus, the provincial government sought to ensure that the Abitibi reserve and others were separated from development areas, maintaining the dichotomy of Native/non-Native lands as established by Treaty 9.

The Mattagami Indian Reserve also involved considerable negotiations between the federal and provincial governments. In the Schedule of Reserves appended to the original Treaty 9 document, Mattagami Indian Reserve 71 was described as being on the west side of Mattagami Lake.[11] Before the reserve was surveyed, however, a disagreement arose between the Mattagami First Nation and the federal and Ontario governments. In a letter dated 5 January 1908, James Miller, the Hudson's Bay Company agent at Fort Mattagami who was writing on behalf of the Indian signators of the Mattagami Band, explained the problem to the Treaty 9 commissioner, D.C. Scott:

> On reading the report of the transactions at Metagami [sic] to the men of the tribe, I found them unanimous in disgust and indignation at the reserve laid aside for them within the boundaries mentioned in the report. I myself was as certain as they that this was not the tract of land promised and to convince myself I communicated with three of the witnesses of the Treaty ... and found them all of our opinion here ... Their reserve promised lies East of the Metagami River immediately north of the [Hudson's Bay Company] Post.[12]

Scott and the other treaty commissioners, Samuel Stewart and Daniel MacMartin, attributed the confusion to a 'clerical error,' and in their letter to Frank Pedley, deputy superintendent general of Indian affairs, wrote:

> We beg to submit that no clerical error should operate to deprive the Indians of the land which they themselves chose and which was confirmed by the Commissioners and promised them on the spot as the consideration under which they gave their adherence to the terms of the Treaty.[13]

The Department of Indian Affairs complied with the request of the Mattagami people and the Treaty 9 commissioners to have the Indian reserve at Mattagami changed to the east side of the Mattagami River. The Ontario government also agreed to this change, but only after securing the rights to all timber over eight inches in diameter on those lands for a period of ten years, effective from 1907.[14]

In approving the new description of Indian Reserve 71, the provincial government had succeeded in exerting its control over a valuable resource even within a reserve. Although the Mattagami negotiation was an unusual situation, it demonstrates that, even if natural resources were found within Indian reserves, the province tried to separate them from First Nations to ensure their development. Thus the province acted as if development activities would or could only be undertaken by non-Natives on non-Native land. Perhaps it was in this policy that the seeds of the 'welfare Indian' were planted. There was no recognition on the part of non-Native governments that Aboriginal culture might include developing an industrial economy, despite the knowledge that Aboriginal people did take employment as construction workers, lumberers, and transporters.

This point needs further elaboration. To be Aboriginal as defined by non-Native governments meant, among other things, to pursue an economic lifestyle of hunting game, trapping furs, and fishing for subsistence rather than commercial purposes. If an Aboriginal person were to participate in the industrial economy, he or she was viewed as someone assimilating into, rather than adapting to, the non-Native 'mainstream.' In other words, to non-Native officials, an Aboriginal construction worker was less 'Indian' than an Aboriginal trapper. 'Aboriginality' was something frozen in time: there could be no change without a concurrent loss of Aboriginal identity.

By examining the process of confirmations, we have a clear record of Treaty 9 fulfilling its purpose of dividing the land into Native and non-Native areas just as the federal and provincial governments intended it to do. In the examples provided, the provincial government insisted, and the federal government concurred, that areas of development, potential or real, be excluded from Indian reserves. Yet even though the land was ostensibly categorized neatly as either Native or non-Native, the First Nations in the area continued to pursue their usual harvesting activities both on and off reserve. Thus Native and non-Native activities seemingly were not as easily divided as Native and non-Native lands. This point can be demonstrated by looking at the activities of the northeastern First Nations after the signing of Treaty 9.

According to Jim Morrison, the boundary separating the traditional territories of the Cree and Anishnabe in the Moose/Mattagami watershed was located in the Smoky Falls area near the Kapuskasing and Groundhog River junctions.[15] After the treaty, these two groups of peoples continued to traverse much the same area harvesting fish, fur, and game, but also seeking seasonal employment with the Hudson's Bay Company, Revillon Frères, the railways, and the pulp and paper industries. People from the Matachewan Band continued to trap in the eastern portions of the Porcupine, while members of the Mattagami Band trapped northwest of Timmins and along the Northern Transcontinental Line at Driftwood, Hunta, and Smooth Rock Falls. Others spent most of their time in newly established communities at Mattice and Smoky Falls. From Mattice, many spread out to traplines north of Kapuskasing. In the Abitibi area, trapping and other harvesting activities continued along the Abitibi and Mehkwanegon rivers. Certainly, there was some movement of families and of traplines from 1906 onwards because of hydroelectric generation, mining, and pulp and paper activities, yet, despite these site-specific developments that destroyed various wildlife habitats or drove wildlife away, the harvesting activities of the northern First Nations continued, in combination with industrial employment.

Oral testimonies taken from elders in the late 1980s portray not only the variety of activities pursued by the First Nations but their extensive use of the resources of the land and the vast territory they covered in order to do so. Consider the testimony of Jane Louttit of the Moose Factory First Nation, who was born in 1922.[16] She spent all her childhood summers in the bush, frequenting areas such as Kesagami River, Hannah Bay River, Missinaibi River, and Kapuskasing. She wintered in Moose Factory. Her father's trapline was located at Wash-Ush-Gaw, or South Bluff Creek, which is 12 miles south of Moosonee. Her father caught fish and sold them at Wetabohigan River to the Ontario Northern Railway cookery. She also remembers:

> We used to stay all together and set nets in an area known as Niskinneau, which is two or three miles down river from Moose Factory. There would be a lot of tents. We would catch fish and salt them in barrels. We would smoke them until they would turn dry and crisp ... Another place that we caught fish was located directly down the river from Moose Factory. That place we called Muncie ... We would leave Moose Factory in August and get to Kapuskasing in September. We would go up the Mattagami River and then up the Kapuskasing River. I did this three times in the 1930s. I would walk most of the way.[17]

Louttit also mentioned that her father trapped at a place called Big Stone, half way between Moose Factory Island and the Harricinaw River.[18]

George Cheena, who was born in 1928 and was also a member of the Moose Factory First Nation, testified that he moved his traplines from the Moose River to Fraserdale because the dams lowered the waters and the area became too dry. Cheena's father trapped 'all over the place including at James and Hannah Bays ... He used to spend eight months in the bush and four months in Moose Factory.'[19]

James Roderique, who was born in Hearst in 1924, grew up in Mattice with his parents until 1943, when he went to live with his grandparents along the Smoky Line, a railroad that used to run from Kapuskasing to the Smoky Falls Dam. He, too, was a member of the Moose Factory First Nation. James's experiences following the traditional way of life were extensive. He reported:

> I lived in the bush from 1943 to the 1960s, trapping along both sides of the Smoky Line, going north along the Kapuskasing River to about 15 miles from Smoky [sic] Falls ... I spent the winters in the bush, and also parts of the summer ...
>
> The Becks, a Cree family ... had their trapping grounds close to our family, on the east side of the Mattagami River near to where the Harmon and Kipling dams are located now. The Becks and the Cheenas trapped around Smoky Falls and up to Mileage 35 on the Smoky Line.[20]

His testimony also revealed that the traditional activities of berry picking, hunting, and fishing continued to be important economic activities for him and his extended family. They caught fish in abundance, including sturgeon, whitefish, and trout along the Kapuskasing River and on many creeks that flowed into that river. Another gathering place for him and other Cree families was at Remi Lake in what is now René Brunelle Provincial Park. They would meet there during the summer as their forebears had done for 'hundreds and hundreds of years.'[21]

Peter Sutherland, a member of New Post First Nation, had his trapping territory east of Fraserdale. It used to stretch from the mouth of the New Post Creek right up to the dam at Island Falls. He reminisced:

> Our ground was around the lake across the Little Abitibi River and the head waters of New Post Creek ... During the 1930s and 1940s my foster father Thomas Sutherland and I trapped to the east of Island Falls and worked as labourers on the railway in the summer ... I trapped there until 1956 when I moved to Moosonee.[22]

The above examples amply illustrate that Native people continued to hunt and fish, to exercise their Aboriginal rights, both on and off reserve. They also illustrate the interaction between the Native and non-Native economies, an interaction that complemented, rather than replaced, the Aboriginal practice of hunting and fishing. For Aboriginal people, Indian lands were, in a practical sense at least, not limited to Indian reserves.

There are even instances where bands never settled on their allotted reserves or where they left them for long periods of time. It appears from the historical record that the Moose Band never lived on the original reserve set aside for it under the treaty. In fact, by 1912, with the assistance of the Rt Rev. John G. Anderson, Anglican bishop of the diocese of Moosonee, the Moose Band requested a different reserve. In a letter to the secretary of the Department of Indian Affairs, the chief and councillors explained their request:

> When the treaty was made with us, a reserve on French Creek was given us, about seven miles south of Moose Fort. We find on examination that the above reserve is a poor one, not suitable for wood or farming. The wood has been largely cut down or destroyed and the land is too stony for agricultural purposes. Besides there is very poor hunting there. The arrangements were too hurriedly made and did not give us time to investigate. We much prefer and do hereby apply for a reserve extending from North Bluff to Navy Creek about nine miles N.W. from Moose Fort along the coast towards Albany. This is most suitable for all purposes – for farming and hunting and wood supply. Though rather swampy further back, it is far ahead of the French Creek Reserve. The hunting is especially good and we could leave our old and infirm there while the hunters are away in the winter, and they would be comfortable – there being also good fishing in the various creeks and streams.[23]

On 7 October 1912 J.D. McLean referred the petition to Aubrey White. McLean stated that his department had no trouble agreeing to the Indians' request and asked White if the provincial government would agree to the change.[24] White's initial reaction was unfavourable, stating in a letter to McLean that the province was not given sufficient reasons to make the change.[25] Apparently, the Band Council's petition had not been forwarded to White along with the letter of 7 October 1912.[26]

The matter of getting suitable reserve land for the Moose Band was still an issue in 1930. W.C. Cain, White's successor, informed A.F. MacKenzie, McLean's assistant, that his department would be glad to give the matter further consideration, although, he noted:

> While the Department is always glad to co-operate with the Indian Depart-ment in matters pertaining to the Indians, I do feel that after a Reserve has been duly established and laid out in accordance with the terms of Treaty, some hesitation should be shown in undertaking to make any substitution therefor.[27]

The provincial department's hesitation continued until 25 January 1956. On that date, Factory Island 1 was confirmed as a reserve for the Moose Band by order in council. During all this time and beyond, the Moose Band Cree had continued to visit their usual fishing spots and traplines, most of which were off reserve.

Thus, by examining the administrative history of reserves and contrasting it with Aboriginal off-reserve activities, it is apparent that there is an administrative history that supports the government goal of opening up land for development. Yet, despite this development agenda, there is also a history of use by the First Nations in the Treaty 9 territory, with continued visits to family hunting grounds and seasonal migrations.

The other area of significant cognitive dissonance over the meaning of Treaty 9 is illustrated by the history of Brunswick House Indian Reserve 76. To the provincial and, at times, the federal government, Treaty 9 extinguished Aboriginal rights to hunt and fish off reserve except on crown lands on which there was no industrial development. However, the province also believed it had the responsibility to protect fish and game species from depletion. Part of this responsibility arose from the knowledge that many non-Native people also engaged in hunting and fishing activities, further blurring the distinction between Native and non-Native pursuits. Consequently, the province passed legislation for the conservation of these living resources not only over areas that were settled or developed but also over those that were undeveloped. As long as these living resources were plentiful – which generally meant there was little or no non-Native activity – then Indians could harvest them. When they became scarce, however, the province felt obliged to restrict Aboriginal rights to hunt and fish on unsettled portions of the Treaty 9 territory.

Wildlife scarcity had become a concern by the time the Department of Game and Fisheries made its annual report in 1919. The department noted that 'great inroads have been made upon the fur-bearing animals, as well as the game and birds of the province during the past few years, and more attention must be given by the Department to the existing conditions.'[28] In particular, the Ontario deputy minister of game and fisheries strongly recommended in this report that 'one or more suitable areas of considerable extent be set aside by the Government for the establishment of a Game Sanctuary or Sanctuaries which, in my opinion, should be located somewhere in the north or western part of the province where arrangements could be readily made for such purposes and which are suitable for natural conditions.'[29] Towards that end, the Chapleau Game Preserve was established by an Ontario order in council effective 1 June 1925. The preserve comprised about 2600 square miles and completely surrounded New Brunswick House Indian Reserve 76.[30]

While Game and Fisheries staff fretted over declining wildlife resources, members of the New Brunswick House First Nation continued to hunt, trap, and fish, even though they also appeared to hold waged employment off the reserve, at least on a seasonal basis.[31] Once the preserve was established, however, Ontario game wardens administered it as if Indian Reserve 76 were part of the game preserve. All persons, whether Native or not, found hunting or trapping within the boundaries of the game preserve were either removed or charged under the Game and Fisheries Act.[32] The Rev. George Prewer reported to D.C. Scott, deputy superintendent general of Indian affairs, that the Indians, when attempting to enter their trapping areas inside the Game Preserve, were 'halted at these game preserve boundaries and either turned back or stripped of their guns, traps and other paraphanalia [sic] which goes to make up their necessary equipment.'[33]

On 12 November 1925 Scott wrote to W.C. Cain stating that the New Brunswick House Band was 'rightly entitled to some reasonable compensation' because the province of Ontario had 'barred them from enjoyment of the privileges accorded them under the terms of Treaty No. 9, by including within the closed area [game preserve], the New Brunswick House Reserve.'[34] Scott suggested that the band surrender the reserve for sale to the province, and that money from the sale be used for the band's benefit.[35] The province agreed.[36]

The Department of Indian Affairs obtained a surrender of Indian Reserve 76 from the New Brunswick House Band on 18 June 1926. In submitting the surrender documents to the Department of Indian Affairs, T.J. Godfrey, the Indian agent at Chapleau, reported that he

> did not find one objection in the whole band but rather a feeling that they were anxious to dispose of it as the placing of their reserve within the limits of the game sanctuary has imposed a hardship on this band of Indians as they have not only lost the use of their reserve, but all good hunting and trapping grounds which were located all around their reserve, and the action of the Provincial Government in creating this sanctuary has imposed great hardship and distress on this band and many of them are having a hard time to find a place to hunt and trap and are having much difficulty in making a living.[37]

In this instance, it appears that the province's right to conserve wildlife prevailed over Aboriginal rights to hunt and fish. However, statements from several band members of other reserves in the northern portion of Treaty 9 illustrate that the enforcement of the province's conservation laws were at best spotty and in many instances completely unsuccessful. Examining these oral testimonies enables us to comprehend that a different history of the Treaty 9 area also exists from that found in the provincial documented history. The oral testimonies illustrate that, once again, a history of use by Aboriginal peoples was maintained despite legislative restrictions.

James Davey was born at Me-tito-Bostik (Grand Rapids) on the Mattagami River in 1922 and is a member of the Moose Band. He stated in his testimony that he was born in the bush on his family's trapping grounds and that Moose Factory was the family base camp where he and his family spent the summers. When trapping was no longer economically viable because the price of furs had fallen and/or the animals had become scarce, he worked at the Moose Factory hospital power house. 'Even in my lifetime,' he noted, 'Native people did not need the whiteman to tell them where and when to hunt. We did not require permission from the government, such as licenses. Whenever we needed food, we simply went into the bush and hunted, or went to the rivers to fish. Today there are too many rules and regulations.'[38]

Peter Sutherland had this to say about provincial government regulations:

> Some of the game wardens bothered us a lot. I recall one time when a game warden took away my net when I had it set in a lake while I was trapping. I had set it in the lake, not the river, so I would not be seen, but the warden was spying on me with binoculars. When he came to get the net, he asked me what I had a gun for, and who had caught the pike ... I told him I knew I had a right to do that, but he took my net. I told him I was going to keep on fighting to know more about my rights for hunting and fishing. Four days after he took my net, I got word from him saying he was sorry, they had made a mistake in taking my net, and then they shipped it back to me. This incident made me feel very hurt, because I was being stopped from living as an Indian.[39]

Bert Jeffries, who was born in 1924, remembered

> people being upset by the government's plans to build the bird sanctuary on Ship Sands Island in the 1940s at the mouth of the river. That was a very big issue. The people were worried that they would not be able to go to Ship Sands Island any more. When the document was signed, the game warden, Aleck Hunter, told us that native people would be allowed to hunt on the sanctuary, that it would be closed only to white hunters. We found out later that anybody caught hunting in the sanctuary would be taken to court by the Ministry of Natural Resources. The document was signed around 1949, but the sanctuary was not officially in use until ten years later. Once it was in use, Daniel Wesley was arrested after shooting a moose on Ship Sands Island. The moose and his equipment were confiscated and were later returned to him.[40]

The experiences of these individuals illustrate that the provincial government did on occasion attempt to prevent Native people from hunting and fishing off reserve, but was often unsuccessful in doing so. Additionally, within the past twenty years, First Nations have increasingly asserted their rights to hunt and fish. At the same time, the ambiguous status of Aboriginal rights and title within Canadian law has made the issue of land use and access a lot more cloudy for the provincial and federal governments.

In this century, several cases involving charges laid against Aboriginal people for hunting illegally have reached the Supreme Court of Canada. Often, if the charges were laid by provincial authorities in the name of conservation, the court rejected their ability to deny Aboriginal rights to hunt and fish. If, on the other hand, federal authorities laid the charges, usually under the Migratory Birds Convention Act, the Supreme Court acknowledged the federal authority to deny these rights in situations where conservation of a particular species was deemed necessary.[41]

Other Supreme Court cases involving more than hunting or fishing rights have also tended to support the Aboriginal view of land and resource use. In *Sioui v. R*, 1990, the Supreme Court recognized that treaties need not be limited to agreements over land; they could also include a recognition of political or cultural rights.[42] Thus, First Nations who were hunting to carry out a religious ceremony, for example, could have the right to do so even in off-reserve areas.

The *Sparrow* case, heard in late 1990, elaborated on the findings of the *Sioui* case to give recognition to the new status of Aboriginal rights as stipulated in the Constitution Act of 1982. In *Sparrow*, the court ruled that Aboriginal fishing rights were not traditional property rights. They were rights held by a collective and were in keeping with the culture and existence of that group.[43] Also, Aboriginal rights were not frozen in time, but could evolve with 'the changing needs, customs and lifestyles of Aboriginal Peoples.' Aboriginal peoples were to be given first priority in the allocation of renewable natural resources.[44] Although not every court case in recent years has ruled in a manner that supported or enlarged Aboriginal rights, many have reinforced the idea that the First Nations continue to enjoy Aboriginal hunting and fishing rights off reserve, despite a history of legislative rules and regulations that have tried to eliminate them.

In conclusion, there are many ways in which people 'know' the land. In the examples given above, varying interpretations over the concept of Indian lands stem not only from cultural dissonance or ethnocentrism but also from a variety of other factors: the ability of the First Nations to continue to use the land according to their ancient customs, and the ability of the federal government and, more especially, the provincial government to control or administer the land through legislation. Although Native and non-Native ways of knowing the land are disparate, clashes between the two views occurred only when non-Native activities destroyed natural habitats or depleted the living resources of fish and game. In recent years, these clashes have at times been mediated by the court system, with considerable, though not unanimous, support being given to the First Nations' interpretation of what their treaty and Aboriginal rights mean.

Today, with self-government negotiations taking place at the highest levels, co-management agreements being negotiated, and the Supreme Court of Canada reversing some of the ethnocentric decisions of the nineteenth century, the opposing ways of knowing the land are better shared and understood. It is interesting to note that through these various processes, the Aboriginal political leaders are now negotiating for administrative powers or control of the land, while the federal and provincial governments are recognizing Aboriginal uses of the land. This historic coming together of Native and non-Native viewpoints is always threatened by a public backlash, by citizens who feel threatened by the monetary cost of these negotiations or by the loss of access and privileges to selected areas of what they know as crown land. Many non-Native citizens feel that their way of knowing the land has not been adequately considered by the politicians. Their opposition to this coming together has resurfaced particularly in Ontario and British Columbia,[45] where provincial politicians are once again expressing sympathy with the concerns of these citizens, thereby threatening a process of reconciliation that has taken over a century to develop.

NOTES

1 For the purposes of this essay, cognitive dissonance occurs when individuals or groups have different knowledge and understandings about a given subject as a result of their experiences, training, or culture.
2 Anishnabe is the preferred appellation by those in northern Ontario who have been known historically as Ojibwa.
3 E.S. Rogers, 'Southeastern Ojibwa,' *Handbook of North American Indians*, vol. 15: *Northeast*, ed. Bruce G. Trigger (Washington, DC: Smithsonian Institution, 1978), 760–2.
4 E.A. Mitchell, *Fort Temiskaming and the Fur Trade* (Toronto: University of Toronto Press, 1977), 94.
5 E.E. Rich, *The History of the Hudson's Bay Company* (Toronto: 1960), 888; Ontario, Department of Lands and Forests, District History Series, 'A History of Gogama District, No. 11,' 1964, 29–30.

6 S.A. Pain, *The Way North: Men, Mines and Minerals, Being an Account of the Curious History of the Ancient Route between North Bay and Hudson Bay in Ontario* (Toronto: Ryerson Press, 1964), 99.

7 Canada, *Treaty 9, James Bay Treaty*, Report by the Treaty Commissioners, 5 October 1906 (reprinted 1962).

8 Ontario Native Affairs Secretariat (ONAS), Ministry of Natural Resources (MNR), Indian Land File 91551, Abitibi Indian Reserve 7, J.D. McLean, secretary, Department of Indian Affairs, to Aubrey White, deputy minister, Lands, Mines and Forests, 29 May 1908.

9 Ibid.

10 Ibid., Abitibi Indian Reserve 70, J.D. McLean, assistant deputy superintendent general, to T.W. Gibson, deputy minister of mines, 13 July 1909.

11 Ibid., MNR Indian Land File 39414, Mattagami Indian Reserve 71, 'Schedule of Reserves,' 1906.

12 Ibid., James Miller, Hudson's Bay Company (HBC) agent, Fort Mattagami, to D.C. Scott, acting deputy superintendent general of Indian Affairs, 5 January 1908.

13 Ibid., Treaty 9 Commissioners Scott, Stewart, and MacMartin to Frank Pedley, deputy superintendent general, Indian Affairs, 22 January 1908.

14 Ibid., Ontario Order in Council 3291/09, dated 20 January 1909. Ironically, the Mattagami Indian Band had chosen this eastern location with the intention of harvesting the timber themselves. See James Morrison, *Treaty 9: The James Bay Treaty* (Ottawa: DIAND, 1986), 56. The ten-year time limit elapsed before Ontario was able to remove the timber. Ontario requested an extension, but was turned down by the Department of Indian Affairs at the request of the Mattagami Indian Band. ONAS, MNR Indian Land File 91551, memorandum re Indian Reserves Treaty No. 9, 17 October 1919, from L.V. Rorke, director of surveys, Department of Lands, Forests, and Mines, to Albert Grigg, deputy minister of lands, forests and mines 4.

15 James Morrison, 'Colonization, Resource Extraction and Hydroelectric Development in the Moose River Basin: A Preliminary History of the Implications for Aboriginal People,' Report for Moose River/James Bay Coalition, Environmental Assessment, Ontario Hydro Demand Supply Plan (OH/DSP), November 1992.

16 Ontario Hydro Public Information Centre (OH/PIC), OH/DSP, witness statement of Jane Louttit.

17 Ibid.

18 Ibid.

19 OH/PIC, OH/DSP, witness statement of George Cheena.

20 Ibid., witness statement of James Roderique.

21 Ibid.

22 Ibid., witness statement of Peter Sutherland.

23 ONAS, MNR Indian land File 185901, Indian Reserve 68, Moose Factory, Chief and Councillors of Moose Factory Band to Secretary of the Indian Department, 2 October 1912.

24 Ibid., J.D. McLean, assistant deputy and secretary, to Aubrey White, deputy minister of lands, 7 October 1912.

25 Ibid., Deputy Minister to J.D. McLean, assistant deputy minister of Indian affairs, 10 October 1912.

26 Ibid., S. Stewart, assistant secretary, Department of Indian Affairs, to Aubrey White, deputy minister, Department of Lands, Forests and Mines, 14 October 1912.

27 Ibid., Deputy Minister to A.F. MacKenzie, acting assistant deputy and secretary, Department of Indian Affairs, 12 March 1930.

28 Mary-Lynn Murphy, 'Brunswick House Indian Band Land Claim with respect to the Chapleau Game Preserve and Brunswick House Indian Reserve 76, Treaty 9,' ONAS Research Report, 1987, 13.

29 Ibid.

30 Ontario, Sessional Papers vol. LXIV, no. 36, Department of Game and Fisheries, 1930.

31 Murphy, 'Brunswick House Indian Band Land Claim,' 14.

32 Ibid., 17.

33 Ibid.

34 National Archives of Canada (NA), RG 10, vol. 6745, file 420-8A, D.C. Scott, deputy superintendent general of Indian affairs, to W.C. Cain, deputy minister, Department of Lands and Forests, 12 November 1925.

35 Ibid.

36 NA, RG 10, vol. 6745, file 420–8A, D. McDonald, deputy minister of game and fisheries, to D.C. Scott, deputy superintendent general of Indian affairs, 27 November 1925.

37 David T. McNab, 'Research Report on the Chapleau Game Preserve and New Brunswick House Indian Reserve 76, Treaty 9,' ONAS Research Report, 1980, 6.

38 OH/PIC, OH/DSP, witness statement of James Davey.

39 Ibid., witness statement of Peter Sutherland.

40 Ibid., witness statement of Bert Jeffries.

41 Peter Cumming and Neil Mickenberg, eds., Native Rights in Canada (Toronto: Indian-Eskimo Association of Canada/General, 1972), 209.

42 Brian Slattery, 'Understanding Aboriginal Rights,' unpublished paper, 1986, 58.

43 Ibid., 19.

44 Larry Chartrand, 'R. v. Van der Peet: A Legal Leap Backward for Aboriginal Peoples,' unpublished paper, Ottawa 1996, 7.

45 Since writing this paper, tensions between Native and non-Native people have

also increased in New Brunswick, following the Supreme Court ruling on *R v. Marshall*. Some people interpreted this ruling as a recognition of a Mi'kmaq right to fish anywhere at anytime. The Supreme Court, in its response to a motion for a rehearing and stay of their judgment, denied that this was the meaning of their ruling and reasserted the authority of the federal government to regulate fisheries for the purpose of, among other things, conservation.

'Salvaging War's Waste': The University of Toronto and the 'Physical Reconstruction' of Disabled Soldiers during the First World War

RUBY HEAP

'Salvaging War's Waste,' the title of an article published in October 1917 in the *Red Cross Magazine*, the official organ of the American Red Cross, illustrated the impressive work being done by the Canadian government to restore 'wounded and disabled soldiers to health so that they can become self supporting.'[1] Canada's outstanding record in this area was also established two years later by Douglas C. McMurtrie, director of the American Red Cross Institute for Crippled and Disabled Men and editor of the *American Journal of Care for Cripples*. 'Great credit is due to our neighbor on [sic] the north for her promptness in making provision for her disabled men,' he wrote in *The Disabled Soldier*, a study in which he reviewed the various schemes adopted during the Great War by the Allied countries to take care of disabled soldiers and to facilitate their re-entry into civilian life.[2]

Indeed, McMurtrie's account pointed to the essential feature of Canadian policy: soon after the country entered the war, the federal government assumed a central and directing role in the formulation and implementation of policy concerning the rehabilitation of disabled soldiers. It acted as planner, organizer, trainer, and employer in the two major areas making up the federal scheme: the physical rehabilitation of wounded and disabled soldiers and, if necessary, their vocational training in a new trade. In order to fulfil its mission, the federal government had rapidly to mobilize its provincial counterparts as well as a wide array of institutions, organizations, and individual citizens in various arenas. With considerable human and material resources at their disposition, universities were among the first to be sollicited. Not surprisingly, the University of Toronto, as Ontario's provincial university and Canada's leading institution of higher education, was expected to make a significant contribution. Under the leadership of its president, Robert Falconer, who was totally committed to the war effort, the university readily obliged. It became the site where political, military, medical, and educational interests converged to deal with a problem that soon became a national crisis. This essay will discuss the key role played by the University of Toronto in the rehabilitation of Canada's disabled soldiers; it will focus specifically on the university's contribution to the 'physical reconstruction' of injured and disabled soldiers through the organization and delivery of those medical services which, as McMurtrie indicated, constituted the first of the two major features of the Canadian rehabilitation scheme.

So far, historians of education in Ontario have paid little or no attention to this significant dimension of the University of Toronto's contribution to the war effort.[3] In fact, as Brian McKillop recently observed in his groundbreaking study of Ontario universities, the intellectual and social history of the University of Toronto remains largely untold.[4] Our examination of the provincial university's direct involvement in the federal rehabilitation scheme sheds light on some of the most important issues raised by McKillop, including the university's evolving role as a social institution, its relationship with the state, the impact of the war on curricular and research developments, and the growing importance of the professional ideal in postwar Ontario. As we shall see, this ideal affected not only men but also a rising generation of middle-class single women who eagerly sought higher education as a means of entering those professions open to them.[5] Finally, this essay addresses themes that remain largely unexplored by Canadian medical historians: it considers the development of wartime orthopaedics, and touches on the history of disability by illustrating the interplay of wartime images, politics, institutions, and policies centred on the disabled soldier and the 'rebuilding' of his injured body.

What transpires throughout this discussion is the predominance of the University of Toronto on the provincial academic scene and the leading role it played in the national arena during this time of international crisis. In 1914 the editor of the Toronto's *Globe* wondered how 'the greatest Canadian university' would contribute to the war effort: 'Has war brought it no new occasion? no fresh fields? no widening horizons? no enlarged responsibilities for the Nation, for the Empire, for the World?' He went on to raise the fundamental question: 'What, indeed, is a university?'[6]

Disability Becomes an Object of National Policy

In 1914 Canada automatically entered the war on Great Britain's side. The federal government's immediate task was to mobilize a mass contingent of volunteers for overseas service in the Canadian Expeditionary Force (CEF).

More than 619,000 Canadians served in the CEF during the war, at first on a voluntary basis and then under compulsory conscription following the landslide victory of Robert Borden's Union Government in the 1917 federal election. Close to 52,000 men were killed in action or died of wounds. Three times as many were hospitalized for sickness or for wounds. The majority returned home, a novel situation that called for new policies with regard to their treatment and reinsertion as civilians. The problem of disabled veterans was especially formidable. At the end of 1919, more than 8000 were still in hospital. Although these servicemen suffered from a wide range of afflictions, including venereal diseases, tuberculosis, and 'shell-shock,' the amputees symbolized most visibly the destructive power of modern technological warfare. In 1922 some 3600 CEF veterans belonged to this group, the majority of whom had lost an arm or a leg.[7]

These war-maimed men formed a new constituency of disabled citizens. Before the war, disability was identified mainly with poor, working-class children and with adult male workers who had been injured on the job. Although groups of philanthropists and social reformers were growing more interested in the 'problem' of crippled children in the late nineteenth and early twentieth century, and workmen's compensation legislation was gradually adopted during the same period, these two categories of disabled civilians were still largely ignored and marginalized by the general population. The army of disabled soldiers returning home could not be so easily ignored, however, for many were young and otherwise healthy men. The character and severity of these battlefield injuries also struck the public eye. In sum, the physical devastation associated with the Great War spread the experience of disability through a larger segment of the population in addition to making it more visible.[8]

As a result, there was a significant shift in the perceptions of disability in both Western Europe and North America. Popular images of dismembered soldiers, as well as the painful reality of their new existence, raised public sympathy for the men who had sacrificed so much to defend their country. The nation, people believed, owed them a debt that could not be discharged by a mere pension award. In addition, the Great War reinforced the argument articulated by social reform advocates that most 'cripples' did not form a natural category of individuals whose physical disability was preordained. Instead, the majority were the products of warfare, industrial violence, disease, and poverty. In other words, disabled people were part of a social category: they were made, not born.[9]

In Canada, the Great War inspired similar sentiments with regard to disabled soldiers. As historians Desmond Morton and Glenn Wright point out in their study of the return of Canadian veterans to civilian life, Canadians would not tolerate seeing disabled veterans become beggars, dependent on family, friends, or public charity, as had been the case after earlier wars: 'That was a small but real social revolution.'[10] Other social and economic factors were also at play, mainly the threat of the 'pension evil' that had afflicted the United States after the Civil War, the fear of social disruption, and the increasing need for manpower. As early as 1915, Canadian Prime Minister Robert Borden declared that the care and rehabilitation of disabled veterans commanded the federal government's immediate attention.[11] The next major issue facing the Canadian state was to determine what kind of agency or agencies would be reponsible for implementing federal policy.

In 1914 the adoption of the War Measures Act by the Canadian Parliament massively increased the powers of the federal government. Furthermore, the British North America Act made Ottawa responsible for the provision of health services to the armed forces, which fell under its jurisdiction. As a result, the Borden government chose to centralize operations at the national level. The Military Hospitals Commission (MHC), a new federal agency headed by the Conservative leader of the Canadian Senate and composed of prominent male citizens, was established by order in council in June 1915. The MHC was given a wide array of responsibilities. First, it would provide wounded and disabled soldiers with the appropriate care to restore them to the best possible physical condition. Second, for those unable to return to military duty or to their previous civilian occupation, it would offer vocational training to restore them as self-sufficient and productive members of the community. The MHC led a highly orchestrated publicity campaign to educate Canadians on its pioneering work and, more fundamentally, to 'convince the ex-serviceman himself that his future prospects are good rather than hopeless, to disabuse the community of the notion that the crippled man is necessarly a helpless dependant, and to promote the most constructive possible spirit toward the disabled soldiers themselves.'[12]

By creating a single administrative body to implement its rehabilitation scheme, Canada took a different route from that chosen by England and France, where early efforts were conducted mainly at the local level by private agencies and municipal authorities.[13] The MHC moved rapidly into unchartered territory as it acquired a large number of institutions to provide for the active and long-term care of sick and wounded soldiers, and set up various mechanisms at the national and provincial levels to dispense vocational training to the disabled.[14] The MHC's performance on the medical front was quite impressive. By the end of 1917, the commission controlled over fifty military convalescent hospitals and nineteen sanatoria for tuberculosis, and had secured space and accommodation in some twenty-one general hospitals.[15]

Despite its success, or probably because of it, the MHC would not survive the war. The main issue was the responsibility for the active medical care of undischarged officers and soldiers in Canadian military hospitals. In 1917 the MHC engaged in a bitter territorial dispute with the Canadian Army Medical Corps (CAMC) over this matter. The CAMC and the military lobby ultimately won the battle. In 1918 the Borden government abolished the MHC, transferred a large number of its hospitals to the Department of Militia and Defence, and put the CAMC in charge of the medical work performed in these institutions. The CAMC, however, did not wish to be involved in the long-term care of soldiers suffering from tuberculosis, paralysis, or mental illness, or in the vocational training of discharged soldiers. In 1918 these responsibilities were assigned to the new Department of Soldiers' Civil Re-establishment (DSCR). For a brief period the DSCR delegated some of these tasks to the MHC's immediate successor, the Invalided Soldiers' Commission (ISC), which was placed under its direction. By the end of the war however, the DSCR was solely responsible for the Canadian state's rehabilitation scheme. The vocational training of returning soldiers constituted a large part of its work, while its medical branch expanded to meet the demand for long-term care.[16]

Ontario, the largest and richest province in the dominion, was expected to be a leading partner in the implementation of the Canadian rehabilitation scheme. The MHC's broad mandate directly touched on health and education, two areas that fell under provincial jurisdiction. In the context of an international crisis, however, a possible constitutional dispute was avoided. In 1915 the provincial premiers, including Ontario's William Hearst, agreed to let Ottawa assume full responsibility for the care and retraining of disabled soldiers; in return, provincial commissions would be created to assist the federal government in the area of job placement.[17] But Ontario soon demanded and secured complete control over vocational training, a sector in which it had invested considerably over the years. This arrangement proved to be the exception to the rule, as other provincial governments readily complied with federal policy in this area.[18]

Ontario did not dispute Ottawa's authority over the medical care and rehabilitation of wounded and disabled soldiers. In fact, the province became Canada's main centre of activity on this front. The largest number of hospitals – general, convalescent and sanitaria – controlled by federal authorities were located in Ontario. The provincial government also offered the MHC the mental hospital recently erected at Cobourg.[19] Toronto, for its part, became the main site for the MHC's artificial limb factory and for the retraining of blinded soldiers. The University of Toronto attracted the widest attention, as it became a leading theatre of activity in the physical rehabilitation of returning soldiers.

Restoring the 'Physical Man' at the University of Toronto

When war broke out there was no doubt in the mind of Robert Falconer that the University of Toronto had a major role to play in the defence of the Allied cause. In several emotional public speeches and articles, the former professor of theology invoked the themes of patriotism, idealism, duty, and sacrifice. That Falconer saw himself as a servant of the state, loyal to the government of the day, reinforced his resolve to serve Canada and the British Empire. Falconer was also drawn to Robert Borden and his Conservative Party. As the war progressed, Falconer came to be closely identified with the prime minister, his government, and his policies, including conscription.[20]

Falconer's contribution to the war effort was also closely identified with the University of Toronto's own record of service. Canada's leading university could readily offer a large pool of human and material resources to the nation. The high numbers of students and staff who enlisted for active service received considerable publicity and praise.[21] Buildings and grounds were taken over by the army and the Red Cross. The university was also soon engaged in the provision of overseas medical services. It rallied to Falconer's call for the mobilization of an entire base hospital for overseas service. In November 1915 No. 4 Canadian General Hospital was established in Salonika, Greece, with a capacity for over 1000 beds. In 1917 it was relocated to Basingstoke, England, where it remained for nearly two years. At No. 4 Canadian General, many prominent surgeons and physicians performed who were teaching at the University of Toronto before the war.[22]

On the home front, the University of Toronto became a key player in the federal government's rehabilitation scheme for returning injured and maimed soldiers. At first, the MHC solicited, and secured, Falconer's support for the extensive campaign it had launched to publicize its scheme. As Major John L. Todd, CAMC, a driving force in these propaganda efforts, conveyed to Falconer, it was imperative to make the general population appreciate the principles underlying the MHC's work, which could be summarized in the title of one of its publications: 'Once a Soldier, Always a Man.'[23]

The University of Toronto's involvement would soon expand. With the number of returning disabled soldiers increasing rapidly, the MHC's most pressing task in the early years of its existence was to provide for their physical rehabilitation. Inspired by the work performed by the Allied countries, especially by France's early implementation of a wide-ranging rehabilitation scheme, the commission, first, and, after 1918, the CAMC and the DSCR, organized and managed services for the soldiers' active medical and surgical treatment; for their 'functional re-education,' defined as the 'retraining' of disabled men on the 'physical side'; and for the provision of artificial limbs for all those who needed them.[24]

The provincial university became a leading participant in this process. Its contribution in this area was threefold. First, groundbreaking work in functional re-education was conducted on campus. Second, prominent members of the medical faculty were actively involved in the organization of wartime orthopaedic services, both inside and outside university walls. Finally, the university became the site where new categories of rehabilitation personnel were trained for the war effort, the two most important of which were physiotherapists and occupational therapists.

Hart House: A National Laboratory in 'Functional Re-education'

Reporting in 1918 to the DSCR on the work performed during the war in the area of physical rehabilitation, the newly established Invalided Soldiers' Commission (ISC) observed that functional re-education, 'a science little studied before the present war,' was now firmly established in Canada and in several European countries as a 'therapeutic method of prime importance in conserving and restoring the physical and mental powers of disabled soldiers.' The ISC then provided a detailed account of the pioneering and fruitful work begun in this new field in the 'psychological laboratory' of the University of Toronto.[25] This laboratory was under the supervision of Edward Alexander Bott, whose name is closely tied to the introduction of applied psychology in Canada. Bott had completed an undergraduate degree in philosophy at the University of Toronto in 1912 and had then begun doctoral work in the same discipline. But he was actually more interested in the emerging field of applied psychology. Based on experimental laboratory work, the 'new' psychology was reorienting the discipline in the United States by distancing it from philosophy. Bott was working as an assistant in the university's nascent pyschological laboratory when war broke out.[26]

The Great War provided Bott with the opportunity to promote this new field at the University of Toronto. Rejected from active service because of poor eyesight, he decided to devote himself fully to the rehabilitation of wounded and disabled soldiers. To this end, he transformed the psychological laboratory into a rehabilitation clinic. Assisted by an increasing number of students, Bott conducted experimental and research work on new treatments designed to hasten the recovery of soldiers afflicted by a derangement or destruction of normal voluntary functions, either physical or mental. He designed specific sets of exercises targeted at various kinds of disabilities, including limitations of joint movement and of muscle strength, paralysis resulting from damage to the nervous system, and physical and mental disturbances related to conditions of 'shock.' He was also strongly influenced by the groundbreaking work conducted by the French, who had successfully designed special devices and appliances aimed at challenging injured soldiers into recovering the use of their limbs. Bott's laboratory built scores of gadgets aimed at helping and encouraging patients to conquer their disabilities as rapidly as possible. Committed to the principles of the new psychology, he attached great importance to the motivational dimensions of his treatments. Functional re-education, he declared, was a 'mental tonic' that made each soldier an active and confident player in his recovery.[27]

In 1916 Bott applied his methods successfully to patients from the Central Military Hospital in Toronto. These results attracted the attention of the MHC, which resolved to organize his work on a much larger scale. Bott's clinic, which had already been enlarged because of increasing demand, was now in need of bigger quarters on the university campus. Fortunately, L-Col. Vincent Massey, who was personnally impressed by Bott's accomplishments, offered the use of Hart House, the new student building, still under construction, which his wealthy family estate had donated to the university. Following its transfer to Hart House in the spring of 1917, Bott's clinic was able to handle hundreds of cases with a strong success rate. These results were highly publicized by the university and by the MHC. The clinic also received recognition south of the border. On announcing the opening in New York of the first endowed American clinic devoted to the functional re-education of maimed soldiers and civilians in 1918, the *New York Times* described the impressive work already accomplished at Hart House. The treatment to be provided in New York would largely be based on that at the University of Toronto.[28]

Research constituted an essential dimension of Bott's war work. Although conducted under MHC sponsorship, it received no government funding during the war. It was supported by private donations, starting with an initial grant of $400 from Massey. Despite its precarious financial position, due mainly to rapidly declining enrolments and lack of proper government funding,[29] the University of Toronto was also willing to support what it considered to be deserving research. During the 1916–17 academic year, the Board of Governors established a special research fund of $15,000, part of which would be devoted to the physiological and psychological aspects of functional re-education.[30] This new fund called for the involvement of members of the medical faculty in Bott's team, thereby promoting closer links between medicine and the emerging discipline of psychology. Bott's appointment in 1918 as honorary captain in the CAMC symbolized this relationship.

The Development of Wartime Orthopaedics

Orthopaedic surgeons were directly involved with the physical restoration of injured soldiers during the Great War. On both sides of the Atlantic, the war spurred the growth of modern orthopaedics.[31] Canadian orthopaedics was still in its infancy before 1914. Along with their American and British counterparts, however, Canadian orthopaedists had made some advances through their involvement in the treatment of physically disabled children. The social 'discovery' of 'crippled children' by philanthropic and reformist interests in the late nineteenth and early twentieth century fostered the promotion of orthopaedists as medical specialists who could 'remake' crippled children. Robert Jones, the internationally known British orthopaedist, was closely associated with the cause of physically handicapped children before he directed his energies to the war effort.[32]

In Canada before 1914, Toronto was the site of considerable activity in this emerging field. Two of the country's most prominent orthopaedic surgeons, Clarence L. Starr and W.E. Gallie, had devoted a large part of their careers to the treatment of disabled children at the Hospital for Sick Children in Toronto. Established in 1875, the hospital had developed over the years as a privileged space for orthopaedics, to which it assigned a crucial role in helping crippled children become 'future useful members of society.'[33] Together, Starr and Gallie had built the hospital's international reputation for the quality and progressive nature of its surgical services. Both graduates of the University of Toronto, they had maintained a close relationship with their alma mater as members of its medical faculty.[34]

Canada's small contingent of orthopaedists grasped the opportunity the war offered them to prove the value of their specialty. The work they had performed on behalf of crippled children could now be directed towards the treatment of mutilated men. Starr's expertise, in particular, was put amply to use by the federal government. He led the Canadian orthopaedic services overseas between 1915 and 1917. Back in Canada, he was appointed as the Department of Militia's chief consultant for orthopaedic surgery and made responsible for organizing this service in Canada's military hospitals.[35] He also played a decisive role in the design of the MHC's rehabilitation plan. Along with his colleague Dr Gallie, he convinced the commission to centralize its orthopaedic work for the dominion in one institution located in Toronto. This goal was accomplished in 1917 when the MHC took over the Salvation Army's Booth Memorial Training College in the northern suburb of Davisville.

Starr and Gallie also secured the establishment of a government-run artificial limb factory, which also opened in 1917 in Davisville. They argued that the manufacturing of limbs, another major dimension of the commission's rehabilitation scheme, would yield better results if it were controlled by the state rather than by profit-driven private enterprise. The MHC promised to produce 'the best arms and legs devised anywhere in the world,' as well as orthopaedic apparatus such as splints, braces, and orthopaedic shoes. The factory would set the example by employing 'limbless soldiers' trained in the art of making artificial limbs and orthopaedic shoes.[36] At the same time, centralization would allow the young specialty of orthopaedics to supervise the work being performed more closely. Starr provided close assistance as the Department of Militia's chief orthopaedic consultant. When the DSCR took over the control of the limb factory in 1918, the plant was attached to the newly created Orthopaedic and Surgical Appliances Branch. An orthopaedic surgeon was appointed to examine all the cases for whom limbs were requested, to suggest any means of improving the appliances, and to instruct doctors from all parts of Canada on the dimensions of orthopaedic work.[37]

By producing a formidable number of injured bodies that had to be rebuilt in a speedy and economical fashion, the Great War gave Starr and Gallie the opportunity to secure state support for the establishment of a specialized and integrated infrastructure conducive to the growth of their specialty. The Toronto surgeons were able to set up wartime orthopaedic services in Canada similar to those organized in Great Britain under the supervision of the celebrated Robert Jones, who acted as director of Military Orthopaedic Services during the war.[38]

The Military School of Orthopaedic Surgery and Physiotherapy

The organization of wartime orthopaedics created the need for a number of auxiliary personnel who would accelerate the convalescence of patients once active treatment had ended. Physiotherapists represented one of the most important groups in this category. The small contingent of surgeons engaged in orthopaedic work on both sides of the Atlantic had for some time been promoting the therapeutic value of massage and remedial gymnastics, especially in the treatment of physically disabled children.[39] Now, when it was realized that surgery and medical care alone could not ensure the satisfactory restoration of severely wounded and disabled men, the Great War prompted the rapid organization of physiotherapy services in military hospitals overseas and on the home front.

Canada joined the Allied countries in this endeavour. The country's 'special' military hospitals in England were the first to provide physiotherapy treatments. Along with massage and gymnastics, these treatments encompassed various methods derived from the use of light, heat, water, and electricity. The Granville Special Hospital in Ramsgate, where Clarence Starr served as senior surgeon during his tour of duty, boasted one of the most advanced physiotherapy departments overseas. Impressed by the beneficial results obtained on the front, the MHC decided to offer physiotherapy services in its numerous hospitals, a process pursued on a larger scale when the CAMC and the DSCR took over these institutions in 1918.[40]

There was, however, a formidable obstacle to the efficient operation of these services: the lack of suitable rehabilitation personnel. While Canadian overseas hospitals relied on nursing sisters, enlisted men, and trained British physiotherapists, the federal government chose to depend at home on a distinct group of civilians specifically trained for rehabilitation work. When war broke out, physiotherapy was practically non-existent, except for a few isolated 'masseurs,' 'masseuses,' and medical gymnasts who had trained outside the country.[41] The MHC decided at first to train military men, but the return of thousands of injured and maimed soldiers created an urgent need for a large number of therapists. This state of emergency opened the door to civilians, and, specifically, to women.[42]

To train this new category of workers, the MHC sollicited the help of Canada's major universities. McGill responded first in 1916 by offering at its School of Physical Education a one-year diploma course in massage and medical gymnastics. The University of Toronto followed suit in 1917, when it allowed the MHC to transfer to Hart House the classes in massage it had set up originally in Whitby, Ontario. Before long, the provincial university was involved in a much larger scheme. In 1918 the federal government authorized the establishment at Hart House of a Military School of Orthopaedic Surgery and Physiotherapy. The name of the new institution illustrates the close association between wartime orthopaedics and the emergence of physiotherapy in Canada. In fact, the school would act mainly as a national centre for the training of doctors and auxiliary personnel in the methods of physiotherapy. It was established as a unit of the Canadian Army and put under the command of a member of the CAMC. Its staff comprised military as well as civilian personnel, both paid and unpaid. The unpaid civilians were members of the University of Toronto's medical faculty who had volunteered their services. They would help train doctors coming from all parts of the country, as well as the first major contingent of physiotherapists employed in Canadian military hospitals.[43]

Over 250 physiotherapists were trained at Hart House before the school closed its doors in July 1919. The majority were women, identified by their commanding officer as his 'salvage crew.'[44] But the Military School of Orthopaedic Surgery and Physiotherapy was also responsible for the training of other categories of rehabilitation personnel. Men selected from the Canadian Army Gymnastic Staff were trained as medical remedial gymnastics instructors. Physical training was taught to army sergeants, who were then assigned to give drill and free exercices to patients on the eve of their discharge. Following the example of St Dunstan's Hostel in London, England, an institution that had acquired international fame by devoting itself to the vocational re-education of soldiers and sailors who had lost their sight, the school was also given the authority to train blinded soldiers as masseurs, with a graduate from St Dunstan's as their instructor.[45] Finally, the establishment of the Military School gave further impetus to the research that Bott had been conducting at Hart House on functional re-education, in collaboration with the university's Department of Physiology. This work was pursued on a much larger scale after 1918. The school also assumed control of the various voluntary contributions awarded to Bott's research team over the years by private individuals, the University of Toronto, the Canadian Red Cross, and various other organizations.[46] The decision to coordinate Bott's research activities and sources of funding illustrates the lack of proper policies and administrative agencies responsible for this kind of academic work during the war.

The Training of Occupational Therapists at the Faculty of Applied Science and Engineering

'Hart House,' as the Military School of Orthopaedic Surgery and Physiotherapy became known, was not the only site at the University of Toronto which was involved in the training of rehabilitation personnel. The Faculty of Applied Science and Engineering was responsible for the training of occupational therapists, another new category of rehabilitation workers which, in this case, was entirely composed of women. Occupational therapy as a specific method of treatment did not exist in Canada before the war. Essentially curative in character, it was based on the principle that occupation provided the best tonic, at both the physical and the mental level, for those disabled and wounded soldiers destined to long periods of con-valescence. The treatment was completed in two consecutive stages: ward occupations and curative workshops. In the hospital wards, the patients began by performing light work such as basketry, embroidery, weaving, toy making, and other simple handicrafts. Then they moved to 'curative work-shops,' where they performed heavier work in trades such as auto mechan-ics, drafting, woodworking, stenography, telegraphy, and commercial design. This kind of activity was expected to benefit the patient in four major ways: to provide mental stimulus, psychological diversion, muscle re-education, and preliminary vocational training. The patient was then ready for indus-trial re-education, the last stage in the rehabilitation program.[47]

Before the war, handicraft work as a therapeutic form of treatment had been introduced in Great Britain by leaders of the crippled children welfare movement.[48] Inspired by these early efforts, in 1916 Jones promoted and secured the creation of curative workshops for injured and maimed service-men. The British were following the example of their Canadian allies, who had already established similar workshops at Ramsgate.[49] In 1917 leaders of the handicraft movement in Quebec introduced ward occupations on an experimental basis in Montreal. Doctors who observed the work were so impressed by the results that the MHC resolved to make crafts an integral part of its rehabilitation scheme. As in the case of physiotherapy, the CAMC and the DSCR expanded the services inaugurated by the MHC in this new field when they assumed control of the commission's hospitals in 1918. The federal government made a far-reaching decision concerning the organiza-tion of the work: occupational therapy would be administered by the Voca-tional Branch of the DSCR, which would provide and control the supplies and the personnel. Because of its curative character, however, occupational therapy would be directed by the CAMC and conducted in hospitals solely under medical supervision.[50]

One of the early moves taken by the DSCR was to solicit the support of the University of Toronto for the training of Canada's first occupational therapists, who were then identified as 'ward aides.' Falconer readily com-plied to this new request. He approached Herbert Haultain, a professor in the Department of Mining Engineering, who agreed to organize classes at the Faculty of Applied Science and Engineering. Haultain and his faculty were actively involved in the vocational retraining of disabled soldiers, the last stage in the federal government's rehabilitation program. Pressed by the federal authorities, and despite Ontario's insistence on controlling voca-tional education at Ottawa's expense, the university had expanded its participation in this area considerably after Haultain's appointment as the MHC's vocational officer for the province of Ontario in 1917. The DSCR later provided funds for space, staff, and equipment. Haultain, who had begun his role with a staff of two stenographers, was administering a personnel of over 400 at the end of 1918.[51]

At Haultain's request, the new classes in occupational therapy were placed under a committee of management that was composed of colleagues and chaired by the dean of the Faculty of Applied Science and Engineering. Girls and women of 'good education and high mental ability' were considered to be the most suitable candidates for this kind of work, which required patience, tact, and diplomacy.[52] Almost all those selected for training had some previous experience in arts and crafts. Courses of three-months' duration, dispensed between June 1918 and February 1919, produced 270 graduates. These 'radiators of sunshine,' to quote the University of Toronto *Varsity*, were sent out to almost every hospital in Canada to care for various categories of patients, including those afflicted with tuberculosis and mental illness. The DSCR also equipped workshops in occupational therapy at Hart House's Military School.[53]

For Haultain, it was logical that his faculty would take charge of the training of 'ward aides,' since 'ward occupations' and 'curative workshops' constituted the preliminary stages in the vocational retraining of disabled soldiers. He also hoped that its involvement in the governement's rehabilitation scheme would help raise the professional and social status of engineers who, in his view, were not getting the recognition they deserved. He urged his colleagues to devote themselves to public service at a time when their expertise could be put on display, reminding them that, 'being engineers, we are very poor hands at window dressing or publicity.'[54] Haultain believed that engineers could probably handle the return of the disabled soldier to civilian life better than anybody else. The engineer's ingenuity and technological know-how had already been demonstrated in the dozens of machines that professors in the Department of Mechanical Engineering had designed to help rebuild injured muscles. Furthermore, engineers promoted the principles of efficiency and speed, on which the state's rehabilitation scheme was based. Finally, Haultain was convinced that with proper help and guidance, the disabled man could be remade physically and mentally: 'The returned man is the most plastic material of which we have had experience ... If handled successfully, he can be made, in most cases, into a better citizen than he was before the war, despite his war shock and his physical disabilities.'[55]

The Legacy of War

Haultain's remarks summarized faithfully the fundamental objective of Canada's rehabilitation scheme during the Great War: to 'reconstruct' the disabled soldier at all levels – physically, mentally, and socially – in order to reinsert him into society as a productive and law-abiding citizen. In Ontario, as in the other provinces, universities were soon involved in the organization and delivery of rehabilitation services. For its part, the University of Toronto clearly led the way in the various activities related to the physical 'rebuilding' of injured servicemen. Hart House, in particular, became a national showcase of rehabilitation work that attracted international attraction. This stature was largely due to Bott's pioneering experimental and practical work in functional re-education and to the various activities conducted at the Military School of Orthopaedic Surgery and Physiotherapy. Meanwhile, prominent professors such as Clarence Starr and Herbert Haultain played key roles in the organization of wartime orthopaedics and soldiers' vocational re-education, respectively. Along with colleagues from the Faculty of Applied Science and Engineering, Haultain was also responsible for the training of Canada's first contingent of occupational therapists. Meanwhile, the University of Toronto became the most important training centre for physiotherapists, another new group of health workers whose services were particularly appreciated during the war by orthopaedic surgeons.

The University of Toronto's participation in the Canadian rehabilitation scheme propelled disciplinary changes and the creation of new academic programs in the 1920s. The postwar evolution of psychology as a distinct discipline is a case in point. Bott's celebrated work at Hart House had necessitated the employment of a growing number of psychologists, with the result that a de facto department of psychology existed at the end of the war. Bott continued to be the guiding force behind further advances of the discipline in its applied form, as indicated by his promotion to assistant professor of psychology in 1920 and his appointment as the first head of the new Department of Psychology in 1926, a position he would hold for more than thirty years.[56] Another direct legacy of the war was the university's decision to create Canada's first academic programs in occupational therapy and in physiotherapy, in 1926 and 1929, respectively. University-based training was eagerly sought by the associations established by these two occupations. Their leaders were supported in their professionalizing efforts by prominent members of the Faculty of Medicine who had familiarized themselves with the new forms of treatment dispensed by these two categories of health workers in Canadian military hospitals.[57]

Orthopaedics also made a significant inroad at the University of Toronto after the war when Clarence Starr was appointed as its first full-time professor of surgery in 1920. Starr promoted the training of specialists as well as clinical instruction in the hospitals. He was also an avid supporter of scientific research – a goal helped by the fact that his professorship was established with the help of a huge grant from the Rockefeller Foundation.[58] Before his appointment, Starr had been involved in research projects directly linked to the work conducted by Bott at the Military School of Orthopaedic Surgery and Physiotherapy. In 1919, on the recommendation of the minister of militia and national defence, the federal government authorized the school to establish a Committee of Research, which could spend a sum not exceeding $12,000 to conduct investigations related to Bott's work and to physiotherapy in general.[59] On the committee sat the school's commanding officer, Lt-Col. Wilson, E.A. Bott, now designated as a 'Professor of Psychology,' Clarence Starr, and four University of Toronto professors representing neurology, physiology, physics, and histology. The control of the funds would be in the hands of the military, and the publications produced from the research would be of a 'strictly military nature.' In recommending the creation of this committee, the Department of Militia and Defence hoped to pursue the 'harmonious and helpful' relationship it had developed with the university during the war.[60]

Supported during the war by private contributions and University of Toronto funds, Bott's work was now receiving direct assistance from the Canadian state. His research career would later benefit from the support of the National Research Council of Canada, established by the federal government in 1916 with the mandate of financially assisting scientific and industrial research in the country. A strong supporter of state-funded research, Falconer, along with the dean of the Faculty of Applied Science and Engineering, had taken part in the discussions leading to the creation of the NRC.[61] Like Herbert Haultain, faculty members now felt that engineers could improve their professional status by engaging in public service, as they had done so effectively during the war. To promote industrial efficiency through research appeared to be a promising strategy to attain this goal, and engineers would continue to campaign for the development of industrial research after the end of the war.[62]

Conclusion

If we consider the questions raised by the *Globe* in 1914 with regard to both the mission of 'the greatest Canadian university' during wartime and the impact of the war on its intellectual activities, there is no doubt that the Great War enlarged the responsibilities of the provincial university. During these years, the Canadian state rapidly mobilized the university for service at home and overseas. This essay has considered one major, yet largely overlooked, dimension of the University of Toronto's contribution to the war effort – the key role it played in the federal government's rehabilitation program. Along with the many other services it rendered, the university's major involvement in this area certainly increased public awareness of its practical value and social usefulness, two attributes that Ontario's provincial university cultivated in the postwar years.[63]

At the same time, the University of Toronto's contribution to the federal rehabilitation scheme had a significant impact on the academic front. In the medical and health sectors specifically, it fostered disciplinary changes, spurred scientific research, and widened the university's role as a site for the training for new professions, including those aimed at women. The Faculty of Applied Science and Engineering's eagerness to participate is also a good illustration of the relationship between university wartime service and the shaping of professional identities.

All these developments, then, constitute important wartime legacies that historians have to consider when they examine the history of the University of Toronto in the postwar era.

NOTES

The author would like to thank the Hannah Institute for the History of Medicine, which funded the research conducted in preparation for this essay.

1 Adam Black, 'Salvaging War's Waste,' *Red Cross Magazine*, October 1917, 98.
2 Douglas McMurtrie, *The Disabled Soldier* (New York: Macmillan, 1919), 195.
3 The role of Canadian universities in the implementation of the federal rehabilitation scheme is briefly discussed in Desmond Morton and Glenn Wright, *Winning the Second Battle: Canadian Veterans and the Return to Civilian Life, 1915–1930* (Toronto: University of Toronto Press, 1987).
4 A.B. McKillop, *Matters of Mind: The University in Ontario, 1791–1951* (Toronto: University of Toronto Press, 1994), 5.
5 For a recent discussion on women and the professions, see the introduction to Elizabeth Smyth et al., eds., *Challenging Professions: Historical and Contemporary Perspectives on Women's Professional Work* (Toronto: University of Toronto Press, 1999), 3–22.
6 'The University and the War,' Toronto *Globe*, 14 September 1914.
7 Morton and Wright, *Winning the Second Battle*, 9–10, 130–1.
8 On this question, see Joanna Bourke, *Dismembering the Male: Men's Bodies, Britain and the Great War* (Chicago: University of Chicago Press, 1996), chapter 1. See also Seth Koven, 'Remembering and Dismemberment: Crippled Children, Wounded Soldiers, and the Great War in Great Britain,' *American Historical Review* (October 1994): 1185–6.

9 Bourke, *Dismembering the Male*, 41–2; Koven, 'Remembering and Dismemberment,' 1175–6.

10 Morton and Wright, *Winning the Second Battle*, np.

11 Ibid., 7.

12 Douglas C. McMurtrie, 'The Canadian Publicity Campaign in the Interest of Crippled Soldiers, Their Re-education and Employment,' *American Journal of Care for Cripples* 5, 1 (1917): 149.

13 On the various schemes adopted by the Allied countries, see McMurtrie, *The Disabled Soldier*, chapters 13 and 14.

14 See J.S. McLennan, *What the Military Hospitals Commission Is Doing* (Ottawa: 1918), King's Printer, 2–3, 8–9.

15 Black, 'Salvaging War's Waste,' 98.

16 On the sequence of events leading to the creation of the DSCR, see Morton and Wright, *Winning the Second Battle*, 84–92. On its increasing postwar responsibilities, see ibid., 130–1. See also Colonel G.W.L. Nicholson, *Seventy Years of Service: A History of the Royal Canadian Army Medical Corps* (Ottawa: Borealis Press, 1977), 114–15.

17 Morton and Wright, *Winning the Second Battle*, 7–8, 18.

18 Ibid., 34–5.

19 Canada, Department of the DSCR, *Report of the Work of the Invalided Soldiers' Commission* (Ottawa: The Commission, May 1918), 10–11. Morton and Wright, *Winning the Second Battle*, 277.

20 James G. Greenlee, *Sir Robert Falconer: A Biography* (Toronto: University of Toronto Press, 1988), 204–26.

21 See, for example, 'The Canadian Universities and the War,' *The Varsity Magazine Supplement*, 4th ed., 1918, 87–8.

22 McKillop, *Matters of Mind*, 269–70. See also W.G. Cosbie, *The Toronto General Hospital, 1819–1965: A Chronicle* (Toronto: Macmillan, 1975), 152–5.

23 University of Toronto Archives (UTA), Office of the President, A67-0007, box 45(a), doc. 348, J.L. Todd to Robert Falconer, 14 September 1916.

24 National Archives of Canada, RG 38, Department of Veterans' Affairs, vol. 225, Minutes of the Military Affairs Committee, 15 November 1915. For a detailed examination of the French scheme, see Major John L. Todd, 'The French System for Return to Civilian Life of Crippled and Discharged Soldiers,' *American Journal of Care for Cripples* 5, 1 (1917): 5–68. In the area of vocational re-education, the MHC was inspired by the French scheme, which called for 'professional re-training' aimed at providing disabled soldiers with 'technical training for new occupations,' and for their re-establishment in civilian life. These last two stages had an educational, social, and economic dimension, a feature that also characterized Canada's rehabiliation policy.

25 DSCR, *Report of the Work of the Invalided Soldiers' Commission*, 22–3.

26 See Michael Gauvreau, 'Philosophy, Psychology and History: George Sidney

Brett and the Quest for a Social Science at the University of Toronto, 1910–1940,' Canadian Historical Association, *Historical Papers*, 1988, 225–6; and C.R. Myers, 'Edward Alexander Bott (1877–1974),' *Canadian Psychologist* 15, 3 (July 1974): 292.

27 'Disabled Soldiers Get Training at Hart House,' *The Varsity*, 5 October 1917; DSCR, *Report of the Work of the Invalided Soldiers' Commission*, 23. See also C. Roger Myers, 'Psychology at Toronto,' in Mary J. Wright and C. Roger Myers, eds., *History of Academic Psychology in Canada* (Toronto: Hogrete, 1982), 81–2.

28 MHC, 'Function Re-education,' *Reconstruction*, July 1918, 10.

29 McKillop, *Matters of Mind*, 280–8.

30 'Dr. Bott's Great Work of Re-education,' *The Varsity*, 7 November 1917, 1; University of Toronto, *President's Annual Report for 1918*, 10; UTA, A67-0007, box 51(a), Office of the President, doc. # 266, E.A. Bott to Professor J.J. Mackenzie, 14 May 1919.

31 Concerned at first with congenital osseous deformities, orthopaedics became orthopaedic surgery when it extended its territory to development anomalies and to disabilities due to age, infections, or injuries of the locomotor apparatus. See W.F. Bynum and Roy Porter, eds., *Companion Encyclopedia of the History of Medicine*, vol. 2 (London: Routledge, 1996), 1011.

32 On the relationship between the cause of crippled children and the growth of orthopaedics, see Roger Cooter, *Surgery and Society in Peace and War: Orthopaedics and the Organization of Modern Medicine, 1880–1948* (London: Macmillan, 1993), chapter 4. See also Koven, 'Remembering and Dismemberment,' 1172–84.

33 Toronto, Archives of the Toronto Hospital for Sick Children, Hospital for Sick Children, *Annual Report*, 1899–1900, 8.

34 David Le Vay, *The History of Orthopaedics* (Park Ridge, N.J.: Parthenon Publishing Group, 1990), 367–8; Cosbie, *The Toronto General Hospital*, 173.

35 Le Vay, *The History of Orthopaedics*, 367.

36 MHC, 'Canada's Method of Facing Debt to Soldiers Who Have Lost Limbs in Battle Is Described,' *Reconstruction*, January 1918, 8.

37 Canada, *Sessional Papers* 56, 5, 1920, Sessional Paper 14, 'Report of the Soldiers' Civil Re-establishment, 1919,' 17–18.

38 Their scheme was largely inspired by Jones's cardinal principles of organization: segregation of patients, uniformity in surgical control, standardization of procedures and supplies, and continuity of treatment and after-care. See Cooter, *Surgery and Society*, 121.

39 See Jean Barclay, *In Good Hands: The History of the Chartered Society of Physiotherapy, 1894–1994* (Oxford: Butterworth-Heineman, 1994), chapter 2, for the development of British physiotherapy before the First World War. On the beginnings of American physiotherapy, see Wendy Murphy, *Healing the Generations: A History of Physical Therapy and the American Physical Therapy Association* (Lyme, Conn.: APTA, 1995), chapter 1.

40 Robert Wilson, *Report on the Physiotherapeutic Work in the Various Military Hospitals throughout Canada* (Ottawa: King's Printer, 1920), 7.

41 Archives of the Canadian Physiotherapy Association, Mrs Duncan Graham, 'Canadian Physiotherapy Association: An Historical Sketch,' *Journal of the Canadian Physiotherapy Association* (*JCPA*), 1, 1 (1939): 9, and 'CPA. Recollections and Reflections,' ibid., 22, 2 (1970): 57.

42 'Dearth of Qualified Masseurs in Canada Met by Establishment of M.H.C. Training School,' *Reconstruction*, March 1918, 6. See also Sir Andrew Macphail, *The Medical Services: Offical History of the Canadian Forces in the Great War, 1914–19* (Ottawa: King's Printer, 1925), 210.

43 Robert Wilson, *Report on the Organization of the Work of the Military School of Orthopaedic Surgery and Physiotherapy* (Ottawa: King's Printer, 1920), 11; Walter E. Segsworth, *Canada's Disabled Soldiers* (Ottawa: King's Printer, 1920), 45.

44 Wilson, *Report on the Organization of the Work*, 16. J.D. McDougall, 'Hart House,' *Journal of the Canadian Association of Massage and Remedial Gymnastics*, 1923, 7–8.

45 Wilson, *Report on the Organization of the Work*, 13–15; Archives of the Canadian Physiotherapy Association, 'The Early Days,' *CPA* 22, 2 (1970): 64.

46 Wilson, *Report on the Organization of the Work*, 17. These contributions had been regrouped in two separate funds, the Hart House School of Therapy Fund and the Hart House Special Research Fund. A total amount of $14,284,06 had been injected into these funds between November 1916 and October 1918.

47 Segsworth, *Canada's Disabled Soldiers*, chapters 4 and 5; Canada, *Sessional Papers* 56, 5, 1920, Sessional Paper 14, 'Report of the DSCR for 1919,' 35–8; R. Tait Mckenzie, *Reclaiming the Maimed: A Handbook of Physical Therapy* (New York: Macmillan, 1918), 105–6.

48 Koven, 'Remembering and Dismemberment,' 1175.

49 Cooter, *Surgery and Society*, 118–19.

50 Sessional Papers, 1920, 'Report of the DSCR for 1919,' 34–7.

51 Segsworth, *Canada's Disabled Soldiers*, 24; H.W. Price, 'Training Disabled Soldiers at the University in the Faculty of Applied Science and Engineering,' *The Varsity Magazine Supplement*, 4th ed., 1918, 137–9. On Ontario's attitude towards Haultain's involvement in vocational retraining at the University of Toronto, see Morton and Wright, *Winning the Second Battle*, 94–5.

52 Segsworth, *Canada's Disabled Soldiers*, 24.

53 Price, 'Training Disabled Soldiers,' 137–9; Wilson, *Report on the Physiotherapic Work*, 15.

54 UTA, B72-0005, Haultain Papers, box 1, file: Industrial Rehabilitation, Post World War I, 'This is an SOS Call from an Engineer to Engineers,' 15 April 1918.

55 Ibid.; address by Haultain, 1918.

56 Gauvreau, 'Philosophy, Psychology and History,' 230.

57 Dr Starr and Dr Gallie headed this group, which also included Dr Alexander Primrose, who became dean of the faculty in 1920, and of Dr Duncan Graham, a bacteriologist who, in 1919, was appointed the faculty's first full-time professor of medicine. On the establishment of the program in physiotherapy, see Ruby Heap, 'Training Women for a new "Women's Profession": Physiotherapy Education at the University of Toronto, 1917–1940,' *History of Education Quarterly* 35, 1 (1995): 135–58. On the creation of the program in occupational therapy, see *The Varsity*, 20 January 1926, 'New Course Will Be Only Thing of Its Kind in Dominion,' and 2 November 1927, 'New Course Opens Fine Opportunities for Professionals.'

58 McKillop, *Matters of Mind*, 351–2.

59 Wilson, *Report on the Organization of the Work*, 17–18.

60 UTA, A67-0007, Office of the President, box 52(a), doc. 309, 'Report of the Committee of the Privy Council, approved by His Excellency the Governor-General on the 24th of April, 1919.'

61 See Mel Thistle, *The Inner Ring: The Early History of the National Research Council of Canada* (Toronto: University of Toronto Press, 1966), 4–5. In 1919 Bott was appointed to the Research Committee on Industrial Fatigue, established the same year by the National Research Council. See *Report of the Administrative Chairman of the Honorary Advisory Council for Scientific and Industrial Research of Canada for the Year Ending March 31, 1919* (Ottawa: King's Printer, 1919), 8, 22.

62 Thistle, *The Inner Ring*, 8–9. On the engineers' quest for a better professional status, see McKillop, *Matters of Mind*, 334–42, and J. Rodney Millard, *The Master Spirit of the Age: Canadian Engineers and the Politics of Professionalism, 1887–1922* (Toronto: University of Toronto Press, 1988), chapter 7.

63 On this issue, see McKillop, *Matters of Mind*, chapter 13.

Illegitimate Children and the Children of Unmarried Parents Act

LORI CHAMBERS

Although children themselves play no role in creating the circumstances of their birth, illegitimate children have long been viewed as beyond the pale of respectable society.[1] Leontine Young, the foremost American social worker specializing in work with unwed mothers in the 1950s, asserted that 'the out-of-wedlock child remain[s] a hopeless outsider without equal legal rights or even equal legal recognition as an individual, stigmatized throughout his life by the fact of his birth ... without regard for his helplessness or his innocence.'[2] At law, the illegitimate child, the *filius nullius*, was 'no one's child,' although in practice most children born out of wedlock remained de facto under the guardianship of their mothers. Illegitimate children had no rights of inheritance and, when illegitimate adults died childless, they were regarded as 'without kin' and their property could devolve upon the state.[3] Illegitimate children were denied basic legal rights and recognition in Ontario until 1980, when the term *illegitimate* was formally removed from law.[4]

In Ontario, the initial steps towards improving the status, rights, and opportunities of children born outside 'lawful' wedlock originated in the nascent child welfare movement of the early twentieth century.[5] Three pieces of legislation, passed in 1921, determined the legal conditions under which illegitimate children would live throughout most of this century. The Legitimation Act allowed for the subsequent legitimation of children born outside wedlock, but whose biological parents later married.[6] Such children would thereafter have all the rights and privileges of legitimate children. This measure was intended not only to improve the status of children but to provide an incentive for common law couples to formalize their relationships. The state rewarded conformity rather than explicitly punishing non-marital cohabitation.[7]

The Adoption Act provided a mechanism for the permanent adoption of children either by strangers or by kin.[8] Until 1921 all adoption proceedings had been the responsibility of the legislature;[9] after this time, adoptions could be formalized quickly and cheaply through the county court system. This act facilitated the adoption of both orphaned and illegitimate children, providing them with rights more nearly parallel to those of children born in lawful wedlock. Adoption, of course, also served state interests because adoptive parents assumed legal responsibility for their new children, making these infants and youngsters less likely to become charges on the public purse.[10] It was hoped that this legislation would encourage unwed mothers to release their children for adoption, either to strangers or to their own kin network, or to adopt such children themselves if and when they married men other than the putative fathers of their illegitimate children.

The third act, An Act for the Protection of the Children of Unmarried Parents, provided a mechanism by which unwed mothers could obtain financial support from the putative fathers of their children.[11] This act was only to be invoked as a last resort. Legislators, Children's Aid Society (CAS) social workers, and family court judges all preferred that children were legitimated or adopted. Moreover, the support that was granted to unwed mothers was punitive and degrading. This act explicitly undermined the common law assumption that the mother was de facto guardian of her illegitimate child, instead providing that 'the provincial officer may upon his own application be appointed guardian of a child born out of wedlock either alone or jointly with the mother of such child.'[12] The state, not the mother, had the right to sue the putative father of the child for support. To qualify for such support, a mother had to be willing to name the father of her 'bastard' publicly and to prove to both the CAS[13] and the court that no other man could possibly have fathered the child.[14] This act was intended to privatize the costs of reproduction – to prevent illegitimate children, as one judge put it, from 'becoming a burden' on society.[15] Although ostensibly about child welfare, these three acts were also intended to save the state money and to encourage adherence to middle-class standards of morality – in particular the ideals of chastity, except within legal marriage, and the patriarchal, male-headed, family model.[16]

Thousands of children were born outside wedlock in Ontario between 1921 and 1969. This essay is based on an examination of the 3172 extant case files from investigations of paternity held under the Children of Unmarried Parents Act between 1921 and 1969.[17] Using these files, I sought to understand the impact of the act on children themselves. As a strange hybrid of morality legislation and nascent welfarism, it is not surprising that the acts failed to improve significantly either the status or the opportunities of illegitimate children.[18] Children legitimated under the Legitimation Act benefited most from these legislative changes, but only forty of the parents in these cases are known to have opted to formalize their relationships through legal marriage. This low number is not surprising as those who wished to marry would in most cases have done so before the birth of the child thereby removing the necessity of recourse to the state.[19]

The 273 illegitimate children in this sample who are known to have been released for adoption by strangers[20] had greater security within their new families than they had been accorded in the past under informal adoption, but they did not achieve parity with children living with their biological families. The adopted child's legal status was, and is, ambiguous, for 'the obligations of blood relatives toward it are unclear.'[21] Moreover, adoption could potentially be the source of considerable trauma for these children. Children who were not adopted or legitimated remained legally stigmatized by the circumstances of their birth and were much more likely than their legitimate peers to die young,[22] to be institutionalized,[23] or to grow up in poverty in single-parent, female-headed households. Mothers raising illegitimate children alone faced social ostracism and material deprivation, and the Children of Unmarried Parents Act did little to improve this situation. Tragically, poverty drove many women to release their children, either temporarily or permanently, into the care of the state. Children placed in foster care or in specialized government institutions could be denied not only adequate material care but love and emotional support as well.

These acts failed, fundamentally, because they did not address directly the central issue of child poverty, and because the stigma attached to illegitimacy, and to unwed motherhood itself, was not challenged. Under these acts, children born outside relationships sanctioned by the state remained 'bastards,' and their mothers were, by definition, 'illegitimate' and therefore suspect as parents and as citizens.[24] How could policies intended to reinforce 'proper' families ever meet the needs of those still deemed outside the bounds of respectable society?[25] As Linda Gordon has argued with regard to the development of welfare policies in the United States during this same period, single mothers, and by implication their children, might be pitied, but they were not viewed as entitled to much help.[26] The purpose of this essay is to reconstruct the social consequences of such beliefs. E.C. Drury, premier of Ontario in 1921, described the child welfare reforms enacted under his administration as 'such a program of social legislation as Ontario and indeed all of Canada and North America had never seen, or perhaps thought possible.'[27] As Michael Katz has argued forcefully, however, 'the history of welfare looks very different when the historian perches on the shoulders of a [child] and looks outward than it does when the story is told from the perspective of governments, agencies or reformers.'[28]

Adoption

A significant percentage of illegitimate children were adopted. Of the 3468 children in this sample, a minimum of 273 are known to have been released for adoption by strangers and another 219 to have been adopted by kin, either unwed mothers and their new husbands[29] or other members of the maternal family.[30] Ostensibly, the purpose of adoption was 'the promotion of the welfare of adopted children in part through removal of the stigma attaching to such terms as bastard and illegitimacy and the clarification of the legal relationship of the adopted child to both his/her natural and legal adoptive parents and thus making the rights of succession to property more certain.'[31] Much of the stigma attached to illegitimacy was mitigated by adoption, since the adopted child assumed, with regard to his or her new parents, all the rights of care, protection, and inheritance attendant on legitimate children.[32]

When a white[33] unmarried mother could not, or would not, marry the putative father of her child, adoption was perceived by CAS workers as the ideal solution to her social problem.[34] Adoption also met the needs of infertile, middle-class white couples, and for this reason had wide social support. From the 1930s onwards, and particularly in the postwar period, the heterosexual nuclear family ideal created a growing demand for adoptable, white, and healthy infants. The 'availability of white illegitimate babies met an overwhelming demand from white childless couples who wanted to create normative ... families.'[35] As one American social scientist argued in the 1950s, white illegitimacy was a blessing for the 'involuntarily childless': 'Over one in ten of all marriages are involuntarily childless. Since most of these couples desire to adopt a baby, illegitimacy is a blessing to [them]. Curiously, from their standpoint there are not enough illegitimate births because most of these couples must wait one or two or three years in order to adopt a baby, and some are never able to have one because there is [sic] not enough for all who want them.'[36]

In a society that prejudged the unwed mother as, by definition, an unfit mother, adoption, it was believed, offered the unfortunate illegitimate child the brightest possible future. Couples desiring to adopt were, in theory, screened to ensure that children would be given loving care and economic advantages in the context of a 'normal' heterosexual, two-parent family. The child, even when born of economically disadvantaged parents, could be accepted without question into the ranks of a middle-class family and raised 'by a couple prejudged to possess all the attributes and resources necessary for successful parenthood.'[37] Children's Aids Society workers were well aware that even the most dedicated and loving of unwed mothers faced enormous material challenges in supporting their children alone. Child poverty could be avoided, they asserted, through adoption placement.

It was widely believed that adoption was good not only for the child but also for the unwed mother. As Leontine Young, a prominent authority on casework with unwed mothers, argued, adoption 'is an opportunity, the best life chance for both mother and child in the great majority of cases.'[38] There is considerable evidence in the extant Children of Unmarried Parents Act (CUPA) files that representatives of the CAS in Ontario shared this perspective, and that pressure was brought to bear upon unwed mothers to encourage them to relinquish their children for adoption.

Although it was, and is, a 'commonly shared belief about adoption ... that mothers freely choose to relinquish their children,'[39] it is important to appraise the conditions under which this 'free choice' was exercised. Unwed mothers were very vulnerable: the CAS controlled the claims against putative fathers as well as decisions with regard to the fitness of any individual to 'mother' a child in the sociological sense. This agency also had control over the adoption process. An unwed mother faced hostility, social stigma, and the prospect that her material needs, and those of her baby, would be inadequately met. As other authors have also recognized, 'she had to seek help and then was virtually dependent on the same bodies who acted as agents for adoption. This proximity was not always unrelated to the decision to relinquish a child.'[40] While CAS workers had a responsibility to ensure that mothers were aware of the financial difficulties they would confront raising children alone, they could use this knowledge to scare women into releasing children against their own best judgment.[41] One distraught mother asserted, 'all social agencies are anxious that all unmarried mothers give up their children.' The social worker who had reviewed her case retorted that this mother was economically unable to support her twins in comfort. Instead of considering any means by which the state might mitigate the economic hardships this mother acknowledged she would face, her material disadvantage was seen as simply another reason why her children should be given up for adoption: 'We regret that Miss W. has undertaken the responsibility of these babies before she had a permanent plan or even a permanent job for herself, but we have been unable to help her in her confusion.'[42]

In the majority of these cases, mothers did not leave any record of why they elected to relinquish their children for adoption, but it is clear that economic considerations were paramount for many of them. As one mother expressed her dilemma, 'I'd like to keep her, if I could, but without money I just can't.'[43] Often financial and emotional support from parents determined whether young women would be able to keep their children. Women who felt they had to hide pregnancy from parents used adoption as a means to escape from family disapproval and perhaps wrath and violence; as one mother argued, she was having her baby 'placed out, to keep knowledge from her father ... an exceedingly violent man.'[44] In another case, a fourteen-year-old girl was forced by her parents to release her child for adoption against her own wishes; the parents were unwilling either to support the baby or to allow the girl, who was still a minor, to marry the baby's father, although this was the solution to the dilemma favoured by both parents of the new baby.[45]

Supportive families could greatly widen the options available to distraught young women. In one case, a mother who bore an illegitimate child in 1945 was reported by her CAS social worker to be 'very disappointed to think Mr. L. has taken this attitude, as she wants to keep the baby and does not know how she can finance her support without his help.' Although the CAS ultimately persuaded this man to enter into a voluntary agreement to support the child, he fled the jurisdiction of the court and the young woman was successful in supporting her child only because her parents provided both her and the baby with a home.[46] Even very poor families could at least provide mothers and their children with a place to live and with help in caring for children; one poverty-stricken widower whose sixteen-year-old daughter bore a child out of wedlock in 1945 took both mother and child into the family home, although he was himself already burdened with the care of eleven dependent children. He argued that despite the hardships his family faced, the pregnancy was a 'family problem and adoption was undesirable.'[47]

Without such family support, women were very vulnerable. An unwed mother might not share the social work perspective that she could be a proper mother only 'by relinquishing the child,' that 'if you love your baby you will give him up' because this is 'best for our babies, best for the lovely couple who would be the best people to have our baby, best for our family and best for society,' but most realistically acknowledged their limited financial ability to raise children themselves.[48] Women who were desperate and alone were more readily influenced or coerced. In this context, many potentially loving mothers were encouraged to relinquish their children for adoption in the hope that the adoptive home would provide materially for the child in a way that it was impossible for the mother herself to do.

Some mothers who wanted to keep their children released them for adoption only after they had struggled in vain to support them alone. For example, one mother worked in a series of low-paying jobs, with her child in the care of her landlady, for eighty-five weeks. When she lost her third job, however, and with the putative father having fled the jurisdiction, she released her baby for adoption, although she asserted that this occasioned 'great distress.'[49] It also reduced the chances that the child would be adopted, since the greatest demand was for infants. Instead of acting to help such mothers to support their children, or pressing for increased state financial support for unwed mothers, CAS workers encouraged mothers to release their children immediately after birth to avoid such eventualities and to ensure immediate placement of infants.

Regardless of when and why women released children for adoption, it is clear that the decision to do so was difficult and relinquishing mothers experienced a profound sense of loss. This sense of loss, eloquently described in other sources as a feeling of being 'haunted by fear for their child's welfare, [and of] guilt both for abandoning their child and for continuing to love and long for him,'[50] and as 'the most stressful event of their lives,'[51] is also illustrated in the CUPA records. One mother, who decided to keep a second illegitimate child after she had relinquished her first ten years earlier, described the trauma of having parted with a child and being denied knowledge of the child's welfare:[52]

Q: When I inquired if you had a child previous to the one in question, you said yes and also that you had given up the child. To whom?
A. I don't know. When these people came to me I was quite young. I didn't even see the baby. They said the best thing was for the child to be adopted.
Q: Who are the people?
A: I don't know, but all this happened in the hospital, through the Children's Aid Society.
Q: Did you on that occasion sign any papers?
A: I signed. A lady came in and I signed my name to a paper. That's all. Nothing was read to me. I didn't see the child or anything and that's the reason I want to keep my child. I feel I have a right to keep my child. I know what it is like to give up a child.
Q: Would you explain that?
A: There are things that go on in your mind. You think about it. You wonder if the child is alright.[62]

In 33 of the 273 cases in which children were relinquished for adoption by strangers, mothers later sought information about the welfare and/or placement of their offspring. Their concerns were dismissed, however, and they were told that they had no right to such information, that their relationships with the children had been permanently and irrevocably severed. Despite this refusal to reassure concerned birth mothers, once the child was relinquished there was no guarantee that he or she was placed immediately or into a loving home. As Young asserted, 'for the child, [such placements] were as good and as bad as the kind of adoptive parents selected. That selection offers social work one of its greatest opportunities and one of its greatest responsibilities.'[53] There is little evidence in the extant case files with which to assess the success of the placements facilitated by local Children's Aid Societies, each of which acted independently. Once a child 'had been adopted,'[54] the financial obligation of the putative father ceased, and the CUPA file was closed and all supervision of the adoptive family ceased. However, the rapidity of placements and adoption,[55] and the failure to conduct post-placement assessments, suggests that this 'great responsibility' was at times discharged in a superficial manner that was not necessarily conducive to the best interests of the children concerned.

Records about adopted children in Canada are abysmal, and it is impossible to know whether the adopted children in these cases had happy family lives. As June Callwood lamented in a popular 1976 exposé of the adoption 'racket,' 'we don't even know how many Canadians have been adopted. Canada keeps better records on its animal population ... We don't know if adopted children are high risk or if they are happier than other children ... The ignorance about the well-being of adopted children is even more unsettling than the lack of a head-count.'[56] Fragmented evidence in the CUPA files, however, suggests that adoption could create emotional stress not only for birth mothers but for adopted children themselves. In seventeen cases in these files, adopted children are known to have sought information about their birth mothers before they reached the age of sixteen. One child, born and adopted in 1960, started writing letters to the CAS in 1971 requesting information about her biological parents. Although it is unclear what response she was ultimately given, she wrote a minimum of eleven letters of inquiry between 1971 and 1977.[57] Although adoption placements may have been happy and successful in this and other cases, such quests for information about birth parents reveal that 'adoption raises subtle and imponderable questions from the child's point of view.'[58] Adoption can provide wonderful opportunities for children, but a lack of information about birth parents can be unsettling. The widespread belief that mothers freely choose relinquishment ensures that the birth mother is perceived as 'profoundly unmotherly and untroubled by her action,'[59] and this belief, not surprisingly, has potentially traumatic implications for adopted children. It also, of course, denigrates the role that society has played in denying such mothers the means by which to support their children alone.

Children Who Remained with Unwed Mothers

Despite the preferences of the CAS, a large proportion of mothers resisted the adoption mandate. Of the 3468 children in these 3172 cases, 1218 remained in the care of their mothers. Mothers made this choice at a cost. Illegitimate children who remained with unwed mothers were, and are, disproportionately likely to live in poverty.[60] Perhaps the greatest disadvantage that such children face is the fact that they are dependent for survival on the parent who, historically, has the lowest earning potential: 'The illegitimate infant's total or partial dependence on its mother, the economically weaker parent, has always been the source of its most serious material disabilities.'[61] Women who sought support for their illegitimate children under the CUPA were aware of their limited earning capacity. One woman asserted during a hearing of the court in which she sought an increase in child support payments from the father of her illegitimate twins: 'He didn't tell me how much he was earning. Women's wages are not as much as men's wages and I supported the two children.'[62] Financial support from the state was non-existent,[63] and it is not surprising that women viewed acknowledgment of paternity and financial agreements or court orders for child support as an essential prerequisite for raising children in decency and comfort. Such support, however, was rarely forthcoming.

The support granted to unwed mothers under the CUPA was inadequate for several reasons. First, many mothers who lacked corroborative evidence with regard to paternity were denied the right to pursue maintenance orders; unless the woman could prove unequivocally that the putative father of her child was indeed the biological father, the CAS remained unwilling to prosecute. Moreover, even when orders were granted or settlements were reached out of court, the amount of such support was insufficient to raise a child. Under the CUPA, in determining support orders, judges were to 'take into consideration the ability to provide and the prospective means of such father.'[64] Judges were to be 'governed in their findings by the consideration of what the child would have enjoyed had he been born to his parents in lawful wedlock.'[65] Although in theory this was an equitable way in which to determine support, in practice many of the working-class men who were called into court under the CUPA earned insufficient wages to support two households adequately.[66] So long as men remained single, if they did not flee the jurisdiction,[67] women might receive an amount of support that, while not adequate, was of significant assistance in maintaining a child. However, married men who had sired children during extramarital affairs were always perceived to owe their first responsibility to their legitimate families; mothers of their illegitimate children were told that no support was possible 'because this man cannot afford it.'[68] The unwed mother always faced the prospect that support payments might be reduced to reflect the changed circumstances of the putative father; if he lost his job, or if he married and fathered legitimate children, a variation of the original order could be obtained by the father. The court always asserted that 'a man's first responsibility [is] to his own family,' irrespective of when such a family had been acquired.[69] This policy reflected and reinforced the hierarchical valuing of families.

Mothers resented the fact that subsequent legitimate children received priority over illegitimate children; as one indignant mother asserted, 'Could you please explain to me why it is that he can afford to support a wife and child but *CANNOT* send $7/wk for the support of his *daughter* that is his *first* responsibility?'[70] Another mother put her anger bluntly in a letter to the court in 1950. Her ex-lover had been ordered to pay her $4 a week, but was unreliable with regard to payment:

> H goes free. He wasn't married when he first had his payments but now he is married and he has excuses and gets away with it. It sure looks to me that you are not all working for the child welfare ... Pay for a few months then miss and until time for a court case then pay a few more months and stop again ... He [the baby] would sure go hungry if he had to depend on the welfare of H to help him ... I make only a small wage and my health is not as good as it should be and I had to take housework to pay my debts. Yet H can't pay his small part and I can ... I think myself he enjoys defying the law and making a joke of the whole concern. The fact that he could not previously keep up the payments for such a length of time, but as soon as he was advised to appear in court he made up three pays all in one month.[71]

Such patterns were typical. The repeated letters of one mother to the Department of Public Welfare illustrate the financial difficulties that non-payment created for custodial mothers. Her twins, born in 1947, were entitled to support from their putative father at the rate of $10 per week. The father, however, paid only intermittently under this order and the mother worked at a variety of cleaning jobs, all of which paid very low wages, to support her children. Her children were in ill health, yet she could not afford medical care without assistance: 'I do not take my children to clinics, which are free, because I cannot get off work to do so, therefore any medical attention is costly. I still cannot see why my children have to *wait* for THEIR money so I can give them necessary medical care.'[72] Even so, women, such as this mother, who received any money from putative fathers were in the minority. Fully 51 per cent of putative fathers disappeared entirely when ordered to pay ongoing child support.[73]

Without adequate support from the putative fathers of their children, and denied state-sponsored relief, women faced an uphill battle in maintaining their families. For most of them, it was imperative that they work outside the home, though they could earn only inadequate wages,[74] child care was costly, and they were reviled as bad mothers simply because they 'chose' not to remain at home.[75] Child care arrangements were often complicated. Whenever possible, women seem to have given children over to their own mothers or sisters for care during working hours. In 130 cases, mothers and babies are known to have returned to the family home or to the homes of married sisters. The presence of supportive parents – as one mother put it, 'Of course, my dear, we will stand by you in every way'[76] – made an enormous difference not only in the options available to the unwed mother but in the material and emotional future of her child. Providing respectable and loving care for the child was a central concern of any mother, and of particular importance to unwed mothers who were under constant surveillance by the CAS. These women were haunted by the possibility that they might be deemed unfit, since the CAS, with the approval of a county court judge, had the power 'to make such order in respect to the care and custody of the child ... as he may deem just.'[77] In a society organized around the 'complementary' roles of male breadwinning and female domesticity, unwed working mothers were susceptible to negative stereotypes about their ability as parents.

Frequently, mothers who did not have families to turn to had to board out their children. In such cases, mothers paid a set amount per week for the care of the child in someone else's home; often they were able spend only to weekends with children because of employment responsibilities.[78] Such boarding homes varied widely with regard to the quality of care that children received. The primary reason people boarded children, after all, was for economic gain. Boarding homes, at best, were homes in the true sense, and boarding home 'mothers' could express considerable concern about and affection for their charges. At times, however, they did so in a manner invasive of the rights of birth mothers. For example, one boarding home mother wrote to the CAS that during visits with her birth mother, the child suffered from neglect: 'The environment was not good ... R. [the mother] went to work on Sunday and the child played in the street or went to call on her father who is in the neighbourhood.' She recommended that the mother should be allowed to take the girl only on outings or to visit her at the boarding home. Although the CAS seems not to have imposed such restrictions on the mother, the boarding home system could mean that mothers endured long absences from children as well as an additional layer of surveillance.[79]

Boarding homes could also be very mercenary operations – undoubtedly a source of even greater concern for mothers. For example, one distraught young mother, who had limited earning potential because she had left school at sixteen when she became pregnant, was trying to support her baby alone. Her parents were unable to assist her financially or to provide her or the baby with a home; she was forced to board the baby while she worked. When the putative father of her child failed to make payments under their agreement, she found herself unable to pay this board and wrote to the CAS in desperation: 'I don't like to be forever complaining to you about the matter, but right now I am at my wits end as to know what to do ... As of today I am boarding her in a private home for the summer and I don't have a cent to pay the lady for her care, and won't have until I receive some of the money that's owed me by Mr. J. The lady won't keep her for more than a couple of weeks without being paid and I don't know what I am going to do with her then. It isn't that Mr. J can't afford to pay and I don't see why he isn't doing so.'[80]

For most of these single mothers it was an all-consuming struggle to scrape together enough money to ensure the basic survival of their children. The double burden of single parenthood and long hours of work meant that mothers felt they were denied the opportunity to raise their children as they desired; in a society that venerated the at-home mother, it is not surprising that working moms at times internalized attitudes critical of mothers who laboured outside the home.[81] One mother described her circumstances to the CAS in a detailed letter in 1954. The putative father of her child was paying only intermittent support and she was in dire straits trying to support her child: 'I am working now six days a week from 7am to 7pm and Sunday I go for three hours as a waitress and still I earn not more than $150 a month. How long can I do this only a make a living for us and be a good mother too ... My girl will be 8 in November and she has to come after school to the nursing home where I am working and wait there until 7pm when I can go home with her ... Please do help me. I moved to a small town as everyone said it would be cheaper, but still I cannot keep up and I am so tired.'[82] Another mother asserted that after eight years of supporting her child alone she 'was getting a little weary now. For some years we have lived in one room – we have advanced now to an apartment and to us it is a palace. We wouldn't even entertain the thought of living in a house or owning a piece of land like G (the putative father). As nice as it might be, it is beyond our dreams.'[83]

In this context, it is not surprising that many young women looked on marriage as the best solution to their economic problems. Women who married men who were willing to formally adopt their illegitimate children, or at least to care for them materially, considered themselves fortunate. Marriage itself, however, did not make new husbands legally responsible for the support of illegitimate children. Without formal adoption proceedings, such children remained outside the new family unit. The court was adamant that while husbands might be expected to play some role in the support of their wives' children, this responsibility remained primarily with the putative father until adoption. CAS workers expressed concern that new husbands might resent illegitimate children and that requiring them to support children they had not fathered might impede happy marital relations: 'Mrs. I's husband is not liable for the support of these children and it seemed that this defendant wanted to get out of his responsibilities completely ... How can this woman live happily with this man while asking him to support the children of another man.'[84]

It is evident that in a minimum of eighty-nine cases, new husbands adopted illegitimate children, thereby assuming full responsibility for their financial support.[85] Given the stigma attached to illegitimacy, it is not surprising that mothers expressed relief when husbands adopted their children; adoption, moreover, sometimes allowed mothers the luxury of conforming to societal ideals by retiring from the paid workforce. For example, one young mother, who had brought her relationship with the putative father of her child to an end when she learned he was already married, refused to give her child up for adoption, despite the hardships she knew would be attendant on raising the child herself. Her ex-boyfriend, however, who already had to pay $15 a week in support to his estranged wife and child, was less than dependable in making payments for his illegitimate daughter's support, paying on average less than $4 a week on an order for $7 a week. The mother lamented that she could not 'support her daughter on her own,' but found a job in a factory and made arrangements to have her child cared for by her landlady each day. In 1950, when the child was five years old, she married another man who sought to adopt the little girl. In a letter in which the mother released the putative father of the child from any further financial responsibility, she described her new husband as a 'man in good financial standing' and expressed happiness that she would no longer be obligated to work in the factory.[86]

Tragically, however, material deprivation forced some women to relinquish their children against their will. For example, one mother who had a legitimate son by a previous marriage and a daughter born out of wedlock, attempted to keep her family together. She tolerated drunken interference on the part of the putative father of her daughter in the hope that he would pay support. The circumstances of the case were recorded by the CAS:

> She states that this man comes to her home in an intoxicated state and she
> does not want him to do this. He annoys her landlady and puts her in an
> awkward position. If she allows him to see the baby for a short time he stays
> much longer. One night recently he hit this girl because she would not allow
> him in. At Christmas time he was very good and gave additional money for
> the baby and for her own son by marriage and she had the man for Xmas
> dinner to repay his assistance. However, he brought liquor to her home and
> was very drunk while there and she could not deal with him.

When, after too many such episodes, she denied him access to their child,
he fled the province. She was caught in a no-win situation. She refused to
allow him to see the child to protect herself and the baby from potential
violence, but once he had been denied visitation rights he lost interest in
supporting the baby. The mother lacked the resources necessary to support
two children on her own. By 1949, when her baby was only a year old, she
had been forced to place her in an infant's home. Her son went to summer
camp while she worked, hoping to earn sufficient money to reclaim both
children in the fall. In 1954, however, both children were made wards of the
Children's Aid Society. This young mother, whom the CAS workers deemed
'decent and caring,' had lost custody of her children solely because of her
poverty.[87] Other women were constantly haunted by the possibility that
they would be unable to support their children adequately and would be
forced to release them into the care of the state. As one mother lamented in
a letter to the CAS in 1957, 'I'm haunted by bills even in my sleep ... Must I
give up my son?'[88]

In the Care of the State

Illegitimate children were disproportionately likely to end up in institutional care; a minimum of 128 of these children are known to have come
temporarily into care, and at least 25 became permanent wards of the state.
Children who ended up in institutional care faced a bleak future.[89] It is
widely accepted that institutional care, and often the foster home experience as well, have negative consequences for children's psychological development:

> Loneliness, insecurity, violent rages and self-hate ... are mentioned as among
> the psychological problems which [experts] believe to have been partly caused
> by childhood years spent in institutions ... empirical evidence ... tends to

support the general picture presented by illegitimate individuals and by writers from Dickens to Frank Norman; as does common sense and the observation of ordinary people. It shows that the separation of an infant from its kin involves a variety of possible mental and physical hazards and confirms that on the whole children's homes and similar institutions are not good places in which to be reared.[90]

Institutional care is inevitably impersonal, and foster care, until the 1970s and even beyond, was largely unregulated and unsupervised in Ontario.[91] Institutional and foster care experiences could vary dramatically, but the potential for abuse, neglect, and unhappiness was enormous. It is difficult, however, to piece together the experiences of the illegitimate children who remained in the care of the state. The CUPA files themselves document only the movement in and out of state care and foster homes; rarely are the reasons for placement given or the opinions of the children recorded.

Many children moved in and out of state care as the ebb and flow of economic circumstances dictated.[92] One mother, for example, placed her child with the CAS temporarily while she awaited the arrival of her mother, a German citizen, who emigrated to Canada to care for the child while the mother worked to support the family.[93] The policies of the court at times directly contributed to the need of women to place their children in the temporary care of the state. For example, one mother, who bore her child in 1946, had been involved with a married man. They cohabited for a period of months, but his wife sued him for non-support and he was placed on probation, 'one of the terms being that he must stay away from Miss H.' When he resumed cohabitation with the unwed mother, in defiance of the court order, he was jailed for thirty days and lost his job. Once released, he once again resumed cohabitation with his wife, although they separated within months; after this separation they reached a support agreement that allowed the father to live with his lover and their child. In the meantime, however, the unfortunate child had lived for eleven months in a foster home, as the mother could not afford to support the child on her own.[94]

Mothers who could not afford boarding care or private placements for their children and who could not depend on help from their families, but hoped some day to reclaim their children, left them temporarily in CAS facilities. To leave a child for too long, however, whatever the financial circumstances that dictated such a course of action, was to risk losing custody of the child. For example, one mother was described by the CAS as 'a girl of slightly sub-normal intelligence who is employed as a waitress and earns on average $9.50 per week from which she has made some contribution toward the support of her child. She has tried to interest relatives in G without success. Her mother is dead and there is no family home to which she can take him.' After three years, during which the mother consistently visited and attempted to pay for her child, the CAS sought ward action. They removed the child from the custody of the mother, not because she had been a disinterested or neglectful parent, or because adoption was believed to be possible, but simply because 'this child is born out of wedlock and his mother is unable to maintain him.'[95] It is unclear whether or not such mothers would have retained rights of visitation while their children were in public institutions. The policies of the state, despite the ostensible purpose of legislation, did not serve the best interests of children.

Conclusion

Although Ontario society changed dramatically over the period in question in these cases, the prospects for illegitimate children did not. Women who found themselves pregnant out of wedlock, and the children they produced, continued to face ostracism and social marginalization into the 1960s, despite the sexual revolution. Single mothers remained economically disadvantaged (as they do even to this day) and were explicitly excluded from aid programs in Ontario until 1956. Adoption placements remained ad hoc and unregulated. Institutions for children were unpleasant and impersonal. And judges in family court, perhaps because in some jurisdictions the same men held these positions for extended periods of time, continued to be distrustful of the word of the unwed mother.

The Legitimation Act, the Adoption Act, and the Children of Unmarried Parents Act failed as child welfare legislation. By continuing to discriminate between legitimate and illegitimate children in an effort to encourage the formation of state-sanctioned, traditional families, the acts perpetuated stereotypes that condemned and marginalized both unwed mothers and their innocent children. Legitimated children benefited individually from the Legitimation Act, but it upheld and reinforced the very stereotypes and social distinctions that undermined the viability of 'illegitimate' families. Adopted children escaped some of the worst consequences of having been born out of wedlock, but adoption could raise difficult psychological questions for unwed mothers and their children. Those children who remained with their unwed mothers were a stigmatized minority.

The greatest disadvantage that illegitimate children faced was that they were likely to suffer material deprivation and, for this reason, be released into the care of the state. Although we have, as a society, addressed the issue of the legal stigmatization of children born outside wedlock by eliminating the designation 'illegitimate' from formal law, the history of the treatment of unwed mothers and their children should illustrate that such legal change is of minimal value unless accompanied by a social commitment to eliminate child poverty. Privatizing the costs of reproduction represents an abdication of our communal responsibility to ensure the well-being of all children. Recent policy decisions of the Harris government illustrate that we have yet to make a commitment to the eradication of childhood hunger and want. We continue to condemn children, through no fault of their own, to suffer for the so-called sins of their parents.

NOTES

1 It should be noted that the use of the word *illegitimate* throughout this essay does not reflect any moral judgment of children born out of wedlock or of the parents who begot them. The term is used because it was the contemporary term used to describe such children. In law, the meaning of the term *illegitimacy* was very precise; the only other word that could convey the same meaning is bastard, an even more derogatory term. As one legal commentator put it, 'He is the child whose "nice" legal designation means "unlawful" and whose traditional legal designation [bastard] is a swear word for the use of which an action lies in tort.' Harry D. Krause, 'The Non-Marital Child – New Conceptions for the Law of Unlawfulness,' *Family Law Quarterly* 1, 2(1967): 114–28.

2 Leontine Young, *Out of Wedlock: A Study of the Problems of the Unmarried Mother and Her Child* (New York: McGraw-Hill, 1954), 10 and 127.

3 For a full description of the law of 'bastardy,' see Alan Macfarlane, 'Illegitimacy and Illegitimates in English History,' in P. Laslett, K. Oosterveen, and R.M. Smith, eds., *Bastardy and Its Comparative History* (Cambridge, Mass.: Harvard University Press, 1980), 71–6.

4 Family Law Reform Act, RSO, 1980, c. 152, s. 1(a). Despite the fact that the designation *illegitimate* has been removed from law, children born outside stable heterosexual relationships remain materially disadvantaged. For example, a child born out of wedlock or common law marriage has no claim on the property of his or her father unless the child is explicitly acknowledged by such father.

5 For further information on the child welfare movement, see Neil Sutherland, *Children in English-Canadian Society: Framing the Twentieth-Century Consensus* (Toronto: University of Toronto Press, 1976); Joy Parr, *Labouring Children: British Immigrant Apprentices to Canada, 1869–1924* (Toronto: University of Toronto Press, 1980, 1994); Andrew Jones and Leonard Rutman, *In the Children's Aid: J.J. Kelso and Child Welfare in Ontario* (Toronto: University of Toronto Press, 1987); Joy Parr, ed., *Childhood and Family in Canadian History* (Toronto: McClelland & Stewart, 1982).

6 An Act respecting the Legitimation of Children, SO, 1921, c. 53.

7 In the early decades of the twentieth century, more punitive legislation had considerable support. For example, the Presbyterian Church called for 'adultery and lewd cohabitation' to be made punishable offences under the Criminal Code. The federal Department of Justice gave some consideration to such legislation, although it was ultimately deemed unwise, largely because it would have been completely unenforceable. For further information on this subject, see James Snell, 'The White Life for Two': The Defence of Marriage and Sexual Morality in Canada, 1890–1914,' *Histoire sociale/Social History* 16, 31 (1983): 111–28.

8 An Act respecting the Adoption of Children, SO, 1921, c. 55.

9 Of course, in a manner that parallels the situation with regard to legislative divorce, this responsibility ensured that poorer families, while they might well have a non-kin child within the household, were denied the opportunity to bestow familial status on such a child. For information on legislative divorce in Canada, see James Snell, *In the Shadow of the Law: Divorce in Canada, 1900–1939* (Toronto: University of Toronto Press, 1991). For information on informal adoption among the poor in the early twentieth century in Great Britain, see Ellen Ross, *Love and Toil: Motherhood in Outcast London, 1870–1918* (New York: Oxford University Press, 1993).

10 Although the adopted child assumed rights with regard to inheritance and maintenance by the adoptive parents which were exactly the same as those of legitimate children, the responsibilities of more distant kin towards the adopted child, and the right of the adopted child to inherit from cousins, grandparents, uncles, aunts, and other relatives, were not defined. The adopted child, while acquiring a status clearly superior to that of the illegitimate child, was not made a child like any other within the family.

11 An Act for the Protection of the Children of Unmarried Parents, SO, 1921, c. 54. Before 1921 a much less state-determined mechanism for creating affiliation orders had been in place. In Upper Canada, until 1859, the father of an illegitimate child could be ordered to pay restitution, not to the mother, but to her guardians, to compensate them for a presumed loss of service during the period of pregnancy. In 1859 this act was amended, and the legal basis of restitution was changed from loss of services to responsibility for one's progeny. Moreover, from 1859 onward the mother herself could name the father of her child in an affirmation of bastardy and sue for restitution in her own right. This perogative recognized her as de facto legal guardian of her child and as an independent legal being. Such recognition was denied, however, under the Children of Unmarried Parents Act. For information on unwed motherhood in the nineteenth century in English Canada, see Peter Ward, 'Unwed Motherhood in Nineteenth-Century English Canada,' Canadian Historical Association, *Historical Papers*, 1981: 46–63.

12 An Act for the Protection of the Children of Unmarried Parents, SO, 1921, c. 54, s. 10.

13 The Children's Aid Society was a unique institution. It assumed responsibility for a wide range of child welfare legislation and was empowered to claim custody of children as well as to enforce the acts of 1921. It was a quasi-state agency, partially financed by the state, yet operating as a private charity run by its own board with considerable variation in policy from one jurisdiction to the next. Although enforcing state policies and receiving state funding, the CAS experienced only minimal government regulation.

14 Not surprisingly, the procedure involved in enforcing this legislation exposed women to humiliating questions about their personal lives and to invasive supervision of their ability as mothers. See Lori Chambers, 'Unwed Mothers and the State,' paper presented at the Berkshire Conference on the History of Women, Chapel Hill, North Carolina, June 1996.

15 Case 585.

16 It is no coincidence that when the Deserted Wives' Maintenance Act, 1888, was overhauled in 1922, the major reform enacted was that the children's right to maintenance was, for the first time, explicitly elaborated. Deserted Wives' and Children's Maintenance Act, SO, 1922, c. 57.

17 These cases involved a total of 3468 children, as some mothers had more than one illegitimate child with the same putative father. All files are held at the Archives of Ontario.

18 I am indebted to Jack Choules of the Archives of Ontario for bringing these files to my attention. Because of the requirements of the Freedom of Information Act, pseudonyms are used throughout and the case files are numbered only internally. Although some of these cases eventually made their way into the law reports, or individuals in such cases had other interactions with the legal and social work system, no connections are drawn between these files and documents in the public domain which might reveal the identity of individuals.

19 It is clear, however, that women were encouraged to marry the putative fathers of their children, whether they loved these men or not. Not being willing to marry the father was held as evidence that the mother was undeserving of financial aid from the putative father. One judge asserted: 'I have pointed out to the woman that her marriage with H would legitimize the child and relieve him for the rest of his life of a handicapping stigma. She, however, persists in her refusal to marry the man and insists on keeping the child. Under these circumstances I think H should pay a reasonable sum of cash, but I do not think he should be tied up to a periodic payment.' Case 1025.

20 This number undoubtedly represents only a small fraction of those formally adopted. In many files it was noted that a small settlement had been reached, suggesting that adoption had taken place and that the putative father had been

released from further financial obligation in the case. In the majority of such cases, however, the outcome for the child is not explicitly noted, and I have included here only those cases in which adoption is certain.

21 H. Philips Hepsworth, *Foster Care and Adoption in Canada* (Ottawa: Canadian Council on Social Development, 1980), 185.

22 Of the 3468 children in this sample, 211 are known to have died within the first few months of life. This number represents an infant mortality rate of 60 per 1000 live births. The national infant mortality rate was 43 per 1000 live births in 1921, rose to 48 in 1926, and dropped relatively steadily to 30 in 1940. F.H. Leacy, ed., *Historical Statistics of Canada*, 2nd ed. (Ottawa: 1983), B51–8. Statistics Canada. This sample covers the period up until 1969, by which time these rates had dropped even further. This higher death rate seems to be the typical fate of illegitimate children. For example, in Great Britain, infant mortality rates were as follows: 1914 – illegitimate 207 per 1000, legitimate 100; 1973 – illegitimate 23 per 1000, legitimate 16. Jenny Teichman, *Illegitimacy: An Examination of Bastardy* (Ithaca: Cornell University Press, 1982), 105. As late as 1960, statistics for the United Kingdom illustrate that children of unwed mothers had a mortality rate 27 per cent higher than that of the general population. See Virginia Wimperis, *The Unmarried Mother and Her Child* (London: Allen & Unwin, 1960), 123.

23 Of these 3468 children, a minimum of 128 are known to have become wards of the state, at least temporarily.

24 The way in which mothers of illegitimate chlidren were marginalized and considered 'not mothers' is clearly indicated in the Toronto Stork Derby contest. For information on this event and its interpretation by the court and in the media, see Mariana Valverde, 'Families, Private Property and the State: The Dionnes and the Toronto Stork Derby,' *Journal of Canadian Studies* 29, 4 (1994–5): 15–35.

25 Linda Gordon, *Heroes of Their Own Lives: The Politics and History of Family Violence* (Boston: Penguin Books, 1988), 83.

26 Linda Gordon, *Pitied but Not Entitled: Single Mothers and the History of Welfare, 1890–1935* (New York: Free Press, 1994). For further information on this topic, see Veronica Strong-Boag, 'Wages for Housework: Mothers' Allowances and the Beginnings of Social Security in Canada,' *Journal of Canadian Studies* 14, 1 (1979): 24–34; Margaret Hillyard Little, 'A Fit and Proper Person: The Moral Regulation of Single Mothers in Ontario, 1920–1940,' paper presented to the Canadian Women's Studies Association, Kingston, 30 May 1991; Suzanne Morton, 'Women on Their Own: Single Mothers in Working-Class Halifax in the 1920s,' *Acadiensis* 21, 2 (1992): 90–107; and Jane Lewis, *The Politics of Motherhood: Child and Maternal Welfare in England, 1900–1939* (London: Croom Helm, 1980).

27 E.C. Drury, *Farmer Premier* (Toronto: McClelland & Stewart, 1966), 108. This

case study of Ontario is particularly important because his contemporaries shared this view, and legislative changes in Ontario became the model on which 'progressive' reform in other jurisdictions, in the Canadian West and in the United States, was based.

28 Michael Katz, *In the Shadow of the Poorhouse: A Social History of Welfare in America* (New York: Basic Books, 1986), 293.

29 A minimum of eighty-nine of the mothers who opted to raise children alone ultimately married and adopted, jointly with their husbands, their illegitimate offspring. Children who were adopted by their own mothers and their new husbands are discussed later in this essay, since such mothers usually had first to endure a period of time raising such children alone, often under very trying material circumstances.

30 It is known that 130 children were adopted by other kin, most often maternal grandparents and siblings of the mother. In three other cases it is known that paternal grandparents formally adopted illegitimate offspring.

31 Hepsworth, *Foster Care and Adoption*, 131.

32 Adoption Act, SO, 1921, c. 55.

33 In only one of the 273 cases in which children were released for adoption by strangers is the child known to have been non-white. In this case the social worker asserted: 'there may be some delay in finding a family who will accept the part negro background. This child is not negroid in appearance. He is quite attractive with a full little face, small regular features, ovile complexion, very dark brown eyes, medium brown hair which may curl. He is small but sturdily built. Therefore we feel he has a good chance of achieving adoption.' Case 407. This statement suggests that racism in Canada, as in the United States, profoundly influenced the experiences of Black and white unwed mothers, imposing on Black mothers an obligation to keep their children. See Rickie Solinger, *Wake Up Little Susie: Single Pregnancy and Race before Roe v. Wade* (New York: Routledge, 1992).

34 In Ontario, during this period, 70 per cent of children discharged from care because of adoption were children of unwed parents. Hepsworth, *Foster Care and Adoption*, 149.

35 Solinger, *Wake Up Little Susie*, 154.

36 Winston Ehrmann, 'Illegitimacy in Florida II: Social and Psychological Aspects of Illegitimacy,' *Eugenics Quarterly* 3 (December 1956): 227.

37 Solinger, *Wake Up Little Susie*, 155.

38 Young, *Out of Wedlock*, 160.

39 Kate Inglis, *Living Mistakes: Mothers Who Consented to Adoption* (Sydney: George Allen & Unwin, 1984), 15.

40 Ibid., 5.

41 One woman went so far as to assert that babies were being sold to the United States without the consent of their mothers. She wanted maternity homes, and

the Children's Aid Society, to be investigated on this count. Case 295. In the
United States, there is ample evidence that such a racket in babies existed. See
Solinger, *Wake Up Little Susie.*

42 Case 498.

43 Case 111.

44 Case 340.

45 Case 392.

46 Her mother babysat the child while the young woman, only sixteen years of
age, worked in a factory. Case 79.

47 Case 344.

48 This finding is consistent with those of other authors who have investigated
the reasons for relinquishment of children born out of wedlock. See Inglis,
Living Mistakes, 191, and E.K. Rynearson, 'Relinquishment and Its Maternal
Complications: A Preliminary Study,' *American Journal of Psychiatry,* no. 123
(1982): 338–40.

49 Case 165.

50 Inglis, *Living Mistakes,* 294.

51 Ibid., 191.

52 Case 976.

53 Young, *Out of Wedlock,* 160.

54 Case 6.

55 Although under the law, adoptions were not to be formalized until a two-year
period had elapsed, it seems to have been routine for judges to approve that
the CAS dispense with such formalities, asserting that 'it is to the advantage of
the said child in every respect that the two year period of residence be dispensed with.' Case 1018.

56 June Callwood, 'Adoption: Not All Hearts and Flowers,' *Chatelaine,* April 1976,
41.

57 Case 455.

58 Callwood, 'Adoption,' 108.

59 Inglis, *Living Mistakes,* 15.

60 Today, this description applies equally well to children born outside traditional
two-parent families and to children of divorce, who overwhelmingly remain
in the care of mothers. As early as 1971, 'close to 43% of female-headed one-
parent families with children under 18 were receiving social assistance ... It
may be seen, therefore, that the bulk of single-parent families with young
children experience financial difficulties whether the parents are employed or
not, as well as the other difficulties contingent on trying to raise a family single-
handed.' Hepsworth, *Foster Care and Adoption,* 25. The major difference between the present and the past is not the issue of the poverty of female-headed
households, but the number of such households within our society. American
statistics reveal that, before 1960, the number of single-parent, female-headed

households was relatively stable at approximately 9 per cent of all families, although this figure did not include those single mothers who lived within other households. In recent decades, however, the number of such families has exploded. See Gordon, *Pitied but Not Entitled*, 18.

61 Teichman, *Illegitimacy*, 105.

62 Case 613.

63 For example, unwed mothers were explicitly denied the mother's allowance, established in Ontario in 1920. SO, 1920, c. 89. This injustice was amended only in 1956. For further information, see Margaret Little, '"No Car, No Radio, No Liquor Permit": The Moral Regulation of Single Mothers in Ontario, 1920–1993' (PhD dissertation, York University, 1994), and James Struthers, *The Limits of Affluence: Welfare in Ontario, 1920–1970* (Toronto: University of Toronto Press, 1994).

64 Children of Unmarried Parents Act, s. 18(2).

65 Ibid., s. 20.

66 Both the men and the women represented in these cases were working class, and many of them earned only subsistence wages. The women who listed any form of employment were usually waitresses, domestic servants, or factory workers. Men also worked in marginal forms of employment.

67 Only a small minority of women ever collected the money owed to them under support orders or agreements for on-going maintenance. See Lori Chambers, 'You Have No Rights, Only Obligations: Putative Fathers and the *Children of Unmarried Parents Act*,' in Lori Chambers and Edgar-André Montigny, eds., *Family Matters: Papers in Post-Confederation Canadian Family History* (Toronto: Canadian Scholars' Press, 1998).

68 Case 101.

69 Only one child in this sample of 3172 cases seems to have received financial support, while living with a single mother, that exceeded a minimal level required for mere subsistence. It is significant that this is also the only case in which the mother was involved with a putative father outside her own social class. She was a saleslady, but the putative father of her child was the president of a large factory and owned an expensive home. He was also a married man with five legitimate children. When she threatened him with public humiliation through affiliation proceedings, he hired a lawyer and granted her a generous private allowance for the child; while court orders and agreements with the CAS were rarely more than $10 a week, this father paid the mother's hospital expenses, which were exceptionally high because the baby had been very ill at birth, and $40 a week in support. He also paid the child's school fees when she attended Havergal College pre-school. The baby was born blind and the father supported her, not only until the age of sixteen as required under legislation, but until she completed high school at the Brantford School for the Blind. Because of his social position, and the fact that he did not want his wife

to learn of his sexual 'indiscretion,' this man could not, like so many other fathers, simply flee the jurisdiction. Instead, the threat of court proceedings was a valuable weapon for this mother. Case 410.

70 Case 468 (emphasis in original).

71 Case 296.

72 Case 498 (emphasis in original).

73 They were much more likely to pay finite debts, which were usually incurred when children were adopted. Most fathers were willing to pay these debts to be able to stay in their communities. In contrast to the rate of pay under support orders, 83 per cent of fathers paid debts in their entirety. See Chambers, 'You Have No Rights, Only Obligations.'

74 Throughout this period, the occupational opportunities afforded to women remained very limited, and their potential earnings were never more than about 60 per cent of what a man could reasonably hope to earn.

75 For more information on attitudes towards working mothers, see Joan Sangster, 'Doing Two Jobs: The Wage Earning Mother, 1945–1970,' in Joy Parr, ed., *A Diversity of Women: Ontario, 1945–1980* (Toronto: University of Toronto Press, 1995), 98–134.

76 Case 508.

77 Children of Unmarried Parents Act, s. 19.

78 Case 128.

79 Case 228.

80 Case 315.

81 As Sangster has argued, married women who worked outside the home also suffered guilt and anxiety in this context. Sangster, 'Doing Two Jobs,' 98–134.

82 Case 923.

83 Case 2472.

84 Case 459.

85 In only five cases does it appear that husbands refused to accept the illegitimate child into the new family home, and in all such cases the children remained with maternal grandparents, with whom they had resided since birth.

86 Case 79.

87 Case 414.

88 Case 872.

89 Even the CAS workers admitted that institutional care was problematic. One child, who as a toddler was being released for adoption, was described as 'somewhat backward in development owing to institutional care.' Case 2389.

90 Hepsworth, *Foster Care and Adoption*, 116.

91 Only in the early 1970s were policies for evaluating foster homes and for training foster parents established in Ontario. Ibid., 102–9.

92 For a description of a similar pattern in the temporary use of orphanages by desperate women in nineteenth-century Montreal, see Bettina Bradbury, 'The

Fragmented Family: Family Strategies in the Face of Death, Illness and Poverty, Montreal, 1860–1885,' in Parr, ed., *Childhood and Family in Canadian History*, 135–52.
93 Case 703.
94 Case 81.

'That Repulsive Abnormal Creature I Heard of in That Book': Lesbians and Families in Ontario, 1920–1965

KAREN DUDER

In 1926 Helene Fraser remarked to her daughter, Frieda: 'It is pleasant for you to have Bud. I am glad the interns like her & I shall also be glad if she will like them & not concentrate all her affections on poor little you.'[1] She was commenting on a visit Frieda's partner was making to her while Frieda was working in New York as a doctor. Mrs Fraser's reactions to Bud were not always as 'beneficent' as they were on this occasion. Frieda conveyed her mother's words while writing to Bud in England, where she had been sent to get her away from Frieda. Their relationship continued through letters, sometimes several in a single day, as they successfully thwarted their families' attempts to keep them apart.

This paper uses correspondence between and interviews with Ontario lesbians to examine the relationships between lesbians and their families of origin in Ontario between 1920 and 1965.[2] It might be assumed that lesbians in that period, because of their sexuality, usually had difficult relationships with their families. It would be tempting to view today's relatively 'liberal' attitudes towards lesbianism as contributing to higher-quality and longer-maintained family ties, and the attitudes of the past as deleterious to family relationships. In some cases a general improvement did occur, but many lesbians growing up and forming relationships between 1920 and 1965 remained close to their families, with sexuality forming a site of conflict but not of irrevocable division. This paper argues that, in many instances, lesbians before 1965 had stronger ties to their families of origin than those who came out in the 1970s into the lesbian movement.

Lesbians, before the advent of the communes, the feminist movement, and the gay and lesbian rights movements of the late 1960s and 1970s, negotiated the boundaries of their sexuality in a situation that did not include the notions of 'alternative' family structure and lesbian 'community' which would later emerge with political activism and greater social tolerance of same-sex partnerships. What little community did exist was based on social connection rather than political agenda. Although many longer-term lesbian relationships were phrased in terms similar to those of heterosexual marriage, there was little theorizing of these relationships as representing alternative families. These ideas would come later in the century.

In the period 1920–65, Ontario was the site of considerable gay and lesbian community-building and, indeed, of regulatory and discursive re-actions to it. Montreal also had a significant gay and lesbian population, but it was Toronto that became the destination for many a young lesbian seeking others of her kind, especially after the Second World War. Police and municipal authorities had increasingly to deal with the presence of larger numbers of lesbians on the streets, in clubs and bars, and in residen-tial areas. Ontario was also the site of much mainstream and medical publishing on the subject of deviant sexualities in the postwar period. As Mary Louise Adams argues, Toronto was the centre of English-language publishing, broadcasting, and cultural production in Canada and was 'en-twined with the definition of "national culture."'[3] Ontario is therefore an ideal geographical focus for a study of the tensions between lesbians and their families, acting as it did as a crucible of conflict between rebellious sexualities and hegemonic social norms in a rapidly changing nation.

In this essay, I suggest that Ontario lesbians before 1965, and especially before the 1950s, remained closer to their families of origin, even after becoming sexually active as lesbians, than did many later lesbians. The context of their lives was, in many ways, fundamentally different: not only were the ideological constructs of the lesbian community and the alterna-tive family not yet in place, but earlier lesbians had less financial independ-ence on the basis of which they could break their familial ties. Furthermore, while societal approval of close relationships between women began to wane as early as the turn of the century, and was all but gone by the 1930s,[4] Canadian society did not, until at least the mid-1950s, have a publicly available discourse of pathological homosexuality on which to base its reactions to women who transgressed heteronormativity. With the arrival of such a discourse, family reactions towards lesbians began to change.

It cannot be said that the 1950s and 1960s saw a sudden swing towards family intolerance of lesbians; nor did lesbians abruptly sever family ties once they became aware of their sexual orientation. In only some families were lesbians suddenly the target of rejection and isolation. What this small study of Ontario lesbians suggests is that, even within a context of increas-ing societal discussion of and hostility towards lesbians, many families remained very tolerant of their wayward daughters. Other factors militated against the tendency for lesbian sexuality to involve family condemnation. The mid-twentieth century was, however, a time at which a significant break occurred between lesbian and family life. The formation of urban lesbian communities, the structures of which would gradually replace many of the functions of the family, and from which would arise the alternative family structures of 1970s' and 1980s' lesbianism, was the key moment in the changing relationship between lesbian identity and the family.

Little is known about the lives of lesbians in Canada before the late 1960s. The dearth of information is hardly surprising, given the limited availability of lesbians' personal records and the equally limited purview of the state in the area of lesbian sexuality. What little scholarship does exist focuses largely on the public discourses concerning lesbian sexuality and the public lives of lesbians in Canadian cities. The Canadian public had few sources of information about lesbianism before the mid-twentieth century. By the 1920s, many authors were writing about homosexuality, and their works were being read by a broader section of the public. Those works were, however, primarily available to medical professionals. After the volumes of *Studies in the Psychology of Sex* were banned in Britain, Havelock Ellis published them in the United States, where they received wide distribution.[5] The extent of the availability of this and other such material to a Canadian lay readership is unknown, but there are indications that some sexological works were being read by heterosexual as well as homosexual people. Readers of the *Canadian Forum* would also have been aware of the furore caused by the publication and obscenity trial of Radclyffe Hall's *Well of Loneliness* in 1928.[6] Such information was most likely available to only a small proportion of the Canadian public and, before the Second World War, lesbians in particular remained virtually invisible in Canadian society.

Steven Maynard's extensive research on the surveillance and prosecution of mostly working-class male homosexual subcultures in Toronto before 1930 reveals that gay men were increasingly part of what Maynard calls 'a dialectics of discovery' in which the subculture of male-male public sex was simultaneously observed and produced by the very judicial forces that sought to control it. Those men who sought out other men with whom to have sex may have known where to find them, but Maynard argues that 'the reciprocal or dialectical relationship between the activity of the men and the maneuvers of the police ... forged and contributed to the growth and knowledge of a sexual underground.'[7]

No similar dialectics of discovery occurred for lesbian women before the Second World War. The focus of legal authorities and urban policing was on sexual activity between men, and few beyond the walls of asylums and prisons considered lesbian sexuality a major threat to social order. There existed no law under which a woman could be convicted for specifically lesbian activity, unless she were arrested under a broader category such as gross indecency, fraud, vagrancy, or disorderly conduct. Moreover, even though women's mobility and independence increased as the century wore on, women had fewer opportunities to form the same kinds of sexual subcultures as did men. Lesbian sexuality was for the most part *ultra vires*. Even within the prison system, where lesbians formed a somewhat visible group, it would seem that lesbianism was largely ignored until at least the 1950s or 1960s. Robin Brownlie suggests that there was, until the mid-twentieth century, a 'continuing inclination to downplay and disregard prison lesbianism.'[8]

Lesbian Relationships of the 1920s and 1930s

From the 1920s to the 1950s, the level of acceptance of relationships between women gradually changed in Canada, as it did in the United States. Long gone were the halcyon days of the romantic friendship, although many middle-class lesbians still used the language of this type of relationship.[9] Only just emerging were the decades of psychotherapy and notions of family 'dysfunction.' Within this period of transition, lesbian relationships were disapproved of by the general public, but without the psychiatric and psychological discourses that were yet to become hegemonic within Canadian society. Family condemnation rested, therefore, on somewhat vague and unspecified grounds.

Frieda Fraser and Edith Bickerton (Bud) Williams, whose relationship lasted from the age of nineteen to Bud's death in 1979 at the age of eighty, had constantly to negotiate the waters of family disapproval. Bud left Ontario for Britain in 1925 to work in a bank. She was encouraged by her mother to stay there, but returned in 1927 to be with Frieda. Their letters during the time they were apart reveal the degree to which their families were opposed to their relationship and the strength with which they had to resist all attempts to keep them apart.[10]

In January 1926 Frieda went to visit Bud's family for reasons not entirely obvious to the reader. It would appear that Frieda attempted to elicit from Bud's mother and sister some information about their perspective on Bud's temporary return to Canada. The resulting argument involved Frieda and Bud in lengthy discussions in their subsequent letters. On 11 January, Bud wrote to Frieda that she had received letters from her mother and sister and commented: 'You have got me into a nice mess with them. Mother is hurt that I would discuss my family with an out-sider and Mary is perfectly furious and wants to know what the hell I mean by it. And of course they didn't say anything to you about what they really thought apparently.' She further lamented, 'Darling, don't they see that you are not an out-sider to me?'[11] She admonished Frieda for thinking that she could have found out more information, and urged her to be more careful in the future.

It was Frieda's mother who proved the more hostile to their relationship, however, and around whom Frieda and Bud most often had to plan their meetings. Frieda's father had died in 1916, and Frieda seemed to feel a great responsibility towards her mother, despite their ambivalent relationship. After a trip home for Christmas, Frieda wrote: 'By the way, when I was at home I took careful soundings as to your status in the home. Mother doesn't seem to mind your being talked of now – she did a bit when she was here – rather likes it up to a point.'[12] By the middle of 1926, however, when Frieda and Bud were planning their next meeting, the situation was tense once again. Frieda wrote to Bud: 'Either you arrive just before Mother & we greet her arm in arm, or Mother arrives just before you & will want me out of arm's [sic] way. I rather hope for the former. It would be a nightmare if it weren't so funny.'[13]

Both families posed problems. Bud wrote to Frieda: 'It seems such an appalling waste of time to have to go and see my family first and for most of the time. It isn't as if they wanted to see me particularly. They would bear up if I wanted to stay in any other place but N.Y. to see anyone else but you.'[14] And the next day, she complained: 'What rotten luck that Mrs. Fraser is coming back in July! You must tell me when, so that we can see what can be arranged. It is an awful thought, but I feel that N.Y. is not big enough for both of us.'[15] Bud rearranged her schedule so as to be able to visit Frieda when Mrs Fraser was not there.

It would appear that the Williams family was not quite as concerned about the relationship as was Frieda's mother. In July 1926, Bud asked:

I suppose you wouldn't think of coming here to see me instead of Montreal? It is further I know, but the Williams family would treat you agreeably and give you a bed for the night you'd be here. There wouldn't be much entertainment to offer you but I would do my best to be agreeable too! I know it's a mad idea but I have the horrid feeling that we should see each other before Mrs. Fraser comes, or something will happen. I really know that it won't but I would like to see you *now*. Also, it would be quite possible not to mention the fact that you had been, if it would make you unpopular afterwards.[16]

It seems that each of the women visited their family individually during the summer of 1926. Bud attempted to resolve things with her family, but was unsuccessful. She told Frieda:

> The whole thing came up quite soon after I got back when I said I was going to see you, and they said that they hoped I had got over that absurd business and that as you weren't here to pursue me – isn't it odd that both our families think that the other does the pursuing? – there was no point in my running down to N.Y. to put my self in your way. So I said that I was fond of you and it *wasn't* entirely on your side ... She [Bud's mother] said that it was such an unusual relationship, to which I agreed, that she had nothing against you personally, in fact rather liked you, and that she could never approve but I would no longer be badgered about it.[17]

They were to see each other late in the summer. In early August, Frieda prepared Bud for the worst, commenting:

> The only thing, dear, that is likely to occur is the one that you didn't mention – perhaps you knew it – & that is that I will get annoyed & be unpleasant to Mother. Then she will point out that that is the evil effect etc. If I could see enough of you beforehand it mightn't happen. You see we are bound to have words about something anyway & if you are there it will be blamed on my liking you. The only thing that improves my good nature is our affection for each other & having seen a good bit of you helps a lot.[18]

By the end of 1926 matters had become difficult. Frieda wrote: 'Your being away hasn't been of the slightest good to Mother apparently. We exchanged a few words several days ago. The essence of it was in the end that "something or some one has come between us" & that she thinks is you. Whereupon I pointed out that the condition existed long before I knew you. Which surprised her & made her quite miserable I'm afraid.'[19]

Frieda's mother was concerned about the relationship from its inception, but became especially concerned at the prospect of Bud returning to Canada on a permanent basis in 1927. She wrote to her friend Nettie for advice and, while her letter is not available, Nettie's response is revealing:

> If I can *only* transfer to you, unbroken, my dear old friend, the vision which stands in my own mind with *increasingly persistent clearness and vigour* as a sure, safe, and upright method of meeting this rare problem – and, what is more, though God forbid that it should fail! – it seems to me looking at it in every way possible – it seems to me to be the *one and only* way which will bring everything around in the end!
>
> As to Bud, the reaction that I have felt in realizing that she was not after all

of the nature of that repulsive abnormal creature I heard of in that book, has resulted in a more tolerant leniency (perhaps that is expressing it a bit too strongly – as it might seem to you) – even you yourself could not help being conscious if you had read the thing![20]

It is unclear precisely to which book she was referring, but Nettie, in her guidance to Helene on how to deal with the relationship between Frieda and Bud, clearly reveals the availability in the 1920s of at least some works attesting to the existence of 'abnormal' sexualities. The degree to which Helene herself was familiar with such ideas is unknown, but it may be said that she held the relationship to be unhealthy and unnatural, even if she did not use any of the new sexological terminology with which to describe it.

Despite the obvious tensions involved in the relationships of Bud and Frieda with their respective families, the daughters maintained regular contact with family members and seemed to feel a duty to familial ties. During their separation and when they were able to live once again in Canada, their social worlds consisted primarily of women, some of whom were in same-sex relationships, yet these female social groups did not draw them away from their families.

Scholars suggest that lesbian communities, in which large numbers of women socialized together and even lived in close proximity to one another, based on their shared sexuality, formed in some areas of the United States as early as the 1920s and 1930s.[21] It is difficult to determine whether embryonic forms of lesbian community formed at this time in Canada. The evidence we do have suggests that the urban centres of entertainment, around which community often formed, did not begin as early in Canada as they did in the United States. How, then, were Canadian lesbians to recognize each other during these decades?

Frieda and Bud were both able to 'spot' other lesbians while they worked in the United States and Britain, but it is clear that they had an idea there were other women like themselves before they left Canada. Middle-class lesbian women were able to recognize each other within middle-class social milieux. Precisely what 'signs' they looked for in other women is difficult to determine, however. For example, while travelling with her friend Bess on a cruise ship in Europe, Bud reported:

Bess picked up the nicest women from the hospital on board – two nurses, Miss B and Miss S. They are head nurses at T.G.H. and quite old – about 45!! – They are *very* devoted to each other which is enough to make me interested in them even if they weren't such perfect lambs. We have been playing bridge with them a bit and this morning I had a long conversation with them when

Bess was being professional. I was quite thrilled when they said that they had known each other for years and had always planned this trip, and had only managed it this year, and you could tell by the way they looked at each other, just *how* thrilled *they* were.[22]

How exactly Bess was 'spotted' by the Misses B. and S. is not known, but it would seem that they became reasonably friendly towards Bud, in whom they confided that 'their families had been awfully against their being together so much when they were young but after 20 years they are beginning to get used to it. It is an awfully difficult subject to chat about and it would never be approached if I had to do it, but they suddenly began to talk about it to-day.' Bud commented to Frieda that her new friends 'seem to agree with all we think about it, and also that there is no use trying to convince any other people about it – they simply can't see it.'[23]

During her stay in England in 1925, Bud wrote to Frieda about her aunt's cook and housemaid, revealing that her aunt

told me that her cook and housemaid – who are by way of being ladies – had never had jobs before, but that their families had been rather disagreeable about their being awfully devoted and so they had up and left, and this was the only thing they could do. However, they loved it as it meant living together. So there seems to be a fair amount of it about. And they were certainly the happiest looking creatures. I simply pined to talk to them about it. Aunt F. didn't like it much, but at the time she was ill and couldn't get anyone else who could get on with her nurse and her companion, but she seems to be quite satisfied now. I asked her what her objection was and she said that is wasn't natural! Isn't it funny?[24]

Frieda discovered women who were 'devoted' to one another while she was working as an intern in New York during the late 1920s. She wrote to Bud concerning 'two middle-aged & very good looking females that spend all their week-ends together here.'[25] In the social milieux in which Frieda and Bud moved, it was likely that all of these same-sex couples were 'by way of being ladies' and were able to identify, in nuances of middle-class dress and language, others like themselves.

The Changing Discourse: Lesbians as Enemies of the Family

It is difficult to determine the precise degree to which the increasingly medicalized discourse of sexuality infiltrated Ontario society beyond the medical profession and the educated elite. Emerging ideas about lesbianism, having their origin in the sexological and Freudian thinking of the early twentieth century, had both positive and negative effects for lesbians. Some women were able to frame their feelings within the new discourse without internalizing its more negative aspects. Bunny, writing passionately to her partner in Toronto, said:

> You have all the things that would, and did, hoist you almost beyond reach of my earthly eyes ... social poise, academic honours that are staggering in comparison to mine, achievement and prestige in the top drawer of social work ... teaching. Even those dizzy heights couldn't deter me, or send me ricocheting away from you as they might easily have ... Instead we reached out to each other from the ... to be analytical about this ... from *the libidinal level* ... the warm altogether pleasure of our emotional reaction to each other.[26]

Acknowledging that she and Elisabeth could not 'avoid the usual implications of the conservative school ... the biddies who frown upon close attachments between women,' Betty commented: 'I faced the prospect of matrimony once, and decided with a cool sort of half logical knowledge, that I would never be able to face the drudge, nor able to measure up to the usual expectations ... and once that was decided the rest has been easy ... lacking in conflict, I mean.'[27] The tide clearly was turning against lesbian relationships, yet Bunny and many other women of the 1940s were able to decide not to get married but to follow their passions, with only moderate public condemnation compared with that which would come later.

The Canadian public had to be trained slowly to view female relationships with an eye to lesbian content. Many parents remained ignorant of the possibility or saw it as something that could exist outside their family, but not within it. Consequently, many lesbians were able to begin their sexual lives with other girls or women without fear of being caught. This may particularly have been the case for girls growing up lesbian in rural Ontario, which remained somewhat out of the reach of magazines and tabloid newspapers. Moreover, gender-bending was often more tolerated in rural settings, at least before the 1950s. Barb, a tomboyish young woman, was active around the farm, helping with the manual work: 'Always known as a tomboy in the family ... always like to wear my over-hauls, and my plaid shirts, and a straw hat. Oh boy. Spiffy!'[28] Her gender-bending behaviour was tolerated by her parents, who saw nothing unusual in it. She played most often with the boys, and did not care for the traditional pursuits of girls. She preferred the world of westerns, and would sometimes go into town to see a Roy Rogers or Gene Autry film:

Oh, loved those, and then came home and if the neighbour's kids came up then we'd play cops and robbers or cowboys and Indians, or something like that. We'd play all over the farm, hide and seek. Always had to have our little belt on with our guns and our, you know, and our cowboy hat. After watching those movies I had to go home and play. I would be Gene Autry or I'd be Roy Rogers ... my sisters were a little more, mmm, ladylike around home with Mum, you know ... they liked to sew and knit ... I tried it all, I tried ... never could work out very well, so I gave that up.[29]

Barb 'hated putting on a dress, or a skirt, or stockings, you know, nylons, and shoes shined up and, oh, boy. I didn't like that at all ... and my sisters were always in their skirt or dresses. Had my hair cut, squared off, like cut short. Just showing my ears.'[30] While it can be said that young women in farm families were often allowed to do more manual labour than their city counterparts, and could dress appropriately, Barb's appearance would, in the following decade, have been likely to cause suspicion and comment. In the 1930s and 1940s, however, Barb was merely a curiosity. Mary Louise Adams reveals that advice literature and films of the 1940s rarely explicitly linked 'sissy' and 'tomboy' behaviour with homosexuality because, she argues, to do so would have given credence to biological arguments about homosexuality and suggested the futility of the recent regulatory measures and sex education as a prophylaxis against social deviancy. Rather, gender-bending behaviour among children was portrayed as an adolescent condition, often the result of poor parenting, that could be reversed.[31] As Christabelle Sethna suggests, sex education was often conflated with gender instruction for girls. N. Rae Speirs, director of physical education for Toronto schools, argued in 1947 for the discouragement of antagonism towards the opposite sex; girls and boys 'needed to develop desirable attitudes toward each other.'[32]

Barb began her first lesbian relationship with a friend while she was in high school in the late 1940s and recalls spending every available moment with her girlfriend, without her family, friends, or teachers being any the wiser. She states that after their first night together:

I got more intimate with her ... And then we used to go, back and forth, to our homes. She would come and stay a Saturday night and we'd be going to a show or something, and I'd go over to her house and stay. And then we got more intimate with touching the rest of our bodies ... It'd be every weekend ... and we'd have at least a night together, whether it would be a Friday or a Saturday night ... so that went on for, oh, quite some time ... probably two full summers and all the seasons through.[33]

When asked if she thought that her parents had figured out what was going on, Barb replied:

No, or her parents, this girl's parents either. No, I'm sure they didn't. Or even the kids that we went to ... school with in the classroom and stuff. I don't think, I don't know that anyone ever picked up anything. We were always trying, I was always trying to be close with her. Whenever we left school, we'd walk home together, or coming to school ... so ... I never heard anyone, no-one had ever said anything to me about 'What are you two together for all the time?' There was never anything of that said.[34]

It was not until Barb joined the armed services in 1952 that she heard much of lesbianism. She made friends with a group of five other lesbian women. In 1954 one of the women, under questioning, offered up the names of the rest of the group. Barb was hauled in to see a psychiatrist and, after an attempt to cover up her sexuality, was forced to admit that she was a lesbian. She was discharged. When asked how she had known what would be the consequences of telling the truth, Barb said that she could not remember specifically reading anything, but she had the distinct impression that, 'at that time, that was bad, bad, bad. Anybody caught you on your job, or any place, you know, that wasn't the right thing. In other words, you were queer, that was the whole thing, I think, you just weren't a normal person.'[35]

The armed services in the postwar period were the focus of much antagonism towards same-sex relationships. As representatives of the nation, of courage and honour, and of respectability, servicemen and servicewomen were subject to intense scrutiny of their sexual behaviour and gender performances. Any suspicion of a gay or lesbian relationship could provoke severe censure, if not immediate dismissal.[36] Fortunately, Barb was not asked to explain her military discharge to her family, as she had voluntarily left and received an honourable discharge, and she remained close to them throughout this period of her life.

'Lesbians Who Flaunt Themselves in Public'

Although it is impossible to determine with certainty the proportion of the Canadian population that had heard of lesbian relationships in this period, it can be argued that, by the middle of the twentieth century, images of same-sex relationships and social worlds were increasingly available through mainstream media. This was particularly the case in Toronto, where a large gay and lesbian population congregated in the Yonge Street and Chinatown areas and was the cause of much comment. Lesbians became the subject of many a magazine or newspaper article. While some were vaguely sympathetic, many were lurid in their hyperbole about the 'homosexual lifestyle.' With the growth of the 'yellow press' in the 1950s, scare-mongering about homosexuality became *de rigueur*. The scandal sheets printed local and international material about lesbians and gay men. In 1955, for example, the *Justice Weekly* printed a story about two women in London, England, who had married. Violet Jones, who had desired for some time to change her sex, dressed as a man and married Joan Lee. The judge's comment to the two 'lesbians' was that 'the fact remains that you made a grave false statement to cover your unnatural passions with a false air of respectability.'[37] They were fined £25 each.

By 1964 homosexuality had become a more widespread concern. The *Telegram* published a series entitled 'Society and the Homosexual,' which aimed, after two months' research on the subject, to present 'accurate' information to the public. The first article in the series quoted the Toronto Forensic Clinic as believing that there were 15,000 active homosexual men in the metropolitan Toronto area, and a further 150,000 who were latent homosexuals or bisexuals. The article added: 'This deviate population is swelled by 6,000 Lesbians and 30,000 other women who live outwardly heterosexual lives but are sporadic or latent homosexuals.' The article went on to chronicle the torrid goings-on in a homosexual club on Yonge Street, where 'one pale, ethereal looking Lesbian danced with another who looked and moved like a sack of potatoes rolling downhill. To the homosexual, particularly, beauty is in the eye of the beholder.'[38] The newspaper reporter then tied the problem of homosexuality to the perceived breakdown in family life. Reporting that Toronto experts disagreed with rumours that the proportion of male homosexuals to heterosexuals had increased since the war, the paper nevertheless stated that the time was ripe for an increase. The cause? The author stated that 'the patriarchal society has become the matriarchal society and the lines of familial authority are blurring.'[39]

Such opinions echoed wartime fears of reversal in the 'natural' gender relationships of Canadian society. The presence of large numbers of women in the paid workforce during the war had produced considerable anxiety about the erosion of appropriate gender roles and, as Ruth Roach Pierson indicates, had particularly aroused fears of the masculinization of women. The Canadian military and the government had been at pains to emphasize the temporary nature and the femininity of the work involved.[40] The fears remained in the postwar period, however, and found their expression in an increasing range of regulatory and discursive measures aimed at controlling the behaviour of women and young people.[41]

While images of lesbians were becoming more widespread in Canada, the common assumptions about them were still largely negative, and many lesbians remained reticent about revealing their sexual orientation. This was particularly the case with middle-class and professional women, who kept their relationships out of public view and often condemned those lesbians who did not. An article reputedly from the Los Angeles gay newspaper *One*, reproduced in *Justice Weekly*, portrays some condemnation of the more overt, butch lesbians of the bar scene. An editor's note precedes the text which, even if really a *One* article, seems to have been printed in *Justice Weekly* for reasons other than the acknowledgment of diversity within the lesbian community. The author, Inez Wagner, 'addressing herself apparently to Lesbians who flaunt themselves in public,' comments on the lesbian habit of wearing men's clothing and bragging about it. She further asks, 'What about the girl who is presently standing by the juke box? She's attractive, intelligent looking and seems to have a fine sense of humor – but the way she's table hopping makes you wonder if she wasn't bitten by a frog when a child! In fact, not 10 in the place seem to stay at the same table or booth for more than one drink! (Musical chairs, anyone?)' She claims that lesbians such as these are demanding acceptance while making it impossible to achieve it, stating 'O.K. – go ahead, fight – you may win, but the cause of the homosexual to prove that he or she is a decent citizen of good character, that IMPORTANT fight, takes the 10 count for the umpteenth time.'[42]

Ross Higgins and Line Chamberland have shown that the yellow press of the 1950s and 1960s, while supporting and disseminating negative stereotypes of gays and lesbians, also helped to form the very communities they were describing. These papers, they say, not only described where the bars were but portrayed men and women of same-sex orientation, however strangely. Their study of Montreal scandal sheets shows that lesbians and gay men used the papers to give them access to personal contacts and to the bar scene, even while many papers were adopting a tone of moral outrage to sell more copies to a prurient heterosexual public.[43] The same dual function of the yellow press occurred in Toronto.[44]

Valerie Korinek's study of *Chatelaine* in the 1950s and 1960s has revealed that the magazine, unlike its American counterparts, published several articles on lesbians.[45] Many of these pieces perpetuated the psychological stereotypes of lesbians as neurotic and immature. Yet the few articles Korinek discovered which were directly related to lesbians avoided the turgid approach of the tabloid press in their attempt to provide an authoritative, scientific, and balanced viewpoint. The magazine interviewed lesbians to publicize their perspective. Korinek also argues that *Chatelaine* contained a number of stories, articles, and advertisements that were open to what she calls 'perverse readings,' in which 'lesbian readers could easily resist the preferred meanings of the material and opt for alternate interpretations which more aptly reflected their sense of themselves.'[46]

These media images, then, were available both to lesbians and to their families. But while open to the perverse readings of which Korinek writes, the new discourse of sexuality began to posit lesbians more forcefully as antagonists to the family, as both the result and the agents of family breakdown. Adams's *Trouble with Normal* sets the increasing normalization of matrimonial heterosexuality within a framework of a postwar domestic 'revival,' in which deviance 'precluded the homogenization that was seen to be central to Canada's strength as a nation.'[47] Homogenization had to involve the protection of the young, who were believed to be particularly vulnerable to persuasion by popular images. The lesbian pulp novels of the 1950s, popular reading material for many a lesbian, were held in this context to 'sway normal girls toward the abnormal, making the latter seem both attractive and possible.'[48] Not only were young lesbians having their identities affirmed by popular material, it would seem, but lesbians were also being *created* by literature.[49]

Lesbians' relationship to family life began fundamentally to change in this new era of coercive heteronormativity. Whereas in earlier times the concept of family obligation and the lack of female financial independence (or, indeed, the family's need to rely on a daughter's income) might have militated against a family's wish to expel a daughter because of her sexuality, the new discourse allowed families to see their lesbian daughters increasingly as enemies, as threats to the further stability of the family home.

Lesbians themselves took advantage of the new employment opportunities and sought work and refuge from their families in the burgeoning metropolises of Toronto, Montreal, and Vancouver. Both middle- and working-class women sought new opportunities, which included the ability to live by themselves or with other women rather than with family. For the butch women, who most clearly transgressed the boundaries of gender, employment opportunities were few. In Toronto they were restricted to such jobs as driving trucks and labouring.[50] They were often supported financially by femmes or by other butch women in the community.

The most visible world of lesbians in postwar Canada was the predominantly working-class butch and femme bar culture of Toronto, Montreal, and Vancouver. There is little documentation of this culture in Canadian society. We know that there were many lesbian-friendly bars in Canadian cities in the 1960s, but fewer social outlets of this kind can be found for the previous decades.[51] Perhaps the most extensive study of a single Canadian butch and femme culture is Elise Chenier's examination of Toronto's public lesbian community from 1955 to 1965.[52] Chenier interviewed seven women, in addition to examining the Lesbians Making History Project interviews also used in this paper. She discusses the Continental Hotel, the main lesbian bar in the 1950s, and the lesbian community that used it. The Continental, like many other lesbian haunts, was in an area already associated in the minds of the police and the public with prostitution, drugs, and other illicit activities: Chinatown. Chenier argues that the lesbians involved in the bar culture in Toronto 'inadvertently helped to give shape to the postwar feminine ideal and provided medical experts with ammunition to launch an effective ideological war against women's social and economic emancipation.'[53] Despite these negative effects, however, the bar women also created for themselves a social environment based on their shared sexuality.

That the Ontario community was part of a wider trend is indicated by Chamberland's research into the Montreal lesbian community. Chamberland charts the bar scene of Montreal from 1955 to 1975 in an article that shows that the lesbian bar culture was structured along the same butch and femme lines as that of the United States.[54] She argues that Canadian butches and femmes, like their American counterparts, used their roles 'as a way of living [their] lesbian identity during an extremely repressive era by juggling gender categories and thus making visible or concealing lesbian existence, depending on the circumstances.'[55] Her research also indicates that butch and femme roles were strategies for securing and defending public space, in which she is in agreement with the Kennedy and Davis argument that butch/femme couples were the precursors to the lesbian-feminist movement of the 1970s in fighting for women's right to live openly and publicly as lesbians.[56] As Chamberland states, 'exposure was needed in order to ensure that lesbian bars became known and accessible. Knowing that such places existed and discovering where they were was a problem. On the other hand, concealment was necessary in order to escape repression.'[57]

The mid-twentieth-century bar culture provided women with a sense of community: they knew where they could go to be with women like themselves; and they had a support group of women who trained them in the roles of the community, saw them through relationships and through struggles with the police and employers, and fought with them for public lesbian space. There was not necessarily a sense of community based on identity shared across class and other lines, however. Jerry, one of the women interviewed in the Lesbians Making History Project, argued that there was no lesbian community in the 1950s and 1960s. 'You survive, you survive,' she said.[58]

While their pre-war predecessors had been forced to deal with an emerging but still vague disapproval of their relationships, Ontario lesbians in the postwar era were faced with more hostile reactions from families informed by the new, public discourse of homosexuality and sexual pathology. In an examination of popular pscyhology in postwar Canada, Mona Gleason clearly demonstrates that psychologists, wishing to sustain the professional prestige established by their employment in the military, broadened their scope to take psychology into the innermost recesses of the public mind.[59] Via newspapers, magazines, and radio, psychologists gradually increased their hold on the Canadian psyche.

The new era made images of lesbians and their social worlds more available to young women coming to terms with their sexuality; it also meant that many families now had a name to put to their daughters' behaviours, and a socially approved framework within which to respond. That framework often involved psychiatric or psychological treatment. Jackie reported: 'They phoned my family up and they said, "Did you know that your sister's been seen in Toronto and she's dressing like a man?" My brother came looking for me, my older brother and my older sister. And I met them and they said, "We're going to put you in the fucking nuthouse: look at you!"'[60]

Pat came out to her family accidentally. Her mother's tone during a telephone conversation had suggested to Pat that she knew of her daughter's lesbianism, when in fact her mother had assumed that Pat was going out with a black man. Thinking that her mother had guessed her sexual orientation, Pat started talking about it. She had been a tomboy when she was growing up and later had been given a copy of *The Well of Loneliness* by her mother, a gift that might have suggested to Pat that her mother had some suspicions.[61] On revealing her sexual orientation, Pat was told to see a psychiatrist.

Jerry moved to Toronto at the age of fifteen, after receiving a hostile reaction to her sexuality. 'I was accused of being a lesbian at the age of 13 by my mother in the waiting room,' Jerry said. She continued: 'And this woman, her name was S. She had a pyjama party one night and there was 2 other, 3 other women I think. And S. and I got pretty heavy duty on the chesterfield.'[62] Jerry had known fully what lesbianism was, and had two books beneath her mattress at home about lesbian relationships, yet she was careful to deny knowledge when asked by her father and several doctors. After she left home, Jerry's father said to her sister: 'Your sister's a lesbian and I don't want her anywhere near my house. I don't want her anywhere near you.'[63] Jerry's father was in the airforce and might reasonably be expected to have had somewhat greater knowledge of homosexuality than many in the general public, given the high-profile purging of gay men and later of lesbians in the military.[64] He certainly was in command of a wider range of terminology for homosexuality than many others would have had, and he frequently lamented the fact that his daughter was 'queer.'[65]

Arlene discovered lesbians in the psychiatric hospital, after her mother had her committed at sixteen. She had been 'fooling around' with girls since the age of nine, but had not known what a lesbian was until she met several lesbian patients on the ward.[66] At nine, she and her best friend had started acting out the love scenes they saw at the movies. When she was ten, her friend's mother walked in on them making love, asked 'What are you doing?' and started to scream. Arlene fled the house, went home, and overdosed on her mother's sleeping pills. Although it would appear that her friend's mother did not discuss the matter with Arlene's mother, her friend was put in another school and Arlene ceased most of her lesbian activity until her introduction to lesbians in the hospital.[67]

Arlene revealed that she was committed the same year that she came out to her family as a lesbian, but said the reason for the committal was that she was leaving home and her mother did not want her to go. Despite the fact that her mother abused her physically, Arlene described her family as a 'great one.' She was able to tell her whole family, including her grandparents, 'This is the way it is: I am a lesbian. I intend to stay one. You can either like me or not see me again.'[68] As Chenier comments, however, it is quite likely that her sexual preference was a factor in her mother's decision to have her committed.[69] Another Toronto lesbian, Alice, mentioned a friend who was kicked out of a convent when she was sixteen after she had been discovered in bed with another girl: 'And they threw her out because she wasn't Catholic. And her mother sent her to a psychiatrist and Betty lied to him.'[70]

Parents who regarded lesbianism negatively did not all send their wayward daughters to psychiatrists, however. Deborah, whose first relationship occurred in 1950, when she was sixteen years of age, had a very close relationship with her family. She had been told when she was growing up that homosexual men and lesbians were 'sick, deprived, mentally deprived.'[71] This comment had not deterred her from exploring a relationship with her teacher, who appeared regularly at the sports events Deborah was playing in. 'She made me feel whole – like I was the only person in the world and I was very special,' Deborah commented, though she knew that her relationship was risky: 'I used to think that if anybody ever knew that I was making love to a woman they would think I was crazy. They would think I was out of my mind. So we did everything we possibly could do to hide that, and we successfully did it, and I don't know how we did it. I really don't.' There were not even any close calls, 'because we always had a reason, and ... I always had some backup ... Although my family caught us lying in bed, looking through the crack of the door or something, you know, I found out that years and years later. But we were very cautious.'[72]

Veronica, who in 1956 began a relationship with a school friend, is sure that her girlfriend's mother knew of the relationship: 'There was her poor mother downstairs, you know, I'm sure. You know, we'd be up there ... we're 16 years old. We were just so enraptured and so carried away, we could have carried on. And I'm sure her mother knew. And I'm sure her mother used to talk to her, Marilyn's aunt, whose daughter is [also a lesbian]. Maybe this was going on at the same time, you know, in her life, yeah. Yeah, so that was basically it, like in each other's homes. We never went anywhere and expressed anything.'[73]

These members of Ontario's lesbian culture reveal that even those lesbians who most clearly transgressed the boundaries of heteronormativity were not necessarily cast outside the family, but that attitudes towards lesbians had changed dramatically from the previous decades. Even though many women remained in touch with their families, concern about their sexuality could be explicit and overt. The new arguments of homosexual pathology were clearly available to parents and were part of their reactions to their daughters' behaviour.

For many lesbians, coming out meant giving up their own children. Jerry recalled that 90 per cent of women who were gay gave up their children. When asked why they did so, she replied: 'Because they figured they couldn't give them the proper life, the proper upbringing, give them what they needed while they were growing up or possibly the love and affection they needed because they were too fucked up in their own mind.'[74] Arlene confirmed that there were many lesbians who had children and had to give them up: 'I don't know any gay women at the time, that if the Children's Aid got hold of the kids, they ever got them back.'[75] In Ontario, all sexuality deemed 'deviant,' from unwed motherhood to homosexuality, was subject to moral regulation, which might take informal forms but was also policed by the province. Margaret Little clearly indicates that sexual morality was explicitly linked to deservedness in the case of the Ontario Mothers' Allowance in the postwar era.[76]

Because the discourse of the postwar era condemned lesbians as the products of dysfunctional families, it is axiomatic that they were held to be bad parents. It was therefore not possible for lesbians to maintain relationships with their children, since society held that exposure to the lesbian lifestyle would 'make' children homosexual. Even lesbian mothers themselves doubted their ability to be good parents to their children. It was not until the social movements of the late 1960s and the 1970s that a reverse discourse emerged. This discourse challenged the traditional, heterosexual family and welcomed new ways of interpreting 'family,' notions that would allow lesbians to conceptualize themselves as at least as fit as heterosexual parents.

Examining the period 1920 to 1965, one sees a gradual shift in the relationship between lesbians and their families. In the early twentieth century, several factors militated against families of origin rejecting outright their lesbian daughters. There existed perhaps a stronger sense of obligation within some families, although it would be difficult to assess the degree to which this comparison was true across class boundaries, given the paucity of records of working-class women for the years before the Second World War. This is not to suggest that there were not cases in which women were thrown out of the family home because of lesbianism. Doubtless there were, but this study of lesbian lives has revealed that family ties remained important for many lesbians even into the 1960s.

What is more important, however, is the impact of the postwar discourse about homosexuality. Whereas, before the war, families often condemned lesbian relationships with vague reasons for their views, the postwar era gave families a new terminology, and an extremely hostile one, with which to reject their daughters' sexuality. In addition, one might suggest that the expanding world of women's work allowed a diminishing of family obligation, in the sense that more women could be financially independent. For families, this made the expulsion of the lesbian daughter from the family home less objectionable. The rising standard of living in the postwar era might also have made it easier for some families to give up their daughters' incomes. For lesbians themselves, it meant the opening up of the possibility of living their own lives without the scrutiny of family members. Many working-class women in particular moved to Canada's cities both for employment opportunities and for the chance to live as lesbians within the emerging lesbian communities.

Ideologues of the postwar era in Canada tried to instil in family life an antagonism towards those who strayed from the path of heterosexual matrimony, yet they were only partially successful. Many lesbians suffered the consequences of the new, psychological arguments and were marginalized and institutionalized on the basis of their sexuality. Yet, as the sources for this essay indicate, family remained important in the lives of many lesbians. Few families absorbed the new discourse to the degree that they cut ties with their daughters absolutely.

With the advent of the social movements of the late 1960s, however, change occurred in lesbians' relationships with their families of origin. Society had come, over the preceding two decades, to see lesbians as anti-thetical to the family, and lesbians began to see the traditional family as heterosexist. By the 1970s lesbians could be singing 'Family of Womon We've Begun.'[77] By the 1980s and 1990s one could speak of 'lesbian parenting' and 'lesbian families' as viable alternatives to the traditional normative family.[78] These ideas are a positive interpretation of lesbian life, in which lesbians are seen once again as capable of family life, albeit with a twist, and yet this positive development has its origin in the gradual separation of lesbians from the family unit in the postwar era. Born in antagonism, the alternative lesbian family is the result of a decades-old struggle between lesbian identity and notions of family life.

NOTES

1 University of Toronto Archives, Fraser Family Personal Records, Acc. No. B95-0044 (Fraser Records), sous-fonds III, box 036, file 8, Frieda Fraser to Edith Bickerton Williams, 5 March 1926. Frieda moved temporarily from Ontario between 1925 and late 1926 to gain her medical internship at the New York Infirmary for Women. She then moved to Philadelphia to complete her training and returned to Toronto in 1928.

2 This essay uses two archival collections of correspondence. Pseudonyms have been used in the case of one and its accession information is not included. Also used are interviews conducted by the author as well as several interviews conducted by the Lesbians Making History Project. Pseudonyms have been used to disguise the identities of the narrators. The author is indebted to Maureen Fitzgerald for access to the Lesbians Making History Project interviews.

3 Mary Louise Adams, *The Trouble with Normal: Postwar Youth and the Making of Heterosexuality* (Toronto: University of Toronto Press, 1997), 5.

4 Lillian Faderman, *Odd Girls and Twilight Lovers: A History of Lesbian Life in Twentieth-Century America* (New York: Penguin, 1991), 93–4.

5 Jeffrey Weeks, *Sexuality and Its Discontents: Meanings, Myths, and Modern Sexualities* (London and New York: Routledge, 1985), 76.

6 Radclyffe Hall, *The Well of Loneliness* (London: Cape, 1928). The book was reviewed in the *Canadian Forum* 9, 103 (1929), 243–4. See also Steven Maynard, 'Radclyffe Hall in Canada,' *Centre/Fold* 6 (1994), 9.

7 Steven Maynard, 'Through a Hole in the Lavatory Wall: Homosexual Subcul-tures, Police Surveillance, and the Dialectics of Discovery, Toronto, 1890–1930,' in Joy Parr and Mark Rosenfeld, eds., *Gender and History in Canada* (Toronto: Copp Clark, 1996), 178.

8 Robin Brownlie, 'Crimes of Passion: Lesbians and Lesbianism in Canadian Prisons, 1960–1994,' paper delivered at the Canadian Historical Association Conference, Ottawa, 1998, 13.

9 Lillian Faderman argues that tolerance of romantic friendships between women began to erode at the beginning of the twentieth century with the gradual popularization of sexological theories. See, for example, Lillian Faderman, *Surpassing the Love of Men: Romantic Friendship and Love between Women from the Renaissance to the Present* (New York: William Morrow, 1981), and *Odd Girls and Twilight Lovers*. It can be shown, however, that the distinct vocabulary of the romantic friendship was still in use in the mid-twentieth century. The Elizabeth Govan/Bunny correspondence discussed in this paper and that between Ontario social welfare administrator and politician Charlotte Whitton and Margaret Grier clearly indicate that the language of the romantic friendship was being used by Canadian women well into the twentieth century. Whitton's relationships with women are discussed in Patricia T. Rooke, 'Public Figure, Private Woman: Same-Sex Support Structures in the Life of Charlotte Whitton,' *International Journal of Women's Studies* 6, 5 (1983): 205–28, and in P.T. Rooke and R.L. Schnell, *No Bleeding Heart: Charlotte Whitton, A Feminist on the Right* (Vancouver: UBC Press, 1987).

10 This extremely large collection of letters is one of the most significant discoveries in Canadian lesbian history. The collection follows the entire course of their relationship, although the major part of the collection comprises the letters written between Frieda and Bud during their years apart in the 1920s. The author is indebted to Donald Fraser and Nancy Fraser Brooks, nephew and niece of Frieda Fraser and executors of her estate, whose assistance with this collection has been extremely helpful and whose realization of the historical importance of the letters has given to Canadian scholars the stories of two very interesting lives.

11 Fraser Records, sous-fonds II, box 010, file 4, Edith Bickerton Williams to Frieda Fraser, 11 January 1925. Although the letter is dated 1925, all the contextual information suggests that it was actually written in 1926 and that she had made an error in the dating.

12 Ibid., sous-fonds III, box 036, file 7, Frieda Fraser to Edith Bickerton Williams, 1 January 1926.

13 Ibid., file 9, Frieda Fraser to Edith Bickerton Williams, 13 June 1926.

14 Ibid., Box 010, file 4, Edith Bickerton Williams to Frieda Fraser, 11 June 1926.

15 Ibid., Edith Bickerton Williams to Frieda Fraser, 12 June 1926.

16 Ibid., file 5, Edith Bickerton Williams to Frieda Fraser, 10 July 1926.

17 Ibid., Edith Bickerton Williams to Frieda Fraser, 17 July 1926.

18 Ibid., sous-fonds III, box 036, file 9, Frieda Fraser to Edith Bickerton Williams, 2 August 1926.

19 Ibid., file 10, Frieda Fraser to Edith Bickerton Williams, 22 December 1926.

20 Ibid., sous-fonds II, box 001, file 17, Nettie Bryant to Helene Fraser, 23 April 1927.

21 See, for example, Faderman, *Odd Girls and Twilight Lovers*; Elizabeth Lapovsky Kennedy and Madeline D. Davis, *Boots of Leather, Slippers of Gold: The History of a Lesbian Community* (New York and London: Routledge, 1993); and Esther Newton, *Cherry Grove, Fire Island: Sixty Years in America's First Gay and Lesbian Town* (Boston: Beacon Press, 1993). George Chauncey, although writing mainly of the gay male world, reveals lesbian social community in New York in this period in his excellent *Gay New York: Gender, Urban Culture, and the Making of the Gay Male World 1890–1940* (New York: Basic Books, 1994).

22 Fraser Records, sous-fonds II, box 010, file 3, Edith Bickerton Williams to Frieda Fraser, 30 June 1925.

23 Ibid., Edith Bickerton Williams to Frieda Fraser, 2 July 1925.

24 Ibid., 22 August 1925.

25 Ibid., sous-fonds III, box 036, file 11, Frieda Fraser to Edith Bickerton Williams, 5 March 1927.

26 University of Toronto Archives, Elisabeth Steel Govan Papers, Acc. No. B79-0027, box 003, file 4, 'Bunny' to Elisabeth Govan, nd., prob. 1945.

27 Bunny to Elisabeth Govan, nd.

28 Interview with Barb, 15 May 1998.

29 Ibid.

30 Ibid.

31 Adams, *The Trouble with Normal*, 95–8.

32 Christabelle Sethna, 'The Facts of Life: The Sex Instruction of Ontario Public School Children, 1900–1950' (PhD thesis, University of Toronto, 1995), 253.

33 Interview with Barb, 15 May 1998.

34 Ibid.

35 Ibid.

36 Little work has yet been done on the experiences of lesbians in the Canadian military. Ruth Roach Pierson reveals, in *They're Still Women after All: The Second World War and Canadian Womanhood* (Toronto: McClelland & Stewart, 1986), 275 n. 83, that lesbians were forced to leave the military during the war. Much greater detail on the armed services during the war and the postwar period is offered by Gary Kinsman, *The Regulation of Desire: Homo and Hetero Sexualities*, 2nd ed. (Montreal: Black Rose Books, 1996), 148–54, 181–3. Kinsman and Patrizia Gentile are at present working on an examination of the national security campaigns in Canada, the preliminary findings of which have been published as *In the Interests of the State: The Anti-gay, Anti-lesbian National Security Campaign in Canada. A Preliminary Research Report* (Sudbury, Ont.: Laurentian University, 1998). The subject of the security campaigns has also been explored in Daniel J. Robinson and David Kimmel, 'The Queer Career of Homosexual Security Vetting in Cold War Canada,' *Canadian Historical Review* 75, 3 (1994): 319–45.

37 *Justice Weekly*, 15 January 1955, 14.

38 *The Telegram*, 11 April 1964, 7.

39 Ibid.

40 Pierson *They're Still Women after All*, 129–68.

41 See, for example, those measures discussed in Mariana Valverde, 'Building Anti-delinquent Communities: Morality, Gender, and Generation in the City,' in Joy Parr, ed., *A Diversity of Women: Ontario, 1945–1980* (Toronto: University of Toronto Press, 1995), 19–45.

42 *Justice Weekly*, 3 April 1954, 12.

43 Ross Higgins and Line Chamberland, 'Mixed Messages: Gays and Lesbians in Montreal Yellow Papers in the 1950s,' in Ian McKay, ed., *The Challenge of Modernity: A Reader on Post-Confederation Canada* (Toronto: McGraw-Hill Ryerson, 1992), 428–30.

44 Kinsman, *The Regulation of Desire*, 168.

45 Valerie Korinek, '"Don't Let Your Girlfriends Ruin Your Marriage": Lesbian Imagery in *Chatelaine* Magazine, 1950–1969,' paper presented at the Canadian Historical Association Conference, 1998.

46 Ibid., 27.

47 Adams, *The Trouble with Normal*, 23.

48 Mary Louise Adams, 'Youth, Corruptibility, and English-Canadian Postwar Campaigns against Indecency, 1948–1955,' *Journal of the History of Sexuality* 6, 1 (1995): 113.

49 For an examination of representations of lesbians in literature in the United States, see Sherrie A. Inness, *The Lesbian Menace: Ideology, Identity, and the Representation of Lesbian Life* (Amherst: University of Massachusetts Press, 1997). Some of the works that Inness examines probably found their way into Ontario via the Buffalo lesbian community, which was frequently visited by Ontario lesbians.

50 Elise Chenier, 'Tough Ladies and Troublemakers: Toronto's Public Lesbian Community, 1955–1965' (MA thesis, Queen's University, 1995), 133–4.

51 Donald W. McLeod, *Lesbian and Gay Liberation in Canada: A Selected Annotated Chronology, 1964–1975* (Toronto: ECW Press/Homewood Books, 1996), 277–86.

52 Chenier, 'Tough Ladies and Troublemakers.'

53 Ibid., 229.

54 Line Chamberland, 'Remembering Lesbian Bars: Montreal, 1955–1975,' in Wendy Mitchinson et al., eds., *Canadian Women: A Reader* (Toronto: Harcourt Brace, 1996), 354–58.

55 Ibid., 361.

56 Kennedy and Davis, *Boots of Leather, Slippers of Gold*, 378–80.

57 Chamberland, 'Remembering Lesbian Bars,' 363.

58 Jerry, interview conducted by Elise Chenier, Lesbians Making History Project

Collection (LMH), 23 November 1992. Chenier donated this interview to the
LMH Collection after completion of her MA thesis.

59 Mona Gleason, 'Psychology and the Construction of the "Normal" Family in
Postwar Canada, 1945–60,' *Canadian Historical Review* 78, 3 (1997): 447.

60 Interview with Jackie, LMH, 19 October 1985.

61 Interview with Pat, LMH, 21 September 1986.

62 Jerry, interview conducted by Elise Chenier, LMH, 23 November 1992.

63 Ibid.

64 See Kinsman, *The Regulation of Desire*, 148–212; and Robinson and David
Kimmel, 'The Queer Career of Homosexual Security Vetting in Cold War
Canada.'

65 Jerry, interview conducted by Elise Chenier, LMH, 23 November 1992.

66 Interview with Arlene, LHM, 6 May 1987.

67 Ibid.

68 Ibid.

69 Chenier, 'Tough Ladies and Troublemakers,' 84.

70 Interview with Alice, LHM, 16 November 1985.

71 Deborah, e-mail interview, 10 June 1998.

72 Interview with Deborah, 29 September 1998.

73 Interview with Veronica, 27 September 1998.

74 Jerry, interview conducted by Elise Chenier, LMH, 23 November 1992.

75 Interview with Arlene, LHM, 6 May 1987.

76 Margaret Jane Hillyard Little, *'No Car, No Radio, No Liquor Permit': The Moral
Regulation of Single Mothers in Ontario, 1920–1997* (Toronto: Oxford University
Press, 1998), 130.

77 Title of a Linda Shear song, cited in Becki Ross, *The House That Jill Built: A
Lesbian Nation in Formation* (Toronto: University of Toronto Press, 1995), 57,
n.258.

78 Katherine Arnup, ed., *Lesbian Parenting: Living with Pride and Prejudice*
(Charlottetown: Gynergy Books, 1995), is the most recent Canadian work
to explore the creation of alternative families on the basis of parenting by
lesbians.

'A Barren Cupboard at Home': Ontario Families Confront the Premiers during the Great Depression

LARA CAMPBELL

On 9 October 1933, Mr T. Frith of Pembroke, Ontario, wrote his fourth of six letters to Premier George Henry. Unemployed and supporting a family, he unsuccessfully petitioned Henry for a job: 'I am getting fed up with everything. It looks strange to me men that never did anything for the Government can be holding down permanent jobs and the likes of me face poverty ... I would just like too [sic] know how you would like it yourself if you fought 3½ years for your government ... do you think you would be getting a fair deal if they didn't give you a little work to keep your wife and family.'[1]

Unemployed citizens of Ontario wrote thousands of similar letters to Premiers George Henry and Mitchell Hepburn during the Great Depression. In 1931, 18 per cent of wage earners in the province were officially out of work, and by 1935 in some cities, such as Niagara Falls, Windsor, and the Toronto suburbs, 33–45 per cent of the population relied on relief.[2] At the beginning of the Depression, state-run social welfare programs were limited in scope, consisting of Mothers' Allowance, Workmen's Compensation, and a means-tested Old Age Pension. Unemployment relief, funded by the federal government and administered by the municipalities, was inadequate and stigmatizing, and was viewed by the federal and provincial governments as a temporary emergency measure. To qualify for relief, the unemployed had to be completely destitute, and were forced to forfeit cars, radios, phones, and liquor permits. Relief payments were often made in kind or by a voucher system, and were different in each community across Canada.[3]

In response to high unemployment and inadequate and stigmatizing relief policies, many Ontario citizens wrote directly to the premier of Ontario. Some of these letters consist of criticisms of government policy, complaints against those on relief, or proposed economic solutions to the Depression, but most are requests from unemployed, white, working-class men and women for jobs or financial aid. The only Canadian study looking at similar sources is *The Wretched of Canada*, a collection of letters to Prime Minister R.B. Bennett. The editors, Michael Bliss and L.M. Grayson, argue that these letters were written by the poorest of the population, those whose lives were 'a single-minded struggle for survival, monotonous and dreary.' They claim that 'the Canadian people had too much discipline, too much individualism ... too little political sophistication to fight back in a radical protest against a whole economic and social system.'[4] While some of the letters to the prime minister and the premiers were indeed desperate pleas for help, many were clearly articulated demands based on notions of rights and entitlement. As citizens, letter writers believed that, in return for service and duty to the state, they and their families were entitled to economic security. Letters written by breadwinners, wives and mothers, homeowners, veterans, and Canadians of British background used the idea of a reciprocal relationship between citizen and state, and the language of respectability, service, and duty, to claim entitlement to jobs and financial aid. Rather than interpreting these letters as expressions of helplessness, this essay examines them as a fundamental part of the shift to the postwar welfare state.

The history of the welfare state has been well documented in Canada, but most historians have used a top-down approach to debate the development of policies, institutions, and the origins and objectives of welfare state programs. Historians have discussed the influence of government, business, religion, and party politics, the role of intellectuals and the social sciences, and the desire of the state to preserve the capitalist economic order and to avoid social disorder. Written mainly from an institutional approach, this history leaves little room in which to locate the agency of welfare recipients or to understand their role in the development of the postwar welfare state.[5] Most people in the 1930s did not belong to an organized political party or protest group, but they voiced concerns and criticisms to friends and neighbours, and in letters written to politicians. Letters to the premiers demonstrate that popular pressure must not be overlooked as a major source of political influence. In Canada, the thousands of letters received by federal and provincial governments demanding that the state take moral responsibility to protect and nurture its citizens, along with relief protests, strikes, and other forms of unrest, helped to push the government towards a more interventionist rights-based welfare state.[6] A broad consensus of public opinion began to develop around the belief that the stigma of charity-based relief was no longer acceptable for Canadian citizens.

The concept of 'rights' articulated by the letter writers was not one of universal entitlement to economic security. Although letter writers thought that every citizen was entitled to a set of rights, they also believed that citizenship itself had to be earned. One way that people attempted to influence the government and assert their fundamental sense of belonging and status as citizens was by making claims on the state,[7] through which they defined the meaning and limits of citizenship. A proper citizen was understood as someone who had a strong work ethic, fulfilled proper gender roles, was married and raising a family, and was white and of British background. Meeting most or all of these requirements meant that one was a citizen and had a right to enter into a moral relationship with the state. In return, the state had a duty and a responsibility to protect its citizens from poverty and unemployment, both of which interfered with the ability to practise good citizenship. Letter writers explicitly used the language of citizenship, a powerful word connoting 'respect, rights, and dignity,'[8] to argue that the government should take the problems of unemployment and poverty seriously. Writers understood themselves to be fully participating members of a larger community; as such, they were entitled to formulate demands and claim a central place in the social and economic order.[9]

Linda Gordon and Nancy Fraser argue that social welfare policy is based on the dichotomous principles of contract or charity. They define charity as a stigmatizing handout symbolizing dependence, 'a gift on which the recipient had no claim, and for which the donor had no obligation.'[10] Contract, however, is associated with rights and dignity; it is based on the free-market economy and the historic rights of free male citizens to own their property and their labour power.[11] This opposition between charity and contract has formed the basis of the twentieth-century welfare state, and runs throughout most social welfare programs and policies in Canada.[12] Whether social welfare should be temporary, minimal, and stigmatizing, or a 'guarantee of a decent standard of living, economic security and honorable entitlement,'[13] is still a topic of debate in late twentieth-century politics.

Feminist historians have argued that this contrast between contract and charity is gendered, creating a two-tiered welfare state intended to uphold the traditional family model of the male breadwinner and the dependent female homemaker. Programs that serve a mainly female constituency, such as Mothers' Allowances or Family Benefits, are, they argue, charity-based programs that are low-paying, stigmatizing, intrusive, and based on the applicant meeting a particular moral standard of female propriety.[14] Programs that develop in the tradition of contract and are based on male patterns of participation in the paid labour force, such as Workmen's Compensation and Unemployment Insurance, are less stigmatizing and more generous. However, it is important to remember that there is no neat division between charity and contract-based social welfare programs. Even in the contract-based model, concerns over upholding the work ethic and preserving the difference between the deserving and the undeserving are often incorporated into the programs.[15]

A comparison of the principles of contract and charity is helpful in interpreting how specific welfare state programs were implemented and how claimants articulated their demands. By examining the grassroots level in the development of social welfare, such as letters written to the premiers, it is possible to develop a more complex and nuanced appreciation of the relationship between the citizen and the state. It is useful to think of charity and contract not as dichotomous categories, but as a continuum with a variety of positions in between. Where particular claimants fit themselves, or are situated by the state, is mediated by such characteristics as class, race, gender, and marital status. In the Depression years, both men and women attempted to incorporate the dignity and sense of entitlement associated with the language of citizenship and a rights-based discourse in order to negotiate a space of greater equality and security for themselves and their families. The language of charity and of entitlement co-exist in these letters, and historians should not assume that writers envisioned themselves solely as supplicants because some of the language is deferential.

The letters, read carefully and as a whole, clearly demonstrate that the Depression years were a meeting point between traditional values of character, duty, and charity and developing ideas of entitlement and state-sponsored welfare in opposition to government bureaucracy and charity. What emerged was both a desire to reform rather than completely eradicate the capitalist economic structure, and a discourse that never completely challenged deeply held inequities and hierarchies of gender, ethnicity and race, and marital status.[16] While recognizing that the welfare state was limited in scope, and was never intended to create full social and economic equality, the postwar welfare state was still an important shift in policy that recognized a right to a certain minimum level of income. Programs such as unemployment insurance or family allowances, and, later, universal old age security and health insurance, were non–means-tested social programs that, at a minimum, 'have been crucial breakthroughs in the fight against poverty and insecurity, and have helped to create a sense of social rights linked to national citizenship.'[17] The language and values of service, duty, and respectability framed writers' demands for economic security and helped to shape the extent of government responsibility for social welfare.

To most letter writers, having a job was crucial to feeling fully human.

Unemployed men in particular claimed that working and earning a wage was central to maintaining responsible citizenship, pride, and self-worth. This 'right' to a job, however, was not unconditional. Unemployed people, either those on relief or those refusing to take it, were careful to point out their strong work ethic and willingness to perform any type of labour for good pay. Because the stereotype of the lazy, unemployed worker persisted into the 1930s, the jobless were careful to distance themselves from such images.[18] There was little agreement on who, exactly, deserved employment or had the right to it. In the fight for limited jobs, forceful divisions based on gender and marital status existed among those who were unemployed. It is clear, however, that most men believed they had a right to work before women, and that both men and women thought that married men were the most entitled to jobs. Ideally, men were the breadwinners who would support their dependent wives and children.[19]

Men articulated their demands for jobs or financial aid through a discourse of independent breadwinner status, claiming they had never needed help and insisting they wanted work, not relief. Although it was usually considered humiliating to ask for relief, men did not feel it was shameful to remind the government of its responsibility to help them find work. They consistently reminded the government that they were 'entitled, deserving and in dire need of work.'[20] This demand for work was based on a powerful sense of masculine entitlement, one that enabled a man to claim respectable status and avoid the shame of charity. The state, men declared, had an obligation to help them fulfil their manly duties, as it would 'lift a man up to be given work instead off [sic] charity.'[21]

Not surprisingly, letters clearly indicate that men's status and self-esteem was intricately bound up with the ability to work.[22] As one man pointed out, 'I love to work ... But, if I work or run the race, I want to win some sort of prize.'[23] The ideal prize, for many, was a family wage and the opportunity to marry and raise new citizens. For married men, masculinity and self-respect were linked to the right to work and the ability to support a family. Even though the family wage was a reality for only a small minority of the population, the idea of the man as the main monetary contributor to the family economy was dominant in the 1930s. As one unemployed man stated: 'I respectfully request that the Government will give me the opportunity to work ... and provide fully all that is needed for the support of my wife and child ... for whose welfare, both the Government and myself are legally and morally responsible.'[24]

Indeed, while men argued for entitlement from the contract and rights-based position of employment, it is crucial to remember that they spoke of these rights within a familial context. Their rights as wage-earners drew additional strength from their role as providers and were inseparable from their position as husband and father within the family. Men continually referred to their obligations and duties as family providers, and to the emotional and psychological trauma of failing in these roles. By the inter-war period, the representation of fatherhood had shifted slightly to accommodate the more involved roles expected of men in the ideal companionate family. The father's main contribution to the family was still breadwinning, but he was also expected to take on a more active and involved role with his children.[25] Cynthia Comacchio argues that breadwinning came to symbolize the emotional ideals of 'fatherly devotion' and 'paternal protection' as well as material provision.[26] For fathers, seeing their children going hungry was a visible and painful reminder of their failure as providers, a challenge to the duties surrounding the societal definitions of respectable manhood.[27]

Unemployment could lead not only to the loss of 'manhood and self-respect' but to a serious threat to the social order, once men could no longer be rewarded for fulfilling the expected roles of husband, father, and provider. 'You can readily understand [that] a hungry man,' claimed Sam Harris, president of the Navy League, 'especially if he has children, is dangerous. Holdups, robberies, purse-snatchings, porch-climbings, and other things, might easily happen.'[28] Men could use their role as father to remind the government that the stability of the state and the security of the family were intricately bound together. 'It will be a strong man patriotically who this winter will drown out the cries of his children for bread with the strains of The Maple Leaf Forever,' claimed one unemployed veteran.[29] Another unemployed man told Hepburn: 'We hear our little ones crying for many things that they cannot have under this wave of charity, they do not get enough to eat and they have to starve and suffer these evictions ... and see Bailiffs throwing their home on the street their toys and Belongings can you wonder why men are clamering [sic] for a Revolution.'[30]

The argument that the state's fundamental responsibility was to protect families from instability created a powerful demand for increased state support of welfare programs. As Analee Golz argues, by the postwar reconstruction period the state accepted a moral obligation to protect and ensure the stability and welfare of the Canadian family.[31] This concern over the stability of the family did not exist only in social welfare or state discourse, however. Part of the powerful rhetoric of postwar welfare programs, such as the Family Allowance Act, was rooted in the demands of Depression-era families for their right to protection by the state.

Women wrote to the premiers as frequently as men, but the basis of their arguments for entitlement differed. While men consistently referred to their status as breadwinners, women were viewed as wives and mothers who had no rightful claim to a position in the paid labour force, especially when male unemployment was so high. But women used the language of rights and entitlement even though these rights were not based on their position within the market economy. As wives and mothers, women demanded help on behalf of their husbands' and families' well-being and independence. Like men, women viewed the family as an independent and self-supporting unit that was, ideally, free from dependence on charity. They were careful to point out the respectable status of their families and their husbands' strong work ethic. 'We want work, not charity' was the refrain from women on behalf of their families just as much as it was from unemployed men.[32]

Married women in particular were labelled as dependants of men and were located in the private sphere where domestic reproduction and caregiving work was unpaid and privatized.[33] Women tended, therefore, to make indirect claims on the state, rooted in their position as wife, mother, and dependant.[34] They asked for jobs for husbands and aid for children, so as to maintain the pride and security of the family. 'My husband feels terrible he loves his family, is willing to work hard,' wrote a mother of seven whose university-educated husband lost his job as a salesman. Her husband, and many other men, she claimed, were 'people who have always paid their way people unaccustomed to hardship [and] are losing everything they ever worked for through no fault of theirs.'[35] Although the claims women made for their families' right to economic security were not as strong as men's, their requests for help should not be interpreted as a form of begging or charity. Certainly, male breadwinners claimed a more direct form of entitlement predicated on independent wage-earning status and a broad public consensus around their right to paid employment. But women still found room to argue for their right to economic security, even within a position of subordination and the framework of a familial status that defined them primarily as dependants.[36]

Even though the idea of the family wage excluded women from the public sphere, women could draw on the rights associated with it to criticize government unemployment policy and the lack of adequate relief, and to argue for their families' right to economic security. As one woman wrote: 'It is almost winter and our men have had no work for ages and we have no winter clothes and no prospects of any my own children have no clothes ... Its work we want not relief. We don't our living [sic] for nothing we want work and lots of it.'[37] Women repeatedly insisted on their children's need for adequate food and clothing as well as school books and medicine, reminding the premiers that their husbands required jobs to meet these necessities. Protesting on behalf of husbands and children by using the rhetoric of 'militant mothering' was one way that women could subvert assumptions of female domesticity to make claims on the state.[38]

The Great Depression drove home the disparity between idealized prescriptions for womanhood and the reality of taking care of a family on a limited budget. As women's ability to manage households and raise children grew increasingly constrained due to high male unemployment, women challenged the traditional roles in which they held a sense of pride and accomplishment.[39] In doing so, they politicized the rhetoric associated with the family wage and with family duties and obligations. A letter signed by the 'mothers of Sturgeon Falls' illustrates women's ability as wives and mothers to make collective demands on the state:

> There are many fathers without work, some with only three days a week. Fathers have these young, unemployed men to care for. As a father, Hon. Sir, you will understand the situation, we mothers are up against, who have our young sons on our hands, who cannot get employment ... the people will need relief money, or some means given by the Government that the people may have a way of living to keep body and soul together.[40]

Wives and mothers expected men to protest against the unemployment that robbed them of their ability to provide and made it difficult to manage the household. One woman from Welland observed: 'There are millions of men driven to being red. A man can stand a good deal but when his wife and children suffer if *he is a man* he becomes desperate.'[41] When men protested against low wages or inadequate relief, their wives clearly framed those actions within the proper duties and responsibilities of manhood. After the arrest of Stratford relief strikers in 1936, one of many wives wrote to Hepburn in protest: 'Surely it is no crime to ask for more food that our children may not suffer from malnutrition.'[42] Another wife asked the premier, 'Why should our children and I be denied having a good husband and father in our home just because he protested against the low standard of relief?'[43]

The arguments made by women on behalf of their families may not have challenged traditional gender roles, but their actions demonstrate that they did not see themselves as passive victims. These letters were a form of political resistance, where women actively voiced opposition to the way the government handled unemployment, threatened to withhold their vote in the next election, and demanded political accountability.[44] As one woman admonished Henry, after writing him three times in vain to request a farm loan and school books for her daughter, there was 'one vote here the last time and will be three this time if i get no help i give none.'[45] Although women were generally excluded from higher-paying administrative positions and policy making, and were labelled as dependants or excluded from the better-paying and less-stigmatizing welfare programs, they were still pivotal in 'shaping the broad outlines of the welfare state.'[46] As Linda Gordon points out, when women made demands for relief, they were rejecting charity, 'inventing rights,' and claiming the status of rightful citizen.[47] Married women were not accorded the same respect and status as men, but their demands for respectability and security should be recognized as a crucial factor in transforming state obligations for social welfare.

Women with husbands could make claims on the government based on the family wage, but women who were deserted or widowed also used the language of entitlement to claim the right to Mothers' Allowance. Mothers' Allowance may have been a form of moral regulation, yet these letters indicate that women understood it as a form of entitlement,[48] not charity. They adopted the language of contract to clothe their claims in a discourse of rights that validated their needs as legitimate entitlements tied to marriage and motherhood. 'To raise a future Canadian in the way he should be raised,' claimed one widow, 'is an important and full time job, enough responsibility for any woman however strong, without the added burden of trying to find a job.'[49] Women drew on the gendered expectations of womanhood to legitimate their requests and to demand recognition,[50] arguing that the state owed them support in return for fulfilling their proper roles as wives and mothers. A deserted wife whose remarriage disqualified her from a veteran's pension drew on her status as a mother as well as the language of service and sacrifice used by veterans, claiming, 'at the same time after I have struggled to raise my boys up to manhood the Government would expect my boys to step out and do their share to protect the country should a war break out; that go [sic] to show how much respect the Government has for the citizens of the country.'[51] Women protested when allowances were cut off or denied, contacted local Mothers' Allowances Boards, and wrote to politicians. 'Why do innocent children have to suffer the loss of a good home,' asked one woman, '... when we are Canadians, and our parents before us.'[52] While not always successful, their determination indicates that women were serious in attempting to force the state to recognize their maternal concerns and duties.

Historians have argued that Mothers' Allowance acted as a form of state moral regulation by making women's eligibility dependent on their moral propriety and respectability, such as proper housekeeping standards and the cleanliness and behaviour of their children.[53] Sexual standards were of particular concern to administrators, and many women were cut off from the allowance after being accused of immorality.[54] But even those recipients who were accused of impropriety could draw on the rhetoric of some reformers who had originally envisioned the allowance as a form of entitlement that recognized that 'the reproductive work of women merited some degree of entitlement.'[55] A woman accused of moral impropriety for keeping a male boarder in her home unsuccessfully protested the removal of her allowance by claiming, 'I am a member of the Church of England and a conservative and I am trying to bring my children up right.'[56] In some cases, however, being a good mother was enough to maintain the allowance, even in the face of sexual scandal. A woman from Toronto, whose application for a mother's allowance was rejected because she had two children by a man who turned out to be a bigamist, appealed successfully, saying: 'I am a Canadian girl born and raised in Toronto and I am a Mother. I think I am deserving of that allowance.'[57] Claiming entitlement based on fulfilling the gendered duties of wife and mother could be a source of power for women, who could use those accomplishments to demand financial aid from the state. Like most women who wrote to the premiers, single mothers believed they and their children were entitled to economic and family security.

Letter writers used the language of respectability to claim that the proper relationship between the citizen and the state was reciprocal, and they emphasized certain moral qualities as necessary preconditions of citizenship. One argument closely associated with respectability and the demand for work was the declaration by many letter writers that homes were in danger.[58] To both men and women, owning their own home was a clear sign of moral worth within the community. In her study of male workers in Hanover, Joy Parr shows how home ownership gave families economic security and a sense of pride rooted in community respectability.[59] Men and women took great satisfaction in the presentation of their homes, since a home was where a family could 'live in a sanitary condition,' and where a man could fulfil his obligation to his family and 'bring my wife, and children up right.'[60] Suzanne Morton argues that workers in Halifax achieved respectability by establishing privacy and meeting common standards of good taste, reflected in consumer purchases and the decoration of the family home.[61] While most of the people in her study were tenants rather than owners, homeownership would have further increased the pride and self-worth of men and women within the community. Letter writers were determined to maintain their homes at great cost, and were worried about the possibility of foreclosure and eviction.

Homeowners placed themselves within the circle of respectability by emphasizing such values as thrift and economic responsibility. City councils and homeowners' associations worried that men were 'becoming ill in mind and body for want of their regular employment, and the happiness and peace of our homelife is almost destroyed through the enforced idleness of the breadwinners.'[62] Councils passed resolutions that explicitly linked homeownership to respectability, pride, and self-respect, and demanded that unemployed homeowners be given special opportunities to work off tax arrears and mortgage payments. Homeowners were praised for thriftiness and savings 'at a considerable sacrifice,' for paying taxes and taking 'a pride in the Municipality,' and for their 'praiseworthy efforts [at] maintaining themselves without recourse to relief.'[63] Homes were important because they were a powerful symbol of a person's position in the social order and the most visible evidence of hard work and thrift, the very moral qualities needed to be a good citizen. To be evicted from one's home, citizens claimed, destroyed the 'family's self-respect and morale.'[64] Women could also appeal to the government as homeowners, since they were an essential part of the family economy when buying and maintaining a home. One woman told Henry: 'I worked like a man on our place to help my husband and saved every cent I could to help get along ... it is no fault of ours that we cannot meet our way.'[65] For a married woman, the home was the centre of domestic production and the heart of her responsibilities as a wife and mother. 'Making do' was a skill many women perfected in order to stretch a man's low wage and to manage the household on limited resources.[66] Preventing foreclosure was a crucial job for women in the Depression years, and letters indicate that women saved and spent money carefully, took in sewing and boarders, sold their own produce and baking, and performed domestic service to help save their homes.[67]

While men and their wives made claims on the state based on fulfilling proper gender roles, respectability, and home ownership, First World War veterans and their families were also able to draw on the language of sacrifice and service to the country. To veterans, service in the Great War set their demands apart from all other claims on the state. The letters of unemployed veterans carefully pointed out their years of service and duty, claiming that patriotic loyalty was the duty of the soldier, but that the government had a moral obligation to protect and support them in return. Many unemployed veterans felt abandoned and ignored by a government that was reluctant to offer them special status in recognition of their sacrifices. 'It certainly does not make me feel very nice,' explained one unemployed man, 'to think I helped to defend a country that will not help me in times when I and my family need it badly.'[68] Veterans' associations complained to the government that veterans' dismissals from jobs were contrary to 'British justice,' and that returned men should be given preference for employment.[69] One veterans' group protested the arrests of Etobicoke relief strikers because some of the men were vets 'who at the country's call willingly went through hell, believing they were fighting for Justice, Peace and Freedom and now when they dare Fight for even a miseryable [sic] existence for themselves and their wives and Families you have them thrown into prison cells.'[70] Jobs and economic security, veterans claimed, were basic rights that they had earned overseas while proving themselves as worthy Canadian men and citizens.

Veterans' criticisms of the government in the 1930s were rooted in their collective protest against inadequate government compensation after First World War, when they began to mobilize against poor training programs, inadequate pensions for disabled soldiers, and unfair differentials in pensions based on rank.[71] They made their claims for compensation, Desmond Morton argues, on the basis of 'moral entitlement,' not charity.[72] By 1919 the Great War Veterans' Association advocated state policies such as public housing, minimum wage, nationalization of primary resources, profit controls, and age, sickness, and unemployment insurance.[73] Veterans insisted that their wartime sacrifices of lost wages and family separations had yet to be properly rewarded,[74] and linked their status as soldiers to the respectability associated with manly breadwinning and family duty. Their fulfilment of the masculine call to sacrifice deserved special recognition, they believed, particularly when high unemployment made it increasingly difficult to support their families. 'When MEN were needed to save our nation,' claimed the Canadian Legion, 'the boys responded to the call unselfishly, upholding the best traditions of our Empire. They gave their all. Promises of Freedom and Security have been broken or forgotten.'[75] The discourse of sacrifice and duty, combined with the privilege associated with the role of breadwinner, was, for many veterans, a powerful argument for their right to employment. One veteran with an ill wife and four children told Henry to give the men who 'wallowed in the mud of Flanders a chance to make a few dollars and keep the Respectability of ourselves and our families.'[76]

Veterans' families also used the concepts of duty and sacrifice to make claims on the government, often linking war service to the powerful image of protecting the home. Some families were literally on the verge of foreclosure, but, for others, the word *home* represented economic security. One mother reminded Henry: 'If this country ever has to fight again it can call on my eight boys to protect it well you cannot expect them to protect homes they haven't got.'[77] Future soldiers were the same young men who were unemployed and unable to fulfil the basic duties of citizenship. Their families reminded the government that its success in future international conflicts depended on the willingness of young men to serve, and, therefore, they expected protection on the home front in times of economic crisis. As one father reminded Henry, 'We thought that when two of our boys went overseas, that they went to protect our home.'[78]

Closely tied to values of duty and respectability were particular notions of ethnicity. It is not surprising that in a time of social and economic upheaval, an affirmation of Canadian national identity should appear in popular discourse. Although historians have discussed the rise of an independent Canadian cultural nationalism beginning in the 1920s, few have looked at how national identity was formed outside the intellectual elite.[79] Yet, if a nation is an 'imagined community,' it is crucial to understand how conceptions of nationality were shaped and understood at the popular level.[80] Letter writers used the discourse of national identity to place themselves, along with the politicians they were addressing, within a collective, although narrowly defined, Canadian identity. Anyone who was white and of British heritage was a true Canadian, and therefore worthy of financial aid and economic justice. Letter writers clearly indicated who was and was not included in a hierarchy of entitlement. Those who were 'Canadian by Birth'[81] or of British heritage were seen as the only truly deserving citizens of Canada. For many, true Canadian identity was established through generations of Canadian ancestry. To letter writers, the United Empire Loyalists and the early pioneers symbolized the belief in an organic community where generations of Canadians were linked together in the creation of the Canadian nation. An unemployed man on the verge of foreclosure wrote to Henry to ask for help in saving his family's home, saying: 'My wife is a Canadian of three generations back and myself I am forty-five years in Canada a British subject at that.'[82] United Empire Loyalist 'stock' was a vital signifier of status to both men and women, and to Conservative and Liberal supporters. One woman explicitly linked the Hepburn government with 'pioneer British stock' from 'the Stirring days of Alexander McKenzie.'[83]

By drawing on the status of ethnicity, women could be true Canadians on an equal basis with men and could claim a crucial place for themselves within the national narrative.[84] A woman's status as a member of the Anglo-Canadian community could be used to argue for greater recognition and entitlement, and a stronger position on the continuum of charity and contract. The native-born, according to female letter writers, played a crucial role in building the nation, and should therefore receive recognition from the state. Genealogy became a calling card and signifier of special status. 'I am no foreigner,' wrote a widow who was facing foreclosure. 'I was born in Ontario from parents that [were] also born in Ontario. My grandfather was a U. E. L. my grandparents on my mothers side were Irish. My husband was also a good Canadian born in Canada from English blood.'[85] Another woman wrote: 'Are we not true, loyal Canadians from the same descent as your wife Mrs. Henry. Her ancestry [sic] Laura Secord was mine also as well as Sir Allen McNab and the other faithful early settlers.'[86] Single mothers could also call on Canadian ethnicity to more forcefully argue their status of respectability. A woman who was turned down for Mothers' Allowance wrote to say: 'We are respectable citizens of Canada and have been for generations back. I am bringing up my family deasent and respectabel [sic] and educating them the best I can ... I feel I have been dealt out of my rights by some-one who thinks it there [sic] duty to save government money.'[87]

This tendency to use ethnicity as a claim for entitlement can be seen as both a radical and a conservative impulse. Canadian identity became a way for the unemployed and poor to claim respectability and to make demands for economic and political justice. But the narrow definition of a true Canadian excluded the non-Canadian born and those 'foreigners' who were not of British background, and were therefore unable to demand the entitlements claimed by those considered full members of the Canadian state.[88] 'Is there a chance,' asked one unemployed man, 'for a good honest Canadian Citizen to make an honest living for himself and Family ... Why do our Governments ... permit our own Canadians to be shut out and all classes of foreigners placed in their positions.'[89] Writers complained with bitterness and hostility that 'foreigners' were taking away Canadians' rightful place in the labour force and stealing away potential opportunities. As one unemployed woman stated: 'It is impossible for a single man, during the last five years, to have any hope of marriage ... It is the foreigner and the Jew who are taking our trades and work from us, who can afford to marry and start a home.'[90]

In the public imagination, the fear of immigrants was also associated with the fear of communist protest against the capitalist system. The rhetoric of 'British justice' was commonly used to set criticism of the government and claims for entitlement apart from more radical critiques of the economic and political system, although the distinction between radical and 'British justice' could be ambiguous. 'I don't want any Czar of Russia methods in what I have always been taught was a free Canada for Canadians,' claimed an unemployed miner from Cobalt. 'But in my case it is far from being a free country ... I do not want you to think I am a Red or an agitator, but I do feel that I have been very unfairly dealt with.'[91] Many individuals wrote to say they were not communist agitators or radicals, just ordinary people who desired 'British justice,' which they defined variously as 'the Right to work in a man's own country,'[92] to receive a living wage and provide for a wife and family, to criticize government relief and policy measures freely, and to receive priority for jobs if a veteran or Canadian born. Using the threat of communism or 'turning red' within their letters was one way that writers expressed the depth of their concerns about the economic condition. An unemployed veteran told Henry in 1931, 'I am no extremist or radical,' but 'starvation breeds revolution,' particularly when 'my children are receiving less nourishment than I received while in a Soviet prison in Moscow.'[93] A woman with an unemployed husband and a sick child, and who proudly claimed Loyalist descent, asked Henry, 'Do you wonder in the face of such suffering that people become radicals?'[94]

As men and women wrote formal requests to the government, they were attempting to establish their needs as legitimate political concerns and participating in a debate to define how those needs should be properly met.[95] Using the language of rights and entitlement, letter writers attempted to link their demands to the dignity associated with the principle of contract, claiming that economic security and stability should be provided in return for service to the state. This language of contract, rights, and entitlement was at once progressive and limiting. While it argued for greater government responsibility for the welfare of its citizens, expanded government obligation for social welfare was never intended to eradicate economic inequality completely, and many people were excluded from the status of a fully entitled and deserving citizen. The dignity associated with a rights-based discourse in this era still presumed the existence of the oppositional categories of charity and dependence.[96] The assertions by letter writers that they were entitled citizens who had fulfilled certain duties implied that others had failed to meet the obligations required of citizenship, and were therefore not entitled to aid. The way that claimants understood state responsibility and individual obligation left little room for a conception of state welfare beyond contractual obligations based on individual duties.[97]

Yet individuals did have some room to act and to manoeuvre. While some letters received a formulaic response, others obtained some form of help. After a direct appeal to the premier, some men were given temporary work on government public works projects in the early 1930s. Many others received answers to their questions on government policy and legislation, or promises of investigation into denial of, for example, relief payments or Old Age Pensions or Mothers' Allowance Benefits. With a few notable exceptions, however, most people who wrote to the premiers did not offer a radical critique of the capitalist economic order or demand sweeping changes to the political system. Still, their actions should be seen as no less important than those of organized political parties or labour unions. They made their demands and criticisms on a basis of duties, obligations, and moral values, including a willingness to work, proper gender roles, and a moral character emphasizing thrift, sobriety, and honesty. Recommendations to Henry and Hepburn from reeves, ministers, and prominent members of the community, remarking on workers' responsibility and honesty, demonstrated that good character was considered an essential component of good citizenship. Letter writers used traditional notions of hard work, good character, and duty to make claims on the state and to argue for increased state responsibility for its citizens. Within a limited discourse and range of possibilities, writers were attempting to create a positive vision of a society where citizens within an industrial capitalist order could expect protection from the economic insecurity and instability produced by unemployment. Ultimately, viewing these letters as political actions means re-evaluating the way historians have defined the meaning of the word *political*. Taken seriously, these letters suggest an active and politically aware population determined to write to politicians and government officials to keep them accountable, and to ensure that their claims were seriously acknowledged. In Depression-era Canada, the letters and appeals of unemployed men and women for a reciprocal relationship between citizen and state should be viewed as an important force in the transition to the postwar welfare state.

NOTES

I would like to thank Karen Dubinsky, Catherine Gidney, and Eric Wredenhagen for their helpful comments and encouragement, and the Queen's University School of Graduate Studies for financial support.

1 Archives of Ontario (AO), RG 3-8, G.S. Henry Papers, MS 1759, file Department of Public Works, Mr T.F. to Henry, 9 October 1933.

2 John T. Saywell, 'Just Call Me Mitch': The Life of Mitchell F. Hepburn (Toronto: University of Toronto Press, 1991), 84; James Struthers, The Limits of Affluence: Welfare in Ontario, 1920–1970 (Toronto: University of Toronto Press, 1994), 92.

3 See James Struthers, No Fault of Their Own: Unemployment and the Canadian Welfare State, 1914–1941 (Toronto: University of Toronto Press, 1983); and Dennis Guest, The Emergence of Social Security in Canada (Vancouver: UBC Press, 1985), 84–5.

4 Michael Bliss and L.M. Grayson, eds. The Wretched of Canada: Letters to R.B. Bennett, 1930–1935 (Toronto: University of Toronto Press, 1971), xxv.

5 See, for example, Alvin Finkel, Business and Social Reform in the Thirties (Toronto: James Lorimer, 1979); Allan Moscovitch and J. Albert, The Benevolent State: The Growth of Welfare in Canada (Toronto: Garamond Press, 1987); Struthers, No Fault of Their Own and The Limits of Affluence; Doug Owram, The Government Generation: Canadian Intellectuals and the State (Toronto: University

of Toronto Press, 1986); Michiel Horn, *The League for Social Reconstruction* (Toronto: University of Toronto Press, 1980); Larry Glassford, *Reaction and Reform: The Politics of the Conservative Party under R.B. Bennett, 1927–1938* (Toronto: University of Toronto Press, 1992); Walter Young, *Anatomy of a Party: The National CCF, 1932–61* (Toronto: University of Toronto Press, 1969); and Nancy Christie and Michael Gauvreau, *A Full-Orbed Christianity: The Protestant Churches and Social Welfare in Canada, 1900–1940* (Toronto: McGill-Queen's University Press, 1996). For an examination of grassroots activism, see Frances Fox Piven and Richard A. Cloward, *Regulating the Poor: The Functions of Public Welfare* (New York: Random House, 1971). In Canada, see Victor Howard, '*We Were the Salt of the Earth': The On-to-Ottawa Trek and the Regina Riot* (Regina: Canadian Plains Research Center, 1985); Ronald Liversedge, *Recollections of the On-to-Ottawa Trek* (Toronto: McClelland & Stewart, 1973); Dominique Marshall, 'The Language of Children's Rights, the Formation of the Welfare State, and the Democratic Experience of Poor Families in Quebec, 1940–55,' *Canadian Historical Review* 78, 3 (1997): 409–39; and Shirley Tillotson, 'Citizen Participation in the Welfare State: An Experiment, 1945–57,' *Canadian Historical Review* 75, 4 (1994), 511–42.

6 See Craig Jenkins and Barbara G. Brents, 'Social Protest, Hegemonic Competition, and Social Reform: A Political Struggle Interpretation of the Origins of the American Welfare State,' *American Sociological Review* 54 (1989): 891–909; Saywell, *Just Call Me Mitch*, 265–6; and Linda Gordon, *Pitied but Not Entitled: Single Mothers and the History of Welfare, 1890–1935* (Cambridge: Harvard University Press, 1994), 241–51.

7 Gordon, *Pitied but Not Entitled*, 274.

8 Nancy Fraser and Linda Gordon, 'Contract versus Charity: Why Is There No Social Citizenship in the United States?' *Socialist Review* 22, 3 (1992): 45.

9 T.H. Marshall argues that social citizenship ranges from the 'right to a modicum of economic welfare and security to the right to share in the social heritage and to live the life of a civilized being according to the standards prevailing in the society.' T.H. Marshall, *Citizenship and Social Class* (London: Pluto Press, 1992), 6. For a critique of Marshall, see Gordon and Fraser, 'Contract versus Charity,' 48–56, and Carol Pateman, *The Disorder of Women: Democracy, Feminism and Political Theory* (Stanford: Stanford University Press, 1989), 184–5.

10 Gordon and Fraser, 'Contract versus Charity,' 59.

11 Ibid., 55, and Pateman, *Disorder of Women*, 185.

12 See Guest, *The Emergence of Social Security*, and Michael Katz, *In the Shadow of the Poorhouse: A Social History of Welfare in America* (New York: Basic Books, 1986), ix–xiv.

13 Fraser and Gordon, 'Contract versus Charity,' 48.

14 See Veronica Strong-Boag, 'Wages for Housework: Mothers' Allowance and the Beginning of Social Security in Canada,' *Journal of Canadian Studies* 14

(1979–80): 24–34; Struthers, *Limits of Affluence*, 19–49; Margaret Little, 'The Blurring of Boundaries: Private and Public Welfare for Single Mothers in Ontario,' *Studies in Political Economy* 47 (summer 1995): 89–109; Jane Ursel, *Private Lives, Public Policy: 100 Years of State Intervention in the Family* (Toronto: Women's Press, 1992); Ruth Roach Pierson, 'Gender and the Unemployment Insurance Debates in Canada,' *Labour/Le Travail* 25 (spring 1990): 77–103; Dominique Jean, 'Family Allowances and Family Autonomy: Quebec Families Encounter the Welfare State, 1945–1955,' in Bettina Bradbury, ed., *Canadian Family History: Selected Readings* (Toronto: Copp Clark Pitman, 1992), 401–37; Analee Golz, 'Family Matters: The Canadian Family and the State in Postwar Canada,' *left history* 1, 2 (1993): 9–50. For the United States, see the essays in Linda Gordon, ed., *Women, the State and Welfare* (Madison: University of Wisconsin Press, 1990); Ann Shorla Orloff, 'Gender and the Social Rights of Citizenship: The Comparative Analysis of Gender Relations and Welfare States,' *American Sociological Review* 58 (1993): 303–28; Mimi Abramovitz, *Regulating the Lives of Women: Social Welfare Policy from Colonial Times to the Present* (Boston: South End Press, 1988).

15 James Struthers argues that the principle of less eligibility was written into unemployment insurance by making benefits lower than market-based wage rates and by favouring those who had steady, full-time employment. See Struthers, *No Fault of Their Own*, 211–12; Pierson, 'Gender and the Unemployment Insurance Debates'; Guest, *Emergence of Social Security*, 146–7.

16 See Tillotson, 'Citizen Participation in the Welfare State,' where she argues that a form of citizen participation can be found in the early years of Brantford's recreation movement.

17 Struthers, *Limits of Affluence*, 4. Family Allowance benefits were never adequate, argues Dominique Jean, but they still 'led parents to incorporate the idea of an adequate allowance into their concept of their rights as Canadians ... [and] to enlarge their concepts of their rights as citizens.' Jean, 'Family Allowances and Family Autonomy,' 430.

18 Struthers, *Limits of Affluence*, 94–5.

19 Margaret Hobbs, 'Gendering Work and Welfare: Women's Relationship to Wage-Work and Social Policy in Canada during the Great Depression' (PhD thesis, University of Toronto, 1995), and 'Rethinking Antifeminism in the 1930s: Gender Crisis or Workplace Justice? A Response to Alice Kessler-Harris,' *Gender and History* 5, 1 (1993): 4–15; Lois Scharf, *To Work and to Wed: Female Employment, Feminism, and the Great Depression* (Westport: Greenwood Press, 1980).

20 AO, RG 3-8, Henry Papers, MS 1759, file Department of Public Works, Mr G.D. to Henry, 20 July 1933.

21 Ibid., MS 1752, file Department of Public Works, Mr S.J. to Henry, 11 May 1932.

22 For a discussion of the importance of the male breadwinner ideal, see Cynthia Comacchio, 'A Postscript for Father: Defining a New Fatherhood in Interwar Canada,' *Canadian Historical Review* 78, 3 (1997): 305–408; Robert Griswold, *Fatherhood in America: A History* (New York: Basic Books, 1993); and Joy Parr, *The Gender of Breadwinners: Women, Men, and Change in Two Industrial Towns, 1880–1950* (Toronto: University of Toronto Press, 1990); and Suzanne Morton, *Ideal Surroundings: Domestic Life in a Working-Class Suburb in the 1920s* (Toronto: University of Toronto Press, 1995).

23 AO, RG 3-8, Henry Papers, MS 1755, file Legislation, mortgage, Mr R.H. to Henry, 7 January, 1932.

24 Ibid., MS 1759, file Department of Public Works, T.H.G. to Henry, 3 October 1933.

25 Morton, *Ideal Surroundings*, 72; Comacchio, 'Postscript for Father'; Parr, *Gender of Breadwinners*, 82.

26 Comacchio, 'Postscript for Father,' 395.

27 Michael Roper and John Tosh argue that male power is continually 'contested and transformed,' partly because the ideal of financial self-sufficiency has always been hard to achieve. Michael Roper and John Tosh, *Manful Assertions: Masculinities in Britain since 1800* (London: Routledge, 1991), 18. See also the essays in Mark Carnes and Clyde Griffen, *Meanings for Manhood: Constructions of Masculinity in Victorian America* (Chicago: University of Chicago Press, 1990); and Morton, *Ideal Surroundings*, 82.

28 AO, RG 3-8, Henry Papers, MS 1757, file Navy League, Sam Harris, president, Navy League of Canada, to Henry, 27 March 1933.

29 Ibid., MS 1747, file Unemployment Relief no. 3, Lt. W.J.O. to Henry, 8 October 1931.

30 AO, RG 3, Series 9, M.F. Hepburn Papers, no. 180, file Unemployment Relief, no. 2, L.W. to Hepburn, 24 June 1934.

31 Analee Golz, 'Family Matters,' 11.

32 AO, RG 3, Series 9, Hepburn Papers, no. 180, file Unemployment Relief no. 2, Mrs M.G. to Hepburn, 27 July 1934.

33 Pierson, 'Gender and the Unemployment Insurance Debates'; Pateman, *Disorder of Women*, 182–5, 192–5.

34 Evans, 'Divided Citizenship,' 91, 95.

35 AO, RG 3-8, Henry Papers, MS 1745, file Relief, asked for, Mrs W.A. Rowland to Henry, 1 October 1931.

36 See Linda Gordon, *Heroes of Their Own Lives: The Politics and History of Family Violence, 1880–1960* (New York: Penguin, 1988).

37 AO, RG 3, Series 9, Hepburn Papers, no. 180, file: Unemployment Relief, Mrs W.H. to Hepburn, 1934.

38 See Joan Sangster, *Dreams of Equality: Women on the Canadian Left, 1920–50* (Toronto: McClelland & Stewart, 1989); Irene Howard, 'The Mothers' Council

of Vancouver: Holding the Fort for the Unemployed, 1935–38,' *BC Studies* 69–70 (1988): 249–87; Annelise Orleck, '"We Are That Mythical Thing Called the Public": Militant Housewives during the Great Depression,' *Feminist Studies* 1 (1993): 147–72.

39 See Lois Rita Helmbold, 'Beyond the Family Economy: Black and White Working-Class Women during the Great Depression,' *Feminist Studies* 13, 3 (1987): 629–49.

40 AO, RG 3-8, MS 1747, Henry Papers, file Unemployment relief no. 3, Mrs W.G. on behalf of the mothers of Sturgeon Falls, 29 September 1931.

41 AO, RG 3-10, Hepburn Papers, no. 250, file Comments on unemployment relief, 29 July 1935.

42 Ibid., no. 203, file Provincial Secretary's Department, Mrs J.J. to Hepburn, 14 May 1936.

43 Ibid., Mrs L.M. to Hepburn, 10 May 1936.

44 Ann Snitow, 'A Gender Diary,' in Marianne Hirsch and Evelyn Fox Keller, eds., *Conflicts in Feminism* (New York: Routledge, 1990), 9–43.

45 AO, RG 3-8, Henry Papers, MS 1736, file Agricultural Development Board, Mrs A.S. to Henry, 26 August 1931.

46 Frances Fox Piven and Richard A. Cloward, 'Welfare Doesn't Shore Up Traditional Family Roles: A Reply to Linda Gordon,' *Social Research* 55, 4 (1988): 633.

47 Gordon, *Pitied but Not Entitled*, 627.

48 Margaret Little notes that lobbyists and recipients in British Columbia saw Mothers' Pensions as payment for a service performed. Margaret Little, 'Claiming a Unique Place: The Introduction of Mothers' Pensions in British Columbia,' in Veronica Strong-Boag and Anita Clair Fellman, eds., *Rethinking Canada: The Promise of Women's History* (Don Mills: Oxford University Press, 1993), 285–303. In *No Car, No Radio, No Liquor Permit: The Moral Regulation of Single Mothers in Ontario, 1920–1997* (Toronto: Oxford University Press, 1998), Little notes that women receiving Mothers' Allowances tended to direct complaints to the premier or local politicians rather than risk a direct protest to the investigator (105).

49 AO, RG 3-10, Hepburn Papers, no. 190, file Public Welfare Department, Mothers' Allowance, Mrs R.H. to Hepburn, 21 February 1935. Quoted in Struthers, *Limits of Affluence*, 99.

50 Recent literature has argued that the welfare state can provide a potential escape route for women from dependence on individual men by providing a direct relationship to the state. See Pateman, *Disorder of Women*, 196; Evans, 'Divided Citizenship,' 95; Gordon, 'What Does Welfare Regulate?' *Social Research* 55, 4 (1988): 609–30; Orloff, 'Gender and the Social Rights of Citizenship,' 305.

51 AO, RG 3, Series 9, Hepburn Papers, no. 180, file Unemployment Relief no. 2, Mrs J.W. to Hepburn, 6 September 1934.

52 AO, RG 3-8, Henry Papers, MS 1745, file Relief: asked for, Mrs C.G. to Henry, 9 June 1931. See also Mothers' Allowances files, ibid., MS 1742, 1931, and MS 1757, 1933.

53 Margaret Little, 'The Blurring of Boundaries,' and Little, 'Manhunts and Bingo Blabs: The Moral Regulation of Ontario Single Mothers,' in Mariana Valverde, ed., *Studies in Moral Regulation* (Toronto: Centre of Criminology, 1994).

54 Little, 'Blurring of Boundaries'; Struthers, *Limits of Affluence*, 43.

55 Struthers, *Limits of Affluence*, 48.

56 AO, RG 3-8, Henry Papers, MS 1742, 30 October 1931, file Mothers' Allowances Commission, Mrs C.C. to Henry, 30 October 1931.

57 Ibid, MS 1757, file Mothers' Allowances Commission, Mrs R.C. to Henry, 5 March 1933.

58 In a clipping from a 1934 Perth newspaper, the homes of seventeen people were listed for sale owing to tax arrears; seven of these homes belonged to women. AO, RG 3, Series 9, Hepburn Papers, no. 180, file Unemployment no. 2, Mrs A.F. to Hepburn, 2 August 1934 (enclosure).

59 Parr, *The Gender of Breadwinners*.

60 AO, RG 3-10, Hepburn Papers, no. 225, file M.F. Hepburn, private no. 3, Mrs G.A. to Hepburn, July 1934; AO, RG 3-8, Henry Papers, MS 1759, file Department of Public Works, Mr V.G. to Hepburn, 19 September 1933.

61 Morton, *Ideal Surroundings*, 32–8.

62 AO, RG 3-8, Henry Papers, MS 1760, file Resolutions, Toronto Ward Two Property Owners Joint Executive to Henry, 24 April 1933.

63 Ibid., file Resolutions, Peterborough City Council to Henry, 7 February 1933; file Resolutions, Kitchener City Council, 14 June 1933; and file Resolutions, Hamilton City Council, 13 June 1933.

64 Ibid., MS 1755, file Legislation, mortgage, Mr W.F.P. to Henry, 9 January, 1933.

65 Ibid., MS 1760, file Relief, asked for, Mrs T.P. to Henry, 18 March 1933.

66 Morton, *Ideal Surroundings*, 38. On 'making do,' see Denyse Baillargeon, '"If You Had No Money, You Had No Trouble, Did You?": Montreal Working-Class Housewives in the Great Depression,' *Women's History Review* 1, 2 (1992): 217–37; Laura Hollingsworth and Vappu Tyyska, 'Hidden Producers: Women's Household Production in the Great Depression,' *Critical Sociology* 15, 3 (1988); Jeane Westin, *Making Do: How Women Survived the Thirties* (Chicago: Follet Publishing, 1976).

67 See, for example, AO, RG 3-8, Henry Papers, MS 1760, file Relief, asked for, Mrs T.P. to Henry, 18 March 1933; MS 1759, file Department of Public Works, Mr R.M. to Henry, 24 June 1933; RG 3-10, Hepburn Papers, no. 225, file Hepburn, private no. 3, Mrs G.W.A. to Hepburn, July 1934. For the role of women in the family economy, see Meg Luxton, *More Than a Labour of Love: Three Generations of Women's Work in the Home* (Toronto: Women's Press, 1980); and Bettina Bradbury, *Working Families: Age, Gender and Daily Survival in Industrializing Montreal* (Toronto: McClelland & Stewart, 1993).

68 AO, RG 3, Series 9, Hepburn Papers, no. 180, file Unemployment Relief no. 1, Mr W.K. to Hepburn, 17 December 1934.

69 See letters in AO, RG 3-10, Hepburn Papers, no. 171, file B.E.S.L., 1934.

70 Ibid., no. 205, file Resolutions, Progressive Veterans in Canada to Hepburn, 27 July 1936.

71 Desmond Morton, 'The Canadian Veterans' Heritage from the Great War,' in Peter Neary and J.L. Granatstein, eds., *The Veterans Charter and Post–World War II Canada* (Montreal and Kingston: McGill-Queen's Universtity Press, 1998), 22–3, and Morton, '"Noblest and Best": Retraining Canada's War Disabled 1915–23,' *Journal of Canadian Studies* 16, 3 and 4 (1991): 75–85.

72 Morton, 'Canadian Veterans,' 22.

73 Jeffrey A. Keshen, *Propaganda and Censorship during Canada's Great War* (Edmonton: University of Alberta Press, 1996), 204.

74 Morton, 'Canadian Veterans,' 23.

75 AO, RG 3, Series 9, Hepburn Papers, no. 180, file Unemployment Relief, Canadian Legion Unemployment Committee, B.E.S.L. Hamilton Branch to Hepburn, December 1934.

76 AO, RG 3-8, Henry Papers, MS 1759, file Department of Public Works, East Block, Mr F.K to Henry, 24 May 1933.

77 Ibid., MS1744, file Positions, general, Mrs A.B. to Henry, 27 June 1931.

78 Ibid., MS 1762, file Unemployment Relief, homeowners, Mr H.V.W. to Henry, 8 September 1933.

79 See Carl Berger, *The Writing of Canadian History: Aspects of English Canadian Historical Writing since 1900* (Toronto: University of Toronto Press, 1986); Mary Vipond, 'Nationalism and Nativism: The Native Sons of Canada in the 1930s,' *Canadian Review of Studies in Nationalism* 9, 1 (1982), 81–95; Vipond, 'The Nationalist Network: English Canada's Intellectuals and Artists in the 1920s,' *Canadian Review of Studies in Nationalism* 7, 1 (1980): 32–52.

80 Benedict Anderson, *Imagined Communities: Reflections on the Origins and Spread of Nationalism* (London: Verso, 1983).

81 AO, RG 3-8, Henry Papers, MS 1761, file Soldiers' Aid Commission, Mr E.L. to Henry, 14 January 1933.

82 Ibid., MS 1762, file Unemployment Relief no. 1, Mr T.H. to Henry, 7 August 1933.

83 AO, RG 3-10, Hepburn Papers, no. 225, file M.F. Hepburn, private no. 3, Miss M.E.M. to Hepburn, 3 July 1934.

84 See Antoinette Burton, *Burdens of History: British Feminists, Indian Women, and Imperial Culture, 1865–1915* (Chapel Hill: University of North Carolina Press); and Ann Curthoys, 'Identity Crisis: Colonialism, Nation, and Gender in Australian History,' *Gender and History* 5, 2 (1993): 165–76.

85 AO, RG 3-8, Henry Papers, MS 1750, file Mothers' Allowances Commission, Mrs S.B.S. to Henry, 24 February 1932.

86 Ibid., MS 1760, file Relief, asked for, Mrs C.R.C. to Henry, 2 August 1933.

87 Ibid., MS 1745, file Relief, asked for, Mrs A.H.M., 29 December, 1931.

88 Although it is difficult to assess the exact ethnic background of letter writers, a careful study of the letters reveals few non-British names.

89 AO, RG 3-8, Henry Papers, MS 1744, file Positions, general, Mr B.C. to Henry, 19 November 1931.

90 Ibid., MS 1750, file Mothers' Allowances Commission, Miss A.M. to Henry, 26 August 1932.

91 Ibid., MS 1760, file Relief, asked for, Mr H.L.S. to Henry, 26 July 1933.

92 Ibid.

93 Ibid., MS 1747, file Unemployment Relief no. 7, Lt. W.J.O. to Henry, 8 October 1931.

94 Ibid., MS 1762, file Unemployment Relief: homeowners, Mrs K.H. to Henry, 21 July 1933.

95 Nancy Fraser, 'Struggle Over Needs: Outline of a Socialist-Feminist Critical Theory of Late Capitalist Political Culture,' in Gordon, ed., *Women, the State, and Welfare*, 202.

96 Fraser and Gordon, 'Contract versus Charity,' 59.

97 Ibid., 64, 47.

Citizen Participation in the Welfare State: The Recreation Movement in Brantford, 1945–1957

SHIRLEY TILLOTSON

The goals of the 1990–1 Spicer Commission hearings on the Constitution and the 1965–71 community organization projects of the Company of Young Canadians could hardly have been more different. The more recent exercise was about forming public opinion, whereas the earlier one aspired to foment action for social change. Both exercises, however, aspired to encourage citizen participation in public life and were justified by concerns that some or most Canadians were marginalized, alienated, or apathetic. Each was inspired by hopes that involving more people in public decision making would make collective decisions more representative of people's needs – that is to say, more democratic. Citizen participation would also help people feel that they, and not some far away 'others,' owned their society's institutions.

Such aspirations for a democratic political culture have a long history. In their most far-reaching forms, they have been at the core of democratic socialism since the nineteenth century. In the confusing ideological clamour of the 1990s, new cries for more active citizenship have also been heard from the political right. For instance, conservative social commentator William Gairdner, deploring the effect of welfare state programs on citizen responsibility, calls on Canadians to organize their own local, nongovernmental services of care and relief, services that would reflect citizens' own values.[1] Gairdner's cry comes in part from a concern strangely similar to one articulated by socialist political theorist John Keane: that welfare state bureaucracies have in effect tended 'to encourage the passive consumption of state provision and seriously to undermine citizens' confidence in their ability to direct their own lives.'[2] Both right and left, then, have suggested that the welfare state produces an alienation that citizen participation might correct.

In at least one part of the welfare state's origins, however, social activists attempted to prevent such alienation. The promoters of public recreation saw playgrounds, clubs, night classes, and sports as welfare services whose particular 'helping' role was to foster active citizenship. In the movement for public recreation, in which Brantford, Ontario, played a small but important part, the agents of the state took seriously the notion (like Gairdner's) that local communities should define their own needs and self-reliantly produce their own services. In Brantford, especially, the recreation movement's professionals resisted becoming bureaucrats and tried (as Keane would prefer) to foster organizations in civil society that would hold state policy makers accountable to their constituents. In short, the recreation movement in Brantford, in its early years, wanted citizen participation to be part of the welfare state so that the welfare state would be democratic. After some initial success, however, the Brantford experiment failed in these political goals.

By the late 1950s, recreation in Brantford had become an efficiently and professionally provided municipal service. It ceased being a spearhead of citizen participation and, implicitly, of democratization in civic culture. In examining the causes of that outcome, I will suggest, along with Keane, that the 'molecular networks of everyday power relations' were the foundation of bureaucracy in the welfare state. Bureaucratization was a process that took place over time, and, at certain stages of that process, the hierarchies of the workplace, of wealth, and of family decisively determined whether citizens' attempts at participation would be rewarded with power. When participation did not empower, the ground was readied for the growth of bureaucracy.[3] This connection between social relations and bureaucracy can be seen in the Brantford case, where citizen alienation *preceded* professionals' drive to limit participation. While professionals' motivations contributed to Brantford's change in participation after 1956, the shift away from a relatively broad activism was already under way in 1953. Rather than being imposed by professionals, this shift came from volunteers' own experience of citizen activism. Finding themselves forced to accept a limited range of choices, ordinary citizens ultimately chose bureaucracy.

The Promise of Participation

The postwar recreation services in Brantford came out of a larger phenomenon, the recreation movement. This movement descended from the adult education ideas of the settlement houses and the character-building programs initiated by the YM/YWCAs, the playgrounds movement, and the Boy Scout and Girl Guide movements. As its origins suggest, the recreation movement belonged to social work and was connected only tenuously and sometimes contentiously with sports. By contrast, recreation shared many methods, goals, and even personnel with adult education and community organization. For example, Roby Kidd of the Canadian Association for Adult Education had been a recreation leader in his early career and was active in the recreation movement. Harriet Carr, a former president of the Federation of Women's Teachers' Associations of Ontario, worked first for Kidd's organization and later for the Ontario provincial recreation authority. Mary Needler, a university classics instructor turned recreation director, went from organizing community committees in a recreation program to doing community organization surveys for a Toronto social planning agency.[4] Recreationists, like other social workers in the late 1940s and early 1950s, all laboured to encourage neighbourhoods to organize.[5] Whether community committees were about recreation or other social services, social workers hoped such organization would encourage citizen participation.

The recreation movement's umbrella organizations in Canada included the Canadian Association for Health, Physical Education and Recreation (founded in 1933) and the Recreation Division of the Canadian Welfare Council (1921). These early organizations at first drew their membership only from private social agencies and some big city public services. During and after the Second World War, however, recreation groups welcomed the new government agencies created under the National Physical Fitness Act of 1944. Ontario, while its government rejected federal funding, soon after formed its own recreation service, the Community Programmes Branch. It was the 1949 offspring of the recreation and adult education branches that had been formed by the Department of Education four years earlier.

The Ontario Community Programmes Branch did not run baseball games or regular craft classes; instead, it provided leader training, organizational advice, and modest subsidies to municipal programs. By paying one-third of recreation staff salaries and one-quarter of operating costs, the province encouraged many municipalities, including Brantford, to hire their first recreation director. These directors were not just coaches or craft experts, but, in many cases, social workers and teachers. They were community organizers who learned in the provincial training course that recreation was an institution to 'teach and promote democratic living.'[6] Keeping faith with adult education ideals, recreation directors were intended by government not to impose 'constructive' or other approved programs on the community but to enable citizens to develop programs of their own choice.[7]

All Ontario recreation directors were taught these precepts, but Brantford's John Pearson practised them exceptionally well between 1945 and 1953. Among the various mid-sized Ontario municipalities that attempted to organize elaborate schemes of citizen participation, Brantford was one of the most successful.[8] Its relative success made it atypical, but the system of citizen involvement attempted in Brantford was the kind of social organization the government, through the experts in the Community Programmes Branch, meant to encourage. Indeed, by getting ordinary people involved in planning and providing social services, the recreationists in Brantford were accomplishing a goal that Premier George Drew had set for public recreation. As the premier said in 1948, the recreation movement could be an example of 'how free people live together.'[9]

The precise political potential of citizen participation depended, of course, on exactly how that broad notion was defined. Cold War idealism about democracy animated both conservative and change-oriented political projects. Within the recreation movement, and indeed generally, there were two strands of thinking about the practice of participation. The first of these – and most likely Drew's – was rooted in the activities of service clubs and women's benevolent societies. For these groups, 'democratic living' meant a sort of organized helpfulness. Translated into the terms of the *public* recreation movement, such social involvement had the extra democratic virtue of being inclusive. Whereas private benevolent groups organized as businessmen or as Catholic women or as farmers, in public recreation the chance to help out was open to *all* citizens. Private groups performed valuable social services, but only through *public* recreation did this work become citizen participation in government. By cooperating in a public program, citizens of all sorts would be obliged to find common ground – in effect, to see social decisions from the brokerage standpoint of their elected officials. In addition to this indirect learning, participants in public recreation were also linked by the grant system to the leadership education programs of the provincial recreation office. In this way of thinking, then, citizen participation in public recreation was a means of expanding and informing citizen activity, in a way that would tend to legitimate government. In effect, this kind of participation reduced the distance between government and private groups: citizen groups involved in public recreation became auxiliaries to a state enterprise. Indeed, this conception of participation in government might appropriately be labelled 'auxiliary.'

The political promise of participation was quite different when it was rooted in reformist social work and the labour movement. These areas were the roots of the second strand of recreation movement thinking and practice, one that might be labelled 'insurgent.' In this mode, 'citizen participation' meant cooperation among citizens *in opposition* to government. Although still founded in a faith that democratic government under capitalism could be made to work, this oppositional notion of citizen participation assumed that, for the working class, democracy did not yet work very well at all.[10] In the 1940s a recent and successful example of such citizen participation had been Chicago's 'Back of the Yards' Neighbourhood Council, whose purpose was to support the nascent packinghouse workers' union. The council's organizer, social worker Saul Alinsky, called it an example of 'the people's organization' and intended it to be an opposition force against elite-dominated governments. This sort of organization shared with the 'auxiliary' idea the hope that participation could overcome socially divisive racial and ethnic hatreds, but the 'insurgent' conception accepted that 'the people' were often at odds with their rulers. Alinsky's tactically inventive left populism became famous in the radical politics of the 1960s. Part of what is intriguing about the Brantford story is that it shows an Alinskyite idea of citizen participation at work in an earlier, more conservative political context.

When Pearson came to Brantford, he, like Alinsky, had a working-class background, a sociology education, and work experience in community organization. His previous job had been as the YMCA 'community secretary' in Broadview, a working-class area of Toronto.[11] Once in Brantford, Pearson began to build public recreation on the 'Alinsky formula,' or, as he modestly acknowledged in a letter to its originator, his own 'warped version of it.'[12] The goal of this formula was to generate in city neighbourhoods a form of popular organization that would bring the people together and empower them in relationship to city government, large property owners, powerful merchants, and big businesses. Alinsky proposed that people reject 'charity.' He argued that a community could get what it needed only if its members together made their own decisions about what they wanted and collectively went about satisfying those needs, by whatever means possible.[13]

This formula implied the rejection of some recreation organizations that had previously existed in Brantford. In particular, an organization formed the year before Pearson's arrival violated Alinsky's idea of citizen participation. The city-funded Brantford Playgrounds and Recreational Commission consisted of middle-class women and men representing service groups, such as the Imperial Order Daughters of the Empire (IODE) and the Optimists.[14] Such elite leaders, doing good for other people, were the objects of Alinsky's scorn in his 1946 *Reveille for Radicals*. In this book, Alinsky's first manual for community organizers, he argued that 'the people's organization' had to be led by a community's 'natural' leaders, not its self-appointed upper crust, however benevolent the latter's intentions.[15] The radical organizer's job was to get to know the people of the community and to find out which individuals had authority based in personality rather than position. The organizer could also help find a local issue that mattered to ordinary people, an issue that the fledgling people's organization could fight and win. Victory in 'battle,' followed by agreement on a democratic constitution, would form the basis of an enduring and empowering people's organization.[16]

That John Pearson intended to use the Alinsky method is clear; how closely he meant to adhere to it is unknown.[17] His actual organizing approach, as it appears in the documentary evidence, certainly resembles Alinsky's, especially in the way Pearson sought out new community leaders. The main difference seems to have been that Pearson was less combative, more willing to accept that, although the leaders of existing charitable and service groups should not dominate civic affairs, they could make a useful contribution.[18] In spite of this acceptance, however, Pearson clearly preferred 'natural' leaders. When, in retrospect, he identified one man as 'the model for a volunteer person in the community,' his choice was not a service club representative or a YMCA leader, but a factory worker who came to the recreation movement through joining a neighbourhood community committee.[19]

Pearson's Alinskyite ideas met with a favourable reception in Brantford. Between 1945 and 1948 about three hundred other men and women showed, by joining community committees, that Pearson's way of organizing public recreation worked.[20] Committee membership alone does not prove these individuals' adherence to Alinsky's political methods, but subsequent events, the subject of later parts of this essay, show there was an insurgent element in the volunteers' ideas about participation. And, given Brantford's history, it is not surprising that some of the recreation volunteers were attracted specifically by a populist/socialist style of community organizing. Situated in the rural heartland of the United Farmers Organization and the cooperative movement, Brantford city voters themselves had elected a labourite mayor – M.M. 'Mac' MacBride – for eight terms in the interwar years, and in 1946 had elected another left-labour mayor, stereotyper J.H. Matthews.[21] Successful union organizing in the 1940s meant that, by 1949, roughly 37 per cent of Brantford's paid labour force were unionists.[22] Not surprisingly, then, as Pearson's scheme of citizen participation unfolded, the ideas he brought to Brantford met with an appreciative reception – at least, in some circles. Certainly, at the beginning, Matthews liked Pearson's novel suggestion that the recreation program should be generated from popular requests rather than being predetermined by the recreation director.[23]

Inclusiveness: The Community Committees

Like the recreation experts in the provincial government, Pearson believed that for a recreation director to promote his own ideas about 'wholesome' or 'constructive' recreation activities was to predestine citizen participation to failure. He described his director's role as being initially like radar, finding out 'what's around' by sending out a wave of energy and observing the pattern of its rebound. To some people, he later recalled, this looked as though he was 'sitting on his fanny,' but in fact he was actively seeking a certain kind of initiative.[24] More than individual initiative, Pearson wanted to foster community organization. A principle of 'No activity without a committee' complemented his stand of 'No program without public demand.'[25] He wanted to discourage the notion that, as the main employee of the Recreation Commission, he would busy himself planning activities, coaching teams, and managing building projects. In his view, these were functions a well-organized community could perform itself. Consequently, if someone said, 'We need more tennis in this town,' Pearson would ask, 'Well, what are you doing about it?' And he met demands for new facilities with suggestions that there were other – and better – routes to making more activities possible.[26] At the beginning of all these routes lay the forming of a community committee.

In Pearson's view, the best way to provide recreation was to mobilize neighbourhood energies, to build 'a sense of community.'[27] 'Where do you live?' and not 'What budget do you need?' was his first question to an interested citizen.[28] To illustrate what people could do on their own, Pearson wrote in his first *Recreation Bulletin* that one man, by flooding the lot near his house, had made a rink for the smaller children, and in this way had 'given a lead to [his] community for neighbourhood projects.'[29] The first initiative that truly fit Pearson's ideas was a request from a self-organized neighbourhood committee for a playground rink: what was attractive to Pearson about their request was that, to supplement the city's contribution, they were willing to raise money to pay for instructors, program materials, and event publicity.[30] Such efforts, Pearson believed, would help build community feeling.

In the years that followed, the example of this neighbourhood's committee was duplicated in other parts of the city. By their peak in 1952, Brantford's community recreation committees operated in eighteen different neighbourhoods, scattered evenly throughout the city's residential areas[31] (see figure 1).[31] The members of these committees raised money for recreation and shared the work of organizing and supervising activities. They even built some recreation equipment.[32] Between 1946 and 1954 recreation volunteers also participated in a 'people's organization': the Community Committees' Council. This council was formed at a meeting Pearson arranged near the end of his first year's work to encourage representatives from the

FIGURE 1

Map of Brantford, 1952, showing the location of community committees existing at various times between 1946 and 1952.

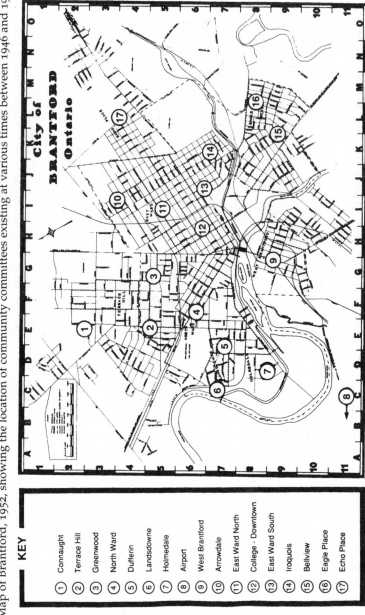

KEY

① Connaught
② Terrace Hill
③ Greenwood
④ North Ward
⑤ Dufferin
⑥ Landsdowne
⑦ Holmedale
⑧ Airport
⑨ West Brantford
⑩ Arrowdale
⑪ East Ward North
⑫ College - Downtown
⑬ East Ward South
⑭ Iroquois
⑮ Bellview
⑯ Eagle Place
⑰ Echo Place

Source: Cartographic and Architectural Archives Division, National Archives of Canada, NMC 12947 S. BRR, Community Committees Council, minutes, 12 January 1949, 1, 5 September 1951.

community committees to plan cooperatively their winter programming. From this discussion of joint activities, the representatives decided to form a community council that would meet monthly, not only to plan programs but also to make representations to the Recreation Commission, the City Council–appointed recreation authority. From this beginning, citizen participation expanded and became more oppositional.

Grassroots citizen participation in the Brantford recreation movement, then, had two levels: neighbourhood committees and a citywide council of committee representatives. Both levels contributed to the recreation movement's democratization goals, but each did so in its own specific way. The council was more specifically Alinskyite, whereas the community committees served a purpose common to both the auxiliary and the insurgent notions of participation. The committees were the primary site for building a new sense of community – for promoting social integration. They were to be inclusive and welcoming bodies that would help transcend social divisions. On a foundation of social integration, decision making would be more democratic, more able to serve common purposes. Every committee member would be a 'citizen.'

At the level of the community committees, this vision seems to have met with substantial success, carefully nurtured by Pearson. To encourage the inclusion of different social groups in the committees, Pearson sent out *Recreation Bulletins*, starting in the winter of 1946, to people who, in his words, were 'actually or potentially leaders in the neighbourhood in which they live.'[33] That working-class leaders were among those whom Pearson hoped to attract to the recreation movement was signalled in his first editorial: 'Labour's demands,' he wrote, were leading to 'a better life for more people.' In the context of the labour climate of 1945–6, when the new industrial unions fought pitched battles against major employers' attempts to hammer them back into Depression-era impotence, this mild observation amounted to a pro-union stance.

Clearly, Pearson was trying to get working-class people involved in the recreation movement. And surviving records indicate that the citizens who became involved in organizing recreation through these committees were, in fact, sociologically diverse, in class status and otherwise. The committees included both women and men, though slightly more men. Members came from all social classes, but the majority were working class (see columns 3 and 4 in table 1).[34] The women were more likely to be working class than the city's male recreation volunteers were: 69 per cent of the women in the sample (including commission members as well as committee members) were working class, compared with 58 per cent of the men. The committees were virtually uniform in one respect: 91 per cent of members were married

TABLE 1
Summary of Class[a] and Sex Distribution of Volunteer Leaders in Brantford's Recreation Movement, 1944–61

Volunteer Leaders (n)	1 Recreation Commission members[b] (n is 87)	2 Key people on community committees[c] (n is 50)	3 Community committee executives[d] (n is 127)	4 Community committee attendance[e] (n is 59)	5 Miscellaneous[f] (n is 59)	Totals[g] (n is 336)		
						Men	Women	Total
Men (%)	91	70	60	54	59			65
Women (%)	9	30	40	46	41			35
Working class (%)	33	73	81	62	61	59	69	62
Professional/Manager (%)	47	17	17	30	29	31	21	28
Owners (%)	20	10	3	8	10	10	10	10
Not identifiable (n)	6	2	3	5	7	19	3	22

[a] Men's class position was determined by the occupation given for them in the city directory. Women's class position was determined either by their own paid work or by their husband's or father's occupation. Because only one occupation was given for married couples, the extent of married women's paid work is undoubtedly understated. Four occupations of ambiguous class status were classified as follows: salesmen's class position was determined by the character of their neighbourhood and the type of commodity they sold; tradesmen who owned their own business were included in the 'owner' category; grocers were labelled 'owners' if their home address was separate from their store address; otherwise, they were categorized as working class; foremen were listed as managers.

[b] The sample includes names of individuals (each counted once) who served on the following commissions: the Postwar Recreational Projects Committee (1944) and Recreation Commissions for 1944, 1945, 1948 to 1954, 1957, and 1959. Names were taken from annual lists usually kept in the minutes binders and in the City Council minutes. Some mid-year changes of service club appointees may have been missed.

[c] The sample includes names of individuals (each counted once) who served as Community Committees' Council delegates or representatives, or who participated in significant committees or special meetings, as follows: individuals chosen in 1948 to lobby aldermen, 1949 constitution committee, 1950 community centre meeting, 1951 community centres' committee, 1953 Crafts and Recreation Fair organizers, 1953 fall and winter programs planning meeting, delegates to the Recreation Commission in 1948–52, and the recreation office's 1955 list of contact names for each community committee.

[d] The sample includes the names of all individuals (each counted once) on existing executive lists. These lists are for the years 1950, 1953 to 1956, and 1961, for the following neighbourhoods: Echo Place, Arrowdale, Eagle Place, North Ward, Bellview, and Iroquois.

[e] The sample consists of fifty-nine names taken from attendance rosters in the minutes of four well-attended meetings in the first three years of the council (November 1946, January 1947, September 1947, and June 1948).

[f] This category includes individuals attending four event-related committees in 1946 and one public organization meeting in 1952.

[g] Some individuals appeared in more than one category; consequently, the total sample number is less than the sum of the sample subsets.

people.[35] Though members' ethnicity is difficult to judge, the presence on committee lists of names such as Camilleri, Schwarzkopf, Papai, Barsotta, Szoke, Souliere, and Romanuk indicate that the non-Anglo-Celtic 23 per cent of Brantford's population were among those involved.[36]

The degree of social mixing in the recreation committees was uneven, depending as it did on the composition of the committees' neighbourhoods. This diversity is apparent in newspaper reports of the formation of three early recreation committees. Of the thirty-six committee members named, thirteen were women and twenty-three were men. Working-class men (twelve) and women (seven), for a total of nineteen, were in the majority of those named (among the thirty-three identifiable individuals). But the county crown attorney was also on one of the committees; he was one of ten men of professional or managerial occupations, and there were two women married to men of this social stratum. Fewest in number were the three small business owners and business owners' wives.[37] In one predominantly working-class suburban neighbourhood (Connaught), six of the seven named committee members (two women, five men) came from working-class homes.[38] More socially diverse was the committee centred on the Spring Street rink. Around this rink were two very different neighbourhoods: at the bottom of the hill were modest Victorian workers' cottages, many without telephones, and at the top were mansions. Residents of both neighbourhoods were on the committee.[39]

Such committees were intended by those who initiated their organization to foster social integration: that is, to establish cooperative relations that transcended religious lines, class differences, and narrow neighbourhood exclusiveness.[40] Reflecting on one committee's success in building a broader community, one of Pearson's two staff organizers found that differences among the members in 'social mores and economic status' provided 'fizz but not disruption.'[41] Some social divisions proved intractable: for instance, 'red' Poles and 'white' Poles both helped with recreation organization in the North Ward area, but they were unwilling to attend the same meetings. However, other social gulfs were narrowed: in a neighbourhood of southeast Brantford, community recreation brought Protestant committee members for the first time into the Catholic Church hall, a step that required them to overcome a certain suspicious fearfulness.[42] Although we cannot assume that all the community committees were equally successful in fostering social integration, most were remarkably stable over the period. Some expired, but only in one area did there seem to have been splintering.[43] Certainly, some of the committees accomplished at least one of the reform objectives of citizen participation, having acted as a means to constructing communities based primarily on citizen status. A state-funded program made this goal comparatively easy because the activities these volunteers supported were funded with 'their' – taxpayers' – money.

Insurgency: Council and Commission

While the community committees contributed to breaking down social exclusiveness, the function of the Community Committees' Council (CCC) was to modify power hierarchies. The committees taught cooperation, but the CCC taught confrontation. At the beginning, the CCC members saw themselves only as an advisory body. However, conflicts in the 1948–52 period showed that, at this council, citizen participation became an attempt to empower subordinate groups. By 1953 the history of the CCC spoke most tellingly about the political meaning of citizen participation in Brantford.

The CCC was hindered more than helped in its democratic goals by its links with a government program. It was incorporated into municipal government in a legally subordinate position and had no power to spend public money: this power was held by the City Council and was partially delegated to the Recreation Commission and the Recreation Department's paid staff. The Recreation Commission itself was a volunteer board, but was appointed by City Council. In the years 1945–61, 67 per cent of commission members were business owners, professionals, or managers (see table 1). In the constitutional arrangement that centred fiscal authority in these bodies, the mainly working-class women and men of the community committees could exert power only by influencing the Recreation Commission.

Their efforts through the CCC to achieve such influence were, to a degree, successful. When the committees began in 1946, they had no say in budget decisions. By 1953, however, their council had six seats on the twenty-four-member Recreation Commission that made the budget. Also, by 1952 the community committees successfully claimed the authority to approve collectively in their council all requests for services and facilities. After 1954, when the Recreation Commission had only seven members, one was a designated woman representative and another a community committee representative. Notably, though, this 'representation' was informal, not the result of delegation by the committees' own council.[44]

In fact, this success in achieving representation, although noteworthy, was counterbalanced after 1953 by a withering of the community committees' *collective* voice. Between 1949 and 1953 a series of conflicts occurred over resources and methods of representation, conflicts that reduced the community committees from an organized council to unconnected groups of petitioners. An organizational structure that had approached participatory democracy was replaced by token representation of 'women' and 'community people' on a mainly middle-class, predominantly male commission.

This change in Brantford's recreation-based experiment in municipal democracy was clearly a class one. Compared with the community committees, the Recreation Commission included relatively few members of the working class. Even more notable, however, is the disparity between women's large participation in the committees and their near absence from the commission (compare column 1 with the other columns in table 1). These class and gender patterns are connected. When the mainly working-class community committees were excluded from the highest decision-making body, so were most of the movement's female members. As previously noted, women in Brantford's recreation movement were a more working-class group than male recreation volunteers. And it was in the CCC and on the local executives, working-class terrain, that women most frequently appeared. If the Brantford recreation movement taught democratic methods, it was in the CCC that women recreation volunteers had their best opportunity to learn and to be empowered. As the CCC declined and disappeared, so did one of working-class Brantford women's avenues for an activist citizenship.

In part, this activism was about community self-reliance, but the conflicts between the CCC and the Recreation Commission showed that some volunteers came to share Pearson's idea about enabling local communities more effectively to direct city government. At first, though, the CCC members imagined their role in relatively modest terms. In a September 1947 statement on the CCC's relationship to the Recreation Commission, the CCCers affirmed that, 'primarily,' their council was 'a place for the exchange of ideas and the review of local problems which might be solved by the experience of other members of the Council.' The Recreation Commission, they allowed, was 'responsible for the overall policy of the municipal recreation programme.' The CCC would implement policy and solve local problems, making representations to the commission only when such problems proved insoluble with the CCC's resources.[45]

This view of the relationship between the committees and the commission reflected manager/worker and breadwinner/housewife hierarchies familiar from daily life. The breadwinner supplies the budget, and the housewife makes it do for the family's needs. The manager sets production goals and quality standards, and the worker makes procedural decisions about how these goals will be met. If the budget is too small or the production goals unreasonable, the subordinates have the power of protest.

Backing this power, one of the 'powers of the weak' that Linda Gordon and Elizabeth Janeway have movingly described, was the fact that the members of community committees did much of the work of providing recreation.[46] By 1948 the Community Committees' Council represented three hundred volunteers who organized street dances, playground supervision, euchre games, movie nights, craft classes, concerts, current events discussions, folk dancing, and garden parties.[47] As many as six community centres, activity groups that met on winter evenings in schools, were managed largely by volunteers.[48] On the basis of this labour, the community committees could and did claim that they were as much recreation 'experts' as the paid staff or the commissioners.[49] But until 1948, they could only offer that expertise through ad hoc delegations to the commission.

In June 1948 this power relationship – part of Keane's 'molecular networks' – began to change, as the community committees began to push the limits of their advisory status. The catalyst for new developments in the CCC's relationship with the commission was community committee members' dissatisfaction with hazardous playground surfaces and shortages of equipment. Convinced that the commission was neglecting 'pressing' needs at the playgrounds, CCC members decided to send a delegation to the commission. One of the delegates, Vern Hamilton,[50] called for reciprocal membership between the CCC and the commission. This suggestion bespoke the council's desire for a real change in their subordination to the commission. In a gesture towards satisfying this wish, the commission agreed to add to its membership one representative from the CCC.[51]

Once the commission had a CCC representative, those who did the bulk of the movement's volunteer work had a voice in budget decisions. The commission soon learned that some of the CCC's interventions cost money. In the fall of 1948 Stephanie Burliuk described to the CCC the problems of families living in her low-income neighbourhood in downtown Brantford: in particular, the lack of safe, attractive play space for children. At the next monthly meeting, representing a newly formed community committee, she said that the downtown needed a rink, a nursery school, and playground supervisors' salaries. The CCC endorsed her request for funding and, at the Recreation Commission meeting the next night, a special CCC delegation told the commissioners that 'the work in their communities could not progress unless their needs were budgeted for.'[52]

This position was accepted by the Recreation Commission, but only with unusual 'discussion.'[53] It was a genuine victory for the CCC to have secured the Recreation Commission's stated support for increased spending by the community committees. Five months earlier, in the summer of 1948, Pearson had told the commissioners that the recreation budget had 'reached its peak.'[54]

In spite of its supposed support for the CCC's budget, however, the commission continued to stymie the downtown improvements. In June 1949 it refused an offer of downtown playground space that would have cost only the amount of the vacant lot's annual property tax. Shortly after this offer was rejected, Burliuk's Central Ward community committee broke up, presumably discouraged by the lack of progress in finding play space. Only after Burliuk again roused the CCC to action the following spring were playgrounds found for downtown children. No new land was purchased for park use; instead, an existing, dirt-surfaced park was seeded for grass, and Central Presbyterian Church allowed its backyard to become a playground.[55]

The problem of downtown playgrounds showed the limits of the CCC's power on the Recreation Commission: with more CCC members, the June 1949 decision on the tax deal would likely have been different. The CCC, in its own meetings, had responded sympathetically to the downtown committee's concerns. The disparity between the commission's response and their own fed into the CCC's feeling that the commission was not sufficiently amenable to suggestion. Consequently, at the 1950 spring conference of community committees, members voted to seek greater representation on the Recreation Commission.[56]

The mover of this motion was Bert Morgen, the factory worker whom Pearson later recalled as 'the model volunteer.' Morgen was energetically involved in community work, not only in the recreation movement but as an active member of the Brantford Co-operative Commonwealth Federation (CCF) Association and an officer of the employee credit union at his place of work.[57] According to Pearson, Morgen worked 'like a dog' and was 'one of the demanding elements in our Community Committees' Council.' Sometimes, Pearson admits, Morgen would 'get us uptight' and involve Recreation Department personnel 'in more than [they] were ready for,' but 'he had appeal' because he worked so hard.[58] Indeed, the documentary evidence shows that Morgen had considerable influence on the CCC until he left it in 1951. He and another factory worker, Harold Williams, attempted to increase the CCC's power in the Recreation Commission when they served as the CCC's representatives in 1950–1.

Morgen and Williams' strategy was to increase the proportion of the commission positions held by members of the CCC. From its single position in 1948, the CCC had come to have two members on the commission in 1950. With the commission at about twenty members, the CCC representatives were a small minority. In the fall of 1950 the commission began discussing the possibility of becoming a smaller, 'more efficient' body. Three proposals were made: for a thirteen-member, ten-member, or nine-member commission. Notably, the thirteen-member proposal was the only one that satisfied the basic demand of the CCC representatives: that 'one less than half of the Recreation Commission' should be CCC representatives.[59]

The politics of the CCC representatives are suggested by the fact that the thirteen-member proposal was, relatively speaking, the 'left-wing' one. It included six CCC representatives, omitted the Board of Trade, and had two 'members at large.' By contrast, the proposed ten-member commission did not include even one labour representative. The nine-member commission was to include a representative from Brantford's Labour Council to 'match' the Board of Trade representative it alone included. None of the members was a 'citizen at large,' and only two were community committee members.

When a new Recreation Commission constitution was finally made law the following spring, the CCC got its six positions. Yet the new bylaw was unfriendly to the CCC's aspirations for a greater voice. The commission in its new form was actually larger than the previous one. Its bylaw provided for twenty-four members, making CCC representation only one-quarter of the total.[60] The commission had rejected the thinking behind the thirteen-member proposal.

That thinking had explicitly challenged the subordination of 'workers' to 'managers' and had even privileged the former over the latter as 'the community.' Morgen and Williams's argument had been that CCC members were 'much closer to the work being carried on and are thus in a better position to serve on the commission.'[61] They claimed that, in relation to the services offered by the Recreation Commission, they, as the volunteer workers, knew more and could serve better on the commission than, say, a member of the Rotary Club, the Board of Trade, or the Knights of Columbus. The committees' community centres were more truly community efforts because they were run by the participants, as distinct from the programs run by service clubs for the benefit of client groups. It was the *self-activity* of the committees that made them 'the community' in public recreation.[62] The influence of this political viewpoint on the revision of the commission's constitution was, in the end, insufficient. The equal share for the CCC in policy making that Morgen and Williams had sought was denied.

Both men served out their terms as CCC representatives on the commission, but with doubts about how seriously the other commissioners viewed the opinions of the CCC.[63] In the enlarged Recreation Commission, the community committees, as the users and direct contributors to public recreation, were subordinated to a larger taxpaying public. The citizenship of the community committees was perhaps seen as insufficiently disinterested. If so, their involvement in the money-spending commission was restricted precisely *because* they wanted to participate in a double-sided way, as both users and managers of public recreation. This interpretation suggests the operation of a principle that, in relation to the welfare state, people must be *either* citizen-constituents *or* consumer-clients. In other words, use of welfare services disqualifies 'citizens' from participation in government as policy makers. Certainly, in Brantford, the commission-council hierarchy separated users from managers and subordinated the former. This power relationship invited the alienation of the user.

Some of the users challenged this relationship. Morgen and others in the CCC fought to get more power for the subaltern elements of the recreation movement. They took a series of steps to make the CCC more powerful, and the CCC, in turn, by revising its own constitution, attempted to give itself a quasi-legal form of authority. Its 1948 constitution required the Recreation Commission to go through the CCC in providing services to community committees. The CCC constitution also required any community committee that wanted services from the city's recreation office to send a representative regularly to CCC meetings, or the CCC would not endorse its service requests. Adopting 'grievance procedures' helped deal with internal weaknesses.[64]

As the relationship between commission and council became more oppositional, the CCC further adjusted its political methods. In 1951, during the debate about the Recreation Commission constitution, the CCC dropped its past practice of rotating chairmanships and adopted instead an annual term. Seeing itself as a policy intervenor, and no longer an apprentice in democratic method, it gave the chairman power based in continuity, rather than providing practice in leading meetings to many members.[65] At the same session, the CCC changed its regular meeting time so that the Recreation Commission's committees would not put off reviewing CCC recommendations until weeks after they were made.[66] Together, these measures suggest that the CCC had come to take a tactical, more than a collegial, approach in its relationship with the commission.

Unfortunately, having failed to gain even near-equal representation on the Recreation Commission, the CCC was without coercive power. Notably, the community committees did not contemplate withdrawing their volunteer labour in support of the CCC representatives on the commission. Consequently, when serious disagreements arose, the commissioners could dismiss CCC objections. This power imbalance was demonstrated in September 1952 when CCC representatives objected to the sale of a city playground to the Board of Education for a building site, an event that raised conflicts over social rights versus property rights. In the debate that followed, the CCC found their motions ignored. Options that would have protected the playground – such as the city's expropriating privately owned vacant lots – were bypassed. Whereas the CCC wanted the social right to recreational space to be given priority over private land uses, the commissioners reflexively, in a class-conditioned manner, defended property rights. And the commissioners' legal position in local government gave them the one-sided power to conclude the issue.[67]

As relations between council and commission developed, it became apparent that the Recreation Commission welcomed the community committees' contributions only when those were offers to raise funds, canvass popular needs, publicize activities, and help with supervision. Here, there were grounds for cooperation: council and commission alike wanted to see better provision for non-commercial recreation. On spending questions, however, the commission would not meet 'public demand,' as articulated by the CCC. The commission also differed from the CCC on the definition of 'the community.' Rooted in the charitable model of community service, the commission welcomed the neighbourhood committees as one more recreation interest group, one that was not perhaps quite responsible on questions of budgets and property. The community committees, founded on an inclusive idea of participation by 'all the people' and directly engaged in providing public services, believed themselves uniquely representative of 'the community.' In the end, their ideal of inclusiveness was used to swamp the representatives of these participant organizations in a sea of service club delegates. The community committees were denied policy-making power commensurate with the labour they contributed.

A Change in the Meaning of Citizen Participation

After September 1952, events and circumstances discouraged any further attempts to make the CCC a vehicle for participant power. In March 1953 John Pearson resigned his position and left Brantford (to study with Saul Alinsky, among other things).[68] Three months later, area director Helen Wilson, who, like Pearson's assistant directors, had worked on developing community committees, also left.[69] Her departure substantially reduced the staff support for the committees. At the time, the community committees expressed appreciation for her past work in 'community organization,' but reported that they now wanted a staff member who would initiate and lead activities.[70]

These parting words reflected the fact that the volunteers had something to do with enlarging the power of professionals. The division of responsibilities between volunteers and paid staff had been at times a point of dispute between Pearson and the community committees. Some committee members wanted Recreation Department staff to take over the administration and operation of the community centres, and even to initiate new program activities. But Pearson argued that to use staff this way would be to undermine 'community' involvement in the centres. His idea had always been to make services contingent on citizen participation. Like Morgen and Williams, Pearson thought that citizen participation meant providing volunteer labour, and getting in return a voice in policy.[71]

For at least the first five or six years of his tenure in Brantford, Pearson had been able to successfully motivate recreation volunteers to participate on these terms. Even a volunteer who wanted to shift some responsibilities to paid staff expressed pride in 'our community set-up,' and he, himself, was a reliable participant in all manner of meetings. Recalling his high school and university days as a seasonal worker under Pearson, another man said that Pearson expected people 'to do virtually impossible things and you did them ... you beefed about it but you did it nonetheless.' Why? 'Because everyone believed [in] him.'[72]

Getting people working for the services they wanted was not necessarily the same as engaging them in political life. After all, pitching in was part of the auxiliary idea of participation, too. Included in the Brantford recreation movement were volunteers interested primarily in getting program activities for their children and themselves. Developments after Pearson's departure suggest that, in the absence of Pearson's assiduous pushing and pulling, many such volunteers became unwilling to work for the larger, Alinskyite project of claiming a voice in policy making. After 1953, the CCC, the volunteers' voice in funding debates, ceased to operate.

The staff departures were only a part of the changing forces that determined the CCC's fate and, with it, the meaning of citizen participation. Militating against the CCC's survival were its earlier defeats on land and representation issues. There had been genuine attempts to exercise collective power, and they had been frustrated by the powers that be on the commission. The CCC had begun to suffer from creeping ineffectiveness: certainly, the CCC's 'endorsing' a community committee's request in the spring of 1953 had not helped the Terrace Hill committee, which, in September, was still waiting for swings and a drinking fountain. A sense of this ineffectiveness must have helped discourage participation in policy meetings. In early 1953 few community committee representatives were going to Recreation Commission meetings, and attendance at the CCC's own monthly sessions was also poor.[73]

Low attendance at meetings was hardly surprising when participation in the committees' winter recreational programs was shrinking. The community centres, which had helped keep community committees active throughout the year, were only minimally active after the winter of 1952–3.[74] Competition came from the school board's new evening classes, which required no supplementary committee work. One group of women interested in rug hooking had simply refused to cooperate when Pearson secured from a local carpet manufacturer a supply of free wool scraps, which needed 'only' to be sorted by hand to be useful. They suggested that it would be better to buy wool. Some participants had said they would go to Craft Guild classes and pay higher fees if the guild offered 'better projects' than the community centres did.[75] Persistent difficulties in organizing a babysitting service at the centres probably discouraged some women with young children from seeking recreation, and, by extension, from attending meetings.[76] The number of adults willing to 'work to play' was also undoubtedly reduced by the increasing number of families with television sets between 1953 and 1955.[77] In 1954 the North Ward committee seems to have been typical in observing that it could not 'commit itself to very much – financially or otherwise.'[78] Pearson's view of citizen participation had required an intense pace of volunteer work. Reasonably enough, then, volunteers looked for a place to reduce their effort. Participation in the CCC became a logical place to cut, once the Recreation Commission had made the CCC powerless.

Already crippled by November 1952, the CCC was dealt a death blow when, late in 1953, the Recreation Commission was remade in a less representative form, with no positions assigned to the CCC. The commission bylaw was amended to shrink the commission to seven members, one to be a city councillor and 'at least one of whom' was to be a woman.[79] With the CCC broken up, citizen participation had, in effect, ceased to be about policy making.

After 1956 this change was consolidated, when the purpose of the community committees themselves was deliberately altered. The new recreation director appointed in 1956 was keen on citizen participation, but he defined it in narrower terms than Pearson had. Reflecting on his time in Brantford, the new director later said, in an unfortunately revealing phrase, that he had approved of the idea that participants would ultimately 'grow up' to be members of policy-making bodies. But, he concluded, that 'never did happen really while [he] was there.'[80]

He had arrived in Brantford as an assistant director in the fall of 1953, at the tail end of the CCC's existence, when it was no longer especially vital.[81] After he became director in 1956, he redefined the community committees:

They were no longer community committees, having [an] interest in the whole government process. I narrowed it down to be a recreation interest because I couldn't see this community committee thing. I know that John [Pearson] still thinks that community committees and community councils having a full concern with the full range of government are important; anyway, we narrowed it down. The people who participated in those committees were making community-building decisions. They helped select where the parks were going to be, what programmes the parks would offer, what kinds of things should be done on them, how they should be designed.[82]

This director, while valuing popular involvement in government, did not push volunteers as far as Pearson had. While the later director wanted to 'support and encourage' community committees, he assigned them a more limited, auxiliary role. This professional's viewpoint did, indeed, shape the development of Brantford's experiment in citizen participation. But by the time of his arrival, the citizens had already made their choices about participation.[83]

The volunteers in the later period were no longer especially interested in testing the limits of citizen participation. Many of the same people continued to be active in public recreation. However, after the frustrations of 1950–2, those who had pushed the limits of social hierarchies turned away from the Alinskyite council model. Having genuine policy power appeared not to have been a real option. So, after 1952, they redirected their hopes. Together with others in the community committees, they turned their attention to providing services for their communities within the limits set by higher authorities. Staff-supplied services took centre stage, supplanting the recreation movement's less efficient self-activity and political insurgency.

Undoubtedly, limiting the role of volunteers made the provision of services more efficient, saving time for both the paid staff and the volunteer workers. But this sensible public administration strategy worked so well in part because it did not modify the power relations many people took for granted. It used socially subordinate people in organizationally subaltern roles. When, in 1952, CCC representatives – factory workers and clerks – had differed with the Recreation Commission on clearly ideological lines, the commission was able to withstand the challenge. Later, volunteers were able to offer advice, but the commission's revised constitution put out of the question any exercise of coordinated power, by bloc voting or otherwise.

The post-1953 structure of the Recreation Commission did not prevent some working-class men and women from becoming commissioners, but they acquired their positions as individuals rather than as representatives of a grassroots organization. The new structure confined significant budgetary decisions to the commission and the City Council. Local committees were restricted to local matters. If, under this new arrangement, recreation volunteers disagreed with some large tendency in municipal policy, they had the usual recourses of voters – recourses taken, again, as individuals or, at best, as members of a neighbourhood committee. The possibility of a larger, collective power had been foreclosed, the project abandoned.

In its most radical dimensions, this project had been Pearson's. But the influence of a social democratic/labour element was apparent in some of the CCC's characteristics: its grievance procedures, its definition of the community's representatives, its affirmation of social rights. That element, an influential one, was not simply pushed along by Pearson's force of personality. Their oppositional stance was of a piece with the rest of their politics. And their abandonment of the CCC seems to have been motivated by a decision that the struggle to make the CCC a power in recreation policy was not a winnable one. This disillusionment, as much as Pearson's departure, led to the CCC's demise.

The end of the CCC was not the end of citizen participation, but only a change in its political meaning. Other committee people carried on, as they had before and during the CCC's life, in the auxiliary mode, helping out the recreation office. They extended municipal services by volunteering their labour, whether by building a portable stage or sewing a canvas shade for a sandbox. When the time came for municipal elections, perhaps they voted. As voters and helpers, Brantford recreation volunteers in the later 1950s were certainly acting as democratic citizens. But they were not intimately involved in the political process in the way that progressive community organizers – not only in recreation, but also in labour, education, and social work – had hoped many Ontarians might be, in a better, more democratic world after the war.

Some volunteers had readily accepted a limited expression of citizenship. To use the word *accepted* is not to say that the choice to accept such constraints was made under identical circumstances by all volunteers. In particular, women and men volunteers acted as citizens in ways shaped by the gender relations of their social world.[84] The lower proportion of women among community committee leaders (see column 2 in table 1) may have reflected not only sexist assumptions about leadership in mixed-sex groups but problems associated with attending meetings for many mothers, with their diffuse and fragmented leisure time.[85] For all volunteers, the time demands of combining helping out and policy making were heavy. But the appeal of participating in the policy fray was reduced most substantially when those volunteers (most often men) who were willing and able to practise oppositional participation had been effectively shackled by the

1951 constitution revision. Brantford's most basic power relations of class and gender, more than the efforts of power-seeking welfare professionals, had so narrowed the potential results of full participation in this part of government that insurgent activism was not worth the effort.

The attempt to build 'a people's organization' around recreation services is part of our political history, even though prime ministers, premiers, and MPs are invisible (or almost so) in the account.[86] The community organizing efforts of the recreation movement were significant as part of a broader undertaking, in a moment of democratic idealism after the Second World War, to remake the relationship between government and the people. As the state expanded old programs or added new activities in welfare provision and economic regulation, more and more Canadians were becoming in different ways clients of the state. Whether, as clients, Canadians would also be constituents – actors in the policy process – depended in part on efforts such as those of the Brantford Community Committees' Council. In the reconstruction mood of the postwar period, such efforts seemed promising. That this promise was, in the Brantford case, only minimally fulfilled can be attributed primarily to the taken-for-granted status of private property rights and persistent class and gender assymetries in access to public administrative authority.

Constrained by these forces, the recreation movement activists succeeded only in a partial way. Undoubtedly, they succeeded in making recreation services a new government responsibility. But efforts towards the broader reform goals of democratic empowerment were largely frustrated. In the coming years, the 'recreation movement' in Ontario would evolve into 'recreation services' directed by professionals. The success of these services would be judged by the numbers of children on playgrounds, the attendance figures for art classes, and the size of crowds taking up square dancing.[87] Participants in public recreation would increasingly be defined as consumers individually voting their preference by attendance, rather than as constituents collectively deciding community priorities. Thus, this realm of social activity came to confirm a market-like model of the citizen's (the consumer's) relation to the state (the supplier). Today, both right and left seem to be agreeing that when 'the public' is reduced to a mass of individuals, both civil society and democratic politics suffer. But the Brantford case should remind us that 'the community,' especially as conservatives such as Gairdner envision it, does not provide an easy alternative to the alienation of our clienthood. Indeed, the hierarchies of our communities helped make the welfare state what it is. That is why democratizing our political culture meant, and continues to mean, tackling the hierarchies of daily life.

NOTES

I would like to thank the recreation director of Brantford in 1990, Eric Finkelstein, and his staff, who generously gave me unrestricted access to the historical records of the Recreation Commission. They also helped me to understand recreation terminology and gave me some idea of present-day issues in municipal recreation. In these ways, they contributed substantially to this research. The views expressed in this essay, however, are entirely my own. Comments from Joy Parr, Margaret McCallum, and other reviewers helped me greatly in formulating those views more clearly.

1 William Gairdner, *The War against the Family: A Parent Speaks Out* (Toronto 1992), 84–5 and passim.
2 John Keane, *Democracy and Civil Society* (London, 1988), 4.
3 The tendency of professional self-interest to produce bureaucracy is by now a set piece of sociology. I do not deny this tendency, but only wish to suggest that it is complemented by the socially constructed agency of clients and by the dynamics of politics in municipal government. Critiques of the welfare professions may be found in Paul Wilding, *Professional Power and Social Welfare* (London, 1982), and John McKnight, 'Professionalized Service and Disabling Help,' *Disabling Professions*, edited by Ivan Illich et al. (London, 1977).
4 Archives of Ontario (AO), Records of the Ministry of Tourism and Information, RG 65, Recreation in Ontario: Historical Resources Collection (RG 65, ROHRC), series A.9, box 16, file 437, interview transcript; AO, RG 2, Records of the Department of Education, series s-1, box 4, J.K. Tett to Roby Kidd, 6 October 1952; AO, RG 65, ROHRC, series A.9, box 16, file 413; interview with former Brantford Recreation Department staff member, 25 June 1992.
5 No one has yet written the history of community organization and its ties to citizen participation in providing welfare. I have found evidence of the breadth and heterogeneity of this organizing spirit in National Archives of Canada (NA), Records of the Canadian Council on Social Development, MG 28, I 10, vol. 49, file 439, Eurith Goold, National Council of the YWCA, to Elizabeth S.L. Govan, Canadian Welfare Council, 11 December 1953; Records of the United Way of the Lower Mainland, Social Planning Section, files 'A' to 'N' 1940–50, file 'Neighbourhood Council Developments, 1953–4' (held at the United Way offices at the date of this research); Jacquelyn Gale Wills, 'Efficiency, Feminism, and Co-operative Democracy: Origins of the Toronto Social Planning Council, 1918–1957' (PhD thesis, University of Toronto, 1989); David Smith, 'First Person Plural: The Community Life Training Institute – Story of an Idea,' *Interchange* 4, 4 (1973): 1–14; Arthur Morgan, *The Small Community: Foundation of Democratic Life, What It Is and How to Achieve It* (New York 1942), especially 279–82; Catherine L. Cleverdon, *The Woman Suffrage Movement in Canada* (Toronto:

University of Toronto Press, 1950), 271–8; J.R. Kidd, ed., *Adult Education in Canada* (Toronto: Canadian Association for Adult Education, 1950), especially 10, 23–4, and 34–6; NA, MG 28, I 10, Papers of the Canadian Council on Social Development, vol. 77, f. 564, 'Labour–General 1942–51,' clipping describing Canadian Congress of Labour study session, Ronald Williams, 'Education – This Is Our Road to Power,' *Financial Post*, 12 February 1949.

6 AO, RG 65, ROHRC, series A.3, box 4, file 96, In-Service Course, second year, 'People,' 3.

7 Ibid., series B.3, box 24, file 872, John K. Tett, director of the Community Programmes Branch, 'Recreation in Ontario,' reprint, circa 1950 (no pagination); series A.9, box 17, file 461, transcript of interview with Bob Secord, 1–2.

8 Small towns and villages needed a less elaborate committee structure, and Toronto entered the postwar period with an elaborate non-participatory public recreation system already in place from the interwar period. Consequently, the most ambitious participation experiments took place in mid-sized cities and one county (a rural munipality). See, for Hamilton, 4316, AO, RG 65, ROHRC, series A.9, box 16, file 459, interview transcript, 9–11; for Guelph, 3126, AO, ROHRC, series B.1, box 20, file 657, T.A. Leishman to J.K. Tett, 10 January 1950; for Toronto Township [Mississauga], 4298, AO, ROHRC, series A.9, box 16, file 433, interview transcript, 4; for Simcoe County, Simcoe County Archives, Recreation Department Records, Louise Colley, 'The Process of Change in the Structure and Functioning of a Rural Agency'; AO, RG 65, ROHRC, series 9, box 16, file 416, interview transcript, passim.

9 Gail Pogue and Bryce Taylor, 'History of Provincial Government Services of the Youth and Recreation Branch (Part I: 1940–1950),' *Recreation Review*, Supplement Number 1 (November 1972): 16–17; 'Drew Sees Youth Plan as Means to Combat Reds,' *Globe and Mail*, 10 April 1948.

10 For an account of this perspective in the previous postwar period, see James Naylor, *The New Democracy: Challenging the Social Order in Industrial Ontario, 1914–1925* (Toronto 1991).

11 AO, RG 65, ROHRC, series A.9, box 16, file 448, interview transcript, 1, 2, 11; City of Brantford Records Office (BRO), City of Brantford scrapbooks, volume for 31 October to 31 December 1945, 1, 'John Pearson New Director of Recreation,' *Brantford Expositor (BE)*, 2 November 1945; W. Kenneth Dunn et al., comp., *Directory of Graduates, 1890–1965* (Montreal: McGill University 1966).

12 Brantford Recreation Records (BRR), Recreation Commission minutes binder, 1952–3, Pearson to Alinsky, 5 January 1953.

13 Donald C. Reitzes and Dietrich C. Reitzes, *The Alinsky Legacy: Alive and Kicking* (Greenwich, Conn.: JAI Press, 1987), biographical information, 1–8, direct quotation quoted from *Current Biography* 4 (1968): 8.

14 BRO, microfilm of City Council minutes, roll 3, 14 February 1944, 619, and 24 April 1944, 670.

15 Saul Alinsky, *Reveille for Radicals* (Chicago 1946), 87–91.

16 Ibid., 219.

17 Pearson is no longer alive, so I was not able to interview him.

18 AO, RG 65, ROHRC, series A.9, box 16, file 448, interview transcript, 2, 18.

19 Ibid., 21.

20 City of Brantford, Records of the Parks and Recreation Department (BRR), Recreation Commission minutes binder, 1948–9, Annual Report for 1948.

21 Ian MacPherson, *Building and Protecting the Co-operative Movement* (Ottawa: Co-operative Union of Canada, 1984), Appendix C; Robert Clark, *A Glimpse of the Past: A Centennial History of Brantford and Brant County* ([Brantford?]: Brant Historical Society, c1966), 56–7; Naylor, *The New Democracy*, 217; Elizabeth Kelly, *Our Expectations: A History of Brantford's Labour Movement* (Brantford 1987), 99; For mayors' terms of office, see Ontario, Department of Municipal Affairs, *Municipal Directory* (for the years 1948–60, inclusive); for mayors' occupations, see *Vernon's City Directory*; for Matthews's political leanings, see AO, RG 65, ROHRC, series A.9, box 16, file 448, interview transcript, 2.

22 *Fortieth Annual Report of Labour Organization in Canada (1950–51 edition)* (Ottawa 1951), 10; *Ninth Census of Canada*, 1951, vol. 4, table 22.

23 AO, RG 65, ROHRC, series A.9, box 16, file 448, interview transcript, 2.

24 Ibid., 3.

25 Interview with former Brantford Recreation Department staff member, 25 June 1992.

26 AO, RG 65, ROHRC, series A.9, box 16, file 448, interview transcript, 18–19.

27 Ibid.

28 Ibid., 4.

29 Ibid., series B.1, box 18, file 537, first issue of *Recreation Bulletin Service* (no pagination), c. February 1946.

30 Ibid., series A.9, box 16, file 448, interview transcript, 3–4.

31 BRR, Community Committees' Council minutes binder, 1946–50, minutes for 12 January 1949, 1; AO, RG 65, ROHRC, series A.9, box 16, file 448, interview transcript, 3–4 (gives figure of sixteen); BRR, Community Committees' Council minutes binder, 1951–3, minutes for 5 September 1951, 1 (lists eighteen committees).

32 The range of common volunteer activities is evident throughout the records of the Community Committees' Council and in the Recreation Office's community committees' files. A particularly detailed single source is the *Eagle Place Community News*, three issues of which (September 1950, March 1951, and September 1951) are located in the Parsons' Park files. The role of adult volunteers as program leaders in the evenings, supplementing the paid daytime supervision, is noted in BRR, Recreation Commission minutes binder, 1952–3, John Pearson to the Ottawa Playgrounds Department director, 21 January 1953, and in the North Ward community committee file, minutes, 9 April 1954;

the Community Committees were also called on to maintain rink discipline by providing supervision at 'nominal cost.' Recreation Commission minutes binder, 1948–9, minutes, 15 January 1948, 1. A general statement on the volunteers' role in running craft courses can be found in the Community Committees' Council minutes binder, 1951–3, minutes, 'Report of the Community Centres committee,' 5 September 1951. The council meeting minutes for 7 July 1948 describe that season's roster of street dances (four) and community concerts (eleven) organized by various member committees; the same minutes also indicate that the council's amateur talent contest, a parade float, and a refreshments concession figured that year in 'Brantford Day' festivities organized by local merchants. The committees were also active in Labour Day celebrations. Community Committees' Council minutes binder, 1951–3, minutes, 6 June 1951, 1). Women's groups tabulated the results of Brantford's first recreation survey: Recreation Commission minutes binder, 1945–7, minutes, 15 March 1945, 1–2; volunteer labour for building equipment (a stage, a sandbox canopy, rinks, and rink shacks) is noted in AO, RG 65, ROHRC, series B.1, box 18, file 537, first issue of *Recreation Bulletin Service* (no pagination), c. February 1946; Recreation Commission minutes binder, 1948–9, minutes, 8 July 1948, 1; Community Committees' Council minutes binder, 1951–3, minutes, 3 January 1951, 3; Recreation Commission minutes binder, minutes, 15 January 1959, 2; and Westdale Community Centre community committee file, letter from committee chairman to Brantford Recreation Commission, 21 January 1957.

33 AO, RG 65, ROHRC, series B.1, box 18, file 537, editorial in first issue of *Recreation Bulletin Service* (no pagination); AO, RG 65, ROHRC, series A.9, box 16, file 448, interview transcript, 6.

34 The committees represented by existing lists do not include the ones from the city's wealthier neighbourhoods, such as Dufferin and Lansdowne, nor the one from the poorest downtown area.

35 Fewer single women than single men were involved in these committees and the commission: nine women versus twenty men. On a percentage basis, the gap is smaller: the nine women represent 8 per cent of the women, while the twenty men were 10 per cent of the men.

36 Percentage of non-Anglo-Celtic Brantford residents was derived from figures given in *Ninth Census of Canada*, 1951, vol. 1.

37 BRO, City of Brantford scrapbooks, volume for 1 January 1946 to 7 June 1947, 5, 'Community Committee Is Formed,' *BE*, 9 January 1946; BRO, City of Brantford scrapbooks, volume for 1 January 1946 to 7 June 1947, 7, 'Victoria Ice Rink Carnival Draws Crowd,' *BE*, 26 January 1946; BRO, City of Brantford scrapbooks, volume for 1 January 1946 to 7 June 1947, 10, 'Ice Carnival Arranged for Spring Street (Holmedale),' *BE*, January 1946; BRO, City of Brantford scrapbooks, volume for 1 January 1946 to 7 June 1947, 13, 'Recreation Rink Carnival Planned,' *BE*, 12 February 1946.

38 BRO, City of Brantford scrapbooks, volume for 1 January 1946 to 7 June 1947, 5, 'Community Committee Is Formed,' *BE*, 9 January 1946.

39 BRO, City of Brantford scrapbooks, volume for 1 January 1946 to 7 June 1947, 10, 'Ice Carnival Arranged for Spring Street (Holmedale),' *BE*, January 1946. The information on telephone service is based on the 1946 *Vernon Directory* street listing for Chestnut Street, a cross street that ran from the bottom to the top of the hill near the park. At the bottom of Chestnut, below Kerr Avenue, sixteen of twenty-three homes had no phone; above Kerr, all had phones.

40 BRR, community committees files, Arrowdale, 'Notes on the Community Committees,' September 1952, by community centres' counsellor.

41 Ibid.

42 Interview with former Brantford Recreation Department staff member, 29 June 1992.

43 This area was Lansdowne/Holmedale/Dufferin. Substantially middle class, with a working-class fringe near adjacent factories, the multiplication and mutation in this area of community committees may have followed from class tensions. The Dufferin committee succeeded the Holmedale committee, the name change signalling a shift in the committee's geographical centre towards the area's more middle-class part. In an intermediate phase, the committee was simply named the 'Spring Street Playground Committee.' A former Recreation Department staff member recalls one working-class Holmedale committee member's feeling that the wealthier members looked down on him. Interview, 25 June 1992. The Lansdowne committee centred on a prosperous neighbourhood, quite near Dufferin. Unfortunately, the changes cannot be precisely dated nor fully explained because few early records survive of these particular committees. The changes described here are inferred from BRR, community committees files, Dufferin (formerly Holmedale), Hallowe'en Parade poster, and BRO, Recreation Commission Annual Report 1955, 'Community Committees December 1955' (no pagination).

44 BRR, Recreation Commission minutes binder, 1952–3, 'Report of the Nominating Committee,' 1953.

45 BRR, Community Committees' Council minutes binder, 1946–50, minutes, September 1947, 1.

46 In the title of the conclusion to *Heroes of Their Own Lives: The Politics and History of Family Violence, Boston, 1880–1960* (New York 1988), Gordon quotes this expression, the 'powers of the weak,' which seems to have been given currency in feminist theory when Elizabeth Janeway used it for the title of her 1980 book (New York: Alfred Knopf).

47 BRR, Community Committees' Council minutes binder, 1946–50, minutes, 22 January 1947, 2, 9 June 1948, 1, and Annual Report 1948.

48 BRR, Recreation Commission minutes binder, 1950–1, 'Report from a Meeting on Community Centre Plans, Oct. 3/50, City Hall,' 1; BRR, Community Com-

mittees' Council minutes binder, 1946–50, minutes, 17 November 1948, 3; BRR, Recreation Commission minutes binder, 1950–1, 'Report of the First Recreation Excursion to Toronto.'

49 AO, RG 65, ROHRC, series A.9, box 16, file 448, interview transcript, 12; file 427, interview transcript, 3–4.

50 The names of Brantford people active as volunteers in the recreation movement were changed, in accordance with the practice I adopted for other municipalities where I had access to records in a provincial collection covered at the time of my research under the Ontario Freedom of Information and Privacy Act. I regret that restrictions imposed by this law have required that I leave anonymous all but a few individuals who contributed to the recreation movement. Excepting civil servants ranked at branch director and higher, and recreation directors and government consultants whose unique public contributions, once described, would make them clearly identifiable, individuals have been given pseudonyms or have been described simply by their occupation or function in recreation.

51 BRR, Community Committees' Council minutes binder, 1946–50, minutes, June 1948, 2, and 7 July 1948, 3; minutes binder, 1948–9, minutes, 10 June and 14 October 1948, 3.

52 BRR, Community Committees' Council minutes binder, 1946–50, minutes, 31 October 1948, 2, and 11 November 1948, 3; BRR, Recreation Commission minutes binder, 1948–9, 10 February 1949, 1.

53 BRR, Recreation Commission minutes binder, 1948–9, minutes, 10 February 1949, 1.

54 Ibid., untitled document summarizing the work of the Recreation Commission from 1945 to 1948; minutes, 10 June 1948.

55 Ibid., 8 June 1949, 3, and 14 July 1949, np; BRR, Community Committees' Council minutes binder, 1946–50, minutes, 10 May 1950, 1; minutes, 6 September 1950, 1.

56 BRR, Community Committees' Council minutes binder, 1946–50, minutes, 31 October 1948, 2, and 9 February 1949, 2; BRR, Recreation Commission minutes binder, 1950–1, 'Resolutions and Recommendations from Community Committees' Conference,' 10 June 1950.

57 'C. Callan Heads Massey-Harris Credit Union,' BE, 23 January 1952, 22; BE, 2 February 1950, 6.

58 AO, RG 65, ROHRC, series A.9, box 16, file 448, interview transcript, 21.

59 BRR, Recreation Commission minutes binder, 1950–1, list of Recreation Commission members and minutes, 12 October 1950, 2.

60 AO, RG 65, ROHRC, series A.9, box 18, file 537, copy of bylaw 3281, 7 May 1951.

61 BRR, Recreation Commission minutes binder, 1950–1, minutes, 12 October 1950, 2.

62 BRR, Community Committees' Council minutes binder, 1951–3, minutes, 'Report of the Community Centres committee,' 5 September 1951, and minutes, 28 March 1951.

63 BRR, Recreation Commission minutes binder, 1950–1, 12 April 1951, 1–2.

64 BRR, Community Committees' Council minutes binder, 1946–50, minutes, 9 March 1949, 2; ibid., 1951–3, minutes, 6 June 1951, 2.

65 This organizational choice indicates an important feature of the recreation volunteers' understanding of their citizenship. Being a 'policy intervenor' is part of what political theorists Samuel Bowles and Herbert Gintis call being a 'chooser.' They point out that this status, in liberal political theory, is opposed to the status of 'learner.' The learner status is held to be appropriate for women, children, native people, or any 'dependent' group, whose alleged incapacities make them temporarily or permanently unable to make decisions about their own or the collective good. When the CCC rejected an organizational structure symbolic of learner status, it implicitly denied that it was dependent. See Samuel Bowles and Herbert Gintis, *Democracy and Capitalism: Property, Community, and the Contradictions of Modern Social Thought* (New York 1987), 121–7.

66 BRR, Community Committees' Council minutes binder, 1951–3, minutes, 3 January 1951, 1–2.

67 BRR, Recreation Commission minutes binder, 1952–3, 11 September 1952, 1–2. Notably, the City Council representative on the commission at this time was United Auto Workers Union officer Charles Ward, and he seems to have been the only commissioner to suggest that not all the possibilities for purchasable land had yet been exhausted.

68 Ibid., Pearson to Alinsky, 5 January 1953; AO, RG 65, ROHRC, series A.9, box 17, file 478, interview transcript, 4.

69 In accordance with practices required under the Freedom of Information and Privacy Act, I have assigned a pseudonym to this individual.

70 BRR, Recreation Commission minutes binder, 1952–3, 'The Area Director,' 2 April 1953.

71 BRR, Community Committees' Council minutes binder, 1946–50, minutes, 17 November 1948, 3, and 'Report of Committee Set Up to Suggest Future Functions of This Council,' 13 December 1950; BRR, Recreation Commission minutes binder, 1950–1, 'Report from a Meeting on Community Centre Plans, Oct. 3/50, City Hall,' 2, and 'Report of the first recreation excursion to Toronto.'

72 BRR, Recreation Commission minutes binder, 1950–1, 'Report of the First Recreation Excursion to Toronto'; AO, RG 65, ROHRC, series A.9, box 17, file 469, interview transcript, 2–3, 20. Given the frequent minor inaccuracies in the transcripts of these interviews, I have assumed that the interviewees' spoken comment included the preposition. But even without the 'in,' the content of the observation is unchanged.

73 BRR, Community Committees' Council minutes binder, 1951–3, minutes,
    9 March and 9 September 1953, 2, and 8 April 1953, 3.

74 BRR, Recreation Commission minutes binder, 1950–1, 'Report from a Meeting
    on Community Centre Plans, Oct. 3/50, City Hall,' 1; BRR, Community
    Committees' Council minutes binder, 1946–50, minutes, 29 September 1948,
    1–2; BRR, Community Committees' Council minutes binder, 1951–3, minutes,
    'Report of Community Centres Committee,' 5 September 1951; BRR,
    Recreation Commission minutes binder, 1954, 'Community Centres –
    1954'.

75 Interviews with former Brantford Recreation Department staff member,
    25 June and 13 July 1992; BRR, Community Committees' Council minutes
    binder, 1951–3, minutes, 'Report of Community Centres Committee,'
    5 September 1951.

76 BRR, Community Committees' Council minutes binder, 1946–50, minutes,
    7 September 1948, 1, and 'Report of Community Centre Special Committee,'
    September 1948; BRR, Community Committees' Council minutes binder, 1951–
    3, 'Special Meeting of Community Committees to Discuss Plans for Fall and
    Winter Community Programmes,' 23 September 1953.

77 Movie-going in Canada declined after 1952, giving one indication of the time
    when television-viewing began to shape leisure pursuits. According to national
    statistics on television ownership, the years 1953–5 showed the greatest two-
    year rate of increase in the period 1953–61, rising from 10 per cent of house-
    holds to 40 per cent in 1955. Paul Rutherford, *When Television Was Young:
    Primetime Canada, 1952–1967* (Toronto 1990), 12, 49. One rural community
    leader in 1955 attributed reduced volunteer participation to the attractions of
    television. AO, RG 65, ROHRC, series B.1, box 19, file 589, report by CPB
    District Representative, 1955. Community television watching seems to have
    been part of public recreation for a time in the early 1950s: one community
    centre in Brantford offered as a special event in 1953 the opportunity to watch
    the coronation of Queen Elizabeth on TV. In Marathon, Ontario, in the early
    1960s, teenagers danced to televised dance shows in the rec centre. (My thanks
    to Ray Desrosiers for telling me about these dances.) For the expression 'work
    to play,' see *Community Courier* 16 (December 1948): 14.

78 BRR, community committees files, North Ward, minutes, 21 September 1953.

79 BRR, Recreation Commission minutes binder, 1952–3, 'Report of the Nominat-
    ing Committee' [re: 1954 commissioners].

80 I was unable to date precisely the change of recreation director in 1956; how-
    ever, the new director appears for the first time in this role in the City Council
    minutes on 12 October 1956, and his predecessor's last appearance in the same
    minutes was 30 January 1956. BRO, microfilm of City Council minutes, roll 1,
    October 1950–1956); quotation from AO, RG 65, ROHRC, series A.9, box 17, file
    474, interview transcript, 3–4.

81 BRR, Community Committees' Council minutes binder, 1951–3, minutes, 9 October 1953, 1.

82 AO, RG 65, ROHRC, series A.9, box 17, file 474, interview transcript, 7.

83 BRO, Annual Reports of Brantford Recreation Commission, 1957 Annual Report, 'Director's Report,' item.

84 For an extended reflection on the gender relations of volunteer work and associated models of citizenship, see chapter 6 of my *The Public at Play: Gender and the Politics of Recreation in Postwar Ontario* (Toronto: University of Toronto Press, 2000).

85 Kathy Peiss, *Cheap Amusements: Working Women and Leisure in Turn-of-the-Century New York* (Philadelphia: Temple University Press, 1986), 12–33; Rosemary Deem, *All Work and No Play? A Study of Women and Leisure* (Milton Keynes, England: Open University Press, 1986), 4–8; Meg Luxton, *More Than a Labour of Love* (Toronto: Women's Press, 1980), 19–21, 195–9; Ruth Millet, 'Women Aren't So Badly Off,' *BE*, 13 September 1952, 8.

86 The importance of citizen participation in the welfare state was recognized by political scientist Leo Panitch when he included an article on the subject in an anthology on the political economy of the Canadian state. However, it appears that neither Panitch nor Martin Loney (the author of that article) knew of the 1945–55 efforts of social activists, some state-funded and some not, to foster citizen participation. Martin Loney, 'A Political Economy of Citizen Participation,' in Leo Panitch, ed., *The Canadian State: Political Economy and Political Power* (Toronto: University of Toronto Press, 1977), 451.

87 This transition is discussed in greater detail in chapter 7 of Tillotson, *The Public at Play*.

Managing Water Quality in the Great Lakes Basin: Sewage Pollution Control, 1951–1960

JENNIFER READ

By the middle of the twentieth century, water pollution control in the Great Lakes basin had become a remarkably complicated issue. Between 1951 and the early 1960s a debate over which level of government would pay for sewage treatment raged among Ontario border municipalities, the province of Ontario, and the federal government. Provincial legislation delegated responsibility for sewerage facilities to the municipalities. At the same time, provincial jurisdiction for health and natural resources under the Constitution Act, 1867, meant that polluted water was also an area of provincial interest. In the Great Lakes basin federal constitutional jurisdiction over navigable waters, and commitments made under the 1909 Boundary Waters Treaty with the United States, further complicated the situation. The treaty established how the two countries would manage their shared water resources from coast to coast, and pledged both of them to avoid polluting the water on either side of the border to the detriment of health and property on the other. At the middle of the century the chief polluting element remained untreated sewage. Clearly, in boundary waters, all three levels of government had some measure of responsibility for correcting the situation.

In 1951 the International Joint Commission (IJC), the binational body created under the Boundary Waters Treaty, reported on the pollution situation in the Great Lakes connecting channels.[1] The two federal governments agreed with the commission's recommendations for pollution remediation, but, because the IJC had no regulatory powers, it relied on the federal, state, and provincial governments' voluntary compliance to implement abatement measures. In Canada, the consent of boundary water municipalities took more than ten years to achieve. Initially, between 1951 and 1956, all three levels of government were reluctant to accept any financial responsibility for much-needed municipal sewerage systems without assurances that at least one other jurisdiction would also participate. Increasing pressure on the Ontario government, both from the federal level and from growing municipal demands, prompted it to create the Ontario Water Resources Commission (OWRC) in 1956. In part the government intended the OWRC to address the province's water quality problems, especially along the boundary waters, but border communities resisted the commission's mandate and insisted that their status should garner them preferential financial treatment from the senior governments. In 1960 the federal government finally succumbed to accusations that it had approved the IJC's recommendations without taking any active steps to help it implement remedial measures. That year, in what proved to be the final act in the decade-long debate, the government amended the National Housing Act to provide financial assistance for municipal sewerage facilities across the country. With federal money in place, the last piece of the multi-jurisdictional puzzle for Great Lakes sewage pollution control fell into place.

The history of water quality policy development in Canada is still somewhat undeveloped. There have been some studies of federal water policy after the Second World War, but they focus on quantity issues rather than quality, and do not explore adequately the provincial influence. There are also some works that briefly examine the Ontario Water Resources Commission, but none place that organization within the larger context of intergovernmental relations.[2] To date, no one has examined the complex, multi-level development of the Ontario boundary water sewerage programs which is a significant step in piecing together the evolution of provincial water quality policy. In the examples of three of the more recalcitrant border communities – Sault Ste Marie, Sarnia, and Windsor – can be seen the range of financial options that finally became available to Ontario municipal governments financing and constructing sewerage systems during the 1960s. This story examines two fundamental questions that have long vexed resource managers in areas of shared jurisdiction: Who will pay for necessary measures, and how will they be implemented?

Water quality management and pollution control were not new concerns in Ontario during the 1950s. Because of the threat and spread of water-borne diseases, such as typhoid fever, water pollution had long been the responsibility of the provincial Department of Health. Early in the twentieth century, provincial public health officials virtually eliminated the spread of water-borne disease by chlorinating municipal water supplies.[3] While chlorinated water helped to protect Ontarians against the dangers of water-borne disease, it did nothing to rehabilitate the Great Lakes basin's polluted waterways. The solution to this problem was adequate sewage treatment, but, during the Great Depression, when many Ontario communities went bankrupt simply providing basic services, such capital-intensive projects were out of the question on the Canadian side of the border.[4] The Second World War, which further diverted resources from municipal infrastructure in order to foster industrial growth in support of Canada's war effort, only added to the sewage burden. After the war the impact of more than twenty years' neglect of basic sewage treatment, combined with the increased sanitary and industrial pollution created by rapid wartime urbanization, could be seen in the smelly, turbid, oily mess flowing downstream from almost every community along the Great Lakes connecting channels.

Official interest in pollution began to resurge with a postwar reference to the International Joint Commission. In 1946 the two federal governments asked the commission to examine pollution in the Great Lakes connecting channels – the St Marys, St Clair, Detroit, and Niagara rivers. Reporting in 1951, the IJC outlined the extent and causes of connecting channels pollution, suggested remedial measures, and identified the municipal and industrial actors responsible for creating the mess. The worst pollution, from both municipal and industrial effluents, occurred between Lake Huron and Lake Erie, with the most degraded sections being the upper St Clair River, the western shore of Lake St Clair, the lower Detroit River, and the western end of Lake Erie.[5]

The IJC used the survey results to create 'Objectives for Boundary Waters Quality Control,' which established effluent standards, including the precise levels at which certain chemical and biological wastes could be discharged by municipal sewerage systems and industries.[6] The IJC then pinpointed those communities, industries, and other pollution sources that were most in need of remedial measures. It also asked that it be authorized to establish and supervise boards of control to ensure that municipalities and industries implemented the recommended remedial measures and met the 'Objectives.'[7]

The two governments responded swiftly to the IJC's report and, late in 1951, authorized the commission to supervise remedial measures to control boundary waters pollution. The IJC quickly created a permanent Technical Advisory Board on Pollution Control, composed primarily of the people who had been seconded to the temporary advisory boards during the pollution reference.[8] Although the board had no power to enforce the IJC's 'Objectives,' it and the commissioners set out to persuade recalcitrant municipalities and industries to adopt them.

Early in 1952 the IJC sent its report to the polluting industries, communities, and the Ontario government and drew attention to the specific abatement measures recommended for each. Ontario border communities recognized the need for sewage treatment facilities, but pleaded weak finances as their excuse for a lack of response. Not one of them could assume the economic burden of remedial measures – generally trunk sewers, a treatment plant, and several pumping stations – and most argued for government funding to help meet the cost of their projects.[9]

In the opinion of the border communities, the sewage treatment problem was not fully a municipal responsibility. As Sarnia's city manager asserted, 'The rapid and continuing development of major industries of national importance in and around Sarnia has greatly overtaxed the City's municipal services.' In view of the importance of Sarnia's industrial base to the national economy, the manager and city council felt justified in seeking financial help from other levels of government and asked the International Joint Commission to take up the 'matter of providing substantial financial aid to enable it [Sarnia] to carry out the works in accordance with the requirements of the Commission.'[10] On their own, Ontario border municipalities were both unable and unwilling to undertake the extensive projects required to comply with the IJC's 'Objectives for Boundary Water Quality.'

In an attempt to respond efficiently to the province's pollution problems, created by both boundary water communities and their inland counterparts, the Ontario government created a Pollution Control Board in 1952. On the recommendation of Dr Albert E. Berry, provincial sanitary engineer and the province's representative on the IJC Technical Advisory Board, the board was composed of senior members from all the government departments with responsibility for pollution control.[11] Its mandate included coordinating all government pollution management functions to avoid duplication of effort, advising the government on all aspects of domestic and industrial waste control, and integrating the existing field and lab facilities involved in pollution abatement research.[12] Although the board energetically pursued its designated activities, Ontario's pollution problem steadily worsened.

Responsibility for deteriorating water quality was not shared equally in Ontario. Industry's favourable response to the pollution report and its cooperation in implementing the recommended remedial measures pleased the IJC. Less satisfactory, by far, was the municipal reaction, especially along the areas identified as most polluted. The IJC's Canadian Section continued to urge the offending border communities to address their pollution problems, but the lack of progress soon attracted other interested governments along the boundary waters. Beginning in 1953, Michigan representatives appeared before the IJC, repeatedly demanding that Ontario border communities install sewage treatment facilities and threatening to sue Canada for damages if they did not comply.[13] Caught between ongoing pressure from the commission's American Section and the apparent indifference of Ontario Premier Leslie Frost, the chairman of the IJC's Canadian Section did all he could to spur further action. This included sending another round of letters to the offending communities and the provincial government late in 1953, reiterating the need for immediate action on the problem. The communities all reported that they lacked the fiscal resources to tackle the problem on their own.[14]

At the same time, a delegation from Sarnia approached Frost in an attempt to secure provincial help with the sewage treatment plant the city required to meet the IJC's effluent standards. Sarnia representatives argued that they required special consideration for provincial funding because of the great burden placed on their city by the rapid wartime industrial development, something that had benefited the province as a whole.[15] To develop a coherent policy response, the premier's advisers solicited advice from both the minister of health, MacKinnon Phillips, and Dr A.E. Berry, who, as provincial sanitary engineer, Ontario representative on the IJC's Technical Advisory Board, and chair of the Pollution Control Board, was most familiar with the province's pollution situation.

Provincial health officials believed that the border communities, especially Sarnia, were deliberately delaying their sewerage facilities in hopes of securing provincial funds.[16] For instance, Sarnia city council had repeatedly refused to begin a much-needed system for a low-lying, flood-prone area on the northern limits of the city. An exasperated investigating engineer reported that the council did not see the situation in terms of the health hazard it presented, but insisted on viewing it as an economic problem. He believed that the health department should again point out, 'in the strongest terms ... [that]the responsibility rests with the municipality for correcting the hazardous condition, rather than the government to provide the money for the correction.'[17] The government's lack of a strong policy only exacerbated the situation. Although the Health Department could order a municipality to adopt proper waste treatment under the Public Health Act, this provision had never been enforced. Provincial health officials therefore had little more than persuasion to aid their pollution abatement efforts. Both Phillips and Berry believed that 'municipalities quite capable of bearing the cost of required sewage plants, are delaying construction in order to discover what assistance the Ontario Government may give and to use the [sewage treatment] money for more attractive vote-catching projects.'[18]

Frost's advisers recommended that the maximum extent of provincial involvement should be to guarantee municipal debentures at a low interest rate. That was as much responsibility as any other jurisdiction, state or province, had assumed to that point. They did urge him to seek federal support to share the cost of debentures issued for boundary waters communities because they believed this was an area of joint responsibility. Finally, they recommended that the government more stringently enforce the Public Health Act.[19]

Despite their strong argument for provincial help, the Sarnia delegation failed to persuade the premier of the political utility of their request. Instead, Frost asserted his government's position that water and sewerage systems were a local responsibility. If the government agreed to help Sarnia, it would set a dangerous precedent for involvement in sewage treatment across the province.[20] Undaunted by Frost's rebuff, Sarnia's mayor initiated an alliance with his counterparts in Windsor, Chatham, and Wallaceburg in February 1954. Calling themselves the Joint Municipal Committee on Sewerage Works, the group determined to secure funding from either the provincial or the federal governments or both, and began efforts to arrange a meeting with the federal minister of national health and welfare.[21]

At the international level, Michigan continued to bring pressure before the International Joint Commission. Clearly embarrassed at the continuing need to explain Ontario's negligent behaviour to his American colleagues, Andrew McNaughton, the IJC's Canadian chairman, sent a stiffly worded message to the Ontario government in July. In it he pointed out that although the Michigan Water Resources Commission (MWRC) had been very successful in forcing its communities to comply with the 'Objectives for Boundary Water Quality,' the state could no longer face them in court when Ontario municipalities across the river continued to pollute with 'impunity.' The time was 'clearly over for persuasion,' McNaughton concluded. What stronger policy did Ontario intend to adopt?[22]

For the time being, Frost decided to wait and see. Then, in October, at the IJC's semi-annual meeting, Michigan's attorney general made another presentation about damages to the people and property of his state by pollution originating in Ontario. He threatened legal action if Ontario did not begin to move more swiftly.[23] Under pressure from the IJC, Prime Minister St Laurent finally wrote Frost in November 1954. He pointed out that Ontario's ongoing pollution represented a contravention of the 1909 Boundary Waters Treaty. 'Such an occurrence would naturally have serious repercussions on Canada's relations with the United States,' he stated. Although the primary fiscal obligation rested with the province in this area, St Laurent admitted that Article 4 of the treaty placed significant responsibility on the federal government. He wanted to know what steps the province had taken to rectify the situation.[24]

In his reply in December, Frost pointed out the complexity of the situation. Both the Depression and the war had a negative impact on Ontario municipalities' sewage treatment plans. First financial stringency, then the scarcity of construction material, had prevented them from undertaking the necessary sewerage works. Industrial growth had played a significant role by concentrating population in Great Lakes communities where new enterprise could take advantage of the abundant water, excellent shipping facilities, and already established businesses. 'This emphasizes a point I have made on occasions at Federal-Provincial conferences,' Frost wrote, 'that a province with a relatively large volume of industrial development requires substantially greater revenues to meet the economic costs of pollution and traffic congestion and other problems in the fields of health and welfare than one which does not experience it.'[25] Frost included sewage treatment within the range of fiscal responsibilities his government faced in administering the nation's foremost industrial centre. For each industrial tax dollar the province earned, it had to extend a number of services, such as hydroelectric and transportation infrastructure, and the larger population associated with industrial growth required a greater investment in education, health care, and social services. The border communities, which had experienced the most rapid growth, faced the largest expenses of all – ones that might prove to be beyond their capacity to meet. 'For this reason,' Frost concluded, 'I firmly believe that the abatement of pollution should be considered as part of the broader Federal-Provincial fiscal problem.'[26] One problem that the premier addressed throughout the 1950s was how his government could secure both the necessary funds and the financial freedom from the federal government to meet provincial needs.[27]

Frost's reply caused consternation within the IJC and the federal government.[28] In January 1955 the undersecretary of state for external affairs called an interdepartmental meeting of the deputy ministers of Finance, National Health and Welfare, and Northern Affairs and Natural Resources, a representative of the Privy Council Office, and the Canadian chair of the IJC. How should the prime minister respond to Frost's proposition that financing sewerage systems be included in federal-provincial fiscal relations? The group decided that St Laurent's reply should be 'somewhat firmer' than his last letter to the Ontario premier. Some even suggested that the prime minister should threaten to build sewage treatment plants in boundary water communities and then sue the province to recover the cost, or perhaps the federal government could use the provincial health act to force action. Clearly it was time, the interdepartmental committee believed, that St Laurent take a tougher stand with Ontario.[29]

Despite the strong advice, cooler heads prevailed in drafting St Laurent's next letter to Frost. The prime minister reiterated the need for immediate action by the offending border communities, and again requested that Frost supply his government with the specific steps the province had taken to ensure municipal cooperation. Continued pollution could, at any moment, constitute a violation of the 1909 treaty which 'would raise questions of considerable importance' to be 'resolved between the Federal and Ontario Governments and the municipalities or persons concerned.' As far as federal financial support went, however, the prime minister regretted that boundary water pollution abatement could not 'usefully be considered within the context of federal-provincial fiscal arrangements.' Although he recognized that the expenditure would challenge the municipalities involved, the number was so small that the federal government could not 'in equity' subsidize boundary water sewage treatment facilities if it did not also offer help to other communities across the country. 'There is an urgent necessity to find a solution to boundary waters pollution,' St Laurent concluded, 'and the prime responsibility for finding the solution rests, we believe, with the Province of Ontario and the municipalities.'[30]

In his response, Frost pointed out that Ontario's pollution problem not only affected boundary waters but compromised inland watersheds as well. He indicated that all offending municipalities had been 'advised' to take remedial measures. Most of them had the planning process well under way, and some had plans already in place. As for the specific boundary waters problem, he acknowledged that the larger communities were the obvious targets for remedial measures, but he was also forced to point out that inland communities on smaller rivers and streams often contributed as much to the problem. Given this fact, the province could not help some communities and ignore the needs of others. He had hoped that the federal government would see the necessity of including sewage treatment within federal-provincial fiscal relations, especially because industrial growth had been the primary cause of the problem. He concluded by reassuring the prime minister that the province recognized the gravity of the situation and would 'do what is feasible to bring about an abatement of this problem.'[31]

Although Frost appeared willing to do little about pollution abatement beyond deflecting criticism from his own government, conditions conspired to move him to action by the middle of the decade. At that time serious water shortages in the southwestern portion of the province, west of a line drawn between Hamilton and Owen Sound, provoked another municipal attempt to engage the provincial government. In April 1955 a fourteen-member committee, led by Waterloo businessman A.M. Snider, presented the premier with a brief outlining the problems associated with the water shortage and recommending government action to ameliorate the situation. The committee asked the government for a survey to determine the best sources of future water supply for their region, how it would be transmitted, and how much the project would cost. The committee also requested legislation to create a provincial water management agency capable of delivering ample clean water at cost, similar to the way the Ontario Hydro-Electric Power Corporation delivered electricity to local utilities. The most popular solution to water shortages was the idea of constructing a pipeline from one or more of the Great Lakes to deliver abundant water to inland communities.[32]

Frost seized the opportunity to couple the nagging pollution issue with the new water supply problem. In May he named Snider to head the five-member Ontario Water Resources and Supply Committee and charged it with investigating the two issues of water quality and quantity, along with related administrative measures, legislation, and financial arrangements. The water resources committee thoroughly investigated the problems outlined in its terms of reference and, over the autumn of 1955, held public meetings across southwestern Ontario to gauge public reaction to the proposed water agency. The committee also met with individuals and organizations which it believed could offer expert help with different aspects of its mandate. These issues included a conference with the IJC's Canadian chairman to discuss diverting water from the Great Lakes to meet inland requirements as well as the ongoing boundary waters pollution situation. The committee met with engineering consultants who had already investigated the needs of some southwestern Ontario communities. They also held a discussion with Dr Otto Holden, chairman of Ontario Hydro. Finally, committee members met with the Pollution Control Board to understand the magnitude and location of pollution problems in the province.[33]

On 26 January 1956 the Water Resources and Supply Committee presented its report to the premier outlining a formidable program of expenditure. In total, it recommended that almost $2.5 billion be spent on water supply and sewage treatment, at least 60 per cent of which would have to be expended within ten years if Ontario expected to bring its water and sewerage infrastructure up to date. As expected, the committee found southwestern Ontario in most immediate need of a dependable water supply and prioritized a Great Lakes pipeline to London, St Thomas, and Aylmer. Sewage treatment needs were more generally felt throughout the urbanized south. The committee gave priority for sewerage works to the rapidly expanding urban centres, such as those on Great Lakes connecting channels, and communities on smaller inland rivers such as London and Kitchener-Waterloo.[34]

Premier Frost introduced a bill to establish the Ontario Water Resources Commission in the Legislative Assembly on 23 February 1956. With no significant opposition, the Ontario Water Resources Commission Act became law in March. The commission consisted of three to five appointed members, one of whom was designated as chairman. They, in turn, could employ any staff they deemed necessary. Not surprisingly, Frost appointed Snider as the first OWRC chairman. The other commissioners were former committee members W.D. Conklin and James Vance, both from southwestern Ontario, and R.M. Simpson from Arnprior and W.H.C. Brien from Sault Ste Marie. Frost also appointed A.E. Berry as the general manager. This appointment made Berry the hub of pollution abatement activity in the province by virtue of his other positions as chairman of the Pollution Control Board and provincial representative on the IJC's technical advisory board.[35] The legislation authorized the new commission to develop water supplies as well as build and operate water purification and sewage treatment systems. It could conduct any research and collect any statistics it required to carry out this duty and any others the government assigned it.[36]

Although the OWRC was greeted as the answer to the province's water supply and pollution control challenges, it was not as successful during its first year as observers had hoped. The Ontario Municipal Board, the provincial agency responsible for approving municipal expenditure, remained committed to enforcing 'fiscal responsibility' and routinely opposed any OWRC project where the community in question had a debenture debt above 15 per cent of its total assessment. In practice, this policy meant that communities most in need of sewerage systems were still unable to afford them and, during its first year, the OWRC proved unable to overrule the municipal board.[37]

In April 1957 the Ontario government amended the OWRC Act to address the commission's problems with the Municipal Board. At the same time, the act transferred specific functions and personnel from the Departments of Health and Mines. Berry's entire Division of Sanitary Engineering, as well as health department authority to suggest changes and approve all municipal and industrial water supply and sewerage system applications, went to the OWRC. From the mining portfolio, the OWRC acquired responsibility for all well drilling and supervision of ground water across the province, along with the staff of the Ground Water Branch.[38] These legislative changes greatly widened the scope of the OWRC's program. As the commission fulfilled its mandate, it expanded from a modest staff of 82 members in 1957 to over 1200 at its peak in the early 1970s.[39]

The OWRC's primary success came with smaller communities. Local politicians' traditional reluctance to commit their communities to costly water and sewerage infrastructure stemmed from the expense of these installations and often their inability to 'sell' the associated debt load to either their rate payers or the Ontario Municipal Board. After the creation of the commission, this process became much easier for smaller communities with the flexible administrative arrangements the OWRC developed. After receiving commission approval for a proposed project, a community could float its own debenture to finance it. It could also make arrangements with the commission for the work to be carried out on its behalf at the lower interest rates charged under the province's credit rating. In most cases the municipality then had thirty years to pay for the works and could defer payments on capital construction for up to five years. Finally, if a municipality could afford neither option, the OWRC would design, finance, build, and operate water or sewerage works, charging only for the services used. This flexibility ensured that sewage treatment facilities were installed in communities that could not afford them before the commission's appearance. By 1962, for instance, expenditure on water and sewerage projects constructed under agreement with the OWRC totalled just under $100 million. Commission projects appear relatively minor when compared with the total annual average spent on water and sewerage works, $113 million, but OWRC projects were generally smaller and were measured in the tens and hundreds of thousands rather than the multimillion-dollar projects that the larger communities undertook. At the same time, the commission regarded the average total annual expenditure with pride because it approached the estimated average $120 million suggested by the water resources and supply committee in 1955.[40]

The larger border communities did not respond as favourably to the OWRC's program as their smaller counterparts. Under Sarnia's leadership, the Joint Municipal Committee on Sewerage Works, which by now included Sault Ste Marie, Windsor, Chatham, Wallaceburg, Amhurstburg, and Niagara Falls, actively opposed the commission's water and sewage treatment proposals. Sarnia's opposition was strengthened when the provincial health department issued a mandatory order in December 1956 threatening the city with a fine of $100 a day unless it started building its sewage treatment system by 1 July 1957. To this point, the government had avoided mandatory orders in order to keep relations with local governments as genial as possible. That the province now issued one indicated the growing significance of boundary water pollution. With the OWRC, the city had the technical and financial means to go ahead with its sewage construction program. The provence, facing federal and international pressure, found Sarnia's continued inactivity politically intolerable. When questioned on the matter in the Legislative Assembly, Frost readily acknowledged these pressures. 'I share with him [Sarnia's mayor] and those municipal representatives their dismay over the fact that the situation is really being forced upon us by direction from Ottawa, coming from a high diplomatic level.'[41]

Sarnia politely refused the OWRC's offer to negotiate an agreement covering the works under the mandatory order. On consideration, city council informed the commission 'that it [the city] is competent to undertake to operate this plant and sewage system itself.'[42] Sarnia's decision to avoid the OWRC was only the first example of a large border community sidestepping the provincial agency.

The major border municipalities, in fact, rejected the OWRC's program outright. They believed that provincial financial help was necessary, but the water commission demanded too much control over a local matter. Initially, Sarnia explored the option of entering an agreement with the provincial agency. After investigation, however, the city council passed a resolution objecting to the fact that, under such an agreement, a municipality had no input into principal, interest, maintenance, or operating costs, yet was required to raise whatever amount the OWRC determined necessary from the local ratepayers. This policy was neither proper nor fair, and the city wished to see a different 'system of assistance for municipalities so that the sewage disposal systems and trunk sewers can be installed, yet controlled by the proper level of Government.'[43] The Windsor city manager came to a similar conclusion a few years later when he informed his council that most of the larger communities had funded their own systems, 'since the advantages of placing this municipal responsibility into the hands of a Provincial Committee [sic] are questionable.'[44] From the border communities' perspective, the commission's program removed control over the details of water and sewerage projects from the municipality while forcing the community to pay for them.

Although the OWRC boasted that its financial arrangements were the best that could be arranged, politicians from communities such as Windsor and Sarnia were unmoved. Long-term debentures were already possible under Ontario Municipal Board regulations that authorized the board to establish thirty-year terms on projects of ongoing benefit to a community, such as water and sewerage works. Although the OWRC claimed it provided a very favourable interest rate, in most cases a municipality in a sound financial position could borrow at no more than ½ per cent higher than the OWRC's own rate. The ability to defer principal payments sounded good for the immediate term, but over the lifetime of the debt meant increased interest costs. And, while an OWRC loan might not be debenture debt, it would still be taken into account by banks and investment houses when calculating future debentures. In reality, no municipality had unlimited, long-term credit and, regardless of how it financed a large project, such as a sewage treatment plant, future borrowing capacity would be reduced accordingly. As for the OWRC's claim that the interest rate on short-term loans would be reduced if the provincial rate fell, municipal politicians knew that such a step would not be taken unless the provincial government could gain some political advantage.[45]

Despite their determination to circumvent the OWRC, border municipalities were still convinced that the senior levels of government should help them finance their sewage treatment facilities. At a March 1957 meeting with Frost, the Joint Municipal Committee on Sewerage Works set out its demands. It wanted outright grants from the federal and provincial governments to cover 50 per cent of total sewerage construction, and provincial loans at a rate of no more than 4 per cent to cover the remaining cost. Frost acknowledged that accelerated urban growth did require further financial assistance from his government to cover social services and education, but he maintained that sewage treatment plants were a municipal responsibility. He reiterated his concern about current federal-provincial fiscal relations, insisting that the province would be unable to 'grant additional aid to municipalities for any purpose, until the Federal Government agreed to give the Province a larger portion of personal and corporate taxes.'[46] Frost assured the municipalities that he would lend moral support to their quest for federal funding, and urged them to seek an audience with the prime minister and his health minister.

In all likelihood the municipal alliance's request for a meeting did not surprise federal officials. In Ottawa, civil servants had been monitoring the national pollution situation closely for some time and considering some measure of national action. In 1955 the St Laurent government appointed an Advisory Committee on Water Uses Policy (ACWUP) to address all water use problems in Canada, and to replace the more narrowly configured water-power committee.[47] From its inception, the ACWUP focused on water pollution, specifically the thorny areas of interprovincial waters, for which there was no remedy at law, and international waters, because of federal obligations under the Boundary Waters Treaty. External Affairs took a particular interest in this latter category and, in 1955, reported the department's deep embarrassment before the International Joint Commission, in part due to the federal government's lack of initiative on the issue. As External Affairs pointed out, the federal government had approved the IJC's 1951 recommendations, but had taken no action to implement them beyond writing letters to the premier of Ontario. The diplomats insisted that 'the need for action in boundary waters was acute, either alone or as part of a broad national policy'; at this urging, the ACWUP gave the problem more thought.[48] Over the next year, a subcommittee on water pollution explored the issue. Late in 1956 it determined that the recent appearance of the OWRC and similar programs in Alberta and Manitoba reduced the need for immediate federal action and advised the federal government to 'defer participation until these provincial programs can be evaluated.'[49] Consequently, the municipal alliance had little success in arranging a meeting with St Laurent and his minister of health.

During the summer of 1957, however, the situation changed dramatically at the federal level. The Liberal Party, which had led the country since 1935, gave way to the Conservatives under John Diefenbaker. Initially, Diefenbaker's government proved just as wary of helping border municipalities to the exclusion of other Canadian communities as had its Liberal predecessors.[50] But the new prime minister had a special interest in interprovincial pollution abatement and, although he was not willing to give the border communities special consideration, his government devised a way to grant federal help to those communities across the country which required greater funding to meet their pollution control obligations.[51]

In the 1960 throne speech, the Diefenbaker government promised to amend the National Housing Act significantly.[52] The aspect of immediate interest to the border municipalities was an amendment authorizing the Central Mortgage and Housing Corporation (CMHC), the federal agency that carried out the act's provisions, to assist municipalities in constructing new or expanded trunk sewage collection systems and treatment plants. Under the new provisions, CMHC loans could be made for as much as two-thirds of the total cost of the project, to a maximum of $100 million. Interest rates were generous and spread out over as many as fifty years. As an impetus to promote immediate construction, especially in border communities, the government would forgive up to 25 per cent of the work completed by 31 March 1963.[53] The municipal response was immediate. The act became law on 2 December 1960 and, by the end of the month, the CMHC had received sixty enquiries and three applications for loans.[54]

Municipal councillors in the border communities were especially happy to see the new federal program. Although the OWRC had already forced Sarnia and Sault Ste Marie to proceed with their respective sewage treatment facilities, the cities hoped to qualify for retroactive funding. Sarnia's project had received Ontario Municipal Board approval in January 1959. The $3.8 million project included interceptor sewers, pumping stations, and a sewage treatment plant to provide secondary treatment and chlorination of Sarnia's effluent.[55] In Sault Ste Marie, the OWRC convinced municipal leaders to enter an agreement providing sewage treatment for the city as well as the two surrounding townships, Tarentorus and Korah. Early in June 1960 the municipal board approved a $1.8 million debenture for this project.[56] With the news that federal money was now available for sewage treatment, Sarnia was among the first communities to inquire about the federal program.[57]

Initially the Central Mortgage and Housing Corporation informed Sarnia and Sault Ste Marie that their communities could not qualify for federal money because the tenders had been let before the act's implementation.[58] Sarnia politicians exploded. Naturally they were angry with the provincial government, especially the OWRC, on whose behalf the Department of Health had issued the mandatory order forcing their sewage treatment program. If the community had not been compelled to begin building its system, one councillor complained, the city would have been able to save at least $1 million. In an attempt to convince the federal government that their city deserved to be worked into the new program, a delegation of Sarnia politicians went to Ottawa in March and met with David Walker, minister of public works. They returned home optimistic that their case had been well received.[59]

At the same time, the provincial minister of municipal affairs, W.K. Warrender, also appealed to David Walker on behalf of both beleaguered border cities. Warrender argued that Sarnia and Sault Ste Marie were being unfairly penalized because of OWRC cooperation with the International Joint Commission to end boundary water pollution. In the course of that work the OWRC had informed the two cities that they must start building their treatment works to meet IJC requirements. The two communities had proceeded 'on good faith at dates earlier than many of the other municipalities which are [now] benefiting by the financial arrangements made under the federal legislation.' Here Warrender's argument echoed Frost's comments about Sarnia's mandatory order. The minister insisted that the OWRC had ordered the two communities to proceed primarily because the federal government and the IJC had pressured them into the action, and now they were being penalized while their more reluctant counterparts benefited from their stubbornness.[60] Warrender's argument, and ongoing pressure from the border communities, won over the federal government. In May 1962 Sarnia City Council learned that the CMHC would be issuing a rebate for the city's sewage system, and in June it applied for and received a CMHC loan for $2.5 million. In November the Ontario Municipal Board approved a CMHC floating debenture for Sault Ste Marie.[61]

It was in Windsor's sewerage program that the three levels of government came together cooperatively and enabled the city to take advantage of the National Housing Act without incident. Here, too, municipal politicians had initially rejected the OWRC and joined Sarnia and Sault Ste Marie in the alliance against the provincial agency's program. But Windsor's anti-

OWRC bluster gradually faded after 1960, when a consultant's report on the city's sewerage needs sobered city council. The report was an update of an earlier one that had become obsolete while the city searched for alternative funding sources. Now consulting engineers reported that the city required an extensive system of main and interceptor sewers as well as a much larger treatment plant, and estimated a total cost of $13.2 million.[62] This figure was well beyond the realm of the possible for the city and, after considering the range of options, Windsor leaders decided to approach the problem from a number of angles. In 1961, with OWRC help, the city worked out an arrangement to share the cost of the treatment plant with a number of the surrounding smaller communities. The riverfront interceptor sewer, needed to collect the effluent from more than thirty existing outfall sewers, was financed by a CMHC loan under the National Housing Act. OWRC expertise helped to balance the carefully phased construction process as the municipal board held the city to $2 million per year in capital expenditure.[63] The Windsor program took longer to implement, but it represented the culmination of federal and provincial help in boundary water pollution abatement.

By 1960 all three levels of government had finally accepted their respective responsibility for sewage treatment. This postwar sewerage debate is a good illustration of how fiscal responsibility in areas of shared jurisdiction has developed in Ontario. It also allows an examination of the two most fundamental questions plaguing resource managers in multi-jurisdictional areas: Who will pay for necessary measures, and how will they be implemented? In the case of the border community sewerage systems, no government readily assumed responsibility for the necessary remedial measures. As a result, an already contentious international situation intensified as the various levels of government jockeyed for fiscal position. At the same time, water quality in the Great Lakes connecting channels continued to deteriorate, making cleanup more difficult when it was finally undertaken in earnest.

The debate also offers an opportunity to explore the growing postwar tension between the economically powerful province of Ontario and the federal government as federal-provincial fiscal relations evolved. This particular story brings the issue down another level by incorporating the municipalities. It demonstrates that the provinces were not the only junior governments during the period to demand financial help from their senior counterparts while simultaneously asserting their independence. Further investigation of intergovernmental relations during this period will reveal that a much more complex evolutionary process was under way than historians have hitherto imagined.

NOTES

I would like to acknowledge the support of the Social Sciences and Humanities Research Council of Canada and the Canada–U.S. Fulbright Program, as well as the comments and critical reading of Gerald Killan and session attendees at the 1998 Ottawa meeting of the Canadian Historical Association.

1 Under the treaty, the IJC had judicial, investigatory, and arbitrational powers on issues related to water diversion along the common boundary as well as other items that might arise from time to time. A clause in Article 4 pledged both sides to avoid polluting boundary waters to the detriment of the health and property of the citizens on the other side.

2 On federal water policy, see Frank Quinn, 'The Evolution of Federal Water Policy,' *Canadian Water Resources Journal* 10, 4 (1985): 21–33; and Peter H. Pearse and Frank Quinn, 'Recent Developments in Federal Water Policy: One Step Forward, Two Steps Back,' ibid., 21, 4 (1996): 329–40. On the OWRC, see Dan Shrubsole, 'The Evolution of Public Water Management Agencies in Ontario: 1946–1988, ibid., 15, 1 (1990): 49–66; Robert C. de Loë's 1991 article, 'The Institutional Pattern for Water Quality Management in Ontario,' ibid., 16, n. 1 (1991): 23–43; and J.K. Rea, *The Prosperous Years: The Economic History of Ontario, 1939–75* (Toronto: University of Toronto Press/Ontario Historical Studies Series, 1985), 40–2. Roger Graham, *Old Man Ontario: Leslie M. Frost* (Toronto: University of Toronto Press, 1990), 205–10, provides a generally good, but brief and occasionally incorrect account of the OWRC's origins. And, because he does not follow up the pollution issue, he misses its significance to federal-provincial and international relations in the Great Lakes basin during Frost's full tenure.

3 For the earlier story, see Jennifer Read, '"A Sort of Destiny": The Multi-jurisdiction Response to Sewage Pollution in the Great Lakes, 1900–1930,' *Scientia Canadiensis* 51 (1999): 103–29.

4 The classic study on municipal difficulty during the Great Depression is James Struthers, *No Fault of Their Own: Unemployment and the Canadian Welfare States, 1914–1941* (Toronto: University of Toronto Press, 1983). See also H. Blair Neatby, *The Politics of Chaos: Canada in the Thirties* (Toronto: Copp, Clark, Pitman, 1986).

5 IJC, *Report of the International Joint Commission, United States, and Canada on the Pollution of Boundary Waters* (Washington: Government Printing Office, 1951).

6 Ibid., p. 20.

7 Ibid., 21–2, 66–7, 174–7, 194–5, 251, 254, and 258.

8 National Archives of Canada (NA), RG 89, Records of the Water Resources Branch, vol. 342, file 192-2-1, Jules Leger, undersecretary of external affairs, to R.G. Robertson, deputy minister of northern affairs and national resources, 20 October 1955.

9 IJC, Canadian Section, Library and Archives, Ottawa, Ontario, docket 54-3-1:9, 'Correspondence – 1952,' E. Royden Colter, Sarnia city manager, to E.M. Sutherland, secretary, Canadian Section, IJC, 6 October 1952. See also earlier letters from Colter, 26 March 1952; the Clerk-Treasurer, Riverside, 27 March 1952; the Clerk-Treasurer, Amherstburg, 26 March 1952; the Clerk-Treasurer, Fort Erie, 19 August 1952; Clerk-Treasurer, Chippewa, 19 August 1952.

10 IJC, docket 54-3-1:9, 'Correspondence – 1952,' E. Royden Colter, Sarnia city manager, to E.M. Sutherland, secretary, Canadian Section, IJC, 6 October 1952.

11 These were the Departments of Health, Lands and Forests, Planning and Development, Municipal Affairs, Mines and Agriculture. Archives of Ontario (AO), Records of the Ontario Water Resources Commission (OWRC), RG 84, Subject Files, 'Pollution Advisory Committee,' brief to Cabinet, 31 January 1952.

12 Ibid., and brief to Cabinet, 2 December 1952, also minutes of meeting, 7 August 1952.

13 IJC, docket 54-2-4:2, 'Statements by N.V. Olds,' 18 September 1953, 9; also Olds' statement in Toronto on 21 August 1953, and docket 54-3-1:10, 'Correspondence – 1953,' Canadian Section memorandum, 11 August 1953, in which the chair of the Canadian Section of the Technical Advisory Boards, J.R. Menzies, warns the Canadian chair, A.G.L. McNaughton, that Michigan is going to 'stir up a fuss.' Michigan State Archives (MSA), RG 74-13, Department of Natural Resources, Environmental Protection Branch, Water Resources Commission, 'Minutes of the Stream Control Commission/Water Resources Commission,' 23 September 1952, 3; 28–29 October 1952; 30 July 1953, 9; 29 September 1953, 3; 29 October 1953, 5; 27–28 January 1954, 9; 24 March 1954, 5; 27 May 1954, 7–8; 26–28 April 1955, 9; and 26–27 October 1955, 2.

14 IJC, docket 54-3-1:1, 'Correspondence, 1954,' A.G.L. McNaughton to Premier Leslie Frost, cc Prime Minister St Laurent, no date. Also AO, RG 3-23, Premiers' Papers, Leslie Frost Papers, box 81, file 138-G, 'International Joint Commission re: Pollution of Rainy River,' memorandum re: Pollution of International and Inland Water Courses, 15 April 1954.

15 Frost Papers, box 148, file 224-G, 'Pollution of Border Waters (Agreement between Canada & U.S.),' Mayor W.C. Nelson to Minister of Health, 11 December 1953, and memorandum of Phillips to Frost, 31 March 1954; also box 81, file 138-G, 'International Joint Commission re: Pollution of Rainy River,' memorandum re: Pollution of International and Inland Water Courses, 15 April 1954.

OWRC, Central Records, 'Correspondence: PM & Health Minister,' memorandum: re. Possible Legal Action Regarding Boundary Water Pollution, Ontario-Michigan, 4 November 1954; Frost to Phillips, 10 November 1954; and memorandum: re. Boundary Waters Pollution, 23 November 1954. Also Sarnia City Hall, Sarnia City Council, Minute Book 26, 1953, 2 March 1953, 474; 23 March 1953, 506; 14 September 1953, 718; 5 October 1953, 736; 14 December 1953, 801; Minute Book 27, 1954, 22 March 1954, 130–1.

16 Frost Papers, box 81, file 138-G, 'International Joint Commission re: Pollution of Rainy River,' memorandum re: Pollution of International and Inland Water Courses, 15 April 1954.

17 OWRC, Water Supply and Pollution Control, 'Sarnia Sewage up to Jan. 1st/59,' Department of Health memo, 24 February 1954.

18 Frost Papers, box 81, file 138-G, 'International Joint Commission re: Pollution of Rainy River,' memorandum re: Pollution of International and Inland Water Courses, 15 April 1954.

19 Ibid.

20 See note 15.

21 Sarnia City Council, Minute Book 27, 1954, 1 February 1954, p. 39; 22 March 1954, 130–1. Also Windsor Public Library, Municipal Archives, RG 2 A III – 4/ 18, Reports: Board of Control, 1954, Report 469, 16 February 1954, and RG 2 A III – 4/19, Reports: Board of Control, 1955, Report 515, 2 November 1955.

22 IJC, docket 54-3-1:1, 'Correspondence, 1954,' A.G.L. McNaughton to MacKinnon Phillips, Ontario minister of health, 26 July 1954. See also NA, Water Resources Branch, vol. 342, file 192–2–1, undersecretary of state for external affairs to the chairman of the Advisory Committee on Water Use Policy, 20 October 1955.

23 IJC, docket 54-2-4:2, 'Statements by H.V. Olds,' 7 October 1954, and OWRC, Central Records, 'Correspondence: PM & Health Minister,' memorandum: re. Possible Legal Action Regarding Boundary Water Pollution, Ontario-Michigan, MacKinnon Phillips to Frost, 4 November 1954, and memorandum: re. Boundary Waters Pollution, MacKinnon Phillips to Frost, 23 November 1954.

24 OWRC, Central Records, 'Correspondence: Frost–St Laurent,' St Laurent to Frost, 16 November 1954. This particular exchange of letters also appears in the records of the IJC, the Premier's Office, and both the federal Water Resources Branch and External Affairs.

25 Ibid., Frost to St Laurent, 23 December 1954.

26 Ibid.

27 See Rea, The Prosperous Years, 22–4; Graham, Old Man Ontario, 317–28; and Robert Bothwell, A Short History of Ontario (Edmonton: Hurtig Publishers, 1986), 177, 182–3.

28 IJC, docket 54-3-1:1, 'Correspondence, 1954,' George Spence to A.G.L. McNaughton, 19 August 1954.

29 NA, Water Resources Branch, vol. 341, file 192-2-1, Undersecretary of State for External Affairs to chair of the Advisory Committee on Water Use Policy, 20 October 1955, and ACC 1988–89/059, box 27, file 7358-1, vol. 1, memorandum, Undersecretary of State for External Affairs to Deputy Ministers of Finance, National Health and Welfare, Northern Affairs and Natural Resources, P. Pelletier, PCO, and chair, Canadian Section, IJC, 6 January 1955; and minutes of meeting, 14 January 1955.

30 OWRC, Central Records, 'Correspondence: Frost–St Laurent,' St Laurent to Frost, 24 March 1955.

31 Ibid., Frost to St Laurent, 24 May 1955.

32 OWRC, Subject Files, 'A Brief Prepared by the Water Resources Committee of South Western Ontario on the Development and Control of Water Resources,' 29 April 1955. Also file 210, 'Reports: Digest Prior to OWRC,' C.F. Owen, 'Brief Submitted to Premier Frost by Dr. Clifford H. Reason,' nd. *Globe and Mail*, 23 and 30 April 1955; *Toronto Daily Star*, 11 May 1955; and *The Kitchener-Waterloo Record*, 30 April 1955.

33 IJC, docket 54-3-1:12, 'Correspondence, 1955,' memorandum re: Ontario Water Resources and Supply Committee, 2 September 1955; OWRC, Subject Files, 'Water Resources and Supply Committee, 1954–56,' meeting of 30 November and 7 December 1955 and 20 February 1956. See also OWRC, *First Annual Report: Ontario Water Resources Commission, 1956* (Toronto 1957), 2.

34 Ontario Water Resources and Supply Committee, 'Water and Sewerage Needs in Ontario, 1955–1975,' *Submission of Ontario to the Royal Commission on Canada's Economic Prospects*, 26 January 1956, 139–41. Also Ontario, Legislative Assembly, *Debates*, 28 February 1956, 561.

35 AO, Frost Papers, Subject Files, 'Water Resources Commission, 1956,' press release, 3 May 1956.

36 OWRC, *First Annual Report*, 2–3.

37 For positive responses, see London *Free Press*, 27 February 1956; *Kitchener-Waterloo Record*, 27 February 1956; *Napanee Beaver*, 11 July 1956; Kingston *Whig Standard*, 5 May 1956; and *Globe and Mail*, 25 February, 11 May, and 3 July 1956. For negative reactions to the OWRC, see Conservation Council of Ontario Library and Archives (Toronto, Ontario), CCO Minutes, 1955–6, vol. 4, 'Draft of Brief to the Ontario Water Resources and Supply Committee,' 8 February 1956. See also OWRC, Subject Files, 'Policy Meeting/Correspondence with Prime Minister,' meeting with prime minister, 10 January 1957. [MSA] Michigan Water Resources Commission, 'Minutes of the Stream Control Commission/Water Resources Commission,' 1 March 1957.

38 Ontario, Legislative Assembly, The Ontario Water Resources Commission Act, 1957, c. 88, 1957, sections 39 (4) and (5), 47, 48, and 49; also OWRC, Subject Files, 'Informational Material – Articles and speeches.'

39 OWRC, *Annual Report* (Toronto 1958–71).

40 OWRC, *1962 Annual Report* (Toronto 1963), 4–5. Also OWRC, *The Story of Water* (Toronto 1965), 5–6, and OWRC, *Ontario Water Resources Commission* (Toronto 1965), 5–7. For specific examples of OWRC projects in smaller communities, see the records remaining in OWRC, Municipal Files, and especially Provincial Projects – Water and Sewage. Unfortunately, these files arrived at the Ontario Archives incomplete, but they do give a good overview of OWRC relations with smaller communities. For later examples of OWRC relations with smaller communities, see AO, Records of the Ministry of the Environment, RG 12, Regional Studies – Water and Sewage Files.

41 Ontario, Legislative Assembly, *Debates*, 28 March 1957, 1778–9. The other community that received a mandatory order was Trenton, on the Bay of Quinte. Sarnia City Hall, Sarnia City Council, Minute Book 29, 1956, 22 May 1956, 180; 10 December 1956, p. 356 and 363. See also newspaper accounts the *Sarnia Observer*, 10–12 December 1956 and 9 September 1958; also the *St. Catharines Standard*, 19 and 21 December 1956.

42 Sarnia City Council, Minute Book 29, 1956, city council resolution, 19 November 1956, and Minute Book 30, 1957, 21 January 1957, 29–31.

43 Ibid., Minute Book 29, 1956, council resolution, 19 November 1956.

44 Windsor Public Library, Municipal Archives, RG 1 B III/103, 'Ontario Water Resources, 1959–1961,' E. Royden Colter, Windsor city manager, to Windsor Municipal Council, 29 September 1959.

45 Ibid., memo re: Ontario Water Resources Commission and Its Policy in regard to Sewage Treatment Plants, Interceptor Sewers, and Other Interrelated Sewers, 1–2. Sarnia City Council, Minute Book 29, 1956, city council resolution, 19 November 1956.

46 NA, RG 25, Records of the Department of External Affairs, vol. 6835, file 2871-A140, pt 1, J.B. Adamac, Windsor city clerk, to Prime Minister John Diefenbaker, 22 August 1957. Sarnia City Council, Minute Book 27, 1954, 1 February 1954, 39; 22 March 1954, 130–1; Minute Book 28, 1955, 6 September 1955, 323; 4 April 1955, 145; 25 April 1955, 180; 9 May 1955, 199–200.

47 Water Resources Branch, vol. 342, file 192–2–1, Advisory Committee on Water Uses Policy minutes, 8 November 1955. Core membership included the deputy ministers of northern affairs and national resources (chair), agriculture, finance, fisheries, mines and technical surveys, trade and commerce, as well as the assistant undersecretary of state for external affairs and the assistant secretary to the Cabinet. This group was augmented as the issue warranted.

48 Ibid.

49 Ibid., vol. 341, file 4.5.4.2.c, part 2, 'Pollution Abatement in Canada,' nd [likely 8 November 1956].

50 Department of External Affairs, vol. 6835, file 2871-A-40, pt. 1, J.B. Adamac, Windsor city manager, to Prime Minister Diefenbaker, 22 August 1957; J.W. Holmes, memorandum for the [prime] minister, 26 August 1957; Minister of

Finance Donald Fleming to Diefenbaker, 6 September 1957; Diefenbaker to Richard Thrasher, MP, 24 September 1957.

51 During the 1956 parliamentary session, Diefenbaker introduced a Criminal Code amendment that would have criminalized pollution and brought it under federal jurisdiction as well as provincial authority. University of Saskatchewan, Diefenbaker Canada Centre, Diefenbaker Archives, John G. Diefenbaker Papers, 1940–56 Series, vol. 71, 'Pollution – Water – n.d. 1949–1956.' Also Charles Clay, 'Is Ottawa Planning to Control River Pollution? Why Was Bill 186 Killed?' *Forest and Outdoors* (September 1955), 10, 21–2.

52 The three-year delay can be explained, in part, by Diefenbaker's initial focus on personal priorities such as the South Saskatchewan Dam and the Bill of Rights. He also appears to have lost some of his decisiveness after his majority win in 1958. See Denis Smith, *Rogue Tory: The Life and Legend of John G. Diefenbaker* (Toronto: Macfarlane Walter and Ross, 1995); Christopher MacLennan, 'Toward the Charter: Canadians and the Demand for a National Bill of Rights, 1929–1960' (PhD thesis, University of Western Ontario, 1996); and Robert Bothwell, Ian Drummond, and John English, *Canada since 1945*, rev. ed. (Toronto: University of Toronto Press, 1989), 184–5.

53 Canada, Department of Resources and Development, *Central Mortgage and Housing Corporation Annual Report, 1960* (Ottawa: Queen's Printer, 1961), 20. The interest rate in 1960 was $5\frac{1}{8}$ per cent, which compared favourably with OWRC rates at $5\frac{1}{2}$ per cent. See Memorandum re: Ontario Water Resources Commission and Its Policy in regard to Sewage Treatment Plants, Interceptor Plants and Other Interrelated Sewers (1959).

54 *CMHC Annual Report, 1960*, 20.

55 AO, RG 37, Records of the Ontario Municipal Board, Series 2, OMB Procedure Books, vol. D 28, Q-S, 1957, file D-7321-57. Primary sewage treatment, which most communities with treatment had to that point, merely settled out the solids and larger suspended particles before releasing the effluent. Secondary treatment meant that some degree of aerobic and anaerobic bacterial digestion, to reduce organic content, occurred before the effluent was released. In Sarnia's case it was also treated with chlorine to help prevent the spread of water-borne diseases.

56 OMB Procedure Books, vol. D&E, S-T, 1958, file D 9351-58.

57 City of Sarnia, Minute Book 34, 1961, 3, 21, and 30 January 1961, 36–7. OWRC, Municipal Files, 'Sarnia 1961–62,' A.E. Berry to Robert Given, Sarnia city manager, 15 May 1961, and Given to Berry, 19 May 1961.

58 City of Sarnia, Minute Book 34, 1961, 30 January 1961, 36–8; 13 February 1961, 66–7.

59 Ibid., 30 January 1961, 36–7; 21 March 1961, 109–10; *Sarnia Observer*, 15–17 March 1961.

60 OWRC, Municipal Files, 'Sarnia 1961–62,' W.K. Warrender to David Walker, 24 July 1961.
61 City of Sarnia, Minute Book 35, 1962, 28 May 1962, 245–6; 13 June 1952, 287–8; and 29 June CMHC approval. OMB, Procedure Books, vol. E 55, S, 1960, file E 6213-60; vol. E 65, S, 1961, file E 6958-61, E 6458-61, and E 7644-61. All entries show CMHC-adjusted amounts dated 11 January 1962. For Sault Ste Marie, see OMB, Procedure Books, vol. D&E, file D 9851-58.
62 Windsor Public Library, Municipal Archives. RG 2 A VI/365, 'City of Windsor Report on Sewerage System,' Gore and Storrie, 9 January 1960; also RG 2 A VI/ 372 and 373, 'Windsor Metropolitan Area Sewerage Report, Parts I, II & III and conclusion,' C.G. Russell Armstrong, 16 June 1960.
63 Windsor City Hall, Windsor Council Minutes, July–December 1961, 8 August 1961. The other communities were Riverside, St Clair Beach, Tecumseh, and Sandwich East Township. AO, OWRC, Municipal Files, 'Windsor 1961–62,' E. Royden Colter, Windsor city manager, to A.E. Berry, 17 January 1961, and Berry to J.D. Adamac, Windsor city clerk, 5 July 1961. Windsor Council Minutes, July–December 1963, 16 September, 1963, 7 October, 4 November, and 12 November 1963.

The CCF and Post–Second World War Politics in Ontario

DAN AZOULAY

One of the more prominent developments in Ontario politics after the Second World War was the sudden decline of the province's democratic socialist party, the Co-operative Commonwealth Federation (CCF). In 1943, riding the wave of war-induced public sympathy for interventionist government and for Canada's besieged Soviet ally, the Ontario CCF came out of nowhere to become the province's official opposition. Four more seats would have made it Canada's first avowedly socialist government, an honour bestowed on its Saskatchewan counterpart the following year. Its enemies on the right were quick to take note. A virulent anti-socialist campaign over the next two years beat back the socialist threat, and, in the 1945 election, the CCF finished a disappointing third. Although it managed to regain its official opposition status three years later, largely on the basis of its program for postwar reconstruction, it is clear that the party's best years were behind it. In 1948 the CCF vote was 5 percentage points below that of 1943, which in turn translated into thirteen fewer seats. In the 1951 election it was virtually eliminated as a legislative force, retaining a beachhead of only two seats. Neither its representation nor its popular support changed much over the next dozen years; not even the much heralded reincarnation of the CCF as the New Democratic Party (NDP) in 1961 could reverse the decline. At its lowest point, in 1963, the party held the affections of fewer than 16 per cent of the voters, and there was talk within the ranks of abandoning the whole enterprise and hooking up with the Liberals. Those who use terms such as 'stability' and 'viable three-party system' to describe Ontario politics between 1945 and 1985 would do well to keep the CCF's postwar experience in mind.[1]

Flowing from and accentuating the CCF's electoral decline was the structural disintegration of the party itself. Devastated by the disappointing results of the provincial and federal elections of June 1945, those who had joined the party in droves when the prospects of victory seemed near fell away just as quickly when prospects faded. The Ontario CCF lost nearly half its members between 1945 and 1947. Even more – and about one-third of its revenues – were lost between 1948 and 1951. These reverses represented a severe drain on the financial and human resources the party needed to spread its message to the voters and to run effective election campaigns, resources that were never ample in the first place. To make matters worse, most of those who remained true to the cause found themselves demoralized to the point of inactivity, so that as many as 30 per cent of the party's riding associations and clubs either disappeared or stopped functioning in the late 1940s.[2] In 1947 a CCF organizer in what was once a party stronghold in Northern Ontario reported, 'There is not a single functioning club in the whole riding,' and even ridings that had elected CCFers in 1943 had 'no functioning riding organization.'[3] Membership, revenues, and morale did not recover to their late 1940s' levels until the early 1960s. Electorally and organizationally, then, the postwar period found the province's democratic socialist movement in a much weakened state.

The first objective of this essay is to explain why this occurred – why the CCF went from being a major player on the Ontario political landscape to what one observer has politely called 'a protest movement becalmed.'[4] It will be argued that various 'external' phenomena – factors beyond the party's control – were ultimately to blame and that intraparty developments, such as apathy and poor organization, while important, were simply contributing factors. The second objective is to explain how the CCF managed to avoid outright extinction. Here the emphasis will be placed on the determined efforts of party leaders to rebuild and extend the CCF's organizational foundations through a series of increasingly sophisticated strategies, culminating in the formation of the NDP.

A Protest Movement Becalmed, 1948–51

Certainly a leading cause of the CCF's decline, if not the main one, was the Cold War atmosphere of the period. The widespread fear of communism tended to mute notions of class divisions, state intervention, and socioeconomic equality on which much of the CCF/NDP's philosophy and program was based. In fact, most Ontarians called for an 'end to ideology' and for a united front in the face of the 'international communist threat.' Dissent was viewed as dangerous, even subversive, especially if it took the form of left-wing agitation. 'Throughout the whole of the Western world,' CCF leader Ted Jolliffe told delegates at the party's 1952 convention, 'constructive popular interest in social welfare, in social ownership, in all forms of social progress, is increasingly overshadowed by the clouds of international uncertainty. Domestic issues ... do not receive the attention they deserve because the world is living in fear – not so much fear of poverty at this time as fear of war.'[5] The CCF also suffered from guilt by association, for despite its long-standing policy of opposing communism at every turn, polls at the time indicated that three-quarters of Canadians saw no difference between socialism and communism. 'To much of the general public,' observe Reginald Whitaker and Gary Marcuse in their massive study of Canada's Cold War, 'social democracy, let alone socialism, could not be readily distinguished from Communism. When the latter became an object of public wrath, socialists of any stripe tended to get lumped in.'[6] Without question, the CCF suffered greatly as a result of the widespread anti-communist phobia of the period, and even more so when its enemies openly linked the party with communism, as they did at various times in the period 1945 to 1963.

Another key factor in the decline of the CCF was the tremendous economic prosperity Ontarians enjoyed between 1945 and 1975, a period in which unemployment averaged below 4 per cent, real incomes tripled, and the amount of available leisure time in which to enjoy these gains increased substantially.[7] However, the relationship between economic growth and the popularity of left-wing parties is not straightforward. The traditional model of this relationship posits that economic growth is inversely related to the success of parties that promise to take the economy in new directions.[8] Even intuitively, this theory makes sense, for voters have little reason to support such parties in times of significant economic growth. But recent studies have questioned this theory as far as Canada is concerned. K. Monroe and L. Erikson, for example, found that although economic developments had a significant impact on the support given to third parties in Canadian federal elections between 1954 and 1974, the relationship between economic growth and CCF/NDP support was the opposite of that predicted by the traditional model.[9] Numerous others, as well, have made the point that the CCF/NDP has done better in good times than in bad, such as during the mid-1940s, early 1970s, and late 1980s. In the end, one is left with the conclusion that economic conditions are a poor predictor of CCF/NDP support.

This essay, while it does not purport to provide a detailed analysis of the relationship between the business cycle and CCF/NDP support, tends to confirm the conventional model – that prosperity hurt the CCF/NDP electorally. After having endured six long years of sacrifice, self-restraint, and government regulation during the Second World War, Ontarians were in no mood come peacetime to create a socialist heaven on earth, especially one directed by bureaucrats. Most wanted only to drive their new cars down one of Ontario's many new expressways, mow their suburban lawns, or watch their new television sets. And many more could afford to do these 'frivolous' things because jobs were plentiful, wages were rising, and inflation was low. 'We seemed to wither on the vine [in the 1950s],' recalls former CCF leader Donald MacDonald, 'partly by reason of the whole atmosphere of the time and the apathy of the Eisenhower period ... Everybody just wanted to relax. The normal apathy of the electorate towards politics became even more pronounced with relatively good times.'[10]

Yet economic growth by itself is an insufficient explanation for the party's decline, as the more recent studies prove. To account for the apparent contradictoriness of the studies surrounding this question, we need to look more closely at how the CCF/NDP was perceived by the voters at various times in its history. It could be argued, for example, that as long as the party's image was largely that of an economic reform party, economic growth tended to hurt the party's support. This connection stands to reason, for voters during good times are unlikely to elect a party whose main goal is to restructure the economy. Such was the case in the immediate postwar period, when the CCF/NDP in Ontario and across much of Canada still emphasized comprehensive economic planning as the answer to society's ills. Since becoming the NDP, however, the party's emphasis has shifted. Realizing the unpopularity of its economic agenda, particularly the concept of state-owned industries, the NDP devoted greater attention to social security issues, such as medicare and pensions, and expanded social services.[11] In any case, the NDP was perceived by voters as being very good on social policy concerns, although less competent with respect to economic questions.[12] This view, in turn, would account for the success the party enjoyed across Canada during the still-prosperous years of the early 1970s and the renewed prosperity of the late 1980s. Studies show that in good times voters seem to be quite comfortable with supporting a democratic socialist party that emphasizes social programs, for they know these benefits can be afforded.[13] Depending on how a democratic socialist party's agenda is perceived by the electorate, therefore, economic growth can either benefit or harm the party.

If this theory is valid, how, then, do we explain the massive support for the CCF during the rapidly rising prosperity of the Second World War, when the CCF was clearly an economic reform party, its ideology still firmly rooted in the Regina Manifesto's call to replace capitalism with a more state-managed system? This can be explained by the unique circumstances of the war, when recent memories of the Depression and widespread fear of postwar recession made voters favour comprehensive economic planning such as the CCF proposed. This feeling of uncertainty about the future simply delayed the negative impact of renewed prosperity on the CCF's popularity. As the fear of recession was slowly dissipated by the tremendous growth of the postwar years, so was support for the CCF. By the early 1950s, the CCF's talk of imminent recession and comprehensive planning seemed very much out of place. The only province in which the party was able to retain its popularity was Saskatchewan, and this success was due to the CCF government's de-emphasis on traditional socialist economic policies.[14] In short, barring the presence of unusual historical circumstances, it is possible that economic growth tends to harm support for socialist parties advocating fundamental economic reforms – the Ontario CCF/NDP situation after the war – while benefiting those favouring government-run, redistributive, social security programs.[15]

It is impossible, in any event, to explain the Ontario CCF/NDP's reduced popularity in the postwar period without reference to international and domestic currents. Yet the existing literature on the party tends to explain much of the decline in terms of internal party dynamics, such as poor organization, low morale, changes in program and ideology, and intraparty divisions.[16] Some of these things were no doubt contributing factors, but they are insufficient in explaining the abyss into which the CCF fell after 1945, and not just in Ontario. After all, the CCF lost seats, members, and popular support in all provinces after the war; even the indomitable Saskatchewan CCF suffered, as its membership fell to less than one-third its 1944 level and it lost fourteen seats in the 1948 election.[17]

Furthermore, many of the internal factors contributing to the Ontario party's decline were themselves simply products of external conditions. The party's weak organization, for example, was largely attributable to the growing East-West tension, which was very demoralizing for grassroots CCF members. As left-wing movements around the world came under attack – thereby destroying the dream of postwar international cooperation, peace, and harmony cherished by many socialists during the bleak days of the Second World War – and especially as support for the CCF began to drop, party members became increasingly disillusioned and apathetic. A large number let their membership lapse, while many of those who remained lost interest. The result was a weakening of efforts to sign up or renew memberships, raise money, hold meetings, and find candidates. Fewer members and financial contributions meant a smaller pool of constituency workers, funds, and capable candidates from which the party could draw during elections. All these factors, in turn, translated into a poorer showing: repeated defeats bred further disillusionment, and so on.[18]

The postwar economic boom can be said to have had the same harmful effect.[19]

The overriding influence of postwar national and international events may also provide the basis for questioning a popular theory concerning the evolution of Ontario's party system in the modern era. The theory, first presented by political scientist John Wilson some twenty-five years ago, holds that urbanization and industrialization, and in particular the growth and concentration of the working class, will tend to benefit social democratic parties because of their more secular, progressive, class-oriented appeal.[20] In view of the province's rapidly expanding urban-industrial base after the war, one might have expected the Ontario CCF's popularity to increase in the urban centres.[21] Yet this was not the case. The CCF's popular vote in those ridings that grew quickest economically and demographically after the war fell at least as much as, and probably more than, its vote in the rest of the province.[22] Why this was so requires a far more sophisticated analysis than can be presented here. It may be, as some have suggested, that proletarian support for the CCF in the growing urban areas was offset by the even more rapid growth of the new middle class, a class more predisposed to liberalism than democratic socialism.[23] Just as likely, though, is the uniformly negative effect that unprecedented prosperity and Cold War paranoia had on the party's potential supporters.

This is not to discount the impact that key structural changes in Ontario may have had on CCF support. It is possible, for example, that socioeconomic changes affected CCF support in rural Ontario as they did in rural areas elsewhere. Studies of the CCF out west have concluded that the loss of the party's rural base of support after the war was due largely to the decline of the small family farm and the rise of larger, more mechanized, farms, where farmers came to see themselves more as entrepreneurs and 'less as victims of capitalism,' particularly with the return of prosperity.[24] Ontario farmers underwent a similar transformation, and electoral returns for the ridings closest to the Hamilton-Toronto nexus in the period 1951 to 1963 indicate that this transformation may have exacerbated the CCF's declining support in rural Ontario.[25] It should be remembered, though, that outside the isolated mining towns of the north, the party's rural base was not significant to begin with.

Another influential factor in the CCF's fall to fringe party status was, without question, the flexibility – some would say opportunism – of the Ontario Conservative Party. If it is true, as some have argued, that third parties flourish when traditional parties fail to represent, or are unresponsive to, the interests of large segments of the electorate,[26] then it is equally true that traditional parties flourish – and protest parties suffer – when they *are* responsive to new public concerns. Ontario Tories were nothing if not responsive in these years. During the war and for a short while after, Ontarians joined many others in the Western world in embracing the concept of 'economic planning,' part of a relatively new economic doctrine called Keynesianism, which emphasized the role of government in maintaining near-full employment through regulation and manipulation of the economy. Alongside this doctrine emerged the belief that governments also had an obligation to buffer the individual from the vissicitudes of life by providing a social safety net for those in need.[27] The meteoric rise of the CCF across Canada in the early 1940s owed almost everything to this new way of thinking.

Unfortunately for the Ontario CCF, the traditional parties proved quite adept at accommodating themselves to the new intellectual climate. One month after the CCF's stunning second-place finish in the 1943 election, the new premier, George Drew, issued his now-famous 'Twenty-two Point Program' promising cradle-to-grave social security and a greater role for government in the economy. It included universal health care insurance, income supplements to mothers and the elderly, a substantial increase in funding for schools and hospitals, increased encouragement and regulation of the province's farming and natural resource sectors, extensive public works projects, and even greater protection to organized labour. It was a far-reaching program for its time, strikingly similar to what the CCF had been preaching for years; and the rapid implementation of a good part of it helped the Tories win re-election in 1945 and again in 1948.[28]

When Leslie Frost took over from Drew in 1949, he continued where his predecessor had left off, pouring millions of dollars into the province's infrastructure and social services. Provincial spending on goods, services, and capital formation as a percentage of the Gross Provincial Product increased from 7.4 per cent in 1951 to 13.5 per cent in 1963, with the bulk going into education, health care, and transfers to individuals.[29] Admittedly such measures were far from the sort of comprehensive economic planning or social security that had been foreseen during the latter part of the war – 'economic planning in this broad sense did not survive the immediate post-war years,' notes Rea[30] – but by then the public mood had changed. A buoyant economy and growing suspicion of centralized economic planning, the latter abetted by the Cold War atmosphere of the day, had made the CCF's program largely passé.[31] A more moderate, pragmatic form of state intervention was in vogue. Focusing increasingly on creating the conditions favourable to private investment and on piecemeal improvements to the social security net, this approach also fit more neatly with the province's long-standing 'progressive conservative' political culture.[32] The successive Frost administrations accommodated the new mood well, or at least well enough to get re-elected time and again. The CCF/NDP, meanwhile, came dangerously close to confirming American historian Richard Hofstadter's well-known maxim that 'third parties, like bees, having stung, must die.'[33]

In addition to the Tory party's skill in stealing the CCF/NDP's thunder, there was Frost's immense personal popularity and cunning. By carefully cultivating the down-to-earth, folksy public image that was his trademark and by diffusing his opponents' assaults with his fulsome stock of charm and anodynes, he carried the Conservative Party to massive victories in these years. Donald MacDonald explains:

> There were many Leslie Frosts. One, the most familiar to the public, was the grandfather figure, usually viewed from afar, but seen in closer proximity only at meetings or on television, rarely attacking his political opponents, but rather chatting about local history and the merits of the province of Ontario in general ... Another was the charmer, who subjected visiting delegations ... to a process of political seduction that became legendary ... They were greeted with warm handshakes, softened with the friendly arm-around-the-shoulder confidentiality, and out-talked from start to finish ... I dubbed him the Great Tranquilizer.[34]

Frost's successor, John Robarts, was also a capable and appealing figure. Although less the politician than Frost, Robarts's low-key, pragmatic management style was appropriate to the even bigger role government was being asked to play by the early 1960s. Both Tory leaders were well served, as well, by skilled provincial organizers: Alex McKenzie and Eddie Goodman under Frost, and Ernie Jackson under Robarts. To some extent, therefore, the decline and stagnation of the CCF/NDP was due to the exceptional political and organizational leadership with which it had to contend in these years.

In view of these powerful external factors – the Cold War, economic prosperity, and co-optation of the left's agenda – circumstances clearly beyond the party's control, it is difficult to see how the Ontario CCF/NDP could have done anything differently to improve its position in this bleak period. 'Looking back,' veteran party activist David Lewis wrote in his memoirs, 'I am confirmed in the feeling I had at the time that the CCF decline could not be reversed. With MacDonald as the leading CCF organizer and [Henry] Weisbach as head of political action in the CCL [Canadian Congress of Labour], our talent simply could not be improved upon.'[35]

What's more, the CCF tried almost everything to revitalize itself, yet the impact on its popular support was minimal.

Reviving the Party, 1952–63

How did the Ontario CCF survive as a political entity in spite of the vicious spiral of rank-and-file apathy and poor election results? Quite simply, it survived because a core of dedicated individuals at the highest levels of the party took it upon themselves to rebuild and expand the party's basic organization. Towards this end, strategies were adopted ranging from the quite rudimentary to the sophisticated and grand, strategies aimed at restoring membership levels, raising money, making members more active on a year-round basis, and extending CCF clubs and riding associations to new areas of the province.[36]

The rebuilding process began shortly after the 1951 election, when the CCF's representation was slashed from twenty-one seats to two. Shocked and disillusioned, party leaders concluded that the main problem was one of weak basic organization. Membership levels, finances, and the number of CCF clubs had all fallen dramatically in a number of ridings since 1948, and the leaders felt that the party lacked an organization strong enough to convey its message, raise much needed funds, recruit appealing candidates, or get its supporters to the polls on election day. The leaders were also aware that this organizational weakness was merely symptomatic of a more serious underlying problem – the severe demoralization and apathy a growing number of party members suffered following the CCF's plunge in popularity after the heady years of the Second World War. The quick reversal in the party's fortunes proved too difficult for many grassroots members to endure and, as a result, they had either allowed their membership to lapse or became inactive.[37] The necessary rebuilding process would have to be directed and largely carried out by the top echelons of the party.

In 1952 the CCF's highest bodies – the Provincial Council and the Executive (which conducted party business out of the Provincial Office in Toronto) – shifted their organizational emphasis from promoting membership education and recreation to recruiting new members, renewing old ones, raising money, and reviving moribund riding associations. The Executive instructed the party's two provincial organizers, Fred Young and C.C. 'Doc' Ames, as well as members of the Provincial Council, to encourage riding associations and clubs in their areas to concentrate on basic organization. Where no CCF group existed, they were to find people willing to start one. The leaders hoped that the party's 'machine' would be sufficiently strengthened in time for the next election. Results in the short term, however, were not encouraging, as few members were willing to carry on the organizers' work or follow through on their advice. 'The present ... picture in regard to membership and organization is not at all satisfactory,' reported the chair of the Executive's organization committee in October of that year. 'The general picture is one of the organizers working hard to maintain the membership at its present level.'[38] It was an assessment that would be heard again and again over the next few years, as one membership or fund-raising drive after another faltered on the shoals of rank-and-file apathy.

Typical of the problem party leaders and organizers faced was the 'CCF Brigade,' a gimmick designed by the party's organization committee in 1954 to double membership levels in two years. All Provincial Council members were asked to pledge themselves to signing up fifty new members each, in turn setting an example for the rank and file to follow. By year's end, more than ninety persons had enlisted in the brigade – half of them council members – and over five hundred new members had been signed up as a result. Unfortunately, these gains were offset, as the organization committee remarked in frustration, by 'the failure of ridings to keep [membership] renewals up-to-date,' so that total party membership had, in fact, fallen during the course of what was otherwise a successful campaign![39] Such a phenomenon was common in these years. The CCF's peripatetic and overextended organizing staff would help revitalize certain riding associations, only to have these groups lapse into inactivity once the organizers moved on to other ridings. The influx of new members for one riding would be regularly offset by losses, through lapsed memberships, in another. Consequently, with local members generally unwilling to assume the responsibilities of sustaining and building constituency organization on their own, membership levels (and hence finances) grew only slowly in the 1950s.

Efforts by the leadership to strengthen the CCF's basic organization were not always as crude as the brigade or the annual spring membership drive. There, the sole object was simply to lengthen the membership lists so as to acquire the much needed workers and funds to conduct at least the semblance of a serious election campaign. Over time, as membership levels slowly recovered, party leaders could afford to develop more sophisticated strategies. One such strategy, adopted in earnest once the brigade wound down, was known as 'zone and poll' organization. Ridings were divided into zones of approximately ten polls each. A handful of party supporters, armed with lists of members and sympathetic contacts, then canvassed a zone, where they distributed party literature and looked for persons willing to assume responsibility for maintaining organization in the zone (and, ideally, in each poll) through zone and poll 'committees.' New recruits willing to form such committees would be trained in canvassing techniques, often through 'regional education conferences.' They were then on their own to organize their zone or poll further, by seeking additional supporters and workers, renewing memberships, distributing literature, and raising money. Meanwhile, the original 'zone captains' would begin organizing adjacent zones in like fashion. The primary goal of the plan was not simply to obtain more members, but to create a more continually active membership, so that at election time the party could mobilize a large corps of experienced volunteers in each zone to perform electioneering duties. As with the brigade, however, the strategy was only of limited success. Although the Provincial Office worked hard to sell the concept to the ridings, it was not embraced as widely, nor was it as enduring, as party leaders had hoped. Local indifference remained a chronic problem.[40]

Without question, the most ambitious project undertaken by the CCF in its drive to stay alive was the formation of a 'New Party,' formally christened the New Democratic Party in the fall of 1961 after three years of frenetic activity. The details of this event have been documented elsewhere and need not be repeated here.[41] Suffice it to say that the New Party was a federal CCF initiative, firmly backed by the Canadian Labour Congress(CLC) and most provincial CCF parties, aimed at reviving the democratic socialist movement across Canada by broadening its base to include new 'liberal-minded' groups, such as farmers, unionists, and especially the urban middle class. What the Ontario CCF saw in the project was a golden opportunity to strengthen its basic organization. As such, it carefully portrayed the party as genuinely new and 'broadly based.' However, it involved the 'liberal-minded' in the gestation phase of the New Party only to the extent needed to support this image and, more important, fill gaps in the CCF's organization. The New Party Clubs, into which the CCF and the CLC hoped to attract urban, middle-class professionals, were promoted only in ridings where the CCF organization was weak. The clubs, in other words, were but an adjunct to the CCF's existing organization. Behind this shrewd, if deceptive strategy was the belief that image alone would attract new members to the NDP, while the CCF could retain its existing members – who had the unfortunate habit of slipping away if neglected – and, further, enter the NDP as the dominant partner in the new left-wing alliance. It almost worked. By the time of the founding convention, the New Party Club section was nearly as large as the CCF itself, and plans were enthusiastically made for integrating club members into regular NDP constituency associations as full party members. However, post-founding fatigue and a string of distracting and costly elections laid waste to these plans. In the end, the NDP's regular membership was no larger than the CCF's had been at the beginning of the New Party project.

In addition to the various schemes devised by party leaders, and carried out with much dedication and personal sacrifice by the party's tiny, underpaid staff, there is one other factor that cannot be ignored in the survival of the CCF/NDP in these years – the role played by Donald C. MacDonald, the party's provincial leader for much of this period. Few, if any, politicians in the province's history have displayed as much energy and enthusiasm for the political game as did MacDonald in his seventeen years as leader, both in the legislature and on the hustings. He was, in a word, indefatigable. Between elections he undertook frequent tours of the province, finding new members, organizing new clubs, seeking out candidates to run for the CCF, addressing the faithful at innumerable party gatherings, and preaching the party gospel on radio and television. But it was at election time that MacDonald really outdid himself. During the 1963 election, for example, he drove close to 20,000 kilometres, addressed forty-one public meetings, issued at least forty press releases, and spent over thirty hours on the phone with his advisers. In addition, he was forced to raise money along the way to finance his own campaign, as party funds were being diverted to the organizing staff and costly advertising.[42]

MacDonald was also the key figure in the party's tiny caucus. From 1955 to 1959 the CCF's three-person caucus had twenty-two government departments to cover as opposition 'critics' – a daunting task indeed. MacDonald covered eighteen of them. Nevertheless, he effectively and relentlessly pursued the Tory governments on many of the issues CCFers had talked about for years, including health insurance, expanded social programs, affordable housing, agricultural marketing schemes, higher corporation taxes, jobs, higher wages, grants to municipalities, and conservation. What's more, he became quite adept at exposing government wrong doing, including the infamous 'highways scandal' of 1954 and the Northern Ontario Natural Gas scandal of 1959. So strong and so persistent were his attacks on these and other occasions that Tory backbenchers quickly dubbed him 'Mac the Knife' and, for the 1950s at least, the CCF gained the reputation as the only real opposition in a perennially lop-sided legislature.[43]

While MacDonald's precise impact on the party and public is difficult to measure, it is clear that he at least attracted new members to the party, inspired existing ones to greater efforts, and gave the CCF/NDP a higher public profile. As the Provincial Council observed shortly after MacDonald's accession as leader, 'his activities have resulted in outstanding publicity in both press and radio throughout the province,' and 'he [has] stimulated renewed enthusiasm for the CCF.'[44] 'Doc' Ames, the party's Northern Ontario organizer, provides further corroboration. 'We are all very proud of the job that you are doing,' he told MacDonald in early 1956. '[It] appears to be giving some of our people more heart for the task ahead.'[45] MacDonald's impact was noticed beyond party circles as well. 'The CCF ... is a very lively party,' wrote columnist Don O'Hearn in 1955: 'This stems primarily from the activities of one man: leader Donald MacDonald. The fact is that for a one-man show, Mr. MacDonald is carrying out a mammoth task. He is organizer, leader and publicity man rolled into one ... The buildings see a lot of Mr. Macdonald. The province sees a lot of him. And the press hears a lot from him. He is always on the go, and he usually has a statement ready on any issue of importance. The impression inevitably is left that the CCF is an active party, and this is going to win it votes.'[46] A more succinct account of MacDonald's impact would be hard to find. As such, Morley's observation that the CCF's tireless leader 'almost single-handedly ... kept the party alive in the darkest days' is only a slight exaggeration.[47]

Notwithstanding the prodigious efforts of people like MacDonald, Young, Ames, and several other key figures at the provincial level – Marjorie Wells as chair of the organization committee and Ken Bryden as provincial secretary, for example – it is tempting to conclude that their efforts to rebuild the party were all for naught. Party membership fluctuated wildly in the 1950s and did not recover to its 1948 level until 1962, in a province whose population had grown substantially in the same period. Yet it is clear that the decision of the leadership to concentrate on restoring the CCF's organizational vitality, despite the indifference and, at times, outright opposition of many grassroots members,[48] brought the CCF back from the brink of extinction in the early 1950s and kept it a viable entity – able to conduct elections and thus retain a public presence and a small foothold in the legislature – until the political winds began shifting in the party's favour in the mid-1960s. When that happened, the party not only had an organization in place to capitalize on the new climate, but had at its disposal a tough and experienced (if somewhat weary) core of organizers who were able to pass their hard-learned lessons down to a new generation of Ontario socialists, including Stephen Lewis, James Renwick, Gerald Caplan, and John Brewin.

Conclusion

There is much about the history of the Ontario CCF/NDP in the period 1948 to 1963 that has not been said in this short account. No effort has been made, for example, to analyse the changes to the party's structure or its program that took place in these years. Nor have the party's changing relations with the labour movement or its internal divisions been discussed. Space limitations are obviously one reason. But another is that such changes as did occur were minor and superficial – the CCF/NDP remained essentially a democratic socialist 'mass' party – compared with the more important alterations in both the strength of the party, internally and at the polls, and in the methods adopted to cope with these changes. The decline of the Ontario CCF after the Second World War, as argued, stemmed primarily from factors beyond the party's control, particularly the Cold War, a vibrant provincial economy, and the efficacy of the Ontario Conservative Party. The resulting drop in the CCF's popularity led to an exodus of party members and a pervasive feeling of hopelessness among those who remained, a situation that further weakened the CCF politically. Only the determined intervention of a small group of party leaders, committed to the notion of reviving the party through organizational means (as opposed to simply preaching socialism to the voters, as CCF 'purists' favoured) saved the party from its death spiral.[49] Over time the methods they devised became more complex and, in the case of the New Party, even somewhat deceptive, but the goal remained the same: to preserve the CCF as a viable political entity so it might live to fight, and eventually win, another day.

NOTES

1 For more on the Ontario CCF's sudden rise during the war and efforts to counter it, see G. Caplan, *The Dilemma of Canadian Socialism: The CCF in Ontario* (Toronto: McClelland & Stewart, 1973). Recent analyses proclaiming the stability and competitiveness of Ontario's 'three-party system' in the postwar years include I. Drummond, 'Voting Behaviour: Counting the Change,' in G. White, ed., *The Government and Politics of Ontario*, 4th ed. (Scarborough, Ont.: Nelson, 1990), 249; K. Brownsey and M. Howlett, 'Class Structure and Political Alliances in an Industrialized Society,' in K. Brownsey and M. Howlett, eds., *The Provincial State: Politics in Canada's Provinces and Territories* (Toronto: Copp Clark Pitman, 1992), 147–74; P. McCormick, 'Provincial Party Systems, 1945–1993,' in A. Tanguay and A. Gagnon, eds., *Canadian Parties in Transition*, 2nd ed. (Scarborough, Ont.: Nelson, 1996), 349–71; and D. MacDonald, 'Ontario's Political Culture: Conservatism with a Progressive Component,' *Ontario History* 86, 4 (December 1994): 297–317. For an older version, see J. Wilson and D. Hoffman, 'Ontario: A Three Party System in Transition,' in M. Robin, ed., *Canadian Provincial Politics* (Scarborough, Ont.: Prentice Hall, 1972).

2 L. Zakuta, *A Protest Movement Becalmed: A Study of Change in the CCF* (Toronto: University of Toronto Press, 1964), 75–6, 82–3, 110; National Archives of Canada (NA), Federal CCF/NDP Papers, CCF/NDP, 'Membership Reports,' appended to Minutes of Ontario CCF/NDP Provincial Council/Executive, 1948–63; Ontario, Chief Electoral Officer, *Returns from General Elections and By-Elections*, 1948–1963; Colin Campbell, *Canadian Political Facts, 1945–1976* (Toronto: Methuen, 1977), 116.

3 Zakuta, *A Protest Movement Becalmed*, 76.

4 Ibid.

5 Federal CCF/NDP Papers, CCF, Ontario, 'Report of the Eighteenth Annual Convention.'

6 R. Whitaker and G. Marcuse, *Cold War Canada: The Making of a National Insecurity State, 1947–1957* (Toronto: University of Toronto Press, 1994), 285.

7 J.K. Rea, *The Prosperous Years: The Economic History of Ontario 1939–1975* (Toronto: University of Toronto Press, 1985), 33, 242.

8 A. Downs, *An Economic Theory of Democracy* (New York: Harper and Row, 1957).

9 K. Monroe and L. Erickson, 'The Economy and Political Support: The Canadian Case,' in J. Wearing, ed., *The Ballot and Its Message: Voting in Canada* (Toronto: Copp Clark Pitman, 1991), 195–222.

10 Archives of Ontario, Ontario Historical Studies Series, Donald MacDonald, interview, 6 June 1972, transcript.

11 D. Morton, *The New Democrats, 1961–1986: The Politics of Change* (Toronto: Copp Clark Pitman, 1986), 65, 90; A. Whitehorn, *Canadian Socialism: Essays on the CCF–NDP* (Toronto: Oxford University Press, 1992), 50–65; L. McDonald, *The Party That Changed Canada: The New Democratic Party Then and Now* (Toronto: Macmillan, 1987), chapter 7.

12 Monroe and Erickson, 'The Economy and Political Support,' 202.

13 As Monroe and Erikson note, 'support for the NDP increases as personal income and employment rise, suggesting the NDP's social welfare programs may be viewed as luxury goods reserved for times of economic prosperity.' Ibid.; A. Whitehorn, 'Audrey McLaughlin and the Decline of the Federal NDP,' in H. Thorburn, ed., *Party Politics in Canada*, 7th ed. (Scarborough, Ont.: Prentice Hall Canada, 1996), 315–35.

14 T. McLeod and I. McLeod, *Tommy Douglas: The Road to Jerusalem* (Edmonton: Hurtig, 1987), 181.

15 This is not to say that the reverse was true – that in hard times, support for the CCF/NDP rose. Severe recessions, as in the 1930s and early 1990s, did not seem to benefit the party. It may be that in situations of severe economic decline, people are primarily concerned about daily survival and less willing to risk their meagre standard of living on untried, radical solutions. Monroe and Erickson speculate, further, that recessions have not benefited the NDP because people doubted it could solve economic problems, and because an extensive social security system was already in place to buffer the recession's impact and keep people from turning to the NDP. Still, as Maurice Pinard has demonstrated for the Social Credit Party in Quebec in the early 1960s, 'economic strain' – the sudden deterioration of economic conditions after relatively long periods of economic prosperity – can work to the benefit of third parties. The significant support given to protest parties generally in the 1930s, parties offering unorthodox solutions to social and economic problems, is further

proof of this suggestion. M. Pinard, *The Rise of a Third Party: A Study in Crisis Politics* (New Jersey: Prentice Hall, 1971); Monroe and Erickson, 'The Economy and Political Support'; N. Penner, 'The Past, Present, and Uneasy Future of the New Democratic Party,' in A. Tanguay and A. Gagnon, eds., *Canadian Parties in Transition* (Scarborough, Ont.: Nelson, 1996), 89–105.

16 See, for example, J.T. Morley, *Secular Socialists: The CCF/NDP in Ontario, A Biography* (Montreal: McGill-Queen's University Press, 1984), 56–9; G. Horowitz, *Canadian Labour in Politics* (Toronto: University of Toronto Press, 1968), 146–57; Zakuta, *A Protest Party Becalmed*, 71–84, 112, 128, who blames the fall on the CCF's 'decline in ideological distinctiveness'; and W. Young, *Anatomy of a Party: The National CCF, 1932–61* (Toronto: University of Toronto Press, 1969), chapter 5.

17 C. Nichol, 'In Pursuit of the Voter: The British Columbia CCF, 1945–50,' in J. Brennan, ed., *'Building the Cooperative Commonwealth': Essays on the Democratic Socialist Tradition in Canada*, (Regina: Canadian Plains Research Center, 1984), 133–4; D. Steeves, *The Compassionate Rebel: Ernest Winch and the Growth of Socialism in Western Canada* (Vancouver: J.J. Douglas, 1960), 176–86; R. Hunter, 'Social Democracy in Alberta: From the CCF to the NDP,' in L. Pratt, ed., *Socialism and Democracy in Alberta: Essays in Honour of Grant Notley* (Edmonton: NeWest Press, 1986), 58; N. Wiseman, *Social Democracy in Manitoba: A History of the CCF/NDP* (Winnipeg: University of Manitoba Press, 1983), 65–6; McLeod and McLeod, *Tommy Douglas*, 184.

18 Federal CCF/NDP Papers, CCF, Ontario, Minutes of Provincial Council, 10 and 11 February, 29 September 1951, 12 and 13 January 1952, and 'Report of the Eighteenth Annual Convention'; Loretta LePalm, Smiths Falls, Ontario, to MacDonald, 19 April 1951.

19 In contrast to this line of argument, political theorist Maurice Duverger argues that membership in mass parties is unaffected by such external forces as economic fluctuations or war and, instead, is 'very much more sensitive to problems that are truly party problems,' especially internal division. In the case of the Ontario CCF/NDP, however, its severe loss of members largely preceded the serious divisions of the early 1950s, and its membership began to increase shortly thereafter. M. Duverger, *Political Parties: Their Organization and Activity in the Modern State*, 3rd ed. (New York: John Wiley and Sons, 1966), 84–5.

20 J. Wilson, 'Towards a Redefinition of the Nature of the Canadian Political System,' *Canadian Journal of Political Science* 7 (September 1974): 438–83; Drummond, 'Voting Behaviour: Counting the Change,' 247–8; Brownsey and Howlett, 'Class Structure and Political Alliances in an Industrialized Society.' An interpretation similar to Wilson's is presented by N.H. Chi and G. Perlin, 'The NDP: A Party in Transition,' in H. Thorburn, ed., *Party Politics in Canada*, 4th ed. (Toronto: Prentice Hall, 1979), chapter 16.

21 The urban population of Canada as a whole increased from 54 per cent of the total population in 1941 to 63 per cent in 1966, with much of the increase occurring in Ontario's Golden Horseshoe region in the south-central part of the province. This area, which contained half of Ontario's population in the 1940s, grew to include two-third's of its residents by the 1960s. It also led the way in terms of industrial growth, with one-third of the increase in the net value of Canadian manufacturing from 1947 to 1961 coming from this region – in particular, from the cities of Toronto, Hamilton, Oshawa, London, and Kitchener. F.H. Leacy, ed., *Historical Statistics of Canada*, 2nd ed. (Ottawa: Statistics Canada, 1983), A67–74; Rea, *The Prosperous Years*, 30; D. Kerr and D. Holdsworth, eds., *The Historical Atlas of Canada*, vol. 3: *Addressing the Twentieth Century* (Toronto: University of Toronto Press, 1990), plate 51.

22 Between the 1951 and 1955 elections, for example, the CCF's popular vote fell by 2.5 per cent across the province, while in Toronto and Hamilton it fell by 2.2 per cent. When the urban centres of Brantford, London, Niagara Falls, and the Yorks (just north of Toronto) are included, the figure jumps to 4 per cent. Ontario, *Returns from General Elections*, 1951 and 1955.

23 J. Richards, 'The Decline and Fall of Agrarian Socialism,' in S.M. Lipset, *Agrarian Socialism: The Cooperative Commonwealth Federation in Saskatchewan*, rev. ed. (Berkeley, Cal.: University of California Press, 1971), 364–92.

24 S. Silverstein, 'Occupational Class and Voting Behaviour: Electoral Support of a Left-Wing Protest Movement in a Period of Prosperity,' in Lipset, *Agrarian Socialism*, 364–92; quote from McLeod and McLeod, *Tommy Douglas*, 211.

25 Between 1951 and 1963, the CCF/NDP's popular vote in the eleven ridings adjacent to the Greater Metropolitan Toronto and Hamilton areas experienced a net loss of 10 percentage points, compared with net loss of 3.6 points across the province. Ontario, *Returns from General Elections, 1951–63*; Rea, *The Prosperous Years*, 134–50.

26 A. Gagnon and A. Tanguay, 'Minor Parties in the Canadian Political System: Origins, Functions, Impact,' in Gagnon and Tanguay, eds., *Canadian Parties in Transition*, 106–34.

27 Rea, *The Prosperous Years*, 11–16.

28 J. Manthorpe, *The Power and the Tories: Ontario Politics – 1943 to the Present* (Toronto: Macmillan, 1974), 31–7; N. Penner, *From Protest to Power: Social Democracy in Canada, 1900–Present* (Toronto: James Lorimer, 1992), 80–3; Rea, *The Prosperous Years*, 17–19,

29 Rea, *The Prosperous Years*, 225.

30 Ibid., 21.

31 Rea notes that, by this point, 'the concern in Ontario soon shifted from unemployment to the ability of the government to provide the infrastructure investment in highways, electric power generating capacity, and municipal services needed to meet the demands of a rapidly expanding and industrializing society.' *The Prosperous Years*, 22.

32 Ibid., 23–4; MacDonald, 'Ontario's Political Culture'; S.F. Wise, 'The Ontario Political Culture: A Study in Complexities,' in G. White, ed., *The Government and Politics of Ontario*, 4th ed. (Scarborough, Ont.: Nelson, 1990), 44–59.

33 Cited in K. McNaught, 'Socialism and the Canadian Political Tradition,' in S. Djwa and R. Macdonald, eds., *On F.R. Scott* (Montreal: McGill-Queen's University Press, 1983), 91.

34 D.C. MacDonald, *The Happy Warrior: Political Memoirs* (Markham, Ont.: Fitzhenry and Whiteside, 1988), 345.

35 D. Lewis, *The Good Fight: Political Memoirs, 1909–1958* (Toronto: Macmillan, 1981), 415.

36 Riding 'clubs' were distinct from riding 'associations.' The party's constitution allowed members in any riding to form clubs for 'social, educational and political purposes ... provided that, for the purposes of electing candidates and fighting election campaigns, members of all clubs in the constituency shall act through the constituency association.' CCF, Ontario, 'Constitution of the CCF (Ontario Section), April 1955,' in Zakuta, *A Protest Movement Becalmed*, appendix B.

37 Zakuta, *A Protest Movement Becalmed*, 112–37; D. Azoulay, *Keeping the Dream Alive: The Survival of the Ontario CCF/NDP, 1950–1963* (Montreal: McGill-Queen's University Press, 1997), 20–1, 26–9.

38 McMaster University Archives, Hamilton, Ontario CCF/NDP Collection, CCF, Ontario, Report of Organization Committee to Provincial Council, 4 and 5 October 1952.

39 *CCF News*, November 1954, January 1955; Federal CCF/NDP Papers, CCF, Ontario, Minutes of Executive Committee, 13 November 1954 (quote); Membership Report, October 1954, appended to Minutes of Executive Committee, 13 November 1954.

40 Federal CCF/NDP Papers, Donald MacDonald, Memorandum on Proposals for Ontario Organization, January 1952, and CCF, Ontario, Minutes of Provincial Council, 8 September, 8 December 1956; *CCF News*, February, November 1956; Ontario CCF/NDP Papers, CCF, Ontario, Minutes of Provincial Executive, 21 November 1956.

41 See D. Azoulay, '"This March Forward to a Genuine People's Party"? Rivalry and Deception in the Founding of the Ontario NDP, 1958–1961,' *Canadian Historical Review* 74, 1 (1993): 1–27.

42 'MacDonald's Day Spent on Foot Greeting Electors in York South,' *Globe and Mail*, 25 September 1963; MacDonald, *The Happy Warrior*, chapters 4–7; Azoulay, *Keeping the Dream Alive*.

43 MacDonald, *Happy Warrior*, 14–15; Azoulay, *Keeping the Dream Alive*, 104–5.

44 Ontario CCF/NDP Papers, CCF, Ontario, 'Report of the Twentieth Annual Convention, May 22–4, 1954.

45 Queen's University Archives, Donald MacDonald Papers, Ames, Organization Report, 29 February 1956.

46 Cited in *CCF News*, December 1955.

47 Morley, *Secular Socialists*, xvii.

48 The strongest opposition within the party to the emphasis on basic organization in this period came from the so-called Ginger Group in the early 1950s. For
more on this phenomenon, see D. Azoulay, 'The Cold War Within: The Ginger
Group, the Woodsworth Foundation, and the Ontario CCF, 1944–53,' *Ontario
History* 84 (June 1992): 79–104.

49 In his master's thesis on the CCF in Northern Ontario, Peter Campbell argues
that academics have placed too much emphasis on the role of party leaders in
'keeping the party together during the lean years between 1945 and 1961,' and
that, in fact, 'rank and file CCFers made an important contribution to the
survival of the CCF as a party.' But Campbell's conclusions are too general and
are based almost entirely on a handful of interviews. Notwithstanding the
efforts of a 'dedicated core of activists,' the hard evidence (especially the
organizers' reports, including Ames in the north) clearly points to an overall
decline in activism at the local level in this period. Campbell himself admits
that much of the local activity in the north was due to the work of Ames and
that the inspiration of the leadership kept the local people going during the
hard times. P. Campbell, '"Truly Grass Roots People,": The Cooperative Commonwealth Federation in Northern Ontario' (MA thesis, Laurentian University, 1986), 1, 55, 117, 131.

The Ontario-Quebec Axis: Postwar Strategies in Intergovernmental Negotiations

P.E. BRYDEN

In the years between Confederation and the Second World War, Ontario developed a fairly consistent pattern in its dealings with Ottawa. Under the early leadership of Oliver Mowat, Ontario positioned itself as the guardian of provincial rights and the first line of defence against the enormous powers the British North America Act granted to the central government. By challenging the extent of federal powers in the courts and by broadening the force of provincial jurisdiction through the careful development of patronage networks, Mowat solidified the position of Ontario in relation to the federal government and more than earned the title of 'father of provincial rights.' The confrontations between the two levels of government were acrimonious, but they played out in the relatively sterile environment of the courtroom and hinged on the sometimes arcane interpretation of constitutional law.

By the 1930s, however, the battle had turned more personal. Although Premier Mitch Hepburn resolutely defended the Mowat position that provincial jurisdiction needed to be extended, the context of depression and war served only to heighten the level of antipathy between the two governments. Convinced that Prime Minister Mackenzie King was dealing ineffectively with both the massive unemployment of the Great Depression and the need for full-scale deployment of resources during the Second World War, Hepburn engaged in an all-out war of his own against the federal government in general and King in particular. It seems, then, that Ontario's strategy in dealing with Ottawa was remarkably well established: using confrontational tactics to defend and extend the power of the province at all costs.[1]

As enduring as this approach seemed from the vantage point of mid-century, Ontario's relationship with Ottawa in the years since the end of the

Second World War has been characterized by a surprising level of cooperation and compromise. In areas of social policy, economic arrangements, and
constitutional renewal, Ontario politicians have generally supported the
national interest. By no means, however, did Ontario become merely a
puppet of the central government, nor did it support Ottawa's initiatives at
the expense of clear provincial priorities. Instead, Ontario began to pursue a
strategy of articulating a 'national' position on issues of contest between the
two levels of government – a position that was sometimes in harmony with
that being taken in Ottawa, but more often was in contrast to the federal
position or in advance of it. This approach, which in many ways saw
Ontario attempting to usurp the role of national government from Ottawa,
demanded the development of alliances at the provincial level. Without
support for their proposals on social, economic, or constitutional change,
Ontario politicians could not hope to have them adopted on the national
stage. The development of a close relationship across provincial boundaries
became far more important to Ontario's overall intergovernmental strategy
in the postwar years than it ever had been before.[2]

The relationship Ontario enjoyed with Quebec, disparagingly referred to
as the Ontario-Quebec Axis, was by far the most important of those links
forged in the postwar years, and it was to have its most lasting significance
on issues of constitutional reform. Growing out of the unlikely alliance that
developed between Ontario's George Drew and Quebec's Maurice Duplessis
at the Dominion-Provincial Conference on Reconstruction in 1945 and 1946,
the axis reached its apotheosis in the late 1960s. Currying favour with
Quebec had two important effects on Ontario's intergovernmental strategy.
First, it allowed Ontario to put some added weight behind its constitutional
proposals and thereby offer serious alternatives to the federal position.
Second, Ontario was forced to modify its own position in light of the
relative strength or weakness of the connection with Quebec. The implications of this alliance for Canadian federalism more generally were profound. By taking the initiative for constitutional negotiation away from
Ottawa in the 1960s, Ontario was responsible for opening a discussion that
has continued, virtually unabated, for more than thirty years.

The election of George Drew as premier of Ontario in 1943, replacing the
Liberal dynasty of Mitch Hepburn, was not in itself an event that suggested
a sea change in the nature of the relationship the province experienced with
Ottawa. While far less erratic in both life and politics than the hard-living
Hepburn, Drew shared his predecessor's view of Mackenzie King. By the
time Drew became premier of Ontario, he had long since reached the
conclusion that King was duplicitous. He denied the existence of a 'feud,'
but noted: 'It is essential that we assert ourselves in provincial matters.'[3]

Conventional wisdom on the Dominion-Provincial Conference on Reconstruction of 1945–6 holds that it was the last gasp of the old rivalry between Ontario and Ottawa. The conference, called to discuss the dominion proposals for postwar reconstruction, ended in the spring of 1946 without any agreement being reached. The blame for the failure of the two levels of government to reach any conclusions on fiscal arrangements, social policies, and a system of equalization grants has generally been placed squarely on Drew's shoulders.[4] Although some revisionist scholarship has contended that the federal government's refusal to separate the social and equalization policies from the continuation of unpleasant wartime tax rental agreements, in conjunction with King's ideological resistance to an active central state, was really to blame for the conference's failure, no one has suggested that Drew was anything other than difficult.[5]

A closer examination of the conference suggests that, rather than being the final chapter in intergovernmental acrimony, it was instead the first verse of a new approach on the part of Ontario to dealing with Ottawa. Drew played a pivotal role in ensuring that there would be an intergovernmental discussion over the shape of postwar Canada. He first broached the subject of holding a conference devoted to considering postwar planning in early January 1944, when the tide had begun to turn in favour of the Allied Powers, but 'before the Dominion and Provincial Governments committed themselves to postwar legislation.' A copy of this letter was sent by the Prime Minister's Office to all provincial premiers, whereupon it became 'the basis for a proposal for a conference' and Drew began to deal more directly with his provincial colleagues.[6] What followed was an eighteen-month period of delay, obfuscation, blame casting, and general confusion. Drew repeatedly called for a conference to be convened; King repeatedly delayed. Federal government officials asked for provincial statistical material to be forwarded to Ottawa to assist in the preparation of their reconstruction proposals; Ontario officials insisted on knowing to what end it would be used, and ended up being charged with impeding the work towards opening a conference.[7] According to Leslie Frost, the provincial treasurer, King was 'beating over some old straw and missing the real point.'[8] Between the time Drew first raised the possibility of intergovernmental discussion on reconstruction in January 1944 and the start of the conference in August 1945, the tenor of Ontario's correspondence shifted from that of polite requests to barely contained fury, but, more than merely becoming enraged, Drew began also to establish a distinctly provincial strategy.

King's reluctance to act in what Drew considered a timely fashion encouraged the provincial leader to propose an alternative means by which agreement could be reached on some sort of plan to deal with the multitude of anticipated postwar challenges. The first tactic Ontario politicians employed in attempting to force King to call the leaders together in conference was soliciting support from the other provincial premiers. He sent copies of his voluminous correspondence to King to the provincial capitals and urged the premiers to contribute to the pressure he was exerting on the prime minister.[9] For months, such efforts resulted only in continued federal stalling. Drew also suggested to the other provincial premiers that they 'might well hold a separate conference of their own after the preliminary conference to determine the measure of unanimity there is as to the general plan submitted to them.'[10] But the failure even to call a preliminary meeting scuttled plans, for the time being at least, of any purely provincial gathering. Neither Drew nor his officials were deterred, however, and continued to develop the Ontario position for the postwar period.

It was absolutely vital for the Ontario representatives that 'Dominion-Provincial relations be clarified before the post-war period is upon us.' The most important issues that needed to be considered were the termination schedule of the Wartime Tax Rental Agreements and a more equitable rearrangement of the tax fields between the federal and provincial governments. To this end, 'it is of the first importance,' declared Ontario's preliminary draft discussion paper on dominion-provincial relations, 'that Ontario and Quebec, representing about two-thirds of our population and resources, should agree upon certain principles and so far as possible present a united front. This would probably carry with it the other provincial governments and would have a tremendous influence on the Dominion Government.'[11] To achieve that united front, however, it would be necessary for talks to open between the governments of the two provinces. This prospect might seem likely, given the similarity of Ontario and Quebec positions in regard to the current fiscal arrangements, but it posed enormous problems owing to the disposition of the premiers of the neighbouring provinces. Drew was a staunch proponent of conscription, and pointed to the anti-conscription sentiment in Quebec as undermining both the war effort and national unity. Duplessis, who returned to power in the fall of 1944 on the crest of that popular opposition to the federal government's about-face on conscription, had never been a favourite of Drew. In fact, while Drew thought that 'much can be done in the way of practical cooperation between the two Provinces' with Adélard Godbout at the helm, he despaired of an 'Anti-British Government headed by either Duplessis or Raymond.'[12] For his part, Duplessis would surely have disagreed with Drew's views on the nature of political community. 'It seems to me,' Drew wrote to a friend in Alberta, that every nation must have some clear central purpose. Ours must clearly be declared. Unity can only be based upon the acceptance of that purpose. I think the longer we appease the isolationists in Quebec, the surer we are of civil war. I think if we act now and leave no doubt about the determination of the English speaking part of Canada, whether of Anglo-Saxon stock or otherwise, to preserve British traditions and maintain the British connection, then we will have laid the foundation of unity, and if it is clear that we are determined in our course I am inclined to think it may not be long before Quebec itself will be offering us some support. Anything else simply means a steady trend toward a Quebec-dominated Canada. That I for one am not prepared to accept. I believe in the British connection and all it means. And I would much rather see my children grow up as citizens of the United States than to be citizens of a Canada which was reduced to the low ethical and moral standard of the people of Quebec.[13]

His flag-waving imperialism and his clear contempt for Quebecers in general made Drew an unlikely ally for the nationalist Duplessis.

Antagonism towards the federal government, however, can make strange bedfellows. Neither Ontario nor Quebec wanted to see the continuation of 'unjust' federal incursions into provincial tax bases, and neither welcomed the possibility of Ottawa spending money in fields that were irrefutably provincial jurisdiction. While the two provinces might disagree on specific legislation, they were in complete accord on the principle of provincial autonomy. The introduction of a system of family allowances, for example, was widely regarded in Ontario as a means of appeasing Quebec. According to the Ontario civil servants charged with preparing the provincial position on dominion-provincial relations, 'when the Federal Government uses revenue from general taxation to finance services specially beneficial to non-Ontario provinces, the matter does not end with taking money from Ontario individuals and corporations and paying it out to the inhabitants of other provinces. Transfers of this nature reduce incomes and spending in Ontario. There is Dominion taxation but no compensatory Dominion expenditure, and the productiveness of the Government of Ontario's own taxes is reduced and its fiscal position impaired.' Despite this concern about the equalization component inherent in the system of universal family allowances, Drew's real opposition was to Ottawa's assumption of responsibility over an aspect of social policy where 'experience shows that ... the more localized the supervision is, the more humane and also the more carefully supervised it is.'[14] Politicians from Ontario and Quebec might disagree over the specifics of family allowances, but they could agree on the general principle that provincial powers were being eroded. Attempts on

the part of others to refute Ontario's position on the need for intergovernmental reform usually ended up lumping Ontario and Quebec together and
served to smooth over some of the specific areas of disagreement between
the two provinces. Premier Stuart Garson of Manitoba was among the most
vocal critics of the Ontario position, reputedly arguing that 'Ontario and
Quebec are credited with corporation income tax which is accumulated on
commodities sold in the Prairies and other non-Ontario and Quebec provinces.' Already sharing a fundamental distrust of the federal government
and a desire to protect provincial jurisdiction, Ontario and Quebec, now
jointly labelled the beneficiaries or spoiled children of Confederation, found
common cause at the Conference on Reconstruction.

The better part of the five days of discussion were occupied with opening
statements from the various government leaders, photo opportunities, and
elegant meals. Most important, the meeting gave the federal government a
chance to table its proposals for postwar reconstruction, contained in a
document widely referred to as the Green Book. Now that the federal
proposals had been made public, it was possible for each of the provinces to
begin the real work of determining the acceptability of those reconstruction
plans and, if necessary, developing counter-proposals. The question of
whether to endorse the Green Book proposals was not a difficult one for
Ontario or Quebec: the federal document outlined a plan for the continued
right of the central government to occupy the corporate, income, and succession tax fields in return for introducing social policies and a system of
equalization grants. It would mean a significant centralization of power
and taxing abilities in the hands of the federal government, and a parallel
reduction in the fiscal and administrative powers of the provinces. The
proposals were clearly anathema to what Drew and Duplessis imagined for
the postwar world and, despite other areas of difference, the two became
allies during the course of the August meeting. Provincial treasurer Leslie
Frost had earlier visited other provincial capitals, to personalize the connections Drew had established through his correspondence with his colleagues,
and was able to introduce his premier to Duplessis at the conference. This
association, which became known as the 'Drew-Duplessis axis,'[15] began
auspiciously. Duplessis reiterated many of the points Drew made, and the
two were regarded with equal suspicion by King.[16] As the Ontario ministers and officials designed the response to the Green Book, they attempted
not only to present an alternative national vision but to ensure that it
included proposals that would keep Quebec firmly in their camp.

Ontario's approach to dealing with the federal proposals was at odds
with its traditional course of action. Rather than respond to the Green Book
through confrontation or outright dismissal, the Ontario officials designed

a completely different set of solutions to the problems facing the federation in the postwar years. There were clear problems with the division of tax powers, for the two levels of government shared rights to the lucrative direct tax fields. Ontario opposed leaving Ottawa with sole jurisdiction, as the Green Book proposed, and instead advocated a fiscal structure in which corporate and personal tax fields would be allotted to the federal government and succession duties to the provinces. In addition, the provinces would take over complete control of the 'nuisance' taxes – gas, amusement, racetrack taxes, and the like. In response to the clear regional inequality, Ontario proposed a system of adjustment grants that would bring the poorer regions a level of income impossible to achieve simply through provincial taxation. The experience of the Depression had left little doubt in anyone's mind that new social welfare programs were necessary to combat the exigencies of old age, unemployment, and poor health, but all these areas fell under the constitutional authority of the provinces. Ontario's reconstruction plan anticipated a system of social security that would see Ottawa footing most of the bill and the provinces retaining administrative control, in line with Drew's thinking that such projects were best left to local authorities.[17]

An alternative to the federal proposal for constitutional change and economic renewal was of little use without some assurances that it met not only the concerns of the Ontario delegation but also those of other provinces. The most important opportunity for developing these relationships occurred during the *in camera* sessions of the coordinating committee and the meetings of the various subcommittees of the Reconstruction Conference. Although each of the provinces was required to make submissions elaborating its particular financial situation and the 'effects of the Dominion proposals on the budgetary position of the provinces,' Ontario's submission went considerably further in outlining alternative arrangements. As a result, it became as much a topic of debate as the proposals outlined by the federal delegation. By taking Ontario's position as a starting point, the provincial alliances became more clear. Certain components of the plan were enthusiastically received: the British Columbia representatives called Ontario's 'a well-proportioned scheme,' and Nova Scotia's Angus L. Macdonald was in agreement with Drew that the provinces must have 'certain definite fields of taxation' reserved for them.[18] Still, for one participant, the only clear alliance that had developed was that between Drew and Duplessis. Although the federal 'experts seem to think that Drew will have to yield his point of view' on the necessity of some provincial taxation autonomy, Prime Minister King remained convinced that he 'will follow Duplessis in opposing the other provinces.'[19]

King probably overstated the degree to which Drew and Duplessis were positioned in opposition to the other seven premiers. During the closed meetings of the coordinating committee at the end of January 1946, premiers from both the West and the Maritimes supported elements of Ontario's proposal and repeatedly pressed for serious consideration of those proposals.[20] However, he was not underestimating the degree to which the premiers of Ontario and Quebec were of one mind. Although Drew was prepared to make some concessions to Ottawa, particularly in respect to the vacation of personal income and corporation taxes, when 'Duplessis came out strongly against allowing the Dominion to have the succession duties ... Drew took a similar stand.'[21] He argued 'that the B.N.A. Act in spirit, if not on strict legal grounds, provided for exclusive provincial jurisdiction in the direct tax fields, and he argued that the cause of the breakdown of every federation in history had been the abandonment of provincial rights of direct taxation.'[22] When it became 'quite apparent that neither Ontario nor Quebec [would] give up this field,' King commented privately that he did 'not blame them.'[23] He later postulated that the unwillingness to give up the field of succession duties was based on a fear that 'if a socialist government came in [in Ottawa] that would make it impossible for the people to leave much for their children.'[24] While agreeing in principle with the stance taken by Ontario and Quebec, King seemed to believe that his civil servants were forcing the issue and making it impossible for him to say anything publicly.

Under pressure from Drew that the closed meetings of the coordinating committee be replaced by open sessions, to eliminate the possibility of views being misrepresented in the press, the full conference reconvened at the end of April 1946.[25] There could not have been much hope for success: neither of the architects of the two main proposals, Ontario and Ottawa, had been able to convince enough of the others of the utility of its position to ensure victory. Drew and Duplessis consistently backed each other up in their arguments against the principle of excessive centralization, although the Ontario premier accompanied his denunciations of the Green Book with solid counter-proposals. When the conference concluded on 3 May with vitriol and acrimony, but without agreement, the public portrayal of the central Canadian premiers as the primary impediments to consensus was unfair. Garson seemed to strike an appealing chord when he declared, 'it is calamitous for Canada that the Ontario and Quebec governments could not have continued with those of the other seven provinces in the negotiation of a compromise of the small area of disagreement which still remains between the seven provinces and the Dominion.'[26] The characterization of the evil Drew-Duplessis axis thwarting the efforts of the

Dominion-Provincial Conference was created at the time and, to a large extent, has remained in the historical literature. This view masks some of the more complex features of the process of negotiation, and paints an inaccurate picture of both the role Ontario was attempting to play and the nature of the relationship between Ontario and Quebec.

Instead of asserting a provincial rights agenda, as had been the tactic of several generations of Ontario premiers before him, Drew sought to articulate an alternative to the Green Book proposals. While this alternative protected provincial taxation jurisdiction to a much greater degree than the federal position, it also included elements designed to address the specific concerns of other regions. The Ontario proposal recognized the need for equalization to redress regional imbalance, allowed federal occupancy of both income and corporate taxes, and included an expanded welfare system. It was not, then, a purely pro-Ontario position, but a first step in the direction of a national plan for reconstruction. The prime minister himself recognized the efforts Drew was making towards establishing a viable alternative, and ultimately blamed his own civil servants for the failure of the conference. He believed that the federal hard line 'might cost the Liberal party power. We were simply allowing Drew to take the Liberal position and to get the support of [Nova Scotia's] Macdonald and others and that we could not hope to win with provinces against us one after the other.'[27] When all was said and done, he lambasted his colleagues by reminding them, 'I had said all along we were taking the wrong course in handing to the provinces an excuse for an attack on us on the score of centralization and not allowing certain tax fields to the provinces.'[28] In the months that followed, Drew's repeated efforts to force the federal government to reconvene the federal-provincial conference attested to his commitment to reach agreement rather than merely scuttle the proceedings.[29] In the end, Drew was left feeling 'convinced that King never had any expectation from the very beginning of reaching agreement and that his main purpose was to make generous promises to the public which would gain favour and then leave the responsibility on Ontario particularly, and Quebec as well if possible, for having prevented them from carrying out their generous intentions.'[30]

The association that was forged with Quebec during the course of the Reconstruction Conference was only the most visible of the numerous relationships the Ontario government attempted to develop with its sister provincial administrations. Far from being an unholy alliance devoted to derailing the federal plans for postwar Canada, it was a natural partnership between two similar provinces and two premiers who distrusted centralization. Ontario and Quebec shared a position within Confederation which necessarily threw them together, and Ontario at least had a vision of how the federation should continue. The condemnation of the pair as the spoilers at the Reconstruction Conference, and Drew's and Duplessis's mutual dislike of Mackenzie King, kept them together.[31] The association would remain an important one if Ontario were ever to claim success in articulating a national vision, and Quebec were to gain a more widely shared understanding of its particular concerns with the Canadian federation.

Although Leslie Frost, who became premier of Ontario in 1948, had cordial relations with Duplessis, the increasing insistence of the Quebec premier in his final decade in office that Ottawa stay out of provincial jurisdiction left little room for alliance between the two premiers. There simply were few occasions in which the Quebec premier even entertained the idea of 'federal-provincial relations,' let alone the need for provincial allies in dealing with Ottawa. But new premiers in both the provinces in the early 1960s opened up the opportunity for a different sort of relationship. In the beginning, Conservative John Robarts and Liberal Jean Lesage forged an association that had all the appearances of being cast in the traditional mould: an axis designed to thwart federal policy. But by establishing linkages between the two provinces and solidifying both friendships and strategies, Ontario and Quebec in the 1960s were able to articulate alternatives to the national policies conceived in Ottawa much more effectively than had been possible in the 1940s. Their role was not simply that of federal antagonist, but a more sophisticated one that envisaged educating the federal government on the appropriate manner of governing. At first this alliance could most clearly be seen in attempts in the social policy field to pressure Ottawa to respect the traditional constitutional jurisdiction; ultimately, Ontario and Quebec dealt with the very heart of the matter by forcing a complete examination and overhaul of the British North America Act.

The decade of the 1960s opened with enthusiasm across Canada, nowhere more obviously than in the two largest provinces. Years of careful economic policies in Ontario had left the province in a strong financial situation and able to contemplate a more generous sharing of the wealth within the province. In Quebec the flurry of government activity soon to be known as the Quiet Revolution was under way, and there was cause for optimism in a province too long dominated by the conservative and isolationist policies of Duplessis. Politicians in both provinces were in the process of examining new roles for government, and their paths not surprisingly crossed. When in 1960 Premier Leslie Frost appointed a commission to examine the pension plans that currently existed in Ontario, with an eye to identifying ways in which the government could offer a portable pensions scheme, Quebec looked on with interest.[32] The first ministers of the two provinces shared thoughts on pension policy at the 1961 Inter-Provincial Conference in Charlottetown, and after Ontario introduced its Pensions Benefits Act, Lesage informed the Ontario premier that he intended to introduce his own portable pension system modelled after it.[33] Such a degree of harmony between the two provinces gave credence to Ontario's largely unspoken wish: that Ottawa would see the wisdom of the Ontario scheme, as Quebec had done, and introduce a similar system that would be in force nationwide. The Chartered Trust Company seemed to speak for many in the government when it predicted that the Ontario legislation 'should have far reaching social significance not only in this province but all across Canada.'[34]

At first, the question of pension reform and the desire on the part of both Ontario and Quebec to introduce legislation that would create provincially based systems of compulsory, contributory, and portable pensions seemed to have little to do with either federal-provincial relations or with the utility of the existing constitutional framework. Even the election of Lester Pearson as prime minister in the spring of 1963, armed with a policy package that included national pension reform, suggested little in the way of intergovernmental conflict. Earlier, new Ontario premier John Robarts had been so disgusted with the ineptitude of Prime Minister John Diefenbaker that he had confided to Liberal leader Pearson in 1962 'that the government of Ontario would concur in and facilitate proper and reasonable plans by your government resulting in a contributory social insurance program becoming a reality.'[35] But the accord was not long-lasting, for, soon after his own election, Pearson indicated that he intended to force the provinces into accepting a pension scheme of national design.[36] The proposed incursion into what was clearly provincial jurisdiction was enough to sound the alarm, and the old Ontario-Quebec axis sprang back into action.

The occasion for the rekindling of the flame of cooperation between the two provinces was a visit to Quebec City from an Ontario parliamentary and press delegation in June 1963. The visitors included the leaders of the three Ontario political parties, Cabinet ministers, and members of the press corps. They were given the red-carpet treatment throughout their several days in the Quebec capital, but nothing was more gratifying than the appearance of agreement on a variety of issues between the two premiers.[37] In welcoming the group, and in outlining Quebec's current constitutional concerns, Lesage remarked on the history of interprovincial relations and his hopes for continued positive relations in the future:

The evolution of our constitutional regime so far has not given to Quebec the possibility of playing its full role as the political expression of French Canada. We know that we are undertaking a very delicate task, which may require time, but mostly a spirit of understanding and co-operation from the English-Canadian nation ... In our eyes, the province of Ontario is probably the Canadian province that is in the best position to understand our situation ... I am sure that Ontario and English-speaking Canada will help us to do our part, the way we feel this part should be done ... Not only do you have to understand the deep motives lying behind the changes you are witnessing, but you have to help us bring it about, so that Canada will become a country in which two nations can live side by side in peace, freedom and security.[38]

For his part, Roberts gave every indication of being a strong ally of the Quebec government. The 'cracks and crevices' in Confederation, he claimed, 'should not cause us to flee and panic and abandon our century-old home.' Instead, Roberts continued, 'let us proceed as good craftsmen and overcome these defects and make it a durable dwelling. For I am certain that we are capable of better political leadership and I am equally certain that the two great peoples who first established our Confederation are ready to make a greater effort to make it work and succeed.'[39]

Ottawa would not see first hand the effects of the renewed Ontario-Quebec commitment to enforcing the constitutional division of powers until discussions over pension policy were well under way. Roberts attended the first meeting called to discuss the national proposals in order to present the Ontario scheme as it had been laid out in the Pension Benefits Act and state the case for provincial control over any pension plan, whether operating on a national level or not. Although it was clear that 'Ontario had dominated the conference,' the 'observers' who attended from Quebec 'left little doubt that, if pushed, [Quebec] was more than prepared to fight the legislation on constitutional grounds.'[40] But if Ontario was the first to attack Ottawa's conception of national pension policy, it was Quebec that dealt the death blow. At a federal-provincial conference called, fittingly, for 1 April 1964, Lesage announced his province's intention to introduce its own pension legislation. The differences between the Canada Pension Plan, as Pearson's government outlined it, and the Quebec Pension Plan, as Lesage explained it, were relatively minor but enormously significant. The Quebec scheme would cover all employed and self-employed persons compulsorily, begin paying benefits at age sixty-five, and be based on a larger proportion of a person's income than Ottawa had envisioned. More important, the fund of contributions would be at the complete disposal of the provincial government. This was the key to the Quebec plan: not only did a provincially sponsored plan fit the letter of the constitution, but the Lesage scheme also benefited the province by establishing a significant fund with which to finance some of the governmental initiatives of the Quiet Revolution. When the contours of the Quebec plan were elaborated, 'the response at the conference was electric ... and [there was] just no question at that moment the Canada Pension Plan was dead.'[41]

The fact that all the premiers were more attracted to the Quebec scheme than they were to the national plan had important ramifications for federal-provincial relations as well as for the shape of the Ontario-Quebec axis.[42] First, in an effort to save the conference, the national pension proposals, and face, Ottawa made two major concessions that were to change the shape of intergovernmental relations. Key Ottawa bureaucrats came up with the idea of striking a tax structure committee that would be a continuing body, composed of representatives of both levels of government, charged with reviewing the entire fiscal structure. While Lesage publicly considered the suggestion nothing more than another federal stalling tactic, it was generally viewed as the first step towards a tax realignment more favourable to the provinces.[43] Some weeks later, the same group of officials met with their counterparts in Quebec City and essentially agreed on a rewriting of the Canada Pension Plan that would have it conform to the Quebec Pension Plan. Ottawa would have its national pension system, Quebec would opt out in favour of its own virtually identical plan, and a system of asymmetrical federalism was born – a key component of Pearson's 'cooperative' approach to federal-provincial relations.

Ontario and Quebec had both entered into negotiations with the federal government with the same goal – respect for their prior constitutional rights in the pension field – and both had used the same body of information to combat federal incursions into provincial jurisdiction. And yet, despite Pearson's efforts to keep Robarts apprised of the state of negotiations with Quebec, there was still a sense that Ontario had been outmanoeuvred.[44] But Quebec's decision to opt out, and Ontario's decision to opt in, merely reoriented the axis rather than severing it. On one level, Quebec's actions in 1964 represented a watershed in intergovernmental relations which paved the way for a new role for Ontario. One participant recalled that, 'after extensive bilateral discussion between Ottawa and Quebec, the Quebec plan was virtually adopted for Canada. Whatever the political reasons behind the decisions, the result was a veritable landmark in federal-provincial financial relations. A province suddenly moved to centre stage on a very complex national issue, and the so-called mysteries of government finance – previously the exclusive domain of the federal civil servants – could be understood by a province with the will to do so. The lesson was not lost on other provinces.'[45] Ontario certainly learned the lesson and took Quebec's position as a legitimation of the role of the provinces in articulating a national vision. On another level, however, the acceptance of the Quebec Pension Plan represented a step towards the isolation of Quebec. It was the only province to opt out of the pension scheme, a decision open to all provinces but taken only by one. The result was the appearance of a special arrangement for Quebec. For Robarts, whose 1963 visit to Quebec had been well received in part because it emphasized that Quebec was not alone, the work of the axis was far from over.

By the end of 1966 much had changed, but the fact that so much remained the same left Canada even closer to crisis. Lesage's fortunes had taken a turn for the worse, in part because of his acceptance of the constitutional amending formula proposed by federal ministers Davie Fulton and Guy Favreau. Work on a means to alter the BNA Act domestically had begun under Diefenbaker, continued through the first years of the Pearson administration, and resulted in a proposal by which each province had to agree to any changes that affected provincial jurisdiction. Lesage had been personally in favour of adopting the Fulton-Favreau formula because it recognized Quebec's right to a veto, but the Quebec public was strongly opposed. This divergence between elite and grassroots sentiment left the provincial Liberals wounded and, despite an impressive record of Quiet Revolution reforms, the Union Nationale under Daniel Johnson was able to step into the breach and assume power in the provincial election of 1966. The new government was equally committed to the spirit of *maître chez nous*, but replaced it with a more aggressive strategy of *indépendence ou égalité*. Thus, despite a new government, its aspirations were essentially the same as those of the Lesage regime, and the rejection of the Fulton-Favreau formula had again set Quebec at odds with Ottawa.[46] The province remained isolated, and insisted on a new relationship with the federal government.

The concerns in Quebec did not go unnoticed. At a federal-provincial conference deadlocked over issues of higher education and the fiscal structure, Robarts reportedly 'astonished' everyone present by calling for a full-blown meeting to discuss the very nature of Confederation.[47] He made clear his intention to spearhead such a discussion some months later during a visit to Montreal, and confirmed that a conference of first ministers would be convened in Ontario to discuss the future of Confederation in the speech from the throne in early 1967.[48] While the prime minister objected to an apparent federal-provincial conference being called at the initiative of a province, Robarts clearly saw it as something much greater.[49] What would become known as the Confederation of Tomorrow Conference was designed not only to end the isolation of Quebec but to restore some of its tarnished prestige to the province of Ontario.

Publicly, Robarts stressed the importance of this conference for the state of the federation, particularly for reaching a pan-Canadian understanding of the situation in Quebec. In the face of suspicions 'that Ontario and Quebec are joining together in some sort of power play to bring about changes in the terms of our Confederation,' Robarts maintained that 'there is no Ontario-Quebec axis.' Ontario had called the conference to facilitate open discussion 'in the widest possible context' and reduce the sense that 'Canadians are not particularly well-acquainted with the problems of the regions of the country other than those in which they live.' He saw certain advantages to a conference with such purposes being called by a province, rather than the federal government, because that genesis might 'diminish the friction' that all too often developed at the more traditional federally chaired intergovernmental conferences. Moreover, Ontario was, in Robarts's mind, the obvious province to initiate a public discussion of the future of Confederation because it 'has a special role to play as an outstanding and an understanding interpreter of the view of Quebec to some of the other parts of Canada.'[50]

But if the conference was publicly portrayed as a generous and selfless initiative on Ontario's part towards greater national unity, privately Robarts seemed to regard the Confederation of Tomorrow Conference as an opportunity to reassert the power of the provinces. Although he assured a somewhat wary Pearson that he had not intended 'to infringe upon the jurisdictional authority of the federal Government,' it was abundantly clear that Robarts did intend to insert the compact theory of Confederation back into the political consciousness.[51] This theory of origin, while having little or no basis in reality, held that either the two founding nations, English Canada and French Canada, or the provinces themselves created the federal government as a result of a compact undertaken in 1864. It is only as a result of agreement between the originators that changes can be made to the union.[52] This theory found its voice in the first Interprovincial Conference of 1887, and was used thereafter as an argument on the part of French Canada to repudiate the extension of federal power or a call for the acceptance of a provincial veto over constitutional change. But Ontario also endorsed the compact theory. Robarts's letter to Pearson explaining his reasons for calling the Confederation of Tomorrow Conference makes clear that this particular Ontario premier was willing to haul out the appealing rhetoric of the compact theory.

It is well to remind ourselves that one hundred or more years ago, only because the provinces existing came together, by conference and finally through legal union, did it become possible to bring about the establishment and creation of the Dominion of Canada ... Today the problems which beset the body politics of Canada cry out for solution. We are in a new era. With the expansion and growth of Canada and its economy, the powers of the Provinces, which created the Canadian Federation, have naturally increased, as have those of the Federal Government. There must be flexibility and understanding if this country of ours is to survive. The one objective I have in mind for this Conference is that it will serve the interests of the Canadian people and their nation which the Provinces created and in whose continued existence, unity and strength, the Provinces are vitally concerned.[53]

It was a sentiment that would have made the ghosts of Oliver Mowat and Honoré Mercier smile, but, interestingly, not one that Robarts was willing to express too publicly. When, during the debate over the motion to host the Confederation of Tomorrow Conference, the Ontario attorney general suggested that 'the provinces originally created Confederation. It is the provinces who must come together and say "this is the type of federation we shall have,"' the premier apparently sat 'red-faced through the speech.' It was certainly a sentiment he shared, but not one he wanted to expose to open debate.[54]

In using the language of the compact theory, Robarts extended the significance of an Ontario-Quebec axis. In his public statement, he made clear that discomfort in Quebec with the existing constitution had been the impetus to calling the Confederation of Tomorrow Conference in the first place. As he stated, 'because our problems are very similar ... we have much in common with the province of Quebec.'[55] The meeting would provide a forum for the discussion of problems most keenly felt by the axis. In his private statements, Robarts underlined the commonalities between the two provinces in a more subtle manner: by using the language of the compact theory, traditionally the preserve of Quebec, he was drawing Pearson's attention to the continued and powerful alliance of the two provinces. The message was not lost on the prime minister, whose initial anxieties about Ontario hosting a dialogue on the future of Confederation did not dissipate. As the conference drew closer, Pearson first refused to participate, then forced Robarts to call it an interprovincial rather than a federal-provincial conference, and finally 'persist[ed] in downgrading [it] by sending along as observers (not participants) four advisors or civil servants.'[56] But the combination of inaction and hostility on the part of the federal government was not enough to derail the conference plans.

In fact, Ottawa's decision to dissociate itself from the conference left open the possibility, probably always imagined, of the provinces, and especially Ontario and Quebec, articulating a 'national' vision in the absence of any contribution from the federal government. The Ontario provincial election just six weeks before the conference opened gave some indication of the role Ontario politicians saw themselves playing in the future of the country. In an election campaign that was devoid of much grassroots participation and instead 'operated on a high level,' Robarts drove home his case for constitutional renewal and a new era of cooperation between English Canada and French Canada.[57] As one observer noted, without Ottawa's presence the conference's two "principal participants" – Robarts and Johnson – could reach a 'deal between Ontario and Quebec which would have far-reaching implication.' Moreover, the 'provincial premiers would be speaking together for the "national" interest, while Ottawa would become the voice of the "federal" interest, and the two would no longer be the same.'[58]

But if the public statements of the two provincial premiers and the media opinion in Ontario and Quebec seemed to support the existence of close ties between the two provinces, the position papers prepared by the Ontario Advisory Committee on Confederation suggested a certain disparity between their constitutional policies. The committee, whose members included historians, legal scholars, political scientists, and opinion makers, had been struck years earlier to spearhead investigations into the nature of Confederation and to propose changes that were deemed necessary.[59] It was natural to assume that the position papers, the first volume of which appeared in the April prior to the Confederation of Tomorrow Conference, would form the basis of the Ontario constitutional position. If this were to be the case, however, there was cause for concern. The collection was immediately described as a 'remarkably negative and reactionary report' with 'scarcely a positive or constructive idea in it.'[60] The contributions dealing specifically with issues anticipated to be part of the discussion at the interprovincial conference were especially unsettling. Eugene Forsey's three pieces on the legislatures, the Crown, and associate states systematically denounced key components of Quebec's position on necessary changes to the constitution. His colleague W.R. Lederman endorsed the already rejected Fulton-Favreau formula and concluded that 'we do not need a major re-writing of the Canadian Constitution at all.'[61] Yet, apart from the pre-conference public posturing of the various participants, the report of the advisory committee remained the only glimpse into an Ontario position until the opening of the Confederation of Tomorrow Conference. Its reactive rather than progressive tone left more than one Quebec spokesman wondering, 'Doesn't Ontario have any ideas of its own?'[62]

Despite evidence that agreement between the premiers would be difficult to achieve, the days leading up to the opening of the conference were filled with optimistic anticipation.[63] The spirit that had motivated the idea of the meeting was positive, so there was no reason that the results should not be too. It was fortunate that the conference was scheduled to last three days, as accord was not immediately apparent. In his opening remarks, Johnson indicated that profound constitutional change was necessary to accommodate Quebec. 'Our present constitution still contains elements which are valid for organizing Canada as a partnership of ten,' he stated, but 'we are forced to conclude that much of this other two-partner Canada remains to be invented.'[64] One again, the rhetoric of the compact theory was being used to underscore the importance of constitutional change: Johnson's 'partnership of ten' was an association of provinces, his 'two-partner Canada' an alliance of the English-speaking Canada and the French-speaking nation. The process of 'invention' that Johnson mentioned would demand a thorough constitutional overhaul, and the line was drawn. Interestingly, it was a line that for the most part had already been drawn in 1867: the original provinces in Confederation tended to agree that constitutional change was necessary, while the 'newcomers' held firm that 'adjustments could be made within the framework of the existing Constitution.'[65]

The second day of the conference opened with an even more serious rift: Roberts and Johnson disagreed over whether amendment to the constitution was sufficient or whether a complete rewriting was necessary. Roberts's statement that Ontario 'was not necessarily anxious for a complete revision' aligned him with Ernest Manning from Alberta and Joey Smallwood from Newfoundland and threatened to break the axis. Yet the relaxation of Johnson's 'hard line' policy went further than mending relations with Ontario. By insisting that a solution could be achieved through a series of amendments that 'could later be consolidated,' Johnson was essentially stating that rewriting the constitution was unnecessary; when he offered a metaphor, the tension broke with laughter. 'Some people in Quebec want to divorce Canada and then remarry the same woman with a new marriage contract,' he declared. 'I want to see if we can't amend the marriage contract, rather than take the chance of a divorce and having the woman meet someone else.'[66]

Any division between Roberts and Johnson was perhaps more apparent to the reporters who were covering the conference than to the principal players. They had been in near constant contact in the days leading up to the opening of the conference, and seemed to be in 'collusion' on how to handle a number of issues that arose during the discussions.[67] In any real sense, the axis was far from the breaking point. But the step that Johnson took towards compromise at the end of the conference was a key moment in transforming the alliance from one of two central Canadian provinces to an alliance of almost all the provinces.[68] It had been clear to observers that the provinces had similar problems with the federal government and were, for example, unanimous in 'deploring the imposition of Medicare on them when they need money for other things';[69] but the conference called to discuss the constitution more generally resulted in a significant agreement to band together in the face of Ottawa's reluctance to initiate a constitutional review process. The conference was a major coup for Robarts, who received congratulations for his 'expert handling' of the 'risky venture.' If it were followed by 'goodwill and continued effort, Confederation may yet be saved.'[70] The conference was also a major coup for the 'axis powers,' who found supporters for their attempt to force the national agenda and assert a national vision.

In a sense, Ontario had already forced the federal government's hand. The decision to hold the Confederation of Tomorrow Conference, and the positive reception that decision received, had already convinced Ottawa of the necessity of convening a full-blown federal-provincial conference to discuss the future of the constitution. Robarts had not imagined that the provinces would have the last say on the issue: as he declared after the fact, 'we believe that our decision to call the Confederation of Tomorrow Conference made it possible for the federal government, if it chose to, to resume its primary role in these matters, and I think that events have proved us to be correct.'[71] In January 1968 Pearson, who had already been accused too often of inaction, convened what was to be the first of a series of seven first-minister constitutional conferences in Ottawa.

In his opening statements, the prime minister attempted to recreate something of the tone of the previous interprovincial conference and, to establish that this new series of discussions would be conciliatory in nature, he acknowledged:

> We all know that French Canada today feels a deep dissatisfaction with its place in Confederation. The reasons for that are complex and of varying significance. I have said in the past, and I repeat now, that I believe most of those reasons to be valid and justified. But this is not the occasion either to try to analyze why there is discontent in French Canada, to assess the responsibility or weigh judiciously everything that has contributed to produce that result. What is far more important is to admit that this dissatisfaction is a fact and recognize that, if it is allowed to continue without remedy, it could lead to separation and the end of Confederation.[72]

Despite the good intentions, the presence of the federal government at this conference, as distinct from the Robarts-convened conference, seemed to loosen the alliances that had formed in Toronto. Provincial premiers, led by

Joey Smallwood, seemed more ready to question the validity of Quebec's position. Even the partnership between Ontario and Quebec was strained, not because their positions had changed but because Quebec was lured into a head-on confrontation with the federal government. The debate between Daniel Johnson and federal minister of justice Pierre Trudeau, the main federal spokesperson, ended as a public and aggressive declaration of the Trudeau vision of Canada. The nationalist agenda was rejected out of hand, and the future of the French language was to be secured through individual participation in the federal system rather than collective autonomy within it.[73] The clash was the turning point: not only did it help in propelling Trudeau into the Prime Minister's Office two months later but, as Robarts said at the time, 'that's the end of Ontario's role as a helpful middle man. From here on in, it is going to be a battle between two varieties of French-speaking Quebeckers.'[74]

Over the next three years, first ministers, departmental chiefs, and continuing committees of officials engaged in a near-constant debate over the constitutional changes necessary. The agenda had shifted from addressing Quebec's concerns, which had been the original impetus to open up the discussions, to debating a broad range of issues including a bill of rights, taxing powers, equalization payments, social policy jurisdiction, and the amending formula. In the eyes of some, the federal government was 'exploiting the English-speaking backlash' and ignoring the Ontario lesson – that 'an ounce of negotiation is worth a pound of confrontation.'[75] The Ontario-Quebec axis seemed to fade into the background.

Although an alliance continued between the two central provinces, circumstances had changed so rapidly after the first constitutional conference that a public axis was difficult to maintain. As one commentator put it, 'it is easy to recall how the first blush of constitutional revision seemed so exciting. It was all a bit lyrical and apocalyptic, like Expo '67 which had just closed its gates.'[76] As the lustre faded, reality set in. While Ontario politicians accepted that the 'real root of the Quebec situation' was 'encroachments and interference of Ottawa,' it became increasingly difficult to acknowledge the commonalities between the two provinces.[77] Despite calls to convene a second Confederation of Tomorrow Conference, to underline that 'Canada is a working partnership, not a "king and his subjects,"' Robarts was 'running into a good deal of opposition' to his constitutional position and found it necessary to 'reassure the people of this province that we are not selling out to Quebec.'[78] The public concerns rested mainly with the extension of French-language rights, which Trudeau had turned into the real issue in the Quebec-Ottawa dialogue.[79]

In the absence of public statements of an alliance with Quebec, which

Ontario officials had always been loath to make, there was still evidence of a working association. Ontario's constitutional proposals, for example, meshed easily with those of Quebec and reiterated suggestions that had been made by Quebec premiers at previous constitutional discussions. In addition to stating bluntly that 'Canada should have a new constitution,' a firmer commitment than Ontario had yet made, the proposals also included a call for a form of asymmetrical federalism. In putting forward the resolution that 'provinces in Canada should have separately or severally a variety of relationships with the federal government,' Ontario was endorsing Johnson's earlier proposition that powers be 'delegated' to the federal government as individual provinces see fit.[80] As the final conference approached, Quebec politicians and commentators could point to a common cause with Ontario, if not an overt alliance.[81]

Sympathetic proposals from Ontario were not enough to secure agreement on changes to the constitution, however. The final episode in this first round of what Peter Russell has termed 'mega-constitutional politics' was held in Victoria amid much fanfare but limited expectations.[82] The new key players had their own concerns that in part prohibited any likelihood of national consensus. John Robarts had been replaced as premier by William Davis, a man with fewer personal connections to Quebec and one more wary of the anti-French sentiment growing in Ontario. Daniel Johnson had retired from public life shortly after the 1968 constitutional conference and died soon after, leaving something of a leadership void in Quebec when it came to confrontations with Ottawa. Prime Minister Trudeau had to protect his reputation in English Canada of being able to 'settle the Quebec questions.'[83] And Quebec premier Robert Bourassa was clearly under pressure at home 'not to agree to the partition and amending formulae ... unless he has a solid promise on the question of income social-security welfare jurisdiction.'[84] It was not surprising, then, that Bourassa issued a press statement on 23 June 1971 indicating that the Quebec government could not accept the Victoria Charter, the constitutional proposal agreed to by the first ministers. The sticking point was the lack of clarity on the issue of jurisdiction over social policy.

Ontario's relationship with Quebec has remained the same over much of the last twenty-five years of constitutional negotiation, and the results of the almost constant discussion have varied little from those witnessed after the Confederation of Tomorrow Conference. While there have been numerous points of common cause, especially over the need for constitutional reform and a greater degree of decentralization, there has been little mention of an Ontario-Quebec axis. The agreements between the provinces have been less obvious than the alliance that formed in the 1960s through personal friendships, the acceptance of the compact theory, and a shared commitment to a new national vision. The result has been the increasing isolation of Quebec, the very situation that prompted Robarts's initiatives in the first place. It has been all too easy in English Canada to regard Quebec's constitutional demands as particular to one geographic area, unwarranted, or excessive. Perhaps the reassertion of the Ontario-Quebec axis is a necessary precondition to constitutional reform that addresses the concerns of all parts of the country.

NOTES

This project has been funded by the Social Sciences and Humanities Research Council of Canada. An earlier version of the article was delivered to the Department of History faculty seminar at Dalhousie University in March 1998. I would like to thank the participants for their helpful comments, and Jennifer Bottos, Andrew Clark, and Christine Clayton for their assistance with the research.

1 On the Mowat legacy, see A. Margaret Evans, *Sir Oliver Mowat* (Toronto: University of Toronto Press, 1992), chapter 6; Christopher Armstrong, *The Politics of Federalism: Ontario's Relations with the Federal Government, 1867–1942* (Toronto: University of Toronto Press, 1981), chapter 1; Christopher Armstrong, 'The Mowat Heritage in Federal-Provincial Relations,' in Donald Swainson, ed., *Oliver Mowat's Ontario* (Toronto: Macmillan, 1972), 93–118; Robert Vipond, *Liberty and Community: Canadian Federalism and the Failure of the Constitution* (Albany: State University of New York Press, 1991), especially chapter 6; and Garth Stevenson, *Ex uno Plures: Federal-Provincial Relations in Canada, 1867–1896* (Montreal and Kingston: McGill-Queen's University Press, 1993), chapters 3 and 11. On Hepburn's feuds with King, see John T. Saywell, *'Just Call Me Mitch': The Life of Mitchell F. Hepburn* (Toronto: University of Toronto Press, 1990).
2 Thomas Courchene argues that Ontario's postwar interest in maintaining a strong central government, the identification of the population with 'Canada' rather than 'Ontario,' and the shift away from defending 'provincial rights' are all characteristic of a 'heartland.' See Thomas Courchene with Colin R. Telman, *From Heartland to North American Region State: The Social, Fiscal and Federal Evolution of Ontario* (Toronto: University of Toronto, Centre for Public Management, 1998), 10–17.
3 Archives of Ontario (AO), George Drew Papers, RG 3-18, box 5, letterbook 10, 12 September to 7 November 1944, Drew to Stanley Hall, MPP, 27 October 1944; box 3, letterbook 6, 18 March to 17 April 1944, Drew to J.H. Cranston, *Midland Free Press*, 31 March 1944.

4 The clearest example of this interpretation can be found in Marc J. Gotlieb, 'George Drew and the Dominion-Provincial Conference on Reconstruction of 1945–46,' *Canadian Historical Review* 66, 1 (March 1985): 27–47.

5 Alvin Finkel, 'Paradise Postponed: A Re-examination of the Green Book Proposals of 1945,' *Journal of the Canadian Historical Association*, 1993, 120–42.

6 National Archives of Canada (NA), Drew Papers, reel M-8990, draft letter to *Financial Post*, 2 August 1944; AO, RG 6–41, Department of Finance Papers, Dominion-Provincial Conferences, 1935–55, vol. 3, file: Interprovincial Confernece, 1945, Drew to King, 6 January 1944.

7 See, for example, AO, Drew Papers, box 3, letterbook 5, 16 February to 17 March 1944, Drew to King, 14 and 16 March 1944; letterbook 6, 18 March to 17 April 1944, Drew to King, 13 April 1944; box 4, letterbook 8, June 1 to July 31, 1944, Drew to King, 20 June 1944; box 5, letterbook 9, 1 August to 11 September 1944, Drew to King, 10 and 21 August 1944.

8 AO, Department of Finance, Dominion-Provincial Conferences, 1935–55, vol. UJ 3-4, file: Interprovincial Conference, 1945, Frost to Drew, 21 August 1944.

9 NA, Drew Papers, vol. 62, file: 556, Drew to Adelard Godbout, 14 April 1944.

10 AO, Drew Papers, box 3, letterbook 5, 16 February to 17 March 1944, Drew to Ernest Manning, 13 March 1944.

11 NA, Drew Papers, vol. 118, file: 1187, memo, 'Dominion-Provincial Relations,' nd.

12 AO, Drew Papers, box 1, letterbook, 16 August to 30 September 1943, Drew to Horace Hunter, 21 September 1943.

13 Ibid., box 5, letterbook 9, 1 August to 11 September 1944, Drew to Hugh C. Farthing, 21 August 1944. See also letterbook 10, 12 September to 7 November 1944, Drew to Norman Dawes, 31 October 1944; Drew to Thornton Purkis, 7 November 1944; Drew to Cecil Birchard, 7 November 1944.

14 AO, RG 6-44, Department of Finance, Policy Division Subject Files, box UF 22, file: Dominion-Provincial Relations, Ontario Bureau of Statistics and Research, 'Facts Pertinent to Dominion-Provincial Relations,' 16 July 1945, 41; AO, Drew Papers, box 5, letterbook 9, 1 August to 11 September 1944, Drew to John Diefenbaker, 24 August 1944.

15 AO, RG 3, box 3, 'Dominion-Provincial Conferences on Various Subjects, 1943–45,' memorandum by Frost, May 1963. Quoted in Roger Graham, *Old Man Ontario: Leslie M. Frost* (Toronto: University of Toronto Press, 1990), 111.

16 King Diaries, 6 and 8 August 1945; Robert Rumilly, *Maurice Duplessis et son temps*, tome 2 (Montréal: Fides, 1973), 84–9; Conrad Black, *Duplessis* (Toronto: McClelland & Stewart, 1977), 457.

17 AO, Department of Finance Papers, Dominion-Provincial Conferences, 1935–55, vol. 7, file: From PMs 'red book'; vol. 2, 'Summary of the Minutes of the Dominion-Provincial Economic Committee, 4–14 December 1945 and 8–17 January 1946,' 1–6.

18 Ibid., vol. 2, 'Summary,' 1–6; King Diaries, 31 January 1946.

19 King Diaries, 23 January 1946.

20 AO, Department of Finance Papers, Dominion-Provincial Conferences, 1935–55, vol. 7, file: From PMs 'red book'; vol. 2, 'Statements by the Ontario Premier at Co-ordinating Committee Meeting January 28 to February 1, 1946.'

21 King Diaries, 31 January 1946.

22 AO, Department of Finance Papers, Dominion-Provincial Conferences, 1935–55, vol. 7, file: From PMs 'red book'; vol. 2, 'Statements by the Ontario Premier at Co-ordinating Committee Meeting January 28 to February 1, 1946.'

23 King Diaries, 31 January 1946.

24 Ibid., 1 February 1946.

25 AO, Department of Finance Papers, Dominion-Provincial Conferences, 1935–55, box 3, file: Dominion-Provincial Conference, 1945 – original letters, Drew to King, 16 April 1946.

26 AO, Policy Division Subject Files, box UF 22, file: 6 'S' Speeches: G.A. Drew, 'Speech by Premier George Drew to Progressive Conservative Business Men's Club, Tuesday, May 14, 1946.'

27 King Diaries, 27 April 1946.

28 Ibid., 6 May 1946.

29 AO, Department of Finance Papers, Dominion-Provincial Conferences, 1935–55, box UJ 3-4, file: Dominion-Provincial Conference, Original letters to and from Mr King and Col. G.A. Drew, 1945, Drew to King, 7 September and 2 October 1946. See also NA, Drew Papers, reel M-9018, Drew to Louis St Laurent, 6 November 1947.

30 NA, Drew Papers, reel M-8956, Drew to John Bassett, 9 May 1946.

31 Ibid., reel M-8976, Duplessis to Drew, 8 and 14 April 1947, and Drew to Duplessis, 10 April 1947.

32 AO, George Gathercole Papers, MU 5330, file: Source Papers, Charles E. Hendry to Gathercole, 25 February 1960.

33 Ibid., MU 5332, file: Portable Pension Correspondence, Gathercole to J.J. Connolly, 1 May 1963.

34 *The Counsellor*, published by Chartered Trust, May 1963, The Ontario government had paid considerable attention to the insurance industry in drafting its pension benefits legislation. By allowing the administration of a compulsory pension system to remain firmly in the hands of private business, the government earned the support of the insurance sector, so it is not surprising that Chartered Trust and others heralded the Ontario scheme as a blueprint for the rest of the nation.

35 Queen's University Archives, Tom Kent Papers, vol. 2, file: Correspondence, June 1963, Robarts to Pearson, 6 February 1962.

36 House of Commons, *Debates*, 21 June 1963.

37 The personal friendships and the festive atmosphere seemed to be equally

gratifying. Those people who participated, and those who heard tales later, commented on the 'good time' enjoyed in Quebec City – a better time than staid Ontario was able to provide when a Quebec delegation paid a courtesy call on Toronto. Interviews, Donald Stevenson, 17 July 1996; Rendell Dick, 15 December 1997.

38 Quoted in *Globe and Mail*, 15 June 1963.

39 Quoted in *Montreal Star*, 17 June 1963.

40 NA, Privy Council Office Papers, RG 2, Cabinet minutes, 12 September 1963, 2; P.E. Bryden, *Planners and Politicians: Liberal Politics and Social Policy, 1957–1968* (Kingston and Montreal: McGill-Queen's University Press, 1997), 97.

41 NA, Peter Stursburg Papers, MG 31, D78, vol. 33, file: Kent, Tom, 1977 interview. On the announcement of the Quebec Pension Plan and the April conference more generally, see John Saywell, ed., *The Canadian Annual Review for 1964* (Toronto: University of Toronto Press, 1965), 64–8; Claude Morin, *Quebec versus Ottawa: The Struggle for Self-Government* (Toronto: University of Toronto Press, 1976); Richard Simeon, *Federal-Provincial Diplomacy: The Making of Recent Policy in Canada* (Toronto: University of Toronto Press, 1972), 54–60.

42 NA, Department of National Health and Welfare Papers, vol. 2114, file: 23-3-6, draft minutes, 'Canada Pension Plan, Federal-Provincial Conference, Quebec, April 1, 1964,' 3–4.

43 Tom Kent, *A Public Purpose: An Experience of Liberal Oppostion and Canadain Government* (Kingston and Montreal: McGill-Queen's University PRess, 1988), 276.

44 Kent Papers, vol. 3, file: Correspondence, April 1964, telegram to Robarts, 15 April 1964; Gathercole Papers, MU 5334, file: Pensions, 1964, Gathercole to John Bassett, 17 April 1964; A.K. McDougall, *John Robarts: His Life and Government* (Toronto: University of Toronto Press, 1986), 133; Wayne Austin Hunt, 'The Federal-Provincial Conference of First Ministers, 1960–1976' (PhD thesis, University of Toronto, 1982), Hunt's interview with Robarts, 25 September 1978; Bruce G. Pollard, *Managing the Interface: Intergovernmental Affairs Agencies in Canada* (Kingston: Institute of Intergovernmetnal Affairs, 1986), 11.

45 AO, Department of Treasury, Economics and Intergovernmental Affairs, RG 75-21-0-20, box 3, file: Role of Ontario in National Policy Formations, H.I. Macdonald, 'The Role of Ontario in the Formation of National Policy,' address delivered at Carleton University, 8 March 1974.

46 On the Fulton Favreau formula, see Gérard Bergeron, 'The Quebecois State under Canadian Federalism,' in Michael Behiels, ed., *Quebec since 1945: Selected Readings* (Toronto: Coppp Clark Pitman, 1987), 178–84; Peter Russell, *Constitutional Odyssey: Can Canadians Become a Sovereign People?* 2nd ed. (Toronto: University of Toronto Press, 1993), 72–4.

47 John Saywell, ed., *Canadian Annual Review for 1966* (Toronto: University of Toronto Press, 1967), 76.

48 Private collection, *Canadian Annual Review* Papers, unorganized material, 'Remarks by the Honourable John Robarts, Prime Minister of Ontario, to the Advertising and Sales Executives' Club in Montreal, Wednesday, November 23rd, 1966'; Ontario, *Legislative Debates*, 18 May 1967, 3566; ibid., speech from the throne, 25 January 1967.

49 Gathercole Papers, MU 5311, file: Corresondence, 1965–71, Pearson to Robarts, 26 January 1967.

50 Ontario, *Legislative Debates*, 18 May 1967, 3570.

51 Gathercole Papers, MU 5311, file: Corresondence, 1965–71, Robarts to Pearson, 1 February 1967.

52 Ramsay Cook, *Provincial Autonomy, Minority Rights and the Compact Theory, 1867–1921* (Ottawa: Queen's Printer, 1969); Russell, *Constitutional Odyssey*, 17–18, 48–50; Robert Vipond, 'Whatever Became of the Compact Theory? Meech Lake and the Politics of Constitutional Amendment in Canada,' *Queen's Quarterly* 96 (1989).

53 Gathercole Papers, MU 5311, file: Correspondence, 1965–71, Robarts to Pearson, 1 February 1967.

54 John Saywell, ed., *The Canadian Annual Review for 1967* (Toronto: University of Toronto Press, 1968), 86; 'PM cites Wishart statement to oppose conference,' *Globe and Mail*, 25 May 1967.

55 Ontario, *Legislative Debates*, 18 May 1967, 3570.

56 'An Unbecoming Shyness,' *Globe and Mail*, 25 September 1967; 'Mr Pearson Avoids Confederation Action,' ibid., 31 October 1967.

57 'Mr Robarts and Confederation,' *Winnipeg Free Press*, 16 October 1967. The election was waged on such a high level, in fact, that this western newspaper characterized it as 'inaudible to people more accustomed to, say, a Saskatchewan type of election.'

58 Peter C. Newman, 'The Great Discussion about Canada's Future,' *Montreal Star*, 25 November 1967.

59 The members of the Ontario Advisory Committee on Confederation were H. Ian Macdonald, Alexander Brady, John Conway, Donald Creighton, Richard Dillon, Eugene Forsey, Paul Fox, George Gathercole, Bora Laskin, W.R. Lederman, Clifford Magone, Lucien Matee, John Meisel, R. Craig McIvor, Edward McWhinney, J. Harvey Perry, Roger Séguin, and T.H.B. Symons.

60 Harold Greer, 'Ontario Accentuates the Negative,' *Montreal Star*, 18 April 1967.

61 Eugene Forsey, 'The Legislatures and Executives of the Federation,' 161–73; Forsey, 'Constitutional Monarchy and the Provinces,' 176–86; Forsey, 'Memorandum on the Associate States,' 189–92; W.R. Lederman, 'The Process of Constitutional Amendment in Canada,' 86, all in *Ontario Advisory Committee on Confederation: Background Papers and Reports* (Toronto: Queen's Printer of Ontario, 1967).

62 Federal forestry minister Maurice Sauvé, quoted in Harold Greer, 'Ontario Radicalism Clearly out of Fashion,' *Montreal Star*, 25 November 1967.

63 Interview, H. Ian Macdonald, 18 December 1996.

64 *Canadian Annual Review Papers*, press releases, 'Opening Statement by the Honourable Daniel Johnson, Prime Minister of Quebec, to the Confederation of Tomorrow Conference,' 27 November 1967.

65 Gordon Pape, 'Confederation Conference: Premiers Badly Divided,' Montreal *Gazette*, 28 November 1967. Of the three original provinces, Ontario was the least firm in its commitment to major constitutional change, a position in keeping with that advanced by the Ontario Advisory Committee on Confederation. See Robarts's opening statement in Government of Ontario, *Preliminary Statement*, Confederation of Tomorrow Conference, Toronto, 27–30 November 1967. New Brunswick premier Louis Robichaud was 'the most emotional voice heard in pleading with the rest of Canada to take action before it's too late to stem the separatist tide in Quebec.' *Gazette*, 1 December 1967.

66 *Canadian Annual Review* Papers, notes on the minutes of the Confederation of Tomorrow Conference, 29 November 1967; Gordon Pape, 'Johnson Relaxes Hard Line Policy,' *Gazette*, 30 November 1967.

67 *Montreal Star*, 2 December 1967.

68 Newfoundland premier Joey Smallwood remained, at the end, the only premier unwilling to accommodate Quebec's need for major constitutional reform.

69 Trent University Archives, Leslie Frost Papers, 77-024, box 76, file: 8 (Political Correspondence, 1967), Frost to Robert Stanfield, 1 December 1967.

70 AO, John Robarts Papers, Series F-15-4-3, MU 7998, box 2, file: Goldenberg, Carl, 1967–9, Goldenberg to Robarts, 4 December 1967.

71 Ontario, *Legislative Debates*, 27 February 1968, 263.

72 *Constitutional Conference: Proceedings*, first meeting, 5–7 February 1968 (Ottawa: Queen's Printer, 1968), 5.

73 Russell, *Constitutional Odyssey*, 79; Kenneth McRoberts, *Misconceiving Canada: The Struggle for National Unity* (Toronto: Oxford University Press, 1997), especially chapter 3.

74 Private collection, Donald W. Stevenson Papers, 'Notes for use by Don Stevenson at the Federal-Provincial Conference simulation, University of Waterloo, December 12, 1988.'

75 NA, Tommy Douglas Papers, MG 32, C28, vol. 7, file: general correspondence, aprt 23, Douglas to Frost, 1 July 1968.

76 John Gray, 'Confederation '71,' *Montreal Star*, 12 June 1971.

77 Frost Papers, box 83, file: 5, Frost to Joe Sullivan, 26 February 1968.

78 Robarts Papers, Series F-14-4-3, box 4, MU 8000, file: MacLeod, A.A., 1967–9, W.A. Rathburn to Robarts, 4 October 1968; box 2, MU 7998, file: Goldenberg, Carl. Robarts to Goldenberg, 1 March 1968.

79 Peter Oliver, 'Ontario,' in John Saywell, ed., *The Canadian Annual Review for 1969* (Toronto: University of Toronto Press, 1970), 81–3.

80 Gathercole Papers, MU 5318, file: Source papers – conferences, Continuing Committee of Officials, 1968–70, Drafts of Ontario's Proposals, 24 June 1968;

Private collection, *Canadian Annual Review* Papers, 'The Ontario Position on the Spending Power Presented by the Government of Ontario,' 3 June 1969, and 'A Briefing Paper on Constitutional Review Activities and Discussions with the Continuing Committee of Officials,' December 1969. At the Confederation of Tomorrow Conference, Johnson had suggested the possibility that areas of provincial jurisdiction, such as health care, could be given to Ottawa by those provinces that were not prepared to legislate effectively in those areas.

81 'L'Ontario s'oppose à la centralisation fédérale,' *Le Devoir*, 29 avril 1971; 'M. Davis continue de critiquer la politique centralisatrice d'Ottawa,' *Le Devoir*, 10 mai 1971. In what appeared to be an attempt to distinguish himself from Robarts, the new Ontario premier, William Davis, 'lashed out at feds and fed policy as Robarts never did,' and was not predisposed to made the federal postiion any easier, 'as Mr. Robarts might have done.' *Canadian Annual Review* Papers, 'The Victoria Conference – notes'; Maxwell Cohen, 'The constitution – it's a priority,' *Gazette*, 1 June 1971.

82 Russell, *Constitutional Odyssey*, 74–6.

83 Gray, 'Confederation '71'; Dominique Clift, 'Quebec'; Harold Greer, 'Ontario' – all in *Montreal Star*, 12 June 1971.

84 Cohen, 'The Constitution – it's a priority.'

'We Want Facts, Not Morals!' Unwanted Pregnancy, the Toronto Women's Caucus, and Sex Education[1]

CHRISTABELLE SETHNA

When a fifteen-year-old member of the High School Fraction of the Toronto Women's Caucus (TWC) met with the trustees of the Toronto Board of Education on 21 January 1971, she recommended that they expand their Family Life Education program to include the topics of birth control, family planning, and abortion and demanded that high schools provide students with contraceptive devices.[2] She urged: 'The high school is where we really need birth control ... It's hard for high school women to get it anywhere else. Students get pregnant and are forced to resign from school. Their whole lives are botched up just because they didn't have access to birth control. They lose their chance for an education, for a decent job, and often end up having to get married when they don't want to.'[3] The board was not swayed. A majority of trustees voted to give principals the power to decide whether to implement the extended version of the Family Life Education program, and then only to students from grade 11 on up. The board's half-hearted response reinforced what several feminist groups had claimed from the late 1960s onward – that inadequate sex education in schools placed girls at serious risk of an unwanted pregnancy.

Scholars, captivated by the fierce battles Canadian second-wave feminists waged for access to safe, legal contraception and abortion in their campaign for reproductive rights, have customarily paid little attention to their demands for sex education.[4] Yet because feminists of every political stripe saw teenaged girls as especially vulnerable to an unwanted pregnancy, they looked to sex education as the first step towards the goal of reproductive control. In Ontario the TWC played a leading role in mobilizing high school girls around the issue of sex education. To do so, the group tapped into a popular discourse that equated unwanted pregnancy in single girls with diminished life opportunities. This discourse was deployed by the TWC to organize high school girls around their sexual and reproductive rights.

The TWC was founded in May 1970 by a few women who broke from the radical New Feminists (NF) following the cross–Canada Abortion Caravan protest. Although the TWC's founders were intent on keeping the group a multi-issue women's organization, the TWC was best known for its contentious decision to make abortion rights its main goal. Dissatisfied with the 1969 Criminal Code revisions to the birth control and abortion laws, TWC members looked successively to abortion on demand, abortion law reform, and abortion law repeal as the key to building a mass-based, activist-oriented movement to win women to revolutionary socialism.[5]

The core of the TWC was made up of white, middle-class, university and high school students, many of whom were simultaneously involved in Old and New Left political parties and in the anti-war, civil rights, and students' rights movements. A significant number of TWC members were also part of the Trotskyist League for Socialist Action (LSA) and its youth arm, the Young Socialists (YS). The TWC's Trotskyist orientation led some feminists to suspect that the group was a front for the Trotskyist movement. Although the TWC typically dismissed the accusation as red-baiting, there was no doubt of the influence of the LSA and the YS on the TWC.[6] Indeed, it was precisely because of these parties' links to youth keen on contraception, abortion, and sex education for high school students that the TWC made the prevention of unwanted pregnancies among single girls central to its abortion rights platform.[7]

'Teenage pregnancy,' the contemporary appellation for pregnancy among single female adolescents, was not coined as a term or identified as a major social problem until the mid-1970s, when, ironically, births to unwed teens declined as the rate of therapeutic abortions rose.[8] However, rates of pregnancy in unwed teenage girls had increased steadily after 1945. The overall Canadian teenage fertility rate after the Second World War peaked in 1959, then continued to dip annually for the next twenty-five years. But the proportion of unwed mothers under the age of twenty increased steadily after 1945, aided by a mid-century drop in the mean age of menarche and by a decline in marriage rates after 1951 for females aged fifteen to nineteen. In Ontario, births to unmarried teens shot up from 27.9 per cent of all out-of-wedlock births in 1945 to 54.8 per cent in 1975, a pattern mirrored in the rest of the country. By the mid-1960s, one-third of the 26,000 unwed mothers in Canada were reported to be teenagers.[9]

The postwar baby boom – in Ontario alone the fifteen to nineteen age group had grown by 72.4 per cent between 1956 and 1966 – heightened the visibility of pregnancy among unwed teens. Larger numbers of unmarried teenage girls had resulted in higher numbers of births. So, too, did the perception of the 'cult of the teenager,' which spotlighted for mass consumption the gyrations of an age-specific, peer-dominated subculture characterized as sexually and politically rebellious.[10] However, shifts in the postwar discourse on unwed pregnancy that were intimately related to the professionalization of social work were also fundamental to constructing unwed motherhood in teenage girls as a cause for concern.

Whereas class had been central to explanations for illegitimacy before the Second World War, after 1945 class and race served as the primary markers of the discourse on unwed pregnancy. Unwed pregnancy among white, middle-class girls was interpreted as a psychologically neurotic act of rebellion against domineering mothers. However, unwed pregnancy among non-white girls was thought to be a culturally acceptable practice in mother-headed families believed to predominate in non-white communities. By the 1960s the discourse on unwed pregnancy had shifted significantly. As concerns over the welfare costs of non-white, unwed motherhood, especially in the United States, dovetailed with widespread anxieties over a presumed global population explosion among the poor and the non-white, girls of colour who became pregnant out of wedlock were deemed hypersexual. Their pregnancies were stigmatized as the result of cultural pathology. In complete contrast, unmarried, white, middle-class girls who became pregnant were viewed as casualties of the sexual revolution. Their unwed pregnancies were understood as the unintended consequence of a new morality that condoned premarital heterosexual sex among youth, and were portrayed as unwanted.[11]

The reframing of unwed pregnancies among white, middle-class girls as unwanted cast them as tragedies to which all women were susceptible, but to which teens were especially vulnerable. This new discourse on the tragedy of an unwanted pregnancy in single teens was grounded in the postwar extension of education and employment advantages to white, middle-class, boomer girls.

While the price of an unwed pregnancy among poor, non-white girls was estimated according to the expense incurred by the state, the high cost of a pregnancy in the single, white teen was calculated in individual terms. Education and employment gains had provided many white, middle-class girls born after 1945 with the scope to fashion careers independent of the traditional roles of wife and mother.[12] By the 1960s an unwanted pregnancy, according to academics, politicians, and feminists alike, threatened to delay at best, to destroy at worst, a girl's opportunity for professional success. Indeed, a number of researchers studying the timing of first births confirmed that single teens who carried to term forfeited their educational and economic futures. Pregnant single girls were said to drop out of school, languish in maternity homes, contract shotgun marriages destined for divorce, or live in poverty and isolation if they raised their child alone.[13] Single mothers who kept their children, a trend on the increase due in part to changes in government maternity benefits, were compared in frightening terms with two other marginalized minorities: 'homosexuals' and 'Negroes.'[14]

The dismal fate to which researchers doomed pregnant, unwed teens proved to be less dependent on the timing of first births and more dependent on the pattern of class and race disadvantages facing an unmarried girl even before pregnancy occurred.[15] Nevertheless, the goal of reproductive control became central to feminist groups like the TWC. TWC members were concerned with the impact of class inequities on women. In keeping with socialist feminists' belief that capitalism lay at the root of women's oppression, the TWC maintained that women's inability to control their reproductive capacities was central to their subservient economic, political, and sexual status in capitalist societies. The group also considered, however marginally, the impact of racial discrimination on women. After appeals from women of colour, TWC members rejected free abortion on demand in favour of abortion law repeal as the issue that all women, regardless of race, would support.[16] Still, the caucus participated uncritically in the essentializing discourse on the tragedy of an unwanted pregnancy among single girls, turning it to their propagandistic advantage. Insisting in their literature on abortion law repeal on the 'tragedy of the thousands of high school women who are forced to drop out of school every year because of prgancy [sic] their life plans aborted by one unfortunate accident,'[17] the TWC incorporated into its abortion rights platform the demand for high school sex education curricula that included information on birth control and abortion and provided students with contraceptive devices.

Although more than seven in ten Canadians polled approved of sex education in high schools, the increase in pregnancy in single girls sparked a heated debate on sex education during the 1960s.[18] Opponents of sex education in schools were often connected to conservative Christian right-wing countermovements to restore traditional moral standards. They insisted on parents' right to manage their children's and, in particular, their daughters' sexuality, arguing that sex education in schools would lead to a rise in unwanted pregnancy.[19] The belief that opponents expressed in the negative socializing power of the curriculum was matched by the faith that advocates of school-based sex education placed in its positive socializing power.[20] Allied with a progressive educational revival that focused on educating the whole child, advocates insisted that sex education in schools could deter unwanted pregnancy. They believed that schools could no longer keep sex a 'State secret.'[21] They insisted that schools had to accept responsibility for sex education because parents, who were either too ignorant, too embarrassed, or too sexually repressed, had neglected to teach their children about sex.[22] Nevertheless, as advocates were unclear whether they wanted to prevent unwanted pregnancy per se or premarital sex in general, they usually ended up supporting sex education curricula that reinforced nuclear family norms.[23]

The Ontario Department of Education was a case in point. At the beginning of the decade, the department warned teachers to exercise caution around any topic 'which may be construed erroneously as sex education.'[24] During the mid-1960s, in the spirit of progressive reform, officials made several important changes to the Health Education guidelines to allow for sex education. Still, because they feared parental opposition, they encouraged schools to segregate health classes, give students only simple physiological information, and establish consultative committees with parental representation.[25] In 1969 the department revised its Health Education guidelines yet again to take a controversial values clarification approach. Adopted after the Hall-Dennis Report and the Report of the Mackay Committee recommended, respectively, that schools focus on the whole child and that public schools eliminate Christian education from the curriculum, values clarification theoretically gave students value-neutral information to enable them to make their own decisions about sex. But at the same time, the department continued to validate the family as 'the basic structural unit in which individuals experience close relationships.'[26]

Sex education curricula, which either ignored mention of birth control or treated contraception and abortion solely as family planning decisions for married couples wishing to regulate the spacing and number of births, seemed to offer the TWC concrete proof that 'our society hates to face the fact of teen-age sexual activity.'[27] Kit Evans's comment, which appeared in the TWC organ the *Velvet Fist*, was typical of its time. It smacked of the pro-teen sexuality/anti-nuclear family argument made principally by Wilhelm Reich and adopted by Old and New Left socialists and feminists in the 1960s. A member of the German Communist Party in the 1920s who would die, for added cachet, in an American jail in 1957, Reich had declared that the family was an authoritarian institution. He theorized that the family was responsible not only for the economic oppression of women but for the sexual repression of youth as well. Because the maintenance of capitalist societies depended on the ongoing reproduction of authoritarian families, sex outside marriage was considered immoral. Consequently, information on sexual pleasure and birth control was often withheld from youth.[28] 'In capitalist society,' Reich concluded, 'there can be no sexual liberation of youth, no healthy, satisfying sex life; if you want to be rid of your sexual troubles, fight for socialism.'[29] However overblown, Reich's thesis exerted a strong appeal for the TWC. It is not difficult to see why.

As contraception and abortion became increasingly medicalized after the 1969 Criminal Code revisions decriminalized birth control and liberalized the abortion law, doctors came to wield tremendous power over single girls' access to these services. Under the new law, birth control information and devices were no longer illegal, but because contraception was intended primarily for married adults for family planning purposes, many doctors were reluctant to provide contraceptives, including the popular birth control pill, to unmarried girls. Despite evidence that single girls seeking contraceptive information and devices were already sexually active, some doctors refused to dispense contraceptives to them because they opposed premarital sexual activity. Others who feared the legal ramifications of treating minors without parental consent declined the girls' requests for contraceptive information and devices. In a national survey of family practitioners and obstetrician/gynecologists, 43 per cent of the respondents said they were unwilling to provide birth control services to minors without parental consent, and 3 per cent reported they might not do so even with parental consent.[30]

Single girls requiring abortions fared slightly better. According to the revised legislation, a qualified general practitioner had to refer a patient for a therapeutic abortion. A qualified doctor could perform the abortion in an accredited hospital only if a Therapeutic Abortion Committee (TAC) composed of at least three physicians at that hospital agreed in writing that the continuation of the pregnancy would endanger the life or health of the patient. The doctor performing the abortion could not be a member of the TAC. These criteria, which hinged on physicians' moral stance on abortion, were compounded by the legal ambiguities over inducing abortion in single girls. Some hospitals required the consent of fathers even when they were separated from or had never married the pregnant girls involved. Furthermore, due to provincial age of consent to medical care laws and age of majority laws, hospitals were often forced to get parental permission for abortions involving minors or had to notify parents of minors' abortions.[31]

After 1970, therapeutic abortions for girls under the age of twenty rose significantly. In Ontario, the province with the largest population and the highest number of TACs, the rise was sharp. In 1970 the Ontario total for births out of wedlock was 10,248. A year later, the total was 8492. Therapeutic abortions were shown to be most effective in reducing the illegitimacy rate in teens aged fifteen to nineteen.[32]

Feminist groups in Ontario attempted to rectify the lack of adequate sex education in schools in various ways. The small, radical NF, which claimed to be 'opposed to a society in which sexuality is destiny,'[33] limited itself to ridiculing trustees at the Toronto Board of Education who opposed sex education for schools.[34] Under the slogan 'WOMEN'S OPPRESSION IS WORRYING ABOUT GETTING PREGNANT. WOMEN'S LIBERATION IS BEING ABLE TO TAKE CARE OF IT BEFORE IT HAPPENS,' the pro-Marxist Toronto Women's Liberation Movement (TWLM) invited high school students to call their birth control and abortion hotline, visit their drop-in centre for more details, or pool their allowances to purchase the *Birth Control Handbook*, a popular but controversial booklet on contraception and abortion originally compiled by McGill University students.[35] TWC members took another tack. They encouraged girls to form high school women's liberation groups and high school birth control committees to lobby for information about contraception and abortion, as well as for contraceptive devices.

Although many radical lesbian feminists had begun to critique the sexual politics of heterosexuality, feminist groups initially steered clear of the issue of lesbianism.[36] Feminist groups were, however, committed to securing for single, young girls both sexual freedom in heterosexual relationships and technological protection against an unwanted pregnancy. High school girls fearing an unwanted pregnancy were simultaneously eager to explore their heterosexual and reproductive options. Indeed, the alliance between adult and teen members in the high school collectives, fractions, and sections of feminist groups took on the kind of symbiotic cast attested to by a TWLM statement: 'We've got a lot to offer [high school girls] and they've got a lot to teach us'[37] But it was clear that feminist groups also viewed those same alliances as a way to nurture in high school girls a budding political identity. Indeed, the TWC saw in the work of high school women's liberation and high school birth control committees an opportunity to promote its brand of socialist feminism among high school 'women,' as the girls came to be very pointedly identified.[38]

Shortly after it was founded, the TWC formed a small High School Fraction. One of the fraction's first tasks was to promote the establishment of women's liberation clubs in high schools. Similar clubs that had sprung up in the United States during the late 1960s were well known for their activist work on sex role steretyping, racism, birth control, and sex education.[39] The first High School Women's Liberation Club in Ontario was kick started in 1970 by three TWC members at York Memorial Collegiate, a school characterized as a 'cauldron' of political activity and situated in a mainly working-class, immigrant neighbourhood in north Toronto. TWC members Liz Barkley and Pam Furlotte were both teachers; Debbie Fraleigh was a student. All three came from secular, white, middle-class homes; only Fraleigh had a family history of left-wing political activism.[40] The first yearbook photo of the club shows thirty smiling, primarily white, young women, dressed in miniskirts and bellbottom pants, gathered on the front steps of the school. Five clenched fists are raised upward in the de rigueur power salute of the time.[41]

Exactly why women's high school liberation was needed was summed up by Ilona Laney, a TWC member. Collapsing the students' rights movement's analysis of the authoritarian structure of high schools and universities into the feminist movement's opposition to sexism, Laney identified the high school as a 'repressive institution' dependent on 'women's oppression and the perpetuation of sexist propaganda.'[42] Members of the club were more concrete. They expressed their dismay at the lack of sports facilities for girls, turned up their noses at history classes for not dealing with women's accomplishments, and complained that courses streamed girls into the stereotypical roles of wife and mother. But the issue that frustrated the girls the most was the lack of adequate information about sex in their health education classes. Club members demanded not only that boys and girls sports receive equal funding, that history classes include information on women's achievements, and that female students take non-traditional courses such as industrial arts. They also insisted that their health education classes be updated and coeducational.[43]

Health education classes, the venue for oblique forms of sex education since the 1930s, had come under attack by the TWC for teaching girls only to groom themselves for dates, boyfriends, and future husbands. Sex-segregated health education classes were held to be even more detrimental to girls' self-realization.[44] Updated, coeducational health education classes, according to the literature produced by the TWC's High School Fraction, 'would inform both the young men and woman [sic] together instead of categorizing knowledge according to sex and would also prevent the teaching of subjects such as "Child Care" to women only.'[45]

Graciela Marandola and Helen Orr, two other club members, went even further. Health education classes at York Memorial Collegiate were sex segregated, but the amount of information students received about sex depended largely on the discretion of the teacher. While some instructors taught girls about menstruation and conception alone, others dealt with birth control by demonstrating how condoms, diaphragms, and the pill worked to prevent pregnancy.[46] Adopting the language of the TWC's abortion rights platform to insist in their high school newspaper that schools should provide students with birth control information, Marandola and Orr wrote: 'The right to control her own body, to choose when she wants to bear children, should be a basic right of all women regardless of age in order to enable them to be free to enter into active participation in all aspects of society.'[47]

A year after the club was founded, Fraleigh ran for student president, campaigning on what she termed a 'students' rights' ticket – freedom of speech and assembly for students, student input into curricula, and access to contraception and abortion information as well as to contraceptive devices in the school. Often approached by frightened peers seeking abortion referrals, Fraleigh denounced sex education in schools as grossly inadequate. She even suggested that school boards fund mobile birth control clinics staffed with doctors and nurses to visit schools on a weekly basis.[48] Despite the large minority of Italian Catholic students at the school (who may have been opposed to contraception and abortion for religious reasons) and the ridicule Fraleigh experienced from her male opponent, who taunted her during campaign speeches with a coat hanger (the well-known feminist protest symbol against illegal abortion), Fraleigh won.[49]

Barkley attributed Fraleigh's triumph to the students' support for access to contraception and abortion. Still, Fraleigh's election to student council president occurred at the same time that club membership began to dwindle. Attrition was one factor; female students' ambivalence about feminism was another. So too was the negative reaction of some male administrators, teachers, and students who, according to student member Wendy Dorrey, 'thought the club was a big joke,' thereby intimidating some members into dropping out.[50] Nevertheless, club members took pains to repeat the TWC's claim that women's liberation was actually about 'human liberation.' Marandola and Orr asserted that far from being anti-male, women's liberation would actually free men from the particular pressure capitalism placed on the male sex: 'Not only will [women's liberation] free women from a double dose of oppression but it will make life easier for men by allowing them to be honest about their masculinity and to be relieved of the pressure on them to compete and succeed in the rat-race for the purpose of supporting a woman.'[51]

Rhetoric aside, opposition to high school women's liberation from male administrators, teachers, and students was common. A befuddled principal refused to allot a room for the club's first meeting. The incensed vice-principal tore down posters advertising its existence. Some teachers teased their female colleagues about their support for the club.[52] Although a few boys had attended the club's initial meetings, male students reassured each other that the women's liberation movement itself would endure only 'until the last day of school.'[53] Male student hostility continued to dog the TWC's efforts to promote high school women's liberation clubs. TWC members who presented the case for feminism in Ontario schools with posters that asked 'Are you dating a male chauvinist pig?' or 'Does sexism happen here?' not surprisingly were met with male students' unfriendly stares, defensive comments, and warnings not to recruit their girlfriends into the movement.[54]

The remaining dozen club members concentrated on surreptitiously distributing the *Birth Control Handbook* to classmates. Described by Barkley as a 'bone of contention' to school administrators, the *Handbook* had been banned from the nurse's office.[55] First published in 1968, when birth control and abortion were still illegal in Canada, the *Handbook* was edited by two McGill university students, Allan Feingold and Donna Cherniak, in response to the concerns of the McGill Students' Society about illegal abortions.

Accusing physicians of humiliating single girls who sought birth control, the editors supported sexual freedom for girls and women, provided readers with information on a wide range of female- and male-dependent contraceptives, and endorsed abortion performed by competent doctors in the event of contraceptive failure. Although the editors agreed with feminists' demands for reproductive rights, they also challenged American population growth experts' fear of a global population explosion among the poor and the non-white. The editors cautioned that the unequal distribution of resources engendered by American capitalist expansion, not overpopulation, was responsible for poverty in the First and Third worlds. Because American population control experts tended to reject family planning in favour of more drastic population control policies to which minority women were often subjected, Cherniak and Feingold branded them racists who used birth control to maintain the supremacy of wealthy whites over poor non-whites.[56]

Ironically, in keeping with their aggressive population control focus, American population control experts were among the most supportive of contraception, abortion, and sex education for young girls. Paul Ehrlich, author of the bestselling *The Population Bomb*, proposed that the United States set an example for the world by establishing a federal Bureau of Population and Environment. As part of its mandate, the bureau would secure abortions for all girls and women who required the procedure and coordinate a mandatory program of sex education in schools. Such a program would include discussion on the need for the regulation of birth rates, display contraceptive techniques, and, with a Reichian twist, identify sex as a pleasureable 'interpersonal relationship.'[57]

Cherniak and Feingold lamented that few copies of the *Handbook* made their way into the high schools owing to student councils' lack of funds and school administrators' 'reactionary nature.'[58] On this latter point they were correct. During the dispute over distribution of the *Handbook*, Fraleigh was warned by teachers to 'be careful or the Mounties will get you.'[59] It was not an idle threat. Declassified documents show that the RCMP conducted regular surveillance of politically active high school students, including Fraleigh, whom they identified as subversives.[60] The public reaction to Fraleigh's exploits was even more unfavourable. She received numerous hate letters, and those threatening her with death were turned over to the police. The more benign appealed to her to 'be her age and live a clean moral and respectable life.' Others insisted she 'be a Lady first and leave to those who are mature the proper thinking and advise [sic] to give to the immature.'[61]

Apart from encouraging the formation of high school women's liberation clubs, the TWC's High School Fraction also urged high school girls to establish student birth control rights committees. Whereas the club had focused attention on distributing the *Handbook* to classmates, student birth control rights committees concentrated their efforts on petitioning Metropolitan Toronto boards of education to have schools provide students with contraceptives. The necessity of directly providing adolescents, especially young girls, with contraceptives had received the full backing of the Royal Commission on the Status of Women (RCSW). Pressured by the high-profile Committee of Equality for Women, the Canadian government had appointed the commission in 1967 to inquire into the status of women in Canadian society. Three years later it delivered a landmark report that provided second-wave feminists with a potentially transformative agenda.[62] Although the commissioners disagreed on the issue of abortion, they remained united on the importance of birth control. Concerned about 'child mothers,' they recommended that primary and secondary school students be taught about human reproduction, that federal and provincial governments print and distribute birth control information to teachers, and that girls have access to birth control counselling and contraceptives.[63]

In February 1971 an ad hoc High School Students Birth Control Rights Committee was struck in Vancouver after the Vancouver and New Westminister school boards denied a high school women's liberation club permission to distribute the *Handbook* on school grounds. To considerable public notoriety, the Committee began demanding free access to birth control information and devices, as well as school-time assemblies on birth control and abortion.[64] That same month, the TWC's High School Fraction formed a Student Birth Control Rights Committee (SBCRC). Operating out of TWC headquarters, the SBCRC invited Toronto high school students to begin campaigning for school-time assemblies on birth control and abortion, mobile birth-control clinics that would dispense contraceptive information and devices to students, and access to contraceptives in schools. 'If you are tired of the mystery, confusion, ignorance and plain old hypocrisy that surrounds the issue of Birth Control,' appealed the SBCRC in stirring fashion, 'join the STUDENT BIRTH CONTROL RIGHTS COMMITTEE.'[65]

Repeating one of the best-known slogans used by the TWC in its call for abortion law repeal – 'Control of Our Bodies-Control of Our Lives!' – the SBCRC began distributing copies of the *Handbook* and petitions to city schools. The petitions, which were intended for presentation at Metropolitan Toronto area school boards, insisted that most sex education courses operating in schools did not fulfil youths' needs because they tended to overemphasize the importance of 'a family structure which is becoming more and more outmoded.' Schools had to be responsible, therefore, 'for distributing birth control devices to students on demand.'[66] For added punch, the SBCRC festooned its literature with a cartoon lampooning the inadequacy of sex education teaching in schools. In it, a flustered male teacher gestures towards a garbled blackboard diagram featuring a stork, a baby, a cloud, and a house and asks his puzzled class: 'Are there any questions so far?'[67]

The SBCRC made the Toronto Board of Education's Family Life Education program one of its prime targets. Concerned with pregnancy among unwed adolescents, a few trustees at the Toronto Board in the early 1960s had displayed a heightened interest in sex education.[68] But because trustees were stymied by the Ontario Department of Education's cautionary approach to the subject, the board settled on a sex-segregated family living course for grades 7–12 with only cursory information on reproduction. This family living course laid the groundwork for the board's 1966 Family Life Education program.[69]

In that year the board, led by chair Barry Lowes, a sex education enthusiast, hired four physical and health education teachers to act as consultants for their grades 7–12 sex-segregated Family Life Education program. The board directed that the consultants give physical and health education teachers in-service training to help them overcome their inexperience, reluctance, or discomfort about teaching sex education. Equipped with kits containing films, books, slides, pamphlets, and guides about anatomy and reproduction intended for classroom teachers, the consultants visited students in every school for two lessons. Students were invited in the first class to ask questions or to write them down and place them in a shoebox. At the second class the consultant discussed the answers. Thereafter, the teacher was expected to devise lessons based on the numerous questions students had asked about pregnancy, venereal disease, masturbation, homosexuality, and pornography.[70]

By 1971 the program had come to include coeducational discussions of veneral disease, birth control, and abortion for the senior grades. But the SBCRC denounced the program, complaining that it presupposed that sex occurred only within the confines of marriage. This presumption, argued SBCRC members, 'is hardly the reality which we all live everyday! Rather than showing us how to take responsibility for our lives and cope with the reality of living, these courses are used to preach to us the ways which a small group thinks we should live.'[71] Pregnant single girls could not have agreed more. When surveyed on their opinions on sex education in schools, they recommended that sex education begin in elementary school, that contraception be discussed as early as grades 8 and 9, that practical demonstrations of contraceptive devices be given, and that information about abortion methods and services in their community be included.[72]

These recommendations seemed to support the SBCRC's belief that value-neutral information on contraception and abortion, as well as access to contraceptives, would go a long way in preventing unwanted pregnancy. Yet contraceptives and the values associated with their use were proving to be an extremely complicated matter for girls, a fact that undoubtedly led those pregnant, single girls surveyed to suggest also that sex education place 'less emphasis on anatomy and more on relationships between the sexes.'[73] Technically speaking, the SBCRC was open to the availability of male- and female-dependent contraceptives in schools, but because of the pragmatic necessity of preventing an unwanted pregnancy, the SBCRC was keen on having schools provide girls with the pill.[74] A pragmatic Fraleigh recalled that it was 'highly unlikely that fellows would take responsibility [for birth control]. They hated condoms and how many teenage kids were going to get vasectomies? Really, I was talking about the girls.'[75]

Highly effective female-dependent contraceptives like the pill had feminized contraception.[76] Although studies showed that more boys than girls were sexually active, girls, not boys, were considered mainly responsible for contraceptive use. But even those girls who did not want to get pregnant, who were somewhat informed about birth control, and who could access contraceptives were not always willing to make use of them, often because they were ambivalent about sexual activity, unaccepting of their own sexual desires, or fearful they would be labelled 'sluts.'[77] The majority of sexually active thirteen-to-nineteen year-old girls surveyed claimed, however, that they did not use contraception at last intercourse because they believed they were unlikely to get pregnant. Although boys also expressed a desire not to impregnate their partners, few used reliable contraceptive methods.[78] Similarly, girls who did become pregnant and could access abortion services did not always do so. A girl's decision to abort or to carry to term was based on a complicated constellation of factors – her attitude towards abortion, the size of her family of origin, her mother's knowledge of her pregnancy, her parents' marital status, her religious background, her country of origin, her desire for a child, her marriage plans, her educational aspirations, and her perception of relatives' attitudes towards unwed motherhood.[79]

In any case, the SBCRC was fighting an uphill battle. The Toronto Board was hardly likely to approve of student access to contraceptives in schools when parents opposed to premarital sex began to attack sex education in schools. The SBCRC had beseiged the board's Family Life Education program from the left, claiming it tied information about sex to the nuclear family. However, parents who feared that sex education classes would encourage girls to engage in premarital sex, thereby weakening the nuclear family, struck at the program from the right.[80]

From 1966 onward the board had hoped to deter parents' objections to its Family Life Education program with the following measures. Consultants hired by the board were required to acquaint parents with the program, inviting them to become familiar with the material and to screen the films intended for their children. The board permitted pupils to be excused from the program on parents' written request. It also printed information about the program in languages other than English for immigrant parents who were believed to be more traditional in their thinking about sex. Despite these precautions, the program became a focal point for parental opposition to sex education in schools.[81]

Parents found a staunch ally in school trustee Mahlon Beach. Elected to the board in 1961, Beach had served overseas with the Royal Canadian Air Force during the Second World War and had spent eleven months in prisoner-of-war camps in Eastern Europe. He was a member of the Riverdale Presbyterian Church, the editor of a masonic magazine, and a Bible teacher. By the time he left the board in 1972, however, he was best known for proclaiming that sex education in schools was 'a Communist plot to undermine the morality of our youth.'[82]

Beach's statement cannot be interpreted as a response to the TWC's demands. His declaration echoed a peculiar red-baiting argument advanced by American Christian right-wing opponents of school-based sex education. Galvanized by the rabidly anti-communist John Birch Society, they denounced sex education in schools as immoral, atheistic, and communistic. Beach was regularly lampooned in the press as a buffoon for his views, and he was largely isolated on the Toronto board. The polls told a different story, however. Beach's repeated electoral success was not due to his distrust of communism. It owed much more to the parents' rights argument that underpinned the American anti-communist rant against sex education.[83]

When Beach protested that school-based sex instruction would drive a wedge between parents and children that communist infiltrators would exploit, he was also responding to many parents' anxiety that advocates of progressive education would usurp parents' prerogative to manage their children's and, particularly, their daughters' sexuality. Progressive educators had maintained that while the proper place to teach children about sex was in the home, parents' neglect of this subject made it necessary for schools to fill the void in many children's sex education. This rationale no longer placated parents. For many parents, progressives who supported the inclusion of information about contraception and abortion information in schools were only too willing to equip girls with the knowledge they needed to engage in premarital sex and to avoid paying the penalty of an unwanted pregnancy.

By the mid-1970s the TWC, along with the High School Women's Liberation Club and the SBCRC, had disbanded. Births to unwed teens began to fall in Ontario in response to the availability of therapeutic abortions. The discourse on the tragedy of an unwanted pregnancy in young girls now devolved into a discourse on teenage pregnancy, due in part to the consternation of American population growth experts over the birth rate among single African American girls. Ironically, the unease Ontario parents continued to experience over the putative alliance between progressive educators and sexually rebellious girls was overshadowed by the fear of a possible partnership between progressive educators and gay rights' activists. The revisions to the Criminal Code which had decriminalized birth control and liberalized the abortion law had also legalized homosexual acts conducted in private between two consenting individuals over the age of twenty-one. Although the revisions did not legalize homosexuality, especially among youth, it set the stage for gay liberation. Taking their cue from the feminist movement, gay rights' activists began to demand equal rights.

The Ontario Department of Education responded by introducing another round of changes to its secondary level Health Education guidelines in 1975. Teachers were now expected to provide students with information on birth control and abortion and to include 'factual data about all the views that are held regarding sexuality.' According to the department, the new clause permitted teachers to apprise students that the American Psychiatric Association no longer considered homosexuality a mental illness and to help them develop respect for a wide range of sexual choices, ranging from homosexuality to marriage to celibacy.[84] Although the department once again permitted parents to remove their children from sex education classes they considered objectionable, the revisions proved too much.[85] Those parents opposed to the new guidelines unleashed a groundswell of protest that would burst into full flower during the early 1990s, when the Toronto board attempted to introduce anti-homophobia education in its schools.[86]

Sex education sensitive to young girls' reproductive needs proved to be an integral part of the second-wave feminist campaign for reproductive rights. During its short period of existence, the TWC used the discourse on the tragedy of an unwanted pregnancy to organize high school girls around their sexual and reproductive rights.

Although the TWC also used this same discourse to advance the group's ideals among a younger generation of women, the High School Women's Liberation Club and the SBCRC remain important examples of alliances forged between adult and teen feminists and of the political activism of young feminists. The TWC may have been overconfident in looking to young girls' access to birth control services as the solution to unwanted pregnancies. Yet in insisting that schools provide students with contraceptive devices, the High School Women's Liberation Club and the SBCRC were ahead of their time. Some Ontario schools have since made considerable progress towards this goal, ironically because of the panic generated over AIDS rather than that over teen pregnancy. Nevertheless, opponents of sex education in schools have also been successful in pressuring local school boards to promote abstinence rather than birth control as the way to curb both sexually transmitted disease and teen pregnancy.

NOTES

I am grateful for the financial support of the Social Sciences and Humanities Research Council of Canada. This paper is for Cindy.

1 'Campaign for High School Birth Control,' *Velvet Fist: A Women's Liberation Newspaper* 1, 4 (1971): 8.
2 Toronto Board of Education, *Minutes of the Board of Education*, 21 January 1971, 20–1.
3 'High School Women Demand Liberation,' *Young Socialist* 2, 2 March 1971, 4.
4 Alison Prentice et al., eds., *Canadian Women: A History* (Toronto: Harcourt Brace Jovanovich, 1988), 352–5; Janine Brodie, Shelley A.M. Gavigan, and Jane Jenson, *The Politics of Abortion* (Toronto: Oxford University Press, 1992); Ruth Roach Pierson, Marjorie Griffin Cohen, Paula Bourne, and Philinda Masters, *Canadian Women's Issues*, vol. 1: *Strong Voices* (Toronto: James Lorimer, 1993): 98–102.

5 Nancy Adamson, Linda Briskin, and Margaret McPhail, *Feminist Organizing for Change: The Contemporary Women's Movement in Canada* (Toronto: Oxford University Press, 1988), 50.

6 Deborah Fraleigh Personal Collection, Corileen North, and Yvonne Trower, 'To Individuals Associated with the Toronto Women's Caucus and/or the Women's Liberation Movement as a Whole,' [28?] March 1971, and 'Socialism and Women's Liberation: A Reply to a Letter of Corileen North and Yvonne Trower,' 1 April 1971.

7 Kate Porter, 'Paper Doll,' *Young Socialist Forum* 4, 6 (December 1967): 3–13.

8 Kristin Luker, *Dubious Conceptions: The Politics of Teenage Pregnancy* (Cambridge, Mass.: Harvard University Press, 1996). For the Canadian situation, see Doris Elise Guyatt, 'Adolescent Pregnancy: A Study of Pregnant Teenagers in a Suburban Community in Ontario' (DSW dissertation, University of Toronto, 1976), 12–18.

9 Compiled from *Selected Birth and Fertility Statistics, Canada, 1921–1990/ Statistiques choisies sur la natalité et la fécondité, Canada, 1921 à 1990*, Statistics Canada, 1993; *Selected Marriage Statistics, 1921–1990/Certains renseignements sur les mariages contractés de 1921 à 1990*, Statistics Canada, 1992; Jack Zackler and Wayne Brandstadt, eds., *The Teenage Pregnant Girl* (Springfield, Ill.: Charles C. Thomas, 1975), 18–19; Guyatt, 'Adolescent Pregnancy,' 6–7; George Anthony, Sheri Craig, Gary Oakes, and Diane Stratas, 'Young, Lonely, Unmarried and Pregnant,' *The Telegram*, 3 July 1967, 6, excerpted in Beth Light and Ruth Roach Pierson, eds., *No Easy Road: Women in Canada 1920s to 1960s* (Toronto: New Hogtown Press, 1990), 116.

10 Doug Owram, *Born at the Right Time: A History of the Baby Boom Generation* (Toronto: University of Toronto Press, 1996), 136–58. Constance Nathanson makes the same point in her *Dangerous Passage: The Social Control of Sexuality in Women's Adolescence* (Philadelphia: Temple University Press, 1991), 26.

11 Ricki Solinger, *Wake Up Little Susie: Single Pregnancy and Race before Roe v. Wade* (New York and London: Routledge, 1992), 205–31, and Regina Kunzel, *Fallen Women, Problem Girls: Unmarried Mothers and the Professionalization of Social Work, 1890–1945* (New Haven and London: Yale University Press, 1993), 144–70.

12 Prentice et al., *Canadian Women*, 319–42. See also Kristin Luker, *Abortion and the Politics of Motherhood* (Berkeley: University of California Press, 1984), 118.

13 Arthur Campbell, 'The Role of Family Planning in the Reduction of Poverty,' *Journal of Marriage and the Family* 30, 2 (1968): 236–45. My thanks to Ann Marie Sorenson for bringing this reference to my attention.

14 Bonnie Buxton, 'The Single-Mother Subculture,' *Chatelaine*, February 1970, 36, 70, 72. For more information on government policies on single mothers, see Margaret Little, *'No Car, No Radio, No Liquor Permit': The Moral Regulation of Single Mothers in Ontario, 1920–1997* (Toronto: Oxford University Press, 1998), 145–6.

15 Luker, *Dubious Conceptions*, 114–15.
16 DFPC, Karen Cunliffe, Toronto Women's Caucus, 'Report of the National Abortion Conference,' Columbia University, New York City, 16–18 July 1971, 1.
17 Canadian Women's Movement Archives, Toronto Women's Caucus Herstory, 'Abortion: A Woman's Right to Choose' (1970?).
18 Canadian Institute of Public Opinion, 'Majority of Adults Favor Sex Education in Our High Schools,' 10 June 1964.
19 TBE, Jean Robinson, 'Sex Education,' *Toronto Telegram*, 13 October 1966. See also Nathanson, *Dangerous Passsage*, 59.
20 George S. Tomkins, *A Common Countenance: Stability and Change in the Canadian Curriculum* (Scarborough, Ont.: Prentice Hall Canada Inc., 1986), 405.
21 John R. Seeley, 'The Facts of Life: A Plea for Their Place in School,' *Toronto Educational Quarterly* 2, 1 (1962): 2–7.
22 W.E. Mann, 'Canadian Trends in Premarital Behaviour: Some Preliminary Studies of Youth in High School and University,' *Bulletin: The Council for Social Service*, December 1967, 22–3.
23 Satu Repo, 'Unwanted Pregnancy: An Issue Out of Focus,' *This Magazine Is about Schools* 1, 1 (1966): 76–89.
24 Canadian Education Association, *The Present Status of Sex Education in Canadian Schools*, Report No. 2, September 1964, 6.
25 Ontario Department of Education, *Physical and Health Education Intermediate Division*, 1966.
26 Ontario Department of Education, *Growing into Maturity in a Changing World and Family Health in a Changing World*, Curriculum S. 29A, 1969, 11.
27 Kit Evans, 'Every Child a Wanted Child,' *Velvet Fist* 1, 1 (1970): 8.
28 Wilhelm Reich, *The Sexual Revolution: Toward a Self-Regulating Character Structure*, trans. Therese Pol (1935; New York: Pocket Books, 1975).
29 'Wilhelm Reich on the Sexual Liberation of Youth,' *Young Socialist*, February 1972, 3, 10.
30 Elise F. Jones et al., eds., *Teenage Pregnancy in Industrialized Countries* (New Haven and London: Yale University Press, 1986), 79.
31 Robin Badgley, Denyse Fortin Caron, and Marion G. Powell, *Report of the Committee on the Operation of the Abortion Law* (Ottawa: Minister of Supply and Services, 1977), 237–45.
32 Guyatt, 'Adolescent Pregnancy,' 13.
33 'Editorial from *The New Feminist*,' a document in Adamson, Briskin, and McPhail, *Feminist Organizing for Change*, 265.
34 'Diddle Diddle Dumpling,' *The New Feminist*, 8 December 1969, 9.
35 CWMA, Women's Liberation Movement files, 'This Is Your Copy of the BIRTH CONTROL HANDBOOK,' and 'Abortion Collective,' [1969?].
36 Becki Ross, *The House That Jill Built: A Lesbian Nation in Formation* (Toronto: University of Toronto Press, 1995).
37 CWMA Women's Liberation Movement files, 'High School Collective,' [1970?].

38 TBE, Lotta Dempsey, 'Abortion Committee Finds Its Support Is Increasing,' *Toronto Star*, 6 February 1971.

39 'High School Women,' in Leslie B. Tanner, ed., *Voices from Women's Liberation* (New York: New American Library, 1971), 215–30.

40 Interviews with Liz Barkley, 29 September 1997; Pam Dineen, 13 June 1996; Debbie Fraleigh, 8 September 1997.

41 Debbie Fraleigh and Katie Curtin, 'High School Women's Liberation,' *Young Socialist* 1, 2 (1970): 3.

42 Ilona Laney, 'High School Women,' *Velvet Fist* 2, 3 (1972): np.

43 Donna Sheehan, 'High School Women's Lib?,' ibid. 1, 1 (1970): np, and DFPC, Helen Orr and Graciela Marandola, 'Women's Liberation,' *Verdad*, 1970, 2–3.

44 Ellie Kirzner, 'Mis-education of Women: Taught to Be "Beautiful,"' *Young Socialist* 1, 1 (1970): 3. See also Christabelle Sethna, 'The Facts of Life: The Sex Instruction of Ontario Public School Children, 1900–1950' (PhD dissertation, University of Toronto, 1995).

45 DFPC, Toronto Women's Caucus, High School Fraction, 'Women's Liberation in the Public Schools,' [1970?].

46 Interview with Liz Barkley, 29 September 1997, and Wendy Dorrey, 19 June 1996.

47 Helen Orr and Graciela Marandola, 'Women's Liberation,' *Verdad*, 1970, 2–3.

48 'School Students Elect Activist,' *Toronto Telegram*, 10 April 1971. Interviews with Liz Barkley, 29 September 1997; Pam Dineen, 13 June 1996; Deborah Fraleigh, 8 September 1997.

49 Interview with Graciela Marandola, 25 July 1997.

50 Interview with Wendy Dorrey, 19 June 1996.

51 Orr and Marandola, 'Women's Liberation, 3.

52 Fraleigh and Curtin, 'High School Women's Liberation,' 3, and interviews with Liz Barkley, 29 September 1997, and Pam Dineen, 13 June 1996.

53 DFPC, Garry Dawe, 'The Movement,' *Verdad* 2, 1 [1971?]: 7.

54 Kathy Ross, 'Invasion,' *The Other Woman/Bellyful/Velvet Fist*, winter 1972, 6.

55 Interview with Liz Barkley, 29 September 1997.

56 Donna Cherniak, Allan Feingold, and the Students' Society of McGill University, eds., *Birth Control Handbook* (1968; Montréal: Journal Offset, August 1970). For further information, see Betsy Hartmann, *Reproductive Rights and Wrongs: The Global Politics of Population Control and Contraceptive Choice* (New York: Harper and Row, 1987).

57 Paul R. Ehrlich, *The Population Bomb* (1968: reprint, New York: Balantine Books, 1971), 134.

58 Donna Cherniak and Allan Feingold, 'Birth Control Handbook,' in *Women Unite! An Anthology of the Canadian Women's Movement* (Toronto: Canadian Women's Educational Press, 1972), 111.

59 Interview with Deborah Fraleigh, 13 June 1995.

60 Christabelle Sethna, 'High School Confidential: RCMP Surveillance of Second-

ary Student Activists,' in Gary Kinsman, Mercedes Steedman, and Dieter Buse, eds., *Whose National Security?* (forthcoming).

61 My thanks to Deborah Fraleigh for providing me with these letters.

62 Prentice et al., *Canadian Women*, 347.

63 *Report of the Royal Commission of the Status of Women in Canada* (Ottawa: Information Canada, 1970), 278.

64 DFPC, High School Students Birth Control Rights C'tee, 'For Immediate Release,' 7 and 22 February 1971.

65 'Campaign for High School Birth Control.'

66 DFPC, Students Birth Control Rights Committee, 'Petition,' nd.

67 'Campaign for High School Birth Control.'

68 TBE, Minutes of the Toronto Board of Education, 22 February 1962, 24; Reports 1940–1962, Family Life Education, 9 April 1962.

69 TBE, Administrative Services Reports, 1966, nos. 1–401, Report 143, 25 March 1966.

70 Ibid.

71 'Campaign for High School Birth Control.'

72 Guyatt, 'Adolescent Pregnancy,' 241.

73 Ibid.

74 Interview with Liz Barkley, 29 September 1997.

75 Interview with Deborah Fraleigh, 8 September 1997.

76 Luker, *Dubious Conceptions*, 146.

77 See Anthony, Craig, Oakes, and Stratas, 'Young, Lonely, Unmarried and Pregnant,' 117.

78 Doris Guyatt, 'Adolescent Sexuality: It's Implications for Social Work,' in Health and Welfare/Santé et Bien-être social Canada, *Family Planning and Social Work* (Ottawa: Ministry of National Health and Welfare, 1976), 191–6.

79 Guyatt, 'Adolescent Pregnancy,' 243–4.

80 TBE, Charles J. Guth, '"Why I Object to the Teaching of Contraception in Schools,"' *Toronto Star*, 5 July 1971.

81 Larry Collins, 'Sex Education for Parents,' *Telegram*, 31 August 1966.

82 Mahlon Beach, quoted in an invitation to an election-day reception for him which appeared in the *Globe and Mail*, 4 October 1969, and reproduced in the *SIECCAN Toronto Newsletter*, 4, 2 (1969): 4.

83 Mary Breasted, *Oh! Sex Education* (New York: Praeger Publishers, 1970).

84 Archives of Ontario (AO), RG 2-82-1, cc. 15689-66, TB6 621-30-4-6, letter to Mesdames Smith and Neidraver from G.M. MacMartin, 19 March 1974.

85 AO, RG 2-82-4, TB 11 621-30-4-11, letter to Robert Welch [misidentified as the minister of education] from Mrs Dorothy Chalmers, 5 May 1975.

86 John Campey, Tim McCaskell, John Miller, and Vanessa Russell, 'Opening the Classroom Closet: Dealing with Sexual Orientation at the Toronto Board of Education,' in Susan Prentice, ed., *Sex in Schools: Canadian Education and Sexual Regulation* (Toronto: Our Schools/Our Selves Education Foundation, 1994), 82–100.

Welfare to Workfare: Poverty and the 'Dependency Debate' in Post–Second World War Ontario

JAMES STRUTHERS

In the spring of 1995 Mike Harris's Conservative Party won a surprise victory in the Ontario provincial election by making welfare reform the most visceral issue of the campaign.[1] Vowing to 'break the cycle of dependency' that he claimed trapped welfare families within a life of poverty, Harris told Ontario's voters that, if elected, his government would give social assistance recipients 'a reason to get out of bed in the morning.' A Conservative government would cut allowances by 25 per cent and impose 'mandatory work-for-welfare requirements' on all the able-bodied. Those who refused to participate would 'lose their benefits entirely.'[2] Harris's ability to capitalize on a groundswell of public dissatisfaction with the welfare system caught most media commentators and Bob Rae's New Democratic Party government by surprise. Ontario's total welfare caseload had more than tripled between 1981 and 1994, rising from 4 per cent to over 12 per cent of the population, or one out of every eight provincial residents. Annual welfare spending had jumped from less than $2 billion to over $6.2 billion over the same period. The driving force behind this explosion, according to Harris, was not recession or economic restructuring, but overly generous welfare benefits that had lured the working poor into chronic dependency. 'The system is broken,' he argued. 'It needs fixing, not tinkering.'[3] Harris's adroit cultivation of a populist welfare backlash played a decisive role in the Conservative's come-from-behind election victory.[4]

On taking power, the Harris government immediately slashed welfare benefits by 21.6 per cent. One year later it unveiled Ontario Works, a new mandatory work-for-welfare regime modelled on American state precedents in New Jersey, Michigan, and Wisconsin, whose goal was to have all employable welfare clients, including single mothers, enrolled in compulsory training, job search, or community work placement schemes by the end of 1998. The 'current welfare system encourages indolence,' social services minister David Tsubouchi told the legislature in justifying the new scheme. Ontario Works, in contrast, would 'demand responsible behavior and individual initiative from people on welfare. For many ... this will be the first time they have had any obligation to work, or even look for work.' Although other parts of the Harris Common Sense Revolution remain mired in controversy, workfare, despite long delays and difficulties in implementation, has the support of 70 per cent of Ontarians, according to public opinion surveys.[5]

Before the Harris victory, welfare had not been a major issue within an Ontario provincial election since the Great Depression. Why did it re-emerge so forcefully six decades later? To what extent have concerns about 'welfare dependency' always surrounded policy debates around social assistance, and in what ways has the discourse been different for men as opposed to women? Why were compulsory work tests abolished in the early 1960s, and why are they now coming back? To what extent does the creation of Ontario Works represent a symbolic turning point within the Canadian welfare state? This essay will attempt to place the Harris government's handling of workfare in context by providing a brief examination of previous cycles of welfare reform and dependency debates within Ontario since the 1930s.

Moral panic around the work ethic during the Great Depression provides the closest parallel to the turbulent welfare politics of the 1990s. It was during the economic crisis of the 1930s that the structure of our welfare bureaucracy first took shape.[6] Then, as now, Ontarians found themselves confronted by exploding relief caseloads, persistent high levels of unemployment, and the stubborn failure of welfare expenditure to decline despite signs of economic recovery.

One common response was to blame the unemployed for preferring relief to work, and to demand compulsory work tests on municipal, provincial, and federal projects as a condition for receiving assistance. 'Cheating is rampant ... [on] direct relief,' Ontario's welfare minister David Croll proclaimed in the autumn of 1934 when Canada's jobless rate stood at almost 22 per cent. Too many of the able-bodied were 'being given rations, shelter, and clothing ... without being required to make any return,' a policy that was 'detrimental to anyone's morale.' Newly elected Liberal premier Mitch Hepburn agreed. 'There's a growing impression among the taxpayers of this province that they are being drained of their money to provide a living for idlers. There's a growing demand for a halt on rising relief costs,' he told the legislature within a year of coming to power. Arguing that 'something for nothing is a dangerous creed,' Croll and Hepburn demanded that local welfare departments require all able-bodied married men to perform work in municipal woodyards or on other city projects as a condition for maintaining their families' eligibility for assistance. Single unemployed men, from 1933 onwards, were already being sent to federal defence department relief camps to perform compulsory work in exchange for their room, board, and a daily 20-cent 'allowance.' The 'moral purpose' of these camps, government officials argued, was to cure a 'state of mind diseased by ... compulsory idleness' by abolishing the men's 'mental attitude that assistance from the State was their inherent right.'[7]

Croll's department also rolled back welfare rates 14 per cent in more than thirty Ontario communities where it believed local councils were paying benefits that were too generous. 'Relief allowances are so close to the amount that can be earned by laborers on full time work that the wages earners' point of view becomes important. What incentive is there for them to work?' senior department officials argued in defence of the cuts. Despite strikes, occupations of local welfare offices, 'hunger marches,' and frequent demonstrations by organizations of the unemployed between 1934 and 1936, Hepburn and Croll stuck to their motto of Relief for Workers, Nothing for Shirkers. For the remainder of the Depression, work tests and surprise home visiting of families – 'to purge exploiters and cheaters' from relief caseloads – remained ongoing features of provincial and municipal welfare administration across Ontario.[8]

Welfare did not disappear as a political issue during the 1940s, even though wartime full employment shrunk relief caseloads to only a fraction of their Depression level. Throughout the war years, welfare was restricted mostly to widows or deserted mothers with children, along with disabled elderly men and women who were still too young to collect a means-tested old age pension.[9] The able-bodied jobless after 1941 were simply cut off relief, although workers could now become eligible for benefits under the new national unemployment insurance scheme launched that same year.

The war experience provided a fertile climate for welfare reform. Detailed research on basic minimum living costs by social planning bodies such as the Toronto Welfare Council proved extremely effective in generating widespread publicity around the glaring inadequacy of provincial and local relief allowances, first formulated during the hard times of the Great Depression. In an era when prices and wages were subjected to stringent wartime regulations, and over one-third of the men volunteering to join the armed forces had been rejected because of poor health, the dangerously low living standards of individuals and families on social assistance were hard to justify. Coordinated pressure from women's organizations, social workers, and nutritionists helped to convince first the City of Toronto, and subsequently the provincial government by 1944, to adopt scientific nutritional standards for pricing welfare food allowances across Ontario.[10] Women on mothers' allowances also received a 20 per cent hike in benefits, the first increase since the program was launched in 1920. By 1945 they would also be getting monthly family allowance payments ranging from $5 to $8 from the federal government for each of their children. In combination, these two policy changes between 1943 and 1945 almost doubled the monthly incomes of many mothers on social assistance, notwithstanding their increased opportunities to gain earnings from part-time work.[11]

Full employment, along with a wartime political climate emphasizing the values of social solidarity, sacrifice, and postwar reconstruction, briefly transformed the context of welfare politics within Ontario, a change signalled most dramatically by the near victory of the socialist CCF in the 1943 provincial election. Demands for work tests and moral alarm over relief dependency, so prevalent during the 1930s, eased once the exceptionally tight labour market of the Second World War put virtually everyone who wanted a job into paid employment. The new Conservative administration of George Drew, elected on a '22 point program' of social reform, appointed a social worker, Burne Heise, as deputy minister of public welfare. Over the next three years Heise enlisted the help of Ontario social work leaders to develop a plan for comprehensive welfare reform. Through the creation of regional welfare units across Ontario, staffed by trained social workers, Heise planned to bring an end to 'aimless policies ... guided by local whims ... or financial expediency,' so that welfare clients, no matter where they lived, would receive 'proper standards of aid.'[12]

Heise's vision of modernizing and consolidating the province's haphazard welfare system was short-lived. Ontario's provincial treasurer, Leslie Frost, warned Drew that any assistance scheme not based on social insurance had a tendency 'to instill into our people the feeling that the country owes them a living.' In a 1946 Cabinet shuffle, Drew appointed a new welfare minister, W.A. Goodfellow, a former rural reeve who believed that postwar social policy reform was moving too fast. 'People are losing their spirit of independence ... and the will to do for themselves ... [They] are only kidding themselves if they think they can get something for nothing,' he warned. Across Ontario, particularly in rural areas where taxes and welfare benefits were kept as low as possible, local politicians quickly mobilized strong opposition against Heise's plan for regionalization of welfare services. As the treasurer of the Ontario Municipal Association reminded a 1947 conference of provincial social workers, the 'primary responsibility' of local officials was 'to those whom they represent and not to the underprivileged.' By 1949, when Frost replaced Drew as Ontario's premier, the brief war-inspired cycle of welfare reform was all but dead. Heise was forced to resign as deputy welfare minister and his ambitious plan for the standardization of Ontario's welfare services remained stillborn. His successor, James Band, was a former relief inspector from the 1930s with no social work training who had carefully worked his way through the ranks of the provincial welfare department with a reputation for vigorous policing of local welfare costs. As deputy minister, Band would dominate the formation of provincial welfare policy for the next two decades.[13]

Ontario's prolonged economic boom throughout most of the 1950s pushed issues of poverty and welfare into the background. Within Toronto, shelter allowances for welfare clients between 1951 and 1961 remained effectively frozen at ceilings set in 1951, despite a 60 per cent jump in the cost of living. Maximum food allowances grew by only 30 per cent. By 1961, according to detailed calculations made by the Toronto Social Planning Council, a mother-led family on welfare with three children was receiving less than half the monthly income needed to reach a basic standard of adequacy. Single people on welfare received only 29 per cent of the council's recommended minimum monthly budget.[14] With annual unemployment rates remaining below 3 per cent, concerns about welfare dependency or the erosion of the work ethic were minimal, particularly since the able-bodied jobless remained ineligible for social assistance. Within the field of welfare, attention focused on the therapeutic adjustment or rehabilitation of 'problem families' through social casework and the incremental expansion of program eligibility to include wider categories of those in need.

Two groups claimed the most attention. The first was single mothers. Since the late 1940s Ontario's mothers' allowance program had undergone a process of incremental liberalization. In 1946 women deserted by their husbands for one year, rather than three years, gained eligibility for benefits, and in 1951 divorced mothers in need were also included. But the most symbolic policy shift occurred in 1956 when unwed mothers were finally brought into the program. Since the inception of mothers' allowances in 1920, the key criteria for determining benefit eligibility was that women be deemed 'fit and proper persons,' a condition interpreted to exclude all mothers who had conceived children outside marriage. Although some advocates for mothers' pensions had never accepted a double standard that punished needy children for the marital status of their parents, most women's groups and social workers, before the 1950s, agreed with the Toronto Social Planning Council's statement that 'plac[ing] the unmarried mother in the same status as the married or widowed mother [would] tend to lower standards rather than raise them.'[15]

Three trends converged by the middle of the 1950s to undercut such moralizing distinctions. The first was the growing demand from municipal authorities to shift the costs of caring for illegitimate children from local taxpayers, who financed the largest share of the work of foster homes and Children's Aid Societies, to the provincial government, which had exclusive responsibility for mothers' allowances. Many unmarried mothers, Toronto's mayor argued in the 1940s, were 'just as capable ... of giving their children good care' as foster parents, whose support, through the CAS, was a 'heavy cost to the municipality.' By the mid-1950s, the dominance of psychiatric theory among social workers employed within child welfare agencies also eroded earlier moral distinctions around who was or was not a 'fit and proper person.' Viewed through the lens of casework, social workers argued, unwed motherhood should be seen 'not ... merely as a sex experience and a violation of the moral code of the community, but as a symptom of behavior expressing the needs of the individual.' Through therapeutic adjustment and with ongoing financial support, some of these women could be rehabilitated to become caring parents. Perhaps the most persuasive argument was simply that illegitimacy rates across Ontario in the 1950s, along with the overall mothers' allowance caseload, were going steadily down.[16] Consequently, the cost of adding unwed mothers to the program was expected to be negligible. 'We have to go slowly ... We don't want to encourage this kind of conduct, but we ought to encourage a mother to bring up her own child,' Ontario's welfare minister Louis Cecile argued when this symbolic change was made in 1956.[17]

Employable men, denied welfare benefits since the end of the Depression, were the second group to gain eligibility in 1957. In contrast with single mothers, who were not expected to seek full-time employment, the problem of what to do about the able-bodied jobless ineligible for federal unemployment insurance benefits revived a different moral debate around welfare rights and the work ethic. About one-third of Ontario's unemployed during the 1950s were recent immigrants, workers in seasonal industries not covered under the Unemployment Insurance (UI) program, or people who had exhausted their insurance benefits through prolonged joblessness. Although their numbers were not large during these years of prosperity, their plight was desperate. The federal, provincial, and local governments were not willing to assume any legal responsibility for their care. As a result, their survival, particularly during the difficult winter months, was dependent on intermittent help from friends, family members, or private charities. Toronto officials reported that many of the married jobless in these years were 'deserting their families so that the women and children could go on straight relief.' Soup kitchens and hostels during winter months were 'full to overflowing,' and heads of families simply could not understand 'why they should not have either work or assistance.' Since many of these men were recent immigrants, they also shared a 'frantic fear of deportation.'[18]

The Ontario government, along with other provinces, argued that since Ottawa had assumed constitutional responsibility for unemployment insurance in 1940, the care of all the able-bodied jobless was a federal problem. Queen's Park wished 'to have nothing to do with unemployment relief.' The federal government of Louis St Laurent replied that its primary responsibility to the jobless was limited only to those who paid UI premiums. Payments for unemployment relief would resume 'only when the problem reached emergency proportions,' something that clearly had not occurred during the 1950s.[19]

This impasse was finally broken in 1955, when the Canadian Welfare Council threatened to organize a national conference on unemployment to publicize the plight of the thousands of unemployed trapped outside of the federal UI scheme. When most of the provinces indicated they were willing to attend, the St Laurent government avoided political embarrassment by agreeing to resume negotiations with the provinces on a shared-cost unemployment relief scheme if the council called off its plans for a national conference. A year later, St Laurent's administration passed the Unemployment Assistance Act which, for the first time since 1941, restored federal funding for employables on provincial and local welfare.[20]

Ontario delayed entering into the new federal unemployment assistance program until 1957, when the Conservative government of John Diefenbaker agreed to share half the cost of all clients on general welfare, not simply the able-bodied, a policy change that would prove critical in the years ahead. Nonetheless, Frost's administration reinstated eligibility for welfare to employables only with reluctance, arguing that it did not wish to 'revert to the dole system of the thirties.' A preferable solution, W.A. Goodfellow argued, would be to allow local governments 'to put a person on relief work rather than on relief and still qualify for Federal aid.' Without some work requirements, government officials pointed out, providing relief to able-bodied men could upset the delicate relationship between welfare and wage rates for low-income workers. When medical care and family allowances were factored in, the maximum welfare allowance for men with families was already higher than what many low-wage earners could make, and most men were 'reluctant to accept employment unless it would afford a higher income than Public Assistance.'[21]

In 1956, when the Unemployment Assistance Act was passed, the Canadian economy was still booming and federal officials did not expect that the cost of the scheme would amount to more than $13 million a year. Instead, the so-called Diefenbaker recession struck Canada in 1958, a cyclical and structural downturn whose effects would persist until the early spring of 1962. Annual unemployment rates shot up to 7 per cent, more than double the levels prevailing throughout most of the 1950s. With the return of significant levels of unemployment came a 150 per cent increase in welfare caseloads, soon to be followed by renewed calls for bringing back compulsory work requirements for the able-bodied jobless.

Ottawa's Unemployment Assistance Act was silent over the question of workfare. Indeed, it contained almost no regulations on welfare standards whatsoever, simply providing 50 per cent federal funding for all local and provincial direct relief spending. It remained up to Ontario's municipalities to decide what conditions they wished to attach to help the able-bodied applying for welfare. By 1959 many had begun to reinstate work tests. In Chippewa, just south of Niagara Falls, women on general welfare assistance were put to work washing the windows and cleaning the floors of the town hall for sixteen hours each month. Scarborough divided the monthly welfare payments of its employables by an hourly rate of $1.55 and demanded that they work it out through eight-hour days 'clearing ... brush from undeveloped township land.' London's mayor told Ontario's premier that the men in his city liked to work out their assistance because 'it took the stigma out of welfare and helped them to retain their self-respect.' The Ontario Welfare Officers' Association claimed that 'the threat of work stimulates people to find other support than welfare.'[22]

Workfare's most powerful advocate within the province was deputy welfare minister James Band, who had perfected such systems during his years as a roving provincial relief inspector during the Great Depression. 'There are many services that can be performed by recipients in return for the assistance granted which do not greatly affect the stream of economic life in the community,' Band told federal officials in justifying the return of workfare to Ontario. 'Most of these projects are basically work tests of a temporary nature such as cutting wood ... road work, brushing, and other projects of this type.' Such tasks kept the jobless 'usefully occupied ... without prejudice to anyone.'[23]

To his great surprise, Band discovered that throughout much of Ontario, and within the federal government itself, the idea of workfare was no longer acceptable. Unlike the 1930s, Ontario by 1960 had a strong trade union movement which, after two decades of high employment and Keynesian economic thinking, viewed unemployment as a national economic problem, not a test of moral character for the jobless. Ontario's unions demanded extended UI benefits and job creation projects with real wages to combat the recession, not the return of punitive practices which, as the National Union of Public Employees argued, would 'create unemployment for regular municipal employees.'[24]

Equally significant was the changed climate of public opinion reflected in newspaper editorials about workfare across the province. 'Older citizens,' the *Belleville Intelligencer* reminded its readers, 'will remember the "make-work" schemes of the Depression, the devices by which relief recipients were required to "earn" the meagre aid received but which so often robbed this work of all dignity because it served no useful social purpose ... Lacking such a purpose, enforced labour comes very near to being a punishment for poverty.' When a local alderman in Peterborough recommended bringing back work tests, the *Peterborough Examiner* argued that giving in to such demands would allow 'penny-pinching municipalities to exploit those on welfare as a cheap source of labour for municipal projects.' It was a 'sure way to bring back the workhouse.' The *Toronto Star* best summed up the way two decades of postwar affluence had changed public thinking about workfare by the early 1960s. 'Our wealthy society has the obligation to provide [the unemployed] with work at a living wage. Failing this, it has the obligation to support them and their families decently – not in exchange for forced labour, not as a matter of charity, but simply as a matter of right.'[25]

Any chance that workfare might make a comeback during the Diefenbaker recession was put to rest by federal officials in Ottawa. Ironically, Canada's auditor general, not usually a friend of social reform, singled out workfare schemes within Ontario as an example of gross fiscal mismanagement within federal financing of the Unemployment Assistance Act, whose costs had ballooned to more than $200 million by the early 1960s. Federal funding provided through this legislation was intended solely for relieving the jobless, not to subsidize cheap labour for municipal improvement schemes, the auditor general argued. Seizing on his critique, social work officials within the federal Department of National Health and Welfare, who detested the idea of workfare as a 'return to Old Poor Law concepts' that reflected a 'punitive approach to relief recipients,' informed the Ontario government that local communities implementing workfare would be ineligible for 50 per cent federal cost sharing. 'Being requested to join a work gang may be physically and emotionally more damaging than being without employment,' Health and Welfare administrators argued; nor would such routine labour 'help the individual to obtain new skills.' They also warned that senior governments would never be able to 'avoid becoming enmeshed in the normal public works and "housekeeping" programs of the municipalities if work for relief projects involving welfare funds were developed.' Deprived of 50 per cent federal dollars, Ontario's brief flirtation with a return to workfare came to a halt by 1961.[26]

With the election of the federal Liberal government of Lester Pearson, campaigning on an activist social policy agenda in 1963,[27] welfare reform underwent its most significant cycle of expansion, culminating in the passage of the Canada Assistance Plan in 1966. A number of divergent factors converged during these years to push the national and provincial governments towards widening welfare entitlement. The first was an unanticipated consequence of the 1956 Unemployment Assistance Act. Ottawa's willingness to finance half the costs of provincial and local general relief caseloads through this program injected a huge stream of new revenue into the field of welfare policy. Within Ontario, for example, this new federal money cut the local government share of general welfare costs in half, from 40 per cent to only 20 per cent. Under these circumstances, municipalities now had the fiscal capacity to meet a wider portion of the unmet budgetary needs of their welfare clients, particularly for burgeoning shelter costs in cities such as Toronto. Provincial governments also had a strong incentive to shift as many people as possible out of other categorical assistance programs such as mothers' allowances, where there was no federal cost sharing, or old age assistance and disability allowances, where federal aid was subject to strict conditions, onto the general relief caseload, where the more open-ended terms of the Unemployment Assistance Act gave Ottawa much weaker control over provincial spending. As a consequence, general welfare costs and caseloads rose dramatically after 1958, and continued to grow even as the economy pulled out of recession. By 1963 unemployment assistance was one of Ottawa's fastest-growing social policy expenditures, yet only one-third of the program's clients were either 'unemployed' or capable of looking for work. This rapid expansion of social spending within a shared-cost program that lacked clear standards, definitions, or accounting procedures pushed federal authorities towards an entirely new legislative framework for public assistance.[28]

Welfare reform also gained great momentum when American president Lyndon Johnson declared a War on Poverty in his January 1964 State of the Union Address. America's War on Poverty, as Gareth Davies argues, 'was a war born of optimism. Abundance created the conditions in which a successful campaign might be launched, while new knowledge encouraged the belief that the causes – and not merely the consequences – could be eliminated.'[29] Within Canada, Pearson lost little time in echoing Johnson's uplifting rhetoric by promising 'the elimination of poverty among our people' in his April 1965 speech from the throne.[30]

Anti-poverty crusaders on both sides of the border described the poor as being trapped within a 'culture of poverty' that prevented them from taking advantage of the opportunities afforded by the economic boom sweeping across North America during the 1960s. There was a 'whole subculture of poverty,' Ontario's New Democratic Party argued, 'of people and their families ... who live within the community but are not part of it and who have developed their own culture of poverty with its own conditions and its own customs.' To break out of this 'vicious circle,' they needed more than money. More important was the provision of 'individual counselling,' 'remedial training and retraining,' and 'rehabilitation services,' all of which should be designed to 'assist them to reestablish themselves as independent, self-reliant citizens.'[31]

In some respects, this early War on Poverty discourse shared assumptions with later workfare campaigns of the 1990s. Within both eras, reformers targeted the cultural values of the poor as a principal cause of poverty and viewed character rehabilitation as a key tool for lifting individuals and families out of poverty. But unlike workfare advocates, most anti-poverty crusaders in the 1960s did not view overly generous welfare entitlement as the principal cause of dependency, particularly given the low benefit levels and narrow eligibility criteria that had surrounded welfare during the previous decade. Nor did they support compulsory work tests as a way out of the welfare system. Instead, reformers sought to liberalize the scope and benefits of government social programs to bring wider categories of the poor within reach of job counselling, skills training, and therapeutic social work intervention. As Ontario's chief economist put it during a 1965 national conference on poverty, expanding opportunity required policies designed to 'lift ... the growing generation out of depressed conditions [through] education, training, or mobility, thereby not only improving their human condition but adding to [their] economic productiveness as well.' From this 'dynamic' viewpoint, 'welfare policies become consistent with growth policies.'[32]

The cause of welfare reform in the 1960s also benefited from the shared social work values and training of senior officials within the federal Department of National Health and Welfare and many provincial welfare departments. Influential members of this policy-making elite had served apprenticeships within the Canadian Welfare Council before moving into government. As Rodney Haddow argues, the Canada Assistance Plan 'emerged from this cooperative group of welfare officials. They reached a general consensus on reform in the [CWC] in the late 1950s, and elaborated this in direct federal-provincial negotiations from 1960 to 1964.'[33]

One key tenet of this consensus was that welfare was a social right. It should be available to any Canadian citizen at a standard sufficient to support health and decency on proof of the fact, not the cause, of need.[34] In other words, older moralizing distinctions between the deserving and the undeserving poor should be jettisoned by public welfare departments in determining eligibility for welfare. It was this belief that led federal welfare officials, along with some of their provincial counterparts, to push hard for the abolition of work tests as a key condition for funding within the Canada Assistance Plan of 1966, as well as for the abolition of the old moral requirement that mothers be 'fit and proper persons' to become eligible for mothers' allowances.[35] They were less successful, however, in achieving meaningful definitions of national minimum standards for benefit levels to be cost shared through the Canada Assistance Plan. Despite official statements that Ottawa's goal through welfare reform was to meet the poor's 'basic needs ... in ways that recognize and preserve [their] rights and dignity,' federal policy makers conceded privately that it was out of the question, politically, for Ottawa to define precisely what those basic needs might be. 'Standards can only be decided upon locally,' the Department of Finance's deputy minister insisted. It should be up to provincial governments to decide what basic level of assistance was appropriate in relation to minimum wage rates within their own borders.[36]

The main significance of the Canada Assistance Plan was to expand the scope of federal cost-sharing for social assistance into entirely new areas. Within Ontario, local Children's Aid Societies, women and children dependent on mothers' allowances, and welfare departments hiring new staff all became eligible for 50 per cent federal subsidization for the first time. Welfare recipients also gained appeal procedures against unfavourable decisions by local authorities, establishing the principle that welfare was indeed a social right of citizenship. Older categorical boundaries separating welfare support for the elderly, the disabled, and single mothers were abolished through the consolidation of all assistance programs into either family benefits for long-term assistance or general welfare assistance for short-term support, principally for the unemployed. On an across-the-board basis, welfare benefits rose 15 to 20 per cent within Ontario when the new legislation came into effect in 1967. It was the most significant single increase since the 1940s, although individual and family benefit levels, even after this increase, ranged from 43 per cent to 66 per cent, respectively, of the minimum budget standards for adequacy recommended by the Toronto Social Planning Council.[37]

Welfare expenditure and caseloads in Ontario continued to rise throughout the remainder of the 1960s, even though the province's economy grew at a record pace and unemployment remained below 4 per cent. By far the largest share of the rising caseload was composed of single mothers. Between 1966 and 1969 the number of families led by women on family benefits more than doubled, from 10,056 to 20,428, boosting the cost of this program by over 200 per cent. By 1972 more than 33,000 mothers in the province would be collecting family benefits, compared with only 7400 in the mid-1950s. Mother-led families on family benefits and general welfare represented one-third of the province's entire welfare caseload.[38] These soaring numbers were fuelled by both liberalized eligibility requirements and a rising rate of family fragmentation.

This 'feminization of poverty' remained one of the most neglected features of the entire debate on welfare during the 1960s. As in the United States, most of the language and program activity flowing out of Ottawa's anti-poverty initiatives in labour market training and regional development 'assumed that the overwhelming majority of those who need jobs, and therefore the skills to obtain jobs, were men,' even though single mothers were the fastest-growing component of the welfare budget. As a consequence, particular structural obstacles such as the absence of affordable daycare, which trapped women within a life of poverty, were ignored. By 1969 Ontario had only 5000 publicly subsidized daycare spaces, at a time when the children of family benefits and general welfare recipients numbered over 100,000. As the province's former director of general welfare assistance pointed out, 'this was like hoisting a small umbrella to shelter a stadium full of people in a downpour.' Across Ontario, only 15 per cent of mothers on family benefits reported any part-time earnings, and the average duration of women on social assistance was over twice the length of men's. Yet Ontario officials refused to see the provision of subsidized daycare as an urgent need for women who wished to escape from poverty. According to Louis Cecile, the province's welfare minister throughout most of the 1960s, it was the desire of too many mothers to combine 'employment and homemaking [that] has contributed to many of the social problems which have to be faced and treated.' Their 'primary responsibility,' he insisted, '[is] for family life.'[39]

For women on social assistance, these arguments were hypocritical. Why did the government 'pay foster mothers more money to look after youngsters than it gives to the natural mothers of these children?' asked Women Trapped in Poverty, an organization of welfare mothers, at the decade's end. 'There is no recognition of our contribution to society.' Harkening back to the origins of mothers' allowances in 1920 as a reward for 'service to the state,' these women demanded that natural mothers on family benefits deserved 'pay for work equal to the foster mother's at least,' as well as 'adequate shelter for our family' and 'greater opportunities and support to ... upgrade our education and eventually phase out of government assistance.' Instead, the level of family benefits to single mothers, as a proportion of the average Ontario family income or the Toronto Social Planning Council's minimum guide for social adequacy, remained virtually unaltered over the course of the 1960s. As Lorna Hurl concludes, 'over time the programme ... changed to ensure more equitable treatment of one group of sole-support ... mothers in relation to another, but not to provide greater adequacy or equality of recipients in relation to the population as a whole.'[40] For women on family benefits, the War on Poverty swelled their ranks but did not substantially alter their prospects for a better life.

One key group bypassed in the 1960s' cycle of welfare reform was the working poor, who laboured intermittently for low wages but were unable to earn enough to bring their living standards close to or above the poverty line. Concern about the relationship between minimum wages and welfare allowances, or the work/welfare tradeoff, had always been a dominant theme within Ontario and Canadian social policy. When the province's welfare benefits were enhanced after the passage of the Canada Assistance Plan, the plight of families living on minimum wage incomes who remained ineligible for social assistance drew growing attention. Two-thirds of the poor, a major study by the Economic Council of Canada revealed in 1968, worked at least part of the year, but could not qualify for needs-tested welfare benefits through the Canada Assistance Plan. Over one million Ontarians – about 13 per cent of the provincial population – were living in poverty, an influential federal government study chaired by Senator David Croll revealed two years later. 'The welfare system is a hopeless failure. The matter is not even controversial,' the Senate report on *Poverty in Canada* concluded.[41] Ontario officials agreed that the tradeoff between work and welfare created major dilemmas in determining a decent standard of social adequacy. 'The problem here [is] in terms of how high the level of allowances may be,' the province's deputy welfare minister told Croll's Senate committee. 'The higher they are, the greater becomes the differential between the person who works full time on low wages and the persons on public assistance ... [T]he person on public assistance begins to be in a position of marked advantage over the person working full time at low wages. If our allowances were higher ... this spread would become even greater than it is at present.' As John Yaremko, Ontario's welfare minister, conceded, 'Our big job now is to solve the problem of how to bring up the income of a family whose head is working full time and who we call, for want of a better term, the working poor.'[42]

The answer put forward by the Senate's 1970 report on *Poverty in Canada*, which borrowed heavily from welfare reform proposals emanating from south of the border, was for a single Guaranteed Annual Income, financed and administered by the federal government, which would replace the complex collection of federal income security programs. The rapid economic growth, and 'opportunity programs' of the 1960s had largely passed over the heads of the poor, the Senate report argued. Education, economic growth, and skills training by themselves were 'insufficient to break the cycle of dependency.' Instead, the poor needed more money. Poverty could 'be eliminated if Canadians so wish,' but only through 'the acceptance ... of an adequate minimum income as a matter of right for all citizens.' Once freed from the struggle of 'meeting the basic needs of survival, [the poor] will be able to take advantage of opportunity programs which will enable them to achieve independence.'[43]

Through a guaranteed annual income, all Canadians, working or otherwise, would receive a basic allowance sufficient to raise them to at least 70 per cent of the poverty line – defined by the Economic Council of Canada as the point at which an individual or family was spending 70 per cent of its income on basic requirements such as food, shelter, and clothing. People would be allowed to retain a proportion of this basic allowance while working, until their earned income reached the existing poverty-line threshold for their household size. All earned income below these thresholds would be exempt from taxation. Through a combination of work and welfare, in other words, everyone would be allowed to enjoy at least a minimum standard of adequacy. Put differently, supplementing the incomes of the working poor through tax-based transfers could reduce or eliminate the discrepancy between their living standards and those of welfare clients, without punishing or humiliating families dependent on social assistance.[44]

These 1970s' proposals for a guaranteed annual income, Gareth Davies argues, represented a major shift 'from opportunity to entitlement' in liberal thinking about poverty. At the start of the 1960s, welfare reformers and politicians who declared War on Poverty had 'shared the general tendency to equate dignity with self-sufficiency' and to define dependency on government support 'as its destructive opposite.' Embedded within the guaranteed income strategies of the early 1970s within both the United States and Canada lay a different assumption. Dignity was now seen as simply 'freedom both from hardship and stigma ... independence, far from connoting self-sufficiency in the conventional sense, meant freedom from want, however achieved.' As Davies concludes, this 'notion of an unconditional right to income' would prove to be a tough sell.[45]

Through the Social Security Review, conducted between 1973 and 1976, Ottawa and the provinces struggled to reach agreement on some form of income supplementation or modified guaranteed income for the working poor. Canada's existing welfare system, the federal government's 1973 orange paper on income security argued, gave the poor 'too little ... incentive to get off social assistance,' since welfare payments were frequently 'higher than what one could earn at or near the minimum wage.' To get people back to work and to encourage the working poor to stay off welfare, the orange paper advocated a 'general income supplementation plan ... to provide them with an incentive to keep on working rather than giving up and living on social aid.'[46]

Despite almost four years of federal-provincial negotiations over ways of boosting the incomes of the working poor, in the end little was accomplished. Rising unemployment and spiralling inflation during the mid-1970s provided a bad fiscal climate for launching an expensive new social program that Ottawa priced at $1 billion annually, but Ontario's treasurer estimated might cost three times as much. Quebec's wariness of any expansion of federal authority in the field of income security also created complications. But the critical opposition that destroyed any chance of success came from Ontario. Officials there had little use for the idea of a guaranteed annual income or for bringing the working poor into the framework of provincial social assistance. The guaranteed income concept, Ontario's veteran deputy welfare minister James Band warned the Cabinet, was 'an extremely costly venture' that was 'unlikely to bring us into the promised land in welfare ... or in any other area.' The key problem remained enforcing the work ethic. Any guarantee scheme that met standards of basic adequacy would provide few incentives to work. One that contained strong work incentives could hardly meet basic needs. 'There is no simple solution to this dilemma.' Supplementing the incomes of the working poor might add up to 1.4 million Ontarians to provincial social assistance caseloads, welfare minister John Yaremko argued, and potentially act like a magnet drawing in the poor from other provinces. Premier John Robarts worried that a guaranteed income might also 'encourage ... "professional" welfare families.'[47]

Throughout the four years of negotiations around the Social Security Review, Ontario's basic opposition to any widening of welfare entitlement through income supplements did not change. 'Ontario cannot ... support this guaranteed income scheme [which would] place another expensive burden on Canadian taxpayers,' provincial treasurer Darcy McKeough flatly told federal officials during the final round of negotiations in 1976. As Rodney Haddow concludes in his analysis of the review, Ontario's hostility towards the potential cost and scope of income supplements for the working poor 'would make agreement virtually impossible.' Instead, provincial officials began pursuing more traditional strategies for restoring the equilibrium between work and welfare. Soon after the collapse of the Social Security Review, Ontario's provincial secretary for justice, Gordon Walker, began lobbying aggressively for the return of compulsory work tests for the able-bodied on social assistance. 'For many able-bodied people welfare has become a right. It's almost a career choice, particularly as it can pay better than regular work,' the Cabinet minister argued. Canada could 'correct this expensive system by introducing a workfare program to replace welfare.'[48]

Although the conditions of the Canada Assistance Plan ruled out any return to work tests, other strategies were employed to restore the emphasis on work. A 1974 Ontario task force recommended that mothers of young children on social assistance should be required to look for work. Another government report one year later argued that the overall proportion of the provincial budget allocated to social security should be lowered. In 1976 Ontario's welfare minister announced a new 'get-tough' approach by vowing that all employables on welfare would be required to take any job that was available or be denied assistance. Most significant, the value of welfare benefits within Ontario was allowed to fall further behind the rapidly rising cost of living. As provincial restraint policies kicked in after 1975, the purchasing power of welfare for a single person, in constant dollars, dropped by 17 per cent over the course of the next eight years. By 1983 the maximum benefits paid to an Ontario mother on welfare with three children was only 57 per cent of Statistic Canada's low-income cutoff line.[49]

Over the next decade, welfare in Ontario underwent the most dramatic series of transformations since the system first emerged during the Great Depression. Welfare policy was buffeted by two severe recessions that saw unemployment within the province double from under 5 per cent to over 10 per cent of the workforce, by political upheaval that placed three different parties in power between 1985 and 1995, and by the abandonment of the Canada Assistance Plan by a national government dedicated to eliminating the federal deficit. Underlying all these changes was the relentlessly upward drift in the percentage of the Ontario population dependent on social assistance: an increase from 4.5 per cent in 1981, to 6.4 per cent in 1988, to a peak of 12.5, or one in eight citizens, by 1994. By that year, welfare spending represented 13 per cent of the total provincial budget, providing income support for almost 1.4 million people.[50]

The key impetus behind a new cycle of welfare reform, launched in the mid-1980s, was the recurring paradox of rising welfare caseloads alongside strong economic growth. Despite an economic boom that dropped unemployment, particularly in southern Ontario, below 5 per cent, the provincial welfare caseload, which had spiked upwards during the 1981–2 recession, continued to climb. More people were not simply coming onto social assistance; they were also staying on it for twice as long, compared with the previous decade. In response, the newly elected Liberal government of

David Peterson, governing in a partnership with the NDP, appointed a Social Assistance Review Committee in 1986 to conduct a sweeping re-examination of the entire welfare system. *Transitions*, its 624-page final report published two years later, contained 274 detailed recommendations for reform. In a scathing indictment of a provincial welfare structure it described as lacking any 'coherent set of principles and objectives,' *Transitions* became the first Ontario government study to acknowledge publicly what private welfare organizations had documented for decades. Welfare benefits within the province 'by any standard ... are inadequate. They provide too little for shelter, too little for food, and too little for other necessities. Perhaps more important, they provide too little for recipients to maintain their dignity and to support the process of transition to autonomy.' Basic allowances needed to be raised immediately by 10 per cent for the disabled, 17.5 per cent for single parents with two children, and 22.5 per cent for single employables, the report argued.[51]

The core theme of the study was the need for finding new ways of moving welfare clients back into the workforce through enhanced job train-ing, better daycare, and other transitional employment supports. In calling for a new child-based income program as well as income supplements for the working poor, *Transitions* echoed the message of many government studies completed since the Senate's report on *Poverty in Canada* about the need to eliminate perverse fiscal disincentives that penalized individuals leaving welfare for low-wage work. The report also placed strong emphasis on the importance of getting single mothers, one of the fastest growing groups within the social assistance caseload, off welfare and into paid employment. At a time when almost 60 per cent of Ontario women with pre-school-age children were active in the labour market, *Transitions*, Katherine Scott argues, articulated a vision of 'greater gender-neutrality in the social assistance system.' In contrast with the original premises of Ontario's mothers' allowance legislation, single mothers were no longer viewed as enjoying any special claim to state support compared with other citizens.[52]

The most immediate argument of the report was that 'the poor need more money.' The total cost of its recommendations was $2.1 billion a year, almost double Ontario's 1988 spending on social assistance. Despite the steep price tag, *Transitions* received strong endorsement from Liberal social services minister John Sweeney and glowing reviews within the provincial media, at a time when Ontario's economy was growing rapidly. It was 'important to dispose of the "myths" that people on welfare do not want to work,' Sweeney argued. As part of its first instalment on welfare reform, just before the provincial election, the Peterson government raised the maximum ceiling on social allowances by 5 per cent in 1989 and in 1990 boosted them by a further 15–16 per cent, respectively, for a single person on General Welfare Assistance and a mother with two children on Family Benefits. NDP leader Bob Rae, the surprise winner of that contest, continued the process. As head of a party with a long tradition of advocacy for a more humane welfare system, Rae increased maximum ceilings on welfare allowances by another 14.2 per cent for a mother with two children, and 16.9 per cent for a single person on general welfare, between 1990 and 1993.[53]

The political and economic timing for these increases could not have been worse. By the fall of 1990, the Canadian economy was sliding into a steep recession that hit Ontario harder than any other province. As unemployment within the province more than doubled to over 10 per cent, welfare caseloads rocketed upwards to a peak of almost 1.4 million people in the spring of 1994, at a cost of over $6.2 billion annually. By that year Ontario was paying welfare benefits that had increased by 33 per cent and were being paid to twice as many people as in 1989. To make matters worse, these benefits were no longer being cost shared equally with the federal government. As part of Ottawa's deficit-reduction strategy, the Conservative government of Brian Mulroney placed a 'cap on CAP' in 1990 which limited annual increases in its cost-sharing of social assistance within Ontario, Alberta, and British Columbia (the three 'have' provinces) to a maximum of 5 per cent, regardless of the actual growth in provincial welfare expenditure. Within Ontario this ceiling pushed down Ottawa's share of provincial welfare spending from 50 per cent to only 28 per cent, at a total cost to the provincial treasury of $3.3 billion between 1990 and 1993. In 1995 the new federal Liberal government of Jean Chrétien went even further, announcing the abolition of the Canada Assistance Plan altogether. It would be replaced by a new block grant, the Canada Health and Social Transfer. Over the next two years this grant would reduce Ottawa's social transfers to the provinces by 23.6 per cent. The end of the Canada Assistance Plan also eliminated almost all national conditions or minimum standards attached to provincial welfare administration, including the prohibition against workfare, which dated back to 1961.[54]

As in the 1930s, a deteriorating economy and exploding social assistance costs provided a fertile climate for a 'welfare backlash.' Any further progress towards implementing the major recommendations of *Transitions* soon came to a dead end. In 1993 the Rae administration, claiming that the current system was 'too passive,' vowed to 'abolish ... welfare as we know it' by implementing phase two of the Social Assistance Review recommendations. A new Ontario Child Income Program would be created to pay monthly income-tested benefits, administered through the tax system, to all low-income families in the province, whether or not they were on welfare. A new Ontario Adult Benefit would replace the existing general welfare and family benefit programs. Employables would be 'encouraged' to participate in JobLink, a third new program designed to 'help people provide an employment plan ... necessary to return to the labour market and to independence.'[55]

Only one year later, Rae's chagrined social services minister, Tony Silipo, announced that Ottawa's 'cap on CAP,' combined with the ballooning provincial deficit, had killed phase two of the plans for welfare reform. 'We've got a $3 billion fiscal hole that we're in because of what the federal government has done to us ... How far welfare reform can go ... will depend on ... the federal government. Right now, we're getting a kick in the teeth.' Over the next year, attitudes towards welfare clients, even within a government previously sympathetic to their plight, began to harden. Shortly after scrapping his plan to 'abolish the welfare system,' Silipo announced he was spending $40 million to create a new 270-person 'anti-fraud squad' within his department. The squad would reinvestigate all welfare cases within Ontario in order to crack down on suspected welfare abuse. Perhaps welfare recipients would also be subjected to compulsory finger-printing. Rae himself declared an 'all-out war against welfare dependency,' arguing that clients should 'no longer be able to just cash cheques,' but might soon be forced into some kind of job-training programs. 'We don't want to see the creation of an underclass in this society where generation after generation after generation of people are relying on welfare.' In order to cope with his ongoing budget crisis, Rae seriously contemplated a 10 per cent rollback in welfare benefits during the spring of 1994, but ultimately abandoned the idea for fear it would split his party wide open.[56] Silipo's fraud squad eventually uncovered only 1029 cases of illegality after auditing more than 266,000 welfare files,[57] and nothing came of the NDP's musings about welfare finger-printing, compulsory job training, or benefit rollbacks. Still, the negative rhetoric served to confirm the public's growing impression that Ontario's $6.2 billion welfare system was far too generous, and encouraged laziness, cheating, and a widening 'cycle of dependency' among its clients.[58]

During the 1995 provincial election, the NDP remained mostly silent on the welfare issue, but the way for Mike Harris's Common Sense Revolution had been well paved. Failure to develop an income supplement program for the working poor during the 1970s and 1980s, a deteriorating economy, Ottawa's fiscal cutbacks to the Canada Assistance Plan along with its ultimate abandonment of welfare standards, and the NDP's own policy confusion and growing frustration with the difficulties of welfare reform all made the public's search for simple answers to the welfare crisis more politically attractive. As in the 1930s, compelling the poor to labour in exchange for their relief re-emerged as a familiar means of reasserting the moral imperative of the work ethic within an economy increasingly unable to provide steady employment.

The close connection between work and welfare, or the fear of creating a 'cycle' or 'culture' of dependency through social assistance, has remained a key concern within Ontario social policy since the Depression. From this perspective the workfare policies of the Harris government represent not so much a sharp break from the past as a return to the punitive traditions and moral categories that dominated welfare policy before the 1960s – and persisted within Ontario Conservative governments well beyond those years. Without the leadership of the federal government on welfare rights during the 1960s, it is clear that work tests might well have returned as a core feature of provincial relief policy more than three decades ago. Ontario's critical opposition to income supplements for the working poor during the 1970s also frustrated Canada's best opportunity for a new income security system, one that might have reduced some of the inherent tensions in balancing the claims of low-wage earners with those of welfare clients. Ironically, after 1988, when a comprehensive blueprint and the political will for such reforms seemed to have emerged within Ontario, a rapidly deteriorating economy undermined any chance of success.

The return of workfare may well have a deterrent effect on potential welfare claimants. If Ontario's previous history of work tests and campaigns against welfare dependency is any guide, however, it will do little to help the jobless find regular employment or to improve the living standards of the working poor. Meanwhile, these standards are worsening with the growth of part-time work, non-standard employment, and deepening wage polarization.[59] Moral panic around the work ethic, as this overview has shown, more typically results from, rather than causes, structural changes within the wider economy. As a consequence, renewed progress in lessening poverty within Ontario will have to await yet another and quite different cycle of welfare reform.

NOTES

1 See, for example, Thomas Walkom, 'Visceral Issue of Campaign Is Welfare "Reform,"' *Toronto Star*, 13 May 1995; William Walker, 'Welfare Watershed,' ibid., 3 June 1995; Fabrice Taylor, 'Working for the Welfare Dollar,' *Globe and Mail*, 3 June 1995.

2 James Rusk, 'Harris Offers Fix for Welfare System,' *Globe and Mail*, 10 May 1995; Lisa Wright, 'Harris Outlines Workfare Program,' *Toronto Star*, 12 May 1995; Walker, 'Welfare Watershed.'

3 Rusk, 'Harris Offers Fix for Welfare System'; Jane Gadd, 'High Rates Were Lure to Welfare,' *Globe and Mail*, 15 November 1995.

4 For an insightful analysis of Harris's astute use of the welfare issue during the 1995 Ontario election, see Ernie Lightman, '"It's Not a Walk in the Park": Workfare in Ontario,' in Eric Shragge, ed., *Workfare: Ideology for a New Underclass* (Toronto: 1997), 85–95.

5 Martin Mittelstaedt, 'Ontario's Welfare Cuts Deeper Than Needed,' *Globe and Mail*, 30 September 1995; 'Tsubouchi Outlines Workfare Scheme,' ibid., 7 February 1996; William Walker, '70% Support Tory Plans for Workfare,' *Toronto Star*, 28 April 1996; Richard Mackie, 'Ontario Works Doesn't, Minister Told: Technical Glitches, Red Tape Foul up Tories' Welfare-Reform Program,' *Globe and Mail*, 30 July 1998.

6 For more details on the formation of Ontario's welfare bureaucracy during the 1930s, see James Struthers, *The Limits of Affluence: Welfare in Ontario, 1920–1970:* (Toronto: University of Toronto Press, 1994), 77–116.

7 For an analysis of the work ethic imperative within federal relief camps, see James Struthers, *No Fault of Their Own: Unemployment and the Canadian Welfare State, 1914–1941* (Toronto: University of Toronto Press, 1983), 99.

8 Struthers, *The Limits of Affluence*, 91–8.

9 By 1943 only 19,000 Ontarians were collecting relief, compared with 450,000 in 1936. See Struthers, *The Limits of Affluence*, 127.

10 Toronto Welfare Council, *The Cost of Living* (Toronto: 1944); E.W. McHenry, *Report on Food Allowances for Relief Recipients in the Province of Ontario* (Toronto: Queen's Printer, 1944). On women's and social work leadership over the struggle for minimum welfare standards in Toronto during the 1940s, see Gayle Wills, *A Marriage of Convenience: Business and Social Work in Toronto, 1918–1957* (Toronto: University of Toronto Press, 1995), 80–106, and Struthers, *The Limits of Affluence*, 101–16.

11 Margaret Hillyard Little, *'No Car, No Radio, No Liquor Permit': The Moral Regulation of Single Mothers in Ontario, 1920–1993* (Toronto: Oxford University Press, 1998), 115.

12 Struthers, *The Limits of Affluence*, 130–1. Heise's main policy adviser was Harry Cassidy, director of the University of Toronto's School of Social Work. For Cassidy's ideas on welfare reform, see Harry Cassidy, *Public Health and Welfare Reorganization in Canada* (Toronto: Ryerson Press, 1945).

13 A more extensive treatment of these events can be found in Struthers, *The Limits of Affluence*, 126–38.

14 Ibid., 191; Social Planning Council of Metropolitan Toronto, *Social Allowances in Ontario: An Historical Analysis of General Welfare Assistance and Family Benefits (with special focus on the adequacy of benefits, 1961–1976)* (Toronto: The Council, 1977).

15 City of Toronto Archives, SC 40, box 168, file 4, 'Interim Report of the Special Committee of the Child and Family Welfare Division set up to study *Survey Recommendations on Services to Unmarried Parents*,' May 1952. For the debate around moral regulation and eligibility criteria during the first decade of Ontario's Mothers' Allowance program, see Little, *'No Car, No Radio, No Liquor Permit,'* 32–50, and Struthers, *The Limits of Affluence*, 19–49.

16 Ontario's highest illegitimacy rate (5.2 per cent of all live births) occurred just after the war. By 1951 the illegitimacy rate was down to 3.3 per cent, and by 1960 it had dropped to 3.2 per cent, one of the lowest rates in the English-speaking world. Ontario's mothers' allowances caseload fell from 12,215 families in 1939 to 7266 families by 1956, when unwed mothers became eligible for benefits. See Little, *'No Car, No Radio, No Liquor Permit,'* 111, 136.

17 Struthers, *The Limits of Affluence*, 159–62. See also Little, *'No Car, No Radio, No Liquor Permit,'* 120–2, 130–6.

18 Struthers, *The Limits of Affluence*, 169–73.

19 Ibid.

20 Ibid., 173–8.

21 Ibid., 149, 176.

22 Ibid., 184.

23 Ibid., 184–5.

24 Ibid., 185–6.

25 Ibid., 186.

26 Ibid., 188–9.

27 See Penny Bryden, *Planners and Politicians: Liberal Politics and Social Policy, 1957–1968* (Montreal and Kingston: McGill-Queen's University Press, 1997), 54–77.

28 Struthers, *The Limits of Affluence*, 190–1.

29 Gareth Davies, *From Opportunity to Entitlement: The Transformation and Decline of Great Society Liberalism* (Lawrence: University Press of Kansas, 1996), 39. Davies's point is captured nicely by a 20 March 1964 Toronto *Globe and Mail* editorial about Johnson's War on Poverty address, which argued, 'No more than they can we be a rich country while the poor are always with us.'

30 Tom Kent, *A Public Purpose: An Experience of Liberal Opposition and the Canadian Government* (Montreal: McGill-Queen's University Press, 1988), 357.

31 Speeches by Ken Bryden and Stephen Lewis, Ontario *Hansard*, 18 March 1964, 1768–74; 14 April 1964, 2020–9. On the importance of 'culture of poverty' theory for the shaping of Canadian debates on welfare reform in this period, see Struthers, *The Limits of Affluence*, 199, 212, 215, 218.

32 Struthers, *The Limits of Affluence*, 224. Or as Ontario's welfare minister, John Yaremko, argued in 1968, 'We intend to lay so much stress on this social service and rehabilitation program that we will eliminate from the minds of the public the fact that there may be somebody on the maintenance rolls that shouldn't be there.' Ibid., 380, n.57.

33 Rodney Haddow, 'The Poverty Policy Community in Canada's Liberal Welfare

State,' in William Coleman and Grace Skogstad, eds., *Policy Communities and Public Policy in Canada: A Structural Approach* (Mississauga: Copp Clark Pitman, 1990), 218. See also Rodney Haddow, *Poverty Reform in Canada, 1958–1978* (Montreal and Kingston: McGill-Queen's University Press, 1993), 66–7.

34 For early statements of this viewpoint, see Canadian Welfare Council, *Public Assistance and the Unemployed* (Ottawa 1953), and *Social Security for Canada* (Ottawa 1958).

35 On the abolition of the 'fit and proper person' criterion in mothers' allowances, see Little, *'No Car, No Radio, No Liquor Permit,'* 142.

36 Struthers, *The Limits of Affluence*, 206–7, 234; Haddow, *Poverty Reform in Canada*, 58.

37 Struthers, *The Limits of Affluence*, 237–8; Social Planning Council of Metropolitan Toronto, *Social Allowances in Ontario*, table 6, 56.

38 Clifford Williams, *Decades of Service: A History of the Ontario Ministry of Community and Social Services, 1930–1980* (Toronto: Queen's Printer, 1984), 81; *Social Allowances in Ontario*, 31–5.

39 Diana Pearce, 'Welfare Is Not for Women: Why the War on Poverty Cannot Conquer the Feminization of Poverty,' in Linda Gordon, ed., *Women, the State, and Welfare* (Madison: University of Wisconsin Press, 1990), 267–71; Williams, *Decades of Service*, 81; *Social Allowances in Ontario*, 31–5; Struthers, *The Limits of Affluence*, 242–3. The divorce rate for women in Ontario jumped by almost 300 per cent over this same time period.

40 Lorna Hurl, 'The Nature of Policy Dynamics: Patterns of Change and Stabililty in a Social Assistance Programme,' paper presented to the Fourth National Conference on Social Welfare Policy, Toronto 24–7 October 1989, 20–1, 28.

41 Economic Council of Canada, *Fifth Annual Review* (Ottawa 1968); Struthers, *The Limits of Affluence*, 248; Special Senate Committee, *Poverty in Canada* (Ottawa 1970), xiii–xviii.

42 Special Senate Committee on Poverty, *Proceedings of Hearings*, 25 May 1970, 43:14–16, 81–4.

43 Senate, *Poverty in Canada*, 169–75, xxix.

44 Ibid., 179–83; Struthers, *The Limits of Affluence*, 248.

45 Davies, *From Opportunity to Entitlement*, 235, 3.

46 Haddow, *Poverty Reform in Canada*, 112.

47 Struthers, *The Limits of Affluence*, 254–6.

48 Haddow, *Poverty Reform in Canada*, 146–7; Christopher Leman, *The Collapse of Welfare Reform: Political Institutions, Policy, and the Poor in Canada and the United States* (Cambridge, Mass.: MIT Press, 1980), 117, 128, 218.

49 Haddow, *Poverty Reform in Canada*, 146–7; Christopher Leman, *The Collapse of Welfare Reform: Political Institutions, Policy, and the Poor in Canada and the United States* (Cambridge: 1980), 117, 128, 218; Allan Irving, 'From No Poor Law to the Social Assistance Review: A History of Social Assistance in Ontario, 1791–1987,' study prepared for the Ontario Social Assistance Review, July 1987, 32–6.

50 Allan Moscovitch, 'Social Assistance in the New Ontario,' in Diana Ralph, André Regimbald, and Nérée St-Amand, eds., *Open for Business, Closed to People: Mike Harris's Ontario* (Halifax: Fernwood, 1997), 81–3; Katherine Scott, 'The Dilemma of Liberal Citizenship: Women and Social Assistance Reform in the 1990s,' *Studies in Political Economy* 50 (summer 1996): 19, 24.

51 Ontario, *Transitions: Report of the Social Assistance Review Committee* (Toronto: Ontario Ministry of Community and Social Services, 1988), 27, 127.

52 Ibid., 112–21; Scott, 'The Dilemma of Liberal Citizenship,' 14–17.

53 'For People on the Treadmill of Poverty,' *Globe and Mail*, Editorial, 8 September 1988; Mary Gooderham, 'Report Urges $2.1 Billion Welfare Increase in Ontario,' ibid., 7 September 1988; Moscovitch, 'Social Assistance in the New Ontario,' 82; Scott, 'The Dilemma of Liberal Citizenship,' 22; Ontario, *Turning Point: New Support Programs for People with Low Incomes* (Toronto: Queen's Printer, 1993), 7; Ontario Ministry of Community and Social Services, Ontario's Maximum Monthly Social Assistance Rates and Percentage Change for Selected Case Types, 1981–95. These are maximum allowance ceilings assuming no other sources of income; the actual assistance paid would vary.

54 Dennis Guest, *The Emergence of Social Security in Canada*, 3rd ed. (Vancouver: UBC Press, 1997), 270–1; Ontario, *Turning Point*, 9–10; David M. Brown, 'Welfare Caseloads Trends in Canada,' in John Richards and Aidan Vining, eds., *Helping the Poor: A Qualified Case for 'Workfare'* (Toronto: C.D. Howe Institute, 1995), figure 6, 60; Allan Moscovitch, 'The Canada Health and Social Transfer,' in Raymond B. Blake, Penny E. Bryden, and J. Frank Strain, eds., *The Welfare State in Canada: Past, Present, and Future* (Concord: Irwin Publishing, 1997), 110.

55 Ontario, *Turning Point*, 9, 13, 16–22.

56 Leslie Papp, 'Welfare Reform Plan Fizzling, NDP Admits,' *Toronto Star*, 3 March 1994; Dale Brazao, 'ID Card Proposal Attacked as Degrading,' ibid., 18 February 1994; William Walker, 'NDP Set to Root out Welfare Cheats,' ibid., 29 March 1994; William Walker, 'Welfare Reliance Must End Rae Vows,' ibid., 7 March 1994; William Walker, 'NDP Puts Welfare Cuts on the Table: Explosive Issue to Be Taken to Caucus amid Deficit Woes,' ibid., 21 March 1994; Thomas Walkom, 'Why the NDP Took a Step Back toward the Left,' ibid., 22 March 1994.

57 James Rusk, 'Ontario Saves $66 Million by Tightening up Welfare,' *Globe and Mail*, 27 October 1994. Ironically, as Rusk noted, 'the primary source of the money saved is to get welfare recipients to claim income from other government programs to which they were entitled but of which they were not aware.'

58 See, for example, 'Welfare Bashing,' *Toronto Star*, Editorial, 3 April 1994.

59 Keith G. Banting and Charles M. Beach, eds., *Labour Market Polarization and Social Policy Reform* (Kingston: School of Policy Studies, Queen's University, 1995).

Contributors

DAN AZOULAY, author of *Keeping the Dream Alive: The Survival of the CCF/NDP in Ontario, 1950–1963*, and editor of *Canadian Political Parties: Historical Readings*, is a sessional instructor in the Department of History at Atkinson College, York University. He is currently writing a history of women in the Canadian consumers movement.

P.E. BRYDEN, author of *Planners and Politicians: Liberal Politics and Social Policy, 1957–1968*, is an assistant professor and chair of the Department of History at Mount Allison University.

DAVID G. BURLEY, author of *A Particular Condition in Life: Self-Employment and Social Mobility in Mid-Victorian Brantford, Ontario*, is a professor in the Department of History of the University of Winnipeg.

CHRISTINA BURR teaches Canadian labour and women's history at the University of Windsor. She is the author of *Spreading the Light*: *Work and Labour Reform in Late Nineteenth-Century Toronto*.

LARA CAMPBELL is a PhD candidate at Queen's University. She is completing a dissertation about the effect of the Great Depression on families, and the relationship among gender, family, and state in Ontario.

LORI CHAMBERS is the author of *Married Women and Property Law in Victorian Ontario* and a forthcoming book on unmarried parents and their children. She co-edited *Family Matters: Papers in Post-Confederation Canadian Family History*. She is an assistant professor in women's studies at Lakehead University.

CYNTHIA R. COMACCHIO teaches at Wilfrid Laurier University. She is the author of *Nations Are Built of Babies: Saving Ontario's Mothers and Children*, and *The Infinite Bonds of Family: Domesticity in Canada, 1850–1940*.

AFUA COOPER is completing a doctoral dissertation on nineteenth-century African-Canadian history at the University of Toronto. She has co-edited *We're Rooted Here and They Can't Pull Us Up: Essays in African Canadian Women's History*. She is also an accomplished poet, and has published four books of poetry.

MARGARET DERRY, an adjunct professor in the Department of History at the University of Guelph, is both a practising farmer who breeds pure-bred cattle and an accomplished artist with a number of gallery exhibits to her credit. She has written many articles on agricultural history as well as a forthcoming monograph, *Ontario's Cattle Kingdom: Purebred Breeders and Their World, 1870–1920*.

KAREN DUDER is a doctoral candidate who teaches in the Department of History at the University of Victoria. Her dissertation, 'The Spreading Depths: Lesbian and Bisexual Women's Sexuality in British Columbia and Ontario, 1920–65,' is a study of lesbian and bisexual women's constructions of their sexual subjectivity.

RUBY HEAP is currently director of the Institute of Women's Studies at the University of Ottawa. She has published extensively on the history of education, women, and the professions in Ontario and Quebec.

ANDREW C. HOLMAN teaches history and Canadian studies at Bridgewater State College in Bridgewater, Massachusetts. He is the author of *A Sense of Their Duty: Middle-Class Formation in Victorian Ontario Towns* and several articles on Canadian and American history.

JEAN L. MANORE, author of *Cross Currents: Hydroelectricity and the Engineering of Northern Ontario*, is currently teaching at Trent University. She is examining the linkages among industrial technologies, wilderness, and Indian land claims.

EDGAR-ANDRÉ MONTIGNY currently teaches in the Department of History at Wilfrid Laurier University. He is the author of *Foisted upon the Government: State Responsibilities, Family Obligations, and the Care of the Dependent Aged in Late Nineteenth-Century Ontario*, and co-editor of *Family Matters: Papers in Post-Confederation Canadian Family History*.

s.j.r. noel is a professor of political science at the University of Western Ontario. He has written widely on Canadian and Ontario politics.

mona-margaret pon is a PhD candidate in history at the University of Toronto. Her dissertation examines the history of the Chinese in Ontario from 1900 to 1940.

jennifer read completed her doctoral dissertation, 'Addressing a Quiet Horror: A History of Ontario Pollution Control Policy in the Great Lakes, 1909–72,' in 1999. She was a Fullbright Doctoral Fellow at the University of Michigan and the Great Lakes Commission in Ann Arbor. She is currently a research associate at the Great Lakes Institute, University of Windsor.

christabelle sethna is an assistant professor appointed to the Institute for Women's Studies and the Faculty of Education at the University of Ottawa. She has published numerous articles on the history of sex education, birth control, and women's reproductive rights. She is preparing a manuscript on the history of sex education in Ontario.

james struthers, author of *No Fault of Their Own: Unemployment and the Canadian Welfare State, 1914–1941* and *The Limits of Affluence: Welfare in Ontario, 1920–1970*, teaches Canadian studies at Trent University.

rhonda telford has a PhD from the University of Toronto. She has been involved in land and resources disputes research since 1985.

shirley tillotson, author of *The Public at Play: Gender and the Politics of Recreation in Postwar Canada*, teaches Canadian history at Dalhousie University.